KRoll

Please remember that this is a library book,
and that it belongs only temporarily to each
person who uses it. Be considerate. Do
not write in this, or any, library book.

THE CONSCIENCE OF THE REVOLUTION

Communist Opposition in Soviet Russia

Robert Vincent Daniels

A CLARION BOOK
PUBLISHED BY SIMON AND SCHUSTER

Originally published as Russian Research Center Studies, 40.
The Russian Research Center of Harvard University is supported by a grant from
the Carnegie Corporation. The Center carries out interdisciplinary study of Russian institutions and behavior and related subjects.

This volume was prepared under a grant from the Carnegie Corporation of New
York. That Corporation is not, however, the author, owner, publisher, or proprietor of this publication and is not to be understood as approving by virtue of its
grant any of the statements made or views expressed therein.

To A. M. D.

PREFACE

This book is a history of the differences within the Communist movement in Russia and of all the groups that disputed with the movement's leaders. It is also, naturally, a history of the issues that divided the movement, from the establishment of the Bolshevik Party by Lenin until the last voices of real opposition were stifled by Stalin. The underlying purpose of this work is to examine the changes in the Communist movement which came about during the first decade or so in its initial and primary seat of power.

The study of the Communist Opposition groups in Russia affords a unique opportunity for insight into the Soviet regime, its development, and its real meaning. As successive issues arose and successive divisions occurred among the Russian Communists, the basic forces shaping the revolutionary state were dramatically revealed. The history of the Opposition is a documentary record of political evolution as, one after another, protesting groups of Communists found themselves thrust aside during the profound transformation which Soviet Russia experienced over the years following the revolution.

For some twenty-five years the main political and social characteristics of the Soviet system have been more or less fixed in the form of what is generally described in the West as totalitarianism. The history of the Communist Opposition is primarily significant in explaining how this system took shape. Except as history the Opposition has been dead—figuratively and literally—for twenty years. There is no direct survival of any of the opposition movements, either in the Soviet Union or in the foreign Communist parties, although in Communist Eastern Europe there have been echoes of some of the old issues.

Following the death of Stalin in 1953, the earlier history of the Communist Party of the Soviet Union regained a measure of topical interest, as the succeeding leadership headed by Khrushchev renounced some of the excesses of Stalin's rule and ventured to correct some of the official misconceptions of the party's past. These gestures—above all the attack on Stalin at the Twentieth Party Congress in 1956—have revived interest in the history of the party both abroad and in the Soviet Union itself. At this juncture, Soviet attitudes toward the history of the party and especially of the Opposition deserve to be carefully watched: they are potentially significant as indicators of any change in the dogmatism of the official "mentality." So far, despite the corrections which the government has allowed, the party historians have made only small progress toward a firmly objective view of their own past. If such truth did appear, it would mean an important new departure in Soviet politics.

This book had its beginning as a doctoral dissertation ("The Left Opposition in the Russian Communist Party, to 1924," Harvard University, 1950), written with the support of the Russian Research Center. My debt to the Center for underwriting three years of my work, and to my many friends and colleagues formerly or still associated with the Center for their generous help and criticism, is inestimable. I am also grateful to the Research Project on the History of the Communist Party of the Soviet Union, Columbia University, for permitting me to devote a year's time to the completion and revision of this work in its present form. I am particularly obligated to Mrs. Helen Parsons and the clerical staff of the Russian Research Center for all manner of help. Howard Swearer and Jerry Hough assisted me in checking references, and in many final points of research. Miss Rose Di Benedetto undertook the major portion of the work of typing and correcting the manuscript.

I would like to express special appreciation for the advice and help which I received from the late Professor Michael Karpovich and Professor Merle Fainsod as directors of my work on the dissertation and from Professor Fainsod as director of studies on Soviet administration and politics for the Russian Research Center. To Professor Karpovich I owe my introduction to the intricacies of scholarship in the Russian field. My wife Alice M. Daniels, and Professors Raymond Bauer, E. H. Carr, Alexander Erlich, George Fischer, Harold H. Fisher, Alfred Meyer, Barrington Moore, Jr., Mark Neuweld, Richard Pipes, Adam Ulam, and Robert L. Wolff have read and commented helpfully on all or substantial parts of the manuscript. Needless to say, my conclusions and my shortcomings remain (sometimes obstinately) my own.

Burlington, Vermont   R. V. D.
August 1959

CONTENTS

THE CONSCIENCE OF
THE REVOLUTION

COMMUNIST OPPOSITION IN SOVIET RUSSIA

INTRODUCTION

A band of revolutionaries came to power in Russia in 1917 and established what they presumed to call a dictatorship of the proletariat. Legend has it that these Bolsheviks* were a single-minded, steeled, and disciplined group, dedicated to the execution of what their leader Lenin willed. All that followed, so both adherents and antagonists of the Communist revolution have since contended, was natural, even inevitable. But in the year 1956 it was suddenly admitted within the innermost councils of the Communist Party of the Soviet Union that the revolution had been in a blind alley for almost twenty years—that one determined, power-crazed individual had fastened his grip on the revolutionary society and had inflicted on it violations of every norm of the so-called socialist order.

As embarrassed Communists outside Russia conceded in their pleas for a "Marxist explanation" of this state of affairs, the dictatorship of Stalin was no mere matter of one evil individual. The roots went deeper, to the very origins of Bolshevism. The explanation of Soviet totalitarianism is far from simple, however. It cannot be found in propositions about the basic nature of the Communist movement. Until Stalin transmuted it into his own image, the Communist movement was not simple, homogeneous, and monolithic, but complex, dissentious, and changeable. The history of Soviet Communism falls neatly into two stages—one in which disunity was overcome and the next in which the consequences of this were suffered.

As the history of the Communist Opposition makes clear, basic differences and conflicts existed within the Communist movement during the first or pretotalitarian phase up to 1929. Fundamental changes were taking place in the movement during these years. Present-day Communism must accordingly be regarded as the evolutionary product of circumstances.

It is very important to recognize at the outset this developmental, circumstantial, unforeseen character of Soviet Communism. Otherwise the history

* The name of the party was changed from Russian Social Democratic Workers' Party (Bolshevik) to Russian Communist Party (Bolshevik) at the Seventh Congress of the party in March 1918. In 1924, after the formation of the Union of Soviet Socialist Republics, it became the All-Union Communist Party (Bolshevik). The name was again changed in 1952, becoming simply Communist Party of the Soviet Union. Throughout this work "Bolshevik" and "Communist" are used as virtual synonyms, as they have been by the Communists themselves. There is a slight difference of connotation between the terms as employed after 1918, "Bolshevik" suggesting the less tangible spirit of the movement and "Communist" the organizational entity.

4 THE CONSCIENCE OF THE REVOLUTION

of the factional controversies within the party will be seriously misunderstood, and the significance of these struggles in understanding the ultimate nature of the Soviet regime may be missed altogether. In the opinion of this writer, most misleading views of the Soviet system and Soviet political behavior stem from a static conception of Communism—as a preformed idea, good or bad, in Lenin's brain or Marx's, which was merely put into practice by a group of relentless disciples. In actual fact, the vast majority of the original founders and supporters of the Communist movement sooner or later found that the movement had disappointed their expectations; they then disavowed it or were themselves cast aside by the people in control.

By and large, the changes of direction which precipitated the splits and controversies among the Russian Communists were not planned long ahead of time, as much as the later official history may claim the party's omniscience. Policies changed because new and unanticipated problems had to be dealt with, or because new personalities with different scales of values rose to positions of influence. The resultant direction of Soviet political evolution was the complex product of many factors—historical circumstances, social and economic realities, ideals and ideology, and the quirks, drives, and preferences of leading or contending personalities. As always in history, the actors perform in an immediate situation, without knowledge of the consequences of what they do; their will, their action, is but one additional factor injected into the intricate matrix of causative forces. Friedrich Engels wrote in 1885, "People who boasted that they had made a revolution have always seen the next day that they had no idea what they were doing, that the revolution *made* did not in the least resemble the one they would have liked to make."[1]

In the history of the factional struggles within the Communist Party there are certain recurring patterns of political behavior which can be reduced—at the risk of oversimplification—to a definite thesis. The argument of this book is as follows: The Communist movement, in the form it had assumed by the time of the revolution, was fundamentally dualistic. It embraced two principal currents of thought; each of these enjoyed substantial continuity, and there were consistent differences of outlook between them. If convenience may be put ahead of symmetry, these currents can best be termed as they usually knew themselves—"Leninist" and "Leftist." In essence, the difference between the two tendencies was that of power and principle—of revolutionary pragmatism and revolutionary idealism. The divergence between the two currents was not always sharp or exclusive, but there was a vital difference of emphasis between those whose eyes were on the ends of the revolution and those whose attention was consumed by the means which its success seemed to require.

This tension between program and ideals, on the one hand, and the instrumentalities of power and the pressure of practical necessities, on the other, is a key to early Soviet history. It was resolved in the victory of the Leninist current of Communism over the Leftist, the triumph of reality over program. The people who represented more faithfully the original revolutionary objectives fell from power as their objectives actually proved (in the Russian situation, at least) to be chimerical. Their place was taken by people who represented practical power and the accommodation to circumstances, typified above all by Stalin. The means to the end—the Communist Party dictatorship—became and remains an end in itself.

Once stated, the theme of this work demands careful qualification. The dualistic character of the Communist movement is not an obvious fact, but neither is it an arbitrarily imposed notion. It is a working hypothesis which has arisen out of the data at hand, has by and large been confirmed by the data, and has proved to be of great value as a guide to the collection and interpretation of further data. This is customary social-science method.

As a preliminary to understanding the thesis of Communist duality, it is essential to define what is meant by the political terms "left" and "right." Loose as they are, these epithets cannot be dispensed with, since their use was a characteristic habit of Soviet politics in the period of the Opposition.

"Left" and "right" as political appelations originated in post-Napoleonic France, when the liberals and ultra-royalists in the Restoration Chamber of Deputies came to be so styled in accordance with their customary seating in relation to the speaker. By the 1870s the terms were used throughout Continental Europe to contrast the parliamentary freedom of the liberals with the conservatives' monarchical authoritarianism. With the demise of the latter and the upsurge of socialism of varying hues, "right" and "left" came more and more to designate attitudes toward social change and the distribution of economic wealth. This remains the significance of the two terms in general present-day usage: the political gamut from yesterday's status quo to utopian radicalism.

A more restricted sense of left-right categorization has come into use to describe not political goals but methods and temperaments. Thus, within a given political movement, whatever place on the general spectrum it may occupy, it is possible to discern a "left" wing which is bolder or more doctrinaire and a "right" wing addicted to caution. It was such a difference which distinguished the respective wings of Bolshevism during the period which this work covers. This more restricted sense of "left" and "right" has been the one generally used in the present analysis of Soviet Communism.

Not until just before the 1905 Revolution did the terms gain currency in Russia, where they were used primarily with respect to divisions among the liberals and populists. They were rarely employed by the Marxists to refer to their own internal cleavages; Lenin's attack on the "left" Bogdanov group in 1909 appears to be the first instance of such terminology within the

Bolshevik ranks. After 1918, "left" and "right" were employed incessantly in slogans and charges, until the final suppression of all opposition activity. "Left," of course, bore the positive emotional content for the revolutionaries, and, while fighting the Trotskyists, Stalin tried to appropriate the leftist position for himself: "Rakovsky asserts that the Opposition are the Left sector of our party. That would make a chicken laugh, comrades. . . . Whoever heard of a Menshevik group . . . more left than the Bolsheviks? Is it not obvious that the Opposition are the Right . . . ?"[2]

In recent decades, the left-right spectrum in its broad sense has increasingly suffered from inconsistency and confusion. One need only point to the violently nonconservative character of some of the Fascist movements which are commonly styled "rightist." In many practical respects, regimes of the "extreme right" and of the "extreme left" have converged toward one another, and the applicability of the term "totalitarian" to both illustrates this. One way to resolve this difficulty is to think of it in terms of a circle, according to which the extremes actually meet. This approach takes account of the similarity in the forms of political organization in totalitarian states and movements, which could not be encompassed by the linear left-right classification, but it obscures the differences which are described by the latter. The problem is deeper: politics are not one-dimensional.

The difficulty can be eased by using two independent scales to describe and relate political movements and ideas.[3] One scale is that of political programs and readiness to undertake changes—this is the left-right spectrum in its familiar sense. The other scale is that of political organization and methods: these range from absolute democracy and reliance on persuasion on one side to extreme authoritarianism and use of violence on the other, with various combinations of these in between. This was what the Bolsheviks and Mensheviks split over, and the terms "hard" and "soft" which they employed are particularly apt.

To find clarity in the study of Communist politics, it is vital to keep in mind these two separate dimensions of political variation and controversy.* Attempts to deal with the factional cleavages in the Russian Communist Party in terms of a simple linear scale of political differences will result in serious confusion, as, for example, where Lenin and Stalin are thought to represent the "center" between the deviations to the left and right. Such a conception obscures both the distinctive nature of the line of development from Lenin through Stalin and the points of similarity among all the deviators.

Among the Communists there were five distinct factional positions, each characterized by a particular degree of programmatic boldness (on the left-

* For a graphical representation of this two-dimensional political analysis and its application to Russian Communism, see Appendix III.

right scale) and political scruple (on the hard-soft scale). Individuals could and did shift, but the basic factional tendencies were relatively stable. The Leftist current of Communism, distinguished by its attachment to theory and program, was internally divided into two subtendencies on the issue of political method and expediency. These subgroups shall be termed "Ultra-Left" and "moderate Left"—the one more utopian and emotionally demo-cratic, the other less carried away by enthusiasm and more prepared to resort to force. The distinction, of course, was not sharp, any more than the line between left and right. The critical difference, as these pages will show, was one of emphasis.

On the right, the differences among the Communist subtendencies were more complicated. Three positions stand out, differing sharply on the scale of political method. The most cautious but democratic and legalistic people, the "Ultra-Right," were really very close to the Mensheviks. This tendency was of negligible importance in the Communist Party, and is not considered here in the basic duality of Communist politics. At the other extreme of method were the most aggressively power-conscious and tough-minded peo-ple—the real "Leninists." In between stood people who were cautious about program and practical problems but who inclined toward the dictatorial methods of Leninism in dealing with them—the "moderate Right" or cautious Leninists. Together the moderate Right and the aggressive Leninists make up what shall be termed here the Leninist current of Communism—hard in method and pragmatic regarding program, but divided (indistinctly, like the Leftists) in degree of boldness.

The program which to one extent or another motivated the various Com-munist groups can be labeled (if not defined) as "proletarian socialism," the new social order predicted and encouraged by Marxism. It meant, generally speaking, the political and social supremacy of the industrial working class; the liquidation or assimilation of all other groups (forming the "classless society"); the wide distribution of political power, administrative responsi-bility, and economic benefit among the citizenry; and the realization of a new collectivistic morality, based upon the presumably inherent virtues of the industrial workers. All Communists in the early years of the movement subscribed to this ideal, though with widely varying degrees of fervor and seriousness.

Primary devotion to this ideal distinguished the Leftist current of Com-munism from the Leninist. For the latter, considerations of acquiring and retaining power came first. This emphasis itself became for the Leninists a point of doctrine. Leninism was in fact an independent ideology, a doctrine of organization, stressing discipline, militancy, and the inevitability of vio-lence. As it turned out, the Marxist and Leninist ideals proved to be incom-patible, and the latter eventually displaced the former in all but name.

From the perspective of the sixth decade of the twentieth century, the nineteenth-century ideal of proletarian socialism appears so utopian that many commentators are inclined to be entirely skeptical about early Communist professions of doctrinal belief. This backward projection of present-day disillusionment can lead to serious error. As Isaiah Berlin recently wrote of the Communists in the 1920s, "Whatever the personal shortcomings of Trotsky or Zinoviev or Bukharin or Molotov or the heads of the secret police, and perhaps even of Stalin at this stage, there is no reason for doubting the sincerity or depth of their convictions or principles."[4]

It is not the purpose of this work to assess the virtue or the universal applicability of the proletarian-socialist ideal. The important concern from the standpoint of understanding the development of Communism is to see how the ideal proved to be unrealizable under the particular Russian conditions where it was attempted. The Marxian theory underlying the ideal, whenever applied objectively, actually foretold the failure: proletarian socialism required a strong proletariat and an advanced economy; Russia lacked the strong proletariat and the advanced economy. Therefore the ideal could not be attained, and any claims to the contrary could only mask the establishment of some other kind of social order.

1

THE FORMATION OF THE BOLSHEVIK PARTY

Russian Communism came into existence and acquired its most distinctive characteristics during the decade and a half preceding the revolution. Its founder was Lenin; its embodiment, the Bolshevik Party which he created. Fundamental differences nevertheless appeared at an early stage in the movement. A disparity between power and program developed which was to characterize Bolshevism through all the critical years that followed. When the lines were drawn at the barricades in 1917, the Bolshevik Party contained a major constituent group that was alien to Lenin's philosophy of organization and power. The stage was then set for the decade and more of political strife that was not to end until the Leftist devotion to the revolutionary program had been altogether extirpated from the party by the monolithic political structure which Stalin built on Lenin's foundation.

The Idea of the Party

In July 1903, the Russian Social Democratic Workers' Party came into being as a national organization when fifty-one Russian Marxist leaders met in Brussels for the Second Congress of the party. (The First Congress, held in Minsk in 1898, had been an ephemeral affair of a few individuals who were arrested before they could succeed in establishing a lasting organization.) Dissension broke out immediately among the delegates in Brussels, and continued after they were compelled to move to London. When the question of party rules came up, a fundamental difference appeared.

The matter in dispute was ostensibly a fine point—the definition of a party member. Yuli Osipovich Martov (Tsederbaum), one of the outstanding younger leaders of the party, proposed the text, "Anyone is considered a member of the Russian Social Democratic Workers' Party who accepts its program, supports the party with material means, and gives it regular personal co-operation under the direction of one of its organizations." A subtly different formula was advanced by Vladimir Ilich Ulianov, already better known as Lenin, who at the age of thirty-three had also become one of the movement's most energetic leaders. As Lenin preferred it, "Anyone is considered a member of the party who accepts its program and supports the party both with material means and by personal participation in one of the party organizations."[1] Acrimonious disagreement over the organization and leadership of the Social Democratic Party had already been building up; the membership question merely brought the accumulated tension out into the open. The issue, in essence, was Lenin—his ideas for tight organization, his plans for shaking up the party leadership, his personality as a revolutionary leader, and his drive to dominate the movement.

On the membership question Lenin lost, even though the patriarch of Russian Marxism, Georgi Valentinovich Plekhanov, stood behind him. In portentous words Plekhanov expressed the philosophy of the "hards": "The fundamental principle of democracy is this: *salus populi, suprema lex.* Translated into revolutionary language that means: the health of the revolution is the supreme law. . . . If the safety of the revolution should demand the temporary limitation of one or another of the democratic principles, it would be a crime to hesitate."[2] Opposition mounted against Lenin's organizational ideas, particularly his conception of the party as a narrow, conspiratorial body of active revolutionaries, distinct from the masses whom they led. Martov, supported by another young firebrand, Liov Davidovich Trotsky (Bronshtein), mobilized a bloc of twenty-eight votes to defeat Lenin's "hard" plan of organization.[3]

The last word at the congress was had by Lenin. Adroitly he maneuvered so that the endorsement of central authority in the party prompted the delegates of the Jewish Bund and the revisionist "Economists" to walk out of the meeting. With the departure of these moderates, who had voted with the "softs" on the membership question, Lenin was able to line up on his side a majority of the remaining delegates—hence the term for his faction, "majority men" or Bolsheviks. He pushed through a reorganization of the party paper *Iskra* (The Spark), by a vote of twenty-five to two with seventeen abstaining, and set up an editorial board composed of himself and Plekhanov, with Martov representing the minority faction, the Mensheviks.[4] Martov, protesting against the elimination of three of the former editors, declined his appointment to *Iskra,* and the minority refused to participate further in the proceedings of the congress. Lenin and Plekhanov then proceeded to set up an all "hard" Central Committee to direct underground revolutionary work in Russia. A supreme party council, also of "hards," was headed by Plekhanov.

This victory scored by Lenin was only temporary. His strength depended in great measure on the support of Plekhanov, and the latter soon began to rue his part in the split of the movement which he had founded. He called on his Menshevik colleagues to return to *Iskra,* and now it was Lenin's turn to go; he resigned in a huff. The underground Central Committee had coopted additional "hards," including Lenin's lieutenant, the remarkable Leonid Borisovich Krasin, engineer, party financier, and bomb-fabricator extraordinary. Now, led by Krasin himself, the committee reacted against the "state of siege" caused by Lenin's unremitting efforts to control the Social Democratic organizations in Russia, and steps were taken to re-establish unity with the Mensheviks. Three representatives of the "soft" faction were coopted into the committee, and Lenin's control was gone.[5] But as he and his followers prepared to fight back, they clung to the name Bolshevik. The term had lost its original sense—the Bolshevik faction was usually in the minority until the two Russian Marxist groups went their separate ways—but a new meaning emerged. Bolshevism, as the world knows it, was born.

Lenin's exposition of his doctrine of the party had already appeared in 1902, in the form of a polemic against the trade-union emphasis of the "Economist" faction in the party. This was his famous tract, "What is to be Done?" The party, Lenin insisted, was the *sine qua non* of a revolutionary movement: "The spontaneous struggle of the proletariat will not become a real 'class struggle' until this struggle is led by a strong organization of revolutionaries." The party, in turn, had to meet strict requirements for the successful pursuit of underground revolutionary activity: "The organization of revolutionists must comprise first and foremost people whose profession consists of revolutionary activity."[6] This was the basis for Lenin's definition of a party member.

Lenin's stress on the party and its conspiratorial organization was more than a response to the obviously difficult circumstances of illegal revolutionary groups in a police state. It was derived from, or justified by, a particular estimate of the forces making for revolution. The masses—even the factory workers—could not be relied on to become revolutionary-minded. Said Lenin, in the most famous passage of "What is to be Done?": "The history of all countries testifies that the working class, exclusively by its own effort, is in a position to work out only trade-union consciousness." A disciplined party organization was essential to keep the mass movement in the proper channel: this assumption has remained an underlying constant in Bolshevik thought from that day to this. "No revolutionary movement can be durable without a stable organization of leaders to maintain continuity," Lenin wrote. "The more widely the masses spontaneously drawn into the struggle form the basis of the movement, and participate in it, the more urgent is the necessity for such an organization and the more stable this organization must be."[7]

One of the greatest drawbacks to the success of this army of revolution was, in Lenin's mind, the political habits of the intellectuals who necessarily comprised most of the leadership of the Social Democratic Party. To counteract their characteristic traits of interminable discussion, indecisiveness, and excessive individualism, he urged measures of strict organizational discipline. "The party link," he asserted, "must be founded on formal, 'bureaucratically' (from the point of view of the disorganized intellectual) worded rules, strict observance of which alone can guarantee us from the willfulness and the caprices of the circle spirit, from the circle scramble methods which are termed the free 'process of the ideological struggle.'"[8]

To his organizational ideal Lenin applied the term "democratic centralism."[9] a formula which is still used by Communists today. It has been pointed out many times that democratic centralism, as Lenin understood it, was far more centralism than democratic. Policies were indeed supposed to be decided by the elected representatives of the rank and file, but in the execution of established policies democratic centralism meant absolute discipline and a military hierarchy of command. As Lenin explained in 1906, "The principle of democratic centralism and autonomy of local institutions means specifically *freedom of criticism,* complete and everywhere, as long as this does not disrupt the unity of *action already decided upon*—and the intolerability of any criticism undermining or obstructing the *unity* of action decided on by the party."[10]

Despite Lenin's verbal obeisance to democratic principles, his centralist conceptions when consistently applied rendered the democratic ideal an empty illusion. Once centralism has prevailed, democracy has to keep quiet lest it violate "unity of action." Once a determined group gets control of the organizational machinery set up in accordance with the principles of centralism, no voice of protest can be raised without violating the party's first principles. In Lenin's mind, a dissident became *ipso facto* a counterrevolutionary: "Any belittling of socialist ideology, *any departure from it,* means strengthening bourgeois ideology."[11] But the intellectual discussion necessary to formulate and define such a complex matter as "socialist ideology" was ruled out by Lenin's insistence on organizational rigor and authoritative decision making. In Bolshevik practice, socialist ideology was Lenin's ideology, and those of his adherents who disagreed with him on ideological points had ultimately no recourse but to leave the Bolshevik faction.

During 1904 the pages of *Iskra,* now the Menshevik voice, were filled with indignant attacks on the organizational heresy propounded by Lenin. "The bureaucrat and the revolutionary decidedly prevail in Comrade Lenin over the Social Democrat," wrote one Menshevik spokesman, replying to Lenin's latest call for absolute central authority in the movement. "The chief deficiency of Lenin's letter . . . is the strong emphasis on the *technical* and *military-revolutionary side* of our activity and a complete ignoring of its *social-democratic ends and tasks.*"[12] Plekhanov, having repudiated the "hard" doctrine altogether, accused Lenin of every political sin—Bonapartism, Bakuninism, sectarianism, and the espousal of dictatorship over the proletariat.[13] The other Menshevik leaders echoed these themes; scorn was heaped on Lenin for his "cult of the professional revolutionary."[14] Lenin was as abhorrent to West European Marxists as he was to most of the Russians, if not more so. *Iskra* published an eloquent protest against Lenin's disciplinarian contempt for the mass movement, written by Rosa Luxemburg, a member of the left wing of the German Social Democratic Party. "The ultracentrism advocated by Lenin," she wrote, "is not something born of a positive creative spirit but of the negative sterile spirit of the watchman."[15]

The most biting polemic against Lenin came from the pen of a future Communist, Trotsky. In a lengthy critique, "Our Political Tasks," Trotsky passionately denounced Lenin's idea of the party and the conception of history which it implied. Lenin was not a Marxist but a Jacobin, distrusting the masses and trying to force revolutionary virtue upon them from outside. Lenin would have the party and its prescribed theology substitute for the mass movement in order to force the pace of history. Trotsky set forth the implications of this prophetically: "These methods lead, as we shall yet see, to this: the party organization is substituted for the party, the Central Committee is substituted for the party organization, and finally the 'dictator' is substituted for the Central Committee." Trotsky concluded with a call for freedom: the problems of a socialist regime would require open competition "between many tendencies within socialism." The working class, he said, "will not tolerate dictatorships over itself." Dead wood and bourgeois thinking would have to be cleaned out, "but this complicated task cannot be solved by placing above the proletariat a well-selected group of people or, still better, one person armed with the right to liquidate and demote."[16] Trotsky was overly sanguine, and he was not entirely without responsibility himself for the triumph of the philosophy which here he attacked.

LEFT AND RIGHT BOLSHEVISM

The Bolshevik movement, despite the principle of discipline which was its cornerstone, soon began to suffer, like Russian Marxism as a whole, from the national trait of factionalism. The cleavage between the Bolsheviks and Mensheviks did not exhaust the possibilities for factional division; it was the result of temperamental and organizational disagreements, and cut across left-right differences of programmatic radicalism. Both the Bolsheviks and Mensheviks contained left and right wings (see Appendix III, "The Graphic Analysis of 'Left' and 'Right'"). Between 1905 and 1914 the Bolshevik faction was continuously beset by left-right factional controversies. The divergence thus established in the movement dominated its history down to the revolution and for a full decade thereafter.

Lenin lost little time in trying to recoup his political fortunes after his loss of control over the party paper and the underground Central Committee in 1904. His first step was to organize a conference of those émigré Social Democrats who remained his loyal supporters. It was held in Geneva in August 1904, with a total of twenty-two "hards" in attendance (which included Lenin, his wife, and his sister).[17] Among the participants of later note were the future Commissar of Education, A. V. Lunacharsky; the economist and future state-planning expert, V. A. Bazarov; the future Soviet diplomat, V. V. Vorovsky (assassinated in Switzerland in 1923); the future military commissar and party-machine man, S. I. Gusev; M. N. Liadov, who was prominent in the Leftist deviation after 1907 and much later figured in the Right Opposition of 1928; Maxim Litvinov, of more recent diplomatic fame; and the man who succeeded Lenin as Soviet premier, an educated young revolutionary then twenty-three years of age, Aleksei Ivanovich Rykov.

Lenin was much encouraged by the adherence to his cause of Alexander Aleksandrovich Bogdanov (Malinovsky), a revolutionary patriarch of thirty-one, trained as a physician, who was achieving fame as a party philosopher. Bogdanov was a prophet of the "hard" doctrine in his own right: "The organizational basis of Russian Social Democracy consists of the developing conscious vanguard of the Russian proletariat." The issue for him was simply the discipline of the workers' party against the opportunism of most of the intellectuals.[18] Apparently Bogdanov was instrumental in securing the allegiance of a number of other intellectuals to Lenin's faction, and he himself became Lenin's second-in-command.[19]

The "Conference of the Twenty-two," which can be taken as the real beginning of the Bolshevik movement as a continuously organized entity, gave Lenin the endorsement he desired against the official party organs, and it underwrote his characterization of the soft-hard split as a "conflict of the circle spirit and the party spirit."[20] The Leninists then proceeded to work energetically for support among the Social Democratic organizations in Russia, and by the fall of 1904 they were ready to challenge the authority of the official underground Central Committee over which Lenin had lost control. In November a Bureau of the Committees of the Majority was set up with the sanction of the pro-Bolshevik underground organizations; Bogdanov was its leading figure. Simultaneously the Bolshevik émigrés established a paper, *Vpered* (Forward), which they described as the organ of the bureau.[21] Thus armed, Lenin began to work for the convocation of a new party congress. His task was facilitated as some members of the official Central Committee, including Krasin, once again veered away from the Mensheviks and backed the project.[22]

The congress, counted as the third, met in London in April and May 1905. It proved to be largely an all-Bolshevik affair, though Lenin claimed for the congress, and for the Central Committee which it elected, official decision-making status for the Social Democratic Party as a whole. The cleavage in the party was threatening to become a clear organizational rupture, but Lenin never hesitated to defy authority which was not his own creature. A split was welcome if it would help preserve his control over a hard core of reliable followers. Lenin wrote, "For God's sake, don't trust the Mensheviks and the Central Committee, and everywhere, unconditionally, and in the most determined way, force splits, splits, and more splits."[23]

The emotions which created the Bolshevik movement were amply illustrated at the 1905 congress. As the outbreaks of popular defiance which made up the revolution of 1905 in Russia were mounting toward a climax, the Bolsheviks expressed high hopes for the seizure of power by the revolutionary parties, and declared their intention to press plans for an armed uprising. This inclination for planned and vigorous political action was underscored by a criticism of the Mensheviks for their "tendency to reduce the significance of the elements of consciousness in the proletarian struggle and subordinate them to the elements of spontaneity." [24] The Bolshevik congress sweepingly condemned the bourgeoisie and all its works, and emphatically rejected the Menshevik plan to allow the liberals to take over in a revolutionary regime. The unity of the Bolsheviks on the basis of revolutionary extremism was never more apparent. Lenin epitomized their feelings when he wrote, "Great questions in the life of nations are settled only by force. . . . The constitutional illusions and school exercises in parliamentarianism are becoming only a screen for the bourgeois betrayal of the revolution. . . . The really revolutionary class must then specifically advance the slogan of dictatorship." [25]

In some respects Lenin's followers were even more uncompromising than he was himself. This tendency for extremism to get out of hand was the root of continued trouble in the party. When Lenin decided, in response both to the ripening revolutionary situation and to the embarrassment which the criticism of the Mensheviks was causing him, that his faction should take steps in the direction of organizational democracy, he had a violent controversy on his hands. His own followers were resisting him in the name of revolutionary purity and "true Leninism"! [26]

On the other hand, few of the Bolsheviks were willing to go as far as Lenin toward an open break with the Mensheviks. Though they subscribed wholeheartedly to the "hard" organizational philosophy, they still felt that it was a doctrine for the whole party, one which they would strive to have accepted by all Social Democrats. The underground party men in Russia often found it difficult to understand the differences between the factions or the bitterness which they engendered. As one future Bolshevik explained in an autobiographical sketch, "My first relations with the party on factional lines were with the Mensheviks, but not because I had made any special effort to involve myself in the differences. As a worker-activist, I was not successful in working out theoretically my world view." [27] At the Third Congress Lenin had to beat back a number of proposals for restoring the unity of the party, and finally he was forced to accept, in a secret resolution, an endorsement of unity: "The Third Congress of the RSDWP empowers the Central Committee to take all measures for preparing and working out the conditions of merger with the schismatic [sic] part of the RSDWP." [28]

The "conciliationist" desire for overall Social Democratic unity was an endemic tendency in prerevolutionary Bolshevism; it constantly recurred and was not the property of any one subgroup. None of the early Bolsheviks, save Lenin himself, appeared to anticipate an independent Bolshevik movement under Lenin's unchallenged authority and claiming exclusive Marxist orthodoxy. Conciliationism was specifically espoused by virtually every one of

Lenin's followers who did not fall into the Left deviation—those who were not Left were Right. Neither group worked for a party split as did Lenin. Not until 1912 did Lenin begin to find recruits for the party leadership who would follow his tortuous course to the bitter end.

This pattern of cleavage which the Bolshevik faction displayed within its own ranks is extremely significant. It suggests two different sets of motives among the people who decided to support Lenin, and thereby supplies an important clue for understanding the development of the Communist movement in Russia. The history of Bolshevism for the next twenty-five years was to be dominated by the interaction between two opposing strands of thought, both of which first found expression at this time. One group was animated by zeal for revolutionary ideals and revolutionary action; it was utopian in aims, impatient, and usually prepared to use violent methods. Such was the left wing that began to emerge after the revolution of 1905—rashly antiparliamentarian and convinced that the Leninist party, by striking hard, could rouse the populace for a mass uprising. The other group was marked above all by caution: these were the people to whom Lenin's organizational system appealed not because the forces for revolution among the masses were thought to be so strong, but because they were thought to be so weak. And just as they did not trust the masses, neither did they trust themselves; they preferred to place their political destinies in the hands of a leader in whom they had faith. While Lenin at times encountered points of difference with the Bolshevik Right equally as disruptive as his disputes with the Left, he could in the end count on their submission. To them, the true Leninists, the party organization proved to be less a means for the attainment of a heroic goal than it was an end in itself, a way of life.

In the heat of political battle in 1905 the Bolsheviks and Mensheviks inside Russia appear for the most part to have disregarded their disputes as they united in the common cause. Demands were quickly expressed for an end to the formal organizational split which Lenin had brought about with his factional congress. Bogdanov and Krasin were in the van of the unity movement, and Bogdanov endeavored to show that the Bolsheviks' organizational ideas did not preclude a free range of doctrinal differences.[29] A joint conference was held in Riga in September 1905 to plan party tactics, and when the Bolsheviks met for a conference at Tammerfors, Finland, in December, the sentiment for Social Democratic unity was overriding. Lenin could not prevent the conference from resolving in favor of an immediate organizational merger and the convocation of a party congress to confirm the solidarity of the movement.[30] For about five years thereafter the forms of party unity were studiously observed. Two joint congresses were held (the fourth—by the Bolshevik enumeration—in Stockholm in 1906, and the fifth in London in 1907), as well as four joint party conferences (a type of meeting which became standardized as a smaller and less authoritative congress). A single underground Central Committee was maintained. Krasin and Rykov (both proponents of unity) were among the three Bolsheviks chosen in 1906 to sit on the committee with the Menshevik contingent of seven.[31]

Nevertheless, the identity of the factions was emphatically preserved. The Bolsheviks retained the paper *Proletari* (The Proletarian) which they had authorized at their 1905 congress.[32] When the joint Central Committee established a "military-technical bureau," the Bolsheviks won control of it and imparted to it a strong left-wing emphasis on preparations for an armed uprising.[33] The informal team of Lenin, Krasin, and Bogdanov functioned as a secret Bolshevik staff with its own finances and its own organizational ties with the underground.[34] Lenin openly espoused a double standard of discipline: "We will not permit the idea of unity to tie a noose around our necks, and we shall under no circumstances permit the Mensheviks to lead us by the rope."[35]

The matter of party finances involved an even more sensitive issue between the factions, that of the "partisan units" and "expropriations." Some Bolshevik organizations in Russia had taken to bank robberies, as well as other irregular devices, to finance the movement, much to the distaste of the Mensheviks. The Stockholm congress voted down the Bolsheviks' unconditional defense of the partisan units and condemned the expropriations and acts of violence against private citizens.[36] Again on this question the ranks of the Bolsheviks failed to hold firmly. Krasin, speaking for the conciliationist tendency, accepted the prohibition of such acts, and only the extremist half of the faction stood firmly with Lenin.[37]

The years following the 1905 Revolution were a period of deepening disillusionment and despair for the revolutionaries. The tsarist government had weathered the storm, and by its quasi-constitutional concessions had driven a wedge between the extreme and moderate opposition parties. Painfully, the Social Democratic Party had to adjust its revolutionary hopes to the prospect of a long period of reaction. The Bolshevik Left refused to make the adjustment.

The question of the correct party tactics for the postrevolutionary situation brought the underlying duality in the Bolshevik movement out into the open. The focal point was the issue of participating in the First Duma, the parliamentary body of limited power which the government set up under the terms of its October Manifesto of 1905. Around the Duma issue there arose a protracted controversy between the Leninists and a Left Opposition—the prologue to the great intraparty struggles of the first postrevolutionary decade.

During the political turmoil of late 1905, revolutionary enthusiasm swept virtually the whole of the Social Democratic Party into the movement to

boycott the Duma and to continue inciting direct action against the government. One of the few people to voice skepticism at this early date was Lenin.
Stalin later recounted Lenin's words of caution pronounced at the Bolsheviks'
Tammerfors conference in December 1905 (where Stalin first appeared as a
delegate and first met Lenin face to face): "What was our surprise when,
after our speeches, Lenin came forth and declared that he was a supporter of
participation in the elections, but then he saw that he was mistaken and
joined the delegates from the provinces."[38] Evidently the attempted uprising
in Moscow and the insurrectionary hopes which it fanned persuaded Lenin
to endorse the boycott of the Duma.[39] It was the voice of uncompromising
radicalism which was registered in the official statements of the conference:
"The conference states that the Social Democracy must strive to break up
this police Duma, and reject any participation in it. The conference advises all
party organizations to use the electoral assemblies widely . . . in order to
extend the revolutionary organization of the proletariat and carry on among
all strata of the people agitation for an armed uprising. The uprising must
be prepared immediately, and organized everywhere. . . ."[40]

The elections to the Duma were held in March 1906, despite the defiance
of the revolutionary parties, all of whom stood by the boycott. To their
chagrin, the revolutionaries found that the population had voted for the
most radical parties available, the Constitutional Democrats (Kadets) and
the so-called Labor Group (*Trudoviki*). The Duma, despite the biased and
indirect character of the system of representation, had an antigovernment
majority. The Mensheviks immediately abandoned the boycott as a fruitless
gesture, and made participation in future Duma elections one of the principal
issues at the party congress held in Stockholm in April. Resisting such a
retreat, the Bolsheviks stressed intensive preparations for an uprising and a
revolutionary government. Krasin, in the course of a polemic against the
Mensheviks' sobriety, declared, "The armed uprising has become inevitable
in the objective course of the Russian Revolution."[41] Thus did revolutionary
romanticism seek scientific sanction. Participation in the elections, according
to the Left Bolsheviks, could only disorganize the forces of revolution; the
tactic of using the electoral assemblies solely for revolutionary agitation was
reaffirmed.[42]

At this point, Lenin turned definitely against the idea of the boycott, and
called for the use of the Duma as a revolutionary forum. On the question of
participating in supplementary elections to the First Duma, particularly in
Georgia, Lenin split his faction and voted yes with the Mensheviks, while
most of his erstwhile supporters either abstained or stood in diehard opposition.[43] The new course of action was vindicated by a landslide Social
Democratic victory in the Caucasus. In 1907 the Social Democrats went
on to participate fully in the elections to the Second Duma, with considerable success: sixty-five Social Democratic deputies were elected, including

eighteen pro-Bolsheviks.[44] The adaptability which Lenin had impressed on the Bolsheviks was rewarded by the faction's winning a slight majority among the delegates at the Fifth (London) Congress of the united party.[45]

Even though they now had a slight plurality in the party as a whole, the Bolsheviks maintained and even expanded their factional center. Its membership provides a convenient roster of the Bolshevik leadership at that time: Lenin, Bogdanov, Krasin and Rykov, all familiar figures by this time, and some new men—I. F. Dubrovinsky (a leader of the conciliationists), V. P. Nogin (a prominent Right Bolshevik in 1917–1918), the historians N. A. Rozhkov and M. N. Pokrovsky, and two new figures, both aged twenty-four, who were destined to play an especially prominent part in the Bolshevik movement—Liov Borisovich Rosenfeld and Grigori Yevseyevich Radomyslsky, respectively known to history by their revolutionary pseudonyms, Kamenev and Zinoviev.[46]

Not long after the London congress of the Social Democrats, the revolutionary parties were subjected to a rude shock. Prime Minister Stolypin dissolved the Second Duma in June 1907 and, in what was viewed by the revolutionaries as a *coup d'état,* decreed a new and highly unrepresentative electoral law designed to rid the government of the nuisance of an opposition majority. The boycott question, so recently resolved, broke out all over again. Local Bolshevik organizations voted overwhelmingly in favor of resuming the boycott of the Duma.[47] At the party conference held in Finland in July 1907, eight of the nine Bolshevik delegates present, led by Lenin's second-in-command, Bogdanov, voted to revert to the policy of boycott. Others among the eight included Lunacharsky, A. S. Bubnov (a young Moscow delegate, who adhered to the left wing after 1917 and later became a Stalinist), and G. A. Aleksinsky, one of the Bolshevik Duma deputies. The one Bolshevik who joined with the Mensheviks, Polish Social Democrats, and Bundists to defeat the boycott was Lenin.[48]

Reasoning that mass revolutionary feeling had given way to a protracted period of reaction, Lenin felt that reversion to the boycott would constitute unjustifiable adventurism. With comparative ease he persuaded the cautious wing of his faction to join him in rejecting the idea of the boycott, while the Left stubbornly held out. Most prominent among those who quickly mended their ways was Kamenev.[49] Zinoviev and Rykov, in contrast to all the rest of Lenin's prominent lieutenants, do not appear to have joined the boycott movement. The familiar party leadership of the early Soviet period was beginning to take shape.

When elections were held in the fall of 1907 under the new law, the Social Democrats managed to win thirteen seats—seven Menshevik and six Bolshevik. Nevertheless, opponents of the Duma were still in a majority among the ten Bolshevik delegates to the party conference held in November 1907 (in Finland, as was the custom, to escape the jurisdiction of the secret police). The Bolshevik regional committee of the Central Industrial Region submitted to the conference, which was meeting just as the Third Duma convened, a demand that the Social Democratic deputies to the Duma be recalled.[50] From this demand came the term by which some of the Left oppositionists were known during this stage, "Otzovists" (Russian *otzovisty,* recallists). Maneuvering adroitly between the Mensheviks on the right and the Otzovist Bolsheviks on the left, Lenin was able to secure endorsement of his own policy of using the Duma as a platform for revolutionary agitation.[51]

In 1908 the Otzovist movement gathered organizational strength and became a serious challenge to Lenin's position in the party. Contests were waged between the Leninists and the Otzovists for the allegiance of the party rank and file in the pro-Bolshevik local organizations in Russia. Lenin kept control of the Moscow organization by a narrow margin, but the Bureau of the Central Region, led by Liadov and Stanislav Volsky, remained staunchly in the opposition.[52] Apparently something of a left-wing tradition was established in the latter organization, for in 1917 and 1918 it was a bulwark of the radical branch of the Bolshevik Party.

A less extreme form of the opposition prevailed in St. Petersburg—"Ultimatism," so designated because its adherents demanded that the Social Democratic Duma delegation be served with an ultimatum to make its conduct more uncompromisingly radical. Bogdanov and Aleksinsky were initially the leaders of this group.[53] Until 1910 the Ultimatists remained in control of the St. Petersburg Bolshevik organization, where they took a critical stand not only in relation to parliamentary activity but to participation in trade-union work and other legal channels as well.[54] Lenin, acting through his own loyal followers (particularly Zinoviev, before he escaped abroad in 1908), engaged in a bitter organizational struggle for control of the strategic St. Petersburg organization. So much animosity was generated that even some non-Ultimatists in the organization protested against Lenin's tactics for fear that they would drive the Ultimatists out of the Bolshevik faction altogether.[55]

In the election of delegates to the Social Democratic conference which was held in Paris in January 1909 (December 1908, Old Style), the Otzovists campaigned as a separate group in opposition to Lenin and scored some success. Bogdanov, now the recognized leader of the left wing, spoke on its behalf at the conference.[56] Bolshevik-Menshevik antagonism was overshadowed by the dissensions within each of the major factions. While Lenin contended with his Leftist critics, the Mensheviks were rent by the issue of "liquidationism," as their more conservative wing proposed the curtailment or liquidation of illegal political organization and activity. Lenin's Right Bolsheviks and Plekhanov's Left Mensheviks made common cause.[57]

Meanwhile the rivalry between the Leninists and the left-wing Bolsheviks was complicated by differences about the philosophical implications and presuppositions of Marxism. This divergence arose as a result of Bogdanov's efforts to reconcile with Marxism the positivistic philosophy of Empiriocriticism, associated with the physicist Ernst Mach. As soon as Bogdanov began expounding this idea (shortly after 1900), he was denounced by Plekhanov for deviating in the direction of idealism. Lenin at first took no stand in the philosophical debate. "I didn't consider myself sufficiently competent in these questions," he explained later in a letter to Maxim Gorky.[58] In 1904, Lenin told Gorky, he began to sense that Bogdanov's philosophical views were not compatible with the Marxian orthodoxy, but the two were able to confine their differences in this sphere to a "neutral region" while their agreement on party organization and revolutionary tactics kept them and their followers fully united through the period of revolutionary enthusiasm during and after 1905. With the onset of the tactical controversy about the proper attitude toward the Duma, an issue stemming from contrasting optimistic and pessimistic evaluations of the revolutionary situation, the philosophical question came out into the open. During 1908 and the first half of 1909, the Bolshevik press was filled with philosophical polemics and heated discussions over the political theory of Otzovism. Lenin climaxed his part in the controversy with his chief philosophical excursion, *Materialism and Empiriocriticism*.

The split among the Bolshevik leaders rapidly widened. Early in 1909 the Leftist leaders established a separate school for the theoretical training of underground party workers, in the incongruously idyllic setting of Capri. Officially the school was nonfactional, but the composition of its faculty, headed by Bogdanov, Lunacharsky, Gorky, and Aleksinsky, showed a clear bias in the direction of Otzovism-Ultimatism and the philosophy of Empiriocriticism. Lenin condemned the institution for its heresies, but it flourished for a time and maintained working contact with the underground party organization in Russia.[59] Lenin thereupon copied the idea and established a school of his own near Paris. For the orthodox Marxists the last straw in the philosophical debate was the so-called "god-building" of Lunacharsky and Gorky, who toyed with the mystical notion, derived from the Mach-Bogdanov philosophy, of regarding socialism as a form of religion. Lenin was infuriated by such doctrinal deviations, in part for the quite valid reason that they were damaging the entire Bolshevik faction in the eyes of other Marxists.[60]

The end of the struggle between Lenin and the Bogdanovists came in June 1909, at a conference of Bolshevik leaders in Paris. Those present were the four editors of the factional organ *Proletari* (Lenin, Zinoviev, Kamenev, and Bogdanov), three representatives of local organizations in Russia (including the future Ukrainian leader, N. A. Skrypnik, and a genuine proletarian from St. Petersburg, Mikhail P. Tomsky, who was to become the Soviet trade-union chief in the 1920s), and five Bolshevik members of the Central

Committee (including Rykov and Lenin's wife, Krupskaya).[61] The Left was represented by only two individuals—Bogdanov and one of his lieutenants.[62] The chances for left-wing resistance within the Bolshevik faction were dim. Party emotions were running high over the god-building affair, and also over the question of the Menshevik liquidators. Lenin had agreed to cooperate with Plekhanov in preserving the party organization from the latter heresy, and actually had the conference disapprove formally the idea of a separate Bolshevik congress. Bogdanov condemned this stand vis-à-vis the Mensheviks as "treason to Bolshevism."[63]

The conference disposed of god-building with dispatch. Bogdanov himself joined the Leninists in criticism of the ideas of the god-builders, though he opposed measures of organizational discipline against them. By a vote of nine to one (with Bogdanov abstaining) the Leninists passed a resolution denouncing god-building as un-Marxian, petty-bourgeois, and sufficient ground for expulsion from the Bolshevik faction.[64] Lenin was determined to go further and eliminate the dissidents altogether. The conference endorsed resolutions damning the Otzovists as the product of unproletarian influences in the party, as "pseudo-revolutionary, unreliable, un-Marxist elements."[65] Thus did Lenin characterize most of the men who had helped him form and lead the Bolshevik faction up to 1907.

Bogdanov took a weak stand in attempting to shield himself with the subtle distinction between Otzovism and Ultimatism; he voted in favor of condemning the Otzovist branch of the left wing.[66] This was the first instance of a fatal Opposition mistake: accepting the purge of heterodoxy and sacrificing their more outspoken confreres, while hoping by their profession of solidarity with the movement to keep their own moderate stand within the limits of party respectability. Bogdanov's maneuver to defend his Ultimatism failed completely. "Politically," the conference resolved, "Ultimatism is at the present time in no way different from Otzovism, and even introduces more nonsense and confusion because of the concealed character of its Otzovism." In a fashion which was to become characteristic, Lenin's left-wing critics were lumped together and identified with the enemies of Bolshevism: "Ultimatism and Otzovism are in essence the reverse side of Menshevism."[67] Bogdanov was summarily read out of the Bolshevik faction. A "faction," it was explained in the informational statement issued in the name of the conference, had to be "single-minded"[68]—a criterion Lenin did not apply to a "party" until he had established one of his own. Bogdanov and the "god-builders" had eliminated themselves by their own dissent, which had "become a threat to the unity of the party."[69] Again in a way which was to become typical, the threat to unity was ended as Lenin himself put an end to unity and expelled the Opposition.

The break between Lenin and the left-wing Bolsheviks was complete. Lenin rejoiced over ridding his faction of these "Left-fools" and declared,

"The Bolsheviks have cleansed the ground for party spirit by their relentless struggle against antiparty elements."[70] The tactic of disposing of intractable opposition groups by purging them from the party was a natural corollary of Lenin's centralism. Whenever differences of outlook prevented minority opposition groups from swallowing a distasteful policy of the party leadership, they became *ipso facto* violators of party discipline. There could be no room for such people within the Bolshevik ranks.

After the split which Lenin forced in June 1909, the left-wing Bolsheviks became an independent factional group in the Social Democratic Party. From the Capri school they began to hit back at Lenin. Bogdanov and Krasin drew up a platform stating the group's concern for "preserving the militant revolutionary tendency in our party."[71] They warned that if their radicalism were not endorsed, the Bolsheviks stood in danger of losing their following to the Anarchists and the Socialist Revolutionary Maximalists. (This opened them to the charge that they were becoming anarchistic themselves in the effort to compete with these groups.[72]) Drawing an analogy between themselves and the twenty-two Bolsheviks of 1904, the Leftists claimed to be the real representatives of Bolshevism, and when they started their own factional journal in December 1909, they took the name of the 1904–1905 Bolshevik organ, *Vpered* (Forward).[73] From this the Leftist faction derived its subsequent appellation, *vperedisty* (Vperiodists).

At the Paris meeting of the Social Democratic Central Committee in January 1910 (noted for the last serious effort at Bolshevik-Menshevik cooperation), the Vperiodists were represented as a separate faction. They were highly critical of the moves toward organizational fusion made at that time, and returned equal coin to Lenin by criticizing him for deviating toward Menshevism and "dispersing the Bolshevik faction." The Leninists in turn accused the Vperiodists of failing to take a firm stand against the Menshevik "liquidators" and of defying the Leninist principles of firm party organization.[74]

Actually the Vperiodists were moving toward the principles of a broad party which would tolerate a variety of factional views within its limits and the democratic expression of rank-and-file opinion. Once out from under Lenin's roof, the Left were free to follow their natural inclination and to put democratic ideals ahead of organizational hardness when the two came into conflict. As antidisciplinarians, they could well be described from Lenin's point of view as Menshevik deviationists. (The same holds true by and large for the left wing of the Bolshevik movement throughout its history.) The community of spirit between the Left Bolsheviks and the left wing of the Mensheviks was revealed by the cooperation of these two groups in 1910 in conducting a new party school at Bologna.[75]

When the Otzovist movement was in full swing, the Leftists were inclined even more than Lenin to stress revolutionary conspiracy. In many respects—

especially their refusal to participate in any parliamentary body—the Otzo-vists were akin to the Anarchists.[76] Like Bakunin's followers of thirty and forty years earlier, they disdained prosaic organization and educational work among the populace, and abjured all compromise. "Cut off from the workers' movement, occupied with the dead work of practical military preparations"— thus were the underground activities of the Leftists described in one con-temporary Bolshevik document.[77] From the standpoint of theoretical Marx-ism the left-wing Bolsheviks went beyond Lenin in their stress on the efficacy of political organizations and resolute action, as opposed to the slow working of economic forces. In stark contrast to the drillmaster Lenin, however, the Leftists were devotees of revolutionary romanticism, emphasizing conspira-torial activity not because they had too little faith in the masses but because they had too much. The imminent mass movement, they assumed, needed only a resolute blow against the government to turn it into an uprising.

Bogdanov posed two alternative visions by which the party could be guided: "a new revolutionary wave" or "an organic development." "If we are holding a course toward 'organic devolpment,' then revolutionary-military questions and tasks simply do not exist for our generation, and the tradition connected with them is a harmful survival from the past. . . . But we submit that the long 'organic development' of Russia is only an Octobrist dream."[78] Ruling out the possibility of gradual social evolution, Bogdanov believed that the party's task was simply to call forth and lead the revolutionary mass movement. This, as it turned out, was precisely the position which Lenin took in 1917, and it was not accidental that men of the Leftist frame of mind gave Lenin more support than his own Leninists in his thrust for power.

In the eyes of the Leftists, Lenin's conservatism deprived his principles of organizational hardness of any justification. After the open factional break in June 1909, the Leftists began to attack Lenin's organizational centralism in a manner reminiscent of the Mensheviks in previous years. In various articles Lenin was denounced for "a regime of dictatorship in the party," "party tsarism," and "the monarchic structure of the party."[79] Liadov attacked the cleavage between the leaders and the masses which the Bolshe-vik organizational principles created and asserted that "for Lenin the question of party centralism is reduced to the statutory strengthening of his personal influence in the Russian movement."[80] Bogdanov struck even deeper in commenting on Lenin's manner of debate—"Rudeness and highhandedness toward people whom one holds lower than oneself in position; respectfulness toward those whom one acknowledges as higher than oneself—is a common feature of *authoritarian* psychology in present-day society."[81]

The history of the Otzovist-Vperiodist tendency, as of prerevolutionary Bolshevism as a whole, was intimately affected by theories of the relation between the revolutionary movement and the masses. Prerevolutionary Left

Bolshevism came to grief as a unified group in disputes over questions in this realm, particularly over Bogdanov's idea of "proletarian culture." According to this notion, socialism was not a definite system to be achieved all at once, but rather a variable ingredient in all social relations, "organization on a socialist-comradely basis." This meant that "the struggle for socialism does not at all reduce to one war against capitalism"; socialism would depend on the gradual formation of a new proletarian culture.[82] To this "revisionism" the "orthodox Marxist" wing of the Vperiod group took sharp exception.[83] Ramifying theoretical dissension, coupled with disgust over this wrangling, caused the group to dissolve rapidly.[84]

In spite of the bitterness of the controversy that had raged between the Leninists and the Vperiodists, most of the latter found their way at one time or another back into Lenin's party. Almost immediately after the dissolution of their group, Bogdanov and Aleksinsky began to cooperate with the Bolsheviks. Bogdanov even contributed to the St. Petersburg *Pravda* (the direct ancestor of the present organ bearing that name), until the editors rejected one of his articles with the familiar comment, "Insofar as the policy of the Vperiodists is mixed up with anarchism and syndicalism, every Marxist will call it adventurism."[85] Bogdanov retreated into a loose association with the Mensheviks. After the revolution he gave up politics to devote himself to the expounding of "proletarian culture" and to scientific work in physiology. In 1922 and 1923 Bogdanov's name appeared once again in connection with opposition activity, when he was associated with a small Communist splinter group known as the Workers' Truth. He died in 1926, the victim of a medical experiment which he was performing on himself. (Rumor had it that his death was a suicide.[86])

Aleksinsky's connection with Bolshevism was cut short in 1914 when he became a defensist and announced support of the Russian war effort. He later went all the way to monarchism and anti-Semitism, sided with the Whites during the Civil War, and then settled down as an émigré in Paris.[87] Most of the Vperiod group, however, together with the Leninists and most of the Mensheviks, remained true to the internationalist ideals of the Second International (which were being abandoned by the majority of European socialists in favor of national defense). It was by virtue of this common stand that most of the Vperiodists again drew close to the Bolshevik Party and adhered to it in 1917.

The anticlimactic demise of the first organized Left Bolshevik opposition contrasted tellingly with Lenin's success in keeping his faction strong in the face of all kinds of difficulties. Lenin's organizational ideas were not ill adapted to Russian conditions and the Russian temperament. It was precisely the evils which Lenin warned against—inadequate discipline, overconcern with theory at the expense of practical work, the excessive individualism of the intellectuals, failure to adjust tactics to changes in the political situation—

that proved the undoing of the Left Bolsheviks as an organization. This lesson
was not lost on the people who later made up the Communist Party.

Lenin had no sooner rid himself of the Left deviation in 1909 than trouble
began to break out on the Right. The pattern here was an accurate forecast
of the events of 1927–1928, when Stalin, after expelling the Left, immediately
found himself deep in controversy with the Right Opposition. When Lenin
eliminated the left wing in 1909, the endemic conciliationist tendency among
the rest of the Bolsheviks surged up. At a meeting of the Social Democratic
leadership, held in Paris in January 1910, almost all of the Bolsheviks present
endorsed unity with the Mensheviks.[88] The initial leader of the conciliators
was Lenin's new lieutenant, Dubrovinsky, whose career soon ended in
Siberian exile where he was driven to suicide.[89] Other conciliators of later
prominence included Rykov and Nogin, and some still newer leaders: S. A.
Lozovsky, who fluctuated between Bolsheviks and Mensheviks before establishing his career as head of the Communist trade-union International; and
Grigori Yakovlevich Sokolnikov, a future Soviet finance commissar and
adherent of the Zinoviev opposition. Kamenev apparently also gave some
support to the unity movement.[90]

Measures for party unity were approved in January 1910 going beyond
anything achieved since 1903. The factional press, always a key factor in
émigré political divisions, was suppressed. A new united editorial board for
the organ *Sotsial-Demokrat* was set up, composed of Lenin and Zinoviev
from the Bolsheviks, the Mensheviks Martov and Dan, and the Polish Social
Democrat, Warski. (Lenin and Zinoviev were the only prominent Bolsheviks, since the purge of the Left, who were not conciliators. From this time
on, Zinoviev was Lenin's number-one lieutenant, completely trusted, until
the events of 1917 rudely put their collaboration to the test.) Both the Left
and Right deviations—the Vperiodists who opposed legal activities and the
Liquidators who rejected illegal work—were condemned by the Paris conference, though not in terms sufficiently strong to meet with Lenin's satisfaction.[91]

Enduring unity in the Russian Social Democratic movement was a
mirage, given the conflict of principle and of personalities which had arisen
by this time. Lenin was a man who could bow to no contrary will; by April
1910 he was writing to Gorky that he could not stand the dissension within
the supposedly united party and hoped for a purge of the deviants.[92] Both
Bolsheviks and Mensheviks failed to observe the conditions for unity which
each expected of the other. The Mensheviks avoided taking action to curb
or expell the Liquidators, and the Bolsheviks refused to desist from the
expropriations and other acts of violence which so perturbed their associates.[93]
By the fall of 1910, the factions were again at swords' points. At this juncture Lenin's cause was conveniently advanced when Rykov, who had suc-

ceeded the imprisoned Dubrovinsky as the most active leader of the conciliators, was himself arrested while on a mission inside Russia. Rykov's place was not effectively filled, and the conciliationist movement among the émigrés began to dissolve.[94] Lenin drove ahead to convoke the all-Bolshevik Prague conference of January 1912, which marked the final rupture of Bolshevik-Menshevik unity.

Rather than proclaim the Bolshevik faction as an independent party, Lenin tried again to pretend that his factional meeting was a legal assemblage representing all bona fide Social Democratic elements. A new all-Bolshevik Central Committee, purporting to represent the whole party, was elected. The Bolshevik conciliators were conspicuously excluded from its membership (though they were never formally driven out of the faction, as was the Left deviation). All those on the committee except Lenin and Zinoviev were new men, promoted in reward for their loyalty and organizational capacity— Ordzhonikidze, Goloshchekin, Schwartzman, and Roman Malinovsky, a Moscow worker (unrelated to Malinovsky-Bogdanov) whose fiery agitational talent had caught Lenin's attention. The alternate members were Bubnov, A. P. Smirnov (a future Commissar of Agriculture), and Elena Stasova, all of some slight note already, and two new men, Suren Spandarian and Mikhail Ivanovich Kalinin, the patriarchal peasant who served as Soviet head of state from 1919 until his death in 1946.[95] The election of Malinovsky to the Central Committee brought a representative of a new faction into the high councils of the party: he was a secret agent of the tsarist police. Following the conference, another undergrounder was coopted into the Central Committee— Joseph Vissarionovich Dzhugashvili, then coming to be known by his latest pseudonym, Stalin, the man of steel, exemplar of the metallic virtues of hardness and toughness.

When Lenin called the Prague meeting and designated it an official party conference, the Vperiodists joined the Mensheviks in denouncing the act as a blow to all hopes of restoring Social Democratic unity. "The conference has dared to christen itself All-Russian," declared a Vperiodist publication, which went on to call it "a clear attempt at usurpation of the party banner on the part of a group of people who are consciously leading the party into a split."[96] In keeping with their desire for "a *genuine* party-wide conference," the Vperiodists supported the conference held by the Mensheviks in Vienna in August 1912: the gathering of the so-called August Bloc. Aleksinsky attended this conference as the delegate of the Vperiod group, but he found it impossible to accept the line which was taken at the session, dominated as it was by the right-wing Menshevik frame of mind, and he walked out.[97] These events serve well to illustrate the demarcation of the Left Bolshevik group—too far left to be Mensheviks, too "soft" to be Leninists.

Even the Prague Bolshevik conference and the recriminations which it set off could not kill the idea of one united Social Democratic Party. To force a complete split took the utmost effort on Lenin's part, abetted by Malinovsky and the other police agents with whom the party was by now riddled from top to bottom. The police, to whom revolutionary disunity seemed an obvious desideratum, facilitated Lenin's policy of a split by arresting the leading conciliators—this appears, for example, to be the reason for Rykov's arrest in 1911. Nevertheless, conciliationist sentiment led the Bolshevik deputies elected to the Fourth Duma in the fall of 1912 to pledge respect for the unity of the whole Social Democratic Duma delegation. The editors of the Bolsheviks' new St. Petersburg paper *Pravda*—Stalin and a young Bolshevik undergrounder, Viacheslav Mikhailovich Skriabin (nephew of the composer, later known as Molotov)—felt called upon to tone down the polemics which Lenin was writing against unity. The last straw for Lenin came when, with the approval of the Social Democratic Duma deputies, the Bolshevik and Menshevik papers in St. Petersburg were partially merged.[98]

Lenin thereupon called a meeting of the Bolshevik leaders at Krakow, with the special aim of putting pressure on the editors of *Pravda*. By direct instruction and the dispatch to Russia of new men—one was Yakub Mikhailovich Sverdlov, the first party secretary and head of state after the revolution—Lenin had his way with the paper.[99] Another such meeting, in the fall of 1913, sufficed for forcing the Bolsheviks to realize the necessity of breaking with the Mensheviks once and for all. Malinovsky, who with police connivance had been elected to the Duma as a Bolshevik, and who, thanks to his forensic gift, had been made leader of the Social Democratic faction, new proceeded with relish to execute the task of schism entrusted to him by both Lenin and the police.[100]

Bolshevik-Menshevik unity was finally dead, though hopes for its resuscitation lingered on. Between 1914 and 1917 there was considerable talk of reuniting the party around the internationalist platform of opposition to the war. In March 1917, in the rosy dawn of revolution, hopes for unity blossomed, and negotiations to that end were actually undertaken. But the unity idea was dispelled when Lenin returned to Russia in April 1917 and turned the Bolshevik Party resolutely toward the seizure of power. There was one final but important effect of the idea of uniting all internationalists: the radical Mensheviks, including Trotsky, were absorbed into the Bolshevik Party, where they played a vital role both in the course of the revolution and in the subsequent history of Opposition activity.

INTERNATIONALISM AND THE FACTIONS

Like its sister parties all over Europe, the Russian Social Democratic Party was thrown into consternation by the outbreak of war in 1914. The support of their nations' war efforts by majorities of most of the parties of the Second International in the belligerent countries seemed to the antiwar groups an outright betrayal of the principles of socialism. Emotions ran high over the issue of "defensism"—the justification of national defense as a prerequisite for the continuation of social progress.

Defensism did not prevail so deeply among the Russian Socialists as it did almost everywhere else. The Social Democratic Duma fraction as a whole, Bolsheviks and Mensheviks alike, voted against war credits. There was, however, a great amount of defensist feeling among the Mensheviks, with Plekhanov in the lead. Even some Bolsheviks, notably the ex-Vperiodist Aleksinsky, deserted the internationalist ranks. Two of the five members of the Bolsheviks' Paris committee volunteered for the French army, and one of them was killed in action. Other Bolsheviks in France volunteered or supported the war against Germany, while the antiwar majority among this group had to seek assurances from Lenin that their stand was correct before they could feel secure.[101] The Bolsheviks in Russia were similarly irresolute in their initial stand. When Kamenev and the Bolshevik Duma deputies were arrested in the fall of 1914 as the tsarist government's reply to Lenin's unabashed enunciation of revolution defeatism, they strove to defend themselves by abjuring the extreme stand of their leader.[102]

The question of defensism versus internationalism cut across the familiar factional differences and created an entirely new alignment among the Russian Social Democrats. This proved to be extremely significant, for it was on the lines of this new division—not according to pre-1914 loyalties—that the Bolshevik Party took shape and struck for power in 1917. As Lunacharsky described this in his memoirs: "The convergence of the 'Vperiod' group and the Bolsheviks and the solidification in general of the left wing came about as a result of the war," and it led to "the merger of all Left groups of the former Social Democratic Party in the great united Communist Party."[103] It was not, as is often supposed, the split of 1903 which set the eventual limits of the Bolshevik Party; the movement as it stood in 1917 was not simply the party of those who adhered to Lenin's organizational principles, but primarily a party of antiwar internationalists. Within the Bolshevik embrace were many who had never committed themselves to Lenin's organizational principles. By stages, people from the most varied political backgrounds were included in the Bolshevik ranks. In 1914, Leninists, Left Bolsheviks, and Left Mensheviks rallied around the principle of internationalism. In 1917 this coalition was formally welded into a single party in which the majority of the leaders and the preponderant thinking were not specifically Leninist.

Lenin's Bolshevik organization was one of the two main rallying points for the internationalists among the émigré Russian Social Democrats. The other was the Paris daily paper *Nashe slovo* (Our Word), edited by Trotsky, Martov, the former Vperiodist D. Z. Manuilsky, and V. A. Antonov-Ovseyenko, later a leader of the October insurrection and one of the first three co-Commissars for Military Affairs in the Soviet government. Centered around this publication as contributors, associates, and sympathizers were a large number of non-Leninist internationalists of both Left Bolshevik and Left Menshevik background. Closely associated with the paper were the Vperiodists Lunacharsky and Pokrovsky, and the Bolshevik conciliators Lozovsky and Sokolnikov.[104] Antonov had oscillated between the Mensheviks and the conciliatory wing of the Bolsheviks.[105] D. B. Riazanov, the scholar of Marxism and another frequent contributor, had had connections ranging from Economism through Lenin's faction to the Vperiod group.[106] These backgrounds illustrate the highly individualist nature of the people who were to constitute a major part of the Communist Opposition later on. Contributors to *Nashe slovo* from outside France included the future Foreign Commissar Chicherin, the radical feminist Alexandra Kollontai (who joined the Bolsheviks in 1915), M. S. Uritsky (a leading Left Communist and Cheka official before his assassination in 1918), the Polish socialist Karl Radek, the Rumanian socialist Christian Rakovsky (a Bulgarian by parentage who later became a leading figure in the Russian Communist Opposition), and the future Soviet diplomat Ivan Maisky (who made his peace with the new regime after clinging for some years to the Menshevik cause).[107]

The trend among the *Nashe slovo* group was toward alliance with the Bolsheviks, despite the distaste felt for Lenin's organizational ideas. One of the staff members wrote: "One ought not and one need not share the sectarian narrow-mindedness, . . . but it cannot be denied that . . . in Russia, in the thick of political action, so-called Leninism is freeing itself from its sectarian features . . . and that the workers' groups connected with *Social Democrat* [Lenin's paper] are now in Russia the only active and consistently internationalist force. . . . For those internationalists who belong to no faction there is no way out but to merge with the Leninists."[108] Apparently it was those editors who had been close to Lenin in the past who led the way toward a reunion. Trotsky followed with some caution. Relations between Lenin and Trotsky were still far from cordial. Lenin tried to have Trotsky barred from the Zimmerwald conference of antiwar socialists held in that Swiss village in 1915, and Trotsky was reluctant to abandon his hopes for reuniting the entire Social Democratic Party on an internationalist platform. Martov resisted the Bolshevik appeal altogether; when Trotsky announced his acceptance of the goal of merger, Martov left the *Nashe slovo* group in protest.[109] With this cleavage in the intermediate group, the fragments gravitated quickly toward the Bolshevik and Menshevik poles.

Inside Russia, the Bolshevik organization was the main source of strength for the internationalist position. The Mensheviks were divided over the issue of defensism, and their organizations vacillated. There were, however, some small intermediate groups which took a firmly internationalist position. The most important of these was the so-called Interdistrict Committee (*Mezhduraionny komitet,* from which was derived its members' appellation *Mezh-*

raiontsy) in Petrograd.*[110] This organization was composed mainly of workers who agreed with the Bolshevik program but who opposed Lenin's narrow factionalism and advocated complete rebuilding of the whole Social Democratic Party. The sympathies of these people lay quite naturally with the non-Leninist internationalists of *Nashe slovo*. In 1915 they managed to send a delegation abroad to establish contact with the émigrés, and various members of the *Nashe slovo* group contributed articles for a journal which the Mezhraiontsy planned to establish. (It was suppressed by the police before it had a chance to begin publication.) The slogans of the Mezhraiontsy, "Long Live the Third International! Long Live the United Russian Social Democratic Workers' Party!"[111] exemplified the combination of programmatic leftism and organizational softness which was characteristic of the non-Leninist accessions to the Bolshevik Party.

The Mezhraiontsy were important as the organizational vehicle whereby a considerable number of internationalists made their way into the ranks of the Bolshevik Party in 1917. As the political émigrés returned to Russia en masse after the February Revolution, many of the people of the *Nashe slovo* group, as well as other non-Leninists, associated themselves with the Mezhraiontsy. These included Trotsky, Lunacharsky, Antonov-Ovseyenko, A. A. Ioffe (Trotsky's successor as Soviet foreign commissar in 1918), Sokolnikov, Manuilsky, Lebedev-Poliansky (a former Vperiodist, later a literary figure and a Stalinist), Uritsky, Riazanov, and Pokrovsky. The group formally merged with the Bolsheviks at the Sixth Congress of the party in July 1917. Other internationalists, including Rakovsky, Radek, M. A. Larin, and Lozovsky, joined the Bolsheviks individually in 1917.

The initiative for the "merger of all Left groups," as Lunacharsky described it, came largely from the non-Leninists. Soon after the outbreak of the war they began to call for a new organization embracing all Russian Social Democrats opposed to the war. Typical was the appeal of the revived *Vpered* for "the unification of all revolutionary internationalist elements, regardless of other differences which do not go beyond the limits of the fundamental principles of revolutionary Marxism."[112] The much-desired unity of the internationalists was delayed, however, by the re-emergence of the old organizational question. The non-Leninists wanted to reunite the old Social Democratic Party on a broad basis and to win over as many of the defensists as possible to the position of internationalism.[113] They were sharply criticized by the Leninists for their reluctance to make a clear organizational break with the defensists, to which *Vpered* replied by denouncing Lenin's "pathological schismatic tendency" and "commanding methods."[114] Lenin was admittedly worried about the appeal which the unity idea had for his adher-

---

* St. Petersburg had its name changed to Petrograd in 1914 and to Leningrad in 1924; it is variously referred to here according to the occasion.

ents inside Russia and the threat this posed to his own political influence.[115]

Among the émigré Bolsheviks themselves there were differences over the issue of unity, which came to light at the party conference held in Berne in February and March 1915. The principal criticism of Lenin came from a small group headed by a young Bolshevik theorist, Nikolai Ivanovich Bukharin, who had earlier been an admirer of Bogdanov's philosophy and was later to become an outstanding Opposition leader, first on the left and then on the right.[116] Backing Bukharin on Social Democratic unity was N. V. Krylenko, subsequently a Soviet co-Commissar for Military Affairs and Commissar of Justice, who had previously expressed syndicalist inclinations.[117] They strongly urged that the contemplated preparation of a Third International be undertaken only in cooperation with other Social Democratic internationalists, especially the *Nashe slovo* group. A proposal to establish closer ties with the latter was, however, voted down by the Leninists.[118]

The question of organizational breadth was only one of several differences which began to appear among the Bolsheviks at the time of the Berne conference. A new left-wing opposition group, of which the Bukharin faction at the Berne conference was the first sign, was taking shape within Lenin's own Bolshevik organization. Like the non-Bolshevik internationalists, the new Left Bolshevik group found Lenin's position on the war much too stubborn.

Lenin summed up his stand in such slogans as "Defeat of the tsarist government" and "Transformation of the imperialist war into a civil war." Trotsky countered that this outright defeatism was an oversimplification which actually worked in favor of the equally imperialist German government: "To stand for the defeat of the Russian government is an uncalled for and unjustifiable concession to the political methods of social-patriotism, offering an extremely arbitrary solution along the lines of the 'lesser evil' rather than along the lines of a revolutionary struggle against the war and against the conditions which gave rise to it."[119] Trotsky's opposition to simple defeatism and his espousal of the slogan "The United States of Europe" as the socialist ideal were points even more heavily stressed by the Bukharin group of Left Bolsheviks and by the former Vperiodists. These people favored the much less radical slogan, "A democratic peace without annexations and indemnities."[120]

Bukharin was representative of the left-wing adherents of extreme internationalism in reasoning from the neo-Marxist theory of imperialism. According to this view, finance capitalism had made the world an economic unit, and the anticipated socialist revolution would consequently sweep the globe without regard for national lines. Lenin set himself against this prevailing outlook by stressing the continued importance of nations and of the economic differences between them: "Unevenness of economic and political development is an unconditional law of capitalism. From here it follows that the victory of socialism is possible at first in a few capitalist countries or even in one taken separately. . . . The free unification of nations in socialism is impossible without a more or less prolonged, stubborn struggle of the social-ist republics against the backward states."[121] Consequently, for Lenin, the hope of a simple solution of the problem of national states through a United States of Europe was a "pacifist illusion."

With the idea of the uneven character of the revolutionary process under-lying his thought, Lenin set forth a program of national self-determination, in opposition to the internationalist Social Democrats. Such a concession to nationalist feelings was in flat contradiction to the pure internationalism espoused by almost all the Bolsheviks and left-wing Mensheviks. Bukharin, together with Grigori Leonidovich Piatakov, the future Trotskyist industrial administrator, led the Left Bolsheviks against the self-determination principle. Radek and Kollontai, among others, represented the Left Mensheviks on the same side of the issue, and the remnant of Vperiodist Left Bolsheviks (includ-ing Pokrovsky and Lunacharsky) stood with them.[122] Felix Dzerzhinsky, the fanatical Polish head of the Cheka in the early years of the Soviet regime, made his first appearance as a left-winger on the nationality question; evi-dently he had acquired this point of view under the influence of Rosa Luxemburg.[123]

Reasoning from the theory of imperialism and world revolution, the Leftists argued that self-determination was meaningless under capitalism and a useless impediment under socialism. As Trotsky put it, "The national state has outgrown itself—as the frame for the development of productive forces, as the basis for the class struggle, and especially as the state form of the dic-tatorship of the proletariat."[124] He went on to warn of "that national revo-lutionary messianic mood which prompts one to see one's own nation-state as destined to lead mankind to socialism."[125] The debate waxed bitter, even within the Bolshevik ranks. When Lenin failed to get his party journal, *Kommunist,* to repudiate an article by Radek dismissing the ideal of self-determination as an anachronism, he scuttled the journal.[126] The question of self-determination remained unsettled when more practical revolutionary interests intervened. It arose again, in 1917 and in 1919, to reveal once more the cleavage between the doctrinaire radicalism of the Left and the rather more cynical pragmatism which made Lenin a successful politician.

The First World War and the questions which it raised for the Russian Social Democrats had consequences of the greatest significance for the sub-sequent history of the Bolshevik Party. One effect was the realignment defin-ing the group which was to become the victorious party of the October Revo-lution. Thanks to this, the party embraced two contrasting lines of thought, closely paralleling the Leninist and Leftist subfactions of prewar Bolshevism. The left-wing current, however, was now swelled by a considerable number of radical Mensheviks, never before directly associated with Leninism, and also by the new group of Left Bolsheviks which had diverged from Lenin's following. This motley crew became the core of the Left Opposition in the Communist Party.

2

THE BOLSHEVIK FACTIONS IN THE
REVOLUTION OF 1917

The momentous revolutionary events of 1917 were not sufficient to make the Bolshevik Party forget its internal differences and close ranks to achieve its revolutionary goals. On the contrary, the challenge of revolution only accentuated the differences between the two currents of thought which had been developing within the Bolshevik movement. The left wing, heavily reinforced by the influx of former Left Menshevik and independent Social Democratic leaders during 1917, was distinguished by the firm stand it took for revolutionary internationalism and against any cooperation with the Provisional Government. In social policy the Leftists quickly assumed the maximal revolutionary program, looking toward an early introduction of socialist measures and the goals of anarchistic democracy. The Leninist wing, on the contrary, was unsure of itself. At first, it was not inclined to oppose vigorously either the war or the Provisional Government; in this respect it was closer to the non-Bolshevik socialist parties than to the Bolshevik left wing. During the year, the Leninists were pulled along after the Left, but there were constant signs of reluctance; the Right lacked confidence in the revolutionary potential both of Russia and of Europe.

Lenin shocked the whole party and the Leninist wing in particular by the stand he took in his "April Theses," demanding inalterable opposition to the war and to the Provisional Government and calling for preparations for the establishment of a revolutionary regime based on the soviets. The most enthusiastic support for Lenin's program came from the Bolshevik Left, in spite of their earlier conflicts with him. Graphically speaking, Lenin had moved from his own "Leninist" wing to the Left, a shift which was underscored by its reversal after the October Revolution. Lenin then came once again into conflict with the left wing of the party, this time over the question of making peace with Germany, and reverted to the support of those who had been his closest adherents before 1917.

PERMANENT REVOLUTION

The cleavage among the Bolsheviks in 1917 and the disputes which divided the party both during and after the October Revolution hinged on a subtle but crucial question of the application of Marxian doctrine to Russia.

This was embodied in that forecast and description of revolutionary events in Russia called the"theory of permanent revolution," a set of ideas which played a role of particular importance in the history of the Bolshevik movement. In 1917 it provided the Bolsheviks with the basic doctrinal inspiration and justification for their drive to seize power. When the party divided after 1923 into contending groups of leaders and Opposition, the theory of permanent revolution was central among the issues which divided the factions.

Authorship of the theory is rightly attributed to Trotsky, with credit for inspiration and assistance going to the Russian-born German socialist, A. L. Helphand (Parvus). The two collaborated in the formulation of the idea when Trotsky was in Germany in 1904, and Trotsky worked the proposition out in full while in prison after his arrest in December 1905 as a leader of the original St. Petersburg Soviet.[1] The theory appeared in print in 1906 as an essay, "Results and Prospects—The Driving Forces of the Revolution," in a collection of Trotsky's writings on the revolution of 1905, "Our Revolution."[2]

Trotsky propounded his theory in an effort to solve a problem which plagued all Russian Marxists. According to the ordinary Marxian analysis, Russia was not supposed to be economically and politically ripe for a socialist revolution; the country was at a stage of social and economic development where only a "bourgeois" revolution, such as the West had experienced in earlier centuries, could occur. But to let the matter rest here was to abandon serious thought of the working class coming to power in the near future and to resign oneself to the role of legal opposition until capitalist democracy paved the way for the next revolutionary advance. This conclusion was obviously not attractive to those who were by temperament revolutionaries first and foremost. Most of the Mensheviks, on the other hand, tended to believe in a long evolution for the same reason that they rejected Lenin's rigorous doctrine of the party: they were liberal, moderate, humane, and not fanatical devotees of revolution as an end in itself.

Lenin was a Marxist because he was a revolutionary. When Marxism led to conclusions of an insufficiently revolutionary nature, he refused to accept them and contrived out of Marxist materials a different justification for his unshakable revolutionary stand. The Russian bourgeoisie, according to Lenin, was both too weak and too reactionary to be relied on. The bourgeois revolution would have to be accomplished by the workers and the party which stood for them. A "democratic dictatorship of the proletariat and the peasantry" would be set up to administer the affairs of state in the interests of the revolutionary classes until such time as the country would become ready for the transition to socialism. Lenin would have his revolution whatever the circumstances: determined leadership and the conquest of political power were the historically decisive factors. In 1905 he wrote, "The outcome of the revolution depends on whether the working class will play . . . the role of leader of the people's revolution. . . . First let ruthless struggle decide the question of choosing the path. . . . The workers . . . are striving to crush the reactionary forces without mercy."[3] A remark Lenin made in 1917 sums up his political philosophy in one line;—"The question at the root of any revolution is the question of governmental power."[4]

The difficulty of reconciling the Marxian philosophy of history with revolutionary fervor under Russian conditions was clearly manifested in the contrasting doctrinal manipulations of the Mensheviks and Lenin. The one group abandoned the fervor; the other, verbal professions to the contrary, sacrificed the philosophy of history. There remained, however, a third position, of little note when it was originated but of crucial significance for the Bolshevik movement when it prepared to take power. This was Trotsky's thesis of "permanent revolution," which managed to reconcile the Marxian strictures on the conditions for proletarian revolution and the Russian radicals' desire for immediate action.

Trotsky's argument began with the observation, conceded by the other Marxists, that Russia's economic and social development, inspired and accelerated by contact with the more advanced West, had proceeded unevenly. The middle class was not the only revolutionary force in Russia. The Russian economy, growing with the help of Western capital and technology, acquired amidst its prevalent peasant backwardness the most modern forms of large-scale industry.[5] In consequence, the working class grew quickly, both in numbers and in revolutionary sentiment. A compound social struggle had begun to emerge—the government and part of the landlords versus almost everyone else, on the one hand; and the industrialists versus the workers, on the other.

This situation led both Lenin and Trotsky to conclude in 1905 that the middle class was likely to desert the revolution in order to protect its property interests, and that the "bourgeois" revolution—meaning the attainment of democracy and civil liberties and the expropriation of the landlords—would have to be carried through by the proletariat. To reconcile this necessity with the prognosis of extended capitalist development for Russia, Lenin advanced the formula of the "democratic dictatorship of the proletariat and the peasantry." Trotsky found a different solution of the problem by viewing the Russian proletariat in the context of an international revolutionary movement. He theorized that after the Russian proletariat was called upon to take the lead in the bourgeois revolution, it could install a socialist regime in power. Here is the first sense of the "permanency" of the revolution—the revolution is permanent or continuous over the period when the bourgeois revolution is completed and the socialist revolution begun. Such a socialist regime could not endure in Russia alone, because of the social and economic backwardness of the country, but help from abroad would be automatic; the revolution in Russia would be the signal for a general socialist revolution in Europe. This is the second sense of the "permanency" of the revolution—a permanently revolutionary situation as the revolution spreads from Russia to the advanced countries. Industrial Russia would become an integral part of socialist Europe. Backward Russia would become a common problem for all of Europe and thus would be reduced to relatively manageable proportions.

Between 1905 and 1917 the theory of permanent revolution or kindred ideas became increasingly popular in leftist circles within the Russian Marxist movement. One of its most vigorous exponents was Rosa Luxemburg.[6] Pokrovsky, the Vperiodist and Bolshevik historian, though later an archcritic of Trotsky, evidenced sympathy with the concept.[7] Bukharin and Radek, among others, expressed their adherence to the theory during the war.[8] "Permanent revolution" was the only satisfactory intellectual solution for those Russian Marxists who tried to retain the spirit of Western Marxism while remaining vigorously revolutionary.

As anti-Trotsky polemics later stressed, Lenin did—at first—take sharp exception to Trotsky's view. During the war years, however, Lenin's intense antiwar internationalism brought him to a position that was for all practical purposes close to Trotsky's.[9] "The task of the proletariat of Russia," Lenin wrote in 1915, "is to complete the bourgeois-democratic revolution in Russia, in order to kindle the socialist revolution in Europe."[10] The outbreak of revolution and the fall of the tsar in February 1917 prompted Lenin to proclaim, "Only a special coincidence of historical conditions has made the proletariat of Russia, *for a certain, perhaps very short time,* the advance skirmishers of the revolutionary proletariat of the whole world."[11] Lenin had now fully embraced permanent revolution in its international sense.

The February Revolution caught the Bolsheviks completely off guard. The assumption of power by a conservative middle-class regime, supposedly impossible, made Lenin's doctrine of the "democratic dictatorship" meaningless. Events were proceeding more nearly according to the Menshevik expectation. The Mensheviks, together with most of the Socialist Revolutionary Party, reacted as they had planned by becoming a loyal opposition. The soviets, which these parties initially dominated, were guided in this direction.

In their responses to the establishment of the Provisional Government, the Bolsheviks divided, and the basic cleavage between the cautious and the bold was dramatically revealed. Most of the old-line Leninist leadership in Russia tacitly admitted that the Menshevik analysis had been borne out; they accepted the "bourgeois" Provisional Government as the most advanced possible, and took on for themselves the role of watchdog and occasional prod in the interests of the democratic revolution. However, Lenin and the left-wingers, both Bolshevik and Menshevik, refused to let the revolution coast along in this manner. Openly or implicitly they embraced Trotsky's theory of permanent revolution, with all the ultrarevolutionary hopes for Russia which this idea implied. In his "April Theses" Lenin announced the program which he had worked out for Russia on the basis of his dream of international revolution—"All power to the soviets" and the overthrow of the Provisional Government, which was to Lenin an integral part of international imperialism.

The immediate test issue was the prosecution of the war. Peace was a widespread demand among the Russian populace, but to achieve it, Lenin maintained, "We need a workers' government, allied in the first place with the mass of the poorest village population, and secondly with the revolutionary workers of all the warring countries."[12] At the same time, Trotsky—in New York—was independently expressing himself in the same fashion: "At the head of the popular masses the Russian revolutionary proletariat will fulfill its historic task. . . . It is necessary to liquidate not only tsarism, but also the war. . . . It is the duty of the revolutionary proletariat of Russia to show that behind the evil imperialist will of the liberal bourgeoisie there is no strength, for it has no support in the worker masses."[13]

The theory of permanent revolution had a dual significance for the year of revolution. As the guide for Bolshevik strategy it encouraged the seizure of power and gave doctrinal sanction to this "workers'" revolution in a country professedly unripe for socialism. At the same time it constituted a remarkably accurate forecast and description of the course of revolutionary events—internally, that is. To this extent it was no doubt unique as an example of the pragmatic testing of a social theory: certain actions were called for which, by their success, upheld the theory.

The Bolsheviks were carried into power on the wave of mass dissatisfaction with the Provisional Government, and then, after completing the "bourgeois" reforms such as land distribution and church disestablishment, they proceeded to such socialistic measures as nationalization of the banks and workers' control of industry. In October 1917, it was firmly believed, particularly in the left wing of the Bolshevik Party, that the international extension of the revolution was certain to follow. Bukharin's fancies of 1918 exemplified the party's endorsement of Trotsky's theory: "The permanent revolution in Russia is passing into the European proletarian revolution."[14] This was a necessity, according to the theory, if the socialist regime in Russia were to survive. But in this vital respect events failed to conform to the theory. The spark did not set off the conflagration; the eagerly anticipated revolution in the West never materialized. In default of the success of international socialism, the Marxian premises of the theory left Russia no hope: the industrial prerequisites for socialism were lacking in sufficient quantity, and an isolated effort to establish socialism in Russia was bound to fail.

Such conclusions were arrived at before long by various Bolshevik groups. Even before the October uprising, when the cautious wing of the party under Zinoviev and Kamenev opposed the venture, they argued that the revolution in Europe was not likely and that the Bolshevik Party was consequently bound to fail if it tried to rule. After the coup it was the turn of the left wing of the party to invoke the internationalist promise: the Left Communists took their stand against peace with Germany on the grounds that revolutionary war was called for to precipitate the European socialist revolution, and that a Russian regime which preserved itself by avoiding such action would, by its isolation, be compelled to assume a nonsocialist form. Lenin's decision to make peace prevailed, though the entire party still looked forward eagerly to the day when the proletarians of Europe would come to the aid of their Russian comrades. That day never came.

That the socialist regime should have survived in Russia under these circumstances was, according to the theory, impossible. That it did was to be variously explained. Did the persistence of the regime imply that it had conformed to circumstantial limitations and ceased to be socialist? The Left Opposition argued in this vein after 1923 with more and more insistence until they were silenced in 1927. Or could the survival of the Soviet regime be taken as evidence that the material conditions of Russian life were no serious bar, given the will and the effort, to the construction of a socialist society in the Soviet Union independently of events abroad? Such was the theoretical solution which Stalin advanced; it had its appeal, but it could not in any atmosphere of free discussion be defended as orthodox Marxism.

"REARMING THE PARTY"

The fall of Nicholas II released the Russian nation into the dazzling unfamiliar light of political freedom. The police were gone and the underground groups became legal. Surprised but excited, political exiles of all hues flocked to the capital from Siberian detention or refuges abroad. The atmosphere was one of tumultuous hope and incipient chaos. Doctrines were thrown askew, and few political figures had clear notions of where they were headed. During the interval between the February Revolution and Lenin's return, no group was more confused and disorganized than the Bolsheviks in Russia. With its leading lights still abroad, the group had no one who could supply authoritative leadership. On the pressing questions of the proper attitude toward the new Provisional Government and the war, the party soon found itself divided into three distinct factions—Left, Right, and Center.

The left-wing Bolsheviks, numerically weak but influential in Petrograd, assumed an antigovernment and antiwar stand that chanced to be very close to that of Lenin and the left-wing émigrés. Most of the better-known Bolsheviks in Russia, and especially the Siberian exiles, took a much less uncompromising position. Still another group decided that with the advent of the Republic, defensism had finally become justified. Such were the Ultra-Right Bolsheviks led by N. P. Avilov, V. S. Voytinsky, and V. Bazarov; with the exception of Avilov, they soon left the ranks of the Bolshevik Party altogether.[15]

For a short time after the February Revolution the left-wing Bolsheviks, led by the previously underground bureau of the Central Committee (consisting of Molotov, A. G. Shliapnikov, and P. A. Zalutsky), were in the ascendency in the Petrograd organization of the party. They took it upon themselves to denounce the Provisional Government and urge the soviets to take power into their hands: "The fundamental task of the revolutionary Social Democracy is, as before, the struggle for the transformation of the present antipopular imperialist war into a civil war of the peoples against their oppressors, the ruling classes."[16] The Mezhraiontsy (the "interdistrict" Menshevik group) supported this left-wing Bolshevik position and proclaimed to the soldiers, "Take the power into your own hands."[17] Such fervor, however, was offset by unsureness, and the Bolshevik leaders failed to take the most extreme stand in the forum of the soviet.[18] Negotiations for left-wing unity were in progress with the Mezhraiontsy and, according to Shliapnikov, a complete merger with that group had almost been reached: "In the middle of March this question was settled positively, and only the appearance within our party of differences with the comrades returning from Siberia and the jump to the side of defensism of our *Pravda* prevented a merger then."[19]

The return of the "comrades from Siberia" was the occasion of a virtual *coup d'état* within the Bolshevik organization. Among the new arrivals were Bolshevik dignitaries who far outranked the party workers previously in charge of the Petrograd organization: M. K. Muranov had been a Duma deputy; Stalin was a member of the Central Committee; prior to his arrest in 1914, Kamenev had been one of Lenin's principal lieutenants. The first act of the new group, as they assumed the reins of leadership, was to reverse the editorial policy of *Pravda*. They adopted the Menshevik and Socialist Revolutionary (SR) formula of supporting the Provisional Government "insofar as" it did not directly violate the interests of the masses, and they abandoned unqualified opposition to the war.[20] "The solution," wrote Stalin, "is the course of pressure on the Provisional Government with a demand for it to declare its agreement to open peace negotiations immediately."[21]

The factional differences among the Bolsheviks appeared even more clearly at the conference of Bolshevik delegates who had come to the capital for the First All-Russian Conference of Soviets, held at the end of March.[22] The Center leadership of Kamenev and Stalin drew the backing of the Moscow city Bolshevik organization and much of the Petrograd membership, and was supported by two former conciliators, Rykov and Nogin, who were to become leading figures in the Bolshevik Right during 1917. On the Left, with the Petrograd Bureau, stood the Moscow Regional Bureau (representing the party organization throughout the central part of European Russia); the latter was the primary left-wing stronghold during the ensuing year. Alexandra Kollontai, who had been in close touch with Lenin before her return to Russia, arrived in time to join the critics on the Left.[23]

The left-wingers at the conference boldly proclaimed the internationalist premises of permanent revolution: "The Russian Revolution . . . can secure for the people of Russia a maximum of democratic liberties and social reforms only if it becomes the point of departure for the revolutionary movement of the west European proletariat against their bourgeois governments." The Provisional Government, as far as the Leftists were concerned, was nothing but a nest of counterrevolutionary treachery: "There is a conspiracy of the Provisional Government against the people and the Revolution, and it is necessary to prepare for a struggle against it."[24] A "Workers' Red Guard" was the means that they urged to this end, and they hailed the soviets as the "embryo of revolutionary power."[25]

The Kamenev-Stalin Center group equivocated. It put through a resolution calling for all peoples to revolt against their warring governments and for "the real transfer of power into the hands of the proletariat and the revolutionary democracy." At the same time the resolution stated that only the eventuality of the enemy governments' refusal to make peace would "compel the people, who have risen up, to take the war into their own hands as a war for the liberty of the peoples, in alliance with the proletariat of Western Europe. Up to that moment, rejecting the disorganization of the army and considering the preservation of its strength to be essential as a bulwark against counterrevolution, we call on all soldiers and workers to remain at their posts and to maintain firm organization."[26] Stalin expressed the same ambivalence in speaking of the Provisional Government as "the fortifier of the conquests of the revolutionary people." Under proper control by the soviets, Stalin maintained, the Provisional Government could prove to be of considerable though temporary usefulness; once the government had "exhausted" itself, the time would be ripe for the soviets to take power.[27] But the idea of "support" for the Provisional Government proved to be too much for the conference, and Stalin's draft resolution was amended to delete such a reference.[28]

It is clear that a majority of the Bolsheviks in Russia at the time of the February Revolution were at a loss when it came to evaluating the new regime. Differing basically with Lenin, the Bolshevik moderates hesitated to take a radical stand on the Provisional Government or the war lest such a course of action disrupt the democratic revolution. Wrote the Menshevik observer Sukhanov, "I had no doubt that Kamenev . . . was trying to follow a line of genuine struggle for peace in the concrete circumstances of the moment. All the actions of the then leader of the Bolshevik Party had just this kind of 'possibilist,' sometimes too moderate, character."[29]

Lenin reached Petrograd via Finland on April 3, 1917, after his celebrated "sealed car" trip across Germany. The effect on the Bolsheviks was volcanic: the party was shaken to its foundations as Lenin imposed his relentless will to refashion it into an instrument of successful revolution. On that day the course of history was laid out for decades to come.

Received by his Bolshevik associates and by other leaders of the soviet in a festive mood, Lenin shocked them with his fanatical attitude. His first move was to pounce on Kamenev: "What is this that's being written in *Pravda?* We saw several numbers and really swore at you!"[30] Disdaining the greetings of the moderate leaders of the soviet, Lenin turned to the crowds: "I am happy to greet in your persons the victorious Russian Revolution. . . . The piratical imperialist war is the beginning of civil war throughout Europe. . . . The Russian Revolution accomplished by you has prepared the way and opened a new epoch. Long live the world-wide socialist revolution!"[31] That night and the following day Lenin proclaimed, to the astonishment of the Bolshevik leaders assembled to hear him, his will to take power. This was the essence of his memorable April Theses. "I shall never forget that thunder-like speech," wrote Sukhanov, "which startled and amazed not only me, a heretic who had accidentally dropped in, but all the true believers. I am certain that no one expected anything of the sort."[32]

Tacitly accepting the theory of permanent revolution, Lenin declared, "The peculiarity of the present situation in Russia lies in the *transition* from the first stage of the revolution . . . to its second stage, which is to place power in the hands of the proletariat and the poorest strata of the peasantry." Mercilessly he tore into the current Bolshevik leadership: "*Pravda* demands that the government renounce annexations. To demand that a government of capitalists renounce annexations is nonsense, a crying mockery. . . . Even our own Bolsheviks show confidence in the government. It is the death of socialism. . . . In that case our ways must part. The majority of the Social Democrats have betrayed socialism. . . . Have the will to build a new party!"[33]

A Bolshevik witness has described the consternation occasioned by Lenin's reversal of the party line: "His speech produced on everyone a stupifying impression. No one expected this. On the contrary, they expected Vladimir Ilich to arrive and call to order the Russian Bureau of the Central Committee and especially Comrade Molotov, who occupied a particularly irreconciliable position with respect to the Provisional Government. It appeared, however, that Molotov himself was closest of all to Ilich."[34]

For a time, Lenin met with very little response from his own party, except for the small Molotov-Shliapnikov left wing from the underground and a few returned émigrés such as Kollontai. On April 8, the day after Lenin's April Theses appeared in *Pravda,* Kamenev published a statement explaining that Lenin did not speak for the party and that the proposition of a quick transition from the democratic to the socialist revolution was untenable. "We hope to defend our point of view," Kamenev asserted confidently, "as the only possible one for revolutionary Social Democrats, as long as they want

... to remain a party of the revolutionary masses of the proletariat, and not be transformed into a group of communist propagandists." [35]

The same day the Petrograd City Committee of the party considered Lenin's theses and voted its disapproval, thirteen to two. [36] To one party member Lenin's policy was "Utopian . . . , explained by his prolonged lack of contact with Russian life." Bukharin later recalled this as a time "when part of our own party looked upon [the April Theses] as a virtual betrayal of accepted Marxist ideology." [37]

Lenin, undaunted by the initial rebuff, stood adamantly against the Provisional Government, while he employed the magnetic, almost hypnotic, power of his personal leadership to win the party over to his radical line. Within two weeks he had scored a substantial success at a conference of the Petrograd city organization of the Bolsheviks, attended by all the national leaders of the party. A hard core of resistance to Lenin nonetheless stood firm. Kamenev flatly opposed Lenin's program of power to the soviets and proposed instead "the most watchful control" by the soviets over the Provisional Government. The conference killed this formula by a vote of twenty to six, with nine abstentions. [38]

In the meantime, the Provisional Government, not yet two months old, was splitting apart at the seams. Mass demonstrations against the government's foreign policy—the so-called April Days—precipitated the first cabinet crisis and paved the way for a coalition of Duma and soviet leaders. While the Bolshevik Central Committee rejected a "Down with the Provisional Government" slogan as adventurist, the Moscow organization of the party issued a blazing manifesto for revolutionary demonstrations, workers' guards, and assumption of power by the soviets. [39] As the political atmosphere became more radical, the Bolshevik opposition to Lenin gave way.

This was the mood when, on April 24, Bolshevik leaders from all over the country met formally for the Seventh All-Russian Party Conference. Neither Kamenev nor Stalin, the March leaders, was elected to the presidium of five. [40] Lenin reiterated his stand against the Provisional Government and the war. Kamenev, persisting in his opposition, delivered a minority report: "It is too early to say that bourgeois democracy has exhausted all of its possibilities." He affirmed again the desirability of cooperation with the "petty-bourgeois" groups and urged "control" by the revolutionaries over the actions of a necessarily bourgeois government. [41] Lenin was supported against Kamenev's criticism by Zinoviev, who had returned from Switzerland with him, and by Stalin. [42] Stalin was quick to trim his sails to the new wind; almost alone of the prominent Bolshevik leaders, he never ventured to oppose the clearly expressed will of Lenin.

On matters of practical import Lenin carried all before him at the April Conference. In condemning continuation of the war the assemblage was unanimous, with the exception of seven die hard right-wingers who abstained.[43] When the conference endorsed "prolonged work" to "guarantee the successful transfer of all state power into the hands of the soviets," only three of the one hundred and thirty-three voting delegates voted no, with eight abstaining.[44] For the Ultra-Right Bolsheviks, the April Conference marked the parting of the ways; most of them soon went over to the Mensheviks.

The theoretical implications of permanent revolution (embodied in a proposed resolution) brought forth the most concerted opposition which Lenin met at the conference. Rykov tried to urge caution: "Whence will arise the sun of the socialist overturn? I think that under present conditions, with our standard of living, the initiation of the socialist overturn does not belong to us. We have not the strength, the objective conditions, for this." "Before us stand gigantic revolutionary tasks," he admitted, "but the execution of these tasks does not lead us out of the framework of the bourgeois system."[45] The resolution did concede that "the proletariat of Russia, acting in one of the most backward countries of Europe, among the small-peasant masses of the population, cannot pose for itself the goal of rapid realization of socialist reform." Socialists would indeed come to power—they hoped— and begin measures of control and antibureaucratic reform pointing toward large proportion of the conference failed to be convinced: the resolution car- socialism, though success depended on an early international revolution. A ried by a majority of only twenty-four against the total of no's and abstentions, in a total vote of one hundred and eighteen.[46]

In view of this persisting timidity, Lenin did not press his plans immediately. Further splitting was avoided, but the price Lenin paid was almost equal representation for the right-wing faction in the party leadership. The new Central Committee elected at the close of the April Conference included four Rightists—Kamenev, Nogin, V. P. Miliutin, and G. F. Fedorov —together with Lenin and his supporters Zinoviev, Stalin, Sverdlov, and I. T. Smilga.[47]

Throughout the rest of 1917 the undercurrent of caution was felt in the Bolshevik Party on one critical occasion after another. The party had yielded to Lenin's leadership, but only with great reluctance was the right wing dragged to the point of taking power. Lenin turned to seek more allies, and his quest was well rewarded. Between May and July, the Bolshevik Party drew into its ranks a swarm of illustrious left-wing Mensheviks, with Trotsky at their head. The new recruits, far more resolute than most of Lenin's old henchmen, figured among the key leaders in the seizure of power.

In July the Bolsheviks experienced a serious setback. In the course of the "July Days," popular revolutionary demonstrations got out of hand and became riots. The Bolsheviks were blamed for an attempt to seize power, though actually they had rejected the idea as unseasonable. Conveniently, documents came to light on the basis of which the Provisional Government (now headed by Alexander Kerensky) denounced the Bolshevik leaders as

German agents. (In this famous forgery, the ex-Bolshevik Alexinsky had a hand.) The Bolshevik Party was proscribed and its leaders threatened with arrest. Lenin and Zinoviev went into hiding, where they remained until the eve of the October Revolution. Kamenev was arrested and for a time jailed, as were Trotsky and Lunacharsky when they quixotically demanded treatment equal to that accorded the Bolsheviks with whom they sympathized.[48]

The effort by the Provisional Government to suppress the Bolsheviks was far from thorough, and they were able to proceed with their Sixth Party Congress, which met from July 26 to August 3. This was the first conclave claiming such a status since 1907. With most of the top-ranking leaders absent, however, the congress was reduced to largely inconclusive wrangling about revolutionary strategy and tactics. Its most notable achievement was to formalize the unification of the Bolsheviks and the revolutionary Mensheviks, and thus establish the party on lines which were to hold for the next ten years.

THE ABSORPTION OF THE MENSHEVIK LEFT

During the honeymoon days after the overthrow of Nicholas II, the idea of reunification was on the tip of every Social Democratic tongue. In some local organizations the Bolsheviks and Mensheviks immediately combined. Some Mensheviks proposed that the factions merge fully. The Ultra-Right Bolsheviks, who found themselves in full agreement with the Mensheviks on most issues, were wholeheartedly in favor of the proposed merger. Said Stalin, expressing the "Center" viewpoint of the Bolshevik leadership at the March conference, "We ought to do it. . . . Unification is possible along the line of Zimmerwald-Kienthal."* Only the Bolshevik left wing opposed unity with the Mensheviks. Complained Zalutsky (who had just been displaced from his short-lived prominence with the Petrograd party bureau), "Only a petty-bourgeois and not a Social Democrat can proceed from a mere desire for unification. . . . It is impossible to unite on the basis of superficial adherence to Zimmerwald-Kienthal." Stalin dismissed the objection: "There is no use running ahead and anticipating disagreements. There is no party life without disagreements."[49]

The Bolsheviks' March conference had approved consultations with the Mensheviks on the subject of unification, though a more concrete proposal for ties with the internationalist wing of the Mensheviks passed by only one vote. This seems to have met with disfavor not only among the Bolshevik Left but also among the Ultra-Right Bolsheviks, who apparently feared that it would encourage a split among the Mensheviks and endanger the prospects for reunification of the whole Social Democratic Party.[50] One Menshevik,

* The reference is to the conferences of antiwar European socialist leaders held in Switzerland in 1915 and 1916.

speaking before a joint meeting of the factions, actually proposed an open realignment on the basis of the defensist-internationalist cleavage among both the Bolsheviks and the Mensheviks.[51] As it turned out, this was almost precisely what happened.

The idea of unification was abruptly set back with Lenin's return to Russia. At the conclusion of his April Theses, Lenin bluntly exclaimed, "Unity with the defensists . . . is treason to socialism."[52] Most of the Bolsheviks were unwilling to accept Lenin's intransigence and voted with their Menshevik associates to set up a joint organizing bureau to prepare a unification congress. Then, vacillating, the Bolshevik leaders declined to participate in this bureau, except for the right-wingers Voitinsky and Goldenberg (who were already on their way toward an open shift to the Menshevik side).[53]

Nothing further came of the plan of overall Bolshevik-Menshevik unity, but it left the Bolsheviks and the antiwar left wing of the Mensheviks ready to come to terms. The Bolshevik April Conference resolved that "rapprochement and unification with groups and currents which in fact stand on the ground of internationalism is indispensable, on the basis of a break with the policy of petty-bourgeois treason to socialism."[54] This kept the unification movement alive, but reduced substantially to what it had been in 1915 and 1916: a question of the absorption of the antiwar socialists into the Bolshevik ranks. Here again the organizational issue proved to be a disruptive factor.

The Mezhraiontsy—Mensheviks who were almost Bolsheviks—had been discussing unity with the Bolsheviks ever since the February Revolution. The idea of absorbing the Mezhraiontsy acquired immediate practical import for Lenin when, on May 4, Trotsky returned to Russia and assumed a position of leadership in that group. For both parties the advantages of coalescence were obvious: Trotsky and his associates among the Mezhraiontsy lacked a broad following and could make themselves effective only in Lenin's mass organization; but they would bring to the Bolsheviks valuable talent as agitators and a great deal of revolutionary prestige. Moreover, Lenin had not disposed of the cautious right wing in his own party; union with the Menshevik Left would (and did) provide strategic reinforcement for the revolutionary position within the ranks of the Bolsheviks.

On May 10, the Bolsheviks and Mezhraiontsy met to discuss unification. Trotsky indicated that he had abandoned the hope of bringing all the Russian Social Democrats under one roof and accepted the Bolshevik condition of unity among the antiwar groups alone. Appearing to let by-gones be by-gones, Lenin gave the Mezhraiontsy an unconditional invitation to join the Bolshevik Party, and he promised Trotsky and his associates leading positions in the party organization and on the editorial board of *Pravda*.[55] There were, however, objections on both sides. The Bolshevik leadership turned down Lenin's first proposal that Trotsky be made an editor of *Pravda*.[56] Trotsky, while observing with satisfaction that the Bolsheviks had "de-Bolshevized" themselves, balked at the party label: "I cannot call myself a Bolshevik. Old factional labels are undesirable."[57] Lenin reportedly thought Trotsky's pride was to blame for this.[58]

Certain tactical considerations, as well as the old organizational discords, contributed to the delay of the merger. Both Lenin and the Mezhraiontsy hoped that if they proceeded slowly all the internationalist Mensheviks, particularly Martov and his following, could be brought into the Bolshevik camp. Lunacharsky, who inclined to the Bolshevik Right after he entered the party with the Mezhraiontsy, wanted Martov to join the Bolsheviks in order to become the head of a right wing with decisive influence.[59] These hopes did not materialize. Martov, though he had no substantial programmatic differences with the Bolsheviks, steadfastly refused to be associated with their tactical and organizational habits.

It was not until after the July Days, when Lenin was hiding in Finland and Trotsky was in jail, that the Sixth Party Congress formally accepted the Mezhraiontsy into the Bolshevik ranks. Some of the Bolsheviks were still disgruntled by the move. No doubt Trotsky's dazzling personality and outstanding reputation soured the more pedestrian figures who had been helping Lenin run the Bolshevik Party. The origin of the long and bitter hostility between Trotsky and Zinoviev is without doubt to be found in the natural resentment felt by Zinoviev, Lenin's closest collaborator since 1909, at being overshadowed by the illustrious newcomer. Possibly Zinoviev's chagrin over this situation influenced his shift to the right wing of the party and his opposition to the insurrection, though his oft-mentioned cowardice may well have been a factor too. Opposition to the merger—even after it was consummated at the Sixth Congress—was also prompted by lingering uneasiness about "petty-bourgeois" groups who were not fully committed to the Bolsheviks' principles of organization.[60] On August 4, when the new Central Committee (without Lenin's presence) was reorganizing the party newspaper, a renewed proposal to make Trotsky one of the editors was voted down, eleven to ten. Not until September, when Trotsky had been released from jail and was becoming the dominant figure in the Petrograd Soviet, did the Central Committee reverse itself and accept him as an editor, along with Kamenev, Stalin, and Sokolnikov.[61]

The composition of the new Central Committee which was elected at the Sixth Congress reflected the heterogeneous character of the new Bolshevik leadership which, together with the simultaneous influx of new rank-and-file members, gave the party a complexion substantially different from that of its underground days.[62] Eight members of the Central Committee elected in April kept their positions—Lenin, Zinoviev, Kamenev, Stalin, Sverdlov, Nogin, Miliutin, and Smilga. Fedorov alone was dropped, while one of the candidate members, Bubnov, was promoted to full status. These had all been firm followers of Lenin before 1917, if exception is made for lapses during the boycottist enthusiasm of 1906 and 1907. But the rightist tendency among this group of old leaders was pronounced in March and April of 1917; Kamenev, Stalin, Miliutin, and Nogin were prominent in advancing the early line of caution. While Stalin shifted to follow Lenin, Zinoviev gravitated toward the right. Lenin's leadership depended on new officer material.

Twelve members of the new Central Committee were entirely fresh. For three, Y. A. Berzin, F. A. Artem-Sergeyev and S. G. Shaumian, there is no evidence that they were anything but loyal followers of Lenin; the same applies to the former Duma deputy, Muranov, unless his espousal of the moderate position in March 1917 had more than episodic significance.[63] On the other hand, Rykov, leader of the Bolshevik conciliators before the war, had stood with the right wing consistently. Sokolnikov was the former conciliator who had gone over to the Trotsky-Martov *Nashe slovo* group during the war. Bukharin and Dzerzhinsky represented those Bolsheviks who had criticized Lenin from the left in 1915 and 1916. The future Trotskyist party secretary Nikolai Nikolaevich Krestinsky was a Bolshevik associate of the Left Menshevik paper *Novaya zhizn* (New Life) which Gorky now edited.[64] Three new members of the Central Committee had never been Bolsheviks before the war—Kollontai, who had come over from the Mensheviks in 1915 and was the first to endorse Lenin's April Theses, and two Mezhraiontsy, Uritsky and, most important of all, Trotsky. The new party leadership was anything but a collection of disciplined yes-men.

With the rounding-out of the Bolshevik Party and its leadership that was accomplished in the summer of 1917, the personal basis was laid for the factional controversies that broke out after the revolution. The group of former deviationists whom Lenin rallied to inspire the party onward to revolution was the embodiment of left-wing idealism in political philosophy and the primary source of the series of Left Opposition movements that rent the party between 1918 and 1927.

A glance at the prerevolutionary political careers of some of the later Left Opposition leaders shows their strong reservations about Lenin. Trotsky, as his enemies never tired of pointing out, was a Menshevik or a nonfactional independent until he joined the Bolshevik Party with the Mezhraiontsy in July 1917. Trotsky's close supporters, Rakovsky and Ioffe, had been old associates of his and also did not become Bolsheviks until 1917. Kollontai, one of the principal leaders of the Workers' Opposition in 1920–1921, was a Menshevik until 1915. Larin, a vocal critic of the party leadership from 1921 to 1923, joined the Bolsheviks as a Menshevik-Internationalist in 1917. Antonov-Ovseyenko, a supporter of Trotsky in 1923, had been a Menshevik and a member of the *Nashe slovo* group. Radek, subsequently an active Comintern leader, had participated in the Polish and German Social Democratic parties as an extreme internationalist, and adhered to the Left Bolshevik position during the war. Bukharin, a left-winger up to 1921 and subsequently the leader of the Right Opposition against Stalin, had not only been a Left Bolshevik during the war but previously had by his own admission "a certain heretical partiality to Empiriocriticism." Piatakov, another wartime Left Bolshevik, later one of Trotsky's principal supporters, began his political career as an anarchist and became a Bolshevik only around 1910. V. V. Osinsky, one of the leaders of the Democratic Centralist opposition group from 1919 to 1923, had been an Otzovist. Vladimir Smirnov, another leading Democratic Centralist, had been an associate of Bukharin and Osinsky at Moscow University.[65]

This suggestion of a close relationship between deviation from Lenin's line before the revolution and opposition activity afterwards is strengthened by certain statistical conclusions which arise from consideration of the records of other Bolshevik leaders. The connections between earlier deviation and later opposition, and between both of these and life as an émigré in Western Europe, are also clear.* Of thirty-five Left Oppositionists, sixteen (46 per cent) had records of prerevolutionary deviation. Of thirty-four nonoppositionists, only eight (24 per cent) had been deviators.

The distinction becomes much sharper if the factors of intellectual background and life in the emigration are taken into account. Of thirty-one intellectual-émigrés, twenty-three (74 per cent) were deviators; none of the nondeviators became a Left Oppositionist; those who did become Left Oppositionists had *all* been deviators. On the other hand, only two out of thirty nonintellectual undergrounders had records of deviation (and both became oppositionists); twelve of the nondeviators, however, became Left Oppositionists.

The fact that intellectual undergrounders, like the nonintellectuals, did not often acquire records of deviation leads to the conclusion that life in the emigration was the main stimulus to prerevolutionary deviation; life in the underground, on the contrary, tended to suppress deviation or conceal the record of it. This is undoubtedly why many undergrounders with no record of deviation became Left Oppositionists, while nondeviating émigrés did not. If a man in the emigration had any affinity for the non-Leninist current of Bolshevism, this inclination would have been manifested clearly in the course

---

* The material for this analysis is drawn largely from the biographies of party leaders in the *Encyclopedic Dictionary*, XLI. A total of eighty-five individuals were classified on the following points:
  1. Record of Opposition
     (a) Left Opposition in 1921 or 1923
     (b) Other opposition
     (c) No record of opposition to Lenin or Stalin up to 1928
  2. Record of prerevolutionary deviation
  3. Intellectual (some university education or equivalent)
  4. Experience as émigrés (six months or more)

of the many controversies which took place. This analysis lends only the slightest support to the frequently expressed idea that the Opposition leaders were more intellectual and the nonoppositionists more proletarian. Of thirty-eight oppositionists, twenty-two (58 per cent) were intellectuals; of forty-eight nonoppositionists, twenty-five (52 per cent) were intellectuals. After 1921, however, the Opposition's support was definitely concentrated in intellectual circles.

It is clear that the Left Opposition after the revolution was part of a current of political thought that had constantly been opposed to the strict followers of Lenin since prerevolutionary days. This fact lends some credence to the allegation made by the Stalinists during their struggle with the Opposition in the twenties that their adversaries were not genuine Bolsheviks at all, but essentially Menshevik in outlook. By this time, the charge of Menshevism was almost tantamount to that of treason, and the oppositionists felt themselves obliged to refute the accusation as best they could. As a result, they went far toward complete endorsement of the Leninist organizational system (which only helped strengthen Stalin the more), and the ideological confusion stirred up in the course of the controversy obscured the nature of the Left Opposition movement as a whole.

In the middle of 1917, however, Bolshevik thinking was not centered on the organizational hardness which both originally and later distinguished the movement. With the general Social Democratic realignment, with the entry of new leaders and spokesmen into the Bolshevik Party, and with Lenin's own reorientation, the Bolsheviks came to be distinguished primarily by their revolutionary fervor and by their utopian hopes for immediate world revolution and the rapid realization of unalloyed socialist ideals in Russia. This new spirit of 1917 was the inspiration for ten years of futile opposition by left-wing Communists.

THE PROGRAM OF REVOLUTION

The outstanding spokesman of the revolutionary idealism of 1917 was none other than Lenin himself. Spurring the Bolshevik Party on toward the seizure of power, Lenin put aside his usual obsession with organizational rigor and conspiratorial discipline, and he penned bold visions of the party's success and the new order which it would bring to Russia and the whole civilized world. His old cautious collaborators from the days of the underground and the emigration were left foundering in leaderless hesitancy, while Lenin himself had taken up with all manner of undisciplined radicals who were ready to share the revolutionary gamble with him.

Such were the alignments when, taking refuge in semiautonomous Finland in the fall of 1917, Lenin composed his chief programmatic work, "State and Revolution." The book reads like a manifesto of left-wing Bolshevism, and indeed that is its real significance. To consider "State and Revolution" as the basic statement of Lenin's political philosophy—which non-Communists as well as Communists usually do—is a serious error. Its argument for a utopian anarchism never actually became official policy after the revolution, as the Soviet leadership has always pretended. The Leninism of 1917 was the point of departure for the Left Opposition, and came to grief in a few short years; it was the revived Leninism of 1902 which prevailed as the basis for the political development of the USSR.

The revolutionary utopianism which Lenin expounded in 1917 was inspired by the experience of the Paris Commune of 1871, whose features were exalted by Marx in *The Civil War in France* as the archtype of a proletarian government. Lenin had been guided to this line of thinking shortly before the February Revolution by the Left Bolsheviks, especially Bukharin, who in turn were under the influence of left-wing and semianarchist thought among the European socialists.[66] In 1917 the "Commune state" was incorporated into the Bolshevik program—"a democratic proletarian-peasant republic."[67] The existing state machinery was to be destroyed. Features of the revolutionary government which Lenin stressed were replacement of organized military and police forces by the "armed people," direct popular election of political representatives with full right of recall, and limitation of officials' salaries to the level of workmen's wages—in sum, every possible extension of direct popular participation in political activities.[68] All of the hierarchic and repressive forms attributed to the "bourgeois" state were to be eliminated. "Such a beginning," declared Lenin, "on the basis of large-scale production, of itself leads to the gradual 'withering away' of any officialdom, to the gradual creation of a new order . . . in which the more and more simplified functions of supervision and accounting will be performed by everyone in turn, will then become a habit, and will finally die out as *special* functions of a special stratum of people."[69]

The institutions through which Lenin envisaged the accomplishment of this transformation (or rather annihilation) of the political order in Russia were the soviets. After 1905 Lenin had looked to these popular councils of spontaneous origin as the basis of a revolutionary regime, and he now praised them as "a new, immeasurably higher, incomparably more democratic type of state apparatus."[70] In April 1917 Lenin asserted, "Insofar as these soviets exist, and *insofar as* they constitute authority, to that extent a state of the Paris Commune *type* exists in Russia."[71] The basic Bolshevik slogan followed naturally—"All power to the soviets."

The function of the party in this eagerly anticipated Armageddon was not made entirely explicit. "State and Revolution" contains only a single reference to the party as an element in the process of revolution.[72] But in various writings earlier in the year Lenin did map out a role for the party; it should serve as goad and critic of the Menshevik and Socialist Revolutionary leaders who up to then were steering the revolution. In this way, Lenin suggested in April, "it is possible to make the ground so 'hot' under the feet of the petty-bourgeoisie that, in certain circumstances, it will *have* to seize power."[73] There was as yet no question of a minority dictatorship. On the contrary, Lenin stressed, "To become the power, the class-conscious workers must win the majority over to their side. *As long as* there is no violence against the masses there is no other road to power. We are not Blanquists, we are not supporters of the seizure of power by a minority."[74] This was good democratic rhetoric, and at the time perhaps Lenin could not anticipate how this stricture would be used against him by some of his own followers when he proposed just such a seizure of power.

Justification for the Bolsheviks' drive for power was found more outside Russia than internally. Reasoning from the premises of permanent revolution, the Bolshevik left wing—Lenin now included—envisioned vast but interdependent possibilities of revolution in Europe as well as in Russia. Europe was ripe for revolution, and Russia would shake the tree. This was a role which the left-wing Bolsheviks regarded as a moral imperative; according to a resolution of the Sixth Party Congress, "The liquidation of imperialist rule sets before the working class of that country which first realizes the dictatorship of the proletarians and semiproletarians, the task of supporting by any means (even armed force) the struggling proletariat of other countries. In particular, such a task stands before Russia, if, as is very probable, the new unavoidable upsurge of the Russian Revolution places the workers and poorest peasants in power before an overturn in the capitalist countries of the West."[75]

For the left wing, international imperialism was the great enemy, and, because the Provisional Government was held to be a representative of imperialism, it made no sense to speak of defending the revolutionary gains which had been made under the aegis of that regime. Thus Trotsky asserted in support of the Bolshevik Party even before he joined it, "Only that party can go in step with the movement of history which builds its program and tactics with consideration of the development of the social-revolutionary struggle of the world proletariat and especially that of Europe."[76] The only significant role for the Russian Revolution, from this standpoint, was to strike the heaviest possible blow to begin the world revolution, to gamble everything on winning the support of the European workers.

To Lenin and his supporters a state of war was a revolutionary asset. Impelled by the formula, "Turn the imperialist war into a civil war," the proletarians everywhere would simultaneously put an end to the war and carry out the socialist revolution. Should the imperialists stand firm and reject the peace offers of a revolutionary Russian government, Lenin promised: "We . . . would ourselves wage a revolutionary war, summoning the workers of all countries to join us."[77] Bukharin declared to the Sixth Party Congress in August 1917: "We will wage a holy war in the name of the interests of all the proletariat. . . . By such a revolutionary war we will light the fire of world socialist revolution."[78]

Despite the strength of this internationalist fervor, there were intimations of a contrary attitude which was destined to develop rapidly after the party came to power. Stalin in his report to the Sixth Congress analyzed the alternatives of continuing or stopping the war, but entirely neglected the prospect of "revolutionary war." A resolution on revolutionary war proposed by Bukharin was watered down in committee, on the realistic ground that "we cannot irrevocably assert that we will command the strength to wage a revolutionary war."[79]

The doctrinaire position was exemplified by Yevgeni Alekseyevich Preobrazhensky, a rising theoretician of the Left, who wanted to restore the original Bukharin resolution. Later on, when Stalin was reading his proposed resolution on the prospects of socialist revolution in Russia, Preobrazhensky interrupted him to suggest adding the words, "with the materializing of the proletarian revolution in the West." Stalin's reply gave a hint of the nationalistic doctrine of "socialism in one country" which he was later to expound: "I am against such an ending of the resolution. The possibility is not excluded that Russia itself may be the country which lays down the road to socialism. . . . The base of our revolution is broader than in Western Europe. . . . Here the poorest strata of the peasantry support the workers. . . . We must reject the worn-out assertion that only Europe can show us the way. There exist both dogmatic Marxism and creative Marxism. I stand on the basis of the latter."[80] Preobrazhensky's amendment was rejected.

Nevertheless, the interdependence of the Russian and international revolutions was axiomatic for almost all Bolsheviks in 1917. There was, to be sure, room for differences: the undercurrent of right-wing opinion persistently discounted the possibility of successful revolution either in Russia or in Europe on the grounds that conditions were not ripe. But Lenin's leadership, supported by the internationalism of the party's new adherents and old deviators, carried the day for a course of revolutionary boldness. "All over the globe the storm signals are flying," proclaimed the manifesto issued by the Sixth Congress.[81]

International revolutionary duty seemed to demand of the Bolsheviks that they strike against the representatives of imperialism in Russia, whatever the odds. On October 8, 1917, when he was pressing the party to seize power, Lenin cited reports of mutiny in the German navy and wrote, "We shall be real betrayers of the International if at such a moment, under such favorable conditions, we answer such a call of the German revolutionists merely with—resolutions."[82] The purpose of the October Revolution, in the minds of its most vigorous proponents, was to give the signal for international upheaval by the force of revolutionary example, by appealing for peace, and by standing ready to wage revolutionary war.

THE QUESTION OF INSURRECTION

In the real world—metaphysical webs aside—history is made by people deciding to take action, though whether or not they achieve what they intend is another matter. Such a decision the Bolshevik Party had to make in the fall of 1917: to act or not, to translate revolutionary ferment into a *coup d'état* or let nature take its course. The decision was made at Lenin's insistent prompting but, like every major step the Bolsheviks took in their early years of power, it was made in an atmosphere of anxious soul-searching and in the face of bitter factional recrimination. The lines of cleavage in the party which Lenin had been trying to weld together opened up again, and the cautious wing of Bolshevism almost fell away irretrievably.

The first definite indication that Lenin seriously contemplated a one-party seizure of power and dictatorship by his Bolsheviks came after the July Days, when the Provisional Government attempted to outlaw the party after the wave of rioting which it had led. Lenin decided that the slogan, "All power to the soviets," had outlived its usefulness.[83] He no longer saw the future of the revolution as lying with the soviets, which the Bolsheviks would prod into action as peaceful collaborators of the other socialist parties. The revolution could progress only through a Bolshevik seizure of power: "The revolutionary proletariat itself must independently take governmental power into its hands."[84]

For the moment, Lenin urged caution and careful preparation. Such restraint met with vigorous objection from the hotheads, and M. M. Volodarsky (one of the Mezhraiontsy who had just joined the Bolsheviks) succeeded in getting the Petrograd city organization to approve a much less patient line.[85] The Sixth Party Congress took a determined stand in favor of direct action by the masses: "The task of these revolutionary classes is . . . to exert all their strength to take state power into their hands, and to direct it, in alliance with the revolutionary proletariat of the advanced countries, toward peace and toward the socialist reconstruction of society."[86] The Bolshevik extremists were happy to break with the soviets and make a direct appeal to the masses. Molotov's March radicalism was vindicated. "Power can be acquired only by force," he declared, with emphasis on "the only way out of the existing situation—the dictatorship of the proletariat and the poorest peasantry."[87]

It was not yet clear what the anticipated progress of the revolution would imply for relations between the Bolsheviks and the other socialist parties. Marxists had always assumed that all genuinely proletarian political forces would be united in one party, and this had blocked consideration of the problem of relations between two or more revolutionary parties. In a speech at the Sixth Congress Sokolnikov claimed exclusive revolutionary virtue for the Bolsheviks: "I do not agree with Comrade Stalin as to whether we want to create a united front from the socialist-revolutionaries to the Bolsheviks. With the transfer of power into the hands of the soviets, the power would inevitably go to the Bolsheviks, as the revolutionary vanguard, and the Mensheviks and Socialist Revolutionaries, following the path of compromise with the Kadets, would be squeezed out of the soviets because they would have lost all credit in the eyes of the masses."[88]

In the latter part of August, Kerensky's own chief of staff, General L. G. Kornilov, attempted to overthrow the Provisional Government by a military coup. To meet this threat from the right, the government had to accept whatever support it could muster on the left, and the outlawry of the Bolsheviks ceased to be enforced. On September 4 the Bolshevik leaders who had been jailed after the July Days, including Trotsky and Kamenev, were released. At the same time, popular support for the Bolsheviks and for the comparable left-wing tendency among the SRs was snowballing. The simple Bolshevik program of Bread, Land, and Peace was almost irresistible at this hour of crisis and revolutionary emotion. On August 31, just after Kornilov's movement had collapsed, the practice of unrestricted recall and re-election of deputies to the soviets produced an ominous indication of the shift of sentiment among the workers and garrison troops in the capital: a Bolshevik resolution for the first time received a majority of votes in the Petrograd Soviet.[89]

With this decisive turn in the fortunes of the Bolsheviks, Lenin fleetingly reverted to his earlier expectation of a multiparty revolutionary leadership in the soviets: "Such a sharp and original turn in the Russian Revolution has now occurred that we as a party can offer a voluntary compromise . . .—our return to the pre-July demand of all power to the soviets, a government of SRs and Mensheviks responsible to the soviets. . . . It is overwhelmingly probable that such a government . . . could secure a peaceful *forward* movement of the whole Russian Revolution. . . . Only in the name of this peaceful development of the revolution . . . the Bolsheviks would refrain . . . from revolutionary methods of struggle. . . . We have nothing to fear under a real democracy, for life favors us. . . ."[90]

Nevertheless, Lenin's conciliatory mood was neither consistent nor enduring. Before publishing the article "On Compromises" he added a postscript declaring the idea to be "obsolete,"[91] and he again began to caution the Bolsheviks against illusions of peaceful progress.[92] The vision of cooperation was abandoned by Lenin as suddenly as it occurred to him, though it did leave him espousing once again the slogan, "All power to the soviets."[93] They were now, or soon to be, Bolshevik soviets; the Bolsheviks won a victory in the Moscow Soviet on September 5, and on September 9 the Petrograd Soviet installed a new presidium with a Bolshevik majority.[94]

Responding to this success, Lenin lost no time in making his momentous decision. In two letters[95] to the Bolshevik Central Committee in Petrograd, which he wrote from his Finnish hideout between September 12 and 14, he announced that the time had come for the Bolsheviks to take the destiny of the revolution in their own hands and prepare for an armed seizure of power: "Having obtained a majority in the Soviets of Workers' and Soldiers' Deputies of both capitals, the Bolsheviks can and must take governmental power into their hands. . . . History will not forgive us if we do not assume power now. . . . Take power at once in Moscow and Petrograd . . . ; we will win *absolutely and unquestionably*."[96]

Lenin's party was far from ready to respond as one man to his call to arms. At the time Lenin's appeal for action was received on September 15, the Bolshevik Party was participating in the so-called Democratic Conference, a consultative body convoked by the government parties in an effort to rally support before the elections to the Constituent Assembly were held. The burning issue of the day for the Bolsheviks was posed by a proposition set before the conference by the government, that it sanction the establishment of a quasi-representative body, the Council of the Republic, which would sit until the Constituent Assembly could be elected. Should the Bolsheviks continue participation in the representational schemes of the Provisional Government, or boycott them and prepare for revolutionary action in the name of the soviets?

Lenin's proposal for insurrection went beyond what either the cautious or the bold factions in the party's Central Committee were prepared to undertake at the moment. Zinoviev had already written an article (published by Stalin on August 30) entitled "What Not to Do," in which he warned that the fate of the Paris Commune was in store for anyone who attempted to seize power by force.[97] The party, schooled by Marxism to follow the objective groundswells of revolution, had not yet been taught to regard the "art of insurrection" as the key to political success. Kamenev proposed to the Central Committee that Lenin's call for a deliberate seizure of power by the party be flatly rejected. This open defiance of the leader was rejected by a majority of the committee, but the general reluctance to take the risk of insurrectionary action, in view of the Bolsheviks' weakness in the provinces, inspired a move to disregard Lenin's proposal altogether and destroy the letters. Someone suggested that this step be modified to keep a copy of Lenin's proposals for the party record. The strength of right-wing caution in the party was revealed by the split which this innocuous amendment caused in the Central Committee—the vote was only six to four to preserve the texts, with six members abstaining. Lenin received no reply at all.[98]

Having sidestepped Lenin's first call for an uprising, the Bolshevik leaders in Petrograd returned to the effort to resolve their differences about the Democratic Conference and the Council of the Republic, or Pre-Parliament, as it was usually styled. The Democratic Conference, which sat from September 14 to September 22, was to pass on the establishment of the Pre-

Parliament (which actually convened on October 7). The Bolshevik delegation or fraction in the Democratic Conference sought instructions from the Central Committee as to the attitude it should take. Trotsky spoke for a boycott of the Pre-Parliament; the committee divided nine to eight in favor, but then referred the question back to the Bolshevik fraction in the Democratic Conference. Trotsky and Stalin—in a rare instance of cooperation—reported to the fraction on behalf of the Leftist bloc in the Central Committee, while Rykov and Kamenev spoke for the Right in opposition to the boycott. The discussion ended with a vote by the fraction, and the delegates defeated the boycott, seventy-seven to fifty. Trotsky attributed his defeat to the representatives of the provincial Bolsheviks, whose estimate of the revolutionary situation was appreciably more conservative than that prevailing in the capital.[99]

Meanwhile Lenin was urging radical tactics: "We should have boycotted the Democratic Conference. . . . We must boycott the Pre-Parliament." When he learned of the decision to participate in the Pre-Parliament, he took it as a sign of serious weakness in the party. Ignoring all his own precepts of "democratic centralism," Lenin wrote, "We cannot and must not in any case reconcile ourselves to participation. . . . At the 'top' of our party we note vacillations that may become *ruinous.*" He singled Trotsky out for praise in defending the revolutionary course: "Trotsky was for the boycott. Bravo, Comrade Trotsky! . . . Long live the boycott!"[100]

Lenin then began a feverish campaign of correspondence to persuade his colleagues that the seizure of power could and must be accomplished. The poor response to his proddings enraged him:

In our Central Committee and at the top of our party there is a tendency or opinion for *awaiting* the Congress of Soviets, *against* the immediate seizure of power, *against* an immediate uprising. We must *overcome* this tendency or opinion.

Otherwise the Bolsheviks would *disgrace* themselves forever and would *come to nothing* as a party.

For to miss such a moment and to "await" the Congress of Soviets is *complete idiocy or complete betrayal.*

Here Lenin invoked the international duty of the Russian revolutionaries: delay meant "a complete betrayal of the German workers. Indeed," he declared, "we must not wait for the beginning of their revolution!"[101]

To this blast Lenin added a compelling threat—he would resign from the Central Committee and (disregarding his own organizational rules) appeal directly to the party:

Seeing that the Central Committee has *not even answered* my demands . . . that the Central Organ [edited by Stalin] is *deleting* from my articles references to such glaring errors of the Bolsheviks as the shameful decision to participate in the Pre-Parliament . . . I am compelled to recognize here a "gentle" hint that the Central Committee does not even wish to consider this question, a gentle hint of gagging me and of proposing that I retire.

I am compelled to *tender my resignation from the Central Committee,* which I hereby do, leaving myself freedom of propaganda *in the lower ranks* of the party and at the party congress.

For it is my deepest conviction that if we "await" the Congress of Soviets and let the present moment pass, we will *ruin* the revolution.[102]

Lenin's threat was effective. The bolder group in the Central Committee, simultaneously prodded by Lenin and furnished with his forensic ammunition, won the ascendancy. On October 3 the Central Committee heard G. I. Lomov, representing the radicals of the Moscow organization, urge an immediate insurrection. Still unprepared to accede to the advocates of bold action, the committee did resolve to call upon Lenin to come to Petrograd secretly and meet with them to make a final decision on the seizure of power.[103] This step was followed by action on the question of the Pre-Parliament. Speaking before the Bolshevik delegation which had assembled for the Pre-Parliament, Trotsky urged that they stage a walk-out on the first day of its proceedings. Kamenev and Riazanov opposed this, and suggested that the Bolshevik fraction await an occasion of reasonable justification before leaving the assembly. This time the vote went to Trotsky.[104] Kamenev vainly protested the walk-out decision in a declaration to the Central Committee; he asked to be relieved of all positions wherein he represented the party in public.[105]

When the Pre-Parliament opened on October 7, the Bolsheviks proceeded with their planned defiance. Trotsky rose to make what was virtually a declaration of war against the government: "With this government of traitors to the people and with this council of counterrevolutionary connivance we have nothing in common. . . . Withdrawing from this temporary council, we call on the workers, soldiers, and peasants of all Russia to be brave and vigilant. Petrograd is in danger! The revolution is in danger! The People are in danger! We turn to the People! All power to the soviets!"[106] The Bolsheviks walked out and turned to the business of insurrection.

Events now moved so fast that Lenin failed to keep up with his party. Between October 3 and 7 he was still writing, "The Bolsheviks have no right to wait for the Congress of Soviets; they must *take power immediately.* . . . To wait for the Congress of Soviets is a childish play of formality . . . betrayal of the revolution."[107] But in the meantime the Bolsheviks were at work on preparations for the uprising. On October 9 the Bolshevik-controlled Petrograd Soviet established a Military-Revolutionary Committee with Trotsky at its head. Designed initially to wrest military control of the Petrograd garrison from the Provisional Government, this body became the actual directing staff of the insurrection.[108]

On October 10, the die was cast. Lenin came to Petrograd in disguise, to meet face to face with the Central Committee for the first time since the July Days. He argued passionately for insurrection and proposed a resolution: "The Central Committee recognizes that the international situation of the Russian Revolution . . . as well as the military situation . . . and the fact that the proletarian parties have gained a majority in the soviets . . . coupled with the peasant uprising and with a shift of the people's confidence toward our party (elections in Moscow); finally, the obvious preparation for a second Kornilov affair . . . places the armed uprising on the order of the day." The motion carried by a vote of ten to two, with Zinoviev and Kamenev standing in opposition.[109]

Zinoviev and Kamenev were no more prepared than Lenin had been to bow before what they considered an unwise decision by the majority of the Central Committee. On October 11 they drew up and dispatched a letter to the major Bolshevik organizations, in which they set forth their reasons for opposing the insurrectionary attempt:

We are deeply convinced that to call at present for an armed uprising means to stake on one card not only the fate of our party, but also the fate of the Russian and international revolution.

There is no doubt that there are historical situations when an oppressed class must recognize that it is better to go forward to defeat than to give up without a battle. Does the Russian working class find itself at present in such a situation? *No, a thousand times no!*

A peaceful policy would capitalize on future mass support, and the party should be able to win a commanding position, in alliance with the Left SRs, at the Constituent Assembly. The course of insurrection and revolutionary war only portended military disaster:

The masses of the soldiers support us not because of the slogan of war, but because of the slogan of peace. . . . If we should wage a revolutionary war, the masses of the soldiers will rush away from us. . . .

Having taken power, the workers' party thereby undoubtedly deals a blow to Wilhelm. . . . But will this blow under present conditions, after [the fall of] Riga, etc., be sufficiently powerful to turn away the hand of German imperialism from Russia?

Zinoviev and Kamenev saw little ground for such a hope. Equally they discounted the assumption that "the majority of the international proletariat allegedly is already with us. Unfortunately this is not so." On the other hand, they professed not to be afraid to act when the time came:

The development of the revolution in Europe will make it obligatory for us, without any hesitation whatever, immediately to take power into our own hands. This is also the only guarantee of the victory of an uprising of the proletariat in Russia. It will come, but it is not here yet.[110]

To put an end to all such lingering doubts, and make definite preparations for the uprising, Lenin again came secretly to Petrograd, on October 16, to meet with the Central Committee and a selected group of local party leaders. The debate waxed more bitter than ever. Zinoviev and Kamenev pleaded the prudence of waiting for the election of the Constituent Assembly, and Kamenev made a Marxist appeal to the impersonal forces of history: "The question is not now or never. I have more belief in the Russian revolution. . . . Two tactics are contending here: the tactic of plot and the tactic of belief in the moving forces of the Russian Revolution."[111]

The debate of October 16 in the Central Committee ended with a vote on Lenin's resolution to proceed with the preparation of an uprising. The decision was reached over an opposition no more effective than that of October 10—the vote was nineteen for and two against (again Zinoviev and Kamenev), with four abstentions. Some members of the committee, however, while not daring to oppose Lenin, were prepared to vote at the same time in favor of contradictory motions. When Zinoviev introduced a counter-resolution calling for the suspension of insurrectionary preparations until the Congress of Soviets was ready to meet and its Bolshevik delegation could be consulted, he gathered six votes to fifteen, with three abstaining. Kamenev —following Lenin's precedent of September 28—resigned from the Central Committee in protest.[112]

It was at this session that the Central Committee created a so-called Military Center to serve as a liaison group between the Central Committee of the party and Trotsky's Military Revolutionary Committee of the Petrograd Soviet. Appointed to the new body were Stalin, Sverdlov, Bubnov, Uritsky, and Dzerzhinsky.[113] The center never functioned as a separate group, but the decision establishing it did serve as the textual basis for the legend proclaimed in the official history later on that Stalin was the man in charge of the uprising. (See Chapter 10.)

Lenin, returning to his hiding place, penned a lengthy reply to the opposition. Abandoning his own earlier reservations, he swept aside all scruples about majority support for the party by refusing to allow the question even to be raised: "To doubt now that the majority of the people is following and will follow the Bolsheviks means shamefully to vacillate and in practice to throw overboard all the principles of proletarian revolutionism, to renounce Bolshevism completely." Delay, as he had constantly insisted, was intolerable: "The position of those who, in arguing about the mood of the masses, attribute to the masses their own personal lack of character, is hopeless."[114] Lenin's letter, obviously aimed at Zinoviev and Kamenev without mentioning their names, was published in the party organ *Rabochi put* (The Workers' Path) by installments on October 19, 20, and 21. The issue for October 20 included a rejoinder by Zinoviev, protesting that his views were by no means as pessimistic as those which Lenin had attributed to him. Appended to these statements was a surprisingly conciliatory note by the editor, Stalin: "We . . . hope that the matter will be considered as closed with the statement made by Comrade Zinoviev. . . . The sharp tone of Comrade Lenin's articles does not alter the fact that we are fundamentally in agreement."[115]

In the meantime, the Zinoviev-Kamenev statement of October 11 had leaked out to nonparty circles. On October 17, Gorky's *Novaya zhizn* published a report by the Menshevik-Internationalist (and former Right Bolshevik) Bazarov that "a hand-written leaflet was distributed in the city, speaking in the name of two leading Bolsheviks against the move."[116] Kamenev responded, in Zinoviev's name and his own, with a note in *Novaya zhizn* reiterating their view that an uprising would be a desperate gamble. They denied that the Bolsheviks had set a date for insurrection, and tried to disguise the fact that the Central Committee had, over their opposition, actually decided on the uprising.[117]

No one, evidently, was deceived or mollified. To Lenin, this published statement by Zinoviev and Kamenev was the most heinous offense they had yet committed. He instantly replied in rage, "On the most important question of battle, on the eve of the critical day of October 20 [the date originally scheduled for the uprising], two 'leading Bolsheviks' . . . attack an *unpublished* decision of the party center in the *non*-party press. . . . Can one imagine an action more treacherous, more strikebreaking? . . . I will fight with all my power . . . for the expulsion of them both from the party."[118] The following day, October 19, he denounced the two oppositionists to the Central Committee and, rightly anticipating qualms about expelling them, wrote, "The more *'outstanding'* the strikebreakers, the more imperative it is to punish them immediately with expulsion. Only in this way is it possible to make the workers' party healthy, to cleanse ourselves of a dozen characterless intellectuals, and with solid ranks of revolutionists . . . to march *with the revolutionary workers*."[119] Here was the real Lenin speaking.

On October 20 the available members of the Central Committee assembled —without Lenin or Zinoviev—to deal with the breach of discipline.[120] Sverdlov read Lenin's letters demanding that Kamenev and Zinoviev be disciplined. Trotsky, seconded by his close friend Adolf Ioffe (also a former *mezhraionets* and now a candidate member of the Central Committee), was most vigorous in pressing the attack, though he was content to accept Kamenev's resignation from the Central Committee and stopped short of endorsing Lenin's demand to expel the culprits from the party. Sverdlov and Dzerzhinsky spoke in the same vein. A contrary position was espoused by Stalin, Miliutin, and Uritsky, who attempted to gloss over the issue by proposing to defer it until the full committee could meet. Said Stalin, "Expulsion from the party is not a cure—we must preserve unity." He was to travel a long way from this stand. Trotsky turned his ire upon Stalin, who was vulnerable because of his editorial defense of Kamenev and Zinoviev. Stalin's associate editor on *Rabochi put,* Sokolnikov, joined in the criticism of the note defending Zinoviev. Stalin offered to resign from his editorial post—a tactic he was to employ successfully more than once—and received an implicit vote of confidence when the resignation was turned down. The vote to accept Kamenev's resignation again revealed the serious cleavage in the party leadership: it followed precisely the differences expressed in the debate—five in favor, three opposed.

The Bolshevik leaders then threw themselves into the effort to seize power. Lenin reiterated his insistence (hardly becoming to a Marxist) that success depended on mastering the art of insurrection. Military action, in the last analysis, would be decisive: "The success of both the Russian and the world revolutions depends upon two or three days of struggle.[121] Trotsky and the Military Revolutionary Committee had completed their plans by October 23, and on October 24 the party was ready to move. Kamenev came back shamefacedly to participate in the uprising and to chair the Second Congress of Soviets. On the following day the October Revolution was engraved in the annals of history by armed workers and mutinous peasant-soldiers, and the Bolsheviks were in power. Their swift triumph proved how unfounded were the Marxian qualms of the Bolshevik Right.

Coalition or Dictatorship?

The October Revolution in itself dispelled one of the reasons for the pessimism of the Kamenev-Zinoviev group. The Bolsheviks successfully seized power and organized a new government in the name of the soviets, headed by Lenin as chairman of the Council of People's Commissars. Most of the Bolsheviks expected that events abroad would shortly belie the other reason for the Rightists' pessimism, with the onset of a successful proletarian revolution in the West.

In the meantime, the split between the Bolshevik majority and the right wing, temporarily healed during the critical days of the insurrection, was reopened by the question of dealing with the other parties in the soviets. The left wing of the SRs, alone of all the non-Bolshevik groups in the soviets, had given full support to the October Revolution and had contributed to the majority by which the Second Congress of Soviets ratified the Bolshevik coup. Nevertheless, there was much agitation in the soviets, in some of the trade unions, and among the right-wing Bolsheviks for the formation of a governing cabinet representing all the socialist parties. Negotiations to this end were carried on between the Bolsheviks and the other parties for several days. The Bolsheviks were not yet committed to a one-party government.

Previous objections to the other soviet parties had been that they were insufficiently energetic in furthering the revolution. Hardly more than a week before the actual uprising, Lenin recalled his idea of a compromise with the Mensheviks and the SRs, and placed the blame on them for the collapse of the plan.[122] When the Second Congress of Soviets ratified the Bolshevik seizure of power on October 25, it was broadly assumed even among the Bolsheviks that the new government would include representatives of all the soviet parties. Martov's proposal that the congress should immediately consider the establishment of such a regime was seconded by Lunacharsky and passed by the delegates unanimously.[123]

During the next few days, the most vigorous proponent of a broad coalition government was the national committee of the railroad workers' union (*Vikzhel,* from its Russian initials), which, with its ability to tie up transportation at this critical time, could readily secure a hearing. On October 29, the Bolshevik Central Committee—in the absence of Lenin, Trotsky, and Stalin —made known its willingness to confer on a coalition, as the Vikzhel desired.[124] Kamenev made himself the Bolshevik spokesman and persuaded the Central Executive Committee of the soviets (two thirds Bolshevik and the rest largely Left SR) to authorize the desired conference. The conference duly met, with a Bolshevik delegation headed by the former Menshevik Riazanov and including Kamenev as its most prominent member. On October 30, again without Lenin and Trotsky (Trotsky was in the field to defeat Kerensky's abortive countercoup), the Bolshevik Central Committee voted unanimously to allow all socialist parties to be represented in the Central Executive Committee, which had become the juridical seat of legislative power in the new regime.[125] The Bolshevik Right was again asserting itself. Nevertheless, the success of the coalition idea was rendered extremely problematical by the conditions which the Mensheviks and Right SRs insisted on —exclusion of Lenin and Trotsky from the new cabinet and a virtual repudiation of the insurrection of October 25.

In the meantime, Lenin made the question of participation in the legislative body academic by having the Council of People's Commissars assume the power to rule temporarily by decree.[126] Trotsky, after dispersing Kerensky's forces, hurried to join Lenin in an attack on the coalition idea. This they began at a conference of the Central Committee and representatives of local Bolshevik organizations on November 1. Kamenev and Riazanov, reporting on the coalition negotiations, met with a cold reception. Trotsky declared that the insurrection was pointless if the Bolsheviks were not to keep a majority. He and Dzerzhinsky denounced the negotiators for even considering the Menshevik and Right SR demand that Lenin and Trotsky be excluded from the government. Lunacharsky defended the negotiations on the ground that they presumed a Bolshevik majority. Lenin saw the negotiations only as a delaying action while the regime consolidated its authority; Rykov replied with surprise that he had been taking them quite seriously. Lenin finally proposed breaking off the negotiations but was defeated, four to ten. By a vote of nine to four with one abstention, the Central Committee adopted the alternative proposed by Trotsky, "to permit members of our party . . . to take part today in a last attempt of the 'Left' SRs to create a so-called homogeneous power, with the aim of once more exposing the bankruptcy of this attempt and finally terminating further negotiations on a coalition government."[127]

Still unsatisfied, Lenin went before a meeting of the Petrograd City Committee of the party, where he challenged the Bolshevik Right to defy him: "As for conciliation, I cannot even speak about that seriously. . . . If you want a split—go ahead. If you have a majority, take power in the Central Executive Committee and carry on. But we will go to the sailors"— a naked threat to decide the matter by force. "Our present slogan," Lenin proclaimed, "is: No compromise, i.e., for a homogeneous Bolshevik government." When Lunacharsky submitted his resignation as Commissar of Education to protest the shelling of the Kremlin during the fighting in Moscow, Lenin demanded (unsuccessfully) that he be expelled from the party, and he once again accused Kamenev and Zinoviev of treason.[128] Such was Lenin's frame of mind, already set for a decade and a half: disagreement with his views could only be regarded as betrayal of the revolution. Not many more years were to pass before the frame of mind would be translated into police action.

The secondary Bolshevik leadership was strongly in favor of coalition. Lenin was rebuffed in Petrograd, and the Moscow city organization, led by Rykov and Nogin, openly backed Zinoviev and Kamenev. Even the Moscow Regional Bureau, distinguished by its left-wing coloration, resolved to accept a coalition if the Bolsheviks had a majority of the cabinet posts.[129] On November 2 the coalition issue began to come to a head when a resolution was passed by the Central Executive Committee insisting that Lenin and Trotsky be included in any cabinet and that at least half the portfolios go to the Bolsheviks. In opposition to this minimal condition, the whole Bolshevik Right voted against the party—Kamenev (the chairman of the Central Executive Committee), Zinoviev, almost half the Council of People's Commissars (Rykov, Lunacharsky, Nogin, Miliutin, Teodorovich), and others including Lozovsky and the ex-Mensheviks Riazanov and Yurenev.[130] Lenin in his rage forced through the Central Committee a resolution damning the Opposition as un-Marxist, un-Bolshevik, confused, vacillating, treacherous, and, to top it all, undemocratic because they would have the majority give in to the threats of a minority. While he denied that he would not consider a coalition, he appealed to "all skeptics and vacillators" to give him their unreserved allegiance.[131]

Lenin then drew up an ultimatum: the Opposition was to observe party

discipline and cease criticizing the majority line on coalition, or else leave
the Bolshevik Party and cast in their lot with the Mensheviks and SRs.[132]
He sought signatures for his ultimatum among the available Central Committee members and secured nine supporters—Trotsky, Stalin, Sverdlov,
Uritsky, Dzerzhinsky, Ioffe, Bubnov, Sokolnikov, and Muranov. Five refused
to sign—Zinoviev, Kamenev, Rykov, Miliutin, and Nogin.[133] The cleavage
was identical with the one produced by the issue of insurrection.

The Opposition disregarded all threats, and on November 4 the crisis
erupted. The Central Executive Committee was discussing the moves made
by the government to muzzle the nonsocialist press, and the representatives
of the Bolshevik Opposition, apprehensive over the possibility of dictatorial
rule, joined in condemning restraints on newspapers which were not actually
calling for rebellion. Larin, a former Menshevik and outstanding exponent
of the left-wing program, offered a resolution to this effect. It failed, twenty-
two to thirty-one, with a number of abstentions. A Leninist countered with
a resolution specifically approving control of the press; this carried by a vote
of thirty-four to twenty-four. Only the Bolsheviks furthest to the Right,
Lozovsky and Riazanov, voted in opposition, together with the Left SRs.[134]

The press issue was the last straw. The Bolshevik oppositionists resigned
en masse from their party and government offices, to the accompaniment of
ringing declarations of principle. All five of Lenin's critics within the Central
Committee left—Zinoviev, Kamenev, Rykov, Miliutin, and Nogin. Collectively they declared, "We cannot assume responsibility for this ruinous policy
of the Central Committee, carried out against the will of a large part of the
proletariat and soldiers. . . . We resign, therefore, from the posts of members
of the Central Committee, so that we will have the right to speak our minds
openly to the mass of workers and soldiers and to call on them to support our
slogan: Long live the government of the soviet parties! Immediate agreement on this condition!"[135]

The three among these Central Committee members who were in the
Council of People's Commissars also surrendered their portfolios in protest
against a one-party government—Rykov (Interior), Miliutin (Agriculture),
and Nogin (Commerce and Industry)— as did Teodorovich (Food) and a
number of subcabinet commissars, including Riazanov and Larin. Shliapnikov, the Commissar of Labor, joined this group in a declaration to the
Central Executive Committee: "We take the stand that it is necessary to form
a socialist government of all parties in the soviet. . . . We assert that other
than this there is only one path: the preservation of a purely Bolshevik government by means of political terror. We cannot and will not accept this. We
see that this will lead . . . to the establishment of an irresponsible regime
and to the ruin of the revolution and the country. We cannot assume responsibility for this policy, and, therefore, we renounce before the Central Executive Committee our titles as Peoples' Commissars."[136]

Lozovsky, who had become secretary of the All-Russian Central Council of Trade Unions, issued a separate and even more impassioned statement: "I cannot, in the name of party discipline, remain silent when in the face of common sense and the elemental movement of the masses, Marxists refuse to take into consideration objective conditions which imperiously dictate to us, under the threat of a catastrophe, conciliation with all the socialist parties." He refused to make Lenin's power a condition: "I cannot, in the name of party discipline, submit to the cult of personal worship and stake political conciliation with all socialist parties who agree to our basic demands upon the inclusion of this or that individual in the ministry. . . ."[137]

Lenin's invective rose to a new pitch in the reply to the Rightists which he prepared in the name of the Central Committee: "Several members of our party who formerly occupied responsible posts have flinched in face of the onslaught of the bourgeoisie and fled from our ranks. The bourgeoisie and all its helpers are jubilant over this fact and are maliciously rejoicing. . . . The comrades who have resigned have acted like deserters." But this defection, Lenin assured the party, would no more deflect it from its course than did the "strike-breaking" of two of the deserters, Zinoviev and Kamenev, before the uprising: *"There is not a shadow* of vacillation among the masses." Lenin still affirmed his willingness to enter into a coalition where the soviets and a Bolshevik majority were accepted. He actually criticized the Left SRs for failing to accept the Bolshevik invitation to join the new government on October 25.[138] But with no effective leadership or coherent organization, the opposition to one-party rule quickly collapsed.

On November 7, the Opposition lost one of its principal leaders. Zinoviev came to realize that history had not taken the turn he expected, and he humbly recanted:

Under such a state of affairs we are obliged to reunite with our old comrades in the struggle. This is a difficult time, a time of extreme responsibility. It is our right, our duty, to warn the party from errors. But we remain together with the party, we prefer to make mistakes together with the millions of workers and soldiers and to die together with them, rather than go off to the side at this decisive, historical moment. Dissensions may remain with us. . . . But in the given state of affairs we are obliged . . . to subordinate ourselves to party discipline and to conduct ourselves as did the Left Bolsheviks when they were a minority on the question of participating in the Pre-Parliament and bound themselves on this matter to carry out the policy of the majority.

There will not, there must not be, any split in our party.[139]

Zinoviev's compunctions about a stable and democratic regime had yielded before the fear that he would be excluded from the community of the revolutionary faithful. Such an anxiety, to use the Marxist simile, "runs like a red thread" with curious persistence throughout the history of opposition activity in the Russian Communist Party.

Zinoviev was quickly reinstated in the Central Committee. Considerations of principle were stronger among the other opponents of the one-party government, and they maintained their stance of defiance until late in November. In the meantime, much of the ground for their protest had disappeared, as agreement between the Bolsheviks and Left SRs on a coalition government was finally worked out.

One more crisis was still to be passed before the Right Opposition of 1917 dissolved. This was the final hurdle on the path to unabashed party dictatorship—the question of the Constituent Assembly. Before taking power the Bolsheviks had steadfastly endorsed the convocation of the assembly: not knowing what else to do, they allowed the elections to proceed as scheduled in November. The results were something of a shock—the Bolsheviks won only about one fourth of the votes, against an overwhelming SR majority. Again the Bolshevik Party was beset by the issue of caution and legal scruple versus bold and forceful action.

The Bolshevik Right, including Zinoviev, Riazanov, and Lozovsky, who were joined by Bukharin on this issue, hoped for some kind of quasi-legal solution. The left-winger Uritsky, who had joined the Bolsheviks with Trotsky, complained, "Some comrades are now of the opinion that the Constituent Assembly is the crowning work of the revolution." [140] While it was becoming increasingly apparent that only a forceful solution of some kind could preserve the Bolshevik government (Bukharin proposed expelling the Kadets and having the left wing of the assembly continue to function), the Bolshevik Right won control over the party's delegation to the assembly. In the bureau elected by the Bolshevik delegates on December 2, the most prominent members were Kamenev, Stalin, Rykov, Nogin, Miliutin, Larin, and Riazanov. The Central Committee, with ample justification, declared that the bureau was dominated by right-wing views, and it finally felt constrained summarily to dissolve the bureau. Bukharin and Sokolnikov were *appointed* to lead the Bolshevik fraction, an early instance of a practice destined to assume decisive import. The issue was settled when the fraction endorsed Lenin's theses making plain his intention to disperse the Constituent Assembly by force.[141]

The last echo of the 1917 Opposition came from the diehard right-wingers, Lozovsky and Riazanov. Clinging tenaciously to the principles of democratic legality, they voted no when the Central Executive Committee approved the dispersal of the Constituent Assembly.[142] Since both of them were trade-union officials, they were able to continue their criticism of the government before the First All-Russian Trade Union Congress, which met in January 1918. The issue was trade-union independence from the government—a subject which was to generate much friction in subsequent years. On this first test, the opposition to centralization went under, and the congress resolved, "Trade unions will become instruments of state authority." [143] Lozovsky was expelled from the Bolshevik Party, and not until the end of 1919 did he return, much chastened.[144] His opposition days were over for good, and he survived the purges of the mid-1930s—only to fall victim to Stalin's Jewish purge in 1952.[145]

The Bolshevik Right Opposition of 1917 stemmed from a combination of literal Marxism, political caution, and democratic scruple, qualities which it shared with the Mensheviks. It was a spontaneous rather than an organized affair. In consequence, it was never able to succeed at the moment of crisis, but, on the other hand, defeats could not destroy it. Lenin might overcome the Right on a specific issue, but the psychological traits which disposed certain people to favor the Right welled up again and again.

It is possible to distinguish three contributing groups in the 1917 Opposition, apart from the Bolshevik defensists who left the party in April. The main body of the Bolshevik Right was the group led by Kamenev and Rykov, and after the middle of the year by Zinoviev as well. These people were old Leninists, committed to the hard organizational doctrine but apparently attracted to it out of considerations of conservatism and caution. To others, participation in an engine of power was a virtue in itself, and this accounts for those Leninists such as Stalin and Sverdlov who followed the leader steadfastly after his return to Russia.

A second group consisted of the former Mensheviks who leaned to the right, particularly Lunacharsky, Riazanov, and Lozovsky. In their reasoning legal scruples and democratic principles were paramount. They failed, however, to have any influence apart from their isolated individual protests.

The last group in the 1917 Opposition stood on the left of the party. It was small at the time—Shliapnikov was its only prominent spokesman—but it was destined to grow into a powerfully disruptive force during the next few years. These were the people who were in deadly earnest about the radical idealism contained in the party's programmatic statements. Revolutionary principle, rather than caution, prompted them to eschew the expedients of dictatorship.

3

THE BREST-LITOVSK CONTROVERSY
AND THE LEFT COMMUNISTS

Within three months after its triumph in the October Revolution, the Bolshevik Party, with all its legendary unity and iron discipline, was once again rent by controversy. Lenin's most enthusiastic backers of 1917 found themselves ranged against their leader in bitter dissension, the immediate cause of which was the issue of concluding peace with Germany. But the new split went much deeper, to questions of basic political philosophy and the general prospects for the workers' revolution in Russia and the world.

The Left Communists of 1918 did not organize to oppose Lenin's policies, any more than the right-wing opposition of 1917 had. In both instances the oppositionists represented a continuation of the course which Lenin had been following earlier. It was Lenin himself who shifted, with his wholesale exchange of one set of lieutenants and ideas for another in the spring of 1917 and the corresponding reversal of these changes by early 1918. In a manner of speaking, Lenin deserted his own Leninist current of Bolshevism to accomplish the revolution in conjunction with the Left, and then returned to his old (and much less independent) followers as he abandoned his allies of 1917 in their stance of purist indignation.

There were remarkably few people among the prominent party leaders who followed Lenin both in 1917 and during the Brest-Litovsk controversy. The Right opposed him in the earlier instance, the Left in the later. Those who steered the twisting course of fealty in between were a small band: Sokolnikov, who was neither before nor afterwards distinguished by orthodoxy; Smilga, a Central Committee member who was never particularly prominent until he joined the Trotsky Opposition in 1926; the party secretary, Sverdlov, who died of typhus in 1919; and another organization man destined to achieve particular fame in that specialty—Stalin. When Lenin's health failed in 1922, Stalin was the only man in the Politburo who had never openly defied the leader. He had strong grounds for claiming to be Lenin's political heir.

REVOLUTIONARY WAR VERSUS PEACE WITH GERMANY

When they swept into power, the Bolsheviks appeared to have no doubts at all on the question of war and peace. The early foreign-policy statements of the Bolshevik leaders were strictly in accord with the program enunciated before the coup: a "democratic peace" or war to the death against "imperialism." Speaking to the Second Congress of Soviets, Trotsky affirmed his view of the conditions for victory: "If the peoples of Europe do not arise and crush imperialism, we shall be crushed—that is beyond doubt. Either the Russian Revolution will raise the whirlwind of struggle in the West, or the capitalists of all countries will stifle our struggle." [1]

It was to prove significant that many more declarations in the revolutionary vein emanated from Trotsky than from Lenin. [2] The Decree on Peace of October 26 had a relatively moderate tone: the appeal was for peace through negotiation among existing governments, while the threat of revolution was only implied. [3] On the other hand, violently inflammatory statements were not uncommon; barely a week after the October coup, I. N. Stukov, a member of the Moscow Regional Bureau of the party, addressed to the Central Committee a declaration demanding "revolutionary war" against German imperialism. [4] Trotsky himself declared bluntly that despite the talk of negotiation, "a genuine democratic" peace would come only through revolution. [5]

Negotiations were opened with the Germans less as a step toward peace than as a gesture of revolutionary defiance directed at the "imperialist" governments. On November 14 overtures by the Soviet government elicited from the German military command an agreement to discuss an armistice, which was agreed upon and put in force on December 2. The ensuing peace talks at Brest-Litovsk, behind the German lines, were used by the Russians as a revolutionary sounding board. Trotsky gleefully trampled all the conventions of protocol in the hope of embarrassing the enemy and arousing revolutionary sympathy in Europe. Toward the end of December the delaying tactics of the Soviet negotiators began to try the patience of many Bolsheviks. On December 28 the Moscow Regional Bureau of the party called upon the government to break off negotiations and declare revolutionary war against Germany. [6] Disquiet among the party members prompted the Central Committee to schedule a discussion with local party representatives for January 8.

At this juncture Lenin undertook a major feat of leadership by deciding to abandon the program of revolutionary war and come to terms with the Central Powers instead. This meant a change of course equaled in decisive abruptness only by the acceptance of the Duma in 1906–1907, the April Theses of 1917, and the New Economic Policy of 1921. The opening surprise came on January 7, when Lenin, in his "Theses on the Question of Immediate Conclusion of a Separate and Annexationist Peace," submitted a reasoned rejection of the idea of revolutionary war. Revolutionary war was for the Soviet government neither a moral necessity nor a practical possibility, nor, Lenin contended, had it actually been promised—only "preparation" for such a war had (though even this promise had not been kept). Peace would buy time and spare the new Soviet government from certain collapse in the absence of revolutionary support from Europe: "It would be absolutely impermissible tactics to stake the fate of the socialist revolution which has already begun in Russia merely on the chance that the German revolution may begin in the immediate future, within a period measurable in weeks. Such tactics would be a reckless gamble. We have no right to take such risks."[7] This recalls similar words—"The revolution in Europe ... will come, but it is not here yet. ... We have no right to stake the whole future. ..." But Zinoviev and Kamenev were indicted for strike-breaking when they thus questioned the October coup.

The premise of caution and the canon of political success were shared by Lenin and those disciples who opposed him in 1917. Pragmatism infused with single-minded boldness was the quality which distinguished Lenin as a leader among these doctrinally kindred individuals. Once the leader had pointed the way—or rather, had committed the party to the course he planned—the cautious Bolsheviks devoted themselves with trusting fervor to the furtherance of the party line. Thus it was by no means accidental that by January 1918 Lenin sounded so much like his previously wayward lieutenants, and that they in turn became the staunchest upholders of the new policy of peace at any price.

Lenin's decision to make peace jabbed the idealist Bolsheviks into indignant protest, much as the April Theses had upset the cautious Bolsheviks. The degree of opposition, similarly, was the product of both emotional impulse and doctrinal momentum. In making each shift Lenin contravened the ideological postulates which had been the best articulated among his followers: in April 1917 it was the idea of the democratic dictatorship; in January 1918 it was the premise of permanent revolution.

The first formal discussion of Lenin's peace proposal took place at the Central Committee session of January 8, with a number of lesser party leaders in attendance.[8] The cleavage in the party was immediately apparent, and the weakness of Lenin's new position was obvious. Among some sixty persons present, Lenin was able to garner only fifteen votes for his proposal to make peace on Germany's terms. The Opposition—or rather those who upheld the previous line against Lenin's new opposition—immediately found themselves a leader in the person of Bukharin. Lenin's chief Left Bolshevik critic before the February Revolution, and a devoted believer in revolutionary internationalism, Bukharin was appalled by the thought of shirking his duty to wage revolutionary war.

At the January 8 conference he called openly for revolutionary war, and won thirty-two votes—just about half—for his cause of defiant idealism. A quarter of the participants stood midway between the Lenin and Bukharin positions and subscribed to a compromise formula set forth by Trotsky as the product of his experience at Brest-Litovsk: "no war, no peace." This idea, to which Trotsky adhered until the very end of the controversy, was an awkward effort to meet both the demands of revolutionary principle and the obvious exigencies of political survival. The obstacle on which it foundered was the presence of the German army: of the three plans Trotsky's could least provide any effective answer to the enemy threat. Then, as later, the less extreme left-wingers around Trotsky who tried to reconcile ideals and practical problems were reduced to impotent vacillation.

On January 11, the Central Committee met in regular session to try to reach a binding decision on the issue of peace. This time, in the narrower group, the demand for a declaration of revolutionary war went down to defeat, with only Krestinsky and Lomov supporting it. The words of some of Lenin's supporters verged on a nationalistic dithyramb as they extolled the defense of the new socialist fatherland. Zinoviev (as in October 1917) and Stalin (as in August 1917) stressed the uncertainty of Western revolutionary support and the priority of a socialist program for Russia.[9] Said Stalin, with his usual disdain for the foreigner, "There is no revolutionary movement in the West . . . , only a potential, and we cannot rely in practice on a mere potential."[10] Lenin, while hesitating to go so far, incurred the reproach (from Uritsky) that he was thinking "from the point of view of Russia and not from an international point of view."[11] Trotsky's "no war, no peace" policy provided a temporary solution. Evidently it attracted many of the purists to whom "no peace" meant ultimate war, whatever it was called. The Foreign Commissar's compromise won nine votes, against an opposition of seven which probably included some extremists along with the proponents of peace.[12]

The opposing factions quickly sought support for their respective positions in the local party organizations. The Moscow region was a left-wing stronghold, as it had been throughout 1917.[13] Bukharin and his supporters completely dominated the Moscow Regional Bureau of the party and used it virtually as the central committee of their faction. Steadfastly spurning conventional national interest, and unable to reconcile peace negotiations with their hope for a rapidly spreading revolutionary movement in Western Europe, the Leftists called for guerrilla resistance against the Germans while a supreme propaganda effort was made to evoke the revolution in the West. A conference of the Moscow regional organization resolved on January 13: "A democratic peace . . . will be achieved only by a mass revolutionary struggle of the peoples against the imperialists of both warring groups. . . . The adoption of the conditions dictated by the German imperialists would be an act going contrary to our whole policy of revolutionary socialism; it would lead to the abandonment of the proper line of international socialism, in domestic as well as in foreign policy, and could lead to one of the worst kinds of opportunism." Fearing such internal decay of the Russian Revolution in the event of compromise, the Leftists could easily resolve that, if

worse came to worst, Bolshevik power in Russia should be sacrificed in the
interest of the world revolution. Exhilarated by visions of revolutionary
heroism, the Moscow Leftists likened the situation of the Soviet government
to that of the Paris Commune, and proclaimed, "We unanimously condemn
any possibility of dropping our previous demands; it is better for us to
perish with honor for the cause of socialism than to bow our necks before
Wilhelm."[14] Lenin likened this state of mind to the quixotic pride of the
old Polish nobleman "who said, dying in a beautiful pose with his sword,
'Peace is a disgrace, war is honor.'"[15]

It is by no means clear, however, that the actual military situation was as
ultimately hopeless as the Leninists have since represented it. Germany,
destined for defeat at the hands of the Allies within the year, was far from
omnipotent, and there was no dearth of articulate support in Russia for continuing the war: every Russian political party save the Bolsheviks was unreservedly opposed to the peace. Peace would and did mean a more serious
internal shock to the Soviet government than would continuation of the war.
Indeed, it has been argued that the prime reason behind Lenin's insistence on
peace was his fear that if the war were resumed, the Bolsheviks would have
too many allies and might lose control of the government.[16]

Lenin having been rebuffed for the moment, the Soviet government proceeded in the latter part of January with Trotsky's compromise policy. This
was an impossible attempt to continue the status quo. Refusal to compromise
with the enemy accorded with the extreme left position of the Moscow
Bolsheviks, but in a vain effort to placate the Germans the open proclamation
of a revolutionary war was suspended. Thus the propaganda possibilities of
the Russian position were considerably reduced, while the German army was
restrained not at all. In the end, the decision was dictated by German force.
The German high command, determined to end the farce of negotiations,
notified the Soviet government on February 17* of its intention to resume
the advance. Discussing this news, the Bolshevik Central Committee split
in every conceivable way.[17] First, out-and-out revolutionary war was turned
down by a vote of eight to three: the Leninists present combined with the
moderate Left to defeat Bukharin. But an equally frank espousal of an
ignominious peace was similarly defeated, as Trotsky's group voted with
the extreme Left on this matter of principle. A Leftist proposal to let the
Germans discredit themselves in the eyes of the world by attacking, and
then sue for peace, was passed by a slim margin. Finally, a motion was
adopted to make peace if the revolution failed to materialize in Germany.
Trotsky voted with the Leninists, while most of the Leftists, perhaps refusing
to admit that the German proletariat could fail them, abstained.

* New Style. On February 14, 1918, Russia adopted the Gregorian calendar, and February 1
became February 14. Old Style dates have been observed in the present work up to this point;
New Style is used hereafter.

The next day, February 18, both the earnestness of the German advance and the futility of resisting it became apparent. Petrograd was thrown into a panic at the prospect of capture by the Germans. Revolutionary enthusiasm began to waver, and the safety of the Soviet state took precedence more and more over the tenuous ideal of international revolution. When the Central Committee voted on suing for peace, the negatives barely won: Trotsky, Krestinsky, Dzerzhinsky, Uritsky, Lomov, Bukharin, Ioffe, against Lenin, Stalin, Sverdlov, Zinoviev, Smilga, Sokolnikov. But before the day was out Trotsky bowed to the force of circumstances and changed his vote; he held the balance, and the request for peace terms was dispatched.[18]

The German answer was awaited with trepidation. Efforts to prepare a defense went ahead, and the political air was filled with appeals for last-ditch resistance. "We are ready to defend the conquests of the revolution to the last drop of blood," read a typical proclamation of the Council of People's Commissars.[19] Lenin wrote a commanding appeal, "The Socialist Fatherland is in Danger!"[20] When the enemy terms arrived—in the form of an ultimatum—they were even harsher than expected, with the extensive territorial demands to which Russia soon had to accede. Once again the Central Committee split. On Trotsky alone depended the success of the Leftists' opposition to the peace. He was the one individual whose leadership could have mobilized the superior strength of the faction and added the unity and resolution necessary for a political victory. The Leftists appealed to him to join them formally, but in vain.[21] Trotsky refused to act—an abnegation of the role history offered him which foreshadowed an even more decisive failure of will some five years later. Trotsky hesitated before the prospect of an open rupture in the party. "If only we had unanimity in our midst," he declared to the Central Committee in rebuttal to Lenin, "we could shoulder the task of organizing the defense. . . . We may gain peace, but we shall lose the support of the advanced elements of the proletariat. We shall, in any case, lead the proletariat to disintegration."[22]

Lenin resorted to his effective and by now familiar tactic of threatening to resign if he did not get his way. Some of the Leftists were ready to let him go; Dzerzhinsky could only regret that the party was not strong enough to dispense with Lenin's leadership. Trotsky abandoned his resistance; "We cannot wage revolutionary war with a split in the party. . . . I do not have confidence that [Lenin's] position is right, but I do not want in any way to disrupt the unity of the party." He could neither oppose nor support, and resigned his commissariat: "I am not able to remain and bear personal responsibility for foreign affairs."[23]

When the final vote on the acceptance of the German terms was taken, Lenin still commanded only a minority of the Central Committee—himself, Zinoviev, Stalin, Sverdlov, Sokolnikov, Smilga, and Stasova. Four members voted against the peace—Bukharin, Bubnov, Uritsky, and Lomov. But Trotsky's group—Krestinsky, Dzerzhinsky, Ioffe, and Trotsky himself—abstained and thereby allowed Lenin's position to become law for the party.[24] Lenin had survived the first and greatest political crisis of his career as head of the Soviet state.

ON THE VERGE OF A PARTY SPLIT

To the diehard Leftists, the acceptance of the German peace terms was tantamount to an act of treason against the revolution. Bukharin and his three Central Committee supporters, joined by Piatakov, Vladimir Smirnov, and Varvara Yakovleva (a candidate member of the Central Committee), immediately resigned all their offices. They accompanied this protest with the challenging statement of intention to "retain for ourselves complete freedom to agitate, outside the party as well as within it, for the position which we consider to be the only correct one."[25] Trotsky's three adherents in the Central Committee joined the Bukharin group in declaring their intention to carry the issue of peace to the party membership, though the prospect of a party split soon led them to reconsider just as Trotsky had.[26]

Left-wing defiance in the Central Committee was quickly echoed by the extremists in the Moscow Regional Bureau of the party. On February 24, in response to an inflammatory report by Stukov, this group unanimously resolved: "Having discussed the activities of the Central Committee, the Moscow Regional Bureau of the RSDWP expresses lack of confidence in the Central Committee, in view of its political line and composition, and will at the first opportunity insist on new elections." This was not all. Contrary to every Bolshevik principle, the authority of the constituted party authority was openly defied: "Furthermore, the Moscow Regional Bureau does not consider itself bound to obey, no matter what, those decisions of the Central Committee that are connected with the implementation of the terms of the peace treaty with Austria and Germany." Continuing with an explanatory note, the Moscow Leftists indicated their readiness to face a party split if it were the price for preserving revolutionary purity:

The Moscow Regional Bureau considers a split in the party in the very near future scarcely avoidable and it sets itself the aim of helping to unite all consistent revolutionary-Communist elements who equally oppose both advocates of the conclusion of a separate peace and all moderate, opportunist elements in the party. In the interests of the international revolution, we consider it expedient to accept the possibility of the loss of the Soviet power, which has now become purely formal. We maintain as before that our primary task is to extend the idea of the socialist revolution to all other countries, resolutely to promote the workers' dictatorship, and ruthlessly to suppress bourgeois counterrevolution in Russia.[27]

Meanwhile, Lenin was trying to persuade the Leftist leaders not to go through with their resignations. He had the Central Committee appeal to the dissidents to remain at their posts and at the same time order the party to respect the decision on peace until the coming party congress could convene, "in the name of party duty, in the name of the preservation of unity in our own ranks."[28] The Central Committee passed a resolution proposed by Trotsky guaranteeing the Opposition the right to defend their position before the party membership, and endorsed preparations for revolutionary war in the event that the Germans finally decided against peace.[29] The Leftists were temporarily mollified, except for Bukharin.[30] "We are turning the party into a dung-heap," was his embittered comment.[31]

Several days passed before the negotiations at Brest-Litovsk could be brought to a close, and as late as March 2 the Soviet government remained uncertain about the German response to its acceptance of the peace terms.[32] Meanwhile, preparations for the defense of Petrograd went ahead, and government offices began evacuating to Moscow. *Pravda* sounded the call to arms in twice-daily editions. The populace was exhorted to mobilize every effort to prepare for renewed struggle. Up to the very day the peace was signed (March 3), the deluge of left-wing slogans was kept up; the controversy within the party went almost unnoticed in the press. With each passing day, left-wing intransigence grew. On February 28, the Moscow *Sotsial-Demokrat* published an impassioned condemnation of the treaty terms:

This peace proclaims: All power to the bourgeoisie; all land to the landlords; all the plants and factories to the capitalists. . . .

This peace proclaims: Ruin and death to the power of the soviets, ruin and death to the proletariat and its Red socialist army.

This peace demands the servile silence of revolutionary Russia—it demands the liquidation of the whole October workers' and peasants' revolution. . . .

With all its strength, with all its enthusiasm, with all the deep consciousness of its great historical mission, the working class must cry out: Never! Either death or victory!

To arms!

Workers of the world, unite!

Despite such revolutionary fervor, the combined pressure of the dismal military situation and Lenin's insistence transmitted through the party hierarchy began to swing more and more members in the local organizations over to the side of peace. The treaty was actually signed on March 3; it remained for the party congress and the Congress of Soviets to ratify the act. Two days before the Seventh Party Congress convened, the Leninists won a majority in the Moscow city organization.[33] Simultaneously, the Leftists in Petrograd took one step further away from the norm of a united party with the establishment of a factional journal, the daily *Kommunist,* edited by Bukharin, Radek, and Uritsky.[34] Lenin's polemical reply to "our woebegone

'Lefts'"[35] left scant prospects that a united Bolshevik Party could endure.

The Seventh Party Congress, the first to follow the seizure of power, was a brief (March 6–8) but critical affair. The overriding question was the ratification of the peace, to which almost the entire debate was devoted. Lenin and Bukharin delivered the major speeches for their respective positions, while each was backed up by a series of statements from his supporters. It was an emotional crisis for the party, and a turning point.

Lenin stated his case again in terms of unabashed pragmatism: there was no alternative to peace; the Soviet government had to buy time; any immediate attempt to continue the war would mean the overthrow of the revolutionary regime. Lenin was more than ready to concede that sooner or later revolutionary war with the imperialists would be inevitable. In this he was backed up by Sokolnikov—a short four days after the latter had signed the treaty—but both emphasized the need for time to prepare for the struggle.[36] It was a "Tilsit Peace," Lenin stressed over and over again during these days, but, like Prussia under Napoleon's heel, Russia now would find the strength and the will to rise up and expel the invader when the time came. "Russia is moving toward a new and genuine patriotic war," Lenin wrote in a polemic against the Left Communists just prior to the congress.[37]

Despite this injection of the nationalist theme, there was no suggestion in Lenin's words that the international revolution might be sacrificed in the interest of the Soviet state. Lenin refused to admit the national-international dilemma; preservation of the Soviet state, he claimed, was the best service that could be rendered to the European proletariat, while the future of the revolutionary cause in Russia inescapably depended on the West: "It is the absolute truth that without a German revolution we will perish."[38] But he reiterated his unwillingness to gamble on an immediate German revolution and dismissed as un-Marxist the notion that the Russian example could set it off.[39] Russia would have to buy time while the German revolution ripened. This was implicitly an endorsement of the Zinoviev-Kamenev position of October 1917. Zinoviev, who at least had the virtue of consistency, could enthusiastically support Lenin's refusal to gamble on the German revolution: "We do not have the right to place all our cards exclusively, solely on that possible chance."[40]

As the issue of peace approached a climax, Lenin moderated his claims. His long speech at the congress was in essence a plea for a respite, a "breathing-space," however short it might prove to be. But toward the Opposition he had grown more bitter. He denounced them for creating the illusion that the Germans might not attack, inviting harsher peace terms, and in fact aiding the cause of German imperialism by their utopian stand.[41] For Trotsky's "no war, no peace" policy he had sharp words—"a profound mistake, a bitter overestimation of events."[42] The Left, Lenin declared, suffered from "an attitude of the deepest and everlasting pessimism, a feeling of complete despair—this is the content of the 'theory' that the significance of the Soviet power is purely formal and that tactics which will risk the possible loss of the Soviet power are permissible. There is no salvation anyway—let even the Soviet regime perish—such is the sentiment that dictated this monstrous resolution."[43]

Lenin would not or could not appreciate the internationalist reasoning which prompted the Left to look beyond the immediate fortunes of the Soviet state. As Bubnov explicitly pointed out at the Seventh Congress, Lenin had abandoned the perspective of international civil war which had inspired him up to the October Revolution and was now fighting the people who clung to his own earlier views.[44] Lenin's concern now was with the reality of power; he would struggle to the end to hold on to it. He could not tolerate Marxist qualms about the value of this power.

The true force of Left Communist emotion, as Bukharin exemplified it in his counterreport to the Seventh Party Congress, lay in precisely the opposite direction: utopian fervor and unbounded revolutionary optimism. Bukharin saw the revolution at a turning point. It could drive ahead boldly, drawing the masses throughout the world to its untarnished anti-imperialist standard, or it could turn aside to the path of compromise and then inevitably degenerate. Peace could mean the end of Bolshevik dominance: "Parallel with the return to the point of view of the necessity of signing the peace goes the return to the point of view of the necessity of the Constituent Assembly and the united front."[45]

Trotsky supported Bukharin on this score and pointed out how the peace terms threatened such Soviet policies as nationalization. Concessions meant to Trotsky that the revolutionaries were quitting, but if indeed they did have to quit, he wanted it to be done "like a revolutionary party, i.e. fighting to the last drop of blood for each position."[46] Others who spoke to endorse Bukharin's revolutionary purism were Uritsky, Bubnov, Radek, Riazanov, Osinsky, and Kollontai. Bukharin was convinced that the internal preservation of the revolution would demand the acceptance of the Left policy: "Sooner or later the top will take our line. . . . Only by accepting it will we save the Soviet power and the socialist content of this power."[47] To the question whether Soviet Russia or the world revolution came first, the Leftists gave an unequivocal answer: Soviet power in Russia meant nothing except as a step toward the international upheaval. Russian defeat was nothing to fear. Said Uritsky, "Defeats can promote the development of the socialist revolution in Western Europe much more than this obscene peace."[48] Trotsky likened the Soviet state to the Paris Commune. He was prepared to see it go under, but he saw hope, in contrast to the 1871 uprising, that a heroic gesture by the Russian revolutionaries would not be in vain: "Even if they crush us, there is no doubt that there can be no such historical decline as there was after the Paris Commune."[49] Only on the international plane could the Leftists see meaning in either a defeat or a victory. "We have said and say now," declared Bukharin, "that in the end the whole business depends on whether the international revolution is victorious or not."

Meanwhile, Bukharin argued—again with Trotsky's support—a truce would disrupt Russia's psychological ability to resist far more than would the continuation of the war: "The organization of the struggle will grow in the very process of struggle . . . the course of welding the proletariat under the slogan of a holy war against militarism and imperialism."[50] Trotsky protested that signing the peace meant throwing away all the propaganda advantage that he had scored in the protracted negotiations at Brest-Litovsk.[51] The treaty, in the minds of the Leftists, was a high price for little gain.

Lenin's persuasive power with the rank-and-file organization men who made up the bulk of the voting delegates carried the day. The decisive vote to ratify the treaty gave Lenin a majority of twenty-eight to nine.[52] Recriminations continued to echo, as Trotsky vainly tried to have the congress express itself in more revolutionary terms and as Zinoviev maneuvered to have Trotsky's record of negotiation censured.[53] In the last analysis, only one thing made the Left Communists relax their opposition to the peace: the fear of a party split. While Lenin was quite prepared to force a split in his insistence on accepting the German terms, the Leftists hesitated. Bukharin's fervor failed him in the crisis: "To fight with Lenin? That would mean a revolt against all our past, against our discipline, against the comrades in arms. . . . Am I of sufficient stature to become a leader of a party and to declare war on Lenin and the Bolshevik Party . . . ? No, no . . . I couldn't do that!"[54] Trotsky was held back by the same fear. "I could not take the responsibility for a coming split in the party," he said to the congress in an attempt at self-justification. "We who abstained performed an act of great self-restraint, since we sacrificed our 'Ego' in the name of saving the unity of the party."[55] This asserted virtue was to prove a fatal weakness throughout the subsequent history of the Opposition.

When the congress reached the point of electing a new Central Committee, Lenin used the occasion for a gesture of simultaneous conciliation and authority: the resigned Leftists, over their personal protests, were re-elected, Bukharin as a Central Committee member and Uritsky and Lomov as candidates.[56] This was followed by a resolution of the congress formally rejecting the resignations and expressing the "firm hope" that the dissident comrades would, in the name of unity, return to their posts.[57] Lenin's authority and the pressure of events eventually accomplished this objective, but not until after broad issues of internal social policy had been thrashed out between the factions.

WORKERS' CONTROL VERSUS STATE CAPITALISM

While dissension over the peace treaty was immediately responsible for the split between the Leninists and the Left Communists, the cleavage went deeper. Following the ratification of the peace, these differences were laid bare as the Left Communists turned to the domestic scene to protest the policy course which Lenin and his backers had begun to follow.

In Leftist eyes, foreign and domestic compromises were leading the revolution into mortal peril, and to guard against this the Left Communists assumed the role of watchdogs of revolutionary virtue. Karl Radek—the uniquely international revolutionary of Polish-German background, who became a Bolshevik just before the October Revolution—warned of grave danger: "Withdrawing in the interest of a breathing-space . . . withdrawing in the face of the claims of foreign capital, the government of the Russian Revolution will be compelled not only to stop its conscious work; it will be compelled to tear down the work already begun." To prevent such retrogression was the role he assumed for the Left Communists. "To point out the danger to the proletariat . . . to lead the struggle for the predominance of the proletariat in the revolution—this is the task of *Proletarian Communists,* and we struggle for it." The risk of military defeat would be far less serious than the internal decay of the revolution in its inauspicious Russian surroundings: "If the Russian revolution were overthrown by violence on the part of the bourgeois counterrevolution, it would rise again like a phoenix; if, however, it lost its socialist character and by this disappointed the working masses, this blow would have ten times more terrible consequences for the future of the Russian and the international revolution."[58]

At the center of the new dispute between the Left Communists and the Leninists was the general question of authority and discipline in the revolutionary society, particularly as it applied to the organization of industry. Throughout the early years of the Communist regime, from 1917 to 1921, this issue of industrial administration had crucial significance on two counts. First, it was the most sensitive indicator of the clash of principles about the shaping of the new social order. At the same time, it was the most continuous and provocative focus of actual conflict between the Communist factions. The struggle grew bitter indeed as each group became convinced of the peril to the revolution represented by any solution other than its own.

The starting point of the controversies over industrial administration is to be found in the Bolshevik program of 1917—the utopian vision of a stateless society administered spontaneously and democratically by the working class. Lenin himself was the most eloquent exponent of the dream, though he quickly delivered himself from illusion and ideal after he came to power. For the left-wing party leaders and for large numbers of politically aroused workers, however, the political and economic principles expressed in "State and Revolution" were articles of faith which no distress or disappointment could shake.

The immediate steps which Lenin demanded in his writings of 1917 were the destruction of all bureaucratically organized political authority and the establishment of control by the masses over the existing capitalist economy— "immediate change such that *all* fulfill the functions of control and supervision, that *all* become 'bureaucrats' for a time, and that *no one,* therefore, can become a 'bureaucrat.' "[59] Lenin was sure that such an opportunity would meet with a wave of mass enthusiasm that could overcome any and all obstacles, while on the other hand, with an equally utopian underestimation of the complexity of administration, he assumed that the tasks of industrial control would dissolve into "simple bookkeeping." "Socialism is above all accounting," he declared on the morrow of the October Revolution, and added in words which the purest anarchist could applaud, "Socialism is not created by order from above. State-bureaucratic automatism is alien to its spirit; socialism is living—it is the creation of the mass of the people themselves."[60]

For all this faith, Lenin did not lose his sense of reality. "The key to the matter will not be in the confiscation of capitalist property," he wrote in September 1917, "but specifically in nation-wide, all-embracing workers' control over the capitalists and their possible supporters. By confiscation alone you will do nothing, for in that there is no element of organization."[61] Socialism he defined at the same time as "nothing but state capitalist monopoly *made to benefit the whole people.*"[62] Given this condition, conventional managerial authority, labor discipline, and payment in proportion to skill and responsibility would appear both necessary and justified. Here was material for long and bitter dissension within the Communist movement.

During the season of revolutionary upheaval which brought the Bolsheviks to power, the practice of industrial anarchy ran far ahead of the theory. The organizations which were instrumental in the establishment of workers' control were the factory and plant committees or *fabzavkomy* (*fabrichnozavodnye komitety*) which sprang up in March 1917. An early statement of their claimed authority emanated from a conference of Petrograd factory committees in April 1917: "All orders concerning the internal order of a plant, such as length of the working day, wages, hiring and firing of workers and employees, leaves of absence, etc., should issue from the factory committee."[63] In view of this radicalism it was no surprise that the factory committees were soon aligned with the Bolsheviks. Bolsheviks dominated the all-Russian conference of factory committees held in Petrograd in June 1917, and passed a resolution calling for "the organization of thorough control by labor over production and distribution," to be assured by "a labor majority . . . in all institutions having executive authority."[64] Wherever they were strong enough—before and especially after the October Revolution, when they were abetted by local soviets—factory committees bodily ousted the management and assumed direct control of their respective plants. Chaos reigned within enterprises and in their relations with the economy as a whole.[65] The level of production, already sagging, suffered grievously.

At the time the Bolsheviks seized power, they were not in a position to do anything but recognize the actual state of affairs, however far it went beyond the idea of workers' control over capitalist enterprise. Doctrine was written into law on November 14, 1917, when the Council of People's Commissars approved a decree (authored by Lenin) recognizing the authority of workers' control throughout the economy.[66] Some workers' spokesmen took the Bolshevik victory to mean that complete economic power and responsibility was in the hands of the workers. The working class, wrote one trade-unionist, "by its nature . . . should occupy the central place both in production and especially in its organization. . . . All production in the future will . . . represent a reflection of the proletarian mind and will."[67]

Such claims on the part of the trade unions were looked upon with favor by the new Soviet government, since the unions represented a more stable and less anarchistic force than the factory committees, which had got completely out of hand. The first congress of trade unions ever held in Russia convened in January 1918, with a Bolshevik majority, and resolved overwhelmingly to assume for the unions the primary role in industrial administration: "The trade-union organizations, as class organizations of the proletariat which are constructed according to the industry principle, must take upon themselves the main work of organizing production and restoring the weakened productive forces of the country. Energetic participation in all organs which regulate production, the organization of workers' control . . . such are the tasks of the day. . . . The trade-union organizations must transform themselves into organs of the socialist state."[68] Only the Ultra-Right Bolsheviks Riazanov and Lozovsky—both unsteady recruits from the Mensheviks—tried to oppose this assumption of power by the unions.[69] They were in agreement with the Mensheviks that it was more important for the unions to preserve their independence and concentrate on protecting the workers.

By the beginning of 1918 the problem of workers' control in industry had begun to provoke dissension within the Bolshevik Party leadership. The argument proceeded on Left-Right lines that coincided with the cleavage over the peace treaty, though the latter issue temporarily overshadowed the economic question. The Left favored recognizing and completing the *de facto* nationalization of industry which the factory committees were carrying out, with the establishment of an overall national economic authority based on and representing the organs of workers' control.[70] Lenin, by contrast, preferred to retain the structure of capitalist administration as long as possible and came increasingly to regard workers' control only as a temporary curb on private industrialists, until such time as direct state control could be effected.[71]

The Council of People's Commissars took a step in the direction of the Leftist plan, apparently at the behest of the factory-committee leadership, with the creation of the Supreme Economic Council (and the authorization of similar local councils) in December 1917.[72] The council was initially dominated by Leftists—the first chairman was Osinsky and the governing bureau included Bukharin, Lomov, and Vladimir Smirnov.[73] Despite the dubious success of the central and local councils in the ensuing months, they represented enough doctrinal momentum to evoke from Lenin a final expression of his 1917 anarchism. He declared to the congress of local economic councils held in May 1918: "The apparatus of the old state is doomed to die; but the apparatus of the type of our Supreme Economic Council is destined to grow, develop, and become strong, fulfilling all the most important functions of an organized society."[74]

The turning point in administrative policy came in March 1918, simultaneously with the Brest-Litovsk crisis. The Left Communist leadership of the Supreme Economic Council either resigned or were ousted, and the moderates Miliutin and Rykov, with the planning enthusiast Larin, supplanted them.[75] Immediate steps were taken to shore up managerial authority, restore labor discipline, and apply wage incentives under the supervision of the trade-union organizations.[76] A particularly striking instance of the change was the decree of "dictatorial powers" to the Commissariat of Communications to end workers' control on the railroads and restore effective administration.[77] Replying to this step on behalf of the Left, Preobrazhensky uttered a prophetic warning: "The party apparently will soon have to decide the question, to what degree the dictatorship of individuals will be extended from the railroads and other branches of the economy to the Russian Communist Party."[78] Nevertheless the Leninists proceeded with the restoration of discipline, and endorsed in addition a policy of retaining and rewarding the former managerial personnel and technicians—"bourgeois specialists" or *spetsy*.

Lenin summed up the new policy in a report to the Central Committee, which was published in revised form at the end of April under the title, "The Immediate Tasks of the Soviet Regime." The most pressing need, he argued, was the establishment of orderly administration and effective control over both capitalist and nationalized enterprises. The attack on private property had gone too far; tighter controls and increased productivity were more important. The services of bourgeois experts had to be retained, whatever the cost in violation of the norms of equality; without them, Lenin asserted, "The transition to socialism will be impossible," even though this meant "a retreat from the principles of the Paris Commune . . . , a step backward." The workers would have to accept discipline and the Taylor system of scientific management; industrial anarchy had value only to effect the transition between the old "slave" discipline and the new "conscious" discipline. Implementation of the dictatorship of the proletariat required "the appointment of individual persons, dictators with unlimited powers." Unshakable authority was the *sine qua non* of industrial success: "The . . . revolution demands . . . precisely in the interests of socialism— that the masses *unquestionably obey the single will* of the leaders of the labor process."[79]

Lenin's new industrial policy brought the Left Communists once more rushing to the defense of revolutionary purism. Invited to a discussion with the Central Committee early in April, the Left Communist leaders presented a set of theses which attacked the policy of the party leadership in sweeping terms:

There may very possibly arise a tendency towards a deviation by the majority of the Communist Party and the Soviet power which it directs, into the channel of a petty-bourgeois policy of a new form. In the event that this tendency should be realized, the working class would cease to be the director, the exercisor of hegemony over the socialist revolution. . . . In case of the rejection of an actively proletarian policy, the conquests of the workers' and peasants' revolution would begin to freeze into a system of state capitalism and petty-bourgeois economic relations.[80]

Broadening their campaign against Lenin's domestic policies, the Left Communists established a new theoretical journal, entitled *Kommunist,* under the aegis of the Leftist-controlled Moscow Regional Bureau. Four numbers were published in April and May. Bukharin, Osinsky, Radek, and Vladimir Smirnov were the editors and the principal contributors.

The most extensive and impassioned criticism of the trend of economic policy under Lenin came from Osinsky. With a ringing declaration of faith in the proletariat, Osinsky denounced labor discipline, managerial authority, and the use of *spetsy* in positions of responsibility, all of which pointed to the dangerous prospect of "state capitalism":

We do not stand for the point of view of "construction of socialism under the direction of the organizers of the trusts." We stand for the point of view of the construction of the proletarian society by the class creativity of the workers themselves, not by ukase of "captains of industry." . . . We proceed from trust for the class instinct, to the active class initiative of the proletariat. It cannot be otherwise. If the proletariat itself does not know how to create the necessary prerequisites for the socialist organization of labor—no one can do this for it and no one can compel it to do this. The stick, if raised against the workers, will find itself in the hands of a social force which is either under the influence of another social class or is in the hands of the soviet power; then the soviet power will be forced to seek support against the proletariat from another class (e.g. the peasantry), and by this it will destroy itself as the dictatorship of the proletariat. Socialism and socialist organization must be set up by the proletariat itself, or they will not be set up at all; something else will be set up—state capitalism.[81]

All such opposition to his program of state capitalism Lenin equated with Menshevism. In the Leftist criticism of his labor policy he found "the most graphic proof of how the 'lefts' have fallen into the trap, have given in to the provocation of the . . . Judases of capitalism."[82] Undaunted by Lenin's vituperation, the Left Communists made one more concerted effort to return the party to its original course in social policy. The occasion for this stand was the congress of regional economic councils, held in Moscow in late May and early June 1918, which, despite its designation, served largely as a forum for the top Communist leaders to restate their economic disagreements.

Lenin opened the congress with a plea for practical steps in the face of staggering economic difficulties. He continued to stress labor discipline and the need to employ *spetsy,* and challenged his listeners to meet "the task of transforming the whole amount of the rich supply of culture and knowledge and technique, accumulated by capitalism, and historically indispensable for us . . . from an instrument of capitalism into an instrument of socialism."[83]

Radek followed with a report on the economic consequences of the peace treaty. He dwelt on the heavy strains and losses which it was inflicting on the Russian economy, but he accepted the peace itself as an accomplished fact and abandoned his earlier talk of a perversion of the socialist regime. Instead, he appealed for the vigorous extension of socialist measures to make the most of Russia's weak economic potential and overcome the difficulties imposed by the war and the peace.[84] In so modifying the Left Communist position, Radek foreshadowed the Leninist-Leftist compromise on economic issues which was to prevail during the period of War Communism—authority and discipline, together with complete nationalization, central control, and an attempt at planning.

Other representatives of the Left Communists—above all Osinsky—stood uncompromisingly for the democratization of industry which the revolution had seemed to promise. This pointed to the coming split among the Left Communists, when the purists, refusing to accept the centralization of War Communism, broke away to form the new opposition group of Democratic Centralists. Osinsky demanded a "workers' administration . . . not only from above but from below" as the indispensable economic base for the proletarian government.[85] Lomov, pleading for workers' control, warned, "Nationalization, centralization . . . are strangling the forces of our country. The masses are being cut off from living creative power in all branches of our economy."[86] Osinsky, vainly protesting the whole trend toward discipline and the authority of "commissars," appealed to Lenin's remark about teaching every cook to administer the state. He urged that industrial enterprises be controlled by boards two thirds elected from among the workers.[87] The

congress cut this to one third, and put it in the context of an elaborate hierarchy of administrative boards reaching up to the Supreme Economic Council.[88] The ground was hence prepared so that when the sweeping nationalization of industry came in the months following, it proceeded not on the
anarchistic lines of 1917 but as a process of concentration into one collossal
state trust.

The broadening controversy between Lenin and the Left Communists
revealed that the doctrinal synthesis of 1917 Bolshevism—Leninist drive and
Leftist program—had for a time broken down completely. The whole developing pattern of Communist centralism was now attacked by the Left, as
they gloomily warned of "bureaucratic centralization, the rule of various
commissars, the deprivation of the local soviets' independence, and in practice
the rejection of the type of 'state commune' administered from below."[89]
Osinsky was not far from the truth in warning that "the Soviet power . . .
will destroy itself as the dictatorship of the proletariat." He shared with
the other Left Communists the fear that if the party failed to pursue a vigorously idealistic and proletarian policy, the whole nature of the revolution
could be perverted and the future of Russian society diverted into an entirely
different channel. Such a notion, indeed, can aptly be applied to the subsequent changes in the USSR: although formally retaining its original ideology
in all its rigor, the Soviet state has in practice abandoned almost all of the
ideals of the revolution. Its social structure has scarcely any anticipation in
the corpus of Marxian theory.

The Left Communists were, to be sure, inaccurate in their descriptions.
They spoke of a regression to "petty-bourgeois relations" with a strong
bureaucratic element in the form of "state capitalism." This was the best
they could do in describing the tendencies of the Soviet regime toward
authoritarianism, bureaucratic privilege, and power politics. The error was
due to the limitations of the Marxist frame of reference in which these Communists thought and acted; they could only describe the strange impending
evil in terms of dangers already familiar to them.

THE ESTABLISHMENT OF LENINIST UNITY

The resolution of the party controversy in the spring of 1918 set a pattern
that was to be followed throughout the history of the Communist Opposition in Russia. This was the settlement of the issues not by discussion, persuasion, or compromise, but by a high-pressure campaign in the party organizations, backed by a barrage of violent invective in the party press and in the
pronouncements of the party leaders. Lenin's polemics set the tone, and his
organizational lieutenants brought the membership into line. The most
effective force of all was Lenin's personal authority, which few people had
the temerity to resist for any length of time. Events also had their effect by

making the Left Communists feel that party disunity threatened the whole future of the Soviet regime.

Even before the ratification of the Brest-Litovsk Treaty, the strength of the Left Communists inside the party was rapidly undermined by the appeal which Lenin's faction made to the rank and file in the local organizations. As early as the day after the signing of the peace treaty, the Moscow city organization gave a majority to Lenin's position. Osinsky's resolution, lamenting that "the signing of the present peace . . . is the suicide of the Russian Revolution," was overwhelmingly rejected. Most of the Leftists voted for the Trotsky position, but they were unable to stem the tide toward the acceptance of peace and the maintenance of the unity of the party now that the question of peace had been decided. The majority resolution instructed the city's delegates to the impending Seventh Party Congress "to defend the unity of the party and to condemn sharply the individual attempts to split the party which have taken place in the past."[90]

Soon after the party congress had approved the peace, a Petrograd city party conference produced a majority for Lenin. It ordered the suspension of the newspaper *Kommunist* which had been serving as a Left Communist organ and declared in a vein similar to that demonstrated at Moscow, "The Petrograd conference . . . protests against any attempts whatsoever to split the party at the present difficult moment. The conference demands that the adherents of *Kommunist* cease their separate organizational existence, and suggests to those comrades friendly work in the common party organizations."[91]

It remained only for the Fourth Extraordinary Congress of Soviets, meeting in Moscow in the middle of March, to ratify the treaty and settle the question of peace definitively. In the caucus of the Bolshevik delegates to the congress the Leftists were crushed by the overwhelming vote of four hundred fifty-three to thirty-six, with eight abstentions.[92] The Left Communists abandoned the fight. "Our duty as international revolutionary Communists compels us to declare our position openly," they declared, "but . . . a *split* of the proletarian party would at this time be harmful to the interests of the revolution." Accordingly, they abstained from voting in the congress itself. The non-Bolshevik opponents of the peace—mostly Left SRs—were easily overcome, and the treaty went into effect.

During the spring and early summer of 1918 the Leninists steadily encroached upon the organizational support of the Leftists. A temporary point of Left Communist strength was the preponderantly proletarian party organization in the Ural region, then led by Preobrazhensky.[93] By the end of May, the Ural organization and even the Leftist stronghold in the Moscow Regional Bureau had been won over by the backers of the party leadership.[94] The fourth and final issue of the Moscow *Kommunist* had to be published as a private factional paper rather than as the official organ of a party organization.

Under the conditions of party life established by Lenin, defense of the Opposition position became impossible within the terms of Bolshevik discipline. The reluctance of the Opposition to understand this proved to be their undoing. Once the revolution began to slip from the expected path, it became futile to attempt to act within the old frame of reference. Old loyalties, programs, organizations, needed to be discarded; the unity which might be a prerequisite for a group trying to launch a revolution became a crippling fetter for those who would redirect a revolution already in motion. For a fleeting moment, the Left Communists realized this. They pledged their support to the existing government only for as long as it avoided the petty-bourgeois tendencies which they feared: "In case of such a deviation the left wing of the party will have to take the position of an effective and responsible proletarian opposition."[95]

Beaten and embittered over the peace of Brest-Litovsk, and undermined in the party organizations, the Left Communists considered desperate measures to implement this intention. They overcame their scruples about party unity long enough to enter into conversations with representatives of the Left SRs, the Bolsheviks' erstwhile coalition partners who had just left the government in protest against the peace treaty. The talks probably occurred near the end of March, with the objective of somehow turning Lenin out of office and resuming the war against Germany. In 1938 this "plot" of the Left Communists and the Left SRs was recalled with great fanfare when Bukharin was a defendant in the third of the great purge trials. He was accused of planning to arrest and "physically exterminate" Lenin, Stalin, and Sverdlov, and to take over the government by force—though, in spite of his general readiness to confess, Bukharin consistently refused to admit this charge. The selectivity of Bukharin's admissions and what is independently known of the affair make much of the trial evidence plausible, despite the suspicion which the nature of the trials evokes.

The first evidence of the "plot" on the Communist side was an article by Yaroslavsky, one of the Left Communists, who wrote in *Pravda* on July 3, 1918, to repudiate the idea of Left Communist and Left SR cooperation. He mentioned and denied reports in the "bourgeois press" that the two groups had planned an anti-Lenin bloc for the Fifth Congress of Soviets, which was about to meet at the time.[96] The affair next came to light during the party controversy of late 1923, when the leadership attempted to use it to discredit some of the former Left Communists who figured in the then current Opposition. In this version, the plot had become more serious, involving the contemplated arrest of Lenin while a new Council of People's Commissars was installed. A group of former Left Communists then siding with the Opposition replied with indignation that "the matter is being represented not at all as it was in fact." The idea of a Left SR and Left Communist coalition they attributed entirely to the Left SRs, and claimed that the notion of arresting

Lenin originated simply as a joke.[97] Whatever the truth in the 1923 charges, the 1938 trial does not go beyond them in substance; only detail and invective were added.

The original suggestion of joint Left Communist and Left SR action to unseat Lenin seems to have come from the hotheads of the Moscow Regional Bureau, particularly Stukov, who reportedly spoke for violent action in February while the Brest-Litovsk negotiations were still going on. After the signing of the treaty and its acceptance by the Seventh Party Congress, Bukharin reportedly declared to his Left Communist supporters that to keep fighting against the treaty the group needed to seek Left SR support. It is quite certain that negotiations were undertaken. No difficulty was met in getting the cooperation of the Left SRs—the initiative may have been more on their side. At the end of March agreement was apparently reached on a plan to remove the cabinet, arrest Lenin for a day or so if necessary, and install Piatakov as the chairman of a new Council of People's Commissars representing the Left Communist and Left SR coalition.[98] Except for the possibility of making arrests, the plan was perfectly legal in the context of parliamentary government, to which the Soviet constitution as then conceived was supposed to conform.

The failure to execute the plot rests with the Left Communists. They were never resolute in their opposition to Lenin, and furthermore felt the ground slipping from under them day by day. Reportedly it was the Left Communists' loss of control over the Moscow Regional Bureau in May 1918 which put an end to their ambitions.[99] The Left SRs were not so easily discouraged. On July 6, 1918, they launched an insurrection in Moscow in the hope of overthrowing the Communist government, and tried to promote a resumption of war with Germany by kidnapping and assassinating the German Ambassador, Mirbach. Within a day or two the Soviet government crushed the uprising, and a break with Germany was avoided. The Left SRs had only succeeded in removing themselves from the arena of legal political activity and in giving the Communists the final impulse toward one-party dictatorship.

In retrospect, the Left SR revolt appears to be the direct consequence of the earlier Left Communist and Left SR thinking, pursued by the bolder of the two parties after the other demurred. For the Left Communists the revolt meant the end of any serious effort to challenge Lenin's political authority. The leading Left Communists felt it necessary to disown their former friends explicitly, and they published a series of articles in *Pravda* to affirm that the alliance had been absolutely ended by the anti-Bolshevik venture of the Left SRs. Wrote Yaroslavsky, "We will try to carry out through the party our own views, which we consider more appropriate to the interests of the socialist revolution. But with the Left SRs, against the Communists? No, this road is not for us."[100]

Uprooted as an organization, the Leftists began one by one to return to the Leninist fold. By the end of the summer, the Central Commitee hold-outs had returned to their posts.[101] Far more important problems presented themselves in the summer of 1918 than intraparty doctrinal disputes over problematical social dangers within the regime. A firm alliance between the Leninists and most of the Leftists was established as the party entered the period of War Communism. Nonetheless, the issues of 1918 were only post-poned. They could not be forgotten, thanks to the Left Communists' work of criticism. As soon as a military respite permitted, left-wing oppositionists were ready to raise again the fundamental question of the social nature of the Soviet regime.

4

WAR COMMUNISM AND THE
CENTRALIZATION CONTROVERSIES

The Russian Revolution was still far from its climax when the October coup brought the Bolsheviks to power, and the costly peace with the Central Powers brought only a temporary respite to the new government. Social conflict deepened, and political hatreds intensified, as the pro- and anti-revolutionary extremes gathered strength at the expense of the Menshevik and Socialist Revolutionary moderates. Clashes between government forces and the troops of the Czecho-Slovak Legion in May 1918 were the signal for anti-Bolshevik risings throughout Siberia and the southeastern part of European Russia, and the agony of civil war thus began.

As the revolution unleashed civil war, so the war intensified the revolution. The Communist Party, cementing its dictatorship by suppressing all opposition parties, veered to the left again. The Leninists and most of the Communist Left submerged their differences in the heat of battle and tried to create a new society by state command. The role of opposition now fell to a small minority of extreme idealists, who held to the antiauthoritarian principles enunciated by the Left Communists in the spring of 1918. These left-wing diehards—the Democratic Centralists and the Workers' Opposition —set themselves determinedly against the bureaucratic and dictatorial expedients which war and the fervor of revolution impelled most of the leadership to adopt. The voice of revolutionary conscience welled up insistently in 1919 and 1920, only to be stifled in 1921 in the name of the revolution itself.

THE TRANSITION TO WAR COMMUNISM AND THE ISSUE OF CENTRAL AUTHORITY

On June 28, 1918, the Council of People's Commissars issued a decree on general nationalization in accordance with which all industrial enterprises with a capital of over a million rubles were confiscated by the state. This signaled the beginning of War Communism. The balance between capitalism and communism represented by the formula, "one foot in socialism," had broken down. Permanent revolution, in the sense of a quick transition to socialist internal policies, was being accurately borne out.

Meanwhile, the civil strife of Reds and Whites had become desperate, as anti-Bolshevik groups ranging from monarchists to SRs battled to overthrow the Soviet government. For the Communists, the summer months of 1918

were among the darkest days of the Civil War. White troops striking up the
Volga penetrated dangerously close to Moscow before they were repulsed by
the newly organized units of the Red Army. Most of the border regions were
in the possession of the Whites or under German and Turkish occupation.
The best food-producing areas were for the most part either lost or cut off
from Soviet-controlled central Russia. Allied intervention had commenced.
(This consisted not so much in the actual landing of troops, the military
effect of which was minor, but in furnishing large quantities of supplies and
arms to the White forces.) Communist power was challenged from within
by rival revolutionaries, the Left SRs. These were the circumstances under
which the Soviet government attempted to carry out the most grandiose ideas
of social reconstruction. In this period of life-and-death struggle and of great
sense of purpose, the Communist Party closed its ranks. All shades of opinion
within the party realized the seriousness of the struggle with the counterrevolution, and submitted to extreme centralization of authority and to measures of discipline which amounted to the militarization of the party.

Opposition activity during the Civil War correlated closely with the
military fortunes of the Red forces. Whenever the Soviet state was in serious
danger, the various groupings in the Communist Party tended to unite, sub-
merge their differences temporarily, suspend criticism of the regime, and
devote all their efforts to defense. During the first great crisis, in the summer
of 1918, the breach caused by the Brest-Litovsk controversy was healed. After
the collapse of Germany in November 1918, Red military fortunes took a
pronounced turn for the better. The Ukraine and the Volga region were
reoccupied, and a period of relative stability and recuperation followed. In
March 1919, at the Eighth Party Congress, a wave of Leftist criticism surged
up in protest against the ultra-centralist trend. Mid-1919 was another time
of military crisis, with the threatening advances of Denikin and Yudenich on
Moscow and Petrograd, respectively; intraparty controversy again faded
away. By the time of the Ninth Congress in the spring of 1920, however, the
military balance had definitely been resolved in favor of the Soviet Republic.
The response to this was a strong resurgence of opposition activity.

Between the Eighth and Ninth congresses the focus of issues between the
factions shifted from problems of high-level decision making and long-range
foreign policy toward questions concerning the execution of decisions, the
organization of the lower levels of the governmental structure, and economic
policy in general. The shift reflected the change in circumstances as the Red
forces clinched their victory over the Whites, the international situation became more stabilized, and the party was able to turn to questions of reconstruction and political reorganization.

General acceptance of the measures of War Communism bound the great
majority of Communists together after mid-1918. The Left Communist movement ended as it began, not as a group temporarily built up in opposition to

the party organization and the mainstream of party thought, but as a long-standing current in the party which had momentarily found itself in disagreement with Lenin over his international and internal compromises. Many of the Leftists embraced War Communism with unrestrained enthusiasm.

Under the pressure of civil war, the Russian economy was reorganized into a highly centralized, semimilitary pattern. A sharp reaction quickly set in against the chaos of workers' control, despite resistance among proletarian partisans of the individual factory committees.[1] Falling production was blamed on the influence of heretical anarcho-syndicalist ideas. "Workers' control over industry, effected by the factory and plant committees," wrote one government spokesman, "has shown what can be expected if the plans of the anarchists are realized."[2]

The most severe economic feature of War Communism was the requisitioning—in effect, confiscation—of food supplies from the peasantry. Such violent measures were required to forestall the urban starvation which was threatened by the breakdown of normal trade. To accomplish this end, the Communists made use of the incipient rural class struggle between the landless peasants and their less-impoverished neighbors. "Committees of the village poor" were established in the summer of 1918 to help find and seize agricultural surpluses in the hands of kulaks and middle peasants. This policy marked another sharp turn away from the Communists' initially moderate economic policy. The Soviet regime no longer represented itself as the protagonist of the "bourgeois revolution," winning the land for the peasantry as a whole. It was turning against the so-called petty-bourgeois strata of the peasantry and relying on the proletarianized poor peasants. This meant in terms of Bolshevik theory that the real dictatorship of the proletariat had been launched. The left-wing Communists were elated about this, to the point of occasional attempts at the forcible establishment of collective farms.[3] A limit was soon reached, however. By the end of 1918 it was apparent to the practical Leninist mind that unrestrained class war in the villages was doing the Bolshevik cause more harm than good, and the committees of the poor were disbanded.

At the Eighth Party Congress in March 1919, Lenin defended the need to conciliate the middle peasants and to restrain acts of violence in connection with the grain collections.[4] The practical wisdom of his position was apparently seen by the whole party, for there was no declared opposition to the change of tactics. This modification of peasant policy indicated that the high-water mark of War Communism had been passed; it foreshadowed the New Economic Policy adopted two years later.

To many Leftists, War Communism was the natural and proper course of the revolution. As L. Kritsman, a writer of Leftist sympathies, later described the period, it was "the attempt to make the first steps of the transition to socialism" as "immanent tendencies of the proletarian revolution" began to take form in a "proletaro-natural economic structure."[5] The most ambitious codification of the excesses of War Communism into a law of history was the work of Bukharin, especially in his book, "The Economics of the Transition Period." Bukharin hailed the fall in industrial production as a sign of the breakup of the old society's hierarchical relationships while horizontal ties were being readied to take their place.[6] Kritsman wrote of War Communism as the first attainment of the ideal of a proletarian society: "Granted that the tendencies of development have been realized for the first time in a perverted form. But they have been realized!"[7]

Not all of the left wing of the party accepted War Communism as a near approach to the millenium. During 1919, in opposition to the bureaucratic excesses into which the party leadership had plunged, the Group of Democratic Centralism crystallized as a clear-cut faction, with its own definite program. The leaders of the group, Osinsky, T. V. Sapronov, and Vladimir Smirnov, had all been active Left Communists, and a number of its members had participated in the left-wing Moscow Regional Bureau. Subsequently they parted company with their more power-minded associates in the Communist left wing over the issue of centralization. The faction's appellation was a misnomer; the party leadership correctly criticized the Democratic Centralists for being excessively decentralist. But the leadership departed equally far from the balance of *democratic* centralism.

In 1920 another group, based on the trade-union leadership, organized to resist the centralizing trend of Soviet politics. These people, even more distinguished by Ultra-Left idealism, formed the Workers' Opposition. Under this name they tried vainly to challenge the party leadership and its policies during the trade-union controversy of 1921. These Ultra-Left groups failed completely. Their objective of administrative democracy in government and economy was chimerical in the face of the practical pressures for centralization, and their political appeal was more and more blocked by the centralized power of the party organization. The historical import of the Ultra-Left was that it kept alive a tradition of struggle for the democratic aspect of the 1917 program and underscored by contrast the changes which were proceeding in the political thinking of the majority of Communists. But all thought of restraints upon the power of the organs of proletarian dictatorship was cast to the winds by the party leadership.

International Revolution and the Nationality Question

Between Lenin and his former critics of the moderate Left there still remained after mid-1918 certain issues of a theoretical nature which the Brest-Litovsk controversy had left unresolved. How was the Russian Revolution now related to the anticipated international movement, and what practical conclusions were to be drawn? In particular, what did Marxian internationalism imply with respect to the ethnic problems of a multinational state such as Russia? The positions represented by Lenin and Bukharin in 1915–1916 stood essentially unchanged. The Left saw the revolution as an international process which made the rights and fortunes of individual nations irrelevant. Lenin had by his stand for peace demonstrated the national terms in which he thought about revolution in Russia. Corresponding to this, he had stood firmly for the principle of self-determination, whereby other nations and nationalities would have the right to decide their own political future.

The nationality issue was debated in April 1917, amidst the dissension occasioned by Lenin's April Theses. A resolution on the question of Russia's national minorities, introduced by Stalin, evoked the left-right differences which had arisen in the emigration. The Georgian Stalin defended the right of self-determination; the Ukrainian Piatakov and the Pole Dzerzhinsky attacked it. Exclaimed Dzerzhinsky: "We should not advance the national question, since that retards the moment of social revolution."[8] The final version of the resolution accepted self-determination solely as a point of political expediency,[9] and this was the sense in which it was actually pursued by the Bolsheviks when they forcibly recovered most of the non-Russian territories of the tsarist empire.

International theory and the nationality question came to the fore again at the Eighth Party Congress in March 1919. Bukharin, speaking for the Left, affirmed his view of the Russian Revolution as a part of a single world-wide struggle against "finance capital." Lenin complained of Bukharin's over-abstractness and his neglect of Russia's special problems as a largely backward peasant country.[10] Underlying the debate was the fundamental question which the Brest-Litovsk controversy had only sharpened: which came first, the interest of the socialist national state, or of the world revolution? As before, the Leninists argued for the national interest, the Leftists for the international.

Of more immediate import was the related issue of national self-determination. Again both points of view were hardly changed by the revolution, but the issue was intensified because the fate of the Soviet regime could easily depend on the prosecution of the correct policy. Bukharin showed the characteristic Leftist unwillingness to compromise on questions of principle; he presented as mutually exclusive alternatives national self-determination or the union of proletarians of all nations, and rejected the former as incompatible with proletarian dictatorship. Instead he proposed a formula, the authorship of which he credited to Stalin: "Self-determination of the toiling classes of each nationality."[11] Self-determination as a right to be exercised only by the proletariat of each nation was the solution to which a great many Bolsheviks, including most of the Leninists, apparently inclined after the revolution.[12] This allowed a loophole sufficiently wide for the maintenance of Soviet power wherever it could be militarily established or defended; anti-Soviet reactions among the population concerned would be automatically dismissed as nonproletarian.

Piatakov clung to a view so extremely antinational that even Bukharin found it unacceptable. Not only did he dismiss the simple "right of nations to self-determination" as a counterrevolutionary slogan; he went so far as to oppose the determination of a nation's fate by the proletariat of that nation. He urged instead the centralized control of all proletarian movements by the newly established Communist International, with the interests of the world revolution placed above those of individual nations. As an example he referred to the situation in the Ukraine, where he himself was the Communist Party leader. He asserted that Soviet Russia must, in the interest of the world revolution, maintain the hold of its power over the Ukraine, even if this meant denying national autonomy to the Ukrainian proletariat.[13] This extreme conclusion, although understandable as the position of a man whose office depended on such an arrangement, had ironic results. In 1920, Piatakov's Leftist group, re-elected to power in the Communist Party of the Ukraine, was purged from office by Lenin and replaced by the latter's own adherents. Such was the effect of proletarian internationalism upon the Leftist cause.

The tendency of the Leftists to oversimplify the world situation as they saw it, and to cast their aspirations in the form of a few uncompromising formulas, was brought out by Lenin as he developed his alternative to the Leftist nationality program. He cautioned against the severity and haste of the Bukharin and Piatakov lines, and urged patience and tolerance toward the nationalist aspirations and national differences of various nations as they developed in the direction of an eventual proletarian revolution. The great danger was "Great Russian chauvinism, hidden under the name of Communism." Of the superinternationalist, like Piatakov, who even wanted uniformity of education among nationality groups, Lenin declared, "Such a Communist—is a Great Russian chauvinist."[14] Lenin's kid-glove policy on the nationality question was received favorably by a majority of the party, including such diverse figures as Riazanov and Osinsky, both of whom stressed the value of national self-determination as a slogan in the struggle against imperialism.[15]

Lenin was to show, however, that his concern for self-determination meant no sacrifice of substantial political advantage. He insisted on maintaining the Communist Party as a centralized body embracing the territories of the tsarist empire which remained under the control of the revolutionaries, even extending to areas such as the Ukraine which were at the time under nominally independent Communist governments. With the exception of Finland, whose independence was recognized in 1917, Lenin's policy of self-determination was in practice a fiction.

THE UKRAINE: OPPOSITION STRONGHOLD

It was inevitable that the issue of real self-determination should come to a head in the Ukraine, the most populous and most important non-Great Russian part of the empire. But events in the Ukraine were even more important as an aspect of the basic divergence between the Leninist and Leftist wings of the Communist Party as a whole. The pattern of controversy in the Ukraine proved to be exceptional. The Leninists and the moderate Leftists did not draw together with the inauguration of War Communism as they did in the RSFSR. The Leftists remained more or less united, and waged a vigorous and often successful political contest with the Leninists for another two years.

Policy disputes between the Left and the Right in the Ukraine only underscored the great continuing issue—the problem of Ukrainian national autonomy and the relation of the Ukrainian Communist organization to the Russian Communist Party. Friction was constantly generated among the Ukrainian Communists as the Right strove for centralization while the Left steadfastly upheld regional and local autonomy. Until 1920 this cleavage coincided with a geographical division: typically, the Communists of the "left bank" (east of the Dnieper, centering around Kharkov) were centralist and Moscow-oriented, while the "right bank" faction (in Kiev) was autonomist and sensitive to the emotions of Ukrainian nationalism. The division reflected the concentration of Great Russians in the industrial areas of the eastern Ukraine.

When the Ukrainian Bolsheviks met in April 1918 (at Taganrog, just across the border in the Russian republic) to organize formally as the "Communist Party (Bolshevik) of the Ukraine," they were deeply divided.[16] The German occupation of the whole of the Ukraine in the spring of 1918 made the autonomist-centralist dispute between the Kievans and the Kharkovians an academic one, but at the same time the issue of peace or war was injected into the Ukrainian factional controversy.

Since the Brest-Litovsk Treaty did not apply to any Soviet-recognized regime in the Ukraine, the question of revolutionary war was still an open one for the Ukrainian Bolsheviks. This issue coincided with that of national autonomy: an independent Ukraine appealed to the Leftists as a base from which they could continue to wage war against the Germans without involving Moscow, while to the Rightists it was repugnant for the same reason.[17] As a result, the factional lines for the Ukrainians held as they had prevailed in Russia during the Brest-Litovsk controversy, and the left wing headed by Piatakov and Bubnov enjoyed commensurately sustained strength. The Leftists were bent on organizing an armed uprising against the German occupation forces, while the Rightists rejected this as adventurist disregard of the need for a long and careful effort at underground organization.[18] So fervent was the insurrectionism of the Ukrainian Leftists that they were reluctant to break with the sympathetic Left SRs even after the latter staged their abortive uprising in Moscow in July 1918.[19] With a majority behind them during the spring and summer of 1918, the Ukrainian Left Communists went ahead with their plans for an insurrection, but the attempt, launched in August 1918, was a complete fiasco. This defeat, together with Moscow's pressure represented in the person of Kamenev, sufficed to precipitate an overturn in the Ukrainian organization at its next congress, in the fall of 1918. The pro-Lenin faction led by E. I. Kviring and Y. A. Yakovlev came to power, and with it the policy of cautious centralism.[20]

When Germany collapsed in November 1918, Lenin and the Ukrainian Rightists took a cautious and conciliatory attitude toward the Ukrainian nationalists who assumed power in Kiev. Piatakov and the Left, on the other hand, clamored for Russian intervention to restore Communist rule in the Ukraine. This course prevailed, but when the new government was established at Kharkov in January 1919, Moscow supplied its chief—the Russified Rumanian of Bulgarian parentage, Christian Rakovsky.[21]

The new Ukrainian regime was scarcely functioning when Left-Right dissension broke out again. When the Third Congress of the Communist Party of the Ukraine (CPU) was held in March 1919, the nature of relations with Moscow had become a burning issue between the factions. The year before, when the party was organized, the Leftists had carried their proposal to make it coequal with the Russian Communist Party.[22] The Rightists now had a vested interest in keeping the CPU subordinate to the Central Committee of the RCP in Moscow, since support from the later quarter was the guarantee of right-wing predominance in the Ukrainian party organization. Yakovlev, the chief right-wing spokesman, took the extreme position that the CPU as a mere regional party organization should not have the privilege of formulating its own policies independently of the line laid down by Moscow. This drew down upon his head the wrath of the Leftists, who believed that it was precisely this stand, involving the clumsy application of Russian methods to different Ukrainian conditions, which was causing much of the party's difficulty in governing the Ukraine.[23]

The concrete issue posed by Moscow's leadership was that of peasant policy. When the Ukrainian Soviet Republic was reconstituted early in 1919, under the leadership of Rakovsky and the Moscow-oriented Ukrainian Rightists, the violent measures characteristic of the Russian republic in 1918 were put into effect—requisitioning, committees of the village poor, and hotheaded attempts to force the peasants into agricultural communes.[24] Although the committees of the poor were at that very time being abolished in the Russian republic, the need to send Ukrainian food to other Soviet areas, as well as the sense of class struggle against the well-established kulaks of the Ukraine, impelled the Communist leadership to wage their revolutionary offensive in the Ukrainian countryside.[25]

A year before, the Ukrainian Leftists had warned against any extreme measures against the peasants. Yakovlev replied that such concern was "petty-bourgeois" and "utopianist."[26] One of the Leftists responded in turn that this attitude revealed "the doubly Russian and anti-Ukrainian orientation of the Rights."[27] The consequence of the forceful policy applied against the Ukrainian peasants in 1919 was disastrous, as all sides later conceded.[28] The bulk of the Ukrainian rural population was alienated, and only the hopeless division of the Bolsheviks' antagonists—Whites, Ukrainian nationalists, and Makhno anarchists—permitted the eventual consolidation of Soviet rule in the region.

The March 1919 congress of the CPU registered a decided shift of sentiment toward autonomy, despite the pressure personally exerted by the secretary of the RCP, Sverdlov (just before he died). The elections to the new Ukrainian Central Committee gave a firm majority to the Left, and the Rightist leader Yakovlev was dropped from the committee altogether.[29] This setback to the Leninist forces did not stop the Russian party leadership from proclaiming that henceforth no autonomous national groups within the party were to be recognized. The Eighth Congress of the RCP resolved: "It is essential to have a *unitary* centralized Communist Party with a unitary Central Committee. . . . All decisions of the RCP and its directing institutions are unconditionally binding on all parts of the party, independently of their national composition. The central committees of the Ukrainian, Latvian, Lithuanian Communists are accorded the rights of regional committees of the party and are entirely subordinate to the Central Committee of the RCP."[30] The rights of the center were thus proclaimed in defiance of all the pretenses of national self-determination which were simultaneously reiterated.

The Leftists were equally guilty of self-contradiction. Their spokesmen at the Eighth Congress opposed self-determination as a bourgeois deviation, or, like Osinsky, justified it only as an expedient slogan.[31] But in the Ukraine the same group, and even some of the same people (Piatakov, for one), took exactly the opposite position. They made every effort to resist control by Moscow over the Ukrainian party organization and gingerly avoided offense to the nationalist sentiments of the Ukrainian populace.

The inconsistency of both factions on the question of national self-determination is without doubt attributable to the largely Russian composition of the Ukrainian Communist movement. These Russian-Ukrainians did not have feelings of nationalism complicating their relations with Moscow; hence they were able to look at nation-wide problems as ordinary Russians. Both Leftists and Rightists, when arguing the general question of nationality policy, had in mind not Russian-Ukrainian relations, but the relation of Soviet Russia to national groups and parties in the world revolutionary movement. In keeping with their respective outlooks, the Leftists argued for proletarian internationalism and the Rightists for self-determination. An entirely different set of considerations applied when the Communist leaders in the Ukraine looked at their connection with Moscow from the vantage point of Kharkov or Kiev. Since both factions actually regarded the Ukraine as a part of Russia, the governing issue was that of centralization versus local autonomy within a single party organization. As a result the Left and Right took positions opposite to their respective nationality doctrines—the Rightists upheld subordination to the center (on which they were dependent for political success in the Ukraine), and the Leftists strove to maintain the privileges of autonomy (which enabled them to keep their organizational positions in the Ukraine).

Such autonomy as the Ukrainian Communists did enjoy suffered a serious blow in mid-1919, as the Civil War took a turn for the worse. With his forces revived by the British and French support which was now able to reach him, General Denikin led the White armies in southern Russia in an amazingly successful offensive, which at its height actually threatened Moscow. The Communist position in the Ukraine, based as it was on a wavering population, collapsed completely. Kharkov fell to the Whites in June, and in August they reached Kiev. After fitful efforts to organize a guerrilla campaign behind the White lines, the Central Committee of the CPU, now devoid of any authority, was disbanded by the Russian party leadership. Many of its members were reassigned to party jobs in Russia, and what was left of the Ukrainian Communist membership passed directly under the control of the RCP.[32]

When the Ukraine was once again brought under Soviet control after Denikin's collapse, the Russian Communist leaders took steps to see that the CPU remained under the firm control of Moscow. In December 1919, a new provisional Ukrainian government was set up in Moscow. Headed by Rakovsky, Petrovsky, and Manuilsky, it was dominated by the Leninist faction. The Central Committee of the RCP passed an appropriate resolution which recognized the revived Ukrainian SSR as an independent state federally linked to the Russian Soviet Republic. The resolution also urged encouragement of the Ukrainian language and culture (suggesting that Russian Communists in the Ukraine should take the trouble to learn and speak Ukrainian), and called for a more lenient peasant policy with a limitation on the grain expropriations.[33] Clearly the Russian party leadership had learned much from the Communist collapse in the Ukraine at the time of Denikin's drive. However, in the area of real power—the Communist Party—Moscow tightened its control. While the newly constituted Ukrainian Central Committee was inviting back to the Ukraine all party workers who had formerly served there, the Central Committee of the RCP published a circular letter to all party organizations forbidding any party members to move to the Ukraine for party or government work without being officially assigned by the central secretariat in Moscow. "All those desiring to go to the Ukraine" were directed to make application through the proper channels. Monolithic coordination was as yet far from perfect.

Despite Moscow's preferences, the Ukrainian Left once again experienced a resurgence in 1920. A considerable number of new left-wing sympathizers appeared in the Ukraine for the first time, either because they were voluntarily attracted by the better opportunity to advance their cause there or because Moscow was trying to get rid of them. (Yakovlev complained, "The Ukraine is being transformed into a place of exile."[34]) The Democratic Centralists, led by Sapronov, moved into Kharkov and actually captured this citadel of the Right.[35] Then they packed the Kharkov party organization with new members, to the extent that Kharkov was privileged to elect almost one third of all the delegates to the Fourth Ukrainian Party Conference in March 1920.[36]

This conference was a turbulent affair. Wave after wave of criticism was hurled at the Ukrainian Rightists and at the Moscow party leadership. On economic policy, no less a figure than Stalin went down to defeat when he attempted to uphold Moscow (and Trotsky) on the militarization of critical sectors of the economy and on individual authority in industrial management. Particular rancor was expressed over Moscow's disbanding of the Ukrainian Central Committee during the Denikin offensive the previous fall. One delegate indignantly exclaimed, "The Third All-Ukrainian Congress appointed them, they should have been accountable to it, and no one was supposed to dismiss them." The general principle of subordination to Moscow was sharply attacked, although a majority of the conference remained sufficiently antinationalist to unseat one delegate on the ground of a "federalist" deviation.[37]

Ukrainian anticentralism was carried by Bubnov to the forum of the Ninth Congress of the RCP. He declared before the assembled Russian leaders that the effect of Moscow's policy in the Ukraine had been to weaken the Soviet regime rather than to strengthen it. The best Ukrainian party workers, he charged, had been hounded or transferred because of their oppositionist views. Moscow interference, especially the dissolution of the Ukrainian Central Committee, had wrecked the central party organization in the Ukraine, and the continuance of the rigorous antikulak policy caused the Ukrainian peasantry to become a dangerous base for anti-Soviet forces.[38] The Russian party leadership showed little readiness to compromise with such sentiments. Rakovsky's defense at the Fourth Ukrainian Conference was to denounce the whole CPU—whose governmental chief he was supposed to be—as essentially degenerate. He charged that the organization, dominated as it was by oppositionist and separatist influence, was not really a party of the proletariat but an "intelligentsia-bourgeois party, which is afraid of Com-

munist tasks." Such rebukes were ineffective, however. With the aid of
Sapronov's Kharkov steamroller, the Leftists won all the important votes at
the conference, and once again elected a majority of the new Ukrainian
Central Committee.[39]

Moscow could hardly be expected to react favorably to such an outcome.
Appealed to by the Ukrainian Rightists, the party center prepared to take
action. Lenin stated his views at the Ninth Party Congress in Moscow in no
uncertain terms: "The majority, with Sapronov at its head, expressed itself
against comrade Rakovsky and engaged in absolutely intolerable baiting. We
say that we will not recognize this decision of a regional conference. This is
the decision of the Central Committee. . . . We say that we will not recognize this conference of Comrade Sapronov's."[40]

Dismissing Leftist protests that the Ukrainian Central Committee had
been legally elected in the presence of a Moscow representative (Stalin), the
Central Committee of the RCP decreed the choice of the Ukrainian party
conference to be invalid.[41] The pretext offered was that "the conference was
roughly divided into two parts, as a result of which the conference appeared
incapable of creating a Central Committee of the Ukrainian Party." (By
now Moscow categorically condemned any sign of a two-party system, even
within a Communist context.) "Under these conditions," the order continued,
"the Central Committee of the RCP considers it essential to create a temporary Central Committee of the CPU of such a composition as will reflect the
will of the overwhelming majority of the RCP [*not* of the CPU] as it was
expressed at the last congress of the party, and which is able to take the lead
of all really Communist elements of the Ukrainian working class in the work
of Ukrainian construction." Then a new Ukrainian Central Committee was
appointed. All of the Rightist leaders who had been dropped by the conference were reinstated, and Leftist influence was virtually eliminated. In addition, the Russian Central Committee declared, "The basic condition for
healthy party and soviet work in the Ukraine is a strict purge of the party
ranks of the CPU." The CPU had allegedly become filled with "unprincipled, adventurist fellow-travelers . . . demagogic elements, semi-Makhnoists,
and disrupters," who were to be eliminated or disciplined. Finally, the
instigators of dissension were to be dispersed: "The Central Committee of
the RCP considers it necessary to transfer from the Ukraine for work in
Great Russia those of the responsible party workers whose active participation in the still fresh struggle has unavoidably made it difficult to carry on
agreed-on and friendly work on the staffs of the party and soviet institutions
on the basis of the decisions reached by the Ninth Congress of the party."

The power of purge and transfer meant unrestricted control by Moscow
over the Ukrainian party organization; "the will of the RCP" was to be the
guide for any local action. "Resting on the ideological and material support
of the RCP," as Moscow acidly reminded them, the Ukrainian Communists

lost the last shred of their autonomy. By legitimate transfers to other duties, the central secretariat of the RCP quickly dispersed the Ukrainian opposition-ists throughout Russia. In the fall of 1920, the Ukraine experienced echoes of national party controversies—the reaction against militarization and the Workers' Opposition[42]—but as an independent threat to the Moscow leader-ship, the Ukrainian base of the Left Opposition had been eliminated.

THE MILITARY OPPOSITION

The Civil War between Reds and Whites brought no cessation of contro-versy among the Communists. The issue of central authority raised by the Left Communists persisted, and the conduct of the war itself became a major focus of disagreement. During the first year of civil strife, in 1918 and 1919, while the Red Army was still in its formative stage, bitter dissensions arose within the party and the Soviet military leadership as to the proper organiza-tional form for the military operations of the revolutionary regime. The essence of the military issue was the same clash of anarchistic idealism and pragmatic predilection for traditional organizational forms which divided the Left Communists and the Leninists in respect to industrial and labor policy.

When Trotsky was appointed Commissar of Military Affairs after the resolution of the Brest-Litovsk crisis in March 1918, he began to apply to this field the same standards of organized authority which Lenin was enjoin-ing on the economy—"Work, discipline, and order" was his formula for victory.[43] Trotsky had to overcome opposition at the very beginning, even in the Communist military leadership: in April, 1918, N. V. Krylenko, one of the co-Commissars of Military Affairs appointed after the October Revo-lution, resigned in disgust from the defense establishment and became Commissar of Justice.[44] Energetically Trotsky began to build up an entirely new force—the Red Army—to replace the army which had dissolved in the ferment of revolution. A central military command and staff were set up, and their authority was gradually imposed on the motley assemblage of irregulars and volunteers who made up the Red Army during the critical spring and summer months of 1918. The guerrilla warfare by "flying squads," to which the Left was so partial, was rudely disdained, though by force of circumstance it could not be entirely abandoned. Democratic forms of organ-ization, including the election of officers, were quickly dispensed with. "The elective basis," Trotsky announced at the end of March 1918, "is politically pointless and technically inexpedient, and has in fact already been set aside by decree."[45] The death penalty for disobedience under fire, a target of so much revolutionary moralism, was calmly restored. The Communist Party organizations in the army were brought into line with the military pattern of hierarchical authority through the system of commissars and "political departments."[46] A new officer corps was rapidly formed; one half of it was recruited from former tsarist officers induced or coerced into serving.

The use of tsarist officers—"military specialists"—was long a point of bitter discord. Trotsky proposed this expedient in March 1918 and, like Lenin on the industrial issue, defended the use of "all worthwhile qualified elements from the old apparatus."[47] The response was a cry of revolutionary anguish in every quarter from the Mensheviks through the Left SRs to the Left Communists. One Left Communist adherent complained, "Confirmed counterrevolutionaries are running things in the army again, not elected persons."[48] Even Lenin did not clearly commit himself to the use of the military *spetsy* for many months, and some of the Leninists, particularly people in the party's military organizations, were actively hostile to Trotsky on this issue. The chief of the party organization in the army, M. M. Lashevich, ignored Trotsky's efforts to appease the officers and urged his colleagues to "squeeze them like lemons and then throw them away."[49] Personal animosity was infused into this issue, for Lashevich was a protegé of Trotsky's rival Zinoviev.

The issue of military organization came to a head at the time of the Eighth Party Congress in March 1919, when the Soviet government was enjoying a brief military respite. A heterogeneous group of party members —partly but not entirely of Left Communist background—joined in their common antipathy to Trotsky, formed the so-called Military Opposition. They went down to defeat, but not without striking a blow at the war commissar's political future. The doctrinaire elements in the Military Opposition found their leading spokesman in Vladimir Smirnov, the former Left Communist who was prominent in the newly formed Democratic Centralist group. Smirnov conceded the need to employ the *spetsy*,[50] but beyond this he would not yield. He pleaded for the party to resist the secondary features of traditional military organization which had returned with discipline and the tsarist officers—the salute, special forms of address, separate living quarters and special privileges for officers, conventional military regulations. "Regulations are necessary," he admitted, "but need to be made in correspondence with the experience which has been acquired, rejecting everything that has been evoked by the specific conditions of the prerevolutionary period."[51]

The party leadership, striving to ward off embarrassing criticism and avoid any restrictions on its freedom, countered by exaggerating the position of the Opposition and then denouncing its heresy: "Counterposing the idea of partisan units to a systematically organized and centralized army . . . represents a caricature-like product of the political thought or lack of thought of the petty-bourgeois intelligentsia. . . . To preach guerrilla warfare as a military program is the same as to recommend turning back from large-scale industry to handicraft trades."[52] In Trotsky's dialectical eloquence, garnished with the wisdom of hindsight: "The chaos of irregular warfare expressed the peasant element that lay beneath the revolution, whereas the struggle against it was also a struggle in favor of the proletarian state organization as opposed to the elemental, petty-bourgeois anarchy that was undermining it."[53]

In secret debate at the Eighth Congress, the criticism of Trotsky was sharp.[54] Sokolnikov, replying on Trotsky's behalf, contended that the virtues of guerrilla warfare were heavily outweighed by its vices, that it amounted ultimately to "banditry and marauding" and was "a bulwark of adventurism."[55] Nevertheless, the Opposition mustered unusual strength—the vote for Smirnov's resolution was 95 against 174 upholding Trotsky's policies.[56] A secret instruction was then passed and (no doubt gleefully) communicated to the absent war commissar by Zinoviev, to pay more heed to the party functionaries in the army. Trotsky rejected this so-called "warning," with a blast at K. Y. Voroshilov (then a partisan leader), to whom he attributed the gesture.[57]

The published resolution of the Eighth Congress on the military question was in its practical details a complete endorsement of Trotsky's centralism. Nevertheless, the tone of its generalities was to a remarkable degree a concession to the old revolutionary idealism. The militia ideal of an army without barracks was affirmed for the future, and even the principle of electing officers was accepted as a desideratum when the maturity and stability of the army should permit it.[58]

The surprising amount of strength which accrued to the Opposition on the military issue must be attributed to an unusual combination of political forces, involving both high principle and petty backbiting. Trotsky's own analysis is undoubtedly near the mark. One element of the Military Opposition included idealists like Smirnov, who suffered from "uncertainty that the new class which had come to power would be able to dominate and control the broad circles of the old intelligentsia." Balancing this reservoir of overzealous revolutionary energy was the other component of the Military Opposition, which included "the numerous underground workers who were utterly worn out by prison and exile, and who now could not find a place for themselves in the building of the army and the State. They looked with great disfavor on all sorts of upstarts."[59] It is not hard to see here Trotsky's view of Stalin and his supporters of the Tsaritsyn group.

The Tsaritsyn affair has been celebrated (and exaggerated) as the origin of the Stalin-Trotsky duel. In the summer of 1918 Stalin had been dispatched to the lower Volga to ensure the transit of food supplies northward to central Russia. At Tsaritsyn (now Stalingrad) he took charge of the defense of the city against the encircling White armies. The Red military forces there were under the tactical command of Voroshilov, with Ordzhonikidze as political commissar. Serious discord arose as the local Tsaritsyn leaders ventured to defy the orders of the Revolutionary Military Council of the republic (the military high command headed by Trotsky). The Tsaritsyn group was

particularly hostile to the policy of using tsarist officers. Stalin, on this occasion suspending his penchant for centralism, sided with the local leaders
against Trotsky. Matters reached the point where Trotsky threatened to
court-martial Voroshilov. After a contest of appeals to Lenin, Stalin was recalled and Trotsky's central military authority was upheld.

Trotsky's victory was costly. While he was busy consolidating the Soviet
forces in southern Russia late in 1918, Stalin had joined Zinoviev in intriguing against him in Moscow. Trotsky was criticized for coddling the
tsarist officers. Zinoviev's friends, Commissars Smilga and Lashevich,
made the then grave charge that Trotsky had ordered Communist Party
members summarily shot.[60] All this contributed to the anti-Trotsky sentiment that appeared at the Eighth Congress. From this time on, Trotsky was
destined to grow steadily more unpopular among most of the men who
surrounded Lenin in the top party leadership.

Not even among the strictly military leadership was Trotsky able to keep
a firm following. During the course of the Civil War he was involved in
acrid frictions with the top military commanders and with most of the high-
ranking political commissars. He suffered particularly stinging blows in
July 1919, when Stalin managed to have Trotsky's adversary, General S. M.
Kamenev (no relation to the party figure, L. B. Kamenev), made com-
mander-in-chief, and when the Revolutionary Military Council was reshuffled
to eliminate most of Trotsky's friends.[61] Despite the brilliance of his leadership, Trotsky only antagonized his colleagues all the more by his success.
The issues of militia organization and of guerrilla tactics were kept alive
and were driven hard by anti-Trotsky military figures, including Voroshilov
and M. V. Frunze, the man who ultimately relieved Trotsky as war commissar. Trotsky remained outstandingly popular among the lower-ranking
officers, but the army as a political factor was run by the military organs of
the party, under the firm control of Trotsky's enemies.[62]

INDUSTRIAL ADMINISTRATION

Russian industry, like the army, had experienced a revolutionary disintegration in the traditional forms of authority and discipline. As with the
army, the issue of industrial organization had been brought to a focus during
the controversy between Lenin and the Left Communists in the spring of
1918. Were the factories to be turned into autonomous, democratic communes, or were the industrial workers to be subjected again to managerial
authority, labor discipline, wage incentives, scientific management—to the
familiar forms of capitalistic industrial organization with the same bourgeois
managers, qualified only by the state's holding title to the property?

During the critical period of the Civil War—from mid-1918 to the end
of 1919—the centralization of economic administration in the hands of the
"chief committees" (*glavnye komitety* or *glavki*) went on apace. The dis-

tastefulness of this trend to the purists of the left wing was ameliorated by two conditions—the participation of the trade unions or their representatives in industrial management and the conduct of administrative operations at all levels by boards (collegia) rather than by individuals. Open left-wing protests were provoked when the party leadership began to turn away from these two revolutionary norms in the direction of a hierarchy of appointed individuals. A vigorous debate commenced early in 1920 over the form of industrial management and the role of the unions. (The latter question so rocked the party that it requires special consideration in the following chapter.) The implications of the industrial issue were broad: the defeat of the Opposition meant a major departure from the original social program of the revolution.

The Leftist administrative ideal was exemplified by the trade-union chief Tomsky in the theses which he prepared for the Ninth Party Congress: "The basic principle in building the organs for regulating and administering industry, the only one capable of guaranteeing the participation of the broad nonparty working masses through the trade unions, is the presently existing principle of the collegial administration of industry, beginning with the presidium of the Supreme Economic Council and concluding with the plant administration."[63] Kritsman termed collegial administration "the specific distinctive mark of the proletariat, distinguishing it from *all* other social classes . . . the most democratic principle of organization."[64]

So strong was the collegial tradition in the party that even Lenin felt compelled to acknowledge the principle, though his partiality to individual authority had been clear since his polemics with the Left Communists. "Collegial administration is essential when we have participation by the trade unions," he conceded in December 1918, but with an immediate qualification: "Collegial administration must not become an obstacle to practical matters."[65] As late as December 1919, the Seventh Congress of Soviets passed as a routine matter a resolution endorsing collegial management.[66] By this time, however, Lenin (strongly supported by Trotsky) was preparing to take a stronger stand. In January 1920, he sharply stated: "The collegial principle . . . represents something rudimentary, necessary for the first stage, when it is necessary to build anew. . . . The transition to practical work is connected with individual authority, as the system which more than any other assures the best utilization of human resources and a real, not merely verbal, checkup on work."[67]

If this was what socialism was going to mean, the Left would have none of it. The Central Trade Union Council twice rejected Lenin's defense of individual management, and a number of trade unions and local party organizations did likewise.[68] Lenin replied in ever-stronger terms: the party and the country would have to turn to "iron discipline," "labor obedience," "centralization of economic administration." In sum, he contended, "The elective principle must be replaced by the principle of *selection*."[69] Carrying the issue to the floor of the Ninth Party Congress, Lenin characterized the collegial principle as "utopian," "impractical," and "injurious."[70]

Trotsky backed up Lenin's contention that the collegial principle represented an outgrown phase of the revolution: "Elected collegia, composed of the very best representatives of the working class, but not possessing basic technical knowledge, cannot replace one technician who has gone to a special school and who knows how to handle a given special job. . . . Collegial management . . . is an entirely natural reaction of a young, revolutionary, recently oppressed class, which rejects the individual command of yesterday's masters, bosses, commanders. . . . But this is not the last word in building the state economy of the proletarian class."[71] The collegial idea, Trotsky charged, was really of Menshevik origin.[72]

The Democratic Centralist group tried to effect a compromise. The resolution which they voted through the earlier Moscow provincial party conference minimized the whole issue: "The question of the collegial system and individual authority is not a question of principle, but a practical one, and must be decided in each case according to the circumstances."[73] They claimed practical virtues for collegial management as a "higher school of administration," training proletarians for responsible posts and eliminating the need for bourgeois specialists.[74] (Trotsky denounced such thinking as an invitation to chaos.[75]) Further, the Democratic Centralists hailed the collegial principle as "the strongest weapon against the growth of departmentalism and bureaucratic deadening of the soviet apparatus."[76] As usual, when the critical test came at the Ninth Congress, Lenin's case prevailed. The economic resolution which he pushed through demanded "the actual implementation from top to bottom of . . . definite responsibility of specific individuals for specific work. The *collegial principle,* though it may have a place in discussing or deciding, must unconditionally yield its place to *individual authority* in the process of execution."[77] Once endorsed by the congress, the new policy was rapidly implemented.[78]

In industry, as in the army, the controversy over individual authority and hierarchical organization was closely connected with the issue of employing *spetsy*. The Democratic Centralists, who had participated in the Military Opposition, urged restraints on the use of specialists in economic areas as well. Sapronov stated, "No one disputes the necessity of using the spetsy— the dispute is over how to use them."[79]

Trotsky, when he turned from military to economic concerns in 1920, kept his positive view about the need to use the experts and give them full freedom of action. He brushed the opposition aside: "Those who fear this unconsciously reveal a deep inner distrust of the Soviet regime."[80] This equation of criticism with disaffection was echoed by the Ninth Party Congress in a resolution condemning "the ignorant conceit of believing that the working class could resolve its tasks without the use of specialists from the bourgeois school in the most responsible posts." Foreshadowing the disciplinary measures of the following year against the Ultra-Left, the resolution went on to warn, "There can be no place in the ranks of the party of scientific socialism for those demagogic elements which play upon this sort of prejudice among the backward section of the workers."[81]

The industrial discussions of 1920 wrote an end to the anarchic ideal of 1917 Bolshevism. Henceforth, as far as Soviet Russia was concerned, the economic base of society was to be organized on the lines of hierarchical authority and rank common to both the military services and the corporate enterprises of "bourgeois" society. One must wonder what the revolution had really changed, from the point of view of the "worker at the bench." As War Communism approached a crisis, the dismay among many workers and Communists was unmistakable. In the meantime, however, changes in the political structure of the Soviet regime were already limiting the effect which this reaction could have.

CONCENTRATION OF POLITICAL POWER

Theoretically, the hierarchy of local, regional, and national soviets which the Bolsheviks converted into the government of Russia came close to the political ideal of the Paris Commune and 1917 Bolshevism—decentralized, direct democracy (qualified, to be sure, by the great disproportion in representation accorded the urban population as against the peasants). In practice it was far from this, and the oppositionists who insisted too stubbornly on living up to the ideal came dangerously close to being labeled un-Bolshevik. During the Civil War years, the soviets rapidly became nothing more than a façade, giving official sanction to decisions made by the Communist Party and carried out by Communists serving in the "soviet apparatus," as the departments and agencies of government were collectively termed. The reduction of the soviets to a political cipher was assured by the exclusion from them of representatives of the Mensheviks and SRs, although remnants of these parties managed to endure in a state of occasional semilegality as late as 1920.

At the Eighth Party Congress, when the organization of the party and the government first came under extensive discussion, the decline of the soviets drew special attention. The Democratic Centralists made themselves the champions of the soviets and urged a series of reforms to restore them as functioning democratic organs of the working class. Osinsky proposed that the Council of People's Commissars and the presidium of the Soviet Central Executive Committee be merged and serve in effect as a parliamentary cabinet, while the main body of the Central Executive Committee would resume the legislative power originally vested in it. Local government would be similarly reformed, to restore regional responsibility.[82]

Such reform ideas were never effective. The oppositionists were too weak and disunited, and their conception of political organization ran counter to the basic Communist conception of government as "decision making." Asserted Lenin, "In an epoch of dictatorship a parliament can neither decide questions, nor direct the party or the soviet organizations."[83] Legislative power, not distinguished from the executive function, was engulfed by the latter: the Congress of Soviets and the Central Executive Committee soon lost most of their power to the Council of People's Commissars. The organs of government were simultaneously losing their power to the corresponding Communist Party organs, where most decisions were actually made. In the party itself, power gravitated from the annual congresses to the Central Committee and from there to the new Political Bureau (established by the Eighth Congress). The concentration of power in the hands of smaller and more efficient bodies was irresistably natural. The larger party and government organs had nothing to do but ratify the decisions of the small committees, and under the conditions of Communist Party discipline ratification quickly became an automatic rubber stamp. Soviet political evolution was well on its way toward a logical conclusion: one-man dictatorship.

In theory the Communist Party, like the system of soviets, was exceedingly democratic; all responsible party officials were supposed to be elected by the membership, and policy was to be set by the annual congresses. But thanks to the responsibilities of power, the circumstances of dictatorial rule, and the pressure of civil war, democracy within the party rapidly became an empty form. The need for streamlining the decision-making process in the party was quickly felt even at the Central Committee level. By the time of the Eighth Congress in 1919, all sides were agreed that the fifteen-man Central Committee was inadequate to its tasks. The leadership found it too unwieldy for continuous executive responsibility, while the people concerned with party democracy considered it too small to be representative.

The Opposition ideal was something approaching a genuinely functioning parliament for the party. The Ukrainian Skrypnik complained of the lack of discussion of important questions before decisions were finally made: "It is essential for us to work out a collective party opinion, for the party can be a party only if it collectively works out opinions in order to put them into practice."[84] This idea was embodied by Osinsky in a proposal to elevate the Central Committee into a truly collective body, charged with the real responsibility for making decisions, though he tried to avoid the charge of parliamentarianism. He broached an idea which was to have great significance when it reappeared in 1923: "It is necessary to enroll workers into the Central Committee on a broad scale; it is necessary to introduce there a sufficient quantity of workers in order thereby, so to speak, to proletarianize the Central Committee."[85] Accordingly, he proposed that the committee be expanded from fifteen to twenty-one members.

The congress agreed in principle, and the membership of the committee was increased to nineteen, with eight candidates. Trotsky's moderate Leftist tendency was strongly represented among the new members, who included his firm supporters Radek, Rakovsky, and L. P. Serebriakov. Other new members were Kalinin (who had just become chief of state as chairman of the Soviet Central Executive Committee) and Tomsky, while two figures on opposite sides in the military controversy, Sokolnikov and Lashevich, were dropped. However, the effort to protect rank-and-file control by enlarging the Central Committee was foredoomed to failure, given the concept that government is decision making. Enlargement meant less efficiency in decision making, and responsibility gravitated to a small inner circle within the body formally exercising authority.

Such a concentration of power was officially sanctioned in a major step toward centralization adopted by the Eighth Congress—the creation of the Political Bureau (Politburo) and the Organizational Bureau (Orgburo). Five men were then elected by the Central Committee to serve on the Politburo: Lenin, Trotsky, Stalin, Kamenev, and Trotsky's supporter, Krestinsky. Zinoviev, Bukharin, and Kalinin were chosen as candidate members.[86] The Orgburo did not have a fixed composition during its first year; most of the members of the Central Committee served on it at one time or another during 1919–1920.[87] Notably absent from the Orgburo was the name of Stalin, who at this early date had not yet begun to get the party organization in his pocket.

The Eighth Congress also responded to criticisms of the Central Committee's organizational inadequacies. Sverdlov, who had supervised the party's organizational affairs, died just before the Eighth Congress opened. The party's records, largely stored in his memory, were lost. To forestall any such difficulties in the future, the Secretariat was reorganized on more formal lines, with a technical staff to be headed by a member of the Orgburo.[88] Krestinsky was the man selected for the post, which made him for the moment a powerful figure in the party.[89]

Technically these new bodies were only subcommittees of the Central Committee, but they rapidly became supreme in their respective fields of general policy making and administration of the party organization. The concentration of decision-making power had proceeded one step farther. The country was ruled, in effect, by decree of the Politburo as registered by the Council of People's Commissars, to which the broader soviet bodies had similarly lost their power.

From 1919 to 1921 the top party leadership was relatively stable, and almost evenly balanced between the Leninists and the moderate Left headed by Trotsky. The Rightists who quit in November 1917 over the coalition issue were gradually being restored to membership in the Central Committee (Kamenev in 1919 and Rykov in 1920). Among the new candidate members elected in 1920 was Molotov. The Politburo stood unchanged in 1920, while the Orgburo was finally given a fixed composition: Krestinsky, Preobrazhensky, Serebriakov, Rykov, and now Stalin.[90] At the same time, the Secretariat was expanded, and Preobrazhensky and Serebriakov were delegated to join Krestinsky in running its affairs. All three, significantly, were Trotsky supporters. March 1920 was the high point in the prestige of Trotsky and his group.

Similar authoritarian trends were proceeding at the same time on the lower levels of the Communist Party organization. By the end of 1919 the whole party was virtually a military organization, devoted to the prosecution of the Civil War. Lenin was adamant on the need for absolute discipline: "The experience of the triumphant dictatorship of the proletariat in Russia . . . proves that unqualified centralism and the strictest discipline of the proletariat are among the principal conditions for the victory over the bourgeoisie."[91] Hence, "Whoever in the least weakens the iron discipline of the party of the proletariat (especially during its dictatorship), aids in reality the bourgeoisie against the proletariat."[92]

"All decisions of the higher jurisdiction are absolutely binding for the lower," ruled the Eighth Congress. "Each decision must above all be fulfilled, and only after this is an appeal to the corresponding party organ permissible. . . ." Centralism was reaffirmed in all its prerevolutionary rigor: "The whole matter of assignment of party workers is in the hands of the Central Committee of the party. Its decision is binding for everyone. . . ."[93] Translating this principle into practice, the Secretariat under Krestinsky began deliberately to transfer party officials for political reasons, to end personal conflicts and curb opposition.[94]

Centralization was generally accepted—even by the Democratic Centralists—as an unavoidable wartime necessity. The stumbling block was the reconversion of the party apparatus to a more decentralized, less bureaucratic, basis after the termination of hostilities. This task was in fact never accomplished, and the legacy of the Civil War in matters of organization proved to be one of the most serious obstacles to the fond hopes of the Left Opposition for a democratically constituted party organization.

At the Ninth Party Congress a storm of protest burst forth against the excesses of centralism in the party. The very first delegate to speak in debate, the former *mezhraionets* Yurenev, complained that the Central Committee had made "paper concessions" on the issue of centralism at the previous congress, and then "carried out its own policy . . . completely opposed to what the congress had decided." He demanded that the Central Committee be "a responsible ministry, and not an irresponsible government."[95] On behalf of the party leader p, Kamenev sought justification in the party's circumstances of bitter struggle: "Yes, we have administered with the aid of dictatorship, and if, in view of those colossal events through which we have been living, we summoned plenums and decided questions by parliamentary means, then undoubtedly we would have destroyed the revolution. . . . We must develop a dictatorship based on complete trust that we have taken the correct line. . . ."[96] Such trust indeed prevailed; in the party congresses after the Seventh an overwhelming majority of the delegates were under the spell of Lenin's leadership and the ideal of party unity.

The aspect of centralization over which the Leftists were most aroused was the replacement of local party committees, which were at least democratic in form, by bureaucratically constituted "political departments." With the institution of such bodies, all political activity in the plant, industry, organization, or locality under their jurisdiction was placed under rigid control from above. This innovation was taken from the army; as its origin suggests, it was strictly a military, authoritarian institution, designed for transmitting propaganda downward rather than opinion upward. One of the most vigorous applications of the political department—to curb opposition as well as to improve the industry—was in the coal mines of the Donets Basin. This happened to be the work of Stalin—early evidence of his special predilection for authoritarian procedures.[97]

Sapronov interpreted the spread of political departments as an indication of the ominous overall trend of developments in the party as a whole:

They [the Central Committee] want to replace the party committee in the coal industry with presidents of political departments. . . . The abolition of provincial committees is becoming systematic. . . . The Central Committee finds that the [local] party committee is a bourgeois prejudice, is conservatism bordering on the province of treason, and that the new form is the replacement of party committees by political departments, the heads of which by themselves replace the elected committees. . . . You transform the members of the party into an obedient gramophone, with leaders who order: go and agitate; but they haven't the right to elect their own committee, their own organs.

I then put the question to comrade Lenin: Who will appoint the Central Committee? You see, there can be individual authority here as well. Here also a single commander can be appointed. It does not appear that we will reach this state, but if we do, the revolution will have been gambled away. . . .

Comrade Lenin . . . allow us ignorant ones to ask you a question. If you go according to this system, do you think that the result will be the salvation of the revolution?[98]

Communists who in 1956 suddenly sought an explanation for the evils of Stalinism might well have begun their inquiry here.

Perceptive as the Democratic Centralists were, their awareness fell short of the real evil—the fundamental Bolshevik ideals of party organization. These remained as Lenin had formulated them and continued to guide Communists of all shades—the primacy of unity, the party as a solidly bound spearhead unit in the class war, the need for all members and all local organizations to adhere to party discipline, and in all relations with people outside the party to accept the party line as determined by the congress and by the Central Committee, or by the Politburo and Lenin.

The reform proposals which the Democratic Centralists put forth were well meant, but they failed to strike at the root of the problem. They could think of no real device, for instance, to assure autonomy to local organizations. In this regard, they were able only to protest the failure of the party center to respect the rights of local bodies, as occurred in assigning personnel or in placing the subordinate organs of local party committees directly under the control of the party secretariat in Moscow. The Democratic Centralists made the mistake of concentrating on attempts to rearrange top-level political institutions, to reshuffle the forms of political control, or to introduce new blood into the leadership, while leaving the real sources of power relatively unaffected.

The process of centralization and the curtailment of opposition are clearly revealed in party documents of the Civil War period. But the process was only gradual: Lenin's centralism was never fully realized until long after the revolutionary overturn had disposed of the task which excused it. The boldness of some of the early criticism directed at Lenin provides a refreshing contrast to the stifling atmosphere which later prevailed. By 1923 the oppositionists looked back to 1917 and 1918 as a golden age of party democracy. Indeed, before 1921 the right of opposition was explicitly acknowledged by the party leadership: "Any comrade, if he considers it necessary to steer the party and soviet ship in another direction, can speak up about this—this is his right."[99] There came a brief moment in the history of the Communist Party when the forces of opposition, availing themselves of this right, almost succeeded in changing the organizational course of the ship of state.

THE HIGH TIDE OF PARTY DEMOCRACY

By the fall of 1920 the Communists had won the Civil War. The last major campaigns—the war with Poland and the reduction of the last White stronghold under Wrangel in the Crimea—were nearing an end. As the stress of war disappeared, there arose a new wave of opposition to the authoritarian regime in the Communist Party. Lenin's authority was challenged more seriously than at any time since the Left Communist movement of 1918.

The focus of discontent was the question of bureaucratic organization and the relation between the "top" and "bottom" of the party—that is, the cleavage between the full-time party leaders and functionaries and the rank-and-file members. By the middle of 1920 the party leadership was showing concern over this problem and the reaction which it caused in the ranks.

Preobrazhensky, who remained sensitive to infringements of democracy even though he was now one of the top party secretaries, drafted a set of theses on the problem of bureaucratism. This was revised and distributed to the party as a Central Committee circular letter.[100] The letter conceded that revolutionary idealism was being stifled by pragmatic expedients, bureaucratic routine, and careerist self-seeking. Apart from these generalities, however, the alleged evils were justified more than they were attacked, and the basic problem of a bureaucratically organized party and state was not tackled. Cries for restoring equality were rebuked as demagogy. The reforming concern of the Central Committee was devoted mainly to adjustments within the bureaucracy, with emphasis on tighter control from above, to enforce efficiency and morality, and to promote the meritorious.

The rank and file must have been far from pleased by this statement, for soon afterward a commission was set up to reconsider the organizational problem. As "official representatives of the party opposition," two men from the Ultra-Left were included on the commission: E. N. Ignatov for the Workers' Opposition (as the trade-union Leftists were now termed) and Sapronov for the Democratic Centralists.[101] The designation of these two is noteworthy: it marks the high point in the recognition of the rights of opposition groups by the party leadership and underscores the strength which the Ultra-Left had accumulated during 1920. When the Ninth Party Conference met in September 1920, the democratic opposition was at its peak.

The Ninth Conference opened with a series of scathing attacks on the performance of the party machinery: insufficient ties with local organizations; unsystematic handling of transfers of party workers; insufficient attention to the economic tasks which the party had to lead the nation in fulfilling; lack of centralized direction of the party's educational activities (a rebuke to Preobrazhensky, head of the agit-prop division of the Secretariat); general inadequacy of the organizational machinery to meet the demands placed upon it.[102] Bubnov, who had joined the Democratic Centralists, declared, "For the last half year there has been a complete absence of any organizational policy." In spite of all this discontent, however, the party leadership was able to push through the conference a resolution approving the organizational work of the Central Committee (with the exception of the agit-prop division), and commending its recent achievements in strengthening the party machinery.[103]

Then the tone of criticism changed.[104] Sapronov repeated the Democratic Centralist arguments about "bureaucratic centralism" and the dangers inherent in individual authority whether in industry or political organizations; he observed that "bureaucratism" flourished at all levels of the party machinery. He saw the remedy in combating bourgeois influences in the party and in enforcing collegial authority in party institutions. Y. Lutovinov of the Workers' Opposition denounced the methods used by the party leadership against the Opposition. It was in such abuse of central authority, he asserted, as well as the Central Committee's extension of its functions from "directing" to "administration and execution," that the real cause of the crisis lay.

The actual differences between the leadership and the Opposition at the Ninth Conference were more a matter of emphasis than of principle. Both sides agreed on the twin dangers of bureaucratism and organizational weakness, but they differed over which was the more serious. The party leadership wanted to keep the organization strong in order to combat the Opposition, as the use they subsequently made of their power clearly shows. It was stated openly that the party's number-one task was to fight the "ideological deviation" of people who "purported" to be defending the lower ranks of the party against the top.[105] Contrary to the logic of their position, the Leftists did not oppose strengthening the party machinery—they criticized the operational deficiencies of the Secretariat as resolutely as did the majority. Organization, they naively believed, was the most effective weapon against bureaucratism.

To this end the conference took the concrete measure of establishing a series of "control commissions," one for the center and one for each provincial party organization. Seven men made up the central commission—Preobrazhensky and Dzherzhinsky, both supporters of Trotsky at this point, the Leninist Muranov, and four representatives of local organizations.[106] The commissions were supposed to put an end to all the familiar abuses of bureaucratism and to defend the interests of the party rank and file. The Left gave no indication that it was not heartily in accord with the idea.

The Ninth Conference ended with a rousing manifesto of democratic intent—a resolution on party organization which read more like a platform of the Ultra-Left than a statement by the party leadership. It called for "broader criticism of the central as well as of the local party institutions," cessation of the appointment of local secretaries by the center, and the rejection of "any kind of repression against comrades because they have different ideas." Stressed above all was "the need again to direct the attention of the whole party to the struggle for the realization of greater equality: in the first place, within the party; secondly, within the proletariat, and in addition within the whole toiling mass; finally, in the third place, between the various offices and various groups of workers, especially the 'spetsy' and responsible workers, in relation to the masses."[107]

This was the climax of Communist liberalism, a far cry from the Leninism of 1902. That the party should officially endorse such sweeping democratic principles was compelling testimony to the strength of left-wing thinking at this particular time. The party leadership evidently felt driven to make this timely concession in order to maintain a firm hold on the party machinery and secure a breathing-space. Lenin was not vituperative; he reportedly described the 1920 Opposition as "perfectly sound, necessary, and inevitable," a natural effect of the transition from the military effort to civil reconstruction.[108] But unity was the goal, and concessions were allowed only with this end in view. Before much time was to pass, circumstances would rule out even these concessions.

5

THE TRADE-UNION CONTROVERSY

By 1920 the existence of the Soviet state was no longer seriously in question, though fighting with the White forces and with Poland dragged on through most of the year. It became possible for the Communist leaders once again to give some attention to the ultimate shape of the new society which they were trying to construct. The effect, as usual when the revolutionaries turned to such general problems, was renewed dissension, which happened to be expressed through the trade-union issue. Starting from the question of the proper role of the trade unions, the argument went far beyond this: it involved basic choices about the future of the Soviet state and its relation to its professed objectives. This is why the trade-union issue produced a storm of debate rivaling the acrimonious prelude to the Treaty of Brest-Litovsk. The underlying divergence between the Leninists and the Left emerged once more, and the lines were drawn which generally were to hold for seven years of factional struggle.

War Communism and the Trade Unions

As with most instances of serious political disagreement, the trade-union controversy among the Communists in the winter of 1920–1921 did not arise overnight. Directly or indirectly the trade unions and labor issues had been involved in the party debates ever since the Communists came to power. Like the general question of political and industrial authority, the trade-union issue had its roots in the anarchistic utopianism which Lenin exemplified in "State and Revolution." Again it was the dissidents on the Left who endeavored to maintain the revolutionary ideal with respect to the trade unions and the autonomous and democratic participation of the masses in the functions of economic administration.

When the year of "workers' control" in 1917 and 1918 gave way to all-encompassing nationalization and direct, centralized governmental administration of industry, the trade unions remained the beneficiaries of the syndicalist legacy of 1917 Bolshevism. The party program drawn up at the Eighth Congress in March 1919 proclaimed, "The organizational apparatus of socialized industry must be based primarily on the trade unions. . . . The trade unions must proceed to the actual concentration in their own hands of all the administration of the whole economy, as a single economic unit."[1] Bukharin elaborated on this prospect in his theory of the new society: he accorded the trade unions a primary role in replacing capitalist cartels and trusts as the basic organization of production relations.[2]

The Second Trade Union Congress, in January 1919, endorsed a formula for the future of the unions which was to become a key term in the controversy of the following year: "governmentalizing" (*ogosudarstvlenie*) of the trade unions as their functions broadened and merged with the governmental machinery of industrial administration and control. This would happen more or less spontaneously, "an altogether inevitable result of their closely coordinated joint work and of the preparation of the broad masses by the trade unions for the task of administering the state apparatus and all organs of economic control."[3] The Commissar of Labor, V. V. Shmidt, said in reference to his own department, "Even the organs of the Commissariat of Labor should be built out of the trade-union apparatus."[4] The reverse side of the unions' administrative prerogative was their responsibility for maintaining labor discipline and productivity, and for preventing, rather than conducting, strikes. Incentives, exhortation, and the mobilization of industrial and military recruits also fell in the province of the unions.[5]

In 1918 and 1919, during the interregnum between private ownership and effective governmental control, the trade unions did play a substantial role in industrial administration.[6] The Communists in the trade-union leadership, headed by Tomsky as chairman of the All-Russian Central Council of Trade Unions (ARCCTU), enjoyed much power and considerable autonomy. In the relation between the union leadership and the rank and file, however, the democratic ideal was far from a reality. In practice, the more the trade unions assumed the administrative functions of a conventional managerial bureaucracy, the more bureaucratic they became themselves.[7] Riazanov, who as a Bolshevik of the Ultra-Right was always apprehensive of the consequences of overambitious programs, warned the Eighth Party Congress, "We will not avoid bureaucratism until all the trade unions . . . relinquish . . . every right in the administration of production."[8] Arguments over the future of the unions turned, however, not on the efficiency of production or the responsiveness of union leaders to the rank and file, but upon the basic economic conditions of the country and the overall prospects for the revolutionary program.

In 1920 War Communism had reached an impasse. The economy had broken down; society was in chaos; workers as well as peasants were beginning to turn against the Soviet regime. People high in the party were starting to view War Communism in a more realistic light—as a pattern of harsh but presumably necessary expedients required for the survival of the revolutionary government rather than as a shortcut to the socialist Elysium. The trade unions quickly felt the chill wind of the postrevolutionary dawn.

Trotsky was the man who put the trade unions in the main arena of Communist political discussion. With the critical military danger gone, he turned his energies and his new-grown habits of command to the field of economic reconstruction, where he proposed to overcome the obstacles to Communist success by the tried-and-tested military methods of central command and discipline. Trotsky's proposals were hardly well received, and the debate which he precipitated spread in broadening circles until the entire party was wracked with factional dissension about basic principles of social organization.

By 1920 conventional labor discipline and incentives to promote productivity were more or less accepted by the party leadership, though not without grumbling among many workers' spokesmen. Trotsky's innovation, early in 1920, was to use military units and military discipline for tasks of civilian labor. Now that the worst of the Civil War was over, Trotsky was especially hopeful of employing the organizational resources of the Red Army, so painfully built up, for peaceful purposes. He warmly endorsed the employment of troops as labor armies, in preference to seeing them demobilized in a chaotic economy.[9] In a longer perspective, Trotsky began to view the militarization of labor as an effective system for mobilizing the masses to solve the country's critical economic problems: "If we seriously speak of planned economy, which is to acquire its unity of purpose from the center, when labor forces are assigned in accordance with the economic plan at the given stage of development, the working masses cannot be wandering all over Russia. They must be thrown here and there, appointed, commanded, just like soldiers. . . . Without this, under conditions of ruin and hunger, we cannot speak seriously of any industry on new foundations."[10]

Militarization had major implications for the trade unions: "The young socialist state requires trade unions, not for a struggle for better conditions of labor . . . but to organize the working class for the ends of production, to educate, discipline . . . to exercise their authority hand in hand with the state in order to lead the workers into the framework of a single economic plan."[11] The unions, in short, were to be fused with the government, deprived of their undisciplined autonomy, and converted into instruments of economic militarization.

Trotsky conceded that the system of administration of labor which he envisioned, with its complicated system of government, trade-union, and army controls, its high degree of bureaucratization, inevitably entailed "measures of compulsion" when applied to the population as a whole. These he justified not simply as temporary expedients for meeting the economic crisis, but as the only way to build socialism in a land of backward peasants and indifferent workers.[12] "The foundations of militarization," he frankly asserted, "are those forms of state compulsion without which the replacement of capitalist economy by the socialist will forever remain an empty sound."[13] The logical extension of the case for centralization pointed to the goal of complete economic planning. Trotsky, who was the most ardent of all centralizers to appear during the first decade of the Soviet regime, complained to the Ninth Congress: "As yet we still do not have a single economic plan which will replace the spontaneous work of the laws of competition. From this stem the difficulties of the Supreme Economic Council."[14]

Trotsky's advocacy of planning was glibly endorsed by the Ninth Congress, although under the circumstances little specific content could be suggested save the enumeration of critical economic problems which were already obvious.[15] Such resistance as there was to the idea of an overall plan seems to have been the product of political differences in the leadership. The Supreme Economic Council was headed by Rykov, always a cautious man. He naturally felt threatened by Trotsky, whose planning idea he protested as an impractical abstraction.[16] Rykov lost; Trotsky's Council of Workers' and Peasants' Defense, renamed the Council of Labor and Defense, was decreed to be the top economic authority, and Rykov, mistakenly supporting the collegial principle, was soon relieved from the Supreme Economic Council and the industrial responsibilities which it still held.[17] Trotsky had made another enemy. Trotsky had no tolerance for Communists whose scruples or fears led them to oppose the drastic measures which he recommended. He said of militarization: "This term at once brings us into the region of the greatest possible superstitions and outcries from the opposition."[18] The opposition, Trotsky maintained, was largely motivated by bourgeois and trade-unionist prejudices on the part of people who were unable to understand the nature and tasks of a socialist society. He called his opponents Mensheviks, and it is clear that he was quite as ready to use compulsion against them as against the reluctant peasantry. If the laboring majority was unable to understand how its real interests must be pursued, that was unfortunate, but it remained no less necessary for the Communist leader, visualizing himself someday before the bar of history, to forge ahead in the direction he believed correct. Socialism, in a backward country unsupported by revolution in the more advanced parts of the globe, had to receive its initial impetus by being forced on the people against their short-term wishes.

In his economic thinking, Trotsky was the earliest Stalinist. His program for the trade unions, stressing their responsibility for productivity and labor discipline, gave a foretaste of Stalin's *Gleichschaltung* of the unions after 1929. More broadly, Trotsky's apology for authority and compulsion in economic life foreshadowed the totalitarian economics of the five-year plans. There were differences, to be sure, and two more dissimilar personalities than Trotsky and Stalin can hardly be imagined. Real conviction underlay Trotsky's rigor: "Our revolution," he wrote in 1919, "will fully justify itself only when every toiling man, every toiling woman feels that life on this earth is easier, freer, cleaner, and more dignified for him. . . . A difficult road still separates us from the achievement of this, our basic and exclusive goal."[19] The kinship between Trotsky's ideas and Stalin's reality can be traced to the circumstances with which both had to deal in attempting to build an industrial power out of the political and economic materials at hand in Russia. From these deep roots grew the social system which the world has come to identify with the term "Communism"—industrial society organized on military lines.

Trotsky's militarization proposal stirred up a veritable hornets' nest of criticism. Much of the protest came from the Ultra-Left, prompted by ideological antipathy to the authoritarianism and centralization which Trotsky advocated. Vladimir Smirnov warned against an excessively authoritarian approach to the more conscious strata of society: "We cannot speak of the militarization of the whole economy. If it were carried out in all branches of industry, it would radically alter the whole physiognomy of our party, smashing that continuous interaction which now exists (although to an insufficient degree) between the upper and lower ranks. In this case the party would resemble a man trying to lift himself up by his hair."[20] To avoid the evils of excessive bureaucracy, discipline and authority should be enforced by existing organs such as the trade unions. Extraordinary controls would destroy the democratic power of the rank and file to influence the leadership, and the party leadership would become responsible only to itself. Smirnov's foresight was exceptional.

Other complaints about militarization came from the right wing of the party, from the cautious Leninists in the economic administration—Rykov, Miliutin, and Nogin.[21] Lenin at first backed Trotsky, for both men were ready to use maximum compulsion and violence to bolster the revolutionary state and make the Russian economy work, and both hoped to use the trade unions to discipline and control the working force.[22] Disagreement over the trade unions between Trotsky's followers and the Leninists began over a fine point of theory. At the Ninth Congress, Bukharin used the term "governmentalizing" to describe the incorporation of the unions into the industrial administration. Molotov objected, preferring to look at this as the use of the unions under the leadership of the party for the purposes of the state. Trade-union autonomy would not fare well in either case, but Molotov claimed to have grounds for criticising Bukharin: "We must not work in a bureaucratic but in a democratic way, the way of organizing the working masses themselves. I think that this is the main objection to the formal governmentalizing of the trade unions; it is necessary to raise the initiative of the working masses through the trade unions, with the aim of raising the productivity of labor."[23] This was the "transmission belt" theory which Lenin soon espoused: the Communist-controlled unions would undertake the political indoctrination of the masses and stimulate them to maximum performance in the building of socialism.

Such a role for the unions conformed neatly with the principle of individual management. Lenin had the Ninth Congress resolve: "The unions must take upon themselves the task of explaining to the broad circles of the working class all the necessities of reconstructing the apparatus of industrial administration in the direction of the greatest elasticity and business ability, which can be achieved only by a transition to the maximum curtailment of administrative collegia and the gradual introduction of individual management in units directly engaged in production."[24] In the pursuit of this objective it was more expedient to keep the unions formally separate from the state and give them the appearance of autonomy, while party control assured their subordination to the top leadership.

Between the spring and the fall of 1920, Trotsky had an opportunity to put his militarization scheme into practice. When disruption in the transportation system, always the Achilles' heel of the Russian economy, became unbearably acute, Trotsky was summoned to rectify the situation and was entrusted with the Commissariat of Transport (in addition to his defense post). The railroad workers had already been put under military discipline, and Trotsky's first act in his new post was to reorganize all political activity on military lines. He established the Chief Political Administration for the Lines of Communication (*Glavpolitput*), an organization of the "political department" type, where the party members were organized in a military structure that could serve as an auxiliary chain of command.[25] With characteristic energy and tactlessness, Trotsky got the wheels turning again, at the cost of much personal friction, especially between his political administrators and the transport union leaders.

Tension in the transport field came to a head in August 1920, when Soviet forces battling in Poland were trying to keep their defeat from turning into a rout. To silence his critics, Trotsky obtained the endorsement of the rest of the party leadership and summarily ousted the heads of the railroad union. In their stead he contrived an institution cast on the lines of his "governmentalizing" idea, the Central Committee for Transport (known by its Russian abbreviation, *Tsektran*). The Tsektran was a fusion of the commissariat, unions, and political apparatus, covering the entire rail and water transport system. With Trotsky himself at its head, it functioned strictly on military and bureaucratic lines. The ideal of one efficient hierarchy was, for this sphere at least, a reality.[26]

At this stage in the evolution of Soviet Communism, such a regime could not escape bitter criticism for its excesses of bureaucratic centralism. The criticism was inspired in large measure by principle, especially on the far left and to a certain extent among the cautious Leninists on the right.

Another factor was personal resentment. The unpopularity of Trotsky's militarization idea and his Tsektran scheme offered a welcome opportunity for political hay-making, and Zinoviev, in particular, snatched it up.[27]

UNION AUTONOMY AND THE WORKERS' OPPOSITION

The sharpest reaction to Trotsky's militarization scheme came from the Ultra-Left. Not only were these people the most doctrinaire defenders of trade-union power and autonomy; they had also dominated the Central Trade Union Council up to this time and thus were the direct beneficiaries of the doctrine of autonomous trade-union responsibility. Throughout 1920 the left-wing union leaders contended with the forces which would subject them to tighter party or governmental authority. Finally the issue reached a point of such intensity that the trade-union extremists formed an avowedly factional organization to fight for trade-union independence in the management of the economy—the self-styled "Workers' Opposition."

At the Ninth Party Congress in March 1920, the trade-unionists made a concerted effort to establish and defend their claim to independent power on the basis of the party program. Tomsky wrote in a precongress statement, "The trade unions are the most competent and interested organizations in the matter of restoring the country's production and its correct functioning."[28] This much was compatible with Trotsky's plans for the unions; the issue between the unionists, on the one hand, and Trotsky (or Bukharin), on the other, turned on whether the unions governed the economy independently or under the orders of the heads of the government. The unions, Bukharin asserted, "must become the foundation and base for the construction of the communist order. Therefore any attempt . . . at reducing the trade unions must meet the firmest resistance. . . ." But, flinging metaphors in all directions, he appended a strict qualification to this strong statement: "The unions participate . . . not as independent apparatuses on the shoulders of which this or that function rests completely, but as an apparatus which ties its organs into the general soviet organs."[29]

Such subordination of the unions to the government was entirely antithetical to the trade-unionists' hopes. Shliapnikov called explicitly for a three-way "separation of powers" between the party, the soviets, and the trade unions, which would separately assume responsibility in their respective fields.[30] Osinsky, speaking for the Democratic Centralists, endorsed Shliapnikov's idea as he observed a "clash of several cultures" among the "military-soviet culture," the "civil-soviet culture," and the trade-union movement, which had "created its own sphere of culture." He held that it was improper to impose the authority of one type of organization on the others or to attempt to apply to all of the "culture's" methods (militarization, for instance) which were appropriate to only one of them.[31] The metalworkers' leader,

Y. Lutovinov, asserted bluntly, "In our opinion, the responsible head of each branch of industry can only be the production union, and of all branches of industry as a whole, the ARCCTU—it cannot be otherwise!"[32]

In reply Lenin and his backers had nothing but invective. Said Lenin, "The Russian Communist Party can in no case agree that political leadership alone should belong to the party, and economic leadership to the trade unions. This is drawn from the views of the bankrupt Second International."[33] In part, the party leaders' opposition to trade-union administrative responsibility was due to the fear of an upsurge of Menshevik and SR influence if the unions should acquire a position of real independence.[34] Krestinsky denounced the unionists' program as "syndicalist contraband" and described the "decisive struggle" which his Secretariat had been conducting against "guild and trade-unionist tendencies."[35] The established principles of party authority could in no way accommodate the idea of independent union power. Meanwhile this had been underscored in a dispute regarding party control in the unions.

The most serious challenge of the trade-unionists to the authority of the party leadership came not in the theoretical debates in the party press and at the congresses, but in their effort to establish an independent center of control over the Communist Party organizations in the trade unions. Friction had developed between the party and trade-union authorities over assignments of Communist Party members in trade-union work, and the Communist Party group in the ARCCTU—dominated by Leftists—was claiming direct authority over the party members in the various industrial unions. Shortly before the Ninth Congress, the party fraction in the ARCCTU passed a resolution which would confirm this claim by making all party fractions in the unions directly subordinate to the party fraction in the ARCCTU, rather than to the geographical organizations of the party.[36] This literally would have created a party within the party, a semiautonomous body embracing a substantial proportion of the party's membership, if not a majority. It would have control over the party's main source of contact with the nonparty workers who supplied most of the Soviet government's popular support. The mere existence of such an inner subparty would be contrary to centralist principles, to say nothing of the prospect of its domination by Leftist opponents of Lenin's leadership. Even the Democratic Centralists took the trade-unionists' plan to be a violation of basic party principles; their resolution which the Moscow organization passed declared that "party discipline in every case takes precedence over trade-union discipline."[37] It was inevitable that the unionists' demands for autonomy within the party would be rejected, and when the resolution was submitted to the Orgburo of the party for confirmation, this was precisely what happened.

The trade-unionists were nonetheless undaunted. In the Ukraine, where the left-wing Communists were returning to power for the last time, the southern bureau of the ARCCTU passed a resolution on autonomy for the trade-union men in the party similar to that drawn up by its parent organization. The proposal won a majority at the Fourth Ukrainian Party Conference and was referred to the Ninth Party Congress in Moscow. In the meantime, the ARCCTU appealed over the Orgburo to the Politburo, where Tomsky and Lutovinov presented the unionists' case. The reception was unprecedently hostile—Krestinsky, the party secretary, actually accused them of counter-revolutionary tendencies, and Kamenev seconded the charge. Lenin and Trotsky opposed the unionists with more moderation but no less firmly, and the autonomy plan was again rejected.[38]

The centralist position of the party leadership was definitively endorsed by the Ninth Congress: "Each party fraction [of a trade union] is a part of a local [party] organization, subordinate to the party committee, and the [Communist] fraction of the ARCCTU is subordinated to the Central Committee of the Russian Communist Party."[39] Bukharin and Radek were installed in the ARCCTU to represent the leadership and apply a restraining influence.[40] Only through a direct appeal to the party membership, in open opposition to the leadership, could the trade-unionists win their case. Organized as the Workers' Opposition, they proceeded to attempt this.

For all the political storm which broke over it, the Workers' Opposition remains a scantily documented affair. The extent of its real support among the rank-and-file factory workers is very difficult to ascertain, but it undeniably drew enough strength within the party to cause the leadership serious alarm. The group embraced a considerable number of genuinely proletarian Communist leaders, mostly in the trade unions: Shliapnikov, the first Commissar of Labor, and Lutovinov and S. Medvedev, the leaders of the metalworkers, were the most prominent. The only important exception to the rule of worker-Bolshevik undergrounders was Alexandra Kollontai, aristocratic intellectual and former Menshevik émigré, mistress of Shliapnikov (among others, as she practiced the free love which she preached).

Geographically the Workers' Opposition was concentrated in the southeastern parts of European Russia—the Donets Basin, the Don and Kuban regions, and the Samara province on the Volga.[41] In Samara the Workers' Opposition was actually in control of the party organization in 1921, and before the party shakeup in the Ukraine in 1920 the oppositionists had won a sympathetic majority in the republic as a whole. Other points of strength were in the Moscow province, where the Workers' Opposition polled about a quarter of the party votes, and in the metalworkers' union throughout the country. The association between the metalworkers' union and the Workers' Opposition was so close that Tomsky (who deserted the trade-unionists and joined Lenin's camp when the controversy grew bitter early in 1921) explained the opposition by the faults of the union—the "metalworkers' ideology . . . of industrialism and syndicalism."[42] It was particularly revealing of the course the revolution had taken that the party leadership could assume this attitude toward the workers of the industry which up to 1917 had outshone all other industries combined in revolutionary militancy.[43]

The program which the Workers' Opposition put forth late in 1920 and early in 1921 was only an extension and elaboration of the ideas for which they had tried to win party approval the year before. By rights, they asserted in their theses prepared for the Tenth Party Congress, "The organization of the administration of the economy belongs to the All-Russian Congress of Producers, united in trade production unions, who elect the central organs which administer the whole economy of the Republic."[44] The main work of explaining the ideology and spirit of the Workers' Opposition fell to Kollontai. This she undertook in a pamphlet, "The Workers' Opposition," written just before the Tenth Party Congress as a defense of the Opposition position. Her thinking could well represent man's highest ascent toward faith in the proletariat.

Kollontai began with the familiar criticisms advanced by Left oppositionists during the previous two and a half years concerning bureaucratism, inequality, and neglect of the interests of the proletariat: "The higher we go up the ladder of the soviet and party hierarchy, the fewer adherents of the Opposition we find. The deeper we penetrate into the masses the more response do we find to the program of the Workers' Opposition. . . . If the masses go away from the 'upper' elements; if there appears a break, a crack, between the directing centers and the 'lower' elements, that means that there is something wrong with the 'upper' elements."[45]

With respect to industrial administration, Kollontai upheld the creativity of the masses against bureaucrats of every description: "Who, after all, shall be called upon to create new forms of economy; shall it be the technicians, businessmen who by their psychology are bound up with the past, and soviet officials with Communists scattered among them, *or the working class collectives which are represented by the unions?*" Kollontai placed her faith in the spontaneous virtue of the proletariat:

The task of the party in its present crisis is to face its mistakes fearlessly and lend its ear to the healthy class call of the broad working masses. Through the creative powers of the rising class in the form of industrial unions we shall go toward the reconstruction and development of the creative forces of the country; toward purification of the party itself from the elements foreign to it; toward correction of the activity of the party by means of going back to democracy, freedom of opinion, and criticism inside the party.[46]

But Lenin had written in 1902, "There can be no talk of an ideology being developed by the working masses on their own."[47] Kollontai's stand was in direct violation of the most fundamental organizational principle of Leninism—the role of the party apparatus as the exclusive leader of all revolutionary forces. A comparison with Rosa Luxemburg readily shows Kollontai's ideological affinities: "The proletariat . . . should . . . exercise a dictatorship . . . of the *class,* not of a party or of a clique . . . that means . . . the most active, unlimited participation of the mass of the people, of unlimited democracy."[48] Kollontai was close to the truth that Lenin's organizational and economic policies were subverting the original goals of the revolution. Pointing to the influence of peasants and former members of the bourgeoisie in the government and economy, she warned, "These are the elements that bring decay into our soviet institutions, breeding there an atmosphere altogether repugnant to the working class."[49]

Not without reason, the Workers' Oppositionists were convinced that the proletarian spirit of the revolution was in danger of being submerged. Medvedev charged the Central Committee with "deviations in the direction of distrust of the creative powers of the working class and concessions to the petty-bourgeoisie and to the bourgeois-official castes."[50] To offset this tendency and preserve the proletarian spirit in the party, the Workers' Opposition proposed at the Tenth Party Congress that every party member be required to live and work for three months out of every year as an ordinary proletarian or peasant, engaged in physical labor.[51]

Basically the Workers' Opposition was inspired by faith; it was sincere in its proletarian idealism and sure that its cause must prevail. Its resounding hopes were illustrated in Kollontai's concluding appeal: "All that part of the party which has been accustomed to reflect the class point of view of the overgrowing giant, the proletariat, will absorb and digest everything that is wholesome, practical, and sound in the Workers' Opposition. Not in vain will the rank-and-file worker speak with assurance and reconciliation: 'Ilich will ponder, think, listen to us, and then will decide to turn the party rudder toward the Opposition. Ilich will be with us yet.' "[52] No follower of Lenin could resist his personal magnetism.

THE TRADE-UNION DEBATE

The fall of 1920 saw the high point of open discussion in the Communist Party and of free opposition to the leaders' authority. The general ferment over the bureaucratization and militarization of the party was compounded by the specific controversy over the role and autonomy of the trade unions, and intensified by deep anxieties over the future of the revolution. That Lenin could escape with his prestige intact may have been due in large measure to Trotsky, who boldly set himself up as a target for the fire of the antibureaucratic forces.

During the fall of 1920 opposition grew in every quarter against Trotsky's administrative strait-jacketing of the trade unions. When the Fifth Trade Union Conference convened early in November, controversy over the trade-union question and the Tsektran issue broke out with renewed vigor. Trotsky greeted the conference with a demand for the total merger of the trade unions and the government industrial administration, and then drew up a statement of the ideal: "The administrative-economic apparatus is nothing but the production organ of the union, i.e., its most important organ." Only such a step, Trotsky argued, would eliminate the parallelism of unions and administrative organs which was responsible for the prevailing confusion. With such a reorganization, the designation and even the very concept of the unions had to be changed—from "trade" (*professionalny*) unions to "production" (*proizvodstvenny*) unions. The pill was to be sweetened with "workers' democracy"—"The systematic consideration in broad mass assemblies of all economic-production measures, election of officials in the whole series of significant economic-administrative posts. . . ." Any objection that this contradicted his militarization plan Trotsky dismissed as "the manifestation of Kautskian-Menshevik-SR prejudices."[53]

A counterproposal, as yet vague, was drawn up by the rising Latvian trade-unionist, Y. E. Rudzutak, who was secretary of the Central Trade Union Council, a member of the presidium of the Tsektran and a Central Committee member since the previous spring.[54] While Rudzutak shared the assumption that the unions would retain an active role in industrial administration,[55] his move was apparently backed by Lenin and the anti-Trotsky members of the Central Committee as they felt their way toward a more definite stand.

The Central Committee met on November 8 and 9, 1920, to iron out its differences and lay down a definite line for the trade-union conference which was still in session. Tomsky, the only member of the Central Committee who had opposed Trotsky's formation of the Tsektran in August, reiterated the trade-unionists' antipathy to that organization.[56] Lenin now turned openly against Trotsky, and the committee voted disapproval of the latter's theses, by the narrow margin of eight to seven. Then, by a vote of ten to four (Trotsky, Krestinsky, Andreyev, and Rykov, with Preobrazhensky abstaining), the committee endorsed the Leninist draft for a resolution to be supplied to the party members in the trade-union conference.[57] This document called for reform in the Tsektran, stressed the bureaucratic dangers inherent in militarization and centralization, and urged the unions to "broaden more and more their role in production."[58] The issue was still cloudy; the major concern of the Leninists seems to have been to delay a decision and silence Trotsky.

This desire was in part responsible for a curious political grouping which took shape at this juncture, the so-called "buffer," an alignment of Central Committee members from both the Leninist and moderate Left tendencies who were either confused about the basic issue or anxious to hush up the controversy. Of Lenin's supporters, it was the cautious individuals of the former right-wing opposition who joined the "buffer"—Zinoviev, Kamenev, and Rykov, together with Sergeyev. The Left was represented by Bukharin, Radek, Dzerzhinsky, and two of the secretaries, Krestinsky and Serebriakov. Tomsky was also a member of the group.[59] The remainder of the nineteenman Central Committee was divided between the Trotskyists—Trotsky, Rakovsky, Ivan Smirnov, Andreyev, and Preobrazhensky—and the out-and-out Leninists, who at first included, besides Lenin himself, only Kalinin, Rudzutak, and Stalin. The underlying split was deep and nearly even.

Prompted by Zinoviev, the buffer group decided on measures to quiet the controversy and postpone a decision. All the members of the Central Committee, including Trotsky, were cautioned not to air their disagreements in public, and a subcommittee, chaired by Zinoviev, was set up to study the whole problem of the trade unions and industrial administration. The subcommittee was at first stacked in favor of the Leninists: Zinoviev, Rudzutak, Rykov, Tomsky, against Trotsky alone.[60] Trotsky promptly announced his intention of boycotting the subcommittee.[61] The subcommittee was broadened with the addition of Lozovsky (now a Leninist), Andreyev (a Trotskyist) and the Workers' Opposition leaders, Shliapnikov and Lutovinov; but the latter two also refused to work with it.[62]

In December the debate welled up more insistently. Trotsky was at loggerheads with the trade-unionist members of the Tsektran, and Zinoviev's subcommittee was ready with a report aimed against Trotsky. The report bluntly proposed that the Central Committee liquidate Trotsky's Tsektran and restore the usual party and trade-union forms of organization in the transport field.[63] Trotsky stood his ground and defended frankly the bureaucratic methods which his party rivals preferred to cloak in democratic phraseology: "Conditions are not always such that there can be recourse to discussion. . . . The question of workers' democracy we have raised before and are raising now: to widen the frame of criticism, discussion, internal polemics, etc. All this, of course, is necessary, but it also depends on general conditions. . . . Militarization of the trade unions and militarization of transport, *which is moreover an internal, ideological militarization,* is dictated by a situation of anxiety, of natural and salutary anxiety about the ruin of the country."[64]

Trotsky's conduct in the Tsektran matter stood out in Lenin's mind (as his "Testament" reveals) as the most striking manifestation of Trotsky's willfulness. Lenin and his supporters, including Stalin and Tomsky, threw their weight behind Zinoviev, but, just as in the Brest-Litovsk controversy, they could not prevail immediately. The Central Committee turned back Zinoviev's proposal by a vote of eight to seven, and the "buffer," now reduced to a group of the moderate Leftists around Bukharin, pushed a conciliatory resolution through.[65] This statement mildly rebuked Trotsky by opposing the reorganization of the unions "from above," but stressed the importance of drawing the masses, through the unions, into the work of administration and the realization of "workers' democracy *in production*." The Tsektran issue itself was simply put off with a provision for new elections in that body and a general appeal for "democratism."

Now, however, it became impossible to prevent public debate on the trade unions, and the Central Committee proclaimed an open discussion of the question. The Eighth Congress of Soviets, held late in December, became the principal forum for airing the clash of views. The grand opening of the debate came on December 30, 1920, at a meeting of the Communist fraction of the soviet congress held in Moscow's Bolshoi Theater. All of the protagonists were on hand to state their respective cases—Lenin and Zinoviev for the Right, Trotsky and Bukharin for the moderate Left, and Shliapnikov for the Ultra-Left Workers' Opposition.[66]

Lenin, while ostensibly concentrating on a criticism of Trotsky, revealed a significant shift in his own position by selectively emphasizing certain points which had appeared in the Central Committee theses presented by Rudzutak. Under the guise of defending orthodoxy, Lenin advanced a trade-union program as different from the accepted one as Trotsky's was, though in the opposite direction. The unions, according to Lenin, were not to be organs of compulsion but of education, the link between the party and the mass of the workers. He ignored altogether the question of making the unions into responsible administrative organs, and he scorned the "production democracy" which was Bukharin's current theme.[67] The most important implication for Communist theory lay in Lenin's objection to one of the "fundamental" errors of Trotsky—the notion that the trade unions did not need to defend the workers because the state was their employer and it was a "workers' state." The validity of this assumption was challenged: "Our present state is such that the entire organized proletariat must defend itself; we must use these workers' organizations for the defense of the workers from their state and for the defense by the workers' of our state."[68]

Lenin's new position was concretized in the "Platform of the Ten," of January 14, 1921, signed by Lenin, Zinoviev, Kamenev, Stalin, Tomsky, Kalinin, Rudzutak, Lozovsky, Petrovsky, and Artem-Sergeyev.[69] This document repeated Lenin's stress on the educational role of the unions, as a "school of communism" and a "support of the proletarian dictatorship." It warned that governmentalization threatened this function by cutting the union leadership off from the masses. The familiar though somewhat specious stress on methods of persuasion in preference to compulsion was echoed, together with the magic words "workers' democracy." The industrial functions of the unions were outlined in some detail: cooperation in economic planning and administration; control and inspection of production (whatever these might mean); wage determination and the defense of the workers against the employer-state. More concrete tasks were "production propaganda" and its complement, the maintenance of labor discipline. There could be no question that the unions would function precisely as the leaders desired: "The Russian Communist Party, in the person of its central and local organizations, unconditionally guides as before the whole ideological side of the work of the trade unions."

In the meantime, the Workers' Opposition was moving toward the opposite extreme. Shliapnikov spoke in the debate of December 30, 1920, to develop his theme of autonomous control over industry by the trade unions. All administrative organs would be elected by, and responsible to, the organized workers. This meant the reorganization of the unions along lines similar to those envisaged by Trotsky, into "production trade unions," and the administration of the whole economy would be concentrated in their hands. To effect this he proposed an All-Russian Congress of Producers. "In this way," Shliapnikov asserted hopefully, "there is created the unity of will which is essential in the organization of the economy, and also a real possibility for the influence of the initiative of the broad working masses on the organization and development of our economy."[70]

Shliapnikov's speech was followed up by the theses on the trade-union question which the Workers' Opposition published in *Pravda* on January 25, 1921.[71] The argument therein was buttressed by pointed references to the old syndicalist phrases of earlier party documents, especially the program of 1919 and the resolutions of the earlier trade-union congresses. At the same time, Kollontai published "The Workers' Opposition," which on a more theoretical plane continued the Ultra-Left attack on the party leadership.

The heat of the controversy increased in proportion to the divergence between the factions, which continued to grow right up to the Tenth Party Congress in March 1921. The buffer group finally disappeared, when its left-wing adherents merged with the Trotskyists to draw up a common platform. This event marked the complete and clear segregation of the Leninist and moderate Leftist views into two sharply opposed camps; the merger effected at the beginning of the period of War Communism was completely undone.

Bukharin had already idealized the "governmentalizing" of the unions as "the state form of workers' socialism": "The 'governmentalizing' of the trade unions and the virtual governmentalizing of all mass organizations of the proletariat result from the inner logic of the transformation process itself."[72] The platform of the Bukharin group drawn up in January 1921 (before the merger with the Trotskyists) linked this theory of a new path for the unions with the ultimate goals of the revolution itself:

If the general progressive line of development is the line of organic union of the trade unions with the organs of state power, i.e., the governmentalizing of the trade unions, then on the other hand that same process is a process of "unionizing" the state. Its logical and historical termination will not be the engulfment

of the unions by the proletarian state, but the disappearance of both categories—
of the unions as well as of the state, and the creation of a third—the communisti-
cally organized society.[73]

The program presented soon afterwards by the Trotsky group expressed
the moderate Leftist ideal somewhat less metaphysically, but it affirmed even
more clearly the ideal of proletarian democracy which was supposed to
come from the rigorous short-term policy which the group espoused:

Developing this system on all sides, linking more and more closely the responsible
role in the union with the responsible role in production, we will arrive sooner
or later at the position in which the union, encompassing a given branch of production as a whole and on all sides, will, by means of a combination of the
methods of election and selection, form out of itself the whole administrative-
economic apparatus, under the general control and direction of the workers' state,
in conformance with the work of all branches of the economy.[74]

Lenin's response to the trade-union programs of the moderate Left was to
sweep them unequivocally into the category of intolerable deviation, already
occupied by the Workers' Opposition. He seized upon the Bukharin platform as "a full break with Communism and a transition to a position of
syndicalism." "So we have 'grown up,'" he observed of the controversy as
a whole, "from small differences to syndicalism, signifying a complete break
with Communism and an unavoidable split of the party."[75] Such language
had not appeared in the party press since the days of Brest-Litovsk.

The trade-union controversy marked a further stage of Soviet political
development in relation to Communist theory. The transition in 1918 from
"one foot in socialism" to complete nationalization and all the rigors of War
Communism had borne out the prognosis of permanent revolution that a
"proletarian" government once in power in Russia would have no choice
but to proceed with a fully socialist policy, despite the country's unreadiness
for it. The ultimate survival of socialism in Russia, according to the theory,
depended on the other aspect of the revolution's permanency, the international socialist revolution. When this failed to materialize, the socialist regime
in Russia was left hanging in mid-air, as it were. In the stress and flux of the
revolutionary years the pendulum of social change had swung far ahead
of the equilibrium point set by existing cultural and economic conditions.
This was the state of affairs which confronted the Communist Party at the
time of the trade-union controversy—impossible to continue but difficult to
withdraw from without political disaster. Such were the circumstances which
made the trade-union debate so intense. For all factions, the trade-union
issue rested on the estimate of the degree of socialism which the Russian
Revolution had attained or could soon reach.

The Workers' Opposition, fired by utopian optimism, were determined to continue the advance. Their program of unfettered workers' democracy and control of the economy by an "association of producers" would mean an attempt at immediate introduction of the forms of social organization which in 1917 the revolutionaries had generally agreed upon as the ultimate institutions of the communist society.

The Trotskyists, taking a much more realistic view of the path toward this goal, stressed the need for authority and discipline to meet the difficult economic problems of the immediate transition period. This meant holding the line where War Communism had drawn it. At the same time the moderate Leftists were working for an institutional structure—the combined government-union administrative edifice—which could (they hoped) be transformed when conditions permitted into the communist ideal of autonomous, democratic, federated collectives.

The Leninists, disabusing themselves of such high expectations for a long time to come, had determined on a strategic retreat. They would concentrate on holding the political strong points of party and government, and carry out a gradual revolution from above through hierarchical controls over a population which had revealed itself to be too backward to share directly in collective administration. The function of the unions, in this context, was to shield the masses against the possible abuses of "state capitalism" and to provide the party with a political link to its presumed clientele in the proletariat.

A decisive psychological difference among the three positions was their sense of the extent to which the masses could help carry out the program of the revolution. Unconditional idealism, producing an optimism difficult to ground in reality, was the spirit of the Workers' Opposition; theirs was the apocalyptic vision of a world remade by the spontaneity of the masses. The Leninists, stressing power, the guidance of the revolution by a close-knit organization of professional revolutionaries, and the necessity of educating and prodding the masses into socialism, reaffirmed the close association of prerevolutionary Leninism with the experience of the Russian past. To this they added a compelling sense of the practical, the necessary, the expedient; the Leninists were the least doctrinaire of all the various strands of Bolshevik thought and yet they were the most dogmatic. They displayed the greatest flexibility in adapting the doctrines of Marxism to the necessities of the situation, but at the same time were adamant in asserting that theirs was the only true interpretation of the Scripture.

A middle stand was taken by the moderate Leftists, Trotsky's adherents; they thought they saw both the possibility of quickly arriving at a socialist society and the necessity of an intense national effort organized on military lines to attain this end. They shared the hopes of the Ultra-Left and at the same time admitted the difficulties and embraced the bureaucratic expedients which the Leninists were so wont to stress.[76]

The dilemma faced by the Communists in 1921 was not entirely unantici-pated by the doctrinal forebears of the Russian Revolution. Engels touched upon it in his history of the German Peasant War of the sixteenth century, though evidently none of his and Marx's disciples paid any attention to this particular possibility:

The worst thing that can befall a leader of an extreme party is to be compelled to take over a government in an epoch when the movement is not yet ripe for the domination of the class which he represents and for the realization of the measures which that domination would imply. . . . He is compelled to represent not his party or his class, but the class for whom conditions are ripe for domination. *In the interest of the movement itself,* he is compelled to defend the interests of an alien class, and to feed his own class with phrases and promises, with the assertion that the interests of that alien class are their own interests.[77]

As a capsule analysis of Soviet Russia, this would be hard to improve upon. What is the alien class whose interests are defended? This is a complex ques-tion, but perhaps the most apt answer is that suggested in many Communist writings of the period—the "technical intelligentsia."[78]

A revolutionary dictatorship identified with the workers but accommo-dating itself to the social paramountcy of the experts, the administrators, and the policemen—such was the sociological basis of the crisis which shook the Communist Party late in 1920 and early in 1921. As the price of survival, the Soviet regime was accepting a managerial social order. Rank-and-file Com-munists were turning against the party leadership because of this, and the Ultra-Left Opposition posed a major challenge. The party leadership (with the Trotskyists joining the Leninists against this threat) had to steer between the Scylla of disillusioned leftism and the Charybdis of anti-Communist rebellion. They insisted that they alone were pursuing the true socialist course—hence their "phrases and promises." Nothing could be more threat-ening than an opposition movement which claimed to be defending the workers and which attacked the government for abandoning the original goals of the revolution. It was vital to the survival of the Soviet regime that the Ultra-Left be silenced and that the fiction of working-class rule be main-tained. To this end Lenin and the party leadership, including the moderate Leftists, bent every effort. In the early months of 1921 they scored a complete success.

6

THE CRISIS OF 1921

The great revolutions—the English, French, and Russian above all—were social convulsions which progressed according to laws of their own. The wills of individual revolutionaries, determined though they might be, could but little govern the torrent of events. When in the early days of their power in Russia the Bolsheviks thought to moderate their measures, they were unable to do so; the tide of revolutionary emotion and social conflict swept them into a mood of extremism. It was equally inevitable, after not so many months had passed, that the exhausted nation should turn against the extremes of revolution and seek to return to normal ways of life.

Early in 1921 the Soviet regime faced its most severe test. Its revolutionary experiments had overreached, and it was simply failing to fulfill the minimum requirements of organized economic life. Popular opposition had culminated in open peasant revolts. The Communist leadership was also in difficulty with respect to its own supporters because it had fallen short of the revolutionary expectation of an equalitarian working-class democracy. The consequence of this was an upsurge in opposition from the Ultra-Left and also from non-Communist socialist groups. Sympathy for the Soviet regime among the rank-and-file workers was gravely threatened.

To keep in power, Lenin had to steer gingerly between the forces of opposition on the left and on the right. The difficulty of this task was underscored by the Kronstadt revolt, in which factors of both proletarian and peasant unrest combined in an open challenge of Communist rule. Both repression and compromise were the response—compromise with the non-proletarian elements whose interests had suffered most under War Communism, but a campaign of extirpation against the critics on the Left, the revolution's most devoted partisans.

The problem of disposing of criticism from the Left was at the root of the crisis within the Communist Party in early 1921. To maneuver as political reality dictated, and yet justify itself as the embodiment of the revolution and keep the allegiance of its doctrinally inspired followers, the party leadership had to destroy the Ultra-Left wing among the Communists and establish guarantees against its recrudescence. Such was the situation which more and more gave shape to the party mentality: divergence of ideal and reality, anxiety to represent action as the correct application of doctrine, and the suppression of free criticism. 1921 was the point at which the Soviet regime began to devour its conscience.

THE REPULSE OF THE ULTRA-LEFT

The formal decisions taken at the Ninth Party Conference in September 1920 did not for long satisfy the Opposition, for it soon became evident that the party leadership intended to leave these broad paper concessions to party democracy unimplemented. Sapronov complained in November that bureaucratism in the party was still spreading: "The course adopted at the last conference must be carried out. Only its bold application will guarantee us from further growth of the 'disease.'"[1]

In the face of the Ultra-Left challenge, the moderate Left around Trotsky and Bukharin stood fast with Lenin on organizational questions, despite their disagreements on the trade-union issue. Bukharin, upbraiding the Moscow organization for its "demagogues" and "methods of struggle unworthy of Communists," invoked the central party authority to discipline and transfer: "The Moscow organization must be *made healthy*. . . . It is necessary to remove . . . the most factious element, to send in *new,* fresh forces . . . and to set up a firm, business-like Moscow committee, which would work and carry out the party line."[2] Now that the military threat to the Soviet regime had passed, the party leaders pointed to the critical economic situation as the justification for tightening the party organization. *Pravda* editorialized, "It is possible to survive this critical time, to reconstruct the apparatuses, etc., only *with the absolute solidarity of our party ranks.* . . . The possibility of internal weakening remains the chief danger, and the chief guarantee against it is *unity of will and action in the ranks of the party of the ruling proletariat.*"[3]

The election of delegates to a Moscow provincial party conference in November revealed a serious challenge to the leadership. Altogether, the Ultra-Left opposition groups—the Workers' Opposition, the Democratic Centralists, and the Ignatov group (a local Moscow faction closely allied to the Workers' Opposition and later to merge with them)—won one hundred twenty-four seats, as against only thirty more, one hundred fifty-four, for the supporters of the Central Committee.[4] Feeling ran so high that the Workers' Opposition and the Ignatov group organized a separate caucus to establish prior agreement in voting on resolutions and candidates for the provincial committee.[5] This action horrified the party leaders, and they repeatedly pointed to it as an example of the perilous violation of party unity which could occur if free opposition were allowed. Endeavoring to work out and justify a retreat from the revolutionary extremes of War Communism, the party leadership found doctrinaire criticism from the Ultra-Left intolerable.

The familiar issue of democracy versus centralized authority and bureaucracy remained the core of the Ultra-Left case. "One of the most immediate causes of the crisis is the uninterrupted, intensified course toward bureaucratic (vertical) centralization," declared the theses which the Democratic Centralists published in January 1921.[6] "Development of initiative and self-activity" among the rank and file was to be insured by "guaranteeing in fact to all tendencies within the party the right of free and complete expression in the press, at party assemblies, and in the responsible organs of the party and soviet apparatus." The same approach was taken by the Workers' Opposition. Declared one of their speakers at the Tenth Congress, "Bureaucratism is a serious question for our party; it is the source of the cleavage between the authority of the soviets and the soviet apparatus as a whole, and the broad working masses."[7] Another drew censure for insulting Lenin as "the greatest chinovnik."[8] The theses of the Ignatov group urged mass pressure by the rank and file to force the party bureaucracy to respect the forms of workers' democracy.[9]

The party leadership was well prepared to face a challenge on the bureaucracy-democracy issue because of the lack of specific proposals from the Opposition and because the issue had long been debated. Much more serious was the newer Ultra-Left theme that the "class content" of the Soviet regime was becoming unproletarian. According to the Ignatov theses, "The mass entry into the ranks of our party of people from bourgeois and petty-bourgeois strata . . . on the one hand, and the heavy losses in the Civil War suffered by the leading vanguard of the proletariat, on the other, have weakened the class unity of the party and in turn have introduced elements of disruption into the midst of our party." The Workers' Opposition stressed heavily the need for a purge to effect the wholesale removal of nonproletarian elements from the party. The Democratic Centralists and the Ignatov group proposed measures to guarantee high proletarian representation on party committees; the Ignatov theses called for a minimum of two thirds of each body to be composed of workers. Of like tenor was the demand of the Workers' Opposition for the requirement of regular periods of manual labor for all party members, to keep them in close contact with the conditions of life among the workers. All these proposals indicated that politically conscious workers felt more and more deserted by the party leadership. The resulting mood of opposition was a serious threat to the hegemony of the party; it culminated in the Kronstadt revolt.

The immediate threat of the Opposition was effectively checked in the course of discussions in the local party organizations leading up to the Tenth Party Congress. By straining every effort in appealing for unity in the party ranks against external dangers and internal difficulties, the Leninists were able to score a series of overwhelming victories at local party conferences. They were aided in their campaign by the use of direct organizational pressure exercised through the rapidly growing central machinery of the party. (Kollantai charged, for example, that the circulation of her pamphlet, "The Workers' Opposition," had been deliberately impeded.[10])

Moscow continued to be a center of Opposition strength. As the pre-congress discussion got under way in January, the Moscow Committee took a vote on the theses of the various factions, and the results give a clear pic-ture of the relative organizational strength of each position: Lenin, nineteen; Trotsky, seven; Bukharin, four; Sapronov (the Democratic Centralists), four; Ignatov, three. A concurrent vote by representatives of the local organ-izations under the jurisdiction of the Moscow Committee yielded roughly similar results: Lenin, fifty-seven; Trotsky, twenty; Bukharin, one; Sapronov, seven; Ignatov, twenty-two; Shliapnikov, four.[11] In both cases the Leninists had only a scant majority over the combined total of the Opposition groups, but the deep cleavage between the moderate and extreme Leftists over the question of centralized authority in the party and in economic life prevented any concerted action to oppose the majority. On organizational issues the moderate Leftists condemned the Ultra-Left Opposition as wholeheartedly as did the Leninists.

In marked contrast to Moscow stood the Petrograd organization, where, under the leadership of Zinoviev, the Leninist forces had firmly established themselves. The Petrograd organization led off in the Leninist campaign early in January 1921 with a sharp criticism of Trotsky for endangering party unity and the tie between the party and the trade unions.[12] Trotsky replied with a defense of his trade-union plan and a plea for settling the issue by open discussion rather than the organizational pressure which was associated with the Petrograd organization.[13] The Moscow Committee at this point actually voted fourteen to thirteen to take a public stand against the Petro-grad organization and censured it for not observing the rules of proper con-troversy.[14] Moscow also criticized the Central Committee and urged it to ensure the equitable distribution of materials, speakers, and such to all local organizations, so that all points of view would be fairly represented. A special danger was indicated in "the tendency of the Petrograd organization to make itself a special center for the preparation of the party congress"[15]—indicating that the Leninists were using the Petrograd organization as a base from which to apply pressure on the rest of the party.

The intensification of the trade-union controversy caused acute division between the Leninists and the moderate Leftists, who between them monop-olized the party command. The regular central machinery was, for once, not available to Lenin. The Central Committee was divided almost evenly, and as for the Secretariat, all three of its members—Preobrazhensky, Kres-tinsky, and Serebriakov—were strong supporters of Trotsky. Some of the Leninists, particularly Zinoviev, made a special point of criticizing the Trotskyist secretaries, who were simultaneously attacked as ineffective and undemocratic.[16] (Actually, Preobrazhensky was probably the most liberal-minded party leader outside of the Ultra-Left.) Focusing charges on the Orgburo, Zinoviev forced the issue before the Central Committee at the end of December 1920. The Orgburo was then composed of five members—the three Trotskyist secretaries together with Rykov and Stalin. A majority of the Central Committee, made up of the Trotskyists and Rykov, voted to defend the Orgburo. Lenin remained aloof; but siding with Zinoviev and the lesser Leninists was the fifth Orgburo member, Stalin.[17] This maneuver was to stand him in good stead.

Despite their weakness in the central party organizations, the Leninists were able to mobilize the strength to score a decisive victory. They appear to have made effective use of the new control commissions. Preobrazhensky, who had no great sympathy with organizational repression of the Ultra-Left, was relieved from the central control commission in November 1920 and replaced by A. A. Solts, an ardent *apparatchik*. Dzerzhinsky (similarly a supporter of Trotsky at this juncture) also left the commission during the controversy.[18] Solts assumed direction of the central control commission and took it upon himself to berate the divided party leadership for its weakness in curtailing the Ultra-Left: "In practice the Central Committee itself refuses to direct this campaign."[19] Further benefit accrued to the Leninists from a rule which they pushed through the Central Committee by the narrow margin of eight to seven, against the opposition of the Trotskyists. The decision was to allow the election of delegates to the forthcoming congress on the basis of separate platforms—the nearest the Communists came to legalizing a multiparty system within their ranks.[20] The Trotskyists opposed the move probably because it made the election a question of confidence in Lenin, whom few were prepared to repudiate.

Mustering all available political resources, and capitalizing to the maximum on the leader's prestige, the Leninists prosecuted a vigorous campaign, as the subsequent record of voting in local party organizations eloquently testifies. Their high-pressure tactics evoked considerable protest, and impelled the Moscow organization to appeal for moderation:

In view of the fact that the discussion . . . has assumed the forms of excessive sharpness and of attacks on individual groups of comrades, the Moscow Committee calls on all party organizations to restrain themselves strictly in the discussion to the substance of the disputed questions, and emphatically warns all comrades against such resort to polemics, which can lead to the weakening of the unity of the party and to the weakening of practical work. Freedom of discussion, freedom of agitation for one or another platform, must not in any event lead to the weakening of the unity of the party, which must and of course does remain inviolate.[21]

Preobrazhensky specifically attacked the Leninists' tactics on the ground that they damaged party unity and thus gave aid and comfort to the enemy:

"The move of the majority of the Petrograd organization was in a tone which would be natural if the party and the trade unions were threatened by some mortal danger. However, it has actually intensified still more the passion and nervousness of the polemics, and leads to madness and evokes a feeling of alarm in the local organizations."[22] But the struggle between the factions continued unabated.

At the party conference of the Baltic Fleet on January 19, the Leninists withstood criticism that they were the faction of the "committee men," and went on to win with 90 per cent of the vote.[23] The artificiality of this result was indicated, however, when opposition welled up the following month. A so-called Fleet Opposition emerged and succeeded in stating its criticism of the authorities at the next party conference: "The political department of the Baltic Fleet has lost contact not only with the masses but with the active political workers as well, and has become a bureaucratic organ without wide authority. . . . Completely cut off from the party masses, the Po-Balt has annihilated all local initiative, has reduced all political work to the level of secretarial correspondence."[24] Delegates returning to the units of the fleet reportedly spoke of "victory over the dictatorship."[25] The emotional powder magazine which blew up at Kronstadt was well stocked.

By and large, even in those local party organizations where the Opposition groups were able to offer substantial resistance, the Leninists won decisive victories. At Tula on January 25, 1921, they won five hundred eighty-seven votes in the city conference against two hundred seventy-two for Trotsky and sixteen for the Workers' Opposition. The strength of the Leninist apparatus in Petrograd was attested by the delivery of the vote in electing delegates to the Petrograd city conference: one hundred seventy-four for Lenin, eleven for Trotsky. Three of the eleven districts in the city actually reported unanimous votes for the Leninist candidates.[26] This success of the Leninists seems too complete to be honest; yet the Opposition never raised charges of actual fraud. In endeavoring to understand this situation one must bear in mind the tremendous impact of Lenin's personal leadership and the great appeal which the tradition of party unity had after the experience of the Civil War. To the extent that additional pressure was applied, it was probably more subtle, such as open balloting with a natural reluctance to defy the local leadership.

In some localities the Leninist machine operated with near perfection: it won all but twenty-seven out of nine hundred votes at the Ivanovo-Voznesensk city conference, and three hundred fifty-eight to eight opposed and ten abstentions at Tver. Sometimes the Leninists even prevailed in the oppositionists' own strongholds. This occurred in two Moscow districts whose committees were dominated by Trotskyists but where the Leninists won large majorities in voting by the rank and file in January.[27]

The final and decisive test was the election of delegates to the Moscow provincial conference late in February. Moscow was not only the most important of all party organizations, but numerically the principal stronghold of the Opposition forces. It was the one great weak point in the otherwise solid front of the Leninist majority. If the oppositionists could displace the Leninists from control of the Moscow organization, they would have won a great strategic and moral victory. They failed the test, however; the Leninists not only managed to hold on to their previously slender margin, but extended it to a two-thirds majority.[28] Ultra-Left delegate strength in the Moscow province had been whittled down from 40 per cent in November to less than 20 per cent in February. "The same process," the Secretariat boasted, was going on in all local organizations.[29]

When the Tenth Party Congress convened on March 8, the Leninists commanded an overwhelming majority. The party leadership had successfully met the challenge posed by the moderate Left and Ultra-Left factions, and it was ready to resolve the party controversy to its own satisfaction. But in the meantime, the national crisis had led to a political upheaval outside the confines of the party which posed a far more immediate and pressing threat to the security of the regime. This was the armed uprising of the sailors and garrison at Kronstadt.

THE KRONSTADT REVOLT

The open rebellion which erupted on March 2, 1921, out of a protest movement at the Kronstadt naval base near Petrograd, was undoubtedly the most serious internal political crisis ever faced by the Soviet government. Kronstadt was a movement of disillusioned revolutionaries, animated by the same kind of grievances expressed by the Ultra-Left Communists but outside the restraints of party loyalty and discipline. The Kronstadters revolted against the Soviet leaders in the name of the October Revolution itself.

Moscow denounced the revolt immediately after word was received of the Kronstadters' defiance of the authority of the Soviet government and their arrest of the leading Communist officials on the island. An official communiqué announced a "new White Guard plot . . . expected and undoubtedly prepared by the French counterrevolution."[30] The main concern of the Soviet leaders was to crush, as soon as possible, all who defied their authority. This attitude surprised many people at the time. Alexander Berkman, an American anarchist then in Petrograd, reported, "Even some Communists are indignant at the tone assumed by the government. It is a fatal error, they say, to interpret the workers' plea for bread as opposition. Kronstadt's sympathy with the strikers and their demand for honest elections have been turned by Zinoviev into a counterrevolutionary plot. . . . All agree that the sailors are the staunchest supporters of the soviets; their object is to compel the authorities to grant needed reforms."[31]

That there was at least some legitimate basis for the Kronstadt reform demands was admitted by Kalinin, who himself had gone to Kronstadt on an unsuccessful mission to restrain the dissidents the day before the revolt broke out. He described a resolution adopted at Kronstadt on March 1, demanding various reforms ranging from free elections to the permission of free trade, as "with certain corrections, more or less acceptable," and based on real organizational abuses within the Communist Party.[32] Undoubtedly the Kronstadt revolt could have been forestalled by timely reforms, but such a course would have been too embarrassing and might well have been a serious blow to the authority of the government. Petrograd was in the throes of a wildcat strike wave, upon which Menshevik and SR undergrounders were allegedly trying to capitalize, and the Soviet authorities had all they could do to keep the situation in hand there.[33] For the Communist leaders it was more natural at this time of crisis to tighten up. Given the state of popular discontent, an admission by the government that the Kronstadters had a case that could be discussed might have brought the Soviet regime crashing down everywhere. It was essential above all for the Communist Party to suppress the idea of Kronstadt as a movement which defended the principles of the October Revolution against the Communists—the idea of the "third revolution."

This concept was the basis of the program which the Kronstadters endeavored to develop in the pages of their journal,[34] the *Izvestiya* of the Temporary Revolutionary Committee:

Waves of uprisings of workers and peasants have testified that their patience has come to an end. The uprising of the laborers has drawn near. The time has come to overthrow the commissarocracy. . . . Kronstadt has raised for the first time the banner of the uprising for the Third Revolution of the toilers. . . . The autocracy has fallen. The Constituent Assembly has departed to the region of the damned. The commissarocracy is crumbling.[35]

"We fight," the rebels proclaimed, "for the genuine power of the laboring people, while the bloody Trotsky and the glutted Zinoviev and their band of adherents fight for the power of the party of the Communist-ravishers."[36] The Bolshevik regime was assailed for repression equaling that of tsarist times. Labor had been made "not into joy," as the Marxist scheme promised, "but into a new slavery." "To be victorious or die!" was the cry.

In their program, though not in their armed defiance, the Kronstadters were closely akin to the Ultra-Left Opposition within the Communist Party. The Kronstadt position on the trade unions was an obvious echo of the Workers' Opposition: "Our trade unions have had absolutely no opportunity to be purely class organizations . . . thanks to the policy of the ruling party, striving for the centralized 'communist' development of the masses." Anarcho-syndicalism of the 1917 vintage was counterposed to bureaucratic centralism:

"If the unions were given rights of broad autonomy, this would unavoidably break down the Communists' whole order of centralist construction, and together with this the necessity for commissars and political departments would fall away. . . . The Soviet Socialist Republic can be strong only when its administration belongs to the toiling classes represented by renovated trade unions."[37]

The number of Communist Party members who joined the revolt testifies to the extent of antibureaucratic emotion among the party rank and file. Statements by defecting Communists published in the *Izvestiya* of the Temporary Revolutionary Committee graphically illustrate this attitude:

The policy of the Communist Party has led the country into a position from which there is no escape—because the party has become bureaucratized, has learned nothing, doesn't wan't to learn or to listen to the voice of the masses.

For three whole years our party has been filled up with self-seekers and careerists, as a result of which there have developed bureaucratism and even a criminal relation to the business of struggling with the breakdown. . . . Long live the Soviet power—the true defender of the rights of the toilers.

Every honorable Communist must mark himself off from those who have found no language for workers and peasants other than the language of bullets and bombs.

Abuses high up in the party . . . spatter mud on the beautiful idea of Communism.[38]

Many of the government troops captured by the Kronstadters in the early days of the defense of the island fortress, on learning that "the sailors and workers had overthrown the power of the commissarocracy," went over to the side of the rebels.[39] Ordinary Communists were indeed so unreliable in the face of the issues raised by the Kronstadt affair that the government did not depend on them, either in the assault on Kronstadt itself or in keeping order in Petrograd, where Kronstadt's hopes for support chiefly rested. The main body of troops employed were Chekists and officer cadets from Red Army training schools. The final assault on Kronstadt was led by the top officialdom of the Communist Party—a large group of the delegates at the Tenth Party Congress was rushed from Moscow for this purpose.[40]

The connection between the Kronstadt revolt and the ideas of the Ultra-Left Communists was compelling evidence to the party leadership that the Opposition could no longer be tolerated. There was, to be sure, no direct tie between the Ultra-Left Opposition and the Kronstadt movement; no Opposition leader failed to support the party leadership against the rebels. Nevertheless, the Opposition within the party and the Kronstadt revolt were manifestations of the same kind of dissatisfaction: both attacked the Communist leadership for violating the spirit of the revolution, for sacrificing democratic

and egalitarian ideals on the altar of expediency, and for inclining to bureaucratic concern with power for its own sake. From the standpoint of the party
leadership, such explosive criticism had to be disarmed permanently.

FORGING PARTY UNITY

The Kronstadt revolt impelled the party leadership to take immediate
and drastic steps to put an end to the challenge of the Ultra-Left Opposition.
Their tactic was to identify the Communist Ultra-Left with the same
counterrevolutionary influences allegedly at work at Kronstadt. The Workers' Opposition, as the most dynamic and threatening segment of the
Opposition, was singled out for the main attack.

In his opening speech to the Tenth Party Congress Lenin denounced the
Workers' Opposition as a threat to the security of the revolution. "It is obvious," he declared in his summary, "that the syndicalist deviation is also an
anarchist deviation, and that the 'Workers' Opposition,' which hides behind
the back of the proletariat, is a petty-bourgeois anarchist element."[41]

The congress took the prosecutor's cue and found the defendants guilty
as charged:

The deviation was caused in part by the entry into the ranks of the party of
elements which have still not completely adopted the Communist world view;
for the most part this deviation was caused by the influence on the proletariat
and on the Russian Communist Party of the petty-bourgeois element, which is
exceptionally strong in our country and which unavoidably causes waverings
on the side of anarchism, especially at moments when the situation of the masses
has badly deteriorated.[42]

The party leadership was certainly aware that this "petty-bourgeois"
charge was a fabrication. Lenin himself remarked that the main trouble
with the proposals of the Workers' Opposition was that they were too
advanced; the Soviet government still had to concentrate on overcoming
the masses' cultural backwardness and petty-bourgeois habits, so-called.[43]
But on the latter ground the party leadership made a second point against
the Workers' Opposition—that it was "objectively" a counterrevolutionary
factor because its extreme demands disrupted the party's efforts to cope with
petty-bourgeois influences and raised hopes among the workers which could
only be disappointed.[44]

A third count against the Workers' Opposition, in addition to the charges
that it was insufficiently revolutionary and excessively revolutionary, was that
it was not revolutionary in the correct manner—that it was deviating toward
anarcho-syndicalism. This allegation brought into play all the emotion connected with the past controversies between Marxists and anarchists since
the split of the First International. Lenin was bent on crushing the Workers'
Opposition even while the Communist regime as a whole was near collapse.

"If we perish," he said privately, "it is all the more important to preserve our ideological line and give a lesson to our continuators. This should *never* be forgotten, even in *hopeless* circumstances."[45] To be sure, there had always been a certain affinity between anarcho-syndicalism and the left-wing strand of Bolshevik thought. Lenin himself was captivated by the anarchistic spirit in 1917, with the programmatic radicalism of his "State and Revolution." But the Ultra-Left had held to the ideal while the party leadership, through the progressive canonization of bureaucratic expedients into the law of the revolution, had departed from the spirit of 1917. The Workers' Opposition actually represented a failure to deviate along with Lenin when he abandoned the anarcho-syndicalist aspects of the Bolshevik program.

The crowning political sin of the Workers' Opposition, in Lenin's eyes, was to question the primacy of the Communist Party. The orthodoxy in this matter was pronounced by the congress: "Marxism teaches"—it was, more strictly speaking, Leninism—

and this teaching . . . is upheld by all the experience of our revolution—that only the political party of the working class, i.e., the Communist Party, is in a position to unite, educate, and organize such a vanguard of the proletariat and all the laboring masses as will be able to counteract the inevitable petty-bourgeois wavering of the masses, to counteract tradition and unavoidable relapses of trade-union narrowness or trade-union prejudices within the proletariat, and to direct all sides of the proletarian movement and hence all the working masses. Without this the dictatorship of the proletariat is meaningless.[46]

The proletariat of itself was held to be incapable of rising above the level of mere trade-union consciousness. To dispute this was an unpardonable theoretical regression from Marxism, which no genuine proletarian could commit.

Granting his premises, Lenin had an air-tight case. Any manifestation of independent revolutionary thought among the workers which would seem to refute Lenin's characterization of them naturally had to challenge the authority of the party which purported to do the proletariat's thinking for it. Such a challenge of the party, given the definition of true proletarian thought as complete loyalty to the authority of the party, was *ipso facto* evidence of "petty-bourgeois," "trade-unionist" thinking or of the "declassing" of the workers in consequence of the economic breakdown. Thus, by 1921, the organizational doctrine of Bolshevism had come full circle, to the primeval Leninism of 1902.

The decisive work of the Tenth Congress was to implement the party's regression to old-style Leninism. The spirit of rigorous centralism and unity characteristic of the earliest Bolshevik organizational doctrine and practice was affirmed as the law of the party—and hence of all Russian political life. The immediate purpose of this was to enforce the condemnation of the

Ultra-Left Opposition groups, particularly the Workers' Opposition. As a result, the future possibilities for open, legal opposition were virtually eliminated. Henceforth every opposition movement was hamstrung by the necessity of denying its own oppositionist nature, of conforming to the new standards of Communist political propriety.

Unity was the all-pervasive theme at the Tenth Congress, as the party leadership capitalized on the Kronstadt menace and the reaction against the bitter factionalism of the precongress debates:

The Congress calls the attention of all members of the party to the fact that the unity and solidarity of its ranks . . . are especially necessary at the present moment, when a series of circumstances intensify the wavering among the petty-bourgeois population of the country. . . .

It is essential that all conscious workers clearly realize the harm and intolerability of any factionalism whatsoever, which unavoidably leads in practice to the weakening of friendly work and to stronger repeated attempts of the enemies of the ruling party who attached themselves to it to deepen the split and utilize it for the ends of counter-revolution.

The next step followed logically, to enforce the new organizational principle:

The Congress prescribes the rapid dispersal of all groups without exception which have formed themselves on one platform or another, and orders all organizations to deal strictly with any factional manifestations by prohibiting them. . . . Failure to execute this decision of the congress will lead to immediate and unconditional expulsion from the party.

To this was added a secret provision giving the Central Committee unlimited disciplinary discretion:

In order to realize strict discipline within the party and attain the greatest unity through the elimination of any factionalism, the congress gives the Central Committee full power to exercise, in cases of violation of discipline or the causing or allowing of factionalism, all measures of party punishment up to expulsion from the party; and regarding members of the Central Committee—demotion of them to candidates and even, as an extreme measure, their expulsion from the party.[47]

A two-thirds vote was "the condition for application of such an extreme measure." The importance of this decision cannot be stressed enough. It was the turning point in the organizational history of the party.

The implication of this change in the party's organizational doctrine was made explicit by Karl Radek in a remarkable speech to the congress. Radek confessed that he was uneasy about the powers which the Central Committee and the Central Control Commission were being given:

I had a feeling that a rule was being established here which left us still uncertain as to whom it might be applied against. For when the Central Committee was chosen, the comrades from the majority composed a list which gave them control, and every comrade knew that this was done at the beginning of the dissension in the party. We still do not know how this will be carried out, what complications may arise, but the comrades who propose this rule think that it is a sword aimed against differently thinking comrades. Although I am voting for this resolution, I feel that it may even be turned against us; but in spite of this, I stand for the resolution.

To explain this paradoxical position Radek referred to the current dangerous situation in which the party and the Soviet regime found themselves:

At such a moment, regardless of whom this sword may be turned against—at such a moment it is necessary to adopt this resolution and to say: let the Central Committee at the moment of danger take the sternest measures against the best comrades, if it finds this necessary. A definite line of the Central Committee is essential. The best Central Committee may make a mistake, but this is less dangerous than the wavering which we see now.[48]

Here is the reasoning which culminated in the confessions during the great purge trials—the act of faith in the party as an institution. With this background, the later opposition movements were never able to muster the single-ness of purpose required to pursue their cause to a successful conclusion.

The affirmation of the principles of centralism by the Tenth Congress did not rule out, at least on the verbal level, the ideal of "workers' democracy." This was meant to "guarantee to all members of the party down to the most backward, active participation in the life of the party, in the deciding of questions, and also an active share in building the party." No violation of the elective principle in choosing party officials was to be allowed, and free discussion and criticism were promised—within the limits of "democratic centralism": "It stands to reason that after a decision has been made, it is binding and must be fulfilled with maximum swiftness and accuracy." Organizational measures of the Civil War period were renounced for peacetime application, as "the system of military orders, which were given by the party's directing institutions and which were obediently fulfilled without discussion by the rank-and-file members of the party."[49]

As a concession to local autonomy the congress provided that "dismissal of lower organizations by higher party organs is permissible only in case of clear violation of decisions of the party congress. . . . In all other cases the higher organ summons the respective conference or gathering of delegates, where the question or conflict which has come to a head is decided. Until the decision of the question in the indicated manner, the execution of the decision of the higher party organ by the lower organ is not ceased." Even in this clause the centralizing tendency is all too apparent. But the congress went still further in its specific measures to strengthen the party's central organs. It declared that the "most immediate task" of the Central Committee was the "stringent effectuation of uniformity in the structure of party committees." It provided for periodic conferences of the heads of the executive departments of the provincial party committees, as well as semiannual party conferences. The membership of the Central Committee was raised from nineteen to twenty-five, of whom five were to devote themselves exclusively to party work (especially by visiting provincial committees and attending provincial party conferences).[50]

The standards of party unity still differed in important respects from what they came to mean in later years. Lenin's insistence on firm party unity was qualified by its inclusive character, and he balanced his abuse of the Workers' Opposition with an appeal for their cooperation: "We don't need an opposition now, comrades. . . . Let them [the oppositionists] call themselves what they please—this is all right; if only they will help the work, if only they will not play with opposition and not defend groups and factions at any price, but will just help us."[51]

Lenin went so far as to admit the Workers' Opposition's contention that "our state is a state with a bureaucratic perversion."[52] On this ground he appealed for the support of the oppositionists to combat the evil. He had the congress place in its resolution "On the Unity of the Party," together with the ban on factional activity, the following provision: "Entrusting to the Central Committee the carrying out of the complete destruction of any factionalism, the congress at the same time declares that regarding questions which attract special attention of members of the party"—and here Lenin interpolated, in reading the resolution to the congress, the words, "for example, groups like the so-called Workers Opposition"—"any practical proposal whatever on the purge of nonproletarian and unreliable elements from the party, on the struggle with bureaucratism, on the development of democratism and the independence of the workers, etc., must be looked over with the greatest attention and tested in practical work."[53]

Even the banning of factional activity was not conceived of as an absolute measure. When Riazanov proposed an amendment to rule out elections to the Central Committee on the basis of separate groups, each standing on its respective platform, Lenin drew the line: "We cannot deprive the party and the members of the Central Committee of the right to turn to the party, if a basic question evokes dissension. . . . We haven't the power to suppress this. . . . If, for example, questions like the Brest-Litovsk peace arise . . . it is possible that it will then be necessary to elect by platform."[54] As a gesture of reconciliation, Shliapnikov was made a member of the Central Committee, as was a lesser Workers' Opposition leader, the unionist I. I. Kutuzov.[55]

In his final speech Lenin rejoiced over the achievements of the congress: "We know that, united at this congress, we will really get rid of our differences, be absolutely united, and have a party which, more tempered, will go on to more and more decisive international victories."[56] Did he not realize that he had only aggravated the issues which had divided the party, and at the same time had created the instruments of power which would eventually be used to extirpate every sort of protest?

The drastic change of organizational policy registered by the Tenth Congress—the return to the organizational tradition of 1902—was reflected by a complete overturn in the leadership of the party Secretariat. At its first meeting after the Tenth Congress, the Central Committee voted out of office the incumbent secretaries Krestinsky, Preobrazhensky, and Serebriakov, and replaced them with Molotov, Yaroslavsky, and V. M. Mikhailov.

The change was a severe blow to Trotsky's moderate Leftist faction, in obvious retaliation for their defiance on the trade-union issue. All three secretaries had supported Trotsky in the trade-union controversy, and Preobrazhensky and Krestinsky, at least, had been Left Communists in 1918. To be sure, the Trotskyists had supported Lenin in taking organizational measures against the Ultra-Left, but hardly with the requisite vigor. Preobrazhensky, in particular, took the idea of party democracy quite seriously. He wrote in January 1921, "This possibility of greater freedom of criticism . . . already underscored by . . . the September party conference, represents one of the victories of the revolution."[57] Such leniency had to stop. The three Trotskyist secretaries were quietly but totally disgraced, and dropped from the Central Committee altogether. Preobrazhensky and Serebriakov were relegated to administrative posts, and Krestinsky was soon afterwards sent off to serve as the Soviet emissary to Germany.

The defeat of the moderate Leftists in 1921 cost them irreparable losses with respect to their power in the party organization. Zinoviev, Trotsky's implacable foe, took Krestinsky's place in the Politburo. The Secretariat and the Orgburo, which the Trotskyists had dominated, were completely lost. Their strength on the Central Committee (which before the Tenth Congress had been almost evenly divided) was decimated. When the congress elected a new and larger Central Committee, four of the Trotskyists were eliminated —the three former secretaries and Andreyev—while one (Ivan Smirnov) was demoted to candidate member. Bukharin and Dzerzhinsky parted company with the Left, and only Trotsky, Rakovsky, and Radek were left to represent the moderate Left point of view in the party's governing council. The two Workers' Oppositionists were brought in as a tactical maneuver, but offsetting this was the selection or promotion of nine new organization men to serve on the new committee. The net result was: Leninists, twenty; Opposition, five. Of the old Orgburo, only Stalin and Rykov remained; they were joined by the three new secretaries and Tomsky (as well as an obscure trade-unionist, N. Komarov). In the shake-up lower down, the Trotskyists lost an important position when Ivan Smirnov was displaced as Petrograd party secretary by N. A. Uglanov.[58]

The organizational shifts of 1921 were a decisive victory for Lenin, the

Leninists, and the Leninist philosophy of party life. The changes worked particularly to the advantage of one individual, who stood primarily behind the scenes—Stalin. He admittedly now became the most influential figure in the party's organizational activities, and his appointment to the post of general secretary the following year was largely the juridical recognition of the *de facto* power which he already enjoyed. Stalin was thenceforth unchallengeable as the dominant personality in the organizational machinery of the party.

The ranking position among the three new secretaries was held by Molotov, who was then only thirty years old. Molotov had seen little of the limelight since his brief occupancy of the center of the stage as a leader, with Shliapnikov, of the Bolshevik left wing in March 1917. During the Civil War he was engrossed in party committee work. In 1920, simultaneously with his inclusion in the Central Committee as a candidate member, he became the secretary of the Ukrainian party organization in the Moscow-directed shake-up which occurred at that time.[59] This superficially dull but capable and methodical functionary was destined to become Stalin's right-hand man and to rise to the highest positions in the Soviet state. His reward for efficient service during the 1920–21 crisis was substantial: he not only became a full member of the Central Committee and one of the three party secretaries, but was also made a candidate member of the Politburo and a full member of the Orgburo.[60]

Mikhailov was lifted from complete obscurity to be made a member of the Central Committee and a secretary. He never distinguished himself and stayed in the Secretariat only a year, but he managed to remain as a member of the Central Committee and part of the time as a candidate member of the Orgburo. In 1928–29, having joined Bukharin's Right Opposition, he was forced publicly to humiliate himself.[61] He was demoted to candidate membership on the Central Committee in 1930, where he remained until he disappeared in the purge of 1938.

Yaroslavsky was a worker from Siberia, active in the Moscow organization where he had been a Left Communist; he became a candidate member of the Central Committee in 1919. After being installed in the Secretariat in 1921 and acquiring full Central Committee membership, he moved on to become a leading figure in the Central Control Commission of the party. In the thirties he achieved some notoriety as director of the Institute of Party History and head of the Union of Militant Atheists. He escaped the purge and died a natural death in 1943.[62]

The accession of the new people who came to power in the party organization in 1921 reflected the triumph of the Bolshevik organizational doctrine of 1902 over the practice of 1917—of military discipline and monolithic unity over mass initiative and factional freedom, of dogma over free controversy. In this manner the Soviet regime drew upon the latent resources of the prerevolutionary Bolshevik tradition to maintain its self-justifications and put an end to the type of criticism advanced by the Ultra-Left Opposition. This pattern set in 1921, of relying on the old organizational tradition of Bolshevism to conceal, rationalize, and explain away the failure of the regime to live up to its original social ideals, epitomizes Soviet politics ever since. In particular it explains the paradox that the further the Soviet regime has departed in its policies from the revolutionary ideal, the more stringently has the letter of the old ideology been imposed.

7

LENINISM RESTORED

The decision to enforce strict unity and discipline in the Communist Party was a major step in resolving the crisis faced by the Soviet regime in 1921. Meanwhile, the tense relations between the party and the country at large were eased by sending the revolution into retreat. The Communist Party parried the threat of counterrevolution and escaped the fate of its French revolutionary prototype by executing its own Ninth Thermidor.

THE NEP—TACTIC OR EVOLUTION?

The heavy cloud of controversy, tension, and uncertainty which hung over the party in the winter of 1920–1921 was dispelled by Lenin at one stroke. Simultaneously with his shake-up of the party, he proposed to the Tenth Congress that the most hated feature of War Communism, the forcible requisitioning of food from the peasants, be abolished. In its stead Lenin introduced a "tax in kind," with a definite scale of obligations, and ended government control of the grain supply. The implication of free trade in grain was soon clear: it meant the end of War Communism. Nevertheless, party reaction was almost unanimously in favor of this step, which marked the beginning of the New Economic Policy. As Lenin reported to the Eleventh Party Congress in 1922, "There was no disagreement among us, there was none because the impossibility in practice of any other approach to the construction of the foundation of a socialist economy was clear to all."[1]

The tax in kind was followed by the revival of a series of old and familiar institutions (though often with new terminology). Private trade was legalized step by step and within a year encompassed three fourths of the total retail volume.[2] Much small-scale industry also reverted to the hands of private entrepreneurs and cooperatives. The notorious new class of "NEP-men" mushroomed overnight. Even within the contracted sphere of state-owned enterprise, extensive changes took place. The top-heavy administrative apparatus was decentralized in favor of the state-owned but autonomous and financially responsible "trusts." Attempts to abolish the use of money were forgotten, and the conventional market and price system were restored, even in transactions between different organs of the government. "State capitalism" was the label which Lenin proposed for the new social order.

Though it was launched with little dissent, the NEP implied an entirely new historical perspective for the Soviet regime. International revolution had clearly failed to materialize, and the Russian revolutionaries now had to contend with, according to the postulates of "permanent revolution," national conditions that made their tenure of power insecure and the realization of their program uncertain. Urging "a whole series of special transitional measures," Lenin declared, "We have gone too far on the road of nationalizing trade and industry. . . . We know that only an agreement with the peasantry can save the socialist revolution in Russia, until the revolution breaks out in other countries."[3] Allowing some elasticity of definition, one can observe the emergence of a regime somewhat akin to Lenin's old formula, "the democratic dictatorship of the proletariat and peasantry."

The NEP remained an unstable compromise, if less for economic reasons than for political ones. In rank-and-file circles of the party there was much emotional disillusionment; the Communist youth organization (the *Komsomol*) lost nearly half its members in two years and suffered an outbreak of suicides.[4] The Ultra-Left groups, despite the blow dealt them by the Tenth Congress, returned to the fray in an effort to make political capital out of the spectacle of a "workers' state" currying the favor of rich peasants and foreign capitalists. A number of "discussion clubs" were organized to debate the new issues, but the party leadership swiftly dissolved them.[5]

More serious were the questions which important party figures of the moderate Leftist persuasion began to pose. Was the NEP temporary or a long-term arrangement? Was it a "tactic" or an "evolution?" Larin balanced the NEP against War Communism: where the latter had been a "bureaucratic perversion" of the revolution, the new line was a "bourgeois perversion." The NEP with all its concessions to capitalism was no achievement, he warned, but "an unavoidable evil, a maneuver or withdrawal . . . in order that the working class can more easily hold out until the revolutionary movement in Europe experiences a new upsurge."[6]

The early discussions about the NEP were largely theoretical, all factions being agreed on the need to proceed slowly and conciliate the peasants, but specific questions of future economic policy were soon faced. How fast could Russian industry be expanded, and how much central economic planning could be undertaken? Preobrazhensky, turning to the field of economic theory after his fall from the party Secretariat, emerged as the leading spokesman for stepped-up planning and industrialization. "Our strength," he declared, "consists in the fact that our petty-bourgeois surroundings . . . don't know . . . what surprises await them on the part of the socialist island."[7] In various writings he began to argue that after "two or three years of peaceful coexistence of the capitalist and the socialist processes of development," the survival of Russian socialism would require a vigorous offensive. This would entail intensive industrialization, supported by exploitation of the peasantry in the interest of the country's economic future.[8]

The new disagreements over the NEP underscored once again the cleavage between the Leninists and the moderate Left. In 1921 these two factions stood together to suppress the opposition of the Ultra-Left, but once the immediate crisis of 1921 was overcome, the question of the future economic course began to drive a deep wedge between them. Both groups were determined to maintain the Communist regime, and both acknowledged the constraints imposed by the isolation of the revolution in Russia. Their approaches, however, diverged widely: one would cautiously retreat, the other boldly advance. The lines were soon drawn for the violence of open controversy that commenced late in 1923. Meanwhile, the immediate problem in intraparty politics was to overcome the effects of the struggle against the Ultra-Left.

DISCIPLINING THE TRADE UNIONS

The introduction of the New Economic Policy settled the trade-union debate. The Leninist program for the unions was based on the least optimistic assumptions and for that reason was most realistic. When the need for retreat was acknowledged with the acceptance of the NEP, the plan to keep the unions out of management followed naturally.

It was a matter of some time, however, before the new trade-union policy was worked out in full detail. Lenin evidently did not give the problem much direct attention, and his followers moved with some caution in breaking with the grandiose conceptions of the role of the unions which prevailed between 1918 and 1920. A long resolution on the trade unions (drawn up by Zinoviev) was passed by the Tenth Congress, by the overwhelming vote of three hundred and thirty-six to fifty for the Trotsky position and eighteen for the Workers' Opposition.[9] Zinoviev took pains in this document to claim absolute continuity with the trade-union doctrine of War Communism, particularly as stated by the First Trade Union Congress and in the party program of 1919. This was the familiar device of generating a smokescreen of orthodoxy to cover the change of course. However, the new emphasis in the trade-union policy of 1921 was fairly clear: "The rapid governmentalizing of the trade unions would be a great political mistake." Union activity, as stressed by the Leninists during the controversy, would revolve around their function as a "school of Communism" and as an auxiliary to management in the furtherance of productive efficiency. The administrative sphere of the unions remained considerable though indefinite. Party control over the unions was proclaimed in absolute terms, which were soon to be implemented in practice: "The Russian Communist Party in the person of its central and local organizations unconditionally guides as before the whole ideological side of the work of the trade unions." Trotsky's administrative devices in the transport field were dismissed as temporary aberrations opposed to the loudly affirmed party line of "workers' democracy."[10] (Actually, the quasi-military pattern of political and trade-union organization in the transport field appears to have been retained.[11])

With the course now set toward unions with curtailed functions and close party supervision, it remained to enjoin the new line on the unions themselves. In some instances, where unions were centers of Workers' Opposition strength, this required a show of political force. A preliminary engagement was fought to decide control of the largest Workers' Opposition union, the metalworkers, of which Medvedev was the head.[12] When the metalworkers' union held its congress in May 1921, the Central Committee of the party handed it a list of recommended candidates for the union leadership. The metalworkers' delegates voted down the party-backed list, but this gesture proved futile: the party leadership boldly appointed their own men to the union offices, and the opposition collapsed. To make the pill more bitter, Shliapnikov was not even permitted to express a protest by resigning his seat on the Central Committee.[13]

The final test on the issue of trade-union autonomy vis-à-vis the party came soon afterwards at the Fourth All-Russian Congress of Trade Unions.[14] At the meeting of delegates who were party members, Tomsky submitted for routine approval a set of theses on the tasks of the trade unions. The approval was a matter of form, but an omission was noted. The theses made no reference to the formula of "proletarian democracy" with which the Tenth Congress had tried to assuage the rank and file. Riazanov, always ready to challenge undemocratic procedures, seized the opportunity and offered an amendment to fill the breach, in language almost identical with the Tenth Congress resolution: "The party must observe with special care the normal methods of proletarian democracy, particularly in the trade unions, where most of all the selection of leaders should be done by the organized party masses themselves."[15] Naturally the delegates saw here no divergence from the official line (neither did Tomsky, apparently), and Riazanov's amendment carried with the usual kind of machine-made vote—fifteen hundred to thirty, as it was recorded.

The party leadership reacted instantaneously to this miscarriage of their plans for curtailing the idea of union autonomy. Tomsky was summarily ejected from the trade-union congress. Lenin put in an appearance together with Bukharin and Stalin to rectify the unionists' action. The offending language was removed from the official theses on the trade unions, and the congress duly adopted the proper version. Quickly asserting the power which they claimed over union officials, the party leaders ordered Riazanov to desist completely from further trade-union activity. Stalin was commissioned to investigate Tomsky's mismanagement of the congress, and as a result the trade-union head was ousted from his position, demoted to mere candidate status on the Central Council of Trade Unions, and packed off on a party mission to Turkestan (a common device of administrative punishment). Similarly, Rudzutak, who had become the secretary of the Trade Union Council in 1920, was removed from that post and sent out with Tomsky to become the head of the Central Asian Bureau of the party.[16]

While the Leninist trade-union leaders, though accepting the new and limited role of the unions, suffered for condoning too much trade-union autonomy, one former exponent of the union-government fusion idea, Andreyev, was restored to favor. He was entrusted with the introduction of a measure giving to the Central Trade Union Council (where party influence was most secure) direct authority over local union organizations (where the Workers' Opposition had been strongest). Resistance to this step was stubborn, and the magnitude of the autonomist opposition as well as the extent of free expression still in effect was attested by the trade-unionists' vote on an attempt to kill Andreyev's plan by amendment—453 to 593. But narrow though the party victory was, it put an end to the question. Andreyev was made the new chairman of the ARCCTU, succeeding Tomsky, and the absolute authority of the party over Communists in the trade unions was confirmed.[17] (Subsequently Andreyev became a follower of Stalin and moved up in the party machinery. In 1926 he was made a candidate member of the Politburo and in 1932 a full member. Despite a colorless administrative record, or perhaps thanks to it, he survived the purges of the thirties and remained a leading figure in party affairs until 1950, when he fell into disgrace after a dispute with Khrushchev over the collective farms. He survives, evidently in semiretirement, and retains his membership in the Central Committee.)

By late 1921, as the implications of the New Economic Policy became clearer, the official conception of the role of the trade unions changed further. The trend of emphasis, in keeping with the restoration of capitalistic economic institutions, was steadily away from the unions' responsibilities in production. Looming much larger was the conventional union role of protecting the interests of the workers, as well as the distinctly Soviet function of the unions as a political auxiliary to the party. Meanwhile Tomsky and Rudzutak came back into favor, and Tomsky (whose exile had evidently turned him into a pliant agent of the leadership) was made secretary of the ARCCTU.

The new labor policy was formally laid down in a resolution of the Politburo in January 1922.[18] It was now established that the primary economic function of the unions was to protect the workers against the elements of capitalism which the Soviet regime had to tolerate for purposes of reconstruction. (Strikes were not formally outlawed, and they actually occurred in significant measure during the early years of the NEP, while the threat of unemployment became a major disciplinary device wielded by Soviet factory managers.[19]) Of course, the unions were also supposed to promote the national interest in increased production, with this qualification: "Any direct interference of the trade unions in the administration of enterprises . . . must be considered unconditionally harmful and impermissable." Politically the unions were charged with linking the masses to the party and combating the "petty-bourgeois influences" ranging from the Mensheviks to the Anarchists, who "continue to believe in the nonclass meaning . . . of 'democracy,' 'equality,' 'freedom' in general." It was conceded that under the conditions of the mixed economy which the NEP brought in, "contradictions" could develop, with consequent disputes in the labor movement. This, however, was but another opportunity to assert the primacy of the party: "It is essential to have a higher authority, sufficiently authoritative, to settle [conflicts] quickly. Such an authority is the Communist Party. . . ."[20]

By the fall of 1922 the trade unions had ceased to be a political problem, and Tomsky was reinstated in his old post as chairman of the Central Council. Andreyev was shunted to the presidency of the railroad workers' union, but he stayed in favor with the party organization and retained the Central Committee seat which had been restored to him at the Eleventh Congress in the spring of 1922.[21] Until 1928 the trade-union machinery was a reliable source of support for the party leadership and their policies of organizational tightness and economic caution. Tomsky had been installed in the Politburo in the spring of 1922 and was a leading member of the party directorate during the later years of the NEP. But when times began to change and as Stalin sought a new course for the ship of state, Tomsky joined the Right Opposition, and the trade unions once again became a center of political controversy and organizational struggle.

TIGHTENING THE PARTY RANKS

Despite the formal condemnation of factions pronounced by the Tenth Party Congress, both the Workers' Opposition and the Democratic Centralist group continued to exist. Of equal concern to the party leadership were several splinter groups which appeared on the fringes of the party. Such were the Workers' Group, headed by Gabriel Miasnikov, a direct offshoot of the Workers' Opposition; the so-called Workers' Truth organization, inspired by the ex-Bolshevik theoretician Alexander Bogdanov; and an ephemeral Workers' and Peasants' Socialist Party.[22]

Less than a month after the Tenth Congress the Central Committee found it necessary to call upon the recently strengthened Central Control Commission to make an investigation of Workers' Opposition activity in certain localities. One of the places singled out was the Ural city of Perm, where a disturbance in the party organization was traceable to the activity of Miasnikov. His virtually single-handed opposition movement drew much of the fire of the party apparatus during the remainder of 1921. Miasnikov's principal offense was to champion freedom of the press. The Central Committee replied by declaring Miasnikov's views to be "incompatible with the interests of the party," and forbade their presentation at a local party conference—one more step in the strengthening of central control over local party organizations.[23]

Lenin wrote to Miasnikov in an effort to dissuade him from his errors:[24] "We don't believe in absolutes. We laugh at pure democracy." In Lenin's mind, the threat of counterrevolution still made freedom dangerous: "Freedom of the press in the RSFSR . . . is freedom of political organization for the bourgeoisie and its most faithful servants—the Mensheviks and SRs. . . . The bourgeoisie (all over the world) is still many times stronger than us. To give it still another weapon, such as freedom of political organization (freedom of press, for the press is the center and foundation of political organization) means to make things easier for the enemy, to help the class enemy." As in the case of the Workers' Opposition, Lenin admitted the evils which evoked the protest but rejected the promised solution. "The breaking away of Communist cells from the party is an evil, a sickness, a misfortune, it is a grave sickness—we see this. But to cure it we need not freedom for the bourgeoisie, but measures directed toward the proletariat and the party."

Miasnikov nevertheless continued to defy party discipline. At length, his activities were investigated by a special commission of the Central Committee, on whose recommendation he was expelled from the party in February 1922.[25] This was the only instance after the Bolsheviks became a party (except for the quasi-Bolshevik Lozovsky in 1918) when Lenin actually expelled a prominent party member. Undaunted, Miasnikov went underground and began to work for a new proletarian opposition movement. Backed by a small group of other former Workers' Oppositionists, Miasnikov issued early in 1923 a lengthy manifesto in the name of "The Workers' Group of the Russian Communist Party." The program was largely that of the Workers' Opposition, with stress on the democratic administration of industry through the unions, coupled with an uncompromising denunciation of the NEP and its concessions to capitalist ways.[26] Repeating the anti-intelligentsia sentiment characteristic of much of the extreme Left, the Workers' Group concluded that the revolution had degenerated into rule by "a bunch of intellectuals." Their demand was for a new movement to protect the workers from the "oligarchy" and bureaucracy of Communist Party rule.[27]

Miasnikov's group apparently played a considerable role in the strike wave which broke out in the summer of 1923, after which the movement was broken by the GPU. Miasnikov escaped from Russia in 1927 and settled in Paris as a factory worker. In 1946, he returned to Russia under mysterious circumstances and has not been heard from since.[28]

Of less political moment but more extreme ideologically was the organization known as the Workers' Truth (*Rabochaya pravda*). It appears to have been composed more of intellectuals than of workers, and in all probability

was an outgrowth of the ostensibly nonpolitical "proletarian culture" movement ("Proletcult") which the Soviet government had permitted Lenin's
old lieutenant Bogdanov to build up.[29] In its tone of uncompromising
radicalism the program of the Workers' Truth was reminiscent of the pre-
1914 Left Bolshevik Opposition which Bogdanov had led.

The Bogdanovists proceeded on the assumption that the revolution had
ended in a complete defeat for the working class and that the "technical intelligentsia" had been brought to power instead.[30] In the manifesto which they
circulated, the Workers' Truth charged that the bureaucracy, along with the
NEPmen, had become a new bourgeoisie, depending on the exploitation of
the workers and taking advantage of their disorganization. The NEP meant
only "the rebirth of normal capitalist relations," while with the trade unions
in the hands of the bureaucracy the workers were more helpless than ever.
"The Communist Party . . . after becoming the ruling party, the party of
the organizers and leaders of the state apparatus and of the capitalist-based
economic life . . . irrevocably lost its tie and community with the proletariat."
(Here Marxism was being pointedly turned against the Communist leadership.) The Workers' Truth frankly appealed for a new "Workers' Party"
to fight for the democratic conditions under which the workers could defend
their interests. Only a new revolutionary spirit, it seems, could redeem the
proletarian cause.[31] But the new circumstances of Soviet political life allowed
no opportunity for such a development, and the Workers' Truth withered on
the vine. Bogdanov abandoned politics for the last time and immersed himself in scientific work until his death in 1926.

During the year following the Tenth Congress, the main source of friction
in the party continued to be the Workers' Opposition. Despite Lenin's conciliatory talk, the party Secretariat was perfecting its technique of dealing
with recalcitrant individuals by the power of removal and transfer, directed
primarily at adherents of the Workers' Opposition.[32] (Of the thirty-seven
Workers' Opposition delegates to the Tenth Congress whom Lenin consulted when he was persuading Shliapnikov and Kutuzov to enter the Central Committee, only four managed to return as voting delegates to the next
congress.[33])

Cooperation between Lenin and the Workers' Opposition representatives
in the Central Committee was short-lived. The affair of the metalworkers'
union had hardly quieted down when, in August 1921, Shliapnikov attacked
the government's economic policy as "antiworker." Lenin seized on this as
an intolerable breach of unity and demanded that the Central Committee
invoke its secret authority to expel one of its members.[34] The ouster failed by
a margin of only one vote short of the necessary two thirds, and Shliapnikov
escaped with a severe warning.[35]

The Workers' Opposition continued to be a real threat partly because of
the response which they found in Communist circles abroad. Now, for the

first time, the Communist International became an important factor in the internal politics of the Russian Communists. Later on, especially between 1925 and 1928, the interaction of the party struggle in Russia and factionalism in the Comintern was to prove of decisive significance in both quarters.

The growth of the Workers' Opposition in Russia coincided with a deviation in the newly formed Comintern which was inspired by much the same emphasis on anarchistic and syndicalist aspects of the left-wing socialist tradition. The most important instance of this tendency was the German Communist Labor Party (KAPD), which split off from the regular Communist organization (KPD) in 1920 and became the nucleus for a short-lived Communist Labor International. These uncompromising revolutionaries made no effort to conceal their sympathy for the Workers' Opposition in Russia, to the evident embarrassment of the latter in their professions of Communist orthodoxy.[36] The Workers' Opposition did seek support, however, from the regular Communist organizations abroad. At the Third Congress of the Comintern Kollontai cautiously sought to rally sympathy for the Opposition cause, while Shliapnikov and Lutovinov went to Germany to contact the left wing of the KPD.[37]

Early in 1922 the Workers' Opposition seized an opportunity to make a forthright appeal to Communists abroad. A statement signed by twenty-two Workers' Opposition leaders, including Kollontai, Shliapnikov, and Lutovinov, was submitted (without the foreknowledge of the Russian party chiefs) to a Comintern conference then considering the question of a "united workers' front."[38] Ostensibly to expose and correct the undemocratic practices in the Russian Communist Party which might embarrass such a policy, this "Declaration of the Twenty-two" reaffirmed the now-familiar Ultra-Left complaint:

Our directing centers are carrying on an unrelenting disruptive campaign against all, especially proletarians, who allow themselves to have their own judgment, and in case of the expression of this within the party they take all kinds of repressive measures.

The effort to draw the proletarian masses closer to the state is declared to be "anarcho-syndicalism," and its adherents are subjected to persecution and discrediting. . . .

The party and trade-union bureaucracy . . . ignore the decisions of our congresses on putting workers' democracy into practice.

Referring to Riazanov's suspension from trade-union activities, the declaration charged, "The tutelage and pressure of the bureaucracy goes so far that it is prescribed for members of the party, under threat of expulsion or other repressive measures, to elect not those whom the Communists want themselves, but those whom the ignorant high places want." Such practices assertedly led to careerism, loss of political enthusiasm on the part of proletarian party members, and general conditions which made the ideal of a united workers' front unattainable. In concluding, the "Twenty-two" appealed to the Comintern to correct the policies of the Russian leadership: "The state of affairs in our party is so serious that it impels us to turn to you for help, and in this way to eliminate the impending threat of a split in our party."

The Russian leadership, represented by Trotsky and Zinoviev, quickly hit back. A special commission of the conference was set up to hear both sides in the controversy, which was decided, not surprisingly, in favor of the Russian leadership.[39] Simultaneously, the executive committee of the Comintern resolved that:

the position taken by the comrades who made the complaint does not at all aid or strengthen the party in the struggle against the objectively existing abnormality, but on the other hand deprives the party of valuable strengh and simultaneously "from the left" presents to the enemies of Communism—the Mensheviks and even the White counterrevolutionaries of the worst type—a weapon against the party and against the dictatorship of the proletariat.[40]

A month later, at the Eleventh Party Congress, a special commission was set up to investigate the activities of the Workers' Opposition. After assembling its evidence and questioning the leaders of the group, the commission concluded, "A number of facts establish beyond doubt that an *illegal factional organization* was preserved, and at its head stood the inspirers and leaders, comrades Shliapnikov, Medvedev, and Kollontai." To the refusal of these three to acknowledge that their declaration to the Comintern had been a breach of party ethics, the commission replied that since the Workers' Opposition leaders would not bow to party and Comintern decisions, they ought to be expelled from the ranks of the RCP.[41] While only expelling two men—Mitin, a recently converted Menshevik, and Kuznetsov, who had allegedly tried to conceal his social background as a grocery-store proprietor—the congress endorsed the commission's charges against the "Twenty-two." These included factional activities in the trade unions, relations with groups attempting to establish a "Fourth International," and action of a "conspiratorial" nature. The condemnation of opposition per se was affirmed, with special censure of Kollontai because "she considers dissent inevitable if the party does not take the way of the views of Comrades Kollontai, Medvedev, and Shliapnikov, which are erroneous and harmful to the working class." Expulsion from the party was promised if the Opposition continued their factional activity.[42]

The Eleventh Congress of the party, held in late March and early April 1922, was the last under Lenin's leadership. Unity and discipline more than ever were the themes foremost in the minds of the party leaders, while the voice of the Opposition was, except for one unforseen moment, hardly more than an echo. The manner in which the proceedings of the congress was conducted, however, shows that the leadership remained in an anxious state about the possible crystallization of an opposition force. Resolutions were rushed through in great haste, especially in the final session, and often votes were called for and secured before the proponents of amendments could bring them to the floor. Nominations for the various committees which the congress set up were carefully prepared ahead of time, and the hand of the party Secretariat was particularly evident in this work.

Lenin wasted no time in affirming the ruthlessness which he felt necessary to maintain the solidarity of the party: "If people begin a panic . . . it is essential to punish the slightest infraction of discipline severely, cruelly, unmercifully." Since the NEP was a retreat, order in the party ranks was all the more essential: "When such a retreat occurs in a real army, they set up machine guns, and when the orderly retreat changes into a disorderly one, they command 'Fire!' And quite correctly."[43] Though Lenin acknowledged a diminution in opposition activity, the delegates were called upon to sanction redoubled efforts to root out factionalism: "It is necessary to wage a decisive struggle with all the authority of the party as a whole and of its local organizations against any kind of manifestations which disrupt the organization of the party. . . . The party as a whole must look upon the introduction of any squabbles and discords as the most serious crime against the party."[44]

The indefatigable spokesmen of the Ultra-Left still returned persistently to their familiar criticisms. Once again, Osinsky complained of "the exaggeration of discipline which gives to our centers the possibility of acting too arbitrarily"; he urged a "shift from military discipline to a strict but genuinely party discipline." Not tightening but relaxation, he insisted, was the way to strengthen the party.[45] The small number of practicing proletarians in the party, and the very limited role which they could play, were pointed out by Kollontai. This she attributed to "the regime which exists in the party. It is necessary to change it in order that the workers will feel 'at home' in the party and will be able to carry out their class, workers' policy." She made a pointed and obviously embarrassing effort to hold the leadership up to their professions of "workers' democracy": "We stand for the decision of the Tenth Congress on workers' democracy and freedom of intraparty criticism, we want it to be put into effect, and we will do everything to confirm workers' democracy, not on paper, not in words, but in deed. . . . In the creativity of the working masses lies our salvation!"[46]

Opposition crystallized in surprising strength on the question of the chief discipline-enforcing agencies, the control commissions. Riazanov, here using his last opportunity to voice a protest in behalf of party democracy, demanded the outright abolition of the commissions.[47] Solts, the chairman of the Central Control Commission, complained that "there exists an opinion among certain groups that the control commissions were appointed for a limited period . . . [or] that the control commissions were a mistake." In reality,

Solts maintained, the work of the control commissions in enforcing doctrinal and moral standards in the party had become more important than ever. Illustrating the trend back to prerevolutionary Bolshevism, Solts specifically cited Lenin's "What is to be Done?" to prove the need for discipline: "Now we need discipline more than before, and it is necessary because the enemy is not as visible as before. When there is a breathing-space, there appears among us the wish to be liberated from the yoke of the party. We begin to think that such a moment has arrived, but it has not arrived."[48] It did not seem to matter that the party had changed from an underground conspiracy to a ruling elite. The old habits of suspicion, dogmatism, intolerance, of a military mode of life and social relationships, were asserting themselves and stamping their image upon the new Soviet state.

The party leaders were manifestly disturbed by the hostility which the control commissions had engendered. Solts called for a vote of confidence in proposing a resolution to the effect that the congress "considers the activity of the Central Control Commission correct, and confirms the necessity for the continued existence at the center and in the provinces of the control commissions." His resolution also urged increased authority for the Central Control Commission to supervise work in the provinces, and stressed the role of the commissions in keeping the party as a whole in line behind the leadership: "On the control commissions rests the serious and important task of warning against, and struggling with, intrigues and groupings."[49]

An Opposition resolution was immediately introduced proposing the abolition of all the local control commissions and the subjection of the Central Control Commission to much more thorough supervision by the Central Committee. A voice vote was first taken, and the two sides appeared to be so equally balanced that someone proposed drawing up a new compromise resolution. However, the chairman declared, "First of all we must establish exactly, so that the congress can know, where lie the majority and the minority, and just how large the majority is." It is clear from these remarks that the voice vote must have been extremely close. Yet when the count was taken, there were 223 votes recorded in favor of retaining the control commissions, and only 89 opposed.[50] Since there were 523 voting delegates present, it is obvious that only abstentions or the losing of ballots saved the day for the control commissions. Never again was the party apparatus to come so close to defeat.

THE PARTY BUREAUCRACY AS A POLITICAL POWER

The renewed stress on party discipline in 1921, and the continued necessity of organizational tightening to put a stop to Ultra-Left deviations claiming sole proletarian virtue, placed a premium on the development of the machinery of organizational control. The entire future evolution of the Soviet regime depended in large measure on what was happening in the realm of organization. More extreme centralization and stricter discipline gave the party leadership the machinery whereby any extensive expression of opposition from the rank and file could be suppressed, if not forestalled altogether. Later on, the only serious Opposition challenges came from splits among the top party leaders themselves. Even in these cases, the outcome was determined by control over the party machinery—and the consequence was the unbroken succession of Stalin's victories.

The trend toward a bureaucratic structure within the party became unmistakable after the shake-up at the Tenth Congress. A resolution of the Eleventh Congress admitted this frankly: "The organizations of the party have begun to be systematically overgrown with a large apparatus which serves the party organizations. This apparatus, gradually expanding, has itself, in turn, begun to make bureaucratic inroads and to engulf an excessive amount of [the party's] forces."[51] Distinctive social effects stemmed from the militarized pattern of party life. The subjection of those party members who performed full-time party work (including party assignments in the government, army, and trade unions) to a special, quasi-military discipline, together with the practice of frequent transfers, began to create a cleavage in outlook, personal associations, influence, and eventually in status between the full-time party worker and the ordinary party member who helped with party work only in his spare time. Party activities came to be dominated by a permanent and distinct group of party officials. These people were further distinguished by economic advantage, thanks to what the Declaration of the Forty-six in the fall of 1923 described as "a sharp divergence in the material position of members of the party in connection with differences in their functions."[52]

Concurrent with the process of bureaucratization in the party was the elaboration and perfection of the institutions of party organization and control. As the result of the development of these organs and the accretion of power to the people who directed them, the Communist Party was speedily transformed into a bureaucratic monolith running far beyond Lenin's own demands for a centralized movement. The evolution of the party's organizational machinery proceeded along three lines, corresponding to three main organizational needs: (1) overall authority and policy making; (2) control over the membership as a whole and the enforcement of party discipline and standards of morality; (3) supervision of local organizations and control over the appointment of party officials and full-time party workers. The centralization of these three functions was completed chronologically roughly in the above order.

In the realm of decision making, by 1921 the party was close to the perfect military pattern of chain of command, with a pyramidal structure of party secretaries, each individually in charge of his territory. At the top, however, authority remained collective, except for Lenin's personal pre-eminence. Until 1922 there was no office within the party which conferred individual authority over the whole movement. Only in 1922, with the creation of the office of general secretary and the appointment to it of Stalin, was the secretarial hierarchy completed at the top. In 1929, when the Opposition had been crushed and the Politburo was packed with Stalin's supporters, the general secretaryship finally emerged as the unchallenged summit of the party structure.

The disciplinary function of the party was embodied in the Central Control Commission which, after the great expansion of its powers and scope at the Tenth Congress, became one of the key weapons of the party leadership. As Gusev, a new member of the commission, put it, "The Central Committee establishes the party line, while the Central Control Commission sees that no one deviates from it, and takes measures to correct deviations and bring the deviators back into line." The means used to accomplish this end were not the most gentle, as Gusev frankly indicated: "Authority is acquired not only by work, but by fear. And now the Central Control Commission and the Workers' and Peasants' Inspection have already succeeded in imposing this fear. In this respect their authority is growing."[53]

The third task of the party organization—controlling local organizations and officials—was performed by the new secretarial apparatus.[54] The Secretariat had two important organizational agencies, both established in 1920 but set in full operation only in 1921 and 1922. These were the Record and Assignment Division (*uchetno-raspredelitelny otdel*), responsible for checking on the individuals who made up the party's corps of full-time officials and recommending their promotion or transfer; and the Organization and Instruction Division (*organizatsionno-instruktorski otdel*), which maintained relations with local party organizations and supervized their work. Stalin asserted in 1923, in describing the work of these agencies, "These organs now have a colossal and primary importance, for this is the greatest real means for keeping all the threads of the economy and the soviet apparatus in the hands of the party."[55] Other measures for the exertion of central influence in the provinces were the dispatch of "responsible instructors" to check on local work and communicate the desires of the center, visits to local conferences by prestigeful Central Committee members, and the appointment of special subcommittees of the Central Committee to make investigations and recommendations whenever serious disturbances occurred in a local party unit. The resources for effective central influence over the local organizations to which the leadership was in theory responsible were impressive.

Of key importance was the practice, well established by 1922, of *de facto* appointment of local party secretaries by the next higher official in the organizational hierarchy. This was done in the guise of "recommendation," while the appearances of election by the local committees were still observed. In the selection of secretaries the work of the new Record and Assignment Division was decisive. The appointment policy of the Secretariat was soon under fire for deliberate discrimination against former oppositionists, "not because they are poor organizers, not because they are bad Communists, but only because, at various times and in various ways, they participated in one or another grouping, took part in controversies against the official line set forth by the Central Committee."[56]

Trotsky launched into a bitter attack on the appointment of secretaries just before he went into open opposition in 1923: "In the fiercest moment of War Communism, the system of appointment within the party did not have one tenth of the extent that it has now. Appointment of the secretaries of provincial committees is now the rule. That creates for the secretary a position essentially independent of the local organization. . . . The bureaucratization of the party apparatus has developed to unheard-of proportions by means of the method of secretarial selection."[57] Since the secretaries were gaining more and more local power, at the expense of committees and conferences, the net result was to confer upon the central Secretariat a potentially absolute power over the whole party.

A particularly graphic instance of the imposition of central control occurred in the party organization of the Samara province on the Volga. Samara was the one case where the Workers' Opposition got control of a provincial organization, when the local strong man, Y. K. Milonov, decided to join the Ultra-Left.[58] In the course of 1921 the central Secretariat, determined to root out the deviationists, alleged all manner of organizational deficiencies in Samara—"a complete absence of party discipline and party ties between the responsible comrades on the one hand and the party masses on the other." Finally, as it had done with the Ukraine in 1920, Moscow applied its appointive power, backed by all the sanctions of party discipline; the Samara Opposition leaders were ordered to jobs elsewhere, and a new organizational staff was sent in. Molotov said in justification of the action, "Leaving the organization any longer in such a situation was intolerable. This was the only provincial organization where the Central Committee removed the whole upper group of party and soviet workers. . . . The Central Committee does not regret it."[59]

With its combined powers of pressure, persuasion, and appointment, the Secretariat could, given a little time, control the politics of any local organization, including the provincial party conferences. These assemblies elected the delegates to the national congresses, the theoretically sovereign institution. Thus the people in control of the central organization could contrive, if they worked patiently enough, to pack and control the party congress.

Stalin was beginning to do precisely this, as early as 1923. The congress, in turn, controlled the Central Committee; or, in more realistic terms, the man who controlled the delegates could swing the choice of new Central Committee members. The final development took a period of years, as Stalin from his base in the Central Commitee went on to dominate the Politburo, purge it of his rivals, and make himself undisputed master of the party.

Roughly by the end of 1922, the party's secretarial machinery, both central and local, was complete and in full operation. Lenin's desire for organizational means to combat the Opposition had been answered in full measure. The apparatus, however, was not simply the unthinking, ready instrument of the party's executive leadership. It had become a core of people with some sense of group interest, and as distinct from the rank-and-file party members as from the population at large.

By a process of natural selection the key jobs in the party apparatus were filled with the kind of people who performed well in a hierarchical, disciplined organization, and who were much less concerned with the Bolshevik ideals of 1917 than with those of 1902. Such were the individuals who made good *apparatchiki*—"apparatus men"—who carried out orders effectively and were resolute in combating opposition activities. Above all, these people were bound by a powerful sense of loyalty to Lenin, evidencing a strong compulsion to have and to enforce an airtight faith. In opposition to the Leftists who retained in varying degrees the idealism of 1917, the more pragmatic followers of Lenin and Stalin began to exemplify in an increasing degree the principles of Bolshevik hardness enunciated by Lenin in the early years of the party's history. In 1920 there appeared what seems to be the first explicit reference made after the revolution to Lenin's "What is to be Done" and "One Step Forward, Two Steps Back"—the most rigorous formulations of the doctrine of organizational hardness. The author of this reference was none other than Stalin, whose opinion was that in these writings Lenin "completely answered Russian reality and masterfully generalized the organizational experience of the best practical workers."[60]

Even before he was appointed to the new office of general secretary in May 1922, Stalin was the party's leading organization man. He was on the Politburo from its inception in 1919 and also served as Commissar of the Workers' and Peasants' Inspection, the governmental organization responsible for bureaucratic rectitude and efficiency. Thanks to the organizational overturn of 1921, Stalin was the dominant man in the Orgburo and the power behind the new Secretariat; he was the logical man for the general secretaryship. In spite of possible qualms about Stalin's character, Lenin valued his organizational talents, as Trotsky later conceded: "Undoubtedly he valued certain of Stalin's traits very highly, his firmness of character, his persistence, even his ruthlessness and conniving," though he "demurred to the candidacy . . . with the observation, 'That cook will concoct nothing but peppery dishes.' "[61] According to one report, Stalin's appointment was not a matter of forethought for Lenin. A meeting of the heads of delegations at the Eleventh Party Congress was considering the organizational question, and made Molotov the butt of much criticism. Someone proposed to drop him as a secretary and appoint Ivan Smirnov as first secretary of the party (he was the Trotskyist ex-secretary of the Petrograd organization, then serving in Siberia). Lenin hesitated, and then replied that Smirnov was "essential" in Siberia. To cries of "Who?" he responded, "Wait till tomorrow." The next day Lenin was ready with his proposal to create the office of general secretary and to appoint Stalin to fill it.[62] Few people openly objected to Stalin's appointment. Only Preobrazhensky, one of the ex-secretaries displaced by the Stalinists, complained about one individual being allowed to hold such a variety of responsible jobs.[63]

Simultaneously with Stalin's elevation to the general secretaryship, the top party organs were shaken up again. Of the three former secretaries only Molotov was retained in that capacity. A new man joined him as Stalin's other deputy—Valerian Kuibyshev, a Bolshevik undergrounder since 1904 (when he was sixteen), who had evidently become attached to Stalin during the Civil War.[64] Kuibyshev was destined to play a key role in the establishment of Stalin's dictatorship. He was chairman of the Central Control Commission from 1923 to 1926 and then became head of the Supreme Economic Council, where he was instrumental in working out the new line of intensive industrialization which Stalin followed after 1928. He came to grief in 1935, allegedly as the victim of a medical murder for which the then Interior Commissar Yagoda and his medical accomplices were tried and executed in 1938.

Possession of the juridical headship of the party organization was extremely important to Stalin in his rise to power. It was not as an individual but as the representative, almost the embodiment, of the secretarial machinery that Stalin accumulated power and prepared the ground for his absolute rule. The loyalty of the secretaries was less to the man than to the duly constituted party authority. While Stalin was certainly concerned with staffing the organization with people who were reliable from his point of view, the converse process was no doubt equally effective: people working in the apparatus and molded by this experience naturally developed a sense of loyalty to the man under whose direction they served and whose favor was necessary to their advancement. Of the prominent party members listed in the index of names in the Protocols of the Eleventh Party Congress, only 16 per cent of those in party work became oppositionists by 1930, whereas 50 per cent of those working in the government and other institutions found themselves in one deviation or another by that time. Personal inclination was also a factor in this divergence; authority and discipline appealed to the nonintellectual undergrounders who were coming up in the party machine, and Stalin was a man of their own type with whom they could readily sympathize. According to the recollections of a "nonreturner" diplomat of the thirties, "All the increasingly numerous members of the party who came from among the masses followed the Stalin group, chiefly because they found in it, in its efforts, in its ideas, in the very psychology of the people composing it, that which was most like their own." [65]

8

THE INTERREGNUM

In 1922, the appalling urgency of fundamental questions facing the Communist Party leaders had abated. Basic decisions were now in effect governing the Soviet regime's economic policy and political life—relaxation and restraint, respectively. The imminence of world revolutionary upheaval had now been discounted, and Soviet Russia was beginning to make its way back into the international community. The underlying issues that had divided the Communist movement were muted, but both the major steps of 1921, economic retreat and political tightening, commanded general support among the party leaders only as temporary measures. When the crisis of succession struck, controversy was ready to erupt anew.

THE SUCCESSION AND THE TROIKA

On May 24, 1922, at the age of fifty-two, Lenin was stricken with a cerebral hemorrhage. From then until the time of his death on January 21, 1924, except for brief periods in the fall and winter of 1922–1923, he was totally removed from the political life of the country.[1] Seven years of political turmoil were to follow before a like degree of personal leadership was restored in Soviet Russia.

Lenin's passing from the scene upset the whole system of Communist authority. Strictly speaking, Lenin had not been a dictator. As far as the rules of the party were concerned, he was only one member of the Politburo. His power was strictly personal, the classical *auctoritas,* the authority of fame, wisdom, incomparable prestige, and personal loyalties. Lenin cast a spell over the whole movement, and a large part of the party—the "Leninists"—instinctively looked to him for the last word on every question. His words were not without weight even for the most diehard oppositionist.

But opposition did exist, even though Lenin himself had sanctioned the organizational steps which were ultimately to stifle all independent thought. Again and again there were bold individuals who attacked Lenin to his face, without suffering personal reprisals. Party business at the top level was decided by vote, and Lenin actually suffered defeats from time to time. He would not defy a vote of the Central Commitee which balked him, as, for example, over expelling Shliapnikov in 1921. Lenin's recourse was persuasion, rather than dictation; he would take his case to the party membership, and in that forum, with the unique prestige he enjoyed, he was always able to get his way.

Lenin was not rancorous as long as he did not feel vitally challenged. He forgave the oppositions of the Right in 1917 and of the Left in 1918, and appealed eloquently to the Workers' Opposition in 1921 for a similar reconciliation, conditional, of course, upon their renunciation of their deviation. In 1920, apropos of the new control commission, Lenin wrote, "There is recommended a deep, individualized relationship with, and sometimes even a type of therapy for, the representatives of the so-called Opposition, those who have experienced a psychological crisis because of failure in their soviet or party career. An effort should be made to quiet them, to explain the matter to them in a way used among comrades."[2]

The nature of Lenin's leadership, commanding but informal, made it all the harder for the dominant Leninist faction to rule without him. They were deprived of his unhesitating power of decision; responsibility was thrust upon them, and they were unused to it. They lacked his ability to convince the hesitant and confute the dissident. The party now functioned on bureaucratic and hierarchical lines predicated on a commanding voice at the top, but Lenin's power could not be transmitted. When he fell ill, the position of *de facto* number-one leader was gone. The logic of Communist politics cried for the gap to be filled. The general secretary was making ready.

During Lenin's absence from the government, which they desperately hoped was temporary, the party leaders fell back upon the letter of the law—the formula of "collective leadership." The party, and hence the government, were to be guided as the statutes read—by authority of the Central Committee, delegated to the Politburo. Informally it came to be understood in the ruling circles that day-to-day executive responsibility would be shared by the senior Politburo members (apart from Trotsky)—the "troika" or triumvirate of Zinoviev, Kamenev, and Stalin.[3] Meanwhile, in the manner of all governments set off balance by illness, outward calm was pretended; *Pravda* belatedly mentioned that Lenin was ill but expressed no alarm.[4]

It is revealing of the intensity of Lenin's leadership that none of the three men who picked up the reins had distingushed himself in character or statesmanship. They were second-rate politicians, anxious and scheming. Lenin never had a follower of stature who was not driven into the Opposition or out of the party altogether. It is particularly evident in the case of Zinoviev that his very mediocrity was the reason for his prominence both under Lenin and afterwards. To Lenin he was a pliable instrument, noted for his readiness to perform dirty jobs for the leader.[5] To the rest of the leaders he was acceptable because he was not strong enough to fear. It was on this shaky foundation that Zinoviev climbed, as *primus inter pares,* to pose as the leader of the Russian Communist Party for the next three years.

Grigori Yevseyevich Zinoviev was still in his thirties when the responsibilities of leadership fell to him. He was born in 1883, of middle-class Jewish antecedents; became a Bolshevik at the age of twenty; and had been one of Lenin's chief henchmen since 1907.[6] He was an orator of formidable endurance, the archtype of the revolutionary agitator and journalist. He avoided administrative work—other than the chairmanship of the Petrograd Soviet, he never held a position in the government as such. With his wild appearance, answering to the bourgeois stereotype of the revolutionary, Zinoviev was well cast in the role of chairman of the Communist International. History has provided few to testify in Zinoviev's defense. By reputation he was unscrupulous and cowardly. Sverdlov reportedly once called him "panic personified," and Lenin is said to have complained of him, "He copies my faults."[7] Lack of nerve no doubt contributed to Zinoviev's lapse into opposition in the fall of 1917, and again in 1925 fear underlay his break with the party leadership. He was always prepared to recant, and no one had more opportunity.

The second member of the troika, Liov Borisovich Kamenev, was Zinoviev's *alter ego* from 1917 to the very end. He was the same age, with much the same background and revolutionary career.[8] There were differences, though: Kamenev was bearded, dignified, and uninteresting. Despite his prominence—he was the first Bolshevik chairman of the Congress of Soviets (in October 1917) and a member of the original Politburo of 1919—he remains a strangely indefinite figure. He busied himself in a variety of administrative jobs (including the deputy chairmanship of the Council of People's Commissars), perennially presided over the Moscow Soviet, and hardly ever made a political move except as Zinoviev's shadow.

Of Stalin little can be said that is not already familiar. He had risen to prominence because he was useful to Lenin, but unlike the other two triumvirs he had established an independent base of power in the secretarial machinery. He was undoubtedly a help to his colleagues and was not famous enough to be considered a political threat. Stalin kept his political ambitions in the background, if he consciously entertained them this early. Trotsky later wrote voluminously on the theme of Stalin's "mediocrity" and obscurity. The contemporary accuracy of this opinion was long afterwards confirmed; as Khrushchev declared in his sensational secret speech to the Twentieth Party Congress in February 1956, "I will probably not sin against the truth when I say that 99 per cent of the persons present here heard and knew very little about Stalin before the year 1924."[9]

Besides the ailing Lenin, Trotsky, and the three triumvirs, there were two others in the Politburo, supporters of the anti-Trotsky coalition, whose bureaucratic reliability had just won them seats in the top party group. The trade-union chief Tomsky was forty-two and Rykov, the chairman of the Supreme Economic Council, forty-one.[10] They were both exemplars of caution, with long right-wing records going back to the "conciliationist" movement between 1907 and 1912. Tomsky's adaptable dependence was dramatized by his sudden removal from the trade-union post and his equally sudden reinstatement.

Thus it was that four and a half years after its birth, the dynamic revolutionary regime of Russian Communism found itself in the hands of three industrious mediocrities, a boring demagogue, and a treacherous schemer. The analogy with France's Directoire is not hard to draw.

The new leadership was by no means secure from the threat of Trotsky. Trotsky was the one leader whose personal prestige approached the order of Lenin's. Trotsky was the leader of the October insurrection, the architect of victory in the Civil War; Trotsky's name was intimately associated with Lenin's in the popular mind. At the time it was possible to conceive of only one person who could succeed, albeit imperfectly, to Lenin's individual leadership, and that person was Trotsky.

The Leninist leaders were determined to forestall such an eventuality. Trotsky's popularity was great among the rank and file, but it did not extend to his colleagues at the top level of the party. He was both disliked and feared. The habit of drawing parallels with revolutionary France caused new alarm about the danger of "Bonapartism."[11] Trotsky was indeed an ambitious politician whose position rested on his military reputation and his command of the armed forces. Moreover, in a strictly Bolshevik context, he was the leader of a potential opposition. In terms of both personalities and programmatic inclinations, the moderate Left Opposition which had last defied the Leninists in 1920–1921 was still largely intact. The secretarial hierarchy was particularly threatened; if Trotsky and his supporters were to prevail in the top councils of the party, it was logical to expect an organizational shake-up to undo the one that was carried out after the Tenth Congress. It was in the compelling interest of the Leninists to close ranks against Trotsky at every level. "The weaker the trio felt in matters of principle," wrote Trotsky afterwards, "the more they feared me—becaused they wanted to get rid of me—and the tighter they had to bolt all the screws and nuts in the state and party system. Much later, in 1925, Bukharin said to me, in answer to my criticism of the party oppression: 'We have no democracy because we are afraid of you.'"[12]

Trotsky himself was not entirely inactive. In the fall of 1922 he succeeded, so it appears, in effecting a shake-up in the political branch of the army. Trotsky's antagonist Gusev was removed as head of the Political Administration of the Revolutionary Military Council (and was shortly afterwards compensated with an appointment to the Central Control Commission, where he steadily supported Stalin). He was replaced by Trotsky's old collaborator, Antonov-Ovseyenko, who had won prominence as a military leader in the October uprising and in the Ukraine.[13]

The hostility between Trotsky and the Leninist leaders, especially Zinoviev and Stalin, was heightened by the background of personal friction and animosity. Ever since he became a Bolshevik in 1917 Trotsky had been antagonizing Zinoviev. Zinoviev, a vain blowhard, could not forgive Trotsky for displacing him from the number-two spot in the party and for oratorically eclipsing him as the tribune of revolution. No two Bolshevik leaders were more consistently in disagreement; in every major party controversy—1917, 1918, 1920–1921, not to mention the military issue—Trotsky and Zinoviev were on opposite sides. Particularly galling to Zinoviev's pride was Trotsky's having to rush to the rescue of Petrograd at the time of the White breakthrough in the fall of 1919.

In comparison with the Zinoviev-Trotsky feud, the frictions between Trotsky and Stalin were of little moment; they have been magnified out of proportion as a natural consequence of the later historic duel between the two men. Stalin did not pretend to outshine Trotsky while Lenin was still in command, and the slights which he suffered at the hands of the domineering War Commissar, as at Tsaritsyn, undoubtedly were like those familiar to many other individuals. Trotsky's character—his arrogance, confidence, brilliance, and brusqueness, together with his inability or unwillingness to indulge in petty personal politiking—served to make him widely disliked, especially among the less colorful, nonintellectual party wheel horses who were coming to staff the organizational machinery. "Trotsky has always been among the impatient comrades," declared Zinoviev later. "He has always thought that everything was going wrong. . . . Trotsky is an expressed individualist. This makes it impossible that he should ever form a firm faction."[14] It was particularly convenient to Trotsky's enemies that he was not an "Old Bolshevik"; this fact was repeatedly employed to stir the resentment of the old-timers who had come all the way with Lenin.

Trotsky's ambitions were restrained by the fact that Lenin, while removed from actual leadership by his stroke, continued to live and, as long as he did, no one could be so presumptuous as to take overt steps toward establishing himself as the official successor. Since the end of the Civil War, Trotsky's prestige had been on the wane, especially as a result of his unsuccessful venture into opposition on the trade-union question in 1920–1921. The Leninists were able to keep Trotsky more or less in partial eclipse during the crucial interregnum while Lenin lived but did not rule.

THE NATIONALITY QUESTION AND THE LENIN-STALIN BREAK

The interregnum was briefly suspended in the fall of 1922. Lenin recovered sufficiently to resume active leadership for three months, until his second stroke in December. He was able to write occasionally until a third stroke in March 1923 eliminated him finally from the Soviet political scene. During his brief return to work Lenin found the conduct of his disciples less than satisfactory. Awakening to some of the dangers inherent in the rigorous intraparty regime which he himself had set up in 1921, he broke openly with Stalin and began to examine the need for fundamental political and social reforms. Time was running out for him, however, and his successors were soon left to their old ways.

Ironically, the matter over which Lenin and Stalin parted company lay in the very field in which the general secretary was supposed to be the party's expert—policy toward the non-Russian national minorities in the Soviet realm. The question at issue was the formation of a new kind of political entity embracing the nominally independent Soviet Republics—Russia (the RSFSR), the Ukraine, Belorussia, Georgia, Armenia, and Azerbaijan— which, though in fact governed as a unit by the Russian Communist Party, had legally been tied together only by treaties. To prepare for a formal union, many people (including Stalin) wished to combine the three small Transcaucasian republics into one federated republic, which would join the new union together with the other three. Ordzhonikidze, as secretary of the Transcaucasian Regional Bureau of the party, was the man locally in charge of putting the federation into effect. The local Georgian Communists, whose country had only been brought under Soviet rule by Red Army intervention early in 1921, were still sensitive on the score of national independence and equality, and they vigorously resisted the planned Transcaucasian federation. The result was a fight which shook the Kremlin.

Soon after Lenin resumed work, his attention was attracted to the situation in Georgia. On September 15, 1922, the Central Commitee of the Communist Party of Georgia (a branch of the RCP) passed a resolution opposing Stalin's plan to tighten the loose Transcaucasian federation which had been set up the previous spring.[15] The leader of the Georgian Opposition, Budu Mdivani, supplemented this by complaining directly to Lenin, and Lenin responded with a note to his colleagues in the party leadership: "In my opinion the question is super-important. Stalin has a little tendency to hurry."[16] Stalin dispatched his rebuttal to the Politburo the same day, and assumed a remarkably independent tone in criticizing Lenin's own "hurriedness" and the plan of separate central executive committees for the Russian republic and for the union.[17] "Lenin is kaputt," Stalin is supposed to have said when he found out for himself the severity of the leader's illness. Relieved of the necessity of toadying to Lenin, Stalin had quickly begun to reach for power.[18]

A week or so later Lenin expressed himself strongly against "Great Russian chauvinism," but he went ahead to endorse the action of the Central Commitee in mid-October in approving Stalin's plan for the Union of Soviet Socialist Republics, to include Transcaucasia.[19] Stalin, in triumph, wired the Georgian rebels that their protests had been unanimously rejected by the Central Committee.[20] The Georgians were incensed, and they disregarded party channels to make an appeal to Bukharin, on whose sympathy they believed they could count.[21] This evidence of insubordination stirred Lenin's ire, and he rebuked the Georgians in a personal reply: "I am astonished at the unseemly tone of the wire. . . . I was sure that the differences were settled by the decision of the Plenum of the Central Committee with my participation, and with the direct participation of Mdivani. Therefore I decidedly condemn the vituperation against Ordzhonikidze, and insist that you submit your conflict in a decent and loyal tone for settlement by the Secretariat of the Central Committee."[22] Lenin still relied on the authority of Stalin as the general secretary to maintain order and discipline within the party. This was probably due to the persistence of his habit of centralized organizational work, rather than to any special desire to appease Stalin, as Trotsky hints.[23] Lenin's telegram is striking evidence of the meagre degree of independence accorded the Communist Party of a supposedly independent republic.

On the very day that Lenin took it to task, the Georgian Central Committee passed another defiant resolution demanding the dissolution of the Transcaucasian federation and the direct entry of Georgia into the USSR. This was the signal for Stalin and Ordzhonikidze to launch their offensive— a sweeping five-months-long purge of the Communist leadership in Georgia. As Lavrenti Beria boasted in his once-official account, "The Transcaucasian party organization, under the leadership of Comrade S. Ordzhonikidze, dealt a crushing blow to national deviationism."[24] Typical methods of central pressure were applied through Ordzhonikidze. His Transcaucasian Regional Committee, operating in the Georgian capital, Tiflis, obstructed the routine work of the Georgian Central Committee, by-passed it to interfere in the subordinate party organizations in Georgia, and encouraged political excesses —"the most 'leftist leftism.' "[25] Armed with Lenin's criticism of their opponents, the Stalin-Ordzhonikidze forces compelled the whole Mdivani Central Committee to resign and replaced it with a new group, subservient to the party apparatus and acquiescent about the Transcaucasian federation.

The struggle was bitter, and Ordzhonikidze was responsible for violence of some sort. There must have been cries of anguish which Moscow could not ignore, for the Central Committee was compelled to dispatch to Georgia a special commission, composed of Dzerzhinsky (a Pole), Manuilsky (sometimes credited with Ukrainian nationality), and Mitskevich-Kapsukas (of Lithuanian and Belorussian descent).[26] The commission found in favor of Ordzhonikidze and the central apparatus, against the Georgian nationalists. Its decision was upheld by the Orgburo, and most of the Georgian leaders were ordered to Moscow.[27] Only action by Lenin could have saved the Georgian Opposition. Meanwhile, the plans for the Transcaucasian federation and for the union of all the Soviet Republics were rushed into effect under Stalin's direction. On December 30, 1922, the Union of Soviet Socialist Republics was formally proclaimed.

Excesses of centralism, uncomplicated by other issues, did not worry Lenin. He had no scruples about deposing the whole Central Committee of the Ukrainian Communist Party in 1920 and seems to have been prepared to go just as far in disciplining the Georgians. What alarmed him was the insult to the forms of national autonomy (even though in party matters he required strict subordination). By the end of December Lenin's views on Georgia had changed completely. At the same time he began to regard Stalin in a new light.

A critical turning point was Lenin's second stroke, which he suffered on December 16. Although less severe than the first, it must have made Lenin and his entourage realize that his days were numbered. In the face of this personal calamity Stalin was scrambling to pick up the keys to power. The result was a clash with Lenin's wife, Krupskaya, which occasioned the following plea from her to Kamenev.[28]

Liov Borisovich!

Because of a short letter which I had written in words dictated to me by Vladimir Ilich by permission of the doctors, Stalin allowed himself yesterday an unusually rude outburst directed at me. This is not my first duty to the party. During all these thirty years I have never heard from any comrade one word of rudeness. The business of the party and of Ilich are not less dear to me than to Stalin. I need at present the maximum of self-control. What one can and what one cannot discuss with Ilich, I know better than any doctor, because I know what makes him nervous and what does not; in any case, I know better than Stalin. I am turning to you and to Grigory [Zinoviev] as to much closer comrades of V. I., and I beg you to protect me from rude interference with my private life and from vile invectives and threats. I have no doubt as to what will be the unanimous decision of the Control Commission, with which Stalin sees fit to threaten me; however, I have neither the strength nor the time to waste on this foolish quarrel. And I am a living person and my nerves are strained to the utmost.

N. Krupskaya
[December 23, 1922]

On December 25, 1922, anticipating the end, Lenin composed the memorandum which has come to be known as his "Testament," in which he expressed his hopes and fears about his successors:

I have in mind stability as a guarantee against a split in the near future, and I intend to examine here a series of considerations of a purely personal character. I think that the fundamental factor in the matter of stability—from this point of view—is such members of the Central Committee as Stalin and Trotsky. The relation between them constitutes, in my opinion, a big half of the danger of that split, which might be avoided. . . .

Comrade Stalin, having become General Secretary, has concentrated an enormous power in his hands; and I am not sure that he always knows how to use that power with sufficient caution. On the other hand, Comrade Trotsky, as was proved by his struggle against the Central Committee in connection with the question of the People's Commissariat of Ways and Communication, is distinguished not only by his exceptional ability—personally, he is, to be sure, the most able man in the present Central Committee—but also by his too far-reaching self-confidence and a disposition to be far too much attracted by the purely administrative side of affairs.

These two qualities of the two most able leaders of the present Central Committee might, quite innocently, lead to a split, and if our party does not take measures to prevent it, a split might arise unexpectedly.[29]

A collective leadership was clearly what Lenin wished for, but he was well aware of how the personalities of his most able lieutenants endangered this solution.

Just after writing this comment on the leadership, Lenin received new information on the Georgian situation. With a personal report from Dzerzhinsky, supplemented by data which his secretaries gathered, Lenin arrived at a radically new view of the matter. On December 30 and 31, he committed his misgivings to paper at some length, in a "Letter on the National Question": "If matters have gone so far that Ordzhonikidze could lose his temper and resort to physical violence, about which Comrade Dzerzhinsky told me, then you can imagine what kind of a bog we have got into. Obviously, all this fiction of 'autonomization' was basically insincere and inopportune."[30] Lenin then discounted the formal protection accorded the national minorities by the union as proposed: " 'The freedom to secede from the Union' . . . is an empty scrap of paper, incapable of defending the other nationalities of Russia from the aggression of that truly Russian man, the Great Russian chauvinist. . . ." Moreover, the execution of the union proposal was unnecessarily harsh:

I think that here Stalin's haste and administrator's impulses have played a fatal role, and also his anger against the notorious "social-nationalism." Anger in general plays the very worst role in politics. I fear also that Comrade Dzerzhinsky, who went to the Caucasus to "investigate" the matter of the "crimes" of these "social-nationalists," is distinguished here only by his truly Russian tendency (it is known that the Russified non-Russian always overdoes things in the truly Russian direction), and that the impartiality of his whole commission is sufficiently illustrated by Ordzhonikidze's violence.

In his second note, on December 31, Lenin distinguished the nationalism of the oppressor nation and that of the oppressed, and underscored the importance of the national question in the class struggle: "For the proletariat it is . . . essentially necessary to guarantee the maximum confidence in the proletarian class struggle on the part of the other nationalities. . . . For this not only is formal equality necessary, for this it is necessary to compensate, in one way or another by our treatment or concessions in regard to the non-Russian, for that distrust, that suspiciousness, those wrongs, which in the

historical past were inflicted upon him by the ruling 'great-power' nation. . . .
It is better to go too far on the side of conciliation and softness toward the
national minorities, than not to go far enough."

Lenin's third note, also of December 31, urged a special code of nationality rights to guard against abuses of Russification and recommended corrective measures: "It is necessary to punish Comrade Ordzhonikidze as an
example . . . and also to inquire into and investigate again all the materials
of Dzerzhinsky's commission, with the object of correcting the vast mass
of incorrect and biased judgments which are undoubtedly contained therein.
We should, of course, make Stalin and Dzerzhinsky politically responsible
for this whole truly Great Russian nationalist campaign." Fortunately for
the comrades here rebuked, the notes remained unpublished for the time
being, and no action was taken along the lines suggested by Lenin.

Following his comments on the Georgian situation, Lenin turned back
to revise his notes on the party leadership, and on January 4, 1923, he added
a postscript to the "Testament." He had become convinced that one of his
leading subordinates was too great a threat to the unified collective leadership which he sought:

Postscript: Stalin is too rude, and this fault, entirely supportable in relations among
us Communists, becomes insupportable in the office of General Secretary. Therefore, I propose to the comrades to find a way to remove Stalin from that position
and appoint another man who in all respects differs from Stalin only in superiority—namely, more patient, more loyal, more polite and more attentive to comrades, less capricious, etc. This circumstance may seem an insignificant trifle, but
I think that from the point of view of the relation between Stalin and Trotsky
which I discussed above, it is not a trifle, or it is such a trifle as may acquire a
decisive significance.

Only in March, it seems, did Lenin learn the full story of Stalin's behavior
toward Krupskaya, and this knowledge prompted him to dictate the following:

To Comrade Stalin:
Copies for: Kamenev and Zinoviev
Dear Comrade Stalin:
    You permitted yourself a rude summons of my wife to the telephone and a
rude reprimand of her. Despite the fact that she told you that she agreed to forget
what was said, nevertheless Zinoviev and Kamenev heard about it from her. I
have no intention to forget so easily that which is being done against me, and
I need not stress here that I consider as directed against me that which is being
done against my wife. I ask you, therefore, that you weigh carefully whether you
are agreeable to retracting your words and apologizing or whether you prefer the
severance of relations between us.

Sincerely,
Lenin [81]

March 5, 1923.

At the same time, since the Georgian party conference that would approve or repeal Stalin's purge was imminent, Lenin turned to Trotsky for support:

Esteemed Comrade Trotsky:

I would very much like to ask you to take upon yourself the defense of the Georgian case in the Central Committee of the party. The case is now under the "prosecution" of Stalin and Dzerzhinsky, and I cannot count on their impartiality. Quite the contrary, even. If you agree to take upon yourself its defense, then I could be at ease. If for some reason you do not agree, then return the whole matter to me. I will consider that the sign of your disagreement.

With the very best comradely greetings,
Lenin[32]

Lenin was by no means sure that Trotsky would uphold his position. Trotsky himself admits that before dispatching his plea for aid, Lenin had his secretary Gliasser make an investigation to determine the probability of Trotsky's opposition to the activities of Stalin.[33] Moreover, it can be seen from the wording of Lenin's note that he was not certain of Trotsky's cooperation— and this doubt was shortly vindicated. Evidently Trotsky gave his immediate assent to Lenin's request for support, and the next day, March 6, Lenin dispatched to Trotsky the text of his "Letter on the National Question." Trotsky's 1927 account follows:

When Fotieva [Lenin's other secretary] brought me the so-called "national" letter of Lenin, I suggested that since Kamenev was leaving that day for Georgia to the party congress [conference], it might be advisable to show him the letter so that he might undertake the necessary measures. Fotieva replied: "I don't know. Vladimir Ilich didn't instruct me to transmit the letter to Comrade Kamenev, but I can ask him." A few minutes later she returned with the following message: "It is entirely out of the question. Vladimir Ilich says that Kamenev would show the letter to Stalin and Stalin would make a rotten compromise in order then to deceive.[34]

In a later account, Trotsky reported the further remarks of Fotieva: "Ilich does not trust Stalin. He wants to come out openly against him before the whole party. He is preparing a bombshell."[35] Within the hour, Lenin decided to change his tactics, and made his position known in the following message:

To Comrades Mdivani, Makharadze and others:
    (Copy to Comrades Trotsky and Kamenev)
Esteemed Comrades:

I am with you in this matter with all my heart. I am outraged at the rudeness of Ordzhonikidze and the connivance of Stalin and Dzerzhinsky. I am preparing for you notes and a speech.

With esteem,
Lenin.[36]

"How do you explain this change?" Trotsky asked Fotieva.

"Evidently Vladimir Ilich is feeling worse and is in haste to do everything he can."[37]

That evening, Trotsky talked with Kamenev, who was about to depart for Tiflis. Kamenev informed him about Lenin's letter rebuking Stalin. Inexplicably, Trotsky decided not to take any action, despite the clear stand which Lenin had made against Stalin. His reply to Kamenev is reconstructed at length in his autobiography:

> The last thing I want is to start a fight at the congress for any changes in organization. I am for preserving the status quo. . . . I am against removing Stalin, and expelling Ordzhonikidze, and displacing Dzerzhinsky from the commissariat of transport. But I do agree with Lenin in substance. I want a radical change in the policy on the national question, a discontinuance of persecutions of the Georgian opponents of Stalin, a discontinuance of the administrative oppression of the party. . . . In addition, it is necessary that Stalin should write to Krupskaya at once to apologize for his rudeness, and that he revise his behavior. Let him not overreach himself. There should be no more intrigues, but honest cooperation. And you . . . when you are at the conference at Tiflis, must arrange a complete reversal of the policy toward Lenin's Georgian supporters on the national question.[38]

Kamenev and Stalin assented to these conditions, but when Lenin was permanently removed from the political scene by his third stroke on March 9, Stalin felt free to pursue his own course.

At the Georgian party conference held in mid-March, the Mdivani-Makharadze faction was overwhelmed, by a vote of one hundred twenty-four to twenty.[39] Though Kamenev tried to conduct the proceedings fairly (even by the Opposition's account),[40] the forces of the central apparatus had no difficulty in imposing their will and in reelecting their own Central Committee. Georgia was an exemplary case of the imposition of central control by the Secretariat. (The victory of the party apparatus was so complete that in the delegation elected to represent Transcaucasia at the Twelfth Party Congress, only one man out of twenty-eight—Makharadze—could be positively identified as an oppositionist. Mdivani attended the congress only as a nonvoting delegate representing the Moscow Central Committee; as a result of the March coup he had been transferred out of Georgia.) Saved from disgrace by Lenin's paralysis, Stalin was assiduously preparing for the decisive advance which he was to score at the coming party congress.

In the latter part of March Trotsky did make some gestures toward upholding Lenin's case on Georgia. He published an article on the nationality question, but confined himself to the vague warning, "We would fall into grave self-deception if we wrongly think that we have already solved the nationality question." He stressed that the younger party members in particular should be made aware that "nationalistic tendencies among Communists of the small nationalities are a sign of the sins of the great-power mentality in the general governmental apparatus and even in corners of the ruling party."[41] This was clearly an echo of Lenin's notes, but Trotsky went no further and named no names. He had warned his enemies and failed to inspire his friends. A few days later, speaking to the Central Committee, Trotsky urged the recall of Ordzhonikidze, denounced the Transcaucasian federation as a centralist perversion of the idea of federalism, and defended the Georgian minority as the protesting victims of an incorrect line. Such was Stalin's facility at covering up his own trail, however, that he managed to have all but the first of Trotsky's propositions stricken from the record.[42]

On the eve of the Twelfth Congress, the nationality question generated new evidence of the growing animosity between Stalin and Trotsky. Trotsky, since receiving the copy of Lenin's explosive article on the nationalities on March 5, had kept the matter to himself. On April 16, Lenin's secretary Fotieva, having returned to work after an illness, communicated to Kamenev and Trotsky an explanation about the article: "V. I. considered his article as a document of guidance and attached great importance to it. On the order of Vladimir Ilich this article was transmitted to Comrade Trotsky to whom V. I. entrusted the defense of his position on this question at the party congress because they have both held identical views in this matter."[43] With this, Trotsky seemed to be exposed before the party as a man who had either betrayed Lenin's trust or plotted secretly against his associates. Kamenev immediately communicated the news to the Central Committee and urged its members to agree to publish the article.[44]

Meanwhile, Trotsky penned a hasty explanation: he had received his copy of the article in confidence from Lenin, with no word as to its author's further intentions, and so felt his silence obligatory, especially because the document contained "a sharp condemnation of three Central Committee members." Now that Fotieva had let the cat out of the bag, he had "no alternative but to make this article known to the Central Committee members" as a document of great importance. More concerned to justify himself than to press an attack, Trotsky concluded, "If, on the basis of motives of an intraparty nature, whose significance is self-evident, no Central Committee member will make this article in one or another form known to the party or to the party congress, I, for my part, will consider this as a decision of silence, a decision which—in connection with the party congress—removes from me personal responsibility for this article."[45]

Lenin's sister, Maria Ulianova, counseled against publication of Lenin's article: it was not in final form and should at most be read only to the delegates at the party congress.[46] On receipt of this news, Stalin drew what must have been a deep breath of relief, and vented his indignation in the following declaration to the Central Committee:

I am greatly surprised that the articles of Comrade Lenin which, without a doubt, are of a distinct basic significance, and which Comrade Trotsky had received already on March 5 of this year, he considers admissible to keep as his own secret for over a month without making their content known to the Political Bureau or to the Central Committee Plenum, until one day before the opening of the Twelfth Congress of the Party. The themes of these articles—as I was informed today by the congress delegates—are subject to discussion and rumors and stories among the delegates; these articles, as I have learned today, are known to people who have nothing in common with the Central Committee; the Central Committee members themselves must seek information from these rumors and stories, while it is self-evident that the content of these articles should have been reported first of all to the Central Committee.

I think that Comrade Lenin's articles should be published in the press. It is only regrettable that—as is clearly evident from Comrade Fotieva's letter—these articles apparently cannot be published because they have not been reviewed by Comrade Lenin.[47]

Trotsky replied the next day with an effort to explain away his circumstantial guilt, by stressing that he had only conformed to what he believed were Lenin's desires. Then, he pointed out, "I referred the matter to the Central Committee. I did it without wasting a minute after I learned that Comrade Lenin had not given any direct and formal instruction." He ended his statement to the Central Committee with a request for a formal investigation if anyone still saw fit to challenge his motives.[48] Buttonholed by Trotsky, Stalin accepted the explanation and promised to give the Central Committee a corrected statement. This was but one instance of Stalin's deceit —the statement never materialized, and the next day Trotsky dispatched a virtual ultimatum to him: "If in reply to this note I do not receive from you a communication to the effect that in the course of today you will send to all members of the Central Committee a declaration that would exclude the possibility of any sort of equivocalness in this matter, then I shall conclude that you have changed your intention of yesterday and will appeal to the conflict commission, requesting an investigation from beginning to end."[49] The gauntlet was thrown down.

The Twelfth Party Congress was in session from April 17 to April 25, 1923. Stalin, undaunted by his narrow escape from censure, boldly assumed his familiar role as the specialist on the nationality question and delivered the principal report on the subject. He made a special effort to justify his policy in Georgia in the face of Lenin's criticism, which he knew was familiar to the delegates: Georgian nationalism had taken the "offensive," and had to be checked by the Transcaucasian federation. This measure, Stalin alleged, was supported by the majority of the Georgian Communists—hence the fall of the Mdivani group at the party conference in March.[50]

In reply, the Georgian oppositionists appealed openly to Lenin's letter on the national question. Mdivani declared, "We need [the policy] which Ilich always taught us and to which he called us in his last letters, which are known to the congress only through individual delegations."[51] Mdivani's associate Makharadze charged that Lenin's earlier critical attitude toward the Georgians was due to deliberate misinformation: "Incorrect information about us, about our organization was systematically sent to the center. Unfortunately, the center believed this information. Hence the center's distrust of the local comrades."[52]

Rakovsky, the Bulgarian premier of the Ukraine, had an obvious interest in joining the critics of the plan for unifying the Soviet republics. He lamented the fact that Lenin was not present to point out "fatal mistakes in the national question." "Comrades," he warned, "I declare that the construction of the union has proceeded by the wrong route. As you know, this is not only my opinion—it is the opinion of Vladimir Ilich."[53] Rakovsky was backed up by Bukharin, who had abandoned his extreme internationalism in favor of concessions to the sensitivities of the non-Russian minorities. Bukharin asserted the need "to buy ourselves the trust of the formerly oppressed nations," and attacked "those Great Russian deviations which have been revealed here." Rhetorically he asked, "Why did Comrade Lenin begin to sound the alarm with such furious energy in the Georgian question? And why did Comrade Lenin say not a word in his letter about the mistakes of the deviators, but on the contrary directed all his words, strong words, against the policy which was being carried out against the deviators?"[54]

The one surprising silence on the nationality issue was Trotsky's. Despite the bountiful opportunity provided by the lengthy and acrimonious debate on the Georgian affair, Trotsky foreswore the whole campaign against Stalin which Lenin had entrusted to him. But this was just one instance of Trotsky's puzzling conduct during these critical months.

The supporters of the troika tried as best they could to explain away the significance of Lenin's letter by attributing it to misinformation. In the face of repeated demands, they steadfastly refused to allow its publication, with the excuse that Lenin had not left the requisite instructions.[55] In spite of the obvious weaknesses in its case, the troika displayed its influence over the congress by winning approval on the nationality issue, and the matter was closed with the complete defeat of the Georgian Opposition. The debate on Georgia revealed that a familiar cleavage within the party was opening up again. Trotsky's former supporters—Bukharin, Rakovsky, and Radek—sympathized with the Georgian Opposition, while the Leninists stood firmly for the authority of the Secretariat. (This was the last occasion on which Bukharin sided with the Left; by the end of the year he stood firmly with the troika against Trotsky.) Aside from Trotsky's curious failure to take part, the split over Georgia was distinguished by the direction of Lenin's sympathy. As once before, in pressing for the seizure of power in 1917, Lenin found himself lined up with the Leftists and opposed to his own close and hence narrow-minded disciples. There were other issues as well, concerning the party and the whole governmental structure, where such a realignment was coming into effect. Had not Lenin's health given way, the fortunes of Soviet politics might have been significantly different.

The Georgian affair did not end the nationality issue. Ukrainian and Moslem dissidents remained to be disposed of, but in both cases Stalin had the last word. Rakovsky and the Ukrainians continued to criticize the constitutional arrangements for the USSR, which, they contended, smacked too much of Great Russian domination.[56] They protested being deprived of their own foreign commissariat[57] (a loss made up, on paper, in 1945). Finally Rakovsky and Stalin clashed directly.[58] Shortly afterwards, Rakovsky suddenly found that he had been appointed as the Soviet representative to Great Britain, and he was quickly relieved as chairman of the Ukrainian Council of People's Commissars by a little-known Ukrainian administrator, V. Y. Chubar. The long arm of the Secretariat reached everywhere, and the potential Left Opposition had lost one of its major political strongpoints.

More acute, and less quietly settled, was the affair of the Tatar Communist leader, Mirza Sultangaliev. Sultangaliev incurred the wrath of the authorities for the vigor of his attacks on "Great Russian chauvinism," which he planned to combat with a project for one vast Soviet Republic unifying all the Moslems in the USSR.[59] With the assent of his partners Kamenev and Zinoviev, Stalin had Sultangaliev arrested, and charged him with treason—the first instance of such a measure against a Communist Party leader.[60] The Central Committee found him guilty of "conspiratorial work . . . in the direction of undermining the confidence of the formerly oppressed nationalities in the revolutionary proletariat," and ordered him expelled from the party.[61] For the union, despite its multinational form, there could be but one line and one authority.

The nationality question was the most spectacular aspect of the interregnum, involving as it did top-level cleavages and the dramatic break between Lenin and Stalin. Other contemporary issues, however, were even more important as factors in the coming party split, indicative of the basic evolution of the Soviet regime. Most disturbing to much of the party and to Lenin himself was the general problem of institutional structure, both in the government and in the party; it was the familiar question of "bureaucratism."

BUREAUCRACY AND PARTY REFORM

The problem of bureaucracy, about which the Ultra-Left Opposition had been warning repeatedly, was suddenly discovered by the party leadership when they undertook to escape from the impasse of War Communism. Sweeping declarations against the evil became a stock feature of official pronouncements. Typical of the new emphasis was Lenin's assertion in 1921, "It is necessary for us to understand that the struggle with bureaucratism is an absolute essential struggle, and it is as complicated as the task of struggling with the petty-bourgeois element. Bureaucratism in our state structure has become such a serious malady that our party program refers to it, and this is because it is connected with this petty-bourgeois element and its diffusion."[62] Underlying the problem of bureacracy was the economic and cultural backwardness of most of the Russian nation. Bitter experience confirmed the Marxists' original analysis that Russia was not sufficiently developed for the success of "socialism." The utopian dreams of War Communism were fated to suffer a rude awakening in the cold dawn of the NEP.

As the Communists labored to construct an administration that could measure up to their self-imposed responsibilities of a nationalized economy, they were compelled to employ both the personnel and the methods of their predecessors. Trotsky admitted frankly that the Soviet apparatus was built largely of tsarist materials: "It was created by us under the pressure of historical necessity, out of such materials as we had at hand. Who is guilty? We all are."[63] Lenin confessed at the Fourth Congress of the Comintern, "We took over the old state apparatus, and this was our misfortune. . . . Down below there are hundreds of thousands of old officials held over from the tsarist regime and bourgeois society, who work against us consciously or unconsciously."[64] The 1917 goal of "smashing" the old governmental machinery and replacing it with direct self-government by the masses lapsed altogether. Lenin now admitted sadly, "We have only a ludicrously small portion of such a [new] apparatus or of even the elements of it, and we must remember that to create it we must not begrudge time and must spend many, many, many years."[65]

In the fall of 1922 Lenin had the unusual opportunity of returning from the grave, so to speak, to observe how his colleagues were carrying on. He came to the alarming realization that the habit of organizing party and governmental work in bureaucratic hierarchies had gotten out of control. To correct the evils of bureaucratism and bring day-to-day policy more closely into line with the party's professed democratic ideals, Lenin embarked on an ambitious plan of criticism and reform. Since his health did not permit him to assume the burden fully, he turned to Trotsky for help.

Lenin's proposal, which he did not keep secret, was that Trotsky should formally become his deputy by assuming the post of vice-chairman of the Council of People's Commissars. According to Trotsky's later account,[66] "Lenin summoned me to his room in the Kremlin, spoke of the terrible growth of bureaucratism in our Soviet apparatus and of the necessity of finding a lever with which to get at that problem. He proposed to create a special commission of the Central Committee and asked me to take active part in the work." Lenin also criticized the performance of the deputy chairmen of the Council of People's Commissars (Kamenev, Tsiurupa, and Rykov), who had been responsible for the conduct of governmental affairs in his absence, and proposed to Trotsky a shake-up in the state leadership: "You must become a deputy. The situation is such that we must have a radical realignment of personnel."

Trotsky declined to become a deputy premier, as he explained to his Politburo colleagues, because the existence of a group of deputy chairmen meant an irrational division of administrative authority, and because the party authorities were making decisions behind the backs of the responsible commissars, including himself. He replied to Lenin:

"Vladimir Ilich, it is my conviction that in the present struggle with bureaucratism in the Soviet apparatus, we must not forget that there is taking place, both in the provinces and in the center, a special selection of functionaries and specialists, party and nonparty, around certain ruling party personalities and groups—in the provinces, in the districts, in the party locals and in the center—that is, the Central Committee. Attacking a functionary you run into the party leader. The specialist is a member of his retinue. Under present circumstances, I would not undertake this work."

Vladimir Ilich reflected a moment and—here I quote him verbatim—said: "That is, I propose a struggle with soviet bureaucratism and you are proposing to include the bureaucratism of the Organization Bureau of the Party?"

I laughed at the unexpectedness of this, because no such finished formulation of the idea was in my mind.

I answered: "I suppose that's it."

Then Vladimir Ilich said: "Very well, then, I propose a bloc."

I said: "It is a pleasure to form a bloc with a good man."

At the end of our conversation, Vladimir Ilich said that he would propose the creation by the Central Committee of a commission to fight bureaucratism "in general," and through that we would be able to reach the Organizational Bureau of the Central Committee. The organizational side he promised to think over "further." At that we parted. . . . Ilich's health became continually worse . . . and so that work was never carried through.

While bedridden between his second and third strokes, Lenin began to outline a program of reform. During the last week of December 1922, he dictated a series of notes—including the "Testament" and the letter on the nationality question—which were apparently intended to serve either as the rough draft for an extended proposal on administrative reorganization, or as guides to the party in the event that Lenin's own health failed before he could elaborate his ideas.[67] On the problems of administration he was able to complete his criticisms and recommendations, which he published in three articles: "On Cooperatives," completed January 6, 1923, and published May

26, 1923; "How We Should Reorganize the Workers' and Peasants' Inspection," completed January 23 and published January 25; and finally, "Better Less but Better," completed March 2 and published March 4, as were the other two, in *Pravda*.

The constantly recurring theme in these notes and articles was the difficulty of pursuing a socialist program under Russian conditions of economic and cultural backwardness. "Complete cooperative organization," Lenin wrote, "is impossible without an entire cultural revolution." History had played an unexpected trick: "For us, the political and social overturn has proved to be a predecessor of the cultural overturn, that cultural revolution in the face of which we nevertheless now stand."[68] The immediate necessity stressed by Lenin was reform of the governmental machinery—"the task of overhauling our apparatus, which is simply good for nothing and which we have taken over *in toto* from an earlier era."[69] Existing checks on bureaucratism had broken down—"The Workers' and Peasants' Inspection, which initially had this function, has proved incapable of coping with it and can be used only as an accessory. . . ."[70] The solution which occurred to Lenin was to expand the Central Committee to fifty or a hundred members, with the inclusion of some rank-and-file workers who, with the control specialists from the staff of the Workers' and Peasants' Inspection (the *Rabkrin*) would constitute a new force to clean up the administration.[71] He made the proposal definite in his article, "How We Should Reorganize the Workers' and Peasants' Inspection," with some modification: the Rabkrin would be replaced by a super-control body merging the governmental control function with the party control responsibilities of the Central Control Commission. This new organ would be staffed with as many as a hundred members, "from the workers and peasants," who would enjoy prestige equal to that of Central Committee members. This authority, combined with the grass-roots connections and interests of the new body, was expected to sweep away the encrusted bureaucratism. In addition, the expanded Central Control Commission would sit jointly with the Central Committee in a plenum, which would assume additional powers as the party's supreme policy-making organ.[72]

Lenin's criticisms and proposals were a shock to most of the other members of the Politburo. According to Trotsky, Lenin sent the article on January 23, 1923, for publication in *Pravda*. Stalin intervened to delay its publication and refer it to the Politburo for consideration. Trotsky thereupon insisted on an immediate Politburo meeting. Present at the meeting were Stalin, Trotsky, Kamenev, and Rykov, the candidates Molotov, Kalinin, and Bukharin, and also Kuibyshev, the third party secretary, who though not a member of the Politburo was apparently allowed by the majority of the group to attend and vote. The majority was opposed to Lenin's reform, and voted six to two (Trotsky and Kamenev) to suspend the printing of the article. Kuibyshev even proposed the printing of a fake number of *Pravda* to appease the sick leader with his article in print. Only by the insistence of Trotsky and Kamenev that Lenin's article could not be kept secret in any case was the majority finally brought around to acquiesce in its publication.[73] It appeared on January 25.[74]

Lenin's reform proposal was evidently regarded by the apparatus group as a real threat to its own power, even though it could not have known definitely of Lenin's attitude toward Stalin expressed in the "Testament." However, Lenin's personal prestige and authority with the rank and file of the party were so vast that his plan could not be attacked directly. It was instead met by supplementary proposals, in an effort to divert the impact of the reform.

On January 29, 1923, the Central Committee received a reform plan which emanated from the Secretariat in the form of a series of amendments to the party statutes.[75] The main proposal paralleled in form a suggestion made by Lenin in his December notes—the Central Committee would be enlarged from twenty-seven to fifty members. This expanded group would exercise increased powers:

For the conduct of current political work the Central Committee sets up the Politburo composed of seven members of the Central Committee, but requires it to hand over political questions of essential importance for decision by the plenum of the Central Committee, regular or special, depending on the circumstances. This change reduces the rights of the Politburo in favor of the plenum of the Central Committee. It is essential because without such a change the broadening of the composition of the Central Committee loses its significance.

This plan would permit the general secretary to use his strength in the local organizations to extend his influence in the highest party organs. The Central Committee would be packed with obscure personalities, ostensibly uncorrupted representatives of the party's rank and file but in reality tools of the Secretariat, which controlled the local organizations that would select the new men. This, indeed, was what Stalin finally did achieve. Increasing the authority of the Central Committee would then partially free the secretarial group from subordination to the Politburo members who had too much personal prestige to be defied openly. Stalin's proposal did not refer at all to the Central Control Commission, which was the keystone of Lenin's plan. An independent antibureaucratic campaign might well infringe upon the power of the secretarial group. Stalin had apparently not yet realized the possibility of getting control of the new Central Control Commission and bending it to his own purposes.

The reorganization plan led to sharp debate among the members of the Central Committee, as Stalin reported: "There is one question—of the expansion of the Central Committee itself—a question which has several times been discussed by us within the Central Committee, and which once evoked serious debate. There are several members within the Central Committee who think that we should not increase the numbers of the Central Committee, but should even reduce it."[76] Trotsky was one of those who firmly opposed the expansion plan. In his statement to the Central Committee on February 22 he declared, "The Central Committee must retain its strict form and its capacity for quick decisions. For this reason its further broadening makes no sense. . . . More complicated relations between the Politburo and the plenum threaten to cause great harm to the accuracy and correctness of the work of the Central Committee." Following Lenin's proposal, Trotsky suggested the establishment of a Central Control Commission consisting of seventy-five members and headed by a presidium of from seven to nine men.[77] Thus reorganized, the commission would have broad responsibility in upholding the party line, enforcing party control over the governmental administration, combating the "petty-bourgeois" and "Thermidorean" influences associated with the NEP, and forestalling adverse influences upon the party from the side of the administrative system.[78]

In the meantime, Lenin finished another article—his last—which amplified his reform proposal and set forth the reasoning behind it. "Better Less but Better," which appeared in *Pravda* on March 4, showed Lenin's deep concern about the general trend of social evolution in the country. Traditional bureaucratic features, feeding on Russia's cultural backwardness, were proliferating in the Soviet governmental machinery. The workers, Lenin now had to admit, lacked the cultural background for successful administrative work. The Workers' and Peasants' Inspection had to bear particular blame—"The Rabkrin does not now enjoy even a shadow of authority. Everyone knows that there are no institutions in worse condition than the institutions of our Rabkrin, and that under present circumstances nothing can be expected from this commissariat." Alleging bad faith on the part of the Rabkrin executives (and by implication criticizing Stalin, who had been the commissar before he became general secretary), Lenin demanded the drastic reform of the Rabkrin into a much smaller institution but in quality a model one: "Any halfway decision would be harmful to the worst degree. All the norms of the employees of the Rabkrin, no matter what considerations they came from, would in essence be based on old bureaucratic considerations, on old prejudices."[79]

In conjunction with the other principal expressions by Lenin in the last few months of his political life—his speech at the Fourth Comintern Congress (warning of excessive Russianism in the Third International), his remarks to Trotsky (which in substance appear to be authentic), his notes on the nationality question, the "Testament," and the other late articles on cooperatives and the Rabkrin—"Better Less but Better" is of fundamental significance. It suggests that Lenin was about to make a political about-face comparable to those which he executed at the beginning and at the end of the year 1917. This can only be guessed at, since Lenin was silenced forever by his third cerebral hemorrhage in March 1923. Nevertheless, he appears to have been shifting again from the "Leninist" group to the Leftist point of view. He now concerned himself less with meeting immediate practical problems and turned his attention to the discrepancy between Soviet reality and the original goals of the revolution.

On fundamentals such as one-party dictatorship, Lenin did not relax in the least. Like the moderate Leftists, he never ceased to stress the monopoly of Communist power or to keep in mind practical problems facing the Soviet government. The new emphasis lay in his recognition that practical expediencies such as individual authority and the suppression of democratic procedures had resulted in a firmly bureaucratic pattern of political organization. Judging that the underlying cause of the bureaucratic trend lay in the nation's cultural backwardness, Lenin tried to work out measures for correcting this basic deficiency. In a sense he was becoming more Marxist, concerning himself more with the effect of the "material conditions of existence" than with his more customary search for a purely organizational solution to all problems. Lenin's break with Stalin was indicative of the limits he wished to apply to high-handed methods of rule. The Man of Steel was too unscrupulously Leninist even for Lenin.

THE PROGRESS OF THE APPARATUS

The Soviet political atmosphere was electric with suspense in April 1923. Lenin lay dying; his lieutenants were intriguing. Problems arose faster than they could be debated. The future was an unsounded void. With the new spring, a profound, inchoate uneasiness was in the air.

This was the setting for the regular annual convocation of the party congress, the Twelfth, which met from April 17 to April 25. It was a memorable assembly—the first Bolshevik conclave without Lenin, the last before his death, and the last when individual delegates spoke their minds without prepared scripts. Henceforth the congresses, excepting the Fourteenth in 1925, would be nothing but staged demonstrations of secretarial manipulation, monolithic and unanimous. But despite the freedom in which the Twelfth Congress met and the discontent which rippled among the delegates, clear factional lines failed to appear, and no one ventured to proclaim his unqualified opposition to the ruling troika. Meanwhile a new force was beginning to reveal its strength.

During the period of "preparation" before the Twelfth Congress, as delegates were being elected by local party conferences, the organizational efforts of the secretarial machinery bore copious fruit. An intensive effort was made to secure the election of delegates loyal to the party apparatus by using all the means of central and local pressure on the rank and file which had been developed during the preceding two years. As Stalin reported to the congress, "For the past six years the Central Committee has never once prepared a congress as it has in the present case."[80] With this experience freshly in mind, the Leftist "Declaration of the Forty-six" (of October 1923) asserted that "the secretarial hierarchy of the party to an ever greater degree selects the membership of conferences and congresses, which to an ever greater degree are becoming executive consultations of this hierarchy."[81] More than half of the provincial party conferences held in March 1923 to elect delegates were attended by members or candidate members of the Central Committee.[82] Though some of the members were still critically inclined, they themselves were under the pressure of party discipline, while on the other hand the overall menace of the Secretariat was still unclear. Trotsky, for example, gave a report to the Ukrainian party conference which was perfectly orthodox in its stress on the need for party unity and discipline, the impossibility of questioning the party's dominant political role, the virtues of the proposed reform of the Central Control Commission, and the importance of maintaining the union of the proletariat and the peasantry as the basis of the NEP.[83]

The preparations for the Twelfth Congress gave Stalin effective control over a majority of the delegates, or at least made him stronger than any likely combination of opposing leaders. On the basis of all the factors affecting power in such a gathering—a nucleus of directly loyal delegates, superior organization, group consciousness, clarity of purpose, influence at the strategic posts—Stalin had quietly become the decisive figure in the party. An open question of titular leadership arose when it had to be decided who would make the political report to the congress. The delivery of this major address had always been Lenin's prerogative, as it was Stalin's in later years. Stalin, preferring to build his power behind the scenes, proposed Trotsky for the honor. Trotsky, however, was equally reluctant to overreach himself at this confused moment.[84] There remained one claimant who was more than eager, Zinoviev, and to him fell the nominal leadership of the party in this and the following year.

The organizational success of the Secretariat did not go unchallenged at the congress. Debate on Stalin's organizational report was opened by the former Democratic Centralist Vladimir Kosior, with a protest against the atmosphere of growing repression: "Comrades, within the party conditions have been created for us which make any practical, organizational criticism more and more difficult." He saw the root of this situation in the unwarranted permanent enforcement of the Tenth Congress resolution against factions, which he regarded as a temporary emergency measure. "Under conditions of peaceful construction why must we now have this exceptional law? . . . Any group life within the party in practice becomes impossible if it does not fit into the framework of the official organs of the party, into the framework of cells and district and city committees."[85] Preobrazhensky made an equally direct attack on the activities of the Secretariat and especially protested the trend toward appointment of local party secretaries: "It is in no case proper to make a system out of that which is exceptional, which is the result of extreme necessity, and which is politically dangerous to the party."[86]

Another individual who spoke out on the organizational issue had not been heard in Bolshevik councils for many years. He was L. B. Krasin, Lenin's former second-in-command, who had returned to the Bolshevik fold after the revolution to serve the Soviet regime in a variety of administrative and diplomatic posts. Currently Krasin was Commissar of Foreign Trade. In 1924, no doubt as an antidote to his critical frame of mind, he was eased out and made Ambassador to France. (He died in 1926 at the age of fifty-six.[87]) Krasin took issue with the general tone of the party leadership's pronouncements on organizational matters, and pointed out an overall deficiency in the party's development since the revolution. He quoted from an article which he had written shortly before: "The superstructure of our party is constructed approximately as it was two decades ago, although now the tasks of the party have changed both quantitatively and qualitatively."

"I say to you," he cautioned the delegates directly, "you are now not an underground party, you are the government of a vast country, working under difficult internal circumstances . . . and complicated international circumstances, under such difficult conditions as not one government in the world has ever faced." He was calling upon the party of conspirators to change itself into one of statesmen. Nevertheless, like virtually every other oppositionist, he firmly upheld the need for the dictatorship of the party: "I believe that until the victory of the world revolution all state work must remain under the strictest control of the party, that only the party, only the Central Committee of the party can be the ultimate organ of decision, which must decide every question of vital significance for our state."[88]

A stern reply to this anticentralist criticism was delivered by various spokesmen of the party leadership. Bukharin called the critics to order for violating what had become the party's cardinal organizational principle: "Comrades like Kosior want to transform our centralized party into a federation of various groupings.[89] One Belenki, a future member of the Zinoviev Opposition, commented, "In a period when we are surrounded by petty-bourgeois elements, unity is especially necessary, and any groupings are inadmissable. Thus it is still premature to speak of changing this law."[90] M. N. Riutin (himself purged in 1932 for Opposition activity) went so far as to express a position of frank authoritarianism—"The party cannot be without leaders. . . . Everything leads into the organizational question. Some comrades are inclined to stress the word 'democratic,' others emphasize the word 'centralism.' The Mensheviks and those petty-bourgeois groups with which we have come to blows, were always inclined to speak a great deal about democratism. We, however, have always subordinated the principles of democratism to revolutionary expediency. We will continue to do this in the future."[91]

To people so inclined, Stalin's conception of the party was a powerful attraction. He spoke of the party as an "organism": as such, it required absolute subordination of its constituent parts to its guiding center. To this end the activity of the Secretariat was directed. It mattered little what the course of action decided upon by the leadership was; as integral parts of an organism the members had no function but to obey. Lenin's dynamic revolutionary scheme with the Communist "vanguard" leading the workers was translated by Stalin into a static pattern for the hierarchical organization of the postrevolutionary regime.[92] Such were the implications stemming from the revived organizational tradition of 1902.

For assurance that the party would continue in the right direction, the party leadership relied on nothing so disruptive as a rank-and-file check on the party's executive organs. The guarantee of correct leadership was found (or was professed to have been found) in the teachings of the party's founder. Opening the congress, Kamenev declaimed: "We know only one antidote for any crisis, against any wrong decision: this is the teaching of Vladimir Ilich, and to this antidote the party will always turn in all difficult moments."[93] Criticism of the professedly Leninist leadership was automatically considered a threat to the pillars of revolutionary orthodoxy. Zinoviev said in his political report, "Any criticism of the party line, even the so-called 'left' one, is now objectively a Menshevik criticism. The 'left' criticism is dangerous, and we must resist it."[94]

It fell upon Stalin to propose concrete steps for implementing the standards of discipline which his colleagues upheld. He was now prepared to call for the establishment of the enlarged and combined Central Control Commission and Workers' and Peasants' Inspection, as recommended by Lenin. Along with this Stalin urged his own plan to expand the Central Committee and subordinate the Politburo to it. Further, he called for the creation of a school for local party secretaries and the training of new leadership "to bring new, fresh workers into the work of the Central Committee and in the course of their work to promote the most able and independent, those who have heads on their shoulders." These qualifications implied, of course, judgment by the Secretariat according to its own criteria. Stalin himself said of his plan, "We need independent people in the Central Committee, but not independent of Leninism . . . not free from our party line. . . . We need independent people free from personal influences, from those habits and traditions of struggle within the Central Committee which have been formed among us and which often cause alarm within the Central Committee."[95]

The new party staff, in other words, would be unfettered by minds of their own and free of the taint of opposition.

All of Stalin's proposals were adopted, though not without resistance. The line-up at the congress on the reorganization question was confused. Trotsky had been on record against the plan to expand the Central Committee, though he supported the new control commission. But the troika itself was apparently split. Zinoviev was obviously unenthusiastic about the reform and pointedly endorsed the existing Central Committee.[96] However, he did not attack the proposals directly, and the troika was still firm enough for Stalin to come effusively to Zinoviev's defense against left-wing criticism.[97] For his own part, Stalin was able to mobilize considerable left-wing support for his reform, on ostensibly antibureaucratic grounds. Stukov, once a fervent Left Communist, endorsed Stalin on the need for new blood in the Central Committee to offset the "castes of priests."[98] Even Osinsky was able to support Stalin's proposals, which he felt would "really establish true unity in our party."[99] Evidently, the support of disaffected Leftists was second in importance only to that delivered by Stalin's secretarial machine in securing passage by the congress of the reform proposals. Confusion among the Leftists was instrumental in setting up the power which caused their own eventual liquidation.

The top leadership of the party was unchanged by the Twelfth Congress —Stalin was biding his time and dared not challenge the position of any of his prominent associates. The Politburo still consisted of, in addition to the ailing Lenin, the Stalin-Zinoviev-Kamenev troika, Trotsky, under a cloud, plus Rykov and Tomsky. One new candidate member, the trade-unionist Rudzutak, joined Bukharin, Kalinin, and Molotov at that level. The Orgburo and Secretariat, already firmly under Stalin's control, were virtually unaltered in their composition. It was in the Central Committee that the great changes occurred, with the expansion from twenty-seven members to forty. Promotion and turnover made room for fourteen new candidate members, and at this level the Secretariat's power of selection was clear: the new men (including Lazar Kaganovich) without exception proved to be loyal Stalinists throughout the twenties.[100]

The new Central Control Commission, vastly enlarged (from five to fifty) and enhanced in its power, proved to be completely under the domination of the Stalinists. Kuibyshev was the new chairman, heading a presidium of nine men who were given the right to attend Politburo meetings. These included Solts, Gusev, Yaroslavsky, and M. F. Shkiriatov, one of the few lesser functionaries to survive all the purges (he was chairman of the Party Control Commission when he died in January 1954). Only one of the nine —N. I. Ilin—threw in his lot with the Left Opposition, and was expelled from the party in 1927.[101] The Stalinists' alarm about the party reform proved to be unfounded; the Central Control Commission became, next to the Secretariat itself, the most solidly reliable instrument at Stalin's command.

The outcome of the Twelfth Congress was an irreparable failure for the forces of genuine reform. Lenin's profound criticisms of the Soviet government had been lost sight of in the quibbling about specific schemes of reorganization, while the Secretariat, with its vested interest in bureaucratic power, was growing steadily more irresistable. Lenin's ideas for reforming the Central Committee and the Central Control Commission actually resulted in nothing but the heightening of the Secretariat's influence. From this time on, Stalin would be hard to stop.

Serious trouble lay ahead for the leadership, however. The Twelfth Congress was the signal for the moderate Leftist elements in the party to rebel against the power of the organization which up to then they had accepted as a necessary evil. This reaction was described afterwards in the Declaration of the Forty-six:

The regime of factional dictatorship within the party, which was objectively set up after the Tenth Congress, has outlived its usefulness. Many of us consciously undertook not to resist such a regime. The turn of events of 1921, and later the illness of Comrade Lenin, demanded, in the opinion of many of us, temporary measures in the nature of a dictatorship within the party. Other comrades [the Democratic Centralists] from the very beginning reacted to this skeptically or negatively. However that may be, at the Twelfth Congress of the party this regime overdid itself. It began to show its reverse side. Intraparty bonds began to weaken. The party began to sink.[102]

THE CLEAVAGE IN ECONOMIC POLICY

By the spring of 1923 the NEP had been in force for two years. Its immediate objectives had been accomplished—the Soviet government had survived the crisis of 1921, the famine was over, and the economy of the country was recovering from the depths to which it had sunk during the Civil War and War Communism. When catastrophe was no longer imminent, however, the original unanimity which attended the NEP ceased to prevail; there were signs of growing uneasiness. The latent cleavage between the Leninist and Leftist groups manifested itself again in issues of present expediency versus long-term goals. Moreover, the voice of the Ultra-Left refused to be stilled. Reduced to a semiunderground status, the spokesmen of this despairing extreme nevertheless managed to proclaim their conviction that the cause of the workers was being betrayed by the party leaders.

The task of the leadership in following through with the NEP was not easy. While the general picture was one of remarkable improvement, in detail the economy was beset with serious imbalances and fluctuations. Agitating the whole party throughout the period of the interregnum was the so-called scissors crisis (falling agricultural prices and rising industrial prices).[103] This disparity was accentuated by the trend of state-owned industrial enterprises to concentrate in syndicates and reap a monopolistic advantage.[104] As a result, by the middle of 1923 state industries were experiencing serious difficulties in disposing of their production at the prices they wished to maintain, and unemployment mounted. The economic situation during 1923 created a new sense of acute crisis just at the time when the party was contending with the delicate political problems of the succession. Responses to the scissors crisis were varied and conflicting, and as individuals and groups maneuvered for influence, technical, economic, and administrative questions inescapably became political footballs. Left-wing boldness and doctrine called for a systematic program of economic development on the basis of a comprehensive plan. Right-wing "Leninist" caution and expediency dictated more concession and conciliation in the face of economic obstacles: the peasants would be appeased still more, at the sacrifice of the urban interest if necessary. Objections from the latter quarter could more easily be kept in hand by the political instruments at the disposal of the party leadership.

Characteristic of the cleavage were the opposing views on currency stabilization. This was an acute problem for a government still financing itself largely through the printing press and trying to cope with one of the most astronomical of all inflations. The Right, represented especially by Sokolnikov as finance commissar, saw the currency problem as a serious impediment to economic progress and were prepared to devote a great effort to its resolution. The Left preferred to view it as the consequence of failing to push planned economic development.[105]

A sharp dispute broke out in the fall of 1922 over foreign-trade policy. Sokolnikov and those inclined to the right-wing view nearly outdid the capitalist world in their financial orthodoxy; a favorable balance of trade was sought to facilitate currency stabilization, and if price advantages pointed to the importation of consumer goods, so be it. In October 1922, under the encouragement of Sokolnikov and with the concurrence of Bukharin and Stalin, the Central Committee passed a resolution against the foreign-trade monopoly then being administered by Krasin, the commissar of foreign trade. This would have been a serious setback, from the point of view of the Left, to the hopes for planned industrial development, while it accorded with the position of those who favored allowing economic development to proceed through the forces of the market. In the end, through the insistence of Krasin and Trotsky and with the intervention of Lenin himself, the foreign-trade monopoly was retained and reaffirmed.[106] Here again Lenin was turning away from his own "Leninist" supporters and toward cooperation with the Left.

Another subject of contention was the inefficiency of the country's slowly recovering industry. In some industries a policy of consolidation had already begun to concentrate production efforts in the most efficient enterprises. This was undertaken in the Donets coal field in 1921,[107] though already with political overtones. Intrigue, evidently engineered by Stalin in defiance of the rest of the leadership, brought about the removal of Trotsky's supporter Piatakov from the Donets coal administration.[108] Trotsky himself gave vigorous support to such measures for the consolidation of industry, even at the cost of creating more unemployment.[109] Political sentiment rebelled, however, when Rykov proposed closing the famous Putilov machinery works in Petrograd. The Putilov plant was both a symbol of the proletarian revolution and a model of the concentrated heavy industry which the party idealized, even though it was operating at a scant 5 per cent of capacity.[110] Zinoviev objected, no doubt taking the Putilov shutdown as a blow to his local prestige, and the Politburo reversed the sentence.[111] Meanwhile, the left-wing sympathizers in economic posts began to advance what was to become a basic opposition principle—state subsidies to industry to hasten its recovery and its further development.

Complicating the economic debate was a new question which became, to one degree or another, a permanent issue in Soviet politics: the relationship between the party organization and the professional managerial personnel in state-owned industry. Within a very brief span of years the new Communist administrators had developed a marked group spirit, and apparently took great pride in the steps they were able to take toward efficiency and profitable management. The syndicate movement of 1922 was largely at their initiative, and they attacked as bureaucratic interference the attempts by the Supreme Economic Council to lay down overall policy. Successful management and the maintenance of high prices made 1923 the first year since the revolution when Russian industry had as a whole operated at a profit.[112] The ramifying operations of the party apparatus, however, were beginning to encroach upon the preserves of the industrial administrators, and serious friction and resentment resulted. Intensifying this feeling was the divergence in attitude between the old undergrounders of the apparatus and the Westernized intellectuals in administrative work.

The administrators found spokesmen for their cause at the Twelfth Party Congress—the so-called "united front" of Krasin, Osinsky, and Larin. These three spoke up vigorously to oppose the proposed merger of the Central Control Commission and the Workers' and Peasants' Inspection, on the ground that this violated the juridical separation of the party and the soviet (governmental) institutions and would lead to unwarranted interference by party officials in administrative affairs.

Krasin had written just before the congress: "I can assert that we managers all await these decisions literally with terror." He drew upon criteria of economic efficiency to support his criticism of political domination by the Secretariat: "The strictly held political line of the party . . . must not be allowed to interfere with the restoration of production." All too frequently,

Krasin charged, administrators were transferred at random for purely party considerations, and often incompetents were assigned to important managerial positions on the same basis.[113] "It will be possible to avoid this," he declared, "only when the directing apparatus of the party includes not just politicians, but organizers, administrators, managers."[114] The one-time arch-conspirator had found that government by professional revolutionaries left much to be desired.

The managerial opposition met with an unusually sharp reaction, voiced principally by Zinoviev and his personal supporters. It was a "bureaucratic deviation" by "individual comrades who are so affected by departmentalism that they forget about party spirit."[115] "Bourgeois elements" allegedly backed this criticism in the hope of prying loose the administrative machinery from Communist Party control. "This is not only a revision of Leninism," asserted G. Y. Yevdokimov, "it is a revision of our whole revolution."[116] Krasin, Osinsky, and Larin, said G. I. Safarov, were "definitely slipping into the Menshevik swamp."[117] The allegations made against the Workers' Opposition were henceforth to apply automatically to anyone who challenged the authority of the party organization.

Preobrazhensky suggested a more sophisticated explanation for the unrest among the managers: their views clashed with overall party control because they were governed by "individual specialties . . . by the short-run interests of most enterprises instead of the long-run interests of the dictatorship of the proletariat." Short-run economic efficiency and large-scale planned development might not coincide, but in the interest of the latter Preobrazhensky urged that the managers be conciliated: "The Central Committee must reconstruct its work so that important questions which require attention are decided or voted on by people who understand them."[118]

The resolution on industry which the Twelfth Congress passed, based on Trotsky's theses, provided both for concessions to the managers and for tighter controls. The party was directed to back up the authority of the manager in the plant and at the same time avoid undue interference in the technical side of plant administration. On the other hand, the overall responsibility of the party for economic success and the execution of the "proletarian line" was emphatically affirmed.[119] The cleavage between the party and administrative bureaucracies was not resolved. When open factional struggle broke out again in the fall of 1923, the antagonism between the administrators and the party officialdom was a major source of dissension.

The contrasting Left and Right orientations toward the NEP revived still another issue which continued to be disputed down to the end of all effective opposition in 1929. This was the broad question of economic planning and the tempo and means of industrial development. Planning, in theory, was a socialist virtue accepted without dissent by the entire party, but in the first years of the NEP it was hardly more than a pious wish.

Limited attempts at planning had been made in some industries, and the State Planning Commission (*Gosplan*) was set up in 1921, although it carried little weight until the later years of the NEP.[120]

As the scissors crisis grew more severe, the adherents of the majority right-wing view made their defense of the NEP all the more absolute. It was not only a correct step but a policy which would remain in effect for an indefinite period. Zinoviev dismissed as "Menshevik" the idea that the peasant could not become a socialist.[121] (Later he himself was to become the victim of just such a charge.) Kamenev steered through the Twelfth Congress a resolution calling for a still more lenient tax policy to cement the "alliance of workers and peasants."[122] The economic reasoning of the Right —to which they adhered until 1927—was based on the cautious assumption that large-scale industry should derive the means for its growth from the demand for its products. This meant that the peasant sector of the economy should first recover and prosper, and then finance the growth of industry by its purchases. Small-scale and consumer-goods industries would benefit first, and these in turn would stimulate the expansion of capital-goods industry.[123] This was diametrically opposed to the Leftist insistence on building industry directly, with complete state planning and financing through the state budget. The overriding consideration, for the Rightist leadership, was to do nothing that might alienate the peasantry.

In the spring of 1922 Trotsky began to press again for a unified economic authority, presumably with himself at the head.[124] He was opposed by most of his colleagues, but in December 1922 he succeeded in winning Lenin's backing to expand the authority of the State Planning Commission.[125] In his "Theses on Industry" prepared in March 1923 for the coming party congress, Trotsky asserted the political importance of a vigorous industrialization program: "Only the development of industry creates an unshakeable foundation for the proletarian dictatorship."[126] He urged a policy of "the correct relating of market and plan" whereby the Soviet government should steer a course between the dangers of inept administrative interference with the market (the evil of which was amply demonstrated by the results of War Communism) and of insufficient regulation of the market when control from above would be advantageous. The implication was that the advantageous moment was arriving. "I hope, I believe," Trotsky affirmed in his report on industry at the congress, "that this congress will declare at this time the initial point of a more harmonious, more concentrated economic offensive."[127]

By this time the issue of economic planning had become the vehicle for personal political rivalries, as the available materials on the Politburo's discussions indicate. Trotsky was obsessed with the rationality of a single plan and a single authority, and he did not hesitate to impute gross inefficiency to his colleagues. Stalin entered into the economic issue in order to embarrass Trotsky and went so far as to allege dereliction of duty on Trotsky's part because he had not become a deputy premier according to Lenin's original plan. Against Trotsky's lone opposition, the Politburo killed the publication of Lenin's article on expanding the powers of the Gosplan.[128] In public, however, the rest of the leadership did not venture to take an open stand directly against Trotsky on the economic issue, and they agreed to accept his position as the official one for the Twelfth Congress.[129]

On the most immediate question, that of credit policy, the cleavage could not be glossed over. The Right favored a policy of tight credit in the interest of currency stabilization and industrial efficiency. Sokolnikov expressed the strict rule that industry should not be allowed to depend on the state, but should pay its own way.[130] This aroused both the managerial groups and the proindustry theorists of the Left, to whom the opposite course was far more appealing. Trotsky urged the formulation of a long-term credit policy whereby the allocation of capital would be governed by the overall investment objectives of the state rather than by the immediate working-capital needs of an enterprise.[131]

A considerably more advanced formulation of the Leftist economic position was currently being worked out by Preobrazhensky. Preobrazhensky found the principal cause for the country's economic difficulties in the "disproportionality" which resulted from Russia's preponderantly peasant economy.[132] The only way out of this difficulty was the rapid development of industry, especially heavy industry. In considering how this could be accomplished, Preobrazhensky worked out the concept of "primary socialist accumulation," an analogy with Marx's analysis of the stage of primary accumulation under capitalism. This implied some form of "exploitation" (or "forcible alienation," "forced saving") of the population by the state in order to accumulate the capital necessary for rapid development of heavy industry. Preobrazhensky envisaged the proletarian state exploiting the peasantry as a sort of "colony."[133] Trotsky accepted the validity of the idea of primary socialist accumulation, and Krasin used it as the point of departure for his highly controversial idea of importing the necessary foreign capital.[134] "Primary socialist accumulation" became one of the basic elements in the economic program of the Left Opposition.

The Twelfth Congress's resolution on industry was ostensibly a victory for Trotsky. It followed his resounding phrases on the importance of heavy industrial development and the need for overall planning: "State activity as a whole must place its primary concern on the planned development of state industry." The progress of industry was the foundation of the Soviet state: "All this work would reveal itself to be built on sand, if there were not underneath it a growing industrial base. Only the development of industry creates an unshakeable foundation for the proletarian dictatorship."[135] With such sentiments no one ventured to take issue, but as a practical move the resolution remained a dead letter. The planning emphasis was branded with the Opposition label, and the leadership succeeded in putting off such an industrialization effort for a full four years, until the Left was at the point of being destroyed.

Lending a note of urgency to the deliberations of the Twelfth Congress was the threat of a movement of protest by the new semiunderground Ultra-Left Opposition. The party leadership was especially perturbed about a so-called "anonymous platform," which had made its appearance in party circles shortly before the congress opened. The platform proclaimed, "We call on all honestly proletarian elements, grouped around Democratic Centralism, the 'Workers' Truth' and the adherents of the Workers' Opposition, those outside the ranks of the party as well as those remaining within it, to unite on the basis of the manifesto of the 'Workers' Group of the Russian Communist Party.' "[136] The authorship of the platform thus apparently lay with the Workers' Group led by Miasnikov. Boldly the platform called for the removal of Zinoviev, Kamenev, and Stalin from the leadership of the party. Osinsky was implicated in this proposal,[137] though on economic questions the Workers' Group and the managerial opposition which he represented were poles apart.

The avowed manifesto of the Workers' Group returned to the original position of the Workers' Opposition and rejected the whole trend of industrial policy since 1919—the specialists and managerial authority were to go, while the ideal of workers' control was held up again: "The organization of this industry since the Ninth Congress of the RCP(b) is carried out without the direct participation of the working class by nominations in a purely bureaucratic way."[138] Another document which was circulating concurrently came from the supporters of the Workers' Truth organization. Their statement was a bitter protest against the exploitation of the rank-and-file workers and the suppression of workers' rights and genuine trade unionism, while the officialdom prospered and the government reverted without scruple to "capitalist methods."[139]

Opposition spokesmen tried to infer from the underground platforms that the worst enemy of real party unity was the repressive activity of the party organization which forced people into dangerous forms of opposition. The former Workers' Opposition leader Lutovinov declared:

As long as all these groupings exist, as long as all these platforms exist, there are obviously reasons for them. If there appear anonymous theses of any kind, if anonymous persons are compelled to issue some kind of platform, this is only because there does not exist in our RCP the possibility of expressing in a normal way one's considerations or points of view on one question or another. This is proved by the fact that if in the RCP you try to criticize not the political line but simply the practical execution of this line, then at once you are quickly counted as a Menshevik, an SR, or anything else convenient.[140]

Far from contemplating the course of concession, the party leadership pointed to the anonymous platform and the Workers' Group as full justification for the policy of banning factions. Zinoviev rejected Opposition protests against the continuation of the ban. The prohibition of factional groupings, he declared, "is not an exceptional law—it is a weapon for the self-defense of the proletarian party, which is surrounded on all sides by the disorganizing influences of the bourgeoisie and the petty-bourgeoisie. . . . In our party there is plenty of freedom for the consideration of any opinion. Only he who wants to disorganize the party is not given freedom."[141]

MANEUVERING FOR THE SUCCESSION

The most decisive aspect of the Twelfth Congress lay in what failed to occur there. Weighty issues were debated, and fateful changes were in the air. The delegates knew that Lenin had fallen out with Stalin, and they had reason to believe that he had turned against the troika as a whole in favor of Trotsky. Dissension flickered intermittently on a variety of issues. All awaited the stroke of defiant criticism which only Trotsky could deliver to galvanize the forces of opposition into action and mobilize them for an assault on the leadership of the troika.[142] That such forces were ready is amply evidenced by the rapidity with which the Opposition took shape when Trotsky finally did launch his attack on the troika in the fall of 1923. But by then the chance of victory had eluded him. The troika was no longer untested and vulnerable as it had been in the spring.

It was not a lack of issues that held Trotsky back. The dispute over economic planning and the emphasis to be given to industry was already clearcut. (The economic issue was a major factor in the break which actually came in the fall of 1923.) Stalin's abuse of the power of the Secretariat was obvious, as both Lenin's "Testament" and much of the left-wing criticism at the Twelfth Congress show. Trotsky himself had already clashed with Stalin over Lenin's reform ideas, and this provided further ammunition against the troika. Most effective of all would have been the nationality question; Lenin's letters were available and might well have caused Stalin's political ruin had they been properly employed by someone sufficiently in authority. Yet Trotsky gingerly avoided any involvement when the congress debated the Georgian question, even though, as he later asserted himself, Lenin had expressly requested him to press the attack against Stalin. Trotsky went so far to avoid controversy that he actually reprimanded people who spoke up to defend him against the troika.[143]

It was certainly not a lack of popularity that kept Trotsky from moving. He was greeted at the congress with tumultuous ovations, as lights blazed and moving-picture cameras turned.[144] With Lenin gone, no one in the party was more the conquering hero. This was the last occasion when Trotsky would appear in such a light. As a rank-and-file member recalled the time, "For us it was merely a question of who was to succeed Lenin, and we were strongly of the opinion that one man, and one man only, had a right to that position, because he was head and shoulders superior to his fellow-claimants and could depend upon our unswerving loyalty. That one was Trotsky."[145] Trotsky's name was first on the lips of every party leader.[146] He had victory within his grasp; yet he did not lift a finger to secure it.

There is no clear explanation for Trotsky's inaction. Perhaps, for all his revolutionary militance, he could not stomach behind-the-scenes personal politics. "He knows how to fight his enemies, but he does not know how to manage his friends," wrote Max Eastman, who had been on the scene at the time.[147] After his exile Trotsky realized and admitted the lost opportunity: "I have no doubt that if I had come forward on the eve of the Twelfth Congress in the spirit of a 'bloc of Lenin and Trotsky,' against the Stalin bureaucracy, I should have been victorious. . . . In 1922–23 . . . it was still possible to capture the commanding position by an open attack on the faction . . . of the epigones of Bolshevism." It should have been easy for Trotsky to decide on a course of action if he really perceived the situation as he did later with the wisdom of hindsight. He was balked, however, by inner fears: "Independent action on my part would have been interpreted, or to be more exact, represented as my personal fight for Lenin's place in the party and the state. The very thought of this made me shudder."[148]

Trotsky's attempt at an explanation only underscores his failure to take advantage of an obvious opportunity. It suggests a lapse in political will power and this may well have been a factor, as it was again at the end of the year when Trotsky failed to take the lead of the opposition which he had encouraged to come out into the open. The one-time Central Committee aide, Bazhanov, thought that Trotsky "considered the struggle with such opponents as beneath his dignity"; he reportedly read novels during sessions of the Politburo.[149]

Could Trotsky's silence have been a sign of a devious political calculation, betraying some kind of intrigue or the misguided notion that he could improve his chances by waiting until his popularity improved? This, or the idea that Trotsky was transfixed by the obligations of party discipline, are less likely possibilities. There is some evidence on yet another point, that Trotsky was distracted from politics by the fascination of economic planning. Zinoviev later criticized him for neglecting other duties in favor of this interest,[150] and Lenin's "Testament" pointed out the same tendency in Trotsky. At the same time he gave his rivals grounds for fearing that he wished to become an industrial dictator and monopolize the entire direction of the country's economy.[151]

Would an opportune thrust for power on Trotsky's part have succeeded, and, if so, would it have made any difference in the long run? It is impossible to escape the feeling that in early 1923 Trotsky held most of the trumps; he failed to play them properly and lost the game. His whole career as the leader of the Left Opposition was anticlimactic, a desperate but vain effort to recoup.

The effect which a Trotsky victory would have had is far more problematical, and the answer depends in large measure on how the subsequent development of the Soviet state is to be explained. To the degree that Stalinism and all its consequences followed from the social and economic circumstances of revolutionary Russia, or from the basic principles and practices of the Bolshevik Party, Trotsky's leadership could not have effected a substantial change. The dictatorship and the rigors of the industrialization drive no doubt would have proceeded as they actually did. But to the extent that personality can influence the course of events—and it is a large extent under any authoritarian system—the difference between Stalin and Trotsky was of momentous importance. Aside from the similarities in strength of ego, two more different personalities can hardly be conceived: Trotsky, the cultured, Westernized intellectual, brilliant, self-confident, and flamboyant; Stalin, the crafty, suspicious, methodical underground party worker, so "rough" that Lenin had called for his removal. The vindictive repressiveness of Soviet totalitarianism and the perverse intricacies of Soviet thought control stemmed directly from the intrigue-ridden mentality of the Caucasus vendetta. A Trotsky regime would have been much less hard on Russia. By the same token, it would have been a much more serious challenge to the non-Communist world.

The Twelfth Congress, which Stalin weathered without mishap, supplied plentiful evidence of the growing influence of the general secretary. Following the congress he assumed a steadily more prominent place in the activities of the party, though he carefully avoided challenging any of his associates openly. A surreptitious campaign was begun to embarrass Trotsky by references to his Menshevik past.[152] Stalin's partner, Zinoviev, who had assumed the position of titular head of the party by undertaking the delivery of the political report to the Twelfth Congress, was himself becoming uneasy. While Trotsky remained his *bête noire,* Zinoviev showed signs of concern about Stalin's growing power and undertook to contrive some means for curtailing the influence of the general secretary.

Towards the end of the summer of 1923, Zinoviev invited a number of other vacationing party leaders to confer with him in the North Caucasus, and a meeting was held, in an oddly conspiratorial fashion, in a cave near the resort of Kislovodsk.[153] Those present, besides Zinoviev and his personal supporters Lashevich and Yevdokimov, included Bukharin and Voroshilov. A plan was advanced by Zinoviev or Bukharin or both to put an end to Stalin's monopoly of organizational power in the Secretariat by "politicalizing" the Secretariat and converting it into a supreme directing body composed of Stalin and Trotsky together with Zinoviev or Kamenev or Bukharin. This reorganization project was communicated to Stalin, who wired a hurried reply to the effect that he was being misunderstood. Then he went to Kislovodsk in person to discuss the idea with Zinoviev and Bukharin. Stalin succeeded in deflecting Zinoviev's attack on the Secretariat and secured agreement on an alternative proposal. This was to give all the leading Politburo members seats in the Orgburo, ostensibly for the purpose of coordination. Actually it was only a gesture recognizing the primacy of the small group which was to sit in both bodies; it did not affect Stalin's organizational power.

In October 1923, pursuant to the Kislovodsk agreement, the Central Committee elected Trotsky and Zinoviev as members of the Orgburo, while Bukharin, still only a candidate member of the Politburo, received the same status in the Orgburo, together with I. I. Korotkov (one of the more obscure Central Committee members, who later served under Stalin on the Central Control Commission until he disappeared in the purges of the thirties).[154] Nothing came of all this maneuvering, however. By Zinoviev's own admission, he did not bother to avail himself of his new right to sit in on the Orgburo more than once or twice, while Trotsky and Bukharin failed to appear at all. The experiment was officially undone when a new Orgburo, almost wholly filled with Stalinists, was elected after the Thirteenth Party Congress in May 1924. Victory was destined for the man who did not feel that mundane organizational work was beneath him.

In the meantime, Zinoviev's concern about Stalin had lapsed when events made the eventuality of a Trotsky-Stalin coalition against him seem remote. By October 1923, the worsening economic situation and the resurgence of the Ultra-Left groups produced the most severe crisis in the party leadership since early 1921. The result was that Trotsky began—or was forced to begin—his venture into open opposition. The four-year drama of public controversy between the party leadership and the Left Opposition was about to commence.

9

THE NEW COURSE CONTROVERSY

The fall of 1923 represents a major turning point in the history of the Communist Opposition. Up to this time the manifestations of Opposition activity had been episodic, though the undercurrents of disagreement were steady. In contrast, the controversy which broke out into the open in December 1923 established the permanent lines of bitter factional struggle between the two major political currents in the Communist movement. The Leninists and the Left Opposition grappled in irreconcilable conflict, a political war to the death which was to end only with the actual liquidation of the vanquished Left.

THE SUMMER CRISIS OF 1923

The dissension which broke out late in 1923 was foreshadowed by growing left-wing concern over the trend of policy as directed by the troika and over the conduct of the party apparatus. These misgivings were brought to the breaking point by the economic straits in which the Soviet government found itself in the summer of 1923. The price imbalance of the scissors crisis was threatening to develop into a total breakdown of economic relations. On the far left the semilegal Opposition groups alarmed the leadership by a renewal of their activity. Among the party leaders the growing divergence on general economic policy was suddenly intensified by the urgent need for firm long-term decisions.

The scissors crisis, with agriculture outrunning demand and industry balked by the difficulties of recovery, took a sudden turn for the worse in July and August 1923. Industry, where prices had been raised artificially by the power of the state monopoly, faced a sales crisis. Unemployment rose, and wages were cut or paid irregularly.[1] In the face of this situation the government decided on the policy of forcing industry to clean house by pressing for the concentration of production in the most efficient plants, and especially by curtailing credit for the nationalized enterprises. Whatever the long-run wisdom of these moves, their immediate effect was to intensify the industrial crisis and throw large numbers of the urban workers into desperate circumstances.

As a result, unrest among the workers increased by leaps and bounds. Political agitation of various persuasions became rife in the factories. According to an official report, "Economic questions . . . are agitating the working masses. . . . Hostile elements have raised their heads. . . . In a series of large enterprises in Moscow and other cities there has been observed a revival of agitation hostile to us, especially in the enterprises with lower wages. Evil demagogy on questions of wages has suddenly increased in these months."[2] A wave of wildcat strikes swept the urban centers of the country in August and September, despite the opposition of the official trade-union leadership and the repeated intervention of the GPU.[3] Thus were industrial relations conducted in the "workers' state."

Especially alarming to the party leadership was the part which the Ultra-Left Opposition groups played or attempted to play in the strikes, with the aim of mobilizing proletarian sentiment against the government. Such influence was felt even within the ranks of the party, as "a process of generating a petty-bourgeois, proprietary ideology, gradual exit from party work, and efforts to become free from party discipline."[4]

By June the activities of the Workers' Group had reached the point where the police felt it necessary to step in, and Miasnikov was arrested. The organization carried on under his lieutenant, Kuznetsov, despite—or perhaps thanks to—the fanciful pretensions which the latter reportedly entertained about the strength of the movement.[5] Contacts were made, though with little effect, with other former leaders of the Workers' Opposition, and efforts were made to build up the organization in Moscow and infiltrate the regular Communist cells there. When the strike wave began in August, the Workers' Group tried to inject its leadership into the movement and agitated for mass political demonstrations. This action recalled the old spirit and tactics of the Bolshevik Party itself, before the possession of power wrought its transformation. The Soviet resources for control and policing, however, were of a different order from their tsarist antecedents, and arrests in September 1923 easily put a final end to the activity of the Workers' Group.[6]

The Workers' Truth was similarly invigorated by the labor crisis. It now professed to be nonpolitical, with the mission of providing the working class with intellectual leadership and cultural enlightenment. This did not secure the group immunity from the police. Even the old Bolshevik Bogdanov, who supplied doctrinal inspiration for the Workers' Truth, was reportedly put under arrest for a time.[7] The Central Control Commission of the party laid down its decision that the Workers' Truth was "both socially and ideologically an enemy . . . a Menshevik conspiracy," having as its express objective "the disorganization of our party." The Communist Party members involved in the Workers' Truth organization were expelled from the party—sentenced to political oblivion—and the ever-effective GPU disposed of the movement as readily as it had the Workers' Group.[8]

The difficulties which beset the party as a result of the economic situation were confined mainly to the rank and file. The party's organizational apparatus, in contrast, continued to strengthen itself and to extend its influence. The monthly reports of the Central Committee referred in an ever-increasing degree to the role of the Secretariat and especially of its Report and Assignment Division in strengthening the party organization, perfecting party control over the state machinery, and weeding out dissidents and incompetents from party and state organs. The intended results were achieved: the party was being made into an increasingly efficient instrument for political control. At the same time, however, the party as a group was rapidly losing to the secretarial apparatus all control over itself; Stalin's machine continued to accumulate power.

The Central Committee of the party met in September 1923 to decide on action to resolve the crisis of industrial dislocation and Ultra-Left criticism. Immediate attention was concentrated on the wage problem, and proper payment and emergency increases were stressed, together with the need for raising productivity and cutting administrative costs.[9] Three special subcommittees were set up—one to continue study of the wage problem, one to propose measures for ending the scissors crisis, and one to deal with the manifestations of extremist opposition in the party.[10] Meanwhile, the Central Committee reaffirmed its belief that the burden of reform lay with the managers of industry. Sokolnikov triumphed in his desire to keep the allocation of credit free from the constraints of long-term planning, and price fixing to protect the peasantry was put into effect.[11] The subcommittee on the scissors crisis was boycotted by the representatives of the Left (Trotsky and Preobrazhensky both declined invitations to participate), and when the group reported in December 1923, it emphatically affirmed the primacy of agriculture and the basic line of conciliating the peasantry at all cost.[12] The scissors crisis was finally brought under control, though the farm-factory price disparity remained an endemic threat throughout the twenties and contributed to the grain-supply crisis of 1928. The measures undertaken in 1923 to "close the scissors" affirmed the NEP considerably beyond the compromise of 1921, and the resulting dismay in left-wing circles could no longer be contained.

The first overt move by the new Opposition was prompted by the Central Committee's subcommittee on the political situation, headed by Dzerzhinsky, the former police chief who had become Commissar of Transport. Dzerzhinsky demonstrated the extent of the party's alarm and contrition over the Ultra-Left challenge by declaring to the Central Committee, "The dying out of our party, the dying out of its internal life, the prevalence of nomination instead of election, is becoming a political danger and is paralyzing our party in its political leadership of the working class."[13] When the subcommittee reported, however, its tone was different. The solution was found in disposing of the protests against repression with more repression; the subcommittee recommended that every party member be compelled to denounce to the GPU anyone known to be associated with an underground factional group.[14] This suggestion that party activities be subjected to one of the regular organs of governmental authority was unprecedented. It suggests a deep sense of insecurity among the party leadership and an increasing reliance on organizational and police force to resolve discomfiting ideological challenges. But the problem was only brought into clearer focus: the Opposition acquired a head, for the Dzerzhinsky recommendation finally caused Trotsky to end his long period of vacillation and take a firm opposition stand.

Any lingering compunctions which Trotsky may have had about taking a forthright position were swept aside when the troika undertook to maneuver him out of his dominant position in the War Commissariat. A proposal was made to expand the Revolutionary Military Council and to add to it a number of leading party figures, including Stalin.[15] According to a functionary who was present at the meeting, Trotsky replied with a threat to resign— he would go off and fight in the German revolution, which at that time was anticipated momentarily. Zinoviev called the bluff by proposing to dispatch Trotsky thither on a conspiratorial mission. Stalin, maneuvering between the two, referred to Trotsky's importance at home and dissuaded the group from such a course. His dignity offended by these proceedings, the proud war commissar rose to effect a dramatic walk-out from the Central Committee session, but his gesture failed, so the report goes, because he was unable to slam the heavy committee-room door as he left.[16]

Trotsky managed to avert a major shake-up of the War Commissariat, but he was compelled to accept on his council two of his old enemies, Voroshilov and Lashevich. Kuibyshev gave Trotsky a frank explanation of the whole maneuver: "We consider it necessary to undertake a struggle against you but cannot declare you an enemy; therefore we must have recourse to such methods."[17] Trotsky was unable to withstand the accumulated provocations on both the personal and policy levels. On October 8 he addressed a letter to the Central Committee and the Central Control Commission in which he openly denounced the whole organizational trend within the party.

Thus the stage was set for open struggle. Meanwhile, critical developments were occurring with respect to the Communist cause abroad, especially in Germany. The setback which the fortunes of the Comintern were shortly to suffer there, while not immediately decisive in Russian Communist politics, was a disturbance of the first magnitude. Within a year the German events were deeply involved in the party controversy.

PROBLEMS OF FOREIGN COMMUNISM—THE CRISIS IN GERMANY

The revolution in its international aspect had been an old stand-by for theoretical controversy among the Bolsheviks. The doctrine of world revolution was of the utmost importance for the Bolsheviks in justifying their effort to take and hold power in Russia, and the Communist International was established in the spring of 1919 amidst high hopes that the flames of revolution would soon race around the entire globe. Yet, despite the vast importance attributed to it, the international revolution was responsible for singularly little of the dissension among the Russian Communists during the early years of the Soviet regime. Only as Russian politics became more stabilized and constrained, toward the mid-twenties, and as the failures of the Comintern became obvious for all to see, did the subject of international Communism take on decisive significance for the controversy among the Russian factions.

Almost simultaneously with the NEP in Russian internal affairs, there was a parallel reassessment of the international scene and a corresponding adaptation in foreign policy. It was becoming clear that the revolutionary wave which followed the end of the First World War had lost its momentum, and that capitalism, as the expression went, had succeeded in stabilizing itself. Lenin moved as resolutely as he had with the NEP to take cognizance of realities and call upon the Comintern to take a defensive stand. A new strategy was adopted by the Comintern—the so-called united front. Direct incitement to revolution was abandoned in favor of trying to build Communist influence and win non-Communist allies. As in the case of the NEP, the issue presented by the Comintern retreat was the extent, duration, and meaning of the maneuver. A similar Left-Right cleavage rose, although the lineup of personalities was quite different. Among the Russian leaders involved in the Comintern, those who joined Lenin in a more cautious appraisal of revolutionary prospects were mostly from the Left—Trotsky, Radek, to some extent Bukharin.[18] The leader of the Comintern Left, hoping to resume the offensive at an early date, was a cautious right-winger at home —the Comintern chairman, Zinoviev, who could still say in mid-1922, "The world revolution is in full swing."[19]

At the Fourth Comintern Congress in 1922, Radek spoke in frankly pessimistic terms: "The broadest masses of the proletariat have lost belief in their ability to conquer power in the foreseeable future."[20] He had become the most outspoken proponent of alliance with non-Communist movements. For Germany (his personal responsibility as a Comintern leader) he urged Communist cooperation not only with the Social Democrats but even with the right-wing nationalists (the idea of "National Bolshevism").[21] "In no way," Radek warned, "can the world revolution win at one blow."[22]

In the middle of 1923 the mood of retrenchment in international revolution was suddenly suspended when the Soviet leaders discovered grounds for believing that Germany, the country they had always looked to as the industrial key to revolutionary success, was on the verge of a Communist victory. Radek, with Bukharin's backing, had been vigorously applying his National Bolshevism line in Germany, in cooperation with the right-wing German Communist leadership under Heinrich Brandler.[23] Zinoviev was growing restive, not only because he disagreed with this cautious course, but also out of anxiety about his political position in Russia—this was near the time of his Kislovodsk intrigue. Followers of his less compromising line had just committed a resounding blunder in Bulgaria, sitting on their hands when a quasi-fascist coup in June 1923 put an end to the democratic peasant regime of Stambulisky. For the sake of his own prestige, Zinoviev urgently needed a revolutionary victory.[24]

The Soviet leadership was confronted in July 1923 with the necessity of a decision for the German Communists, who were debating whether to hold a massive demonstration after the authorities had forbidden it. Zinoviev and now Bukharin were in favor of the move and communicated their endorsement from the North Caucasus. Radek was strongly opposed and with the support of Stalin, who was at this point beginning to show more and more independence in the troika, he had the demonstration canceled.[25] Stalin wrote to Zinoviev and Bukharin, "If today in Germany the power, so to speak, falls, and the Communists seize hold of it, they will fall with a crash. . . . In my opinion, the Germans must be curbed, and not spurred on."[26] However, with the runaway inflation and the French occupation in the Ruhr, the situation in Germany was rapidly approaching a crisis. The ultimate indignity for the German government was a strike of the money printers in August, which paralyzed the financial system and served as the signal for a near-general strike.

It now seemed to the Soviet government that Germany was entering upon a true revolutionary situation, while the Russians' natural desire to take action was fortified by the new Stresemann government and its turn to the West. By mid-September most of the Soviet leaders had swung over to the plan for a German Communist uprising, and gave it their formal endorsement. Most enthusiastic of all was Trotsky, suddenly converted from his conservatism about the Comintern.[27]

The division among the Soviet leaders on the German issue defies all classification. Radek (of the Russian Left, supporting the German Right) was brought together with Stalin (Russian Right, inclined to back the German Left) in opposition to the proposed insurrection. Trotsky (Russian Left, backing the German Right), Bukharin (moving to the Russian Right, also backing the German Right), and Zinoviev (Russian Right, backing the German Left) were united in supporting the venture. This political crazy quilt was the result of political friendships and animosities which cut across ideological lines. Radek had long been closely associated with the German Right Communists and the policy of caution; he was consistent in his international views, at least, even if they did not square with his affiliations in the Russian party. Zinoviev was equally consistent at the opposite pole, with his support of the German Left and their revolutionary hopes. This can be reconciled with his caution respecting Russian internal policy if it is seen as the more strictly Marxist view that little could be accomplished in Russia in the way of socialist progress until the advent of the world revolution.

Trotsky was drawn to the German Right through his association with Radek and his antipathy toward Zinoviev, though this did not prevent his endorsing the revolution. Stalin occupied the reverse position: the course of political intrigue against Trotsky or Zinoviev (or both) led him to favor the German Left, while his natural caution still impelled him to discount the chances of revolution.

This factional confusion had fateful consequences for the movement in Germany. Brandler, the right-wing leader of the German Communists, was thrown into a state of acute anxiety when the Russian leadership shifted in mid-summer to support the insurrectionary line. Fearful of being forced out of his post, Brandler strove to keep himself in favor with Moscow by dissimulating a leftward shift himself and pretending to be optimistic about the revolutionary situation in Germany. His distorted picture of the situation, in turn, fortified Moscow's inclination to press for the revolution, and detailed preparations were undertaken at the Russians' behest and with their assistance.[28]

The critical moment came in October—which gave it a special emotional ring for the Russians—when Germany reached the verge of civil war between the Communist-led workers and the antirepublican forces spearheaded by the army. The German Communists were ready for revolt as never before. One last step remained—the proclamation of a general strike to defend the Communist-Socialist coalition governments in the states of Saxony and Thuringia against the intervention of federal troops. Brandler failed to win Social Democratic assent to the strike, gave way to his personal qualms, and called off the whole insurrection. The Hamburg Communist organization, by mistake getting the word to rise, was bloodily crushed. Disillusionment and division put an end to the revolutionary *élan* of the German Communists. The grounds for faith in the world revolution crumbled.

The immediate effect of this blow upon the Russian leadership was trifling compared to the issue which Trotsky made of it the following year. Moscow was generally in agreement that Brandler's faulty leadership was to blame, and undoubtedly this was correct in fixing responsibility for the failure to stage a real test of strength, to win or go down fighting. Brandler was removed in favor of the German Left. Underlying the whole debacle, however, was the fact that the Russians had asserted their authority but were unable to exercise it with one mind. This fault was shortly to be remedied, though not to the immediate advantage of the international Communist cause—Stalin's obstinate blunders continued on a lavish scale.

Once open controversy had broken out in Russia in December 1923 between the Left and the party leadership, both sides began trying to make capital out of the German fiasco. Radek asserted that Trotsky had the confidence of most of the international movement, a point borne out by much of the debate in the Comintern executive committee the following month.

In reply the leadership denounced the culprits Brandler and Radek, and by implication Trotsky.[29] Radek, who continued to support the German Right, was singled out for special censure in a decision of the Central Committee which was ratified by the Thirteenth Party Conference. He was charged with "incorrect conduct," "incorrect evaluation of class forces in Germany," opportunism, and insubordination, and was warned against "injecting the Russian factional controversy into the Comintern."[30] Radek countered with the argument, in which he was supported by Trotsky and Piatakov, that the retreat in Germany was entirely correct.[31] Trotsky's endorsement of the Radek view, at variance with his own stand both before and afterwards, was obviously a political maneuver. He admitted much later that Radek's theses were "erroneous."[32]

Arguments no longer had much to do with the deciding of the issue. A new Left leadership was installed in Germany, and another long step was taken toward Soviet control of the foreign Communist movement. Inside Russia, the Trotskyist Opposition was being severely beaten. In the first and crucial test of strength between the main Communist factions, the party apparatus proved its own decisive power.

THE CONTROVERSY BEHIND THE SCENES

The immediate occasion for Trotsky's declaring himself against the leadership in his letter of October 8, 1923, was the report by Dzerzhinsky's subcommittee on the internal troubles of the party. Dzerzhinsky had evidently been weaned away from his sympathy with the Left. In his committee recommendation, he was again the policeman rather than the political oppositionist, and denunciation of illicit factionalism was his main prescription. The frame of mind displayed by the Dzerzhinsky subcommittee compelled Trotsky to speak out:

It would seem that to inform the party organizations of the fact that its branches are being used by elements hostile to the party is an obligation of party members so elementary that it ought not to be necessary to introduce a special resolution to that effect six years after the October Revolution. The very demand for such a resolution means: (a) that illegal oppositional groups have been formed in the party; (b) that there exist such states of mind in the party as to permit comrades knowing about such groups not to inform the party organizations. Both these facts testify to an extraordinary deterioration of the situation within the party from the time of the Twelfth Congress.[33]

Trotsky was by no means disposed to condone the existence of the "illegal groupings," the Workers' Group and the Workers' Truth, but he hoped to make political capital by attributing their growth to the conduct of the party apparatus and its repression of honest intraparty criticism. Trotsky admitted that he himself had at first been skeptical of this argument for party democracy. Referring to the Twelfth Congress, he declared:

Many of the speeches at that time spoken in defense of workers' democracy seemed to me exaggerated and to a considerable extent demagoguish, in view of the incompatibility of a fully developed workers' democracy with the regime of dictatorship. But it was perfectly clear that the pressure of the period of War Communism ought to give place to a more lively and broader party responsibility. However, this present regime, which began to form itself before the Twelfth Congress, and which subsequently received its final reinforcement and formulation—is much farther from workers' democracy than the regime of the fiercest period of War Communism. The bureaucratization of the party apparatus has developed to unheard-of proportions by means of the method of secretarial selection. There has been created a very broad stratum of party workers, entering into the apparatus of the government of the party, who completely renounce their own party opinion, at least the open expression of it, as though assuming that the secretarial hierarchy is the apparatus which creates party opinion and party decisions. Beneath this stratum, abstaining from their own opinions, there lies the broad mass of the party, before whom every decision stands in the form of a summons or command. In this foundation-mass of the party there is an unusual amount of dissatisfaction. . . . This dissatisfaction does not dissipate itself by way of influence of the mass upon the party organization (election of party committees, secretaries, etc.), but accumulates in secret and thus leads to interior strains.

Trotsky nevertheless tried to emphasize that his concern was to secure the proper policy rather than to attack the existing leadership. To support this he pointed to his disinclination to make his views public to the whole party:

It is known to the members of the Central Committee and the Central Control Commission that while fighting with all decisiveness and definiteness within the Central Committee against a false policy, I decisively declined to bring the struggle within the Central Committee to the judgment even of a very narrow circle of comrades, in particular those who in the event of a reasonably proper party course ought to occupy prominent places in the Central Committee.

Putting teeth in this scarcely veiled threat of a shake-up, Trotsky made known his intention to carry the issue to the whole party membership, if necessary.

In all of Trotsky's appeal to principle and his warnings of future dangers, his colleagues in the Politburo professed to see nothing but unbridled ambition for personal power:

We consider it necessary to say frankly to the party that at the basis of all the dissatisfaction of Comrade Trotsky, all his irritation, all his attacks against the Central Committee which have continued already for several years, his determination to disturb the party, lies the circumstance that Trotsky wants the Central Committee to place him . . . at the head of our industrial life. . . .

Trotsky is a member of the Council of People's Commissars, a member of the Council of Labor and Defense; Lenin offered him the post of vice-president of the Council of People's Commissars. In all these positions Trotsky might, if he wished to, demonstrate in action, working before the eyes of the whole party, that the party might trust him with those practically unlimited powers in the sphere of industry and military affairs towards which he strives. But Trotsky preferred another method of action. . . .

Trotsky categorically declined the position of substitute for Lenin. That evidently he considers beneath his dignity. He conducts himself according to the formula, "All or nothing."[34]

Trotsky could only reply with a detailed recounting of the issues of the past year in which he had backed Lenin or had been supported by the party chief, against the rest of the leadership—economic planning, foreign trade, the nationality question, the Rabkrin, and the embarrassing episode when the Politburo tried to suppress Lenin's reform plan.[35]

Meanwhile an even more serious challenge was thrown up to the party leadership by the "Declaration of the Forty-six."[36] This was a secret statement submitted to the Politburo on October 15 by forty-six party figures of oppositionist inclination, who set forth a sweeping criticism of the record of the party leadership in the areas of economic policy and intraparty democracy. This document could not be so lightly dismissed as a manifestation of personal ambition; it was symptomatic of real, widespread, and principled discontent within the party. Even more significant was the combination of forces which the lists of signatories represented. For the first time since 1918 the extreme and moderate wings of the Left Opposition were united on a common platform and in a jointly organized effort. Prominent among the moderate Leftists, people who had, for example, stood with Trotsky in the trade-union controversy, were Preobrazhensky, Serebriakov, Piatakov, Antonov-Ovseyenko, and Ivan Smirnov. (Radek expressed solidarity with the Forty-six in a separate declaration.[37]) The former Ultra-Left was represented by a strong contingent of Democratic Centralists, including Osinsky, Sapronov, Bubnov, Vladimir Kosior, Maksimovsky, and Vladimir Smirnov.

In the minds of the Opposition the critical situation in the economy and in the party was closely related to the party leadership and to the need for reform. Regarding economic policy the Forty-six charged,

The casualness, thoughtlessness, lack of system in the decisions of the Central Committee, not making ends meet in the area of the economy, has led to this, that with undoubted large successes in the area of industry, agriculture, finance, and transport, successes achieved by the country's economy essentially not thanks to, but in spite of the unsatisfactory leadership, or rather, in the absence of any leadership— we face the prospect not only of the cessation of this success, but of a serious general economic crisis.

Such was their explanation of the scissors crisis, from which they feared dangerous consequences in default of proper corrective policies:

If broad, considered, planned and energetic measures are not taken quickly, if the present absence of direction continues, we will face the possibility of an unusually sharp economic shock, unavoidably linked with internal political complications and with complete paralysis of our external activity and strength. And the latter, as anyone understands, we need now more than ever; on it depends the fate of the world revolution and of the working class of all countries.

The failure of leadership was attributed to the state of affairs within the party:

The party is to a significant degree ceasing to be that living self-acting collective, which really embraces living activity, being linked by thousands of threads with this activity. Instead of this we observe more and more a progressive division of the party, no longer concealed by hardly anyone, into the secretarial hierarchy and the "laymen," into the professional party functionaries, selected from above, and the simple party masses, who do not participate in its group life. . . .

The regime which has been set up within the party is absolutely intolerable; it kills initiative in the party, subjects the party to an apparatus of appointed officials, which undeniably functions in normal times, but which unavoidably misfires in moments of crisis, and which threatens to reveal itself as completely bankrupt in the face of impending serious events.

This hypertrophy of the organization the Forty-six held responsible, as Trotsky did, for the illegal extremist groupings in the party.

The Central Committee and the Central Control Commission met for a plenary session from October 25 to October 27, and the leadership employed this forum to prepare countermeasures against Trotsky and the Forty-six.[38] Trotsky was kept away from the meeting by the onset of the mysterious illness which afflicted him most of that winter.[39] At the most crucial moment the outstanding Opposition leader was an invalid. Preobrazhensky was the main Opposition spokesman at the plenum, and he continued to carry the major burden of active leadership of the Opposition throughout the period of the New Course controversy. He offered to the Central Committee a resolution embodying the principles of "workers' democracy," including free expression and discussion, real control and elections by the membership, and an end to political bias in the operations of the Secretariat—that is, the political reforms demanded by the Forty-six.[40]

All such pleas were disregarded by the leadership. Instead, they chose the course of counterattack on the issue of factionalism:

The Plenum of the Central Committee and the Central Control Commission . . . considers Comrade Trotsky's move, at a crucial moment in the experience of the party and the world revolution, as a grave political error, especially because Comrade Trotsky's attack, directed at the Politburo, has objectively assumed the character of a factional move, threatening to strike a blow at the unity of the party, and creating a crisis in the party. . . .

The path chosen by Comrade Trotsky has served as a signal for a factional grouping (the Declaration of the Forty-six).

The Plenum of the Central Committee and the Central Control Commission . . .
resolutely condemns the Declaration of the Forty-six as a step of factional-
splitting politics which has assumed this character even if this was not the desire
of the signatories of this declaration. This declaration threatens to place the whole
life of the party for the coming months under the sign of an intraparty struggle
and thereby to weaken the party at a moment which is most crucial for the fate
of the international revolution.[41]

This was the keynote for the campaign against the Opposition which was
shortly to begin.

The state of general unrest in the party in the fall of 1923 is attested to
by the course of action which the leadership followed during November and
early December. They felt it necessary to admit that the party was indeed
experiencing a crisis, and that a "new course" toward workers' democracy
within the party was essential. To the end of working out such a new program, an open party-wide discussion, such as usually took place only immediately before a congress, was proclaimed. Zinoviev opened the debate on
November 7 with concessions that seemed broad on paper: "It is necessary
that intraparty workers' democracy, of which we have spoken so much, begin
to a greater degree to take on flesh and blood. . . . Our chief trouble consists
often in the fact that almost all very important questions go predecided from
above downwards."[42]

Throughout the following month a lively discussion proceeded in the
local party organizations. As reflected in the pages of *Pravda,* the tone of
the rank and file was one of acute concern for the restoration of party democracy. According to one complaint, "the party apparatus is ossifying, it is
beginning to be transformed into a caste of 'party-worker specialists,' of a
special kind of 'priests,' etc., etc."[43] On the other hand, much opinion held
that the apparatus was not strong and effective enough. The bureaucratic
structure of the party organization was not criticized as much as its specific
performance; too often the answer was seen in more and better bureaucracy.

Until December there were almost no public attacks on the record of the
current party leadership. Everyone took a stand in favor of reform. To the
party rank and file (to whom the Opposition declarations of October were
unknown), it seemed that the question was simply one of practical remedies
for the evil of bureaucratism, to which everyone was opposed. By opposing
as supporters of reform, the party leadership allowed much discontent to be
vented and successfully diverted this wrath away from themselves and toward
abstract evils and anonymous bureaucrats. Near the end of November the
tone of the discussion grew sharper. Preobrazhensky extended the scope of
his criticism of the party's organizational policy by attacking the failure to

make necessary structural changes at the end of the War Communism period:

It was necessary to liquidate the military methods within the party, to restore party life in part according to the type of 1917–1918, to develop the activity and initiative of organizations and individual members in the business of posing and discussing all the fundamental questions of party life: it was necessary to give to each member of the party the possibility of taking a more active and conscious part in the decision of all fundamental party and political questions . . . without accusing hands being waved at you . . . and without being called demagogue, Mensheviser, vacillator, "deviationist," etc. . . .

It is characteristic that when we had fronts all around us, party life displayed much more vitality, and the independence of the organizations was much greater. At the time when not only had the objective conditions for invigorating intraparty life and adapting it to new tasks appeared, but when also there existed a real necessity for the party to do this, we not only did not step forward in comparison with the period of War Communism, but on the contrary intensified bureaucratism, petrification, the number of questions predecided from above; we intensified the division of the party, begun in the war period, into those who make decisions and bear responsibility, and the masses who carry out these party decisions in the making of which they have had no part. Instead of a course toward collective initiative of the organizations and the raising of the level of all members of the party in a process of living participation in all intraparty decisions, on the basis of the consciousness of each for each of these decisions, a course was taken toward a good apparatus and toward a good party officialdom.[44]

The party leaders immediately reacted publicly by charging that certain unnamed oppositionists were guilty of advocating freedom for factionalism and of wanting to transform the party into a "parliament of opinions."[45] Stalin, hinting that Trotsky was so inclined, insisted to the contrary that "the party is not only a union of like-minded people, it is . . . a fighting union of common action. . . ." This meant to Stalin, "It is necessary to put limits to discussion, to preserve the party, which is the fighting unit of the proletariat, from degeneration into a discussion club."[46]

Zinoviev also unmasked his real feelings about democracy. Referring to the rule made by the Tenth Congress that only members of at least two years standing could vote for delegates to party gatherings, he explained: "From the point of view of abstract workers' democracy this is a mockery of 'democracy.' But it was necessary for us from the point of view of the fundamental interests of the revolution, from the point of view of the *good of the revolution,* to give the vote only to those who appear to be real guardians of the party. . . . *The good of the revolution—this is the highest law.* Every revolutionist says: to the devil with 'sacred' principles of 'pure' democracy."[47]

While the discussion on "workers' democracy" was in progress, the party leadership made a concerted effort to bring Trotsky into agreement with them, in order to maintain the appearance of unity. Since Trotsky was ill, the Politburo held lengthy sessions in his apartment so that he could participate in drawing up a resolution to serve as the official conclusion to the public discussion.[48] When Trotsky rejected a proposed draft of the resolution, Stalin and Kamenev constituted themselves a subcommittee along with Trotsky to prepare a new statement.[49] The resolution was adopted by the Politburo on December 5 and was published with great fanfare as the promise of real reform.[50] By the evidence of the text, Trotsky's was the main contribution.

The resolution began with a characteristically Leftist analysis of the economic situation in attributing the crisis to the disproportionate weakness of industry. The troubles within the party were also blamed on the circumstances of the NEP:

The objective contradictions of the given stage of the transitional period, stemming from the simultaneous existence of very diverse economic forms, from the presence of market relationships, from the necessity for state institutions to have recourse to capitalistic forms and methods of practical work, from the necessity of relying in this work on a personal staff of functionaries which is still alien to the proletariat, etc.—these objective contradictions are expressed in a whole series of negative tendencies, the struggle with which must be placed on the order of the day. Among such tendencies are: sharp divergences in the material position of members of the party in connection with differences in their functions, and the so-called "excesses" [izlishestva]; the growth of connections with bourgeois elements and ideological influences from the latter; departmental narrowing of horizon, which must be distinguished from necessary specialization, and the appearance on this basis of a weakening of connection between Communists in various branches of work; a danger of losing the perspective of socialist construction as a whole and of the world revolution . . . ; bureaucratization of the party apparatuses and the rise everywhere of a threat of cleavage between the party and the masses.

This was a diagnosis of the party crisis which could not fail to satisfy the most critical oppositionist. On the other hand, the resolution did not give carte blanche to opposition factions:

Workers' democracy signifies freedom of open discussion by all members of the party of the most important questions of party life, freedom of controversy about them, and also electiveness of the leading official individuals and collegia from below upwards. However, it does not at all suggest freedom of factional groupings, which are for a ruling party extremely dangerous, for they always threaten to divide or splinter the government and the state apparatus as a whole. It is self-evident that within the party, which is a voluntary association of people with a definite ideological and practical basis, it is impossible to tolerate groupings, the ideological contents of which are directed against the party as a whole and against the dictatorship of the proletariat (such as, for example, the "Workers' Truth" and the "Workers' Group").

In the deliberations of the editorial subcommittee Trotsky had objected to a provision for the "suppression of groupings," though he accepted a ban on "factions." Stalin and Kamenev proposed as a compromise a simple reference to the Tenth Congress resolution on unity, and Trotsky agreed. Stalin prided himself on a clever maneuver here: Trotsky, he later pointed out, had forgotten that the 1921 resolution condemned "groupings" as well as "factions."[51] The distinction, in any case, was an artificial one, and the antifactional principle was to prove an insuperable obstacle for the Opposition.

A long list of practical reforms was embodied in the resolution, based on the theme of improving the ties between party officials and the membership. This was to be accomplished by enforcing real elections of party officials, with particular reference to secretaries of cells; by discussion of issues by the membership; by facilitating the promotion of new party workers to responsible posts; by better informing the membership about the activities of the Central Committee; by increasing educational efforts; and by doubling the frequency of provincial and nation-wide party conferences to provide a semiannual expression of rank-and-file opinion. The control commissions were charged anew with "the struggle against the bureaucratic perversion of the party apparatus and party practice, and against the penetration into responsible offices of people in the party who are obstructing the carrying out of the principles of workers' democracy in the activity of the party organizations."

The resolution of December 5 appeared to represent a triumph of Opposition views, but its acceptance by the party leadership only signified a tactical withdrawal preparatory to a counterattack. (Some years later a spokesman for the apparatus actually described the resolution as "a mistaken concession to Trotsky."[52]) Preobrazhensky charged explicitly that the passage of the resolution was a mere maneuver: "The members of the Central Committee found the time absolutely ripe to cast upon the waves of party public opinion which had always begun to rage, the document of December 5. This decision could have been made earlier, it could have been made in October, when this transition could have been carried out with much less strain. But thanks to the fact that the Central Committee waited for a push from below, and has here again, if you will excuse the expression, carried on a policy of tailendism, there is now a situation which has been much aggravated in connection with this discussion."[53]

Trotsky, aware of the hostility toward him that was barely concealed behind the resolution, undertook to stress its reform implications in an open letter to a party meeting on December 8.[54] This New Course letter was an enthusiastic endorsement and explanation of the resolution of December 5, with emphasis on the role of the party rank-and-file in its execution:

The resolution of the Political Bureau on the party organization bears an exceptional significance. It indicates that the party has arrived at an important turning point in its historical road.

Trotsky cautioned his audience against covert opponents of the New Course:

Inclined to overestimate the role of the apparatus and to underestimate the initiative of the party, some conservative-minded comrades criticize the resolution of the Political Bureau. The Central Committee, they say, is assuming impossible obligations; the resolution will only engender illusions and produce negative results. It is clear that such an approach reveals a profound bureaucratic distrust of the party. The center of gravity which was mistakenly placed in the apparatus by the old course has now been transferred by the new course, proclaimed in the resolution of the Central Committee, to the activity, the initiative and the critical spirit of all the party members, as the organized vanguard of the proletariat.

Trotsky warned against overestimation of the efficacy of the resolution alone and indicated his concern about the need to "push it from beneath":

The new course does not at all signify that the party apparatus is charted with decreeing, creating, or establishing a democratic regime at such and such a date. No. This regime will be realized by the party itself. To put it briefly: the party must subordinate to itself its own apparatus without for a moment ceasing to be a centralized organization.

In Trotsky's mind, and for the moderate Left in general, this goal was not a contradiction, but only a question of proportions: "Democracy and centralism are two faces of party organization. The question is to harmonize them in the most correct manner. . . . During the last period, there was no such equilibrium. The center of gravity wrongly centered in the apparatus. . . . The idea, or at the very least the feeling, that bureaucratism threatened to get the party into a blind alley had become pretty general. . . . The resolution on the new course is the first official expression of the change that has taken place in the party. It will be realized to the degree that the party, that is, its four hundred thousand members, will want to realize it and will succeed in doing so."

The professions of reforming ardor on the part of the party bureaucracy brought a note of bitterness from Trotsky:

Before the publication of the decision of the Central Committee on the "new course," the mere pointing out of the need of modifying the internal party regime was regarded by bureaucratized apparatus functionaries as heresy, as factionalism, as an infraction of discipline. And now the bureaucrats are ready formally to "take note" of the "new course," that is, *to nullify it bureaucratically.*

To this dangerous charge that the party organization was not acting in good faith Trotsky added an open appeal for a wholesale purge of the leadership:

The renovation of the party apparatus . . . must aim at replacing the mummified bureaucrats with fresh elements. . . . And before anything else, the leading posts must be cleared out of those who, at the first word of criticism, of objection, or of protest, brandish the thunderbolts of penalties before the critic. The "new course" must begin by making everyone feel that from now on nobody will dare terrorize the party.

Now that Trotsky had put himself publicly at the head of the Opposition with his New Course letter, open political combat between the factions became inevitable.

THE OPEN RUPTURE

Trotsky's sympathizers lost no time in translating the paper reforms of December 5 into an open demand for action. Led by Preobrazhensky, the Leftists spoke out strongly at meetings of the district party organizations in the city of Moscow. Preobrazhensky prepared a resolution calling for sweeping reform—"the broad introduction of the elective principle for all leaders of the party apparatus from top to bottom, and also an appropriate refreshing [sic] among the leading comrades in party work, for the practice of the system of military command which they have adopted hinders the transition to the new forms of party structure." These terms were much too strong for the leadership, and Zinoviev, Bukharin, and Sokolnikov, among others, appeared at the district meetings to make sure that the Opposition was rebuffed.[55]

On December 11, the day Trotsky's New Course letter appeared in *Pravda,* the Opposition made a major sally at a city-wide mass meeting of the Moscow party organization. Sapronov was the chief Opposition speaker, answering Kamenev. He repeated the theme of bureaucracy as the cause of factionalism and suggested that the party purge the apparatus instead of the reverse. "We need voting without 'recommendations,'" he added, "without preliminary 'agreements'; the cell must choose its own bureau without any pressure."[56] All the oppositionists protested that they wished only to reform the apparatus, not abolish it, but Preobrazhensky went far toward a repudiation of the authority of the party over its members. He specifically defended the formation of informal "groupings" to express different points of view on any particular question.[57] Radek, with some justification, adduced Lenin's authority for this point of view.[58] Though Preobrazhensky's resolution failed to carry, representatives of the leadership were shouted down, and the general atmosphere at the meeting seems to have been one of oppositionist enthusiasm and reforming zeal.

An immediate counterattack was the indicated move for the leadership. Every effort would have to be bent to turn criticism back at the Opposition. This was the course pursued, daringly and with all the strength at the command of the party leadership. Trotsky has suggested another possible factor in the sudden change.[59] According to this report, Stalin, when he was negotiating with Trotsky before the open break, gave Zinoviev grounds for fearing that he was going to make a deal with Trotsky. Zinoviev thereupon called upon his Petrograd machine to launch the open attack on Trotsky and compelled Stalin to follow suit. *Pravda* changed its tone literally overnight. On December 12 an editorial spoke in familiar generalities of the widespread dissatisfaction with bureaucratism and the improvements which would result from the New Course: It went so far as to say, "Of course, it may happen . . . that certain really bureaucratic elements will resist. But it is clear to all that this resistance will be broken by the single-minded will of the party." An ominous note was sounded, however: "The 'new course' will be carried out as it is necessary to carry it out, not as it could be executed by those who do not know how to defend the foundations of our centralized and disciplined party. The party will be able to preserve both its unity and its apparatus, purging it and reaching that degree of elasticity and flexibility which is necessary for the resolution of the problems next on the order of the day." The next day, December 13, *Pravda* came out openly against the Opposition, which was charged with a variety of sins—opportunism, advocating the destruction of the party apparatus, making the false accusation of "bureaucratic overgrowth," which "has nothing in common with objective analysis of events," and, worst of all, trying to make a distinction between Marxism and Leninism.

This was only a preliminary to the main attack, which began on December 15 with an article in *Pravda* by Stalin and a speech by Zinoviev in Petrograd (published in *Pravda* on December 20 and 21). The party leaders charged that Trotsky in his New Course letter had violated the unanimity of the Politburo by making a public statement in opposition to the unanimously adopted resolution of December 5. This, in effect, was to accuse the Opposition of resisting its own program—an indication of the extent to which the party press was now capable of twisting the truth.

Throughout the second half of December, violent controversy raged in the key party organizations. As Zinoviev described these weeks, "For the first time in the history of our revolution, at least since October, we had a situation when between congresses, in the middle of the year, attempts were made to change the policy of the Central Committee in a fundamental manner and even to change the very composition of the Central Committee, to change horses in mid-stream. . . . The question of 'no confidence' in the Central Committee . . . was the burning question in almost every cell."[60]

In this critical bid for a party endorsement the Opposition was crippled at the outset: Trotsky suddenly withdrew from the struggle. Just as during the crisis of Lenin's break with Stalin, Trotsky allowed himself to be drawn into controversy and then failed to fight in his own cause. Ostensibly the reason this time was illness—the undiagnosed fever which plagued him from November 1923 on through January 1924. In spite of this Trotsky was able to write, criticize, and participate in top-level deliberations, up to mid-

December when the attack against his New Course letter was launched. From that moment on, he appeared to be politically paralyzed, and early in January he left Moscow to recuperate at the Black Sea resort of Sukhum. The leadership of the Opposition fell entirely to Trotsky's sympathizers of the Forty-six group, particularly Preobrazhensky, Osinsky, and Sapronov. These were able and conscientious men, but they were tainted much more than Trotsky by their anti-Leninist records, and they lacked Trotsky's personal prestige. The Opposition had to fight the decisive engagement without their commander.

The party leadership had two unfailing sources of strength in its effort to discredit the Opposition—control of the press and domination of party meetings. The latter was especially important, since in the last analysis it was the votes of the party membership, or those votes as they were counted, which would determine the composition of the responsible party gatherings of delegates. Bukharin himself admitted the steamroller tactics which the supporters of the troika used in many party organizations: "Usually the secretaries of the cells are appointed by the district committees. . . . They simply present the person, and usually the voting takes place according to an established type. When the group has assembled they are asked: 'Who is against?' And since one is more or less afraid to speak out against, the designated individual is appointed secretary of the bureau of the group."[61]

Of particular value to the party leadership in the controversy was the recently strengthened apparatus of the Central Control Commission and its local affiliates. Kuibyshev, the new chairman, boasted about the part which his organization played in "preventing the development of disagreements to a degree dangerous for the unity of the party."[62] The organizational sanctions at the disposal of the party leadership were strongly reinforced by the power of the press, which in turn was kept exclusively on the side of the leadership by the application of party discipline. Certain *Pravda* staff members who favored reporting both sides of the controversy impartially were summarily fired by order of the Central Control Commission.[63] The Opposition found it progressively more difficult to express their views in public; Trotsky's pamphlet, "The New Course," was virtually banned from circulation.[64]

For a time the Opposition managed to retain considerable support in the cells of university students and among party members in Moscow holding positions in the government. The fact that students comprised 25 per cent of the membership of the Moscow party organization helps explain the concentration of Opposition strength there.[65] In the articles which he wrote to elaborate the New Course letter, Trotsky gave special attention to the students and the party youth, in whom he saw the hope of the future. (This point was to draw particular wrath from the party leadership.) The Communist youth organization was badly split by the controversy, and a majority of its Central Committee, having proved insufficiently reliable from the point of view of the party leadership, was ousted.[66]

The Opposition failed to win support among the workers. Both the Trotskyists and the former Democratic Centralists were much more intellectual than proletarian in orientation, and in their economic thinking they inclined to stress the position of industrial management. The leadership jumped at the opportunity to proclaim their superior proletarian qualities, even though their current peasant-oriented economic policy was much more conservative than the Opposition's. Shliapnikov, opting for unity at this juncture, commented bitterly, "In the present controversy the only goal of Comrade Trotsky and the Opposition is simply to seize the apparatus."[67] Neither the leadership nor the Trotsky Opposition made any appeal to the genuine proletarian discontent which the Workers' Group and the Workers' Truth had tried to exploit.

In addition to matters of policy and atmosphere, the organizational factor was a powerful obstacle to Opposition success among the workers. The party apparatus was indeed genuinely proletarian in the sense that the proletarians were the people most susceptible to manipulation and control by the organization.[68] When the test of strength came in December 1923, the cells of factory workers, and the provinces generally, were lined up almost completely on the side of the organization. Whatever the natural leanings of the workers, pressure by the party apparatus prevented any significant Opposition communication with them. Criticism of the apparatus was not so much refuted as buried under an avalanche of propaganda. The Left Opposition after 1923 never got beyond the position of a sect of well-meaning but hopelessly outnumbered intellectuals, except for the *apparatchiki* whom Zinoviev brought over with him when he broke with Stalin and Bukharin in 1925.

Moscow was the only center of real Opposition strength. Only in the capital did anything approaching free discussion take place, but apparently even there irregularities occurred in the elections. According to one observer, "The majority at OGPU headquarters declared for Trotsky. There were some nice manipulations, in which Zinoviev figured, to beat Trotsky."[69] During the debate at the Thirteenth Conference, Sapronov pointed out that the Opposition had won 36 per cent of the representation at the district conferences in the Moscow province, but in the elections for the provincial conference officially received only 18 per cent of the vote. "If the Opposition lost 18 per cent between the district conferences and the provincial conference, then I pose the question: of how many votes was the Opposition deprived in the workers' cells by the pressure of the apparatus, when these votes went to the district conferences?"[70] Reasoning in this manner, Sapronov concluded that the Opposition had been defrauded out of an actual majority in the Moscow province.

The abuses of the party organization were a primary subject of protest by the Opposition, but to the leadership they were the means for smothering the entire controversy. The Secretariat brought into play its power of transfer, which had already proven to be an effective political weapon against the Ukrainian Leftists and the Workers' Opposition. Opposition sympathizers were removed from positions of influence, while pro-Opposition students were expelled from the universities.[71] Most sensational was the removal of Antonov-Ovseyenko from the crucial post of head of the Political Administration of the army, for refusing to carry out the instructions of the leadership during the controversy.[72] The Deputy War Commissar Lashevich called Antonov an "embittered enemy," and justified his removal in strict Leninist terms: "It is wrong to allow the Chief of the Political Administration of the army to be someone who does not support the line of the Central Committee and who cannot therefore carry out its instructions."[73] Antonov was replaced by Bubnov, a former Democratic Centralist and one of the signers of the Declaration of the Forty-six, who now switched to the side of the apparatus and remained a Stalin supporter until he was purged in the 1930s.[74]

While organizational power determined the outcome of the controversy, the Opposition compounded their weakness in this regard with serious tactical blunders. Thanks to the secrecy which they observed until November, they failed to identify themselves in time with the program of reform. During the discussion, as far as the rank-and-file party member could tell, there seemed to be a basic agreement on the necessity of more workers' democracy and less bureaucratism. The debate appeared only to involve means of reaching this desirable state of affairs, and with the resolution of December 5, unity even on practical policy seemed to have been attained. It could only have been with a feeling of complete consternation that party members in the provinces (where the Opposition was not organized as in Moscow) witnessed the outbreak of a violent battle of polemics in mid-December. There was hardly time to appreciate the issues involved before the party apparatus had pronounced the Opposition to be an anti-Leninist deviation which was acting contrary to the party's desire for reform. Under such circumstances, who would resist the demand by the party leadership, strongly backed by all the resources at the command of the apparatus, to close ranks against the Opposition?

Moreover, the Opposition were particularly weak when it came to concrete proposals for making workers' democracy a reality. On more than one occasion they could only repeat the recommendations set forth by the apparatus, with the feeble contention that they, the Opposition, would apply them better or more sincerely. Often they simply expressed the pious wish that the Central Committee would improve upon its past record.[75] The party leadership, by putting themselves on record in the resolution of December 5, had appropriated the credit for all there was of practical import in the Opposition's prescription for the party's ills. To the ordinary rank-and-filer, concerned with practical results and hearing only the official side of the argument, there was little reason to expect any great improvement from putting the Opposition in power. The issues were in this fashion clouded, and the confusion, assiduously cultivated by the party leadership, only increased as the controversy progressed.

The most damaging Opposition mistake was to represent themselves as the best defenders of party unity. The very fact of an opposition arguing for unity was self-contradictory, and everything they said was used against them. The only consistent course for the Opposition would have been complete repudiation of Leninist centralism and the advocacy in substance of a two-party system within the context of the Soviet state. Such a stand could have brought them no worse fate, for this was precisely what they were soon charged with at the Thirteenth Party Conference: "The Bolshevik view of the party as a monolithic whole has been replaced by the Opposition with the view of the party as the sum of all possible tendencies and factions. . . . Such a view has nothing in common with Leninism."[76]

The sudden violence of the campaign against the Opposition during the second half of December is evidence enough that explosive animosity had long been accumulating among the Communist leaders. Issues, rivalries, anxieties, all contributed to the rage with which the leadership responded to the Opposition challenge. Once this storm of factional strife had broken, it became impossible to restore the relatively free discussion within an ostensibly united leadership group which had prevailed up to this time. The methods of struggle brought into play against Trotsky and his followers—the bitter charges and the relentless organizational pressure—put the party into a permanent state of seige. There was no turning back.

Triumph of the Apparatus

December 1923 marked another of the major turning points in the history of the Communist Party in Russia. Political life at the top level of the party took on an altogether different aspect. Heretofore the party had a relatively broad group of leaders among whom discussion and disagreement could freely proceed. Now the lines had hardened and the battle was joined; one side was proscribed and the other hammered into a disciplined phalanx which seemed to speak with one voice and fight at one command. The apparatus of party secretaries, with its principle of hierarchical discipline and its personal embodiment in the leadership of Stalin, had demonstrated its decisive power.

Once the Opposition were on the run, a systematic doctrinal indictment was drawn up against them. This was initially the work of Bukharin, who was now frankly contemptuous of the party democracy which the Opposition demanded: "Bolshevism has always distinguished itself from the formal democratism of the Mensheviks. . . . It does not conceal from the party and the working class the fact that the party is led by leaders. . . . The more conscious lead the less conscious. . . . The less conscious and less active become more and more conscious and active. These internal mechanics constitute real democratism."[77]

Bukharin singled Trotsky out as his main target. Trotsky, he charged, was guilty of a basic deviation from Leninism by denying the principle of discipline and upholding a freedom for "groupings" which made the party a mere "federative body." Bukharin saw nothing but political opportunism as the motive for Trotsky's challenge: "The fact is that for Comrade Trotsky 'democracy' is necessary for strategic purposes, to shake up the 'old cadres' and to 'correct' the policy of the Central Committee."[78]

The record of the moderate Left in trying to compromise revolutionary ideals with authoritarian expedients left them vulnerable when they tried to take a stand against the excesses of the Leninist system. They could be taken to task for their own bureaucratic behavior and at the same time denounced for violating the principles which they had helped to confirm. Trotsky's authoritarian proclivities were especially notorious, and even some of his own supporters in the Opposition, those with Ultra-Left backgrounds, were suspicious of him.[79] Stalin took advantage of Trotsky's inconsistency:

That same Trotsky, who in September, not many days before his factional move, kept silent at the plenum and, in any case, did not express opposition to the decision of the Central Committee, two weeks after this suddenly revealed that the country and party are perishing, and that he, Trotsky, this patriarch of the bureaucrats, cannot live without democracy. . . . Democracy is necessary, as a fad, as a strategic maneuver. . . . It follows that the Opposition was concerned not so much with democracy as with utilizing the idea of democracy to upset the Central Committee, that in the presence of the Opposition we have to deal not with people who wish to help the party, but with a faction which lies in ambush for the Central Committee.[80]

Together with such personal insinuations the party leaders began to fashion a polemical weapon out of party history. This was the start of a pernicious Communist habit—the reinterpretation and rewriting of the past in order to make it fit the immediate political needs of the present. The temptation to make an issue out of Trotsky's pre-1917 independence from the Bolshevik Party was irresistible. Bukharin, quietly ignoring his own sins, hauled out Trotsky's record of opposition to Lenin during the Brest-Litovsk and trade-union controversies, and attributed it to Trotsky's Menshevik background.[81] Squeezing party history for an issue, Bukharin took Trotsky to task for speaking of the "new course" as the beginning of a basic new period in the history of the party. This, according to Bukharin, was evidence of the Opposition's un-Leninist quality, because it exaggerated the periodization of the postrevolutionary history of the party and implicitly slighted the pre-revolutionary work of the party's old guard.[82]

Against other oppositionists the story of the Left Communist and Left SR "plot" of 1918 was recalled and embellished. Bukharin shamelessly prose-cuted his former Opposition colleagues for nothing more than what he had done himself. At this date those attacked were still given a chance to reply, and they protested the exaggeration of the affair as a "perversion of the his-tory of our party."[83] This, however, was only the mild beginning. Party history was manipulated more and more to discredit the Opposition, until finally the party's past was completely rewritten into a fairy tale of heroes and traitors.

With the Opposition under heavy attack, the party leadership grasped the opportunity to make their preferred economic policy the official line. The ground was prepared by earlier insinuations that Trotsky was indifferent to the peasantry and that he had disagreed with Lenin on this subject,[84] a theme which later was to figure prominently in the denunciations of the Opposition. The subcommittee of the Central Committee which had been studying the scissors crisis presented their final recommendations, with a markedly right-wing, propeasant flavor, and the Central Committee gave this view official sanction by incorporating it in a resolution: "The peasant economy is the fundamental basis for the restoration of industry, and, consequently, also for the growth of the working class, since the peasant market is the basic mass market for manufacturing industry. . . . Great support of the peasant econ-omy is demanded not only by the general interests of the Soviet power, but also by the interest in the fastest development of our industry."[85] Various expedients were proposed to raise agricultural prices and promote the well-being of the peasantry, including such measures as price supports, promotion of grain exports, and new marketing devices. Industry was the right-wingers' stepchild, meriting only criticism and reprimands. The industrial aspect of the problem was to be solved—such was the pious hope—by the managers' discovering areas of unnecessary expense, cutting overhead costs, and im-proving efficiency. The notion that the fault lay in a basic deficiency in the industrial plant was sedulously avoided.

The Opposition rejoinder on economics was delivered by Osinsky at a meeting of the Moscow party organization.[86] He reiterated the criticisms made by the Forty-six—"chaos," "lack of system," "spontaneity," and "lack of foresight" in the government's administration of economic affairs. The policies of restricting credit and trying to wipe out industrial profits were singled out for attack as especially injurious to industry. Planned industrial development was Osinsky's prime economic remedy. Such was the position to which the Left adhered as long as they remained a political force, though it continued to be shouted down by the adherents of the apparatus. Not until the Left had been expelled and condemned in 1927 did their ideas gain a hearing, but then Stalin bent them to his own political purposes.

At the Thirteenth Party Conference in January 1924, the Opposition's pleas to stress industry and check the NEP went unheeded. Rykov, restored as head of the Supreme Economic Council in 1923 (and shortly to succeed Lenin as premier), discoursed at length on the impossibility of systematic economic planning in a predominantly peasant economy.[87] He was to continue as an outspoken representative of this view until, to his misfortune, Stalin changed the line in 1928. Economic disagreements between the factions had crystallized; the leadership was determined to implement and justify the cautious course which they had chosen, while the Opposition warned of catastrophe if their protests were not heeded. Technical economic arguments became hopelessly intertwined with the emotions of factional strife.

The Thirteenth Party Conference, in session from January 16 to January 18, 1924, less than a week before Lenin died, was another landmark in the organizational development of the Communist Party. Up to that time, the national party congresses and conferences had been significant gatherings. Even though the party leadership generally had its way, Opposition views were not only heard but commanded real support; decisions were made. Beginning with the Thirteenth Conference, and to this day, every congress and conference has been completely stage-managed, with the partial exception of the Fourteenth Congress in 1925, when Zinoviev's Leningrad organization put up a futile resistance against Stalin.

With relentless efficiency the apparatus prepared for the Thirteenth Conference, using all its resources to crush the Opposition in the election of delegates from local organizations to the regional conferences and from the latter to the nation-wide conference. The process which Stalin had developed and partially applied in preparing the Twelfth Congress now operated with almost perfect results; of one hundred and twenty-eight voting delegates, only three belonged to the Opposition.[88] From the Thirteenth Conference on (with the exception noted), the representation was entirely controlled by the party leadership; decisions were made by higher authority and rubber-stamped by the delegates. Appearances of Opposition speakers were only tactical concessions in the grand strategy of preparing party opinion for the political liquidation of the now powerless deviators.

Stalin came forward at the Thirteenth Conference to take the lead in the attack on the Opposition. He gave the major address on "the immediate tasks of building the party," in the course of which he came down savagely on the Opposition, with biting sarcasm and a creditable, if somewhat forced, display of Marxist logic. He charged the Opposition with a deviation from Leninism on the ground that they believed in absolute democracy, and with cynical

opportunism on the ground that they did not. Opposition criticism of the
party apparatus implied "the anarcho-Menshevik view which denies the very
principle of the direction of party work." The irreparable sin of the Opposition was factionalism—that is, their existence as an opposition—however they
might try to gloss this over by claiming "freedom for groupings." "What
difference is there between a grouping and a faction?" Stalin wanted to know.
"When here, in Moscow, the Opposition created a special bureau, headed by
Serebriakov, and when they dispatched their orators, ordering them to appear at such and such meetings, to speak in such a way, and when the oppositionists in the course of the struggle were compelled to withdraw and change
their resolutions on command, this was, of course, a grouping, and group
discipline. This, they say, was not a faction." In reality, Stalin explained,
"This is an attempt to legalize factions, and above all Trotsky's faction."[89]

Factionalism, Stalin insisted, had nothing to do with the alleged bureaucratic regime in the party. It was rather an expression of, and encouragement
to, the antiproletarian forces in the country: "The Opposition, in its unrestrained agitation for democracy . . . is setting loose the petty-bourgeois
element. . . . The factional work of the Opposition is water in the mill of
the enemies of our party."[90] Many Mensheviks agreed with Stalin's characterization of the Communist Left, and welcomed the Opposition as a
democratic wedge in the one-party dictatorship. (Others, however, feared that
the Leftists were inherently authoritarian and would return to the rigors of
War Communism.[91]) To underscore the importance of discipline, Stalin
publicly announced for the first time the clause of the Tenth Congress resolution on unity which provided that the Central Committee could by a two-
thirds vote expel one of its own members from the committee and even from
the party.[92]

The party conference took its cue from Stalin to label the Opposition as:

not only an attempt at the revision of Bolshevism, not only a direct departure from
Leninism, but also a clearly expressed *petty-bourgeois deviation.* There is no doubt
that this "opposition" objectively reflects the pressure of the petty bourgeoisie on
the position of the proletarian party and its policy. The principle of intraparty
democracy is already beginning to be interpreted broadly beyond the limits of the
party: in the sense of weakening the dictatorship of the proletariat and extending
political rights to the new bourgeoisie.

In this situation where the RCP, embodying the dictatorship of the proletariat,
enjoys a monopoly of legality in the country, it is unavoidable that the least stable
groups of Communists should sometimes give in to nonproletarian influences. The
party as a whole must see these dangers and watchfully guard the proletarian line
of the party.

A systematic and energetic struggle of our whole party against this petty-bourgeois
deviation is essential.[93]

This was the fruition of the campaign against the Opposition and the logical conclusion of the arguments which the party leadership had assembled to rebuff their critics.

By the beginning of 1924 it was clear that the decisive power in the Russian Communist Party was the secretarial apparatus—and the man who headed that apparatus. For all their alarm and attempts to protest, the Opposition had revealed themselves to be essentially impotent when it came to a struggle for power within the party organization. Even before Lenin died, the course of the succession was firmly established. The interregnum, while he lived but could not govern, was the critical period, in which the cards were dealt for a fateful game that could have only one outcome.

10

THE PARTY AFTER LENIN

On January 21, 1924, after nine months of total disability, Lenin suddenly died. Politically his death made little difference, for the successor leadership was already functioning. Emotionally the Communist Party suffered a grievous blow, for they were now on their own.

The year following Lenin's death was a period of low ebb for the Opposition. After their defeat in December 1923, the Left ceased active resistance. Controversy continued at the top level between Trotsky and his rivals, with intermittent acerbity, but attempts at an organized opposition movement ceased. The Trotskyists remained on the whole passive until 1926. Not until the Zinoviev-Kamenev group broke away from the leadership and joined the Left was new life breathed into the Opposition.

UNITY AND DOGMA

Lenin's death was a further setback for Trotsky. Convalescing on the Black Sea coast, Trotsky persisted in his inexplicable inactivity and made no effort to claim the leadership of the party. He was not even present for Lenin's funeral, which prompted the French correspondent Rollin to write, "My God, what an opportunity to miss! Achilles sulking in his tent. . . . If he had come to Moscow . . . he would have stolen the whole show."[1]

Trotsky later claimed that the Politburo deliberately contrived to avoid his presence by falsely informing him that he could not return in time. Apart from this, however, it seems that Trotsky's will was frozen. He could not bring himself to act at all, not even to write an article about Lenin. "I knew only one urgent desire," he later explained, "and that was to be left alone. I could not stretch my hand to lift my pen."[2] The opportunity which Trotsky missed was seized upon by Stalin, who assumed the lead in the funeral proceedings. At a session of the Second All-Union Congress of Soviets held on the evening of January 26, Stalin made his famous speech pledging the party to execute Lenin's desires, with this liturgical refrain, "We swear to thee, Comrade Lenin, that we will fulfill with honor this thy command!"[3]

Stalin's speech was indicative of the trend of thought that was to come, with the ossification of party doctrine into a rigid orthodoxy stressing precision of verbal formulas. In their anxious reaction to the loss of Lenin's firm and reassuring leadership, and beset by the responsibilities of power and an Opposition threat, the party leaders strove to protect themselves by erecting a rampart of dogma and incantation around the name of the deceased leader.[4] As Zinoviev said at the next party congress, "We need not simply unity, but unity based on Leninism, on those views which the party labored to work out during the controversy [of December 1923], and which this congress must confirm in its own name definitively, letter by letter, from word to word, completely and as a whole."[5] "Ilich taught us that . . ." or "Comrade Lenin taught us that . . ." became Stalin's constant refrain.[6] Shortly afterwards, Zinoviev referred to Lenin's "What is to be Done?" as the "Bible of Bolshevism."[7] Trotsky commented, "The attitude toward Lenin as a revolutionary leader gave way to an attitude like that toward the head of an ecclesiastical hierarchy."[8]

In April 1924, Stalin undertook a comprehensive codification of the doctrines of "Leninism" in a series of lectures delivered at the Sverdlov party academy in Moscow. Under the title, "Foundations of Leninism," these talks became a classic of Communist scripture. Stalin explicitly denied the view that Leninism was "the application of Marxism to the peculiar conditions of Russia." He claimed universal validity for the doctrine: "Leninism is an international phenomenon. It is rooted in internationalism, and is not solely Russian. . . . Leninism is the Marxism of the epoch of imperialism and of the proletarian revolution. . . . Leninism is the theory and the tactic of the proletarian revolution in general, and the theory and the tactic of the dictatorship of the proletariat in particular."[9] Nevertheless, Stalin's presentation of Leninism was aimed at justifying absolutely the policies then being followed by the party, as if no other course of action could ever have been conceived of in the context of Leninist thought. This was particularly evident in regard to policy toward the peasantry, as Stalin endeavored to bring all the force and prestige of "Leninism" to bear on the side of the conciliatory line being pursued in the face of Leftist criticism.

In some respects, Stalin was indeed Lenin's best disciple. For Stalin, as for Lenin, the party was the decisive thing in politics. Stalin now elaborated the military conception of the party as an organic fighting unit, which he had first stated the year before: "The party has to guide the proletariat in its struggle . . . it has to instill in the millions of the mass of unorganized nonparty workers a spirit of discipline and planning in the struggle, a spirit of organization and steadfastness. But the party can fulfill these tasks only if it shows itself to be an embodiment of discipline and organization, only if it is the organized detachment of the proletariat. . . . The party is the highest form of the class organization of the proletariat." For Stalin, the party's revolutionary victory made no difference in the need for conspiratorial techniques and dictatorial methods: "The proletariat needs the party for the establishment of the dictatorship. It needs it even more to maintain the dictatorship." The workers lacked proletarian consciousness, which the party had to supply: "The millions of the mass of the proletariat must be imbued with the spirit of discipline and organization . . . must be protected against the corrosive influence of the petty-bourgeois elements and petty-bourgeois habits."

Stalin was following closely in Lenin's footsteps with a drastic though unavowed alteration of the Marxian conception of the historical process. Both really viewed the party—conscious top-level political leadership—as the driving force of history. Thus, it was the party, rather than social forces or broad economic evolution, which must be looked to for the assurance that "conditions be prepared for the inauguration of socialist production." Economic and cultural change, as Stalin was eventually to demonstrate, would be taken care of by command of the party. Stalin thus had abundant reason for asserting the need for "iron discipline" and "unity of will," in addition to the "wholehearted and unconditional unity of action" long since accepted as a party tenet. From this followed the condemnation of any opposition: "The existence of factions within the party is directly inimical to unity and discipline." The purge of "opportunists" became a positive good: "The more drastic the purge, the more likelihood is there of a strong and influential party arising."[10]

During the first half of 1924 the party organization proceeded steadily with the implementation of Stalin's political standards. A major step in making the membership more amenable to organizational controls was the so-called "Lenin Enrollment" in the spring months of 1924. This wholesale admission of approximately two hundred thousand new members (mostly workers)—an increase of more than 40 per cent—swamped the party with political neophytes firmly under the control of the secretarial hierarchy. Though it was an obvious manipulation, the Lenin Enrollment was later used repeatedly by apologists for the party apparatus as evidence of "mass confidence" in the party, and hence as proof that the Opposition complaints about bureaucratism and related sins were unfounded.[11] At the Thirteenth Party Congress in May 1924, Preobrazhensky challenged this explanation boldly: "It would be completely inadmissable optimism to say that by their entry into the party the workers confirm and approve everything that we have done in intraparty politics, including bureaucratic perversions. . . ." On the contrary, he contended, many of the genuinely convinced recruits of the Civil War period were allowing their membership to lapse.[12] To capitalize immediately on the new recruitment, the party leadership had to violate the party statutes and permit probationary members to participate in the process of selecting congress delegates. This was justified on the ground that the congress would certainly legalize the move—and, to be sure, the beneficiaries of this irregular voting did give it their sanction.[13]

Strengthening of the party organization was complemented by unabated pressure against the Opposition during the winter and spring of 1924. According to Preobrazhensky's complaint at the Thirteenth Congress, the Central Control Commission and party purge committees worked systematically to expel Opposition sympathizers from the party. While officially opposition was not a ground for expulsion, the same result was achieved under cover of charges of "opportunism" and personal defects.[14] To supplement the campaign on the ideological level, the party's theoretical journal *Bolshevik* was established in April 1924, with its announced purpose, "the defense and consolidation of *historical* Bolshevism, the struggle against any attempts at distorting or perverting its foundations."[15] Opposition influence in the Commissariat of Military Affairs was cut down when Trotsky's close associate Skliansky was replaced by Frunze in the post of deputy commissar.[16] By the middle of 1924 the Politburo and the Central Committee as well were meeting informally to make decisions without the presence of Opposition members.[17]

When the Thirteenth Party Congress convened in May 1924, the activity of the secretarial machinery had been so effective that not a single oppositionist was elected to the congress as a voting delegate. This success in turn was used to argue that the Opposition were alien to Bolshevism. "The people who were just recently croaking about the ruin of our party actually did not know the party," Stalin charged. "They ought to be called foreigners in the party."[18]

On the eve of the Thirteenth Congress the party leaders were suddenly embarrassed by the appearance of Lenin's "Testament." After keeping the document secret for over a year, Krupskaya revealed it to Kamenev, with the explanation, "Vladimir Ilich expressed the definite wish that this note of his be submitted after his death to the next party congress for its information."[19] The party leadership had no alternative but to allow the "Testament" to be read to the Central Committee and to the congress delegates.[20] Stalin, of course, was placed in an extremely awkward position by the postscript calling for his removal as general secretary. He was extricated by Zinoviev, who declared that "the fears of Ilich have not been confirmed" and went on with, in the words of one witness, "a thousand variations on the theme of the young maiden, who to be sure is with child, but one so small that it is not worth the trouble of speaking about it."[21] Stalin sought a vote of confidence from the Central Committee by offering to resign as general secretary. Zinoviev and Kamenev called for a vote by a show of hands, and since no one, on the spur of the moment, was prepared to defy openly the head of the party apparatus, the result was the unanimous endorsement of which Stalin could later boast.[22]

At the official sessions of the Thirteenth Congress the party leaders drove home their insistence on the monolithic unity of the party against all internal and external threats. Zinoviev, who again came forth as the nominal head of the party by delivering the political report for the Central Committee, verged on hysteria over the theme of unity: "In this hall there is not one man who would not be ready to give up everything for our party to be united, for this is the single serious prerequisite of all further successes of the revolution and all further successes of the Comintern."[23] (Little did he imagine what he himself would be compelled to give up in the party's cause.) The congress, echoing the leader's mania, indicated the source of the party's unity neurosis: "The congress charges the Central Committee to guard, as determinedly and firmly as before, the unity of the party and the established line of Bolshevism from any deviations whatsoever. Since the party has lost Comrade Lenin, the matter of securing full party unity has become still more important and essential than before. The slightest factionalism must be prosecuted most severely. The hardness and the monolithic quality of the RCP, on the basis of the firm principles of Leninism, are the most important prerequisite for the further success of the revolution."[24]

Trotsky and Preobrazhensky, admitted to the congress as consulting delegates without vote, braved a torrent of accusation and invective to defend the Opposition's stand during the December controversy. Trotsky referred back to the resolution of December 5—the conciliatory statement which he had largely written himself—and tried to warn again of underlying dangers which threatened the future of democracy in the party: "The bureaucratization of the apparatus stems from deep social causes. . . . The basic source of bureaucratization is the state apparatus . . . and the unculturedness of the broad masses of toilers. . . ."[25] The party leaders insisted in reply that in the December controversy the Opposition had gravely endangered the Soviet regime. *Bolshevik* called the Opposition a "liquidator deviation."[26] Stalin declared, "The struggle involved the life and death of the party. The Opposition perhaps was most conscious of this. But . . . the question is in the objective results which inevitably flow from the actions of a given group. What does it mean to declare war on the party apparatus? This means the destruction of the party."[27]

The only course open to the Opposition was to recant and to acknowledge the unqualified supremacy of the party. Trotsky undertook to do this, though possibly with sarcastic intent: "Comrades, none of us wishes or is able to be right against his party. The party in the last analysis is always right, because the party is the sole historical instrument given to the proletariat for the solution of its basic problems. . . . I know that one cannot be right against the party. It is only possible to be right with the party and through the party, for history has not created other ways for the realization of what is right."[28] Trotsky's self-abnegation proved to be in vain. He failed to realize the intentions of the forces arrayed against him, which were determined to discredit him no matter what his affirmations of faith. In this case he was denounced for going too far; Stalin and Krupskaya in particular pointed out the obvious absurdity of asserting the infallibility of the party.[29] The congress nonetheless proceeded and ended as it began: the passion for unity had taken on clearly obsessive dimensions. Only Krupskaya spoke in conciliatory terms.[30] Zinoviev's final remarks were replete with typical phrasings of the one formula: "The party is united. . . . There is no man in the world who could split our Russian Communist Party. [Stormy applause] And there is no group, however it might be called, which could split our party. . . . The party must establish a guarantee that in the event of difficulties we will have 100 per cent solidarity."[31]

In 1924, official Communist politics and thinking became both monolithic and monotonous. The very dullness of the Thirteenth Congress and those that followed—the endless repetition of stereotyped arguments and accusations, the interminable rounds of self-praise and applause for the party—was indicative of the rapid change in the Soviet intellectual climate. The empty platitudes, the dogmatic assumption of the infallibility of the party, and the insistence on absolute unity have remained constant features of Communist thought. The substance of party doctrine has changed, but its permanent forms date recognizably from this time.

There are three main reasons for such a definite shift at this point in the history of the party. First, Lenin's death apparently caused an acute sense of insecurity in most of the party. Second, the crystallization of the contest between the party leadership and the Opposition, by institutionalizing for a time the majority-minority cleavage, provided the party apparatus with the anvil upon which the theory and practice of the monolithic party were hammered out. Finally, the progressive divergence of the regime's practical policies and the revolutionary spirit of its professed ideology created a need to cover the discrepancy with a rigidly enforced orthodoxy. This has been the main function of Communist ideology, the "party line," ever since.

The practice of monolithic party unity was being developed concurrently with its theory, as the central organizational machinery of the party continued to be strengthened. The extension of controls over personnel, central schools for party officials, and re-examination of the membership as far down as the cell level in critical places were among the measures which the Thirteenth Congress endorsed after Stalin's report. The Secretariat itself was expanded and partially reorganized. The Report and Assignment Division and the Organization and Instruction Division were merged into an Organization-Assignment Division, which became the principal operating organ of the Secretariat. The activity and power of the responsible instructors in maintaining links with local organizations were further increased.[32]

Particularly effective in enhancing the power of the Secretariat was the dilution of the membership of the Central Committee. From the forty members and seventeen candidates to which the committee had been increased in 1923, the Thirteenth Congress raised the membership to fifty-three, with thirty-four candidates. Again, a long list of virtual unknowns, patently creatures of the Secretariat (except for the old undergrounders Krasin and

Krzhizhanovsky), took their places in the party's governing body. The Central Control Commission was actually tripled, to a total of one hundred and fifty-one members, and its functions of administering discipline and of supervising the local control commissions were correspondingly expanded. The commission, "counteracting any attempt at violating the unity of the party," was especially charged with continuing its selective checkup of the party membership, with emphasis on members in governmental and educational institutions.[33] It was hardly coincidental that these were the major centers of Opposition sympathy.

The top leadership remained almost unchanged. Lenin's six Politburo colleagues—Trotsky, Zinoviev, Kamenev, Stalin, Rykov, and Tomsky—retained their places, while Bukharin was promoted from candidate to full member to fill the vacancy left by Lenin. Three new candidates were added: Dzerzhinsky, head of the Supreme Economic Council in place of Rykov (who had officially taken over as chairman of the Council of Peoples' Commissars); Sokolnikov, the conservative commissar of finance; and Frunze, the new deputy war commissar.[34] In the organizational staff of the party, as in the Central Committee, there was a good deal of new blood—the Orgburo was doubled in size.

Of particular note was the overnight rise of Lazar Moiseyevich Kaganovich to party prominence. Kaganovich, at this time just past thirty years of age, came from a Jewish family in the Ukraine. A worker, he joined the Bolshevik underground when he was seventeen and moved up rapidly as a party functionary during the Civil War years. In June 1922, Stalin made him head of the Organization and Instruction Division of the Secretariat, and the following year he became a candidate member of the Central Committee.[35] He was typical of the new party officials who were being brought into the high command by Stalin. At the time of the Thirteenth Congress he was not only made a full member of the Central Committee but was also placed on the Orgburo as a full member, and made a member of the Secretariat, along with Stalin, Molotov, Andreyev, and I. A. Zelensky (the Moscow secretary, who was tried and shot in 1938).[36] From 1925 to 1928 Kaganovich ran the Ukrainian party organization. He became a full Politburo member in 1930 and remained part of the inner circle until June 1957, when a surprise move by Khrushchev deposed him from the leadership. Without question, Kaganovich was a key man in Stalin's drive to dominate the party.

THE "LESSONS OF OCTOBER" AND THE CAMPAIGN AGAINST TROTSKYISM

Despite their cessation of active resistance, Trotsky and his supporters were still targets in the party press and in the party organizations. The GPU, reportedly, was now used regularly to maintain surveillance over the Opposition.[37] Under the guise of a "reregistration" of the membership, a concerted campaign was undertaken to root out Opposition sympathizers from the party cells where they were most numerous—in the government offices and educational institutions.[38] Kuibyshev, the president of the Central Control Commission, made no denial of this policy but merely argued that the "careerists" whom the party apparatus was bent on expelling sided naturally with the Opposition.[39] A steady effort was also made to demonstrate Trotsky's doctrinal errors and to expose his theoretical differences with Lenin. Trotsky now found silence intolerable; he cast political discretion to the winds and made up his mind to strike with the only effective weapon left to him—his razor-sharp pen.

On the seventh anniversary of the October Revolution, and also just one year after the Communists' debacle in Germany, Trotsky published a lengthy polemical essay entitled "Lessons of October."[40] Trotsky's thesis was that the defeat of the German Communists under Russian leadership was due to the same type of thinking that caused resistance to Lenin's leadership in 1917. "The fundamental question," Trotsky maintained, was "whether or not we should struggle for power." He hurled back the same epithets which the leadership was accustomed to use against him: "These Bolsheviks who . . . were opposed to the seizure of power by the proletariat were, in point of fact, shifting to the prerevolutionary position of the Mensheviks."[41] The "right-wing" attitude, by implication, was responsible for the erroneous course currently being followed by the party leadership domestically, as well as its international failures. Though it named no names, "Lessons of October" was obviously a declaration of political war against Kamenev and Zinoviev, and the party leadership reacted accordingly.

In retrospect, Trotsky's move was a strategic blunder, forcing the Zinoviev-Kamenev partnership to stand with Stalin at a time when differences between the two groups undoubtedly could have been cultivated. It has been suggested that Trotsky actually was trying to split the leadership but, if so, he failed to recognize his real enemy; the strategy, if any, seems to have been to attract Stalin's support to the cause of the Left. (See Chapter 12.) Another theory is that Stalin incited Trotsky's rashness in order to embarrass Zinoviev and Kamenev, make them more dependent on the Secretariat, and pave the way for disposing of them later on.[42] If Trotsky was trying to appeal to the party membership at large and evoke their revolutionary sentiments against the current leadership, he failed completely. His arguments were buried by an avalanche of articles in the controlled press. Trotsky's point-by-point refutation, devastating in its logic, was not even published.[43] Trotsky did not even attempt further defense, for, as he explained, "In the atmosphere of the present discussion, every statement I made on this question . . . would but serve as an impetus to intensify the controversy."[44]

Trotsky's critique did indeed strike the leadership at a sensitive point, and much of the counterargument was an indignant defense. Zinoviev tried crudely to deny that there ever was a "right wing" opposing Lenin in 1917: "Was there a right wing in the Bolshevik Party . . . ? It was not possible—because the fundamental structural principles of the Bolshevik Party according to Lenin excluded the possibility of a right or left wing." He would admit only "episodal differences of opinion" in the Bolshevik past.[45]

Stalin suddenly became broad-minded: the disagreements of 1917 were "of a purely objective nature" and "of a kind without which no active party life and no real party work can exist." This short-lived aberration of tolerance on Stalin's part obviously had to do with the slip in his own past. He had to make a clean breast of the matter, while striving to minimize its significance: "A reorientation of the party under the new conditions of the fight was necessary. The party (its majority) approached this reorientation very cautiously. It adopted the policy of pressure by the soviets on the Provisional Government on the question of peace, and did not at once make up its mind to take the further step from the old slogan of the dictatorship of the proletariat and the peasantry to the new slogan of the power of the soviets. . . . This mistaken attitude I shared at that time with other members of the party, and I only renounced it altogether in the middle of April after I had subscribed to Lenin's theses."[46]

For the counterattack on Trotsky, charges were either entirely fabricated or exaggerated beyond all measure—it was the man that the offended leaders were bent on destroying, not doctrinal error. Trotsky "underestimated the peasantry," a heresy for which the leadership had begun to berate him during the New Course controversy.[47] Conveniently ignoring the rural violence under War Communism for which they all shared responsibility, the leaders used this charge to connect Trotsky's prerevolutionary Menshevism with his current opposition to the appeasement of the peasants at the expense of industry. By implication, the official policy gained the sanction of Leninist orthodoxy.

Trotsky's picture of the "rearming" of the party in 1917 and his well-founded contention that events had largely borne out his theory of permanent revolution were rejected as historical fictions and slanders against Lenin. Kamenev declared that the ideas would mean that the party had had "to renounce what it had taught for the previous fifteen years."[48] Trotsky's worst sin was daring to correct Lenin. In a letter which he wrote in 1921, Trotsky had made the seemingly unexceptional remark, "I by no means believe that I was always in the wrong in my differences of opinion with the Bolsheviks. . . . I believe that my estimate of the driving forces of the revolution was decidedly right."[49] Three years later, the letter was dug up as proof of lèse-majesté. Every word that Trotsky had ever written against Lenin—and there were many—was eagerly recalled in order to convict the heretic. The party was given to understand in no uncertain terms that independent minds were not to be tolerated.

Throughout the onslaught, the new cry of dogmatic belief was sustained —"Leninism or Trotskyism," "Bolshevism or Trotskyism." Trotsky was charged with conspiring to corrupt the Leninist purity of the party's beliefs. Rykov summoned the party to resist "the general campaign of Trotskyism to eliminate Bolshevik ideology from the Bolshevik Party."[50] In Bukharin's vivid metaphor, Trotskyism was "dynamite under the foundations of the party."[51] It was natural to proceed with the identification of Trotskyism and Menshevism. Zinoviev seized on "the notorious theory of the permanent revolution which Comrade Trotsky is now attempting to impose upon Bolshevism. This theory was regarded by Comrade Lenin and all the Bolsheviks as a *variety of Menshevism*. . . . The whole of Trotskyism with its theory of 'permanent' revolution was nothing else than a cleverly thought-out intellectual scheme which was developed according to the requirements of Menshevism."[52]

The net effect of the activity and doctrines of the Opposition, according to the prosecution, was to undermine the party's defenses against the incursion of the dreaded "petty-bourgeois influences." Kamenev associated these with the "weakest link" in the party, a thinly veiled reference to the Opposition, "where people have entered the party without being assimilated to it, and are possessed by a secret conviction . . . that they are more in the right than the party." He concluded explicitly: "It grieves me to say this . . . but it must be said: Comrade Trotsky has become the channel through which petty-bourgeois elements have penetrated into our party."[53] Stalin concurred: "Trotskyism in all its internal content has every possibility of becoming a center and meeting place of the nonproletarian elements which are striving to weaken and disintegrate the dictatorship of the proletariat."[54] Only one of Trotsky's critics showed a disposition to judge fairly. Perhaps it was not without significance that the exception once again was Lenin's widow, Krupskaya, who confessed, "I do not know whether Comrade Trotsky is guilty of all the deadly sins of which he is accused—the matter here is not without polemic heat."[55]

In the case against Trotsky and the Opposition there was nevertheless more than a grain of truth. Leninism and Trotskyism were indeed based on different sources—the contrasting Leninist and Leftist currents of Bolshevism. In combating the bureaucratic trend in the party and the propeasant tendency of the NEP, the Left Opposition was indeed trying to replace Leninism, narrowly construed, with "Trotskyism." The relation between the two currents of thought, however, was not simple; during 1917 Lenin had stood with the Left, and the Leftist school of thought was uppermost when the party swept into power. This fact was seized upon by Trotsky for the thesis of his "Lessons of October," as he tried to discredit the current party leadership and rehabilitate the Leftists by identifying the latter with the April theses, the "rearming" of the party, and the successful execution of the October coup.

It was to prevent just this that the party leadership strove so hard to refute Trotsky's thesis and preserve the oversimplified conception of Lenin and the Opposition in constant disagreement.

The campaign against Trotsky reflected considerably more on the accusers than on the accused. All the party leaders—Stalin, Zinoviev, Kamenev, Bukharin, Rykov—convict themselves with their own words as small and anxious men, terrified by Trotsky's challenge and determined to uphold their self-righteousness at any cost. Max Eastman commented: "Trotsky . . . has undertaken to keep alive the thinking of Lenin after his brain is dead and embalmed. And all the old religious, theological, metaphysical, absolutistical, canonical, scholastic and dogmatic-academic habits of the human race are against him. Only the fool of these habits could fail to detect, in this fanatical panic against Trotsky, the beginning of the transformation of Bolshevism from a science into a religion. . . . It was not only the beginnings of an official caste that Trotsky was attacking, but the beginnings of a priesthood as well."[56] Trotsky himself was on the right track in attributing the "phantom of Trotskyism" to "difficult circumstances . . . certain personal circumstances . . . the suspiciousness evoked by Lenin's death." Trotsky's defense, however, was completely mistaken. He did not once question the new Lenin-worship, but strove only to affirm his own bona fide Leninism and the validity of his "separate path to Bolshevism."[57] By thus accepting orthodoxy as the primary standard of judgment, Trotsky only buttressed the case against himself.

Having condemned Trotsky, the party leaders invoked all the force of the party organization to eradicate disbelief. Cried Bukharin, "We must ideologically liquidate Trotskyism and conquer the whole party under the Leninist banner no matter what."[58] Stalin called for "a developed battle of ideas against the resurrection of Trotskyism."[59] Zinoviev concurred vigorously with this prescription as he advanced the slogans "Bolshevizing of all strata of the party!" and "Ideological struggle against Trotskyism!"[60] Despite all this furor, it is not certain whether the objective of the propaganda campaign was accomplished. According to one report, of December 1924, most of the party rank and file remained *"indubitably* sympathetic to Trotsky."[61] Another participant revealed the importance of the ideological argument in offsetting Trotsky's popularity: "The group to which I belonged took very much to heart these attacks leveled at Trotsky. . . . The 'Permanent Revolution' seemed to me to be a dangerous theory. . . . I deplored the necessity of voting against Trotsky, but, since he persisted in his errors, I felt it to be my duty to do so."[62] The grounds for the leaders' anxiety were clearly not yet removed.

Further action against Trotsky was soon forthcoming. On January 17, 1925, the Central Committee resolved as follows: "The basic prerequisite of all the successes of the Bolshevik Party was always its steel-like unity and iron discipline, its genuine unity of views on the basis of Leninism. Trotsky's unceasing outbursts against Bolshevism confront the party with the necessity either of abandoning this basic prerequisite or of putting an end once and for all to these outbursts. . . . To leave the matter as it has been . . . would mean beginning the de-Bolshevization of the party and even its consequent collapse."[63] Trotsky was compelled to resign from his last post of real power, as war commissar; he was threatened with further disciplinary action should he repeat his defiance and was relegated to petty administrative work dealing with electrification and foreign concessions. The blow was a bitter one, which Trotsky could not recollect without an effort to convince himself that he had really retained some initiative: "I yielded up the military post without a fight, with even a sense of relief, since I was thereby wresting from my opponents' hands their weapons of insinuation concerning my military intentions."[64] But merely evading the accusation of Bonapartism made no improvement in Trotsky's political fortunes.

With the "Lessons of October" controversy, party history became a major weapon used by the leadership in fighting off Opposition challenges. The effect was unprincipled distortion of the past to serve the purposes of the present. Trotsky himself was responsible for introducing history into the party controversy in the fall of 1924, and he used the record effectively. He was aided, of course, by the fact that the truth was on his side. To defend themselves, the party leaders had to begin doctoring the past. Nothing testifies so convincingly to their political vulnerability and their psychological weakness.

Apart from efforts to explain away the Right deviation in 1917, Trotsky's role in the revolution was the principal subject for correction and Stalin was the chief reviser. "I am far from denying the undoubtedly important part played by Comrade Trotsky in the revolution," he began, indicating the vast distance which remained to be traversed before the ultimate fictionalization was reached in the party history of 1938. "I must say, however, that Comrade Trotsky neither did nor could play any special part, that he, as chairman of the Petrograd Soviet, only carried out the will of the party authorities in question who supervised every one of his steps." Stalin supplemented this effort at minimization by the recollection of a minor event which has been the basis for Stalin's replacing Trotsky as the active leader of the October Revolution. This was the selection by the Central Committee of a group composed of Stalin, Sverdlov, Dzerzhinsky, Bubnov, and Uritsky to maintain liaison with Trotsky's Military Revolutionary Committee. Though the group never actually functioned, Stalin now claimed that it had been responsible for "directing all the practical organs of the insurrection."[65] Stalin then went on to challenge Trotsky's role in the Civil War, though he only underscored it in the revision he attempted at this late date: "I am far from denying the important part played by Comrade Trotsky in the Civil War.

I must, however, declare with all firmness that the great honor of being the organizer of our victories belongs to no individual but to the great community of the advanced workers of our country—the Russian Communist Party."[66] The party was then called on to combat "the dissemination of incorrect and exaggerated representations of the personal role of Trotsky in 1917 and in the Civil War."[67]

This was only the beginning. By the end of the next decade, the "genius Stalin" was along with Lenin the director and inspirer of every Bolshevik exploit, and no one could fall from favor without the revelation that he had been a traitor and an imperialist spy from the very start. This practice of keeping history up to date became habitual. As late as 1953, when the man who had directed the Soviet secret police for fourteen years was purged, it was "determined that the beginning of the criminal, treacherous activity of L. P. Beria . . . went back to . . . 1919," when he assertedly connived with the conveniently omnipresent British intelligence service.[68] History, for the Bolsheviks, was the last court of appeal, but the jury was carefully packed.

PERMANENT REVOLUTION VERSUS SOCIALISM IN ONE COUNTRY

The attack on Trotsky's theory of permanent revolution was a bold thrust, for it was aimed at the area in which Trotsky had made his most significant contribution to Bolshevik thinking. Whether acknowledged or not, the theory actually was the basis of Bolshevik reasoning in 1917, and pertaining to developments within Russia it proved to have had a high predictive value. It is not clear exactly how and why the party leaders settled on attacking "permanent revolution," but the strategy proved to be exceptionally clever. The theory of permanent revolution was uniquely apt as a unifying theme for Trotsky's enemies. The attack on it served to bind together the current Opposition and Trotsky's prerevolutionary record of polemics against Lenin; it connected Leftist criticisms of the party's economic policy with Trotsky's alleged theoretical error of underestimating the peasantry; and above all it discredited the notion that the retardation of the world revolution could affect the socialist correctness of the Soviet regime.

It is strange at first glance that the international revolution became a major issue among the Russian Communist factions only when the Opposition had its back to the wall and after the illusion of imminent world upheaval had been thoroughly dispelled. By 1924 Soviet Russia had returned to normal diplomatic relations with most of its neighbors and had secured recognition by most of the major European powers. This very fact of stability in Russia's foreign relations, however, created acute theoretical insecurity for the Communist Party leadership, and the Opposition did not hesitate to take advantage of the situation.

For the doctrinal self-confidence of the party leadership, it was necessary to destroy the idea, so convincingly elaborated in Trotsky's theory, that the firm realization of socialism in revolutionary Russia depended on the victory of the socialist revolution in Western Europe. Kamenev tried to argue that facts had refuted the theory: "If Trotsky's theory had proved correct, then it would mean that the Soviet power had long ago ceased to exist. Ignoring the peasantry and not giving any consideration to the decisive question of the alliance of the proletariat and the peasantry, this theory of 'permanent revolution' places the workers' government in Russia in exclusive and complete dependence on the immediate proletarian revolution in the West."[69] But existence of the "Soviet" power did not necessarily prove that it was "socialist"—and this was the cardinal question still lurking in the background, even though the Ultra-Left oppositionists who raised it in 1920 and 1921 had been suppressed. If permanent revolution were accepted, in the absence of the revolution in the West the survival of the Soviet regime under Russian conditions could only be accounted for as the result of the internal transformation of the regime from a socialist one to some other kind.

The dependence of Russian socialism on the world revolution was a long-held assumption in Bolshevik doctrine, and it could not be attacked directly. A stroke of good fortune was the opportunity for the party leadership to link it, via permanent revolution, with Trotsky and his alleged errors as incompatible with "Leninism." But the effort to show a wide and constant cleavage between Trotsky and Lenin was obviously forced; only by the splitting of hairs and the magnification of minutiae could the argument be constructed, and again the case against Trotsky could be made to stick only by virtue of the party's complete control of the press.

An elaborate distinction was drawn between Trotsky's theory of permanent revolution and what was attributed to Lenin as "the theory of the growing-over of the bourgeois-democratic revolution into the socialist revolution." Stalin himself began to argue this difference in "Foundations of Leninism," when he endeavored to explain away the correspondence between the views of Lenin and Trotsky on the rapid dynamics of the revolutionary process in Russia: "Why . . . did Lenin oppose the idea of 'permanent revolution'? Because he wanted to make the fullest possible use of the revolutionary capacities and energies of the peasantry for the complete liquidation of tsarism and for the transition to the proletarian revolution, whereas the champions of 'permanent revolution' did not understand how important a part the peasantry had and has to play in the Russian Revolution. They underestimated the revolutionary energy of the peasantry."[70] By distorting and magnifying the differences between Lenin and Trotsky, the party leadership managed to dissociate Lenin from his own thinking of 1917—the thrust for power in the hope of international support—and to denounce Trotsky for what had formerly been a universal Bolshevik assumption.

To replace the vanished mirage of international revolution, the Com-

munist leaders turned, like Russian revolutionary heroes of old, to a profession of faith in the Russian peasant. Bukharin completely dismissed the
necessity for European support. It was now the *smychka,* the "union" of
the proletariat and peasantry in the building of socialism under the leadership of the party of the proletariat, which would provide all the social basis
necessary for a victory over Russian backwardness.[71] Bukharin declaimed:
"Lenin taught: Our salvation lies in our coming to an understanding with
the peasantry, and it is possible for us to do this, and to maintain and secure
our position, even if we have to wait a long time for victory in the West. . . .
Leninism contends that the peasantry is to be the *ally* of the working class
during the whole transition period, even if an unwilling ally."[72] This reasoning undoubtedly produced some genuine horror about Trotsky's alleged
underestimation of the peasantry and the Left Opposition's "super-industrialism." The smychka explained the survival of socialism in Russia and
proved the rectitude of the leadership. No wonder that Bukharin could say,
"The question of the worker-peasant bloc is the central question; it is the
question of all questions."[73]

The smychka was in reality sheer farce, though the idea was echoed and
re-echoed throughout the party press as a cardinal element of doctrine.
Neither the peasants nor the workers had any political power. Nevertheless,
the smychka idea was important in the thinking of the Communist Right
during the struggle against the Left Opposition and again when the Right
Opposition defied Stalin in 1928. Bukharin extended the notion of the
smychka to the whole realm of the world revolution, its process and prospects.
He pointed out that the peasantry of the colonial and backward areas greatly
outnumbered the proletariat of the industrialized countries, so that it was
the social situation of Russia, rather than the Western European assumptions
of classical Marxism, which typified the world-wide constellation of class
forces. Hence, for Bukharin, the entire future of the world revolution was at
stake in the success of the smychka formula in Russia. Destroy the possibility
of an international alliance of workers and peasants, and the prospects for
the universal triumph of socialism would grow dim indeed.[74]

On such grounds the right-wing ideologists concluded with evident
sincerity that the Leftists' economic views portended disaster. The secretarial
hierarchy was for its own reasons apprehensive of the Left Opposition, fearing a democratic challenge to its power. This common threat was the basis
for the retrospectively unnatural alliance which persisted between the
Rightists and their cautious program, on the one hand, and the Stalinists and
the organized power of the party apparatus, on the other.

Stalin did not rely entirely on his right-wing colleagues for new doctrinal
formulations. Borrowing Trotsky's device, Stalin took the occasion of the
publication of his own collected writings of the year 1917 to set forth some
new views in a specially written preface, "The October Revolution and the

Tactics of the Russian Communists."[75] Stalin began with the failure of the revolution in Germany in 1923, which, he explained, was due to the fact that the German proletariat lacked the alliance with the peasantry that the Russian proletariat enjoyed in 1917. He concluded that "the dictatorship of the proletariat is a class alliance of the proletariat with the laboring masses of the peasantry." Using an argument parallel to that set forth by Bukharin, if not actually borrowed from him, Stalin confronted the ticklish issue of how socialism could be possible in a peasant country:

According to Lenin the revolution draws its forces above all from among the workers and peasants of Russia itself. According to Trotsky we have it that the indispensable forces can be found *only* "in the arena of a world-wide proletarian revolution. And what if the world revolution is fated to come late? Is there a gleam of hope for our revolution? Comrade Trotsky gives us no hope at all. . . . According to this plan, our revolution has only one prospect: to vegetate in its own contradictions and have its roots rot while waiting for the world-wide revolution.

Stalin was not the man to let a sociological analysis of the Soviet political situation leave him without prospects. Searching back through the pages of Lenin's collected works, he unearthed a passage which provided him with the opportunity to execute a feat of casuistry remarkable both in its boldness and in the extent of the doctrinal refurbishing it afforded. The statement was Lenin's remark of 1915 about fits and starts in the unfolding of world revolution, and the inference that "the victory of socialism is possible at first in a few capitalist countries or even in one taken separately." Stalin was undaunted by the fact that the formula was not meant to apply to Russia, as Lenin's other writings of the period show perfectly well. Citing the one passage as his authority, Stalin leaped to the conclusion that "the victory of socialism in one country alone is entirely possible and probable, even if that country is capitalistically less developed, and even though capitalism remains in other countries which are more developed capitalistically."

In this fashion Stalin provided himself with what was to become a potent doctrinal weapon to counter the charge that under his leadership the Soviet regime was departing from the principles and program of the revolution. He could then dismiss Marxian arguments that Russian backwardness was a serious obstacle to the party's socialist program: Lenin had said that socialism in a single country was possible—therefore the Russian Soviet regime as presently constituted *must* be moving properly toward socialism. In characteristic fashion, the former divinity student rested his case on the now canonized utterances of the party's founder, rather than on independent inferences about the political situation. Bukharin had attempted the latter in imagining that the peasantry could serve as a support for socialism in Russia in lieu of the international revolution. Stalin, however, preferred to base his stand on the pronouncements of authority, meager though they were.

Stalin's case was founded solely on one sentence written by Lenin in his Swiss exile nine years before, taken out of context and distorted to mean something entirely unintended by its author. Thanks to its establishment as doctrine in the face of these facts, "socialism in one country" was a critical turning point in the development of Soviet ideology. It marked the beginning of a pervasive process of reinterpretation and reconstruction, the effect of which has been to bring what is represented as Marxism-Leninism into accordance with the actual evolution of the Soviet state. It inaugurated, furthermore, the practice of proof by textual manipulation, with no questioning of the correctness of the authority, but similarly with no regard for what the authority really meant. Lenin's words were not to be challenged; nor was their manipulation by Stalin. Stalin was soon to show how effectively he could deal with people who attempted to trip him up on his ideological formulations.

11

THE ZINOVIEV OPPOSITION

In the fall of 1925, just one year after the specter of Trotskyism had been exorcised, the Russian Communist Party was again in the throes of factional controversy. Zinoviev and Kamenev, partners of Stalin in the troika, had fallen out with their co-triumvir and were protesting bitterly the course of policy which the party was following under his leadership. This battle of rival Leninists, seeking to outdo one another in quotations from the master, was manifestly the product of a contest for personal political advantage. The issues concerning both theory and policy had become more subordinate with each successive phase in the history of the Opposition; the real stakes now were the domination of the party and the country. Nevertheless, questions of policy and doctrine did play a significant role in the struggle between the Zinoviev Opposition and the Stalin-Bukharin leadership, if only as the field of battle. But the primary importance of the Zinoviev movement was to be realized in the years following: it provided the starting point, both organizationally and ideologically, for the united Trotsky-Zinoviev Opposition of 1926–1927, which undertook the most penetrating criticism ever made of the Soviet regime from within.

THE SPLIT IN THE TROIKA

Signs of dissension within the self-constituted triumvirate date back almost to the original assumption of leadership by Zinoviev, Kamenev, and Stalin. Zinoviev had been cold toward the organizational changes effected at the Twelfth Congress of 1923, which were a major step in Stalin's accumulation of power. The maneuvers in which Zinoviev engaged in the summer of 1923, especially his schemes for reorganizing the Secretariat and the Orgburo, also point to some anxiety on his part about the intentions of his partner. These seem, however, to have been isolated instances; until the end of 1924, Zinoviev was far more worried about Trotsky than about Stalin. Stalin provided useful support to the man who envisaged himself the head of the party.

The victory of late 1923 over the Trotskyists and the organizational tightening sanctioned by the Thirteenth Congress enhanced Stalin's power further, and prompted him to venture some corrections of Zinoviev and Kamenev in matters of theory. Some people, Stalin said in June 1924 (with Zinoviev in mind), were falsely describing the Soviet regime as a "dictatorship of the party," rather than a "dictatorship of the proletariat." In the same speech Stalin criticized Kamenev by name for his erroneous reference to "NEPman Russia," as if the NEPmen were in power. In both these questions Stalin was reacting against overly frank descriptions of reality. Further, Stalin expressed himself against the idea of another great expansion in the membership of the party, a project favored by the Zinovievists and actually endorsed by the Thirteenth Congress.[1]

By the fall of 1924, Stalin had begun to take organizational measures aimed at Zinoviev. He removed the secretary of the Moscow party committee, I. A. Zelensky, and packed him off to Central Asia. Zelensky, though he remains an obscure figure, was a key man in the organization at the time, a member of both the Secretariat and the Orgburo in addition to his Moscow post. He had served in Moscow under the shadow of Kamenev (who was chairman of the Moscow Soviet) since 1921 and was evidently an important member of the Zinoviev bloc. Stalin moved boldly to replace Zelensky with N. A. Uglanov, who as Petrograd party secretary had clashed with Zinoviev in 1921. Zinoviev and Kamenev somehow reasoned that Uglanov's transfer to the Moscow post would be to their advantage, but this illusion was soon dispelled. Uglanov succeeded to Zelensky's seats on the Orgburo and the Secretariat, and took over control of the Moscow party machine.[2] When the crisis came, Kamenev would find himself helpless in his own headquarters. The potential opposition to Stalin had lost one of its major centers of strength.

Trotsky's attack on Zinoviev and Kamenev came at this critical juncture, and the two were driven back into Stalin's arms. The fervor of the ensuing denunciations of Trotskyism appears in part to have stemmed from efforts of the Zinoviev and Stalin factions to keep one another from forming an alliance with Trotsky.[3] Zinoviev's enmity toward Trotsky reached such a pitch that he demanded that the Opposition leader be expelled from the party. Stalin and a majority of the Central Committee opposed this, and even turned down a Leningrad proposal to oust Trotsky from the Politburo; the measures against him were confined to his removal from the Commissariat of War. Stalin's maneuver was rewarded with success: Trotsky repaid the favor by remaining entirely aloof while the leadership did battle with the Zinovievists. By Stalin's own account, the question of expelling Trotsky was the first open disagreement among the troika. "We disagreed with Zinoviev and Kamenev," Stalin commented sanctimoniously, "because we knew that the lopping policy was fraught with grave danger for the party, that the lopping method, the blood-letting method—and they demanded blood—was dangerous, contagious; today you lop off one, tomorrow another, the day after tomorrow a third—what will we have left in the party?"[4]

From the beginning of 1925 skirmishing went on intermittently between the supporters of Zinoviev and the central leadership. In January the Zinovievist Sarkis attacked Bukharin for "syndicalism" because he seemed to encourage peasant organizations insufficiently controlled by the party. Sarkis was forced to retract the charge.[5] In February Stalin began poaching in Zinoviev's Comintern preserve, with advice, promises, and threats designed to exploit the differences in the German Communist Party. Friction arose over control of the Komsomol when Leningrad resisted the authority of the center; Stalin struck the opposition down and had Zinoviev's supporter Safarov removed from the Leningrad Komsomol organization. Zinoviev tried to organize his own theoretical journal; this was blocked, too.[6]

In April new measures dealing with the peasantry were initiated at the plenum of the Central Committee and the Fourteenth Party Conference: the NEP reached its most lenient point in the cultivation of private initiative. This trend alarmed the Zinovievists and aroused their Leninist orthodoxy. Discussions and debates on the state of the NEP continued throughout the rest of the year. In the summer and early fall of 1925 Zinoviev turned to the theoretical plane and shifted to the left to find grounds for attacking the Stalin-Bukharin leadership as an un-Leninist deviation.

Zinoviev's cue was acted on by one of his supporters in the Central Committee, Zalutsky (Molotov's former colleague in the brief Left Bolshevik leadership of March 1917). Zalutsky wrote a pamphlet describing incisively the "state capitalism" of the existing regime and made some remarks on the actual or prospective "Thermidorean degeneration" of the party. The leadership was enraged and ordered the removal of Zalutsky from his post in the Leningrad party committee. This measure evidently took the Zinoviev people somewhat by surprise, for the provincial committee acquiesced, by a vote of nineteen to sixteen. Stalin attempted the *coup de grâce* by having one of his men, N. F. Komarov, installed as Leningrad party secretary. The Zinovievists rallied, curbed Komarov, and protested the interference of the Central Committee. With efficiency equaling Stalin's, Zinoviev began to prepare his machine for a test of strength at the forthcoming party congress.[7]

When the Central Committee met in October, factional lines were sharply drawn. The new Opposition made its first formal appearance, under the leadership of Zinoviev, Kamenev, the finance commissar Sokolnikov, and Lenin's widow Krupskaya. The four complained especially about peasant policy and demanded, unsuccessfully, that an open party debate be officially proclaimed.[8] The party congress, supposed to have been held in the spring, was postponed while Stalin tightened his hold on the party organization. By November the machinery was securely in his grip everywhere except in Leningrad, where Zinoviev's hold was equally tight. At the Leningrad provincial party conference, Zinoviev beat off Stalin's attempted incursions once again. Zinoviev removed every known supporter of the Moscow leadership from the local organization and from the Leningrad delegation to the Fourteenth Congress.[9]

This was the signal for the first public attack on the Leningraders—a resolution passed by the Moscow provincial party conference which was meeting simultaneously.[10] The thrust was expressed in vague terms, without mentioning names, but it was sufficiently clear to the Leningraders to provoke them to a blunt counterstatement: they protested the "unheard-of accusations" which could not possibly be taken seriously because the Leningrad organization was so firmly "proletarian" and "Leninist." [11] Moscow now replied with all the stops pulled out; the Zinovievists' "errors" on everything from "state capitalism" to the party's membership policy were recounted in detail, while the Opposition activity was characterized as "alienation, separatism, hysterical bawling, and intellectualist disbelief in our victory." [12] Moscow rejected a Leningrad overture for settling the controversy amicably, and a steady press campaign against the Opposition continued up to the opening of the Fourteenth Party Congress in mid-December.[13] Trotsky had some ironic comments to make on this battle of the machines—what, he queried, was the social explanation for two great workers' organizations passing unanimous resolutions against each other? [14]

Meanwhile, mysterious events occurred in the army command. The new commissar of war, Frunze, was reportedly at odds with Stalin's closest friend in the military command, the reliable but not particularly competent Voroshilov.[15] Whether because of this or other political reasons, Frunze was rumored to be sympathetic toward the Zinoviev faction. Late in October 1925, Frunze died while undergoing surgery. Although Frunze remains a hero in party history, Stalin's critics allege that the war commissar was deliberately ordered to submit to an operation which his heart could not stand.[16] The death of Frunze precipitated a contest over his successor. Stalin backed Voroshilov (or Ordzhonikidze, according to a different report), while Zinoviev's candidate was Trotsky's old military antagonist, Lashevich. Zinoviev accepted a compromise: Voroshilov became commissar, with Lashevich as his deputy.[17] The Opposition kept a toe hold in the army, though it was to avail them little.

On the eve of the party congress, Stalin undertook a new maneuver designed to avoid an open split. He had no need to make a target of Zinoviev if the latter would acknowledge the supremacy of the general secretary and submit to the discipline of the party. Furthermore, it was to Stalin's advantage to hush up the embarrassing theoretical issues which the Zinovievists were raising. Accordingly, he offered a "compromise": the views of the majority would be accepted as official; Politburo members would not attack each other at the congress; the most glaring doctrinal errors committed by Zinoviev supporters would be condemned; the ouster of the majority men from their posts in the Leningrad organization would be rescinded; and the editor of the Leningrad *Pravda* would be replaced. In return, one Leningrad man would be placed in the party Secretariat and one on the board of *Pravda*.[18] Zinoviev justifiably described these terms not as those of compromise but of capitulation.[19] The Opposition evidently felt they had little to lose in choosing to resist, and proceeded to carry the fight to the floor of the party congress.

Stalin parried the challenge of the Zinovievists with his characteristic adroitness, and made the dispute appear in its true light—a falling out among the leaders, a defection by some because their own voices were not being heeded as they thought they should be. Stalin carefully left the full and formal declaration of struggle to Zinoviev. As for himself, when he delivered the political report at the opening of the Fourteenth Party Congress, he talked around the issues which divided the majority and the Opposition, named no names, and expressed the hope that all disputes would soon come to an end. But to be sure that his provocation of the Opposition took effect, Stalin added, "Since I do not wish to introduce contentious matters, I shall say nothing about the way in which the Leningrad comrades behaved at their conference."[20]

Zinoviev was forced to announce the split. He opted for the privilege of making a minority report (*sodoklad*) to the congress. This was a common practice at local party meetings and in connection with specialized subjects, but such a challenge to the main political report at a national party congress had not been seen since Bukharin led the Left Communists against Lenin in 1918. Zinoviev's defiance was the signal for a torrent of denunciation, which did not end until the Zinoviev Opposition was completely broken.

The Peasantry and the NEP

The peasant problem has always been a source of dissension in the Russian Communist Party. It was a particularly sensitive subject in the middle years of the NEP, when the policy of un-Communist concessions to the private interests of the peasants reached its peak. If the peasant question was not a major cause of the cleavage between Zinoviev and Stalin, it was in any case exploited by both sides to maximum advantage.

The party leadership was attempting to steer through the narrow passage between peasant rebellion and anti-Leninist heresy. In August 1924, armed peasant revolt had broken out in the Georgian republic. On the other side, the Trotsky Opposition had challenged the proletarian orthodoxy of appeasing the peasantry at the expense of industry and the urban workers. Bukharin commented at a session of the Comintern executive committee: "Trotskyism . . . consists of 'more proletarian,' 'more industrial,' 'not too much turning one's face to the village.' And this implies the risk of breaking up the workers' and peasants' bloc, consequently, the risk of destroying the proletarian dictatorship."[21] But the condemnation of Trotsky's "underestimation of the peasantry" still left the leadership insecure in its self-justification. For a time all party leaders were agreed on further concessions to the peasants. In January 1925, Stalin and Kamenev both defended the government's conciliatory peasant policy and warned against Trotskyist underestimation of the worker-peasant smychka.[22] "Face to the village" was the new slogan, verbosely endorsed by Zinoviev. To cultivate more support for the party among the peasantry, he urged the introduction or extension of a series of conciliatory measures—low industrial prices, more stability of land tenure, freer participation in the local soviets, truly voluntary organization of the cooperatives, and tax relief. Zinoviev spoke like a confirmed right-winger, even to the extent of arguing that the conciliatory peasant policy required absolute party unity for its proper execution and control.[23]

The Fourteenth Party Conference met late in April 1925, with peasant policy prominent on the agenda. The Politburo had already worked out its recommendations for the encouragement of agricultural production, and Bukharin, enthusiastically explaining them just before the conference met, proclaimed to the peasantry, "Get rich." This frankness evoked much protest at the conference, and Stalin himself criticized the expression, but Zinoviev joined with the majority in ruling further complaints out of order.[24] Bukharin boldly went ahead to address the conference with a recommendation that the kulaks be "unfettered" so that the state could take advantage of their efforts in the building of socialism.[25] Stalin commented afterwards, "Stakes on the middle peasant in agriculture, the diligent peasant as the central figure of our agricultural upswing . . . is the idea that served as the basis of the decisions and of the concessions to the peasantry that we adopted at the Fourteenth, April, Conference of our party."[26]

The concrete steps taken by the conference did not go as far as the accompanying talk would indicate. Perhaps as a gesture to mollify potential antikulak critics, most of the stress was laid on measures to boost cooperatives and improve party work in the villages.[27] Stalin and Bukharin did not wish to expose the really substantial concessions to criticism at the conference, so they withheld them until April 30, the day after the conference closed, when they had Molotov propose the new policies to the Central Committee. While duly acknowledging efforts to curtail the kulaks and to encourage new collective farms, the Central Committee resolution on Molotov's report called for "the determined elimination of survivals of 'War Communism' in the village" and "the real elimination of any administrative obstacles which put brakes on the growth and strengthening of peasant farms (including the well-to-do stratum of them), with the indispensable introduction of legal measures of struggle (especially economic) against the kulaks." Verbiage aside, the practical steps were all to encourage production by prosperous individual peasants: the terms of land leasing were liberalized, the use of hired labor was officially sanctioned, and the traditional redivision of land by the peasant community was discouraged. State credit assistance, improved machinery supplies, and better village trade were promised. The policy of reducing the prices of industrial products was to be pursued "undeviatingly," while the regulation of agricultural prices was to be eased. Tax relief was repeatedly stressed. For a brief period, the individual farmer had become the government's pet.[28]

Zinoviev was completely deceived. He had desisted from an attack on Bukharin at the opportune moment, since the party conference did not go so far in the propeasant direction as to justify the organizational risks which would be involved in an attack on the party's chief ideologist. Excess caution, here and again in the Comintern, held Zinoviev back until his cause was lost. As soon as the forum of the conference was dispersed, Stalin and Bukharin pushed their program through the Central Committee, and Zinoviev was helpless to resist. Thenceforth the propeasant policy had an official sanction which constantly undercut the Zinovievists' criticism.

Lacking the organizational strength to challenge Stalin and Bukharin head-on, Zinoviev concentrated on an ideological flanking maneuver: he would appeal to Lenin and show by implication that the leaders were guilty of un-Bolshevik aberrations. Accordingly, Zinoviev published in the summer of 1925 a lengthy and incredibly dull volume entitled *Leninism* (in this genre he displayed no more intellectual originality than did Stalin). The work revealed that Zinoviev was seeking a better offensive base by shifting to the left, while simultantiously striving to distract his opponents by stabbing at the dead dragon of Trotskyism. Redefining the NEP to discourage its excessive elaboration, Zinoviev forgot his own earlier attacks on the Left and borrowed their formula of 1921–1923: the NEP was not an "evolution" but a "strategic withdrawal."[29] "We withdrew from War Communism not to socialism," he warned, with profuse reference to Lenin, "but to a special 'state capitalism' in the proletarian state."[30]

Next Zinoviev published a provocative article entitled "The Philosophy of the Epoch."[31] This was a polemic against "Ustrialovism"—the thesis propounded by Professor N. V. Ustrialov, an émigré economist in the employ of the Chinese Eastern Railway, that under the NEP Russia was retrogressing to capitalism and a conventional social order. Like the other Communist leaders, Zinoviev waxed indignant over Ustrialov's contention that the Soviet state was losing its revolutionary character and assuming a "national-democratic" form. Nevertheless, Zinoviev warned that the Soviet regime was indeed subject to dangerous petty-bourgeois influences, against which the party should guard vigilantly. Those who ignored the danger and accepted the idea of the NEP as an evolution, Zinoviev suggested, were dangerously close to Ustrialovism and petty-bourgeois degeneration. Only an appeal to the masses of the proletariat and poor peasants, on the basis of "the destruction of classes, the new life, socialist equality," could guarantee the future of the revolutionary regime.

Stalin reacted to this with a contemptuous indignation that foreshadowed his outright repudiation of equalitarianism in the 1930s: "At the present time the slogan of equality is SR demagogy. There can be no equality as long as there are classes. . . . We must speak not about an undefined equality, but about abolishing classes, about socialism."[32] Nothing could be more intolerable to the right-wing leadership than criticism which implied that their policies represented a petty-bourgeois lapse from Bolshevism. They could endure neither questioning of the propriety of their policies nor challenges to their doctrinal rationalizations. Zinoviev began to threaten them in both respects, while the United Opposition developed this line of attack much further during the next two years. Such was the constellation of organizational forces, however, that the more effective the arguments of the Opposition were, the more they contributed to the destruction of all chance of criticism by inflaming the fanaticism of the anxious holders of power.

During the summer and fall of 1925 the Zinovievists constantly returned to the kulak theme and continued to make Bukharin a target. The leadership responded with both concession and repression: they put more emphasis on the poor peasants and party work to organize them, and at the same time cracked down on the Leningrad Komsomol for manifesting "fear of the middle peasant."[33] Both Zinoviev and Kamenev were criticized for statements in which they neglected to mention the middle peasant, and Zinoviev was taken to task for speaking about "neutralizing" the middle peasants instead of allying himself with them.[34] When the Opposition threatened to make capital out of statistical evidence showing the growth of the kulaks, Stalin procured new figures, reportedly faked, to refute his critics.[35]

At the Central Committee meeting in October 1925, the Zinovievists opened a direct attack on the peasant policy of the leadership, which they accused of overlooking the poor peasants and making concessions to capitalist elements. Stalin charged that the Opposition was trying to violate the April decisions to the detriment of the middle peasants. Zinoviev accused the leadership of the same, in favor of the kulaks.[36] The Central Committee's unanimous passage of a resolution on the peasant question proved to be only a cover for the broadening differences behind the scenes. The Leningraders complained that they were the only people to take the resolution "seriously" and face up to the kulak threat.[37] The Leningrad Komsomol organization distributed a statement on the peasant issue which was especially critical of Bukharin and recalled again his "get rich" error.[38]

For the moment, Stalin and Bukharin were generously conciliatory, in order to keep the controversy behind closed doors until they were ready to strike. Kamenev's report on the economic situation was approved without objection, and a wage increase for low-paid industrial workers was promised.[39] The theme of aiding the poor peasants was especially stressed, while the "decisions of the Fourteenth Conference" were reaffirmed. Twin deviations were warned against—underestimation of the poor peasant and underestimation of the middle peasant.[40] The straight path of orthodoxy was made narrow indeed, the easier to catch the unwary critic in a misstep.

As the result of his political maneuvers during 1925, Zinoviev had brought himself around step by step to the left-wing view of the NEP. He now took it essentially as a temporary period of compromise with nonsocialist forces and conditions—a sort of purgatory on the road to the socialist heaven, as it were. In Politburo debates Zinoviev and Kamenev stressed, much to the indignation of the Rightist leadership, the obstacles which Russia's economic backwardness placed in the path of socialist development.[41] In spite of themselves, the Leningrad Opposition had come close to the Trotskyist theory which they had but lately been villifying. In his minority report to the Fourteenth Congress, Zinoviev ventured, after a few commonplaces, to come out with a vigorous attack on those—and he mentioned Bukharin by name—who contravened Lenin's teachings and idealized the NEP as nascent socialism. State capitalism, not socialism, he asserted with much quotation of Lenin, was the basis of the NEP.[42] This unpleasant fact, as Kamenev argued, should not be covered up: "If in 1925 there has taken shape any tendency in the party representing the distortion of the genuine line of the party, it is the tendency which conceals the negative side of the NEP. . . . We assert that the danger is in the exaggeration of the NEP. . . ."[43] Wage equalization and profit sharing were the main Zinovievist proposals to increase the socialist flavor of nationalized industry.[44]

The party leadership was particularly disturbed by the idea of state capitalism. It seemed to suggest that the Soviet system was hardening into a pattern that fell short of revolutionary ideals, and that the party leaders were exploiting this situation while trying to deny its existence. The remark attributed to Zalutsky about "Thermidorean degeneration" caused a veritable furor, and Zalutsky's stock did not rise with his watered-down warning that nonviolent bourgeois forces were leaving their mark on the country.[45] The Moscow organization thought the question was settled by its repudiation of "liquidator attempts at treating our socialist industry as state-capitalist industry."[46] Stalin declaimed at length on the reasons why Soviet industry could not be called state-capitalist. The use of such a term, he insisted, was as bad as suggesting that the Soviet state could be deficient in its proletarian quality.[47]

Regarding peasant policy the party leadership was equally insistent that expediency was orthodoxy. To the Opposition's complaint that the government was appeasing the kulaks, Stalin replied with irrelevant acidity: "Is that true? I assert that this is untrue, that this is slander upon the party. I assert that a Marxist cannot approach the question this way, that only a liberal can approach the question this way."[48] Stalin again endorsed the agriculture-first economic plans of the right wing, but at the same time he also seized on an opportunity to ascribe to the Opposition excessive reliance on the prospects for agriculture. Sokolnikov, the commissar of finance, had joined the Zinoviev Opposition mainly because of his antipathy toward the political conduct of the Secretariat, on which he expressed himself vigorously. In regard to economic policy, however, he stood on the extreme right of the party, and argued the need to depend on agriculture and foreign trade for a long period while the country's economy was gradually built up. He and his associate, the economist Shanin, provided a useful butt for Stalin, who contemptuously dismissed their ideas as a project for the "Dawesation" of Russia. Boldly Stalin proclaimed the goal—with the means to achieve it as yet undecided—of making Russia industrially self-sufficient, "to prevent our country from becoming an appendage of the world capitalist system."[49] These unimplemented remarks were the sole basis for the appellation later given the Fourteenth Congress, the "Industrialization Congress."[50]

The resolution which the congress passed to endorse Stalin's report did make certain concessions, as Kamenev noted with some satisfaction, toward recognizing the kulak problem and urging measures to boost the socialist sector of the economy.[51] Nevertheless, the prevailing tone of the majority pronouncements was closely in accord with Bukharin's philosophy of gradual evolution toward socialism in Russia on the basis of long-term cooperation with the peasants. "Any underestimation of the middle peasant," the congress resolved, "objectively leads to the undermining of the proletarian dictatorship."[52] In the minds of both the leadership and the Opposition, the issue of peasant policy was connected closely to the whole problem of assessing Russia's future prospects as a socialist nation.

SOCIALISM IN ONE COUNTRY AND THE COMINTERN

The security of socialism in Russia and its relation to the international fortunes of the Communist revolution became a key issue of Russian factional politics during the Zinoviev-Stalin contest. The points of policy which the two sides debated were found to hang upon fundamental—if somewhat theological—questions of interpreting the place of the Russian Revolution in its world setting. Moreover, the Communist International became a decisive political arena—Zinoviev's influence in the Comintern was one of the main sources of his political strength, and Stalin was determined to attack him there.

The key non-Russian force in the Comintern was the German Communist Party. The German party was still under the cloud of the 1923 defeat, in reaction to which the left-wing leaders, Arkady Maslow and Ruth Fischer, had come to the fore. Zinoviev, stressing discipline and caution under the slogan of "Bolshevization," was trying to steer a noncommittal course between what he described as the Right and the Ultra-Left.[53] The unruly German Left, however, was critical both of Russian domination and of Russian internal policies.[54] Stalin's first inclination was to approach the German Left for an alliance against Zinoviev. A Stalin victory, however, seemed even more of a threat to the autonomy which the Germans desired, and Maslow and Fischer rebuffed the overtures. Stalin's alternative was to cultivate other German Left leaders, particularly Ernst Thälmann, and give them his backing.[55]

Early in 1925 Stalin saw his opportunity to by-pass Zinoviev and attack the Maslow-Fischer leadership. The burning issue at this point was the German presidential election: Maslow advocated a bloc with the Social Democrats in the interest of preserving the republic, while Stalin encouraged his man Thälmann to run on a separate Communist ticket. Zinoviev endorsed Maslow's plan, but this policy was defeated; Stalin had scored a major victory in Zinoviev's territory.[56] Right and left were reversed in this curious maneuvering, as political expediency led the right-wing Russian leadership to support the revolutionary romantics in Germany.

Zinoviev's usual reaction when his organizational positions were brought under fire was to counterattack on the theoretical front. By 1924 it had been accepted as doctrine for the Comintern that world capitalism had entered a new phase of "stabilization"—no world revolutionary situation should be expected in the near future. These circumstances had invested Trotsky's theory of permanent revolution with grave implications as to whether Russia could remain socialist. Zinoviev's escape from the quandary was to turn the revolutionary wish into a prediction: "The world position as a whole . . . remains revolutionary." He warned against the pessimistic "Right sickness" of overestimating the stabilization of capitalism, and urged an effort to get more fresh, leftward-leaning leaders at the head of the Comintern parties.[57]

One is tempted to surmise that world revolution was important to Zinoviev chiefly because he feared a diminution in the importance of his own job as chairman of the Comintern. In any event, Zinoviev was soon arguing that the very fact of capitalist stabilization was generating new revolutionary forces. By November 1925, Zinoviev and Kamenev expressed glowing optimism on the progress of the Comintern.[58] "The Comintern is one of the greatest values which has been created by the international working class," asserted Zinoviev at the Fourteenth Congress.[59]

In the meantime Stalin advanced a contrary idea. In April 1925, he had the Fourteenth Party Conference approve a statement which, though obscurely worded, appeared to put the party on record with an endorsement of his new doctrine of socialism in one country.[60] Following the conference Stalin acted boldly on the international issue, just as he had on the peasant question. "Lenin," he declared, invoking the departed prophet in the present tense, "is opposed to the contention that the relatively backward economic condition of Russia would make it impossible for that country to realize socialism. . . . Were this true, there would have been no sense in our seizing power in October 1917 and bringing about the revolution. For if . . . we exclude the possibility and the necessity of building up a fully socialized system of society in Russia, then the October revolution has no meaning. He who denies the possibility of inaugurating socialism in one country alone, must, if he be logical, likewise deny the expediency of the October revolution."[61] Here is an open recognition of the agonizing issue which the theoretical question of the international revolution posed. Reasoning from unadjusted Marxist premises, the party member would be led to the despairing conclusion that decades of struggle and what had passed as triumph in a grueling civil war had all gone for naught—that without the support of the international revolution the Communist Party could not realize its ideals in Russia, no matter how strong its faith and exertions.

Whatever the reasons, this is what actually happened. The Left Opposition had been warning against such an impasse since 1918. It was this contradiction of theory and practice which prompted the rigorous enforcement of the party line since 1921. But the fact that Stalin could now deliberately state the questions which must have worried many people throughout the party—whether the October Revolution had not been in vain and whether the present regime could really be called socialist—is indicative of the secure position which he felt he now held in the party. Without fear of an effective challenge, Stalin was able to reverse the political logic of the party, assert as axiomatic the socialist character of the existing regime, and then proceed to the revision of his theoretical premises in order to account for the alleged survival of socialism in Russia.

In July 1925, the prospect of Russian domination and the conservative trend of Soviet international policy brought the leftist-led German Communists to the verge of revolt against Moscow.[62] Maslow attacked the Soviet leadership along Zinovievist lines but in much stronger terms—the Russian Communists were degenerating under the pressure of the kulaks and perverting the Comintern to serve Russian interests rather than the revolution.[63] To meet this challenge, Stalin assembled a variety of charges against the German leaders, ranging from embezzlement to the contemplation of a Fourth International, and then he had the Politburo force Zinoviev to compose an "Open Letter" repudiating his own German supporters.[64] As on the peasant question at home, Zinoviev was driven from the field before he could resolve to take a stand and defend himself. Stalin installed his leaders in the German party, and the "Bolshevization" of the Comintern proceeded apace. The finishing touches came the following year, when Bukharin, after displacing Zinoviev as Comintern chief, went to Germany to supervise the expulsion of the German left-wing Communists.[65]

Grievously wounded in the Comintern, Zinoviev tried to save himself with ever more leftist-sounding theoretical declarations. In his *Leninism* he finally pronounced himself openly against Stalin's socialism in one country. "The final victory of socialism," Zinoviev wrote, "is impossible in one country. . . . The final victory of the socialist order over the capitalist will be decided on an international scale." [66] He backed up this assertion with an array of quotations from Lenin on the impossibility of the final victory of socialism in one country. [67] On the field of argument Zinoviev triumphed ponderously over Stalin's one frail passage taken out of context. But Stalin was not concerned with scholarly accuracy. What he demanded of the party was an act of faith: "We cannot build up anything unless we have a knowledge of the ultimate aim of our work; no step forward is possible unless we know where we are to place our feet. . . . Are we building under the sign of socialism, in the hope of bringing the work to a triumphant finish? Or are we constructing haphazardly, blindly, in order that, 'while awaiting the advent of the world-wide socialist revolution,' we may fertilize the soil for a bourgeois-democratic harvest?" [68] Thus did Stalin reveal what had become by now the essential pragmatism of the movement as a going concern. It must keep moving—those who might slow it down by questioning its direction must be silenced.

Speaking at the Fourteenth Congress, Zinoviev tried to anticipate the charge that the Opposition "lacked faith" in the building of socialism:

We are in dispute only over whether it is possible to complete the building of socialism . . . in one country. . . . We are not in dispute over whether the building of socialism in one country is impossible: the numbers of the effective proletariat in the Soviet Union are sufficient for this, the economic prerequisites are present, the general political circumstances are altogether favorable for building socialism very successfully, it being remembered that we have the support of the international working class, that our building of socialism will be finally completed on an international scale. [69]

Zinoviev had no lack of faith—he was merely splitting hairs. He was evidently upset about the place being accorded considerations of international revolution and his own center of power in the Comintern. Thus he felt forced to take issue with socialism in one country as Stalin stated it: it is quite all right to pursue the building of socialism in Russia, but remember that Zinoviev's Comintern is important too, for the completion of the building requires international action. It is not likely that such semantic quibbling swayed many minds.

Stalin, for his part, by no means ceased to speak the part of an international revolutionary. Winding up his report to the Fourteenth Congress, he proclaimed: "When the workers of the capitalist countries are infused with faith in their own powers, you can be sure that this will be the beginning of the end of capitalism, and the truest sign of the victory of the proletarian revolution. That is why I believe that in this work we will win on an international scale." [70] It fell to Bukharin to assume the positive defense of the idea of socialism in one country. It was, he contended, the only alternative to Trotsky's heresy of permanent revolution. Thus he lumped the Zinovievist critics of the new doctrine together with the earlier Left Opposition. The crime of which they were all guilty was doubt: "Why did we expose at that time the theory of permanent revolution? We exposed it because it seemed to us . . . that the errors of the Opposition concealed within them the embryo of doubt as to the possibility of building socialism in our country."[71]

Stalin withheld his own direct reply on socialism in one country for his new essay, "Problems of Leninism," which appeared in January 1926. He acknowledged that he had modified the statement in his "Foundations of Leninism" of 1924, when he had repeated what was actually only the currently accepted idea that socialism in Russia depended on the international extension of the revolution. But Stalin asserted that his amendment was only in the interest of clarity: "this [earlier] formulation may give grounds for thinking that the organization of socialist society by the efforts of a single country is impossible—which, of course, is wrong." Stalin's reasoning is a perfect example of the type of thinking which he was soon to make standard for the whole country: changes of doctrine are never to be recognized; people who advance the old interpretation are attacked for committing a new misinterpretation of what was previously supposed to have been said. Thus, Zinoviev's annoying reference to Stalin's own 1924 denial of socialism in one country could mean only "dragging the party back after it has moved forward." Such a move "lands one in a hopeless mire of contradiction, reveals lack of faith in the building of socialism, means abandoning the path of Lenin, and is a confession of one's own defeat."[72] In the same vein the political resolution of the Fourteenth Congress stated as one of the party's primary tasks "the struggle against disbelief in the construction of socialism in our country."[73] Soviet Communism was rapidly on the way to becoming a revealed religion, complete with secretarial infallibility and Inquisition.

Stalin's much-repeated dictum that Marxism "is not a dogma but a guide to action" would stand better if inverted—action is the guide to theory, which nevertheless at any moment stands as dogma in spite of successive modifications. The Stalinist attitude toward theory was not the empirical, flexible one. When experience controverted theory they did not say, "The theory is slightly wrong, it must be adjusted in thus and such respects." The leadership adjusted the theory to fit the facts, to be sure, but then proclaimed that this new version had always been the correct theory and that the old version was a new distortion advanced by the antiproletarian opposition. In initiating this procedure for doctrinal adjustment, the promulgation of the theory of socialism in one country ushered in a new era in the methods of official Soviet thinking—an era which has lasted essentially up to the present. The association of purges with policy changes is an obvious corollary once the new status of theory is appreciated—someone must always be found to blame for the previous anti-Leninist theory. Only in this fashion could the party leadership enjoy complete freedom of action from doctrinal strictures and still use orthodoxy to demand absolute acceptance of the policy of the moment and of the regime as a whole.

THE PARTY AND THE SECRETARIAT

As those in power are disciples of authority, so are those out of power the staunchest believers in democracy. If their fortunes were sufficiently adverse, even Bolsheviks might become devout converts to the cause of political freedom. The worsting of the Leningraders at the hands of Stalin's irresistible party machine awoke them rudely to the imminent threat of one-man dictatorship.

In his volume *Leninism,* Zinoviev began to urge steps to prevent the dictatorship of the proletariat from becoming a dictatorship over the proletariat. In reality, of course, this had been an accomplished fact almost from the beginning of Soviet rule, and the same complaint could have been heard from Lenin's critics six years before—as, for instance, "The structure of the Leninist party must be such as to secure *under all conditions the maximum intraparty proletarian democracy.*"[74] An embarrassing weakness in this appeal was the autocratic reality in the Leningrad party organization, which the Stalinists were quick to point out. The Zinovievists could only rely in kind, with particular reference to Uglanov's iron rule in the Moscow organization.[75] Uglanov, varnishing the truth only a little, explained, "Yes, we do not deny it, in the Moscow organization there is peace and calm, based on the activity of the party masses, on the solidarity of the Moscow organization around the Moscow Committee and the Central Committee of our party."[76]

The Zinovievists' scheme to bolster party democracy and bring the proletarian quality of the dictatorship up to par was to expand party membership rapidly. One of Zinoviev's supporters proposed the immediate recruitment of proletarians into the party until 90 per cent of its membership consisted of "workers at the bench." While such a mass enrollment of workers had been used to good advantage by the secretarial machine the year before, it now seemed to the Zinovievists that the same device, if applied on a sufficiently broad scale, would reinvigorate party democracy and advance their cause. The people in power evidently agreed with this interpretation, for they immediately attacked the expansion project as Menshevism.[77] Stalin cited the real principle of Leninism: "Our party is a party of the elect. . . . Our party has a monopoly among the working class."[78]

Concerning the monopoly of the Secretariat within the party, Stalin was not so frank. The Opposition, however, were driven to challenge the authority of the party leadership directly. By November 1925, their complaints had given the Moscow organization reason to protest "indiscriminate attacks on the 'party apparatus,' which represent a belated repetition of what the Opposition of 1923 said."[79] The prospect of being ground to bits between the millstones of the party apparatus rapidly turned the Leningraders into high-principled exponents of true party democracy. Wrote one of their spokesmen, in acknowledging the authority of the decisions of the Fourteenth Congress, "We cannot replace the collective working out of these decisions on the basis of intraparty workers' democracy, with the naked rejection of any independent thought. . . . Every Bolshevik must have the courage to tell the congress the whole truth, all that it is necessary to say in the interests of the proletarian revolution."[80]

Some Bolsheviks did indeed demonstrate such courage. Speaking at the congress, Kamenev urged the restoration of the freedom for minorities to state their views. "Back to Lenin," he declared, and continued, "We are against creating a theory of the 'Duce,'* we are against making a 'Duce.' We are against the Secretariat, which in practice combined both policy and organization, standing over the political organ. We are for our upper level [verkhushka] being organized in such a fashion that there would be a really all-powerful Politburo, uniting all the policies in our party and, together with that, subordinating to itself the Secretariat which in technical aspects executes its decisions." At this point "noise" is recorded in the stenographic report, and no wonder, for the real issue had at last been brought out into the open. Kamenev concluded: "I have come to the conviction that Comrade Stalin cannot fulfill the role of unifier of the Bolshevik staff. [Disturbance; applause from the Leningrad delegation; cheers and applause for Stalin.]" Amidst the din, Kamenev finished: "We are against the theory of one-man rule; we are against creating a 'Duce.' "[81]

The question was again raised by Sokolnikov, who protested Stalin's dual role as general secretary and member of the Politburo. To the outcry that the party command would be weakened, he responded caustically, "If Comrade Stalin wants to earn such trust as Lenin had, let him win this trust."[82] Collective leadership was the positive alternative around which the Opposition rallied. Differences were to be overcome without repression of dissent, and the top leaders would stand as a team to carry on in place of Lenin.[83] Stalin's supporters took no exception to this ideal. They professed their firm belief that Stalin would never try to assume individual rule.[84] But at the same time they proclaimed (as it was put, for example, by Rudzutak, whom Stalin liquidated in 1938) that "our path is that pointed out by Stalin."[85]

Stalin himself endorsed the collective-leadership idea: "It is impossible to lead the party except by a collegium. After Lenin, it is stupid to dream of anything but this." To turn the tables on the Opposition, Stalin harked back to the Kislovodsk conference of 1923 and Zinoviev's plan for reorganizing the Secretariat. "What is the meaning of this platform . . . ? It means to lead the party without Rykov, without Kalinin, without Tomsky, without

* The word in Russian is vozhd (leader), then a term insulting to the party's pretenses at collective leadership, though later on it became a common designation for Stalin.

Molotov, without Bukharin. . . . It is impossible to lead the party without the comrades I have mentioned." In more recent editions this speech of Stalin's reads, "to lead the party without Kalinin, without Molotov." Stalin was to find that he could, after all, dispense with the others, but at the time he strove to defend his supporters against the Opposition. "Why . . . does all this unwarranted slander of Bukharin continue?" he demanded. "They demand the blood of Comrade Bukharin. . . . You demand Bukharin's blood? We won't give you his blood [applause]." Stalin, having got Bukharin's blood himself in 1938, also found this passage embarrassing later and had to expurgate the last lines.[86]

There was some evidence of the direction which Stalin's political thinking was taking: "Perhaps it is not known to the comrades of the Opposition that for us, for Bolsheviks, formal democracy is a cipher, while the real interests of the party are everything." He qualified collective leadership: "We must not be distracted by discussion. We are a party which is ruling a country—do not forget this. Do not forget that any exchange of words at the top is a minus for us in the country; our differences may reduce our influence."[87] In the last analysis, Stalin observed shortly afterwards, obstructionist minorities would have to be coerced. "Only in this way can we be assured of unity of action in the party . . . and unity of action of the class. . . . Without this there is schism, confusion, and demoralization in the ranks of the workers. . . . Any other conception of leadership is syndicalism, anarchism, bureaucracy, or anything you please: but not Bolshevism, not Leninism."[88]

COLLAPSE OF THE ZINOVIEV OPPOSITION

The defeat of the Zinovievists at the Fourteenth Congress was a foregone conclusion. When the decisive tally was taken on the question of endorsing the Central Committee reports delivered by Stalin and Molotov, sixty-five stood against; in favor were five hundred and fifty-nine.[89]

The most crippling blow against the Zinoviev Opposition came not at the congress but in Leningrad itself. Hardly had the congress completed its sessions, when men from the central apparatus, headed by no less a figure than party secretary Molotov, moved in to take control. The congress sent a communication to the Leningrad party organization, calling for the repudiation of its delegation to the congress on the grounds that it had violated the Leningrad provincial conference's vote for party unity (this having been expressed, of course, as a matter of form). The Leningrad provincial committee was taken to task for violating party democracy by suppressing the wishes of the Vyborg district organization in Leningrad, which had voted with the Stalinists.[90] Vainly did Zinoviev reply that this manifestation of Leningrad discontent was in reality the fruit of efforts by the Secretariat's representatives, already registering some success.[91]

Molotov's team, which included Kirov, Voroshilov, Andreyev, Kalinin, "and others," arrived in Leningrad on January 5, 1926.[92] Zinoviev's forces steeled themselves for the blow and called a city-wide conference at which the representatives of the leadership could report. The strategy of the latter, however, was to circumvent the local party hierarchy and bring their pressure and prestige to bear directly on the party organizations in the factories. Approval of this precedure was secured from the Northwest Bureau of the Central Committee, which overruled the provincial committee. For the next two weeks the party brass toured the factories, to "explain" the decisions of the Fourteenth Congress and mobilize sentiment for the central leadership. No doubt the process was facilitated by rank-and-file antipathy in Leningrad toward what must have been, by all accounts, a particularly burdensome example of the bureaucratic regime in the party. Furthermore, recalcitrant Zinovievist officials faced the ever-effective organizational weapon of transfer to some such area as Turkestan or the Far East. By late January the hold of the Zinovievists was broken at every level in the Leningrad organization.

The climax was the Stalinists' success in winning over the party organization in the famous Putilov machinery plant. The Zinovievists had counted on the Putilov plant most of all and had devoted special organizational efforts to keep it in line. But on January 21, a party meeting at the plant took up the central line, attacked the provincial organization for "repression," and demanded the convocation of conferences to elect new party committees in the Leningrad province. By the time their campaign was concluded, the Stalinists claimed 96 per cent of the total vote in the Leningrad factory organizations. They proceeded from the bottom up, getting control of one district committee after another, replacing oppositionist party functionaries, and (simultaneously with the Putilov victory) taking control in the provincial control commission and in the provincial party committee itself. The final step, in February 1926, was the convocation of a special provincial party conference, which proceeded without a hitch. Bukharin laid down the official line, and the customary unanimous vote was recorded—but this time it gave unqualified endorsement to the Moscow leadership and the resolutions of the Fourteenth Congress, and condemned Leningrad's own former leaders. The oppositionists were all eliminated from the bureau of the provincial party committee, and Zinoviev was removed from the post which had been his almost from the very inception of the Soviet regime—that of chairman of the executive committee of the Leningrad Soviet.[93]

Simultaneous with the extirpation of the Opposition from their only seat of organizational power, the party leadership removed or demoted the Opposition leaders from almost all of the responsible posts which they held in the governmental administration. Kamenev was removed from the presidency of the Council of Labor and Defense (the economic policy-making organ) and from his post as deputy chairman of the Council of Peoples' Commissars; he received instead the portfolio of external and internal trade, which shortly afterwards he lost to Mikoyan. He also lost his chairmanship of the Moscow Soviet. Sokolnikov was demoted from commissar of finance to deputy president of the State Planning Commission.[94]

In the party structure, Zinoviev kept his place, but Kamenev was demoted from Politburo member to candidate, and Sokolnikov, previously a candidate, was dropped altogether. The number of full Politburo members was increased from seven to nine—the first enlargement since 1922—and Molotov, Kalinin, and Voroshilov were advanced to the three vacancies on the top level.[95] Stalin was beginning to place his creatures in the highest party directorate.

From the list of Central Committee members approved by the Fourteenth Congress, three former members, in addition to the deceased Frunze, were missing—Zalutsky, Kharitonov, and Kuklin, all Zinovievists. Two members, including the deputy war commissar Lashevich, were dropped to candidate status. Of the thirty-four candidate members, eleven—almost a third—were dropped. Zinovievist sympathies were evident in only three or four of the cases, and ineffectiveness may have accounted for most of the others. Sixteen new or promoted members joined the Central Committee, now a firm base for Stalin's further moves, and twenty-three men, mostly unknowns, were awarded candidate status. Some of these men achieved considerable fame later on: Generals Gamarnik and Eikhe were purged in 1937; Postyshev rose to become a party secretary and, like Eikhe, a candidate member of the Politburo before his death in 1938; Unshlicht, the deputy chief of the GPU, also disappeared in 1938; Lominadze came to grief in an abortive opposition scheme in 1930; Andrei Zhdanov rose to become one of the leading lights of the party before his unexplained death in 1948.[96]

The defection of the Zinoviev Opposition began entirely as a split within the party leadership. There is no evidence that any bona fide rank-and-file movement was involved; Leningrad went with Zinoviev simply because the proconsul of the northwest was undisputed boss in his own territory. Fundamentally, the Leningrad Opposition originated in the alarm which Zinoviev and Kamenev felt when they perceived the threat of Stalin's growing organizational strength. The two eclipsed triumvirs then began to cast about for issues with which to challenge the Stalin-Bukharin leadership. While ideological motives had previously played a major role in Opposition activity, in the case of the Zinoviev Opposition doctrine was primarily an instrument of political maneuver.

There was no real affinity between the Zinoviev Opposition and the earlier Opposition movements, as the attitude of the Trotskyists at the time of the Fourteenth Congress attests. Trotsky himself took no part in the controversies at the congress, though he was present as a nonvoting delegate. He appears to have been somewhat tempted to intervene, but on the side of

Stalin![97] Trotsky dismissed as a "polemic device" the majority discription of the Zinoviev Opposition as a continuation of the 1923 Opposition movement. However, he did claim that, to acquire support, the Zinovievists had been forced to turn to the Leftists' emphasis on industrialization, which they had so recently been denouncing along with the rest of the party organization.[98]

Viewed in terms of the overall pattern of Communist Party development, the Zinoviev Opposition represented a cleavage within the Leninist or cautious and power-conscious school of thought. One factor in the cleavage was purely personal—the rivalry for number-one position between Zinoviev and Stalin. However, there were also important ideological differences, particularly on the question of socialism in one country, between the more internationalist Zinovievists and the more Russia-oriented Stalinists. This was the interpretation to which Trotsky inclined: "[Zinoviev's and Kamenev's] international outlook, wider than Stalin's, which they acquired under Lenin in foreign exile, did not make their position any stronger; on the contrary, it weakened it. The political tendency was toward a self-contained national development, and the old formula of Russian patriotism. . . . Zinoviev's and Kamenev's attempt to uphold the international viewpoint, if only to a limited degree, turned them into 'Trotskyists' of the second order in the eyes of the bureaucracy."[99]

Finally, there appears to have been an element of temperament in the cleavage: the Zinovievists, rather more doctrinaire and concerned with the literal application of party doctrine, boggled at the liberties which the Stalin-Bukharin group seemed to be taking with the policies laid down by Lenin and with the meaning of his instructions to the party. Among the Zinovievists there was something of the Leftists' attachment to ideas and ideals, and to this extent the alliance which was effected between these two groups in 1926 had a natural foundation. The primary historical significance of the Zinoviev Opposition is that it served as the prelude to this alliance and to the final Left Opposition campaign of 1926–1927. Most of the lower-level support which the Left could then command appears to have been furnished by the Zinovievists. Above all, it was the Zinovievists who had begun to develop the specific issues which supplied the Opposition with most of its political ammunition during 1926 and 1927.

12

THE UNITED OPPOSITION

The years 1926 and 1927 were the high tide of the Opposition movement in Soviet Russia. This is not to suggest that in numerical terms the Opposition was then at its maximum strength. Organizationally, the oppositional challenge was most serious at the very beginning of the Soviet regime, and subsequent manifestations of dissent were progressively weaker and easier to put down. The Opposition of 1926–1927 stands out in the breadth of divergence which arose between the contending factions and in the fever pitch which the controversy attained. At no time before or after did Opposition attacks on those in power assume so bitter a tone or go so far toward outright denunciation of the Communist leadership for betraying the ideals of the revolution.

FORMATION OF THE TROTSKY-ZINOVIEV COALITION

The United Opposition of 1926–1927 issued from a marriage of political convenience: the groups successively worsted by the party apparatus in 1923 and 1925 made natural bedfellows. Before the merger of the Trotsky and Zinoviev groups could be effected, however, a period of adjustment was necessary to assuage the memories of the Zinovievists' part in the campaigns of 1923 and 1924 against Trotskyism. The liaison never lost the marks of its strained beginning, though it had the strength to wage the most dramatic political struggle in Soviet history.

In 1925, while the Zinoviev group was receiving its blows from Stalin's party machine, the Trotskyists sat on their hands. Despite the obvious similarity of the Zinovievists and the Left Opposition in their policy disputes with the Stalin-Bukharin leadership, the Trotskyists still appeared to consider Zinoviev and Kamenev their most confirmed antagonists. They relished the treatment being meted out to the Leningraders who had but lately been chanting imprecations against the heresy of permanent revolution. Zinoviev, in his efforts before the Fourteenth Party Congress, came to see the advantage of letting bygones be bygones. He proposed "to commission the Central Committee to draw into the work all the comrades, all the forces of all the former groups in our party."[1] This drew from Bukharin the charge that Zinoviev was planning an "un-Leninist bloc" of all factions for the purpose of saving his own political skin.[2] Following his debacle at the congress Zinoviev began to suggest explicitly to his associates the necessity for an alliance with Trotsky, on the basis of which, Zinoviev believed, the Opposition could win over a majority of the party and displace Stalin. Negotiations to this end were undertaken.[3]

The Trotskyists divided in their responses to the overtures of Zinoviev and Kamenev. Radek wanted to form a bloc with Stalin against Zinoviev, who was his archenemy in the dispute over the German Communist Party. Serebriakov took the lead in responding positively to Zinoviev's overtures and was instrumental in the eventual establishment of the coalition. Mrachkovsky opposed dealing with either and perspicaciously observed, "Stalin will deceive us, and Zinoviev will run away."[4] There are some indications that Stalin was exploiting the anti-Zinoviev feeling among the Trotskyists by dealing more leniently with them himself. Very little in the way of specific attacks on Trotskyism came from him in the latter part of 1925.

Trotsky, for his part, now found it expedient to repudiate Lenin's "Testament," of which Max Eastman had published excerpts.[5] He wrote in *Bolshevik*, "Vladimir Ilich left no 'testament.' . . . Under the guise of a 'testament' the émigré and foreign bourgeois and Menshevik press habitually refer (with distortion to the point of meaninglessness) to one of the letters of Vladimir Ilich which contains advice of an organizational sort. The Thirteenth Congress attentively considered this letter. . . . All talk about the concealment or violation of the 'testament' is evil fantasy and altogether directed against the actual will of Vladimir Ilich and the interests of the party he created."[6] (Even Krupskaya was dissuaded by Zinoviev's strategy of caution from admitting the real tenor of Lenin's letter—"There is in the letter no distrust at all of those comrades with whom V. I. was joined for long years of common work."[7])

After his expulsion from the party Trotsky pleaded duress as the explanation for his action:

During the time when the Opposition still figured on correcting the party line by strictly internal means without bringing the controversy out in the open, all of us, including myself, were opposed to steps Max Eastman had taken for the defense of the Opposition. In the autumn of 1925 the majority in the Politburo foisted upon me a statement concocted by themselves containing a sharp condemnation of Max Eastman. Insofar as the entire leading group of the Opposition considered it inadvisable at that time to initiate an *open* political struggle, and steered toward making a number of concessions, it naturally could not initiate and develop the struggle over the private question of Eastman who had acted, as I said, on his own accord and at his own risk. That is why, *upon the decision of the leading* group of the Opposition, I signed the statement on Max Eastman *foisted upon me by the majority in the Politburo* with the ultimatum: either sign the statement as written, or enter into an open struggle on this account.

There is no cause to enter here into a discussion whether the general policy of the Opposition in 1925 was correct or not. It is my opinion even now that there

were no other ways during this period. In any case, my then statement on Eastman can be understood only as an integral part of our then line toward conciliation
and peacemaking.[8]

Although Trotsky had reason to think that he might profit from conciliating Stalin, the pressure of the party organization against the Trotskyists did not abate. More Trotsky sympathizers in the armed forces, including
Inspector-General N. I. Muralov, were being removed.[9] Some party organizations, and specifically Uglanov's in Moscow, were abusing Trotsky as a
hireling of the bourgeois press, and allegedly began to use anti-Semitism as
a weapon against the Opposition leaders.[10] Almost any meeting between
Opposition figures was likely to be denounced as an act of factionalism.[11]
The continuation of pressure was such that no convincing alternative to Zinoviev's coalition proposal suggested itself. Certain problems had to be ironed
out before the coalition could be openly proclaimed. These concerned the
abuse which the Trotskyists and Zinovievists had heaped on each other for
the preceding two and a half years. The Stalinists seized upon this material
and devoted a special publication to the attacks which the new allies had
made on each other.[12] "A mutual amnesty," Stalin termed the arrangement,
as well as "a direct and unprincipled bargain."[13]

To mollify the Zinovievists, Trotsky professed to renounce the theory of
permanent revolution, "insofar as it was distinguished from the real views of
Lenin."[14] In return, the Zinoviev group acknowledged that the Trotskyists'
attack on the party apparatus—even when the former participated in it—were
justified. Zinoviev and Kamenev admitted in July 1926, "Now there can be
no doubt that the basic core of the Opposition of 1923 correctly warned about
the danger of a shift from the proletarian line and about the threatening
growth of the apparatus regime." To the Central Committee Zinoviev declared at the same time, "Yes, in the question of back-sliding and in the
question of apparatus-bureaucratic repression Trotsky was right against you."
Reportedly Zinoviev confessed that the whole campaign against "Trotskyism"
in 1923–1924 was a deliberate fabrication on the part of the troika: "There
was a struggle for power. The whole art consisted in linking old disagreements with new questions. For this 'Trotskyism' was put forth."[15] Trotsky
continued to feel that his acceptance of the coalition with the Zinovievists
was justified even after his allies had proved their inconstancy: "Zinoviev
and Kamenev openly avowed that the 'Trotskyists' had been right in the
struggle against them ever since 1923. They accepted the basic principles of
our platform. In such circumstances, it was impossible not to form a bloc
with them, especially since thousands of revolutionary Leningrad workers
were behind them."[16]

The new bloc made its public debut in April 1926 by presenting a common front at the plenum of the Central Committee, with particular emphasis
on the acceleration of planned industrial development.[17] The Zinovievists

were ecstatically optimistic, according to Trotsky's report: "At our very first meeting, Kamenev declared: 'It is enough for you and Zinoviev to appear on the same platform and the party will find its true Central Committee.'" As for himself, Trotsky professed to have been more realistic—"We must aim far ahead . . . we must prepare for a long and serious struggle."[18] Indications of the difficulties awaiting them were not long in coming; no sooner had the United Opposition begun to challenge the leadership when the number-three Zinovievist, Yevdokimov, was removed from the Secretariat and the Orgburo.[19]

The coalition of 1926 was in many respects more directly a continuation of the Leningrad Opposition than of the Trotsky Opposition of 1923–1924. The Zinoviev movement provided the issues (the disputes over economic policy and the Comintern which developed in 1925), most of the organization, and a good deal of the offensive drive of the United Opposition. Not since 1921 had Trotsky stood up to lead an open attack on the leadership; he was inactive in 1923 when his supporters unsuccessfully defended his cause, and since then he had passively endured the abuse which the leadership hurled at him. With the addition of the Zinoviev group the Opposition acquired a distinctly new character; these people were Leninists with undeviating Old Bolshevik records. There were more professional party functionaries among them, since the Zinoviev Opposition was the first case of an open break within the party machinery. The Zinovievists were cautious and disciplined Leninists whom policies and the power issue had driven into a practical alliance with the Trotskyist heirs of left-wing Bolshevism. The union was never entirely harmonious and did not bear up under the strain of adversity.

THE COURSE OF THE STRUGGLE

The first overt moves of the new Opposition were prompted by events abroad. In May 1926, two embarrassing setbacks were suffered by the party leadership in its Comintern policy. Marshal Pilsudski, looked upon benevolently by the Communists, surprised them with the establishment of a military dictatorship in Poland. Fond hopes had been maintained for militant cooperation with British labor groups, through the agency of the curious organization known as the "Anglo-Russian Trade-Union Unity Committee" (ARC), formed in 1925. The Russians were rudely disappointed by the failure of the general strike in Britain in May 1926, which was a severe blow to the "united front" policy enjoined on the Comintern by the Russian leadership.

Trotsky was quick to point out that he had warned of the pitfalls in relying on non-Communist allies, and he followed up this thrust with a general attack on trends in the party under the existing leadership: party democracy was giving way to "the dictatorship of the apparatus."[20] The

Opposition demanded the dissolution of the ARC as a bloc with reformist traitors.[21] The leadership refused to admit any error in the idea of the ARC, though it never did the Rusians any good; criticism of the policy was dismissed as "otzovism."[22] The issue was finally disposed of by the British partners in the ARC, who unilaterally dissolved the organization in September 1927, after the Russian-British diplomatic rupture.

Following the agreement between the Trotsky and Zinoviev groups, the Opposition proceeded with the elaboration of an organization, which under the circumstances necessarily assumed a conspiratorial form. Secret couriers, codes, bodyguards, and clandestine meetings became accustomed practice.[23] For the first time since tsarist days these Bolsheviks found themselves in an atmosphere of underground intrigue. One of the Opposition meetings, where the deputy war commissar Lashevich spoke, was arranged in the woods outside of Moscow.[24] The party leadership quickly learned of this event, and used it as the pretext for a sweeping attack on the Opposition at the next Central Committee session. The furor was anticipated by the Opposition leaders, and they drew up for the plenum a comprehensive statement of their differences with the party leadership. This "Declaration of the Thirteen" was the most penetrating attack yet made by any oppositionists upon the party leadership, and it embodied the essential principles of the Opposition case for the whole period from 1923 to 1927.[25]

To give their case legal foundation, the Opposition leaders appealed to the Politburo resolution of December 5, 1923, for the premise that factionalism in the party was a symptom of grave illness—the disease of "bureaucratism." This malady, they asserted, stemmed from the backwardness of industry, the weakness of the proletariat, and governmental neglect of the workers, which produced a "lowering of the political and cultural self-esteem of the proletariat as the ruling class." Part of the cure would be a general wage increase (a move opposed by the leadership). Above all, the country's political health depended on a vigorous program of planned industrial development to correct the imbalance between industry and agriculture. It followed from this that the policy of concessions to the capitalist instincts of the peasantry had to stop: "The fact is that under the guise of the alliance of the poor peasantry with the middle peasant we observe steadily and regularly the political subordination of the poor to the middle peasants, and through them to the kulaks." The reverse side of proletarian weakness was the ascendency of bureaucratic elements in the government; it was important, despite talk of the proletarian nature of the state, to pursue "the struggle of the proletarian vanguard for real ideological and political subordination of the state apparatus." Bureaucracy in the government infected the party and disillusioned the workers.

In the Comintern, the Thirteen asserted, Russian bureaucratic caution was inhibiting the revolutionary initiative of the foreign militants instead of furthering the world upheaval on which the success of socialism in Russia ultimately depended. The resolution of the Fourteenth Congress on democracy and independence in the Comintern was already being violated, they claimed. The suppression of criticism within and about the Comintern was making possible a series of opportunist errors. Finally, returning to the question of factionalism, the Opposition laid the principal blame on the machinations of the party leadership: repressive measures against left-wing critics were opening the door to bourgeois influence on the government. Such a disaster could be prevented only by a radical change in the party—by the accession of the Opposition to a position of dominance. "Real" unity was promised if repression of the Opposition were suspended: "We address ourselves to the plenum of the Central Committee with the proposal that with our common efforts we restore a party regime which will permit the decision of all disputed questions in full conformity with all the traditions of the party, with the feelings and thoughts of the proletarian vanguard. Only on this foundation is party democracy possible."

At the plenum of July 1926, debate waxed long and bitter, as the small band of oppositionists strove vainly by both reasoned argument and fervent appeal to shake the hold which the leadership had over a great majority of the Central Committee. There was heated wrangling over the key economic issues of industrialization and peasant policy.[26] Dzerzhinsky, now the chairman of the Supreme Economic Council, upheld the official economic policy and reportedly threatened the Opposition with "fresh gunpowder."[27] This was Dzerzhinsky's last effort on behalf of the dictatorship of the proletariat; he collapsed under the strain of the controversy and within a matter of hours the notorious Cheka chief was dead.

The Lashevich affair—the "illegal conspiratorial meeting," as it was styled —was condemned by the Central Committee as a violation of every party principle. The resolution charged that the Opposition was animated by "petty-bourgeois sentiments which often make their appearance under the guise of Left phrases," and that it was encouraging "anti-Soviet agitation among the specialists." Members of the condemned Miasnikov and Workers' Truth groups were said to be involved in disseminating Opposition propaganda. "All these disorganizing steps of the Opposition," the Central Committee concluded, "testify that the Opposition has already decided to go over from the legal defense of their views to the creation of a nation-wide illegal organization opposing itself to the party and thus preparing a split in its ranks."[28] Bukharin charged in a speech following the plenum that the Opposition really proposed to set itself up as a second party, in violation of the fundamentals of Leninism. Its program, he asserted, "is becoming a completely liquidator tendency on the basis of disbelief in the building up of socialism in our country."[29]

In the now customary fashion, the organizational sanctions at the disposal of the apparatus were brought to bear on the Opposition. Lashevich was summarily ousted from his seat in the Central Committee, with the comment that he was lucky not to be expelled from the party. He was also removed as deputy war commissar and forbidden to hold any party office for the next two years. Those involved with him in the meeting in the woods were likewise deprived of the right to hold office. On Zinoviev's head was heaped the blame for masterminding the whole conspiracy. Charged officially with "the actual leadership of the factional struggle of the Opposition," he was thrown out of the Politburo.[30] He retained only his Central Committee seat, while his presidency of the Comintern became purely nominal. Kamenev lost to Anastas Mikoyan his last important government job as commissar of trade. He was relegated to footnote-writing as director of the Lenin Institute.[31] To replace Zinoviev, Rudzutak was promoted from candidate status to full membership in the Politburo. Five new men were brought in at the candidate level—Ordzhonikidze, Andreyev, Kirov, Mikoyan, Kaganovich, all steadfast *apparatchiki,* as their long subsequent tenure in office demonstrated.[32]

A curiosity of this phase of the struggle was the distinction made in the treatment of Zinoviev and Trotsky. Perhaps the leadership hoped to split the allies. Trotsky escaped direct reprisal, and Rykov explained that the kind of action he had engaged in was not as bad as Zinoviev's—"Comrade Trotsky made no such attempt at a split."[33] Nevertheless, the prevailing tone of the Central Committee's decision was ominous—"Unshakable unity of the party is more necessary than ever." Without "greater solidarity and discipline in our proletarian ranks . . . the party would prove incapable of fulfilling the historic task which the October Revolution placed before it . . . to secure the victory of Socialism."[34]

To embarrass the Opposition further and confound their economic criticisms, the leadership unearthed and published a letter written in 1924 by the former Workers' Oppositionist, Medvedev. This "Baku Letter" had expressed acute concern over the country's industrial weakness and, more or less writing off the Communist revolution abroad, called for a vast extension of Lenin's foreign concession idea in order to finance the building of heavy industry.[35] The leadership now raised a storm about Medvedev and Shliapnikov as "the Right danger in our party," and denounced the Trotskyists for contemplating an alliance with "an Ultra-Right group in our party, a group of capitulators to the international financial plutocracy."[36]

In September 1926, the United Opposition determined to endure no longer the pressure of the party apparatus. Trotsky, in a long statement of his position addressed to the forthcoming party conference, protested that "special weight in the Stalin faction is enjoyed by specialists in the erection of unprincipledness into a system."[37] A direct appeal to the rank and file was decided on. "At the end of September," reports the sometime official history by Popov, "the representatives of the Opposition started a simultaneous campaign throughout the entire country at nuclei [cell] meetings with the purpose of forcing a discussion upon the party regarding fundamental questions of policy which had been decided on by the Fourteenth Congress."[38] A notable Opposition demonstration was staged at a Moscow aircraft factory, where Trotsky, Zinoviev, Piatakov, Radek, Sapronov, and Smilga (the Trotskyist deputy chairman of the State Planning Commission) appeared to proclaim their point of view at a party cell meeting.[39] Again the party leadership condemned the Opposition without hesitation: "The petty-bourgeois Opposition is engaged in underground work against the unity of the party and threatens to undermine the practical work of the party and the party itself by a new and embittered discussion. The party will not tolerate this. . . . [It will] prove that the Opposition is not proletarian but petty-bourgeois and that it is serving a class foreign to the proletariat."[40]

The tactics of open defiance failed. Despairing, the Opposition bowed before the force of the party apparatus and on October 4 sued for peace.[41] Nevertheless, still one more attempt was made to appeal to rank-and-file Communist workers. On October 7 Zinoviev and his supporters in Leningrad visited a number of factories and tried to get a hearing for the Opposition point of view. Zinoviev was subjected to the now typical jeering and heckling at the Putilov plant, and a vote by the party organization there was officially recorded as 1375 to 25 against the Opposition. The Politburo condemned Zinoviev's "splitting speech" as "an especially malicious breach of party discipline."[42]

Finally abandoning open resistance, the Opposition leaders—Trotsky, Zinoviev, Kamenev, Piatakov, Sokolnikov, and Yevdokimov—signed a statement of capitulation on October 16. They confessed their guilt in violating party discipline and abjured future factional activity.[43] Leftist dissenters in the Comintern and the remnants of the Workers' Opposition in the USSR were repudiated. Pious hopes for unruffled unity concluded the surrender document.[44] Consternation among rank-and-file oppositionists was the immediate result of their leaders' capitulation.[45] As it turned out, such tactical retreats were cumulatively disastrous to the Opposition cause, and they failed to appease the leadership even temporarily. Organizational conformity was accorded little merit in the absence of the corresponding intellectual conviction. Stalin saw no slackening in the struggle: "The Opposition bloc means to continue to foster disintegrating moods and capitulation ideology in the party and . . . it intends to continue to propagate its erroneous views in the party." The pernicious character of the Opposition was confirmed for Stalin by the sympathy which Russian émigrés of various persuasians allegedly expressed for it.[46] Bukharin, speaking at the Fifteenth Party Conference, denounced the Opposition for not retracting its charges of "bureaucratic degeneration," and he warned of an abrupt end to the argument—the party was growing ever stronger, and those who continued to cry "Thermidor" would simply be struck down.[47]

The blows had begun already. At a session of the Central Committee late in October discipline was meted out to the Opposition leaders. Trotsky was ousted from the Politburo, as Zinoviev had been the summer before, and Kamenev was deprived of the candidate status to which he had been demoted after the Fourteenth Congress. The Central Committee resolved that it "does not find it possible for Comrade Zinoviev to continue work in the Communist International,"[48] and he was replaced as chairman of the Comintern's executive committee by Bukharin. The inevitable promotion of more Stalinists completed the shake-up. Kuibyshev was shifted from the presidency of the Central Control Commission to become a full Politburo member, and he also took over the Supreme Economic Council. Ordzhonikidze replaced Kuibyshev in the Central Control Commission. Promoted to the two vacant Politburo candidacies were Stanislas V. Kosior, a member since 1925 of the central Secretariat, and the Ukrainian premier who had displaced Rakovsky, Vlas Yakovlevich Chubar.[49] They were a noteworthy pair—both were non-Great-Russian (Kosior was of Polish descent and Chubar was a Ukrainian), both later became full members of the Politburo, and both disappeared in the purge of 1938.

During the remainder of 1926 the contest between the Opposition and the party leadership was confined to doctrinal disputation before various party forums, particularly the Fifteenth Party Conference, held from October 26 to November 3, and the Seventh Plenum of the Comintern executive committee in December. Both gatherings witnessed ardent pleas from the Opposition to the effect that their criticisms did not constitute a factional attack on the leadership, and equally emphatic replies by the latter insisting that the Opposition, short of totally dissolving itself, could not cease being an unproletarian deviation.

The Opposition was not bearing up well under pressure. A number of minor supporters of the Opposition foreswore their deviation at this time, and the last of the Workers' Opposition leaders, Shliapnikov and Medvedev, finally signed a full capitulation. They confessed the error of the "Baku Letter," repaid their condemnation by Trotsky and Zinoviev in equal coin, and abjured all further opposition: "We . . . condemn every organizational expression of opinions which contradict the decisions of the party. We appeal to our sympathizers, who have commenced building factional underground groupings, to liquidate these immediately."[50] Alexandra Kollontai, endowed until her death with a curious sort of diplomatic immunity from purging while she filled a series of ambassadorial posts for a quarter-century, had independently abandoned the Opposition cause by this time.

A particular boon to the leadership was the defection of Lenin's widow

Krupskaya from the Opposition. Stalin announced her decision dramatically at the very end of his concluding remarks to the Fifteenth Conference.[51] In a statement published the following spring Krupskaya explained her switch in temperate terms but nonetheless according to the organization line: "The Opposition . . . have gone too far with their criticism." From such attacks as the oppositionists made on the leadership, she feared the masses might be led to think that the party and the Soviet government might not really be representing them.[52] The truth could not be tolerated.

The central issue around which the debates at the Fifteenth Conference turned was once again the theory of socialism in one country. Stalin brought the issue before the meeting deliberately, obviously with the intent of disarming Opposition criticism. He was eminently successful, though hardly on the basis of logic alone. This episode was Stalin's great test in the matter of subordinating party doctrine to his own considerations of power and political expediency. Once having proved his ability to shout down Opposition objections that his theory rested on a bald misinterpretation of Lenin, Stalin was free to pursue the manipulation of Communist theory. He could thereafter fulfill his need for scriptural justification of the policies of the moment and demand the unquestioning acceptance of his successive reinterpretations by all who would qualify as loyal members of the party.

If the Opposition persevered in their errors, this could only be taken as demagogy pointing toward the frightful eventuality of a second, un-Leninist, unproletarian political party. No such tendency was to be tolerated. Declared Rykov, "The Opposition must realize that the party cannot permit anybody to try its patience too long."[53] The one-time Leftist Larin now joined the chorus of anti-Opposition abuse with a warning even more extreme than the leadership was then prepared to make: "Either the Opposition must be excluded and legally suppressed, or the question will be settled with machine guns in the streets, as the Left Socialist Revolutionaries did in Moscow in 1918."[54]

The Opposition again tried to present their defense at the plenum of the ECCI in December, though with little effect. "Trotsky wrapped his exposition of the debate in too great a prudence and diplomacy," reported the Yugoslav Communist observer, Ciliga. "The audience was unable to appreciate . . . the tragedy of the divergences separating the Opposition from the majority. . . . The Opposition . . . was not aware of its weakness; it was also going to underestimate the magnitude of its defeat. . . . Whereas the majority, led by Stalin and Bukharin, maneuvered to obtain the total exclusion of the Opposition, the latter constantly sought for compromise and amicable arrangements. This timid policy of the Opposition was instrumental, if not in bringing about its defeat, certainly in weakening its resistance."[55]

Pravda condemned the Opposition for a new violation of discipline in bringing the controversy before a Comintern body, even though Zinoviev had protested that differences in other Communist parties had always been discussed in the Comintern.[56] Stalin gloried in the struggle: "The fight to overcome internal party differences is the *law of development of our party*."[57] The Opposition, he concluded, was a "Social Democratic deviation" with "a platform for rallying all the opportunist tendencies for the purpose of organizing the struggle against the party, against its unity and against its authority."[58]

After a winter lull, the storm of controversy broke out abruptly in April 1927. The fortunes of the Comintern were responsible, as they were the year before, for reactivating the struggle among the Russian Communists. This time China was the scene of the leadership's embarrassment. The defeat of the Chinese Communists in 1927, a grievous disappointment to the Russians, was the subject of some of the most bitter debate of the entire factional struggle. Since 1923 the "united front" policy had been applied to China, in the form of a close association between the Chinese Communists and the Nationalist Party—the Kuomintang—which the Communists were directed to enter and support as the vehicle for a national revolution against the forces of imperialism. The Moscow party leadership was evidently more interested in the degree of Russian influence over the Kuomintang, as the prospective government of China, than it was in the specific revolutionary fortunes of the Chinese Communists.[59] Growing restiveness among the Chinese Communists about this alliance with Chiang Kai-shek prompted the Russian Opposition to criticize Moscow's insistence on the Kuomintang tie. When the Russian leadership charged "ultra-leftism," Trotsky and Zinoviev replied with allegations of "opportunism" and "organization tail-endism," and likened the Chinese situation to the Anglo-Russian Committee.[60]

On April 12, 1927, Chiang Kai-shek, marching victoriously northward to establish control over the Chinese Republic, turned against his erstwhile Communist allies in Shanghai and massacred a large number of their supporters. The Russian Opposition immediately seized upon this opportunity. Zinoviev had just finished writing a lengthy declaration calling for a break with the "bourgeois nationalists" of the Kuomintang, and to this he exultantly appended the note, "The latest events confirm completely the line that is developed in the accompanying document."[61] The Stalin-Bukharin leadership was charged by the oppositionists with personal responsibility for the blow to Communist prospects in China. Wrote Trotsky, "The April defeat of the Chinese revolution is not only a defeat for the opportunist line but also a defeat for the bureaucratic methods of the leadership."[62] A campaign of petitions, pamphleteering, and speech-making against the policies of the leadership was undertaken.[63] Stalin and Bukharin were acutely embarrassed by this turn of affairs, but they refused to admit even the slightest defect in their "united front" policy.[64] Their first and primary response was to suppress domestic criticism of their failure, while they stubbornly insisted on continuing the Kuomintang alliance.

A suitable pretext for clouding the issue was provided by Zinoviev, who, speaking on May 9 at a meeting which was not a strictly party affair, criticized the China policy of the leadership. The reply was swift, in the form of a decision of the Central Committee and a blast from *Pravda* to the effect that Zinoviev had violated the Opposition's no-factionalism pledge of October 1926, and that at this critical moment (the moment was always critical) the party could not tolerate such "speculation on the difficulties of the international revolution." [65]

In the meantime, the Opposition leaders drew up a comprehensive statement of their case against the leadership. This, the second of the three major political documents of the United Opposition, was the "Declaration of the Eighty-four," put before the Politburo on May 25, 1927.[66] It is clear from the tenor of this document that it was directed to an audience far broader than the Politburo alone. Every step of the leadership, it seems, was a mistake: "The misfortune of our party consists in the fact that in the recent period it was artificially deprived of the possibility of correctly considering and collectively deciding those questions on which depends the fate of the working class and the workers' state."[67] The basic thesis of the declaration was the contention that the series of debacles in Comintern affairs was intimately related, as "any Marxist" would know, to the difficulties and mistakes of the Russian government in internal affairs. The trouble was traced to a doctrinal failing, as the Opposition showed its ability to outdo the leadership in the fervent orthodoxy of its ideological denunciations: "Instead of a Marxist analysis of the real situation of the proletarian dictatorship in the USSR, the party offers the untrue, petty-bourgeois 'theory of socialism in one country,' which has nothing in common with Marxism, with Leninism. This abrupt retreat from Marxism makes it more difficult for the party to see the *class content* of the economic processes which are going on." In peasant policy, industrial development, wage policy, not to speak of international affairs, the Opposition saw the subversive effect of bourgeois influences.

In one aspect of the danger thus perceived there was no illusion. The secretarial apparatus was steadily increasing its pressure against the Opposition, and it is no exaggeration to say that spontaneous political self-expression by genuine proletarians had sunk to a low level. Cries for unity, according to the Opposition, were only designed to conceal the mistakes of the leadership and to avert real proletarian criticism: "Any attempt to place disputed questions before the party is declared to be an assault on the unity of the party. The incorrect line is mechanically imposed from above. Showcase unity and official felicity are being created." "Genuine Leninist unity," was the Opposition's recipe, on the basis of free speech for everyone in the party. A postscript referred to the exclusion of Zinoviev from all contact with the Comintern as evidence of "the absence of political courage on the part of those who prefer to replace ideological struggle with administrative directives." Finally, standing by their criticisms, the oppositionists declared, "We are fulfilling our duty as revolutionaries and party members, as it has always been understood in the ranks of the Bolshevik-Leninists."

By July the leadership had contrived an explanation of the Chinese defeat, which had meanwhile been compounded by a purge of the Communists in the "Left Kuomintang" regime at Hankow. The disaster was blamed on the wrong correlation of class forces (that is, proletarian weakness—though it was not explained why Moscow had not discerned this weakness earlier), and on sabotage of Comintern directives by the Chinese Communist leadership. The latter were appropriately purged. Now that the Russian Opposition had been sufficiently discredited, Stalin and Bukharin felt it possible to take over the Opposition's line without excessive loss of face. They called for the establishment of soviets in China and predicted a "new revolutionary upsurge."[68] Events made it clear that the pronouncements of the leadership were far more relevant to the factional struggle in Russia than to the actual situation in China. Only in the fall of 1927, with the Opposition gripped in the GPU vise, did the Stalin-Bukharin leadership finally acknowledge the complete break with the Kuomintang and order a direct attack upon it. The result was a series of bloody defeats for the Chinese Communists, especially the ill-fated Canton Commune of December, which Kuomintang troops easily crushed.[69] This time, however, there were no voices in Russia free to embarrass the infallible leaders of the party and the Comintern.

The policy of the "united front" ended in a series of unmitigated failures. Whether or not a Leftist policy of revolutionary purism would have succeeded is another matter. The fact remains that the right-wing party leadership had the responsibility of policy making and that it was not graced with success; the leaders maneuvered themselves into a position of extreme vulnerability to Opposition criticism. But the more the attacks of the Opposition hit home, the more anxious the leadership became over the future of their own power and prestige, the more frantically they denounced the Opposition and the more prone they became to take any necessary measures to suppress Opposition criticism. Trotsky and Zinoviev observed trenchantly that Stalin was quite capable of compromising with bourgeois forces but that he could never stand the criticism from a Communist standpoint which the Opposition made.[70] The failures of the party leadership contributed considerably more than their successes to the growth of the dictatorial rule of the Secretariat. Failure brought with it something which for the party leadership was even worse—criticism—and to guarantee themselves against this they took steps to muzzle the last outlets of free thought in the party.

The factional bitterness aroused by the crisis in China was intensified by new anxiety over foreign policy. Just at the time when the Declaration of the

Eighty-four was submitted to the party, a crisis occurred in Soviet relations with Great Britain. In May 1927, a raid by British police on the Soviet trade office in London produced what was alleged to be evidence of espionage operations, and the British Conservative government broke off diplomatic relations. Both the Opposition and the party leadership in Russia jumped to the conclusion that war with Britain was imminent, though the British took the crisis much less seriously.[71] The Declaration of the Eighty-four stressed the war threat and the need to meet it by renouncing the "united front" and appealing to the international proletariat, over the heads of their "traitorous" leaders, to support the Soviet Union. Moreover, the fumbling and repressive leadership of the Soviet regime would have to be replaced. Trotsky continued with attacks in this vein and took the leadership to task for trying to suppress his criticisms—they had even gone to the extent of cutting his remarks out of the official records of party meetings.[72]

The war scare served to justify further repression of Opposition activity. Krupskaya's reasoning was typical: "The Soviet Union is menaced by armed aggression, and in these conditions . . . it is essential that our party be a united whole."[73] Trotsky tried to challenge the genuineness of the leadership's reference to the war danger by citing the simultaneous removals of experienced military leaders on the sole ground of oppositionist sympathy.[74] The leadership darkly hinted that the Opposition, for its own political advantage, might take a defeatist stand in the event of war. Trotsky called this "the identification of the Socialist fatherland with the Stalin group."[75]

More fuel was thrown on the fire in June, when the Trotskyist Smilga was "transferred" to the Far East. When he boarded his train at the Yaroslavl station in Moscow, a group of oppositionists headed by Trotsky and Zinoviev staged a public demonstration, and Trotsky made a speech.[76] By the party's new political standards, this was virtually an act of counterrevolution. The GPU reportedly warned that it could no longer keep order in such cases unless it were given the right to arrest oppositionist party members.[77] The Democratic Centralist splinter group was said to be ready to attempt revolutionary action, though the main body of the Opposition was determined to keep the effort within legal limits as far as possible.[78]

The Central Committee session held in late July and early August was the scene of the most bitter wrangling yet witnessed within the party. Trotsky, determined to scotch the rumors of his "defeatism," affirmed that the Opposition was alone competent to guide the country through its difficult times—the choice was the Opposition or Thermidor. Differences were not to be concealed nor blunders ignored; he found an analogy in wartime France, when Clemenceau in the teeth of catastrophe pursued his opposition to the ministry until his own opportunity came for heroic leadership.[79] The "Clemenceau thesis" immediately produced a furious uproar. Molotov accused the Opposition of "Left SR insurrectionism,"[80] and Stalin warned that the Soviet government was threatened by "a united front from Chamberlain to Trotsky."[81] The leadership demanded that the Opposition leaders unconditionally retract the "semidefeatism" of the Clemenceau thesis and stop their "slander" about Thermidor, on pain of expulsion from the Central Committee. Trotsky and Zinoviev stood fast until the plenum had actually resolved to eject them; then they gave in and accepted a reprimand.[82] In the declaration which they submitted under this pressure, the Opposition declared, "We are absolutely and unreservedly for the defense of our socialist fatherland against the imperialists." They retracted suggestions that the party leadership was infected with Thermidorean tendencies and urged only that the party fight "more systematically" against such Thermidorean elements as were present in the country. Steps leading to a party split were condemned, and the authority of the Central Committee was acknowledged unconditionally.[83]

As usual, retreat by the Opposition yielded no diminution in the pressure brought to bear against them. The final resolution of the plenum continued to condemn the Opposition for the errors which they had just abjured.[84] Nothing short of the total disbanding of the Opposition would satisfy the leadership. Rykov, speaking after the plenum, explained that the Opposition, having been reduced to such insignificant proportions, could not expect any rights within the party. The party, the movement, counted far more in Rykov's estimation than individual leaders who might get in its way: "Whether Zinoviev remains or not, whether Rykov remains or not, the Communist Party will remain."[85] These were prophetic words.

In the course of little more than a year, despite the numerical weakness of the support which they were able to mobilize, the Opposition had succeeded in putting the factional controversy in the center of the Soviet political stage. They generated such a state of political hostility that only a violent solution could put an end to the matter. By the summer of 1927 the fate that was in store for the Opposition was clear; it was only a matter of how long it would take the leadership to prepare public opinion and provoke suitable incidents in order to expel the Opposition from the party and liquidate them as a political force. At the party conference the previous November, Stalin had rejected insinuations of such an intention as another Opposition slander.[86] By June 1927, however, talk of expelling the Opposition was heard openly, and Trotsky commented that Stalin had shifted from a "struggle of exhaustion" to a "struggle of extirpation."[87] Why the leadership had to respond with such vehemence cannot be explained by the organized political strength of the Opposition, which was of little consequence. It was rather the issues raised by the Opposition, the threat of acute political embarrassment which such criticism carried with it, that drove the leadership to such extremes. At

the same time these issues brought into focus some of the fundamental problems facing the Soviet regime in this period and revealed the basic trends of
political and mental evolution which were then under way in Russia.

THE INDUSTRIALIZATION CONTROVERSY

Economic questions consumed the lion's share of the time and volume of
argumentation in the factional debates of 1926 and 1927.[88] Charges and
countercharges were hurled back and forth about every economic matter
which the two sides could unearth to disagree about, from the peasant-horse
ratio to the mathematics of investment yields. Everyone became an economic
expert. In the end, however, the settling of economic questions was governed
by the expediencies of factional politics.

On many of the concrete issues of economic policy, as on the question of
foreign Communist movements, the point of departure for the United Opposition was the stand taken by the Zinovievists in 1925. This was particularly the case with respect to peasant policy and the alleged kulak menace.
Sometimes they suggested that the leadership itself was infected with petty-
bourgeois inclinations and that it was committing a "kulak deviation." (This
was a somewhat diluted imitation of the kind of class-influence argument
which the leadership employed with gusto against the Opposition.) To check
the increasing economic power of the kulaks, the Opposition urged a variety
of measures—curtailment of the concessions regarding land leasing and hired
labor, raising the agricultural tax on prosperous peasants while removing it
entirely from poor peasants, support for the poor peasants through credits
and political organization, encouragement of cooperatives and collective
farms, and even a forced grain loan at the expense of the kulaks, who held a
preponderance of the surplus stocks. Underlying the Opposition view was
the proposition that the lag in the development of socialist industry was responsible for progressive social differentiation among the peasants, and that
the strength of peasant capitalism implied a threat to the political hegemony
(so called) of the workers and poor peasants.

The right-wing position of the party leadership had been developed during the polemics against Trotsky in 1924 and against Zinoviev in 1925. According to this view, the government was economically dependent on the
contentment of the peasantry. Reasonable prosperity and trading oppor-
tunities had to be allowed the peasantry in order to preserve the smychka—
the mythical alliance of workers and peasants—and avoid the threat of the
peasants' withholding their produce from the market. Talk of the "exploitation" of the peasantry in line with Preobrazhensky's theory of "primitive socialist accumulation" evoked sheer horror. On the other hand, preferential treatment of the kulaks was vigorously denied. (The issue seems
to have hinged on the location of the imaginary demarcation line between
the kulak and the middle peasant, whose support was energetically sought.)

Closely connected with the peasant issue was the question of price policy. Here again the lines had become clear in 1925, when the party leaders affirmed their intention of further reducing the ratio of industrial prices to agricultural prices, an effort which had been in progress since the scissors crisis of 1923. The leadership argued that continued price reductions in favor of the peasantry were necessary to guarantee the marketing of food supplies, and that they would also act as a stimulus to industry by compelling it to cut production costs and by assuring the demand for an increased output. The oppositionists were called defeatist for their fear that prosperity would give the peasantry too much purchasing power. For their part, the Opposition saw in the maintenance of relatively high industrial prices the best source for the rapid accumulation of industrial capital which they advocated, as well as the basis for increasing the wages of industrial workers. To meet some of the objection to their high-price policy, the Opposition tried to burn the candle at both ends in contending that retail prices could still be lowered by cutting private-trade margins.

Proposals to cut industrial costs were not appreciated by the Opposition, since they involved the freezing or reduction of wages and the laying off of workers. The Opposition explicitly refused to consider any measure which in their minds relied on exploitation of the industrial workers. Instead they argued that real wages and working conditions were progressively deteriorating, and urged corrective action to protect the proletarian social basis of the regime. The Right contended in reply that wages were already as high as they could safely go and that Opposition demands for a substantial increase were simply "demagogy." The issue was sharpened by a reduction in average real wages when food prices rose in the spring of 1926, but by 1927 workers' income was passing the prewar level and had gained relative to other groups in the population.[89] It is unclear whether this proved the Opposition wrong or resulted from efforts to anticipate their arguments during 1926 and 1927.

Another theme long stressed in various Opposition pronouncements was economic planning. Although there was no difference with the leadership over the ideal, there was complete disagreement over the prerequisite conditions for the actual institution of comprehensive economic planning. Trotsky had been arguing for the planned development of industry since early 1923. The failure to institute planning was cited in the statement of the "Forty-six" as one of the causes of the scissors crisis. At the Thirteenth Party Congress in 1924 Preobrazhensky warned, "If we continue to mark time on the old spot, on the position of no planning in our economy, this would signify an unconscious concession to petty-bourgeois elements."[90] The leadership steadily contended, however, that overall planning was meaningless as long as every effort had to be devoted to restoring the existing economic system.

Underlying the whole range of economic-policy disputes was one core

question: how and at what rate should the country be industrialized?[91]
Urgency was lent this issue by the continued inability of Russian industry
to satisfy consumer demand. This "goods famine" carried with it the constant threat that the peasantry might curtail its grain marketing and endanger
the urban food supply. In the face of the steady need to expand production,
the condition of the country's industrial plant appeared ominous indeed:
there had been almost no new construction since the revolution and not even
enough maintenance and replacement to preserve existing equipment. Up to
1926, the government had been concerned mainly with getting existing industry back into full production. The time was rapidly approaching, however, when output could no longer be expanded without large amounts of
new investment. Thus, the basic inadequacy of Russian industry coupled
with the impending end of the "restoration period" threatened severe economic strains in the near future.

The Left Opposition took the stand that large-scale new investment was
imperative, especially in heavy industry, and that comprehensive planning
and new sources of capital accumulation should be employed immediately to
effect a high rate of industrial expansion. They argued that the basic disproportionality in industry's (especially heavy industry) lagging behind agriculture had to be corrected in order to permit the further advance of the
whole economy. They also stressed the necessity of rapidly overtaking the
capitalist powers in economic strength, both as a guarantee of military security and as a demonstration of the superiority of the socialist system. In
particular they were concerned to see a relative advance in the socialized industries of Russia as compared with the private sector of the economy, to
ward off what they took to be a potentially serious threat to the foundations
of the workers' state.

Preobrazhensky, the outstanding Opposition economist, argued that the
investment needs of industry required very large increments and a high
overall rate of capital formation for a period of years. This necessity was attributed to a number of factors—the anticipated full utilization of existing
facilities and accrued maintenance needs for them, the problem of unemployment, the conditions of indivisibility and complementarity in adding to
the industrial plant at an advanced technological level, and the lowered proportion of rate-of-output increase in relation to the proportion of capital
increase as industry is modernized. Moreover, the existence of a socialist institutional setting and socialist social objectives heightened the need for substantial expansion simultaneously in all branches of industry.[92]

In meeting the vast needs for capital accumulation and investment which
his high-tempo solution implied, Preobrazhensky relied on the formula
paraphrased from Marx which he had advanced as early as 1923—"primitive
socialist accumulation." Before it could realize its organizational merits, the
socialist economy required an initial stock of wealth which, under the condi-

tions of backwardness in Russia, could only be obtained through some form of politically enforced exploitation: "Exactions from the nonsocialist forms [of economy] . . . must inevitably assume a vast, directly decisive role in peasant countries like the Soviet Union. . . . To rely only on accumulation within the socialist sphere means to risk the very existence of socialist economics."[93] The peasant majority of the population was the source from which the necessary wealth was to be obtained (in the form of food for the city workers and for export). This would be extracted by the taxing power of the socialist state and particularly by the monopolistic terms of trade which the government could set up. "Taxation by price" was Preobrazhensky's device for the accumulation of industrial capital.[94] (It is noteworthy that since the onset of the five-year plans and the collectivization of agriculture in the early 1930s, the Soviet regime has obtained most of its capital in precisely this fashion, through the mechanism of the turnover tax on retail sales.)

The gradualist approach was passionately espoused by the party leadership, and harsh words were evoked in response to the Leftist demand for a faster tempo of industrialization. "The super-industrial, 'super-proletarian' program of the Opposition, the program of industrialization at the cost of the peasantry and against the peasantry," *Pravda* declared, "is only a *utopian* superstructure over Social Democratic illusions . . . a demagogic masquerade to cover the right-wing essence of the actual Opposition platform."[95]

The leadership was especially concerned about preserving economic equilibrium to avoid serious dislocations and political stress. Emphasis in economic development was to be placed on technique, efficiency, and investment in the less costly and more quickly completed projects. In the spring of 1926, for example, Stalin objected to the Dneprostroy hydroelectric project as a luxury on the order of a peasant's buying a phonograph when he needed to get his plow fixed.[96] Industry, according to the Rightist argument, should grow in response to stimulation through the market; heavy industry would be encouraged indirectly as the consumer-goods industries prospered and acquired the wherewithal to finance expansion. Socialism would be approached gradually: individual peasant prosperity would be encouraged as the basis for industrial development, and then the competitive success of the socialist part of the economy would win the peasants' allegiance. Every effort would be made to avoid a supply strike by peasants refusing to market their produce, a likely eventuality if the economic desires of the peasantry were not satisfied by the urban sector of the economy.

Almost no one attempted an intermediate position combining the best features of both Left and Right programs. The only important exception was Sokolnikov, who, though a Rightist in economic outlook and in his fiscal policies as finance commissar, joined the Zinoviev Opposition and espoused the Leftist platform on political reform and party democracy. The lines of cleavage and the sharpness of differences in economic policy, if not the issues themselves, were clearly the product of the factional split in the party.

That it was differences in political outlook, rather than economic reasoning, which primarily determined the respective stands is made clear by the nature of the weaknesses in each argument. The Leftists did not prove that industry had to be developed under forced draft—they assumed it. They were really motivated by the belief that an industrial base and economic preferment for the workers were politically essential for maintaining the socialist regime, and that economic gains by the private and individual peasant sector of the economy threatened a bourgeois restoration. This feeling was at the root of the Leftist uneasiness about the NEP from the very beginning; Preobrazhensky was arguing even in 1921 that a prompt "socialist offensive" was required.

The right-wing reasoning was no less grounded in politics. The leadership's basic argument was fallacious—the proposition that market stimulation would provide adequately for industrial expansion. The immediate capital needs for replacement and new construction were overwhelming, but market forces could have their effect on heavy industry only after a considerable lapse of time, during which net disinvestment could result in a major crisis.[97] Bent on appeasing the peasantry, the party leaders all seemed confident that the prosperity of the individual peasant proprietor was not per se a threat to the socialist regime. The political potential of the Russian workers and of foreign revolutionary movements, articles of faith for the Left, were in practice discounted by the leadership, which assumed that the context of the NEP with its particular constellation of social forces and institutional compromises would apply indefinitely. The Left looked beyond, assuming (whether because of insight or wish, it is not clear) that the NEP was inherently unstable. Left boldness clashed again with Right caution.

Both factions were more convincing in their efforts to refute each other than in their positive statements; both sides encountered obstacles which were easy to point out but difficult to dispose of. One man, at least, considered the difficulties of both policies: Preobrazhensky, while concentrating his fire against the right-wing resistance to stepped-up industrialization, was well aware of the explosive consequences that could be entailed by the curtailment of consumption which his program would necessitate. This has been described as the "Preobrazhensky dilemma."[98] The survival of Russian socialism required the shock treatment of intensive industrialization, and yet the shock itself threatened to destroy the semblance of proletarian democracy which (at least in the minds of the Left Opposition) constituted the essence of the socialist system. Economic analysis thus led again to the old Marxian stricture: socialism could not work in a country where prior economic development had not obviated the necessity for the shock treatment. Preobrazhensky's reasoning, like Trotsky's, permitted escape from the impasse only through appeal to the world revolution: "The sum total of these contradictions shows how strongly our development toward socialism is confronted with the necessity of ending our socialist isolation, not only for political but also for economic reasons, and of leaning for support in the future on the material resources of other socialist countries."[99]

Under the pressure of the Opposition, the party leadership made a substantial though unacknowledged modification in their economic policy, in an effort to come to terms with the "Preobrazhensky dilemma." Stalin had nominally accepted the ideal of autarkic industrial development at the time of the Fourteenth Congress,[100] though he generally subscribed to the views of Bukharin and Rykov, and supported them on numerous occasions. When the United Opposition launched their attack in April 1926, the leadership conceded that the planned development of industry to correct the disproportions in the economy was a "decisive task." However, they stressed the dependence of industry on the agricultural base and warned that the program of expansion had to be held within the limits of the available resources. As the main sources of capital accumulation they suggested economizing within industry and borrowing from the population.[101] A measure of the ground being traversed by the party leadership was Trotsky's remark, in July 1926, that the emphasis at last being accorded industry was similar to what had previously been denounced as Trotskyism.[102]

At the Central Committee meeting in February 1927, the leadership at last accepted the necessity for long-term industrial planning, and also approved the Dneprostroy project.[103] But this relaxation of the Right's position only confirmed the Opposition in the correctness of their own diagnosis and program. Throughout 1927, whenever they could secure an audience, they hammered away on the themes of industrial inadequacy, poor planning, the misery of the workers, the goods famine, and the growth of the kulaks. In the fall of 1927, when their expulsion from the party was imminent, the Opposition were still adamant in their condemnation of the leadership. They did note with evident self-satisfaction that the latter had accepted further points first advanced by the Left, particularly their thesis that industry, not agriculture, was the key to economic development, and their policy of pressure on the kulaks. The Central Committee was taken to task by the Opposition for claiming that it had always been fighting the kulaks and thus trying to cover up its change of policy.[104]

By the time of the Fifteenth Party Congress in December 1927, the leaders had changed their line considerably, even though the new industrialization emphasis was qualified by characteristically right-wing views on how it should be accomplished. In substance the leadership acknowledged the Opposition contention that governmental action to effect a jump in the rate of industrial development was required.[105] It was implicitly conceded that the kulaks were a problem; Molotov's theses on the peasantry called for a higher tax rate on the more prosperous peasants, urged encouragement of the cooperatives and restriction of the activity of kulaks in them, the extension of collective farming, and the resticiton of land leasing and the use of hired labor.[106] All of these measures had been demanded by the Opposition. So extensive was the policy shift, in fact, that the economic ideas emanating from the Fifteenth Congress can be described as a synthesis of the earlier Right and Left platforms.[107] Ironically, this came at the same time that the Leftists were expelled from the party.

The change in policy was not without consequent political strains among the leadership. The first suggestion that Stalin was beginning to part company with the right wing came in his report to the Fifteenth Congress. He began to speak there as only the Left Opposition had before, declaring that the goods famine could be cured only by the development of heavy industry and calling for a general "socialist offensive," particularly against the kulaks (though he abjured the use of "administrative methods").[108] Experience proved the correctness of the Leftist economic analysis. The "Preobrazhensky dilemma" could not be avoided. The original Rightist policy of gradualism was appropriate only for the restoration situation which characterized the period of the NEP. Impending new problems demanded new solutions, but the Leftist analysis could reveal no sure channel between Scylla and Charybdis: intensive industrialization was essential and yet there was no way to accomplish it without risking the most violent repercussions. Such is the background of the crisis of industrialization and collectivization of the peasantry through which Stalin relentlessly drove the country during the following years. Stalin's government perfected the means—rigid control and violent repression—to regiment the Soviet population while every available resource was applied to the realization of the long-desired goal of building a modern industrial plant in Russia.

The economic debates of the 1920s showed that Marxian socialism could not work in Russia. The Left demonstrated that the Rightist program of concessions to the peasantry would obstruct the formation of an industrial base and thus fatally weaken the socialist sector of the economy. Both Rightist charges and Leftist admissions, on the other hand, made it clear that the success of the Leftist program of intensive industrialization was extremely dubious without a degree of dictatorial control and violence which was both abhorrent in itself and likely to backfire. Thus the industrialization controversy illustrated in detail the proposition that the revolution in Russia could not retain its proletarian character unless it were quickly conjoined with revolutionary movements elsewhere. Socialism in one country could not really be what the Communists up to then understood by the term: the 1917 ideal of a collectivist order of reasonably free and equal worker-citizens with a government directly responsible to them. Committed to this ideal, the Left Opposition was doomed to fail, however irrefutable their logic might be.

SOCIALISM IN ONE COUNTRY OR THERMIDOREAN DEGENERATION?

The dilemmas of economic policy confronting the Soviet regime made the question of the international revolution, theoretical as it was, vitally sensitive. Without this support, economic analysis led to the conclusion of the propeasant degeneration or the bureaucratic degeneration of Soviet socialism. Marxian presumptions upheld such a prospect: socialism in a single backward country could not survive. This dismal implication, and the temptations to political recrimination which it offered, brought the most general and abstract questions of Communist theory into the forefront of the factional controversy. The disputants sound like medieval scholastics—in a sense they were—but their arguments were no less important on that account. In the course of these debates the official understanding of Communist theory underwent fundamental changes, and the Communist mentality moved closer toward its final solidification under Stalin's dictatorship.

The controversy over socialism in one country did not, as commonly thought, turn on the question of whether to stir up the revolutionaries abroad or abandon the world revolution. Both the Opposition and the party leadership welcomed foreign support, while neither was prepared to take risks with the security of the Soviet state. The issue of socialism in one country was purely a doctrinal repercussion of the Communist Party split and of the divorce between Soviet practice and theory. With strict Marxian logic the Opposition hammered away at the leadership with insinuations that their domestic and international expedients were unsocialist and unproletarian. The leadership tried to readjust party theory to make their expedients seem unchallengeably orthodox. When the Opposition called them down for this, they replied with enraged measures to suppress all criticism whatsoever. "The more openly Stalin's policy is developed," asserted Trotsky, "the more intolerable for Stalin's group becomes the revolutionary Bolshevik criticism on the part of the Opposition." [109]

The Opposition, reasoning that no Russian government could pursue a firmly socialist course without help from foreign revolutionaries, was compelled to place the highest hopes on the international revolution. "We must cast aside all doubting survivals of the innovation which represents the matter as though the victory of socialist construction in our country is not linked indissolubly with the course and outcome of the struggle of the European and world proletariat for power"—thus read the Declaration of the Thirteen of July 1926. In the last analysis, the Opposition saw no threat to the future of socialism in Russia, but only because their faith in the international revolution was unquenchable. As Trotsky explained this, "The Opposition is profoundly convinced of the victory of socialism in our country, not because our country can be torn free of the world economy and world revolution, but because the victory of the proletarian revolution is guaranteed the world over."[110]

On policy toward foreign revolutionaries and the "united front"—as illustrated in the Anglo-Russian Committee and the Kuomintang cases—the Opposition was obliged to be uncompromising, since cooperation with non-Communist movements implied that the fortunes of Communism abroad could be disregarded for the time being. On the other hand, the party leaders, bearing the responsibilities of government, were worried about pursuing a successful foreign policy amidst a hostile world. Here, as in internal affairs, they wanted full freedom to take the course of expediency, yet insisted on covering each move with the mantle of Leninist orthodoxy. Their excuse, accordingly, was the "stabilization of capitalism," a concept already challenged unsuccessfully by Zinoviev in 1925 and now styled by Trotsky as "the theoretical cover of opportunism."[111]

With the world revolution undeniably in abeyance, the disputants turned their main attention to the consequences which this international disappointment implied for the internal character of the Soviet regime. At issue was the old question, debated in 1918, 1921, and 1925, of the nature of "state capitalism," which both sides had agreed on as the designation for the existing social order in Russia. To the leadership state capitalism meant the natural transitional system which would evolve into the socialist society. The Opposition, returning to the theme of the revolution in retreat, saw a great difference between state capitalism and the ultimate ideal or, as Kamenev put it, between "the transference of power and ownership to the proletarian state" and "the actual construction of a truly socialist society."[112]

The system of state capitalism, according to the Opposition, was becoming progressively more bureaucratic, while the influence of the proletariat was dangerously weakening. Thanks to the "backsliding" of the "centrist" leadership, the dangers warned of by Lenin in his last articles were more real than ever. Remedial action was imperative to ward off petty-bourgeois and bureaucratic pressure on the party of the proletariat and to avert a "bureaucratic perversion" of the regime as a whole. The specter of Ustrialovism was paraded forth again, as the émigré professor in his Manchurian exile continued to embarrass the Soviet leadership with predictions of an evolution back to capitalism after the anticipated defeat of the Communist Left. Kamenev thundered against "the Right tendencies . . . which consciously or semiconsciously on the basis of the idea that stabilization has come to stay for decades, drive the party on to the path of a relaxation of the proletarian dictatorship."[113]

A minor Zinovievist, Ossovsky by name, had indiscreetly argued (in an article actually published in *Bolshevik*) that the party ought to rid itself of bourgeois pressures and preserve its unity by ending the Communist monopoly of political legality and tolerating separate parties to represent certain nonproletarian interests. The purified Communist group would then be free to defend the workers against bourgeois influences in the government.[114] Ossovsky was forthwith expelled from the party for his heresy, while an effort was made to impute his extreme view to the Opposition at large.[115]

The leadership's answer to intimations of Thermidorean degeneration was to declare that the Opposition had placed themselves beyond the political pale by questioning the proletarian nature of the Soviet state. This was the cardinal political sin for a Communist. Not since the Kronstadt rebellion had the government been prepared to tolerate even the suggestion that it might not be axiomatically the sole and pure incarnation of the proletarian spirit. "To assert that our state is not a workers' state, that it is already semi-bourgeois," raged Bukharin, "is to assert that our state is already in a condition of degeneration, and to throw doubts upon the existence of the proletarian dictatorship in our country."[116]

To cast such doubts on the political complexion of the Stalin-Bukharin regime was precisely what the Opposition meant to do, though, with the exception of Ossovsky, they hesitated to follow this line of reasoning to the full. Failure to recognize the Thermidorean threat and refusal to admit that concessions to nonproletarian elements had really been made were the most serious charges pressed explicitly against the leadership. The Opposition took great pains to affirm their belief that the state had not yet lost its proletarian character and that they meant only to warn of threatening dangers. In this vein the Opposition leaders stated in August 1927: "We do not doubt that the party and the proletariat of the Soviet Union will overcome these dangers with a correct Leninist line and intraparty democracy. What we demand is that the party leadership fight these phenomena and their influence upon certain parts of the party more systematically. We do not say that our Bolshevik Party, its Central Committee, and its Central Control Commission, are Thermidorean."[117]

No degree of optimism on the part of the Opposition could suffice to protect them against the countercharge that they were undermining the morale of the party. The party leaders were determined to suppress every idea of the possibility that their regime could become the vehicle for a Thermidorean reaction. It was un-Leninist, Stalin contended, to favor building socialism in Russia but to say that it could not be completed: "Such a standpoint weakens the proletariat's will to realize socialism in our country, and thus delays the unleashing of the revolution in other countries." (Even at this early juncture, it appears that revolution elsewhere depended on the Russians' will.) "Socialism in one country" was designed to erase all doubts about the Soviet future. The Opposition, according to Stalin, permitted themselves only two alternative visions—the "ultra-left illusion" that international revolution would salvage Communist hopes in Russia or despair about the degeneration of the Soviet state and the need to form an opposition party representing the workers.[118] Stalin made this dilemma so clear that he had no logical rejoinder. He could only demand an act of faith in his own regime.

The intense emotions which socialism in one country aroused came out dramatically at the Fifteenth Party Conference in November 1926. The debate was a true classic among battles of quotations, as verbal barrages of citations from the collected works of Lenin were furiously hurled at one another by the opposing forces. In this contest the Opposition scored some telling blows, and the day was saved for the leadership only through a remarkable display of forensic wit by Stalin.

Anxiety about the logical foundations of the leadership's theoretical propositions had evidently assumed serious proportions during 1926. On his own initiative Stalin treated the Fifteenth Conference to a detailed review of the idea of socialism in one country, which he asserted to be the main theoretical issue before the party. In the course of his exposition, Stalin endeavored to explain away what Engels had written about the necessity for socialism on an international scale. Stalin claimed that these remarks were no longer valid since Lenin had promulgated the "law of uneven development." Zinoviev thereupon criticized Stalin for correcting Engels, while Trotsky denied that uneven development was a new discovery by Lenin. "Marxism is no dogma but a guide to action," Stalin boldly replied, and for the benefit of any who might still have doubts, he declared, "Engels . . . would welcome our revolution and say: To hell with all old formulas! Long live the victorious revolution in the Soviet Union!"[119]

On this occassion the Opposition, represented by Kamenev, finally pounced upon the fatal flaw in Stalin's reasoning—that the crucial 1915 article by Lenin simply did not refer to Russia. Kamenev backed up his refutation with other citations from Lenin's writings during the same period to show conclusively that Lenin expected nothing but a "bourgeois-democratic" revolution in Russia: "It is the task of the proletariat of Russia to carry the bourgeois-democratic revolution through to its end, in order to arouse socialist revolution in Europe."[120] The Opposition had exposed Stalin's theoretical fabrication, and he did not attempt to answer with logic. "Shouts at Kamenev," the stenographic record reports—it was difficult for the party machine to take this verbal beating in silence.

Trotsky, like Zinoviev previously, seized on Stalin's earlier statement in "Foundations of Leninism" to the effect that the cooperation of several advanced countries was required to achieve the socialist organization of production.[121] Stalin admitted the novelty of socialism in one country, which "was given official expression by the party for the first time in the well-known resolution passed by the Fourteenth Conference," but he protested that self-correction should not be criticized: "I by no means consider myself to be infallible."[122] Trotsky's reply was that Stalin must have been a Trotskyist in denying the possibility of socialism in one country in April 1924. How, Trotsky inquired, could Stalin have made such a mistake if Lenin had really developed the theory of socialism in one country? It was obvious that Stalin had been sharing the internationalist assumptions common to the party ever since the revolution, and that he had contrived socialism in one country on the basis of the single quotation.[123]

Stalin was particularly anxious to rebut denials of the significance which he claimed for Lenin's 1915 article. It contained, he asserted in his reply to the debate at the Fifteenth Conference, "the theses which have determined the whole policy of our revolution and its work of reconstruction, the theses which speak of the possibility of the victory of socialism in one country alone." Stalin was correct at least in the latter part of his statement; he as much as admitted here that his theory hinged on that one quotation from Lenin. To Kamenev's suggestion that Lenin's article was not meant to apply to Russia, Stalin had his answer: "That is unbelievable and unheard of, that sounds like a direct slander against Comrade Lenin . . . a falsification of Lenin."[124] Trotsky cited the entirely unambiguous words of Lenin: "The complete victory of the socialist revolution in one country is unthinkable, and demands the active *cooperation* of at least some advanced countries, *among which we cannot count* Russia." To counter this Stalin improvised a new theoretical distinction, between the "victory" of socialism and the "complete victory" of socialism, and berated Trotsky for confusing the two.[125] Stalin's heavy-handed manipulation of Bolshevik theory was never more obvious; he was clearly caught in a trap and had to use desperate arguments to extricate himself. That he did so is no mean credit to his skill in debate, though he was of course aided by the fact that he could not be answered after he had the last word at the conference and by the fact of his comfortable control of the party press.

The Opposition argument, unanswerable in authentic Marxian terms, was that the achievement of "socialism" in Russia alone was at best a highly dubious prospect because of the country's backwardness. Success could come only as the product of the eventual extension of the proletarian revolutionary movement to the world at large. In the meantime conditions were becoming more and more hazardous for Russian socialism, which had been established, as Trotsky's theory of permanent revolution characterized it, under a unique set of circumstances. Insofar as the same Communist government stayed in power, it was more and more likely to lose its "socialist" character. Thermidor was transpiring without an apparent break in political continuity; the Soviet regime held power, under conditions which made socialism impossible, by becoming unsocialist. Evidence of this transformation, the Opposition contended, was the right-wing caution of the government's policies and the repression of the "proletarian" Opposition. The latter was obviously true. The leadership reacted to the Opposition's charges with manifest anxiety; they intensified their efforts to silence the critics and turned more and more determinedly to the path of ideological manipulation and thought control. The old cleavage between ideology and power, revolutionary objectives and revolutionary instruments, was at the heart of the conflict. The question was soon to be abruptly resolved: the power principle assured its own triumph.

PARTY DEMOCRACY AND BUREAUCRACY

Such was the nature of the Bolshevik Party that every attempt at opposition necessarily involved the issue of party democracy—the question of the very right of opposition to exist and of the ways in which it might be expressed or combated. It was natural that in the ambivalent formula "democratic centralism," the term "centralism" should be stressed by the leadership and the term "democratic" by the oppositionists. There was more to the defense of democracy, however, than sheer calculations of political expediency. Democratic sentiment and antipathy to the extremes of discipline were important motives in impelling people to join the Opposition, particularly during the period of War Communism and in 1923. Moreover, the experience of repression underscored for the Leftists the importance of democratic principles, even apart from their interest in factional success. Not unequivocally but nevertheless with a degree of conviction notable for a professed follower of Lenin, Trotsky proclaimed the necessity for a measure of liberalism in the revolutionary state:

The ruling class must preserve its capacity to reform its ranks under the most difficult conditions—without internal convulsions, without the catastrophic splitting of forces. The dictatorship of the proletariat in a country which is surrounded by capitalist states does not allow either the existence of two parties or the factional splitting of a unified party. But this same dictatorship demands . . . the possibility . . . by the methods of democratic centralism—to control even under the most difficult conditions all its organs, that is, to direct their policies, check them in action, appoint them, and replace them.[126]

The Opposition's political ideal was summed up in the slogan "workers' democracy," which referred particularly to two documents—the resolution of the Ninth Party Conference of September 1920 and the Politburo resolution of December 5, 1923. Both these statements concerned the need to combat "bureaucratism" and implement party democracy, and both had remained dead letters, as the process of disciplining the party went on apace. While the Opposition compromised themselves by accepting the principle of unity as enunciated by the Tenth Party Congress (with the ban on factions), they insisted that a united party required free discussion and the toleration of legitimate differences of opinion. Their fond wish was for a return to the good old days of comradely unity which the party supposedly enjoyed under Lenin.

Constantly they returned to the theme that factionalism was the consequence of the apparatus's choking the normal expression of criticism. To the charges of factionalism pressed against them, the Opposition replied that the leadership itself was behaving as a private faction.[127]

To buttress their protests about the violation of what they held to be fundamental principles of intraparty democracy, the Opposition turned with increasing emphasis to insinuations of Thermidorean degeneration. This connected the issue of party democracy with the prime theoretical question of socialism in one country: the repression which they were suffering was, the Opposition contended, final proof of the unsocialist, unproleterian leanings of the leadership. "The bureaucratization of the party," said Trotsky, "is the expression of the social equilibrium which has been, and is being, upset to the detriment of the proletariat."[128] Persecution of the Opposition, according to the Declaration of the Eighty-four, could only deliver the country into the hands of the forces of the Thermidorean reaction: "Under such conditions, striking a blow at the Opposition signifies nothing less than an attempt, behind hypocritical cries of defending unity . . . to discredit and destroy the *left, proletarian,* Leninist wing of our party."[129]

A new sign of the bureaucratic regime in the party, as the Opposition saw it, was the threat of a one-man dictatorship in violation of the ideal of collective leadership. Here again the United Opposition was taking the course of the Leningrad Opposition in 1925, when Kamenev had openly warned in front of the party congress of the menace of Stalin's personal power. "The further development of the bureaucratic regime," Trotsky asserted in 1926, "leads fatally to individual rule."[130] In mid-1927 Stalin and his faction were charged with "the most extreme usurpation of the supreme rights of the party."[131] Making his last stand, Trotsky warned: "The personal misfortune of Stalin, which is more and more becoming the misfortune of the party, consists of a vast discrepancy between Stalin's intellectual resources and the power which the party apparatus concentrates in his hands."[132] It was, however, no more the man than the system, Trotsky contended. After a pointed reference to the warning in Lenin's "testament" about Stalin's rough tactics, Trotsky cautioned that mere replacement of the individual would still leave the party machine as an independent force, the rule of "factional-bureaucratic centralism."[133]

The party leadership continued to condemn the Opposition and all that they professed. The Opposition, claimed Rykov, had violated "the fundamental principles upon which the Leninist party is built." According to the pseudo-Marxist reasoning in vogue since 1921, the Opposition could only represent an unproletarian force. Their demagogic aim, said Stalin, was "to promote dissatisfaction against the party among the backward sections of the toilers, and to organize this against the working class."[134] As Rykov suggested in the summer of 1926, the Opposition would have to be swept aside so that the party could enjoy the "inflexible and iron unity" necessary for the building of socialism.[135]

Nor was the designation "Left," naturally positive from the Communist point of view, conceded to the Opposition. It was "opportunism masked in revolutionary words," "a Social Democratic deviation, a Right deviation masked by Left phrases."[136] Unity would have to prevail, with the suppression of the Opposition's rightist defeatism, lest the Opposition take the diabolical course of constituting itself a separate party and thus becoming a channel for the forces of bourgeois counterrevolution.[137] The tactic was effective. A participant writes, "How was it possible to see one's way clearly through all these confused issues . . . ? Whatever our hesitations and our doubts, the sentiment of loyalty to the party was always the determining influence in our decisions."[138] From the point of view of the leadership, these charges were not entirely unfounded. The exiled Mensheviks assessed the Opposition as a force favorable to the anti-Communist cause, even if they were not genuinely democratic. Wrote the Menshevik leader Dan, "The 'Opposition' cultivates not only among the working masses but also among the Communist workers the growth of ideas and opinions which with skillful care may easily bear fruit for the Social Democrats."[139]

Anticipating the same effect, Stalin declared in November 1926 that the party "must carry on an energetic ideological campaign against the erroneous ideological views insisted on by the Opposition; it must unmask the opportunist character of these oppositionist ideas, however revolutionary their phraseology may appear, and force the Opposition to abandon their errors out of fear of complete annihilation."[140] Error thus became political crime.

The instrumentalities whereby the party leadership fought against the Opposition were fully formed by 1926. Subsequent changes were only of degree, as the sphere of free activity allowed to dissident elements was progressively constricted to the vanishing point. The protests of the Opposition testify eloquently to the power of the party machinery which was forged to perfection in the course of the struggle. After Zinoviev's Leningrad stronghold was reduced, the secretarial hierarchy worked without a hitch.

New appointees to the Politburo, as to the Central Committee, were hand-picked by Stalin. After bringing Molotov, Kalinin, and Voroshilov in at the time of the Fourteenth Congress in 1925, he was able to promote Rudzutak and Kuibyshev to this pre-eminent status the following year when Trotsky and Zinoviev were dropped. The candidate members were all Stalin men. The general secretary had at last won control of the party's top governing body.

Prominent oppositionists, still treated with circumspection when in the public eye, were removed from the scene by assignment to diplomatic posts abroad. In 1927, Krestinsky was still in Berlin, where he had been sent after his removal from the Secretariat in 1921. Rakovsky, removed from the

Ukrainian government in 1923, had served in London and was now ambassador to France, where Piatakov, Preobrazhensky, and Vladimir Kosior were also sent as trade representatives. Kamenev was made ambassador to Italy for a time; Antonov-Ovseyenko was the Soviet representative in Czechoslovakia.[141] Numerous lesser figures had been disposed of in similar fashion.

The Central Control Commission, together with its local agencies, was primarily responsible for administering disciplinary measures against individual violators of the rule against factionalism. Like the Central Committee, it was solidly packed with organization men by this time and moved with great efficiency against the Opposition. The Opposition complained bitterly, "The Central Control Commission itself has become a purely administrative organ, which assists the repression conducted by other bureaucratic organs, executing for them the most punitive part of the work, prosecuting any independent thought in the party, any voice of criticism, any concern expressed aloud about the fate of the party, any critical remark about certain leaders of the party."[142] Expulsion from the party was the ultimate step, though it was infrequently employed until the controversy built up to its climax in the fall of 1927. Other effective measures were found, however, including the ordeal of interrogation so familiar later on.[143]

The most convenient methods of suasion were administrative and economic. Since every party member was at the disposal of the organization for assignment to whatever employment should be deemed proper, it was easy for the Secretariat, controlling this assignment function, to take such measures of reprisal. Transfers, it was pointed out in one Opposition statement, had become "one of the usual methods of the party leadership," in defiance of an old resolution of the Ninth Party Conference condemning politically motivated transfers.[144] Obstreperous Opposition sympathizers drew the most tedious jobs in the most isolated locations (such as Turkestan or the Far North). Enforced unemployment was but a step further.[145]

Since 1923 the party leadership had had no difficulty (excepting the Leningrad case) in controlling party meetings and the party press, fixing elections with little or no margin of error, and making it progressively harder for the Opposition to get their views across to any audience broader than a small group of party intellectuals. The separate Democratic Centralist platform of 1927 complained of informers sent to party meetings "not to share in their work, but to observe the intervention of militants and indicate to the committees the 'undesirable elements.'"[146] Opposition statements in party bodies like the Central Committee were often cut out of the official reports.[147] By 1927 Opposition speakers at party meetings were literally being shouted down. Party secretaries threatened to have anyone who voted for an Opposition resolution (voting was open) expelled from the party.[148] Strong-arm squads were organized by some party secretaries—particularly by Riutin in Moscow —to prevent oppositionists from speaking publicly and even to break up the private meetings of Opposition sympathizers. "Fascist methods," "Black-hundred gangs," the Opposition cried in righteous but vain protest.[149]

Finally, as the struggle reached a fever pitch, the party leadership yielded to the temptations of anti-Semitism. Utilization of this tactic was officially denied and has continued to be formally repudiated by the Soviet leadership to the present day; Communist tradition was steadfastly against such prejudice. Nevertheless, there was a good deal of rumor and some evidence that anti-Semitism on the local level was condoned by the party leadership as a weapon against the Opposition. The three principal Opposition leaders—Trotsky, Zinoviev, and Kamenev—were all of Jewish background. In some unsophisticated circles the factional struggle was viewed entirely as a battle to stop the Jews.[150] "Benevolent neutrality toward the growing anti-Semitism" was alleged by the Opposition.[151] Trotsky preserved what appears to be an authentic copy of the minutes of a provincial party meeting, in which this bias is but thinly veiled. A speaker was quoted as saying, "Trotsky long ago began to carry on a schismatic policy. Trotsky cannot be a Communist—his very nationality shows that he must favor speculators." As for Zinoviev and Kamenev: "They have made a mistake about the Russian spirit. The Russian worker and peasant will not follow these NEPites [nepachi]."[152] Stalin's comment on the matter, as Trotsky reports it, was only calculated to remind his supporters of the applicability of anti-Semitism: "We are fighting Trotsky, Zinoviev, and Kamenev not because they are Jews, but because they are oppositionists."[153]

THE PSYCHOLOGY OF PARTY UNITY

The most striking facet of the behavior of the party leaders in their contest with the Opposition was their hysterical concern for unity in the Communist Party. Party unity was elevated to the status of a supreme value, while violation of it became a cardinal sin of Communism. Positive acclamation of the ideal of absolute unity became a requirement for all who would remain in favor with the leadership. No policy question was as important as the principle that the party be of one mind and one will. It was Bolshevik tradition to view unity as an absolute, a sharply defined category not subject to gradations of more or less unity. The party was either completely unified or it was wholly split into factions. This attitude corresponded with the Bolsheviks' black-and-white assessment of any particular person—a man was either with them or against them, either absolutely loyal or essentially treacherous.

To convince themselves and their supporters that any opposition was the work of the devil, the party leaders resorted to the Marxian logic of class struggle. Political division, they argued, must reflect class division: any opposition to the will of the proletariat expressed in the Communist Party could only be bourgeois in its ultimate inspiration. To question whether the Communist Party leadership really reflected the will of the proletariat was an act of ultimate political depravity, revealing the true counterrevolutionary. Bukharin said of such doubts, "The logical continuation of this train of thought is bound to lead sooner or later to the idea of the overthrow of the Soviet power—it can lead nowhere else."[154]

Stalin had already indicated in 1923 and 1924 that party unity meant to him an organic whole, dedicated to a common purpose and animated by an undivided will. He was evidently fond of his biological metaphor, for he later employed it again to justify the expulsion of the oppositionists: "Our party is a living organism. As in any organism, a process of exchange of matter is going on in it. The old and worn-out matter drops out [applause], and the new and growing matter lives and develops."[155] Military analogies were even more popular with the party leaders. Lenin had time and again expressed himself in military terms and had praised the martial virtues, notably discipline. This predilection of the party's founder was now hailed again and again. Said Rykov in 1926, "Lenin attached such enormous importance to questions of party discipline, and was so relentless in his condemnation of actions weakening party discipline," that almost any measure of enforcement could be justified.[156] This became an article of faith. "Iron discipline," "unshakeable unity of will"—with such expressions, the fearful and fumbling neophytes whom Lenin left behind to govern one sixth of the globe prided themselves on being, in the best Leninist tradition, tough.

Discipline and unity were looked to not merely as standards of control, but as positive sources of strength and creativity in the party. Even the purge was accorded a positive value, as Lenin and Stalin after him had stressed. The leadership was more than ready to punish the Opposition for their threat to unity by expelling them and making the break complete, though the contradiction in logic here is obvious. Such inconsistency in an emotionally grounded set of beliefs only added to the leaders' anxiety in the face of criticism and to the fury with which they replied to the Opposition challenge. From the premise of unity, doctrinal conformity was deduced as the inescapable corollary. Typical was a resolution of the Moscow Party Committee in the fall of 1926: "Not merely organizational, but also ideological unity on the basis of Leninism are necessary for our party. Organizational unity can only be unshakeable if it is based on a firm ideological solidarity."[157] Vigilance against the Opposition and the enforcement of ideological unity were essential, as Bukharin stated on one occasion in the summer of 1927, to maintain the necessary certainty in the minds of the party's supporters that Soviet Russia was a workers' state.[158]

As this twist indicates, reason was subordinated to faith in the party metaphysics. More than once this irrationalism was proclaimed explicitly. Faith in the "perspectives" of socialist construction, Stalin frequently declared, was a *sine qua non* of the successful progress of the Soviet regime: "We cannot build . . . without the *certainty* that our efforts toward a socialist economy will result in the establishment of socialism." Such certainty could result only from an act of faith. Those who found themselves in a position to criticize and warn of obstacles ahead were doubly damned—they were apostates; and by undermining the beliefs of the faithful, they threatened the prospects of the movement. "Those who seek to disparage the socialist prospects of our construction," warned Stalin, "are quenching the flame of hope of the international proletariat in our victory."[159] Dissent in the Communist world had long been tantamount to error; from this time on, it was treason.

Since the party leaders felt dependent on absolute doctrinal justification, they had to pretend that the party's theoretical maxims and even its current practical policies supposedly deduced therefrom were nothing less than eternal verities. The "ideological purity" represented by unquestioning acceptance of this reasoning became an essential test of loyalty. "The party will know how to preserve the ideological purity of Bolshevism," declared *Pravda* in July 1926. "The party will not tolerate factional attempts against Leninist unity."[160] Any attempt to criticize or modify the official interpretation of the moment was taken as a heretical attack on the whole corpus of Leninism.

"The Opposition bloc must be induced to give up its fundamental errors, and thereby the party and Leninism will be protected against attacks and attempts at revision"—so spoke Stalin at the Fifteenth Conference.[161] The term "revision" naturally recalled all the controversies between the strict Marxists and the gradualist socialists in the Second International, and it helped evoke the sentiments of outraged orthodoxy. When Zinoviev, for example, tried to apply the statements of the Fathers to uphold his critique of socialism in one country, he was criticized for a "revisionist manner in quoting the classics of Marxism." On the other hand, what Zinoviev attacked as revisionism on the part of the party leaders was defended as "improving Marxist science and its formulas."[162]

The formulas of Marxist science were endowed with a significance to which the outside observer has difficulty in giving credence. The party leaders went to fantastic lengths in their hair-splitting definitions of concepts and categories, in their literal standards of ideological correctness. When is some miserable *muzhik* not a poor peasant but a middle peasant or not a middle peasant but a kulak? How can one decide which is more serious— the deviation of underestimating the kulak danger or the deviation of overestimating the danger of the kulak-underestimating deviation? Defying the complexities and infinite gradations of the real world, the party leaders insisted on organizing reality in neat little boxes. He who got his boxes mixed up or did not divide them in the proper fashion himself became categorized among the deviators.

In their concern for verbal correctness, the party leaders manifested habits of thought not usually associated with the metaphysical materialism which they formally acknowledged. The word, the slogan, the formula, were in practice treated as the real thing; the Marxian category became the ultimate reality. Trotsky, on the carpet before the Central Control Commission for his opposition activity in the middle of 1927, replied to Ordzhonikidze's charge of "pessimism": "Your thinking is utterly permeated with fatalism. You differentiate between optimism and pessimism as if they were two immutable categories independent of conditions and politics. According to your way of thinking, one can be only either an 'optimist' or a 'pessimist.' "[163] The party leaders had fallen into the great semantic fallacy of assuming that hard and fast natural entities exist in exact correspondence with every word. Natural or historical events which failed to correspond to the Communist system of thought were regarded as imperfect—mixtures of or transitions between the categories of reality represented by the formulas of Marxism. An unbridgeable qualitative gap was assumed, for example, between the category of middle peasant and the category of kulak; the unfortunate peasant's fate depended completely on how he was classified.

In a word, the official state of mind in the party was scholasticism—the unquestioned authority of a body of scripture; interminably dull exegesis; hair-splitting and logic-chopping in pretending to deduce practice from theory; liturgical fastidiousness of expression; and, above all, the habit of meeting the problems posed by everyday experience and social change by looking to the Books rather than by new study and thought. In the years following the demise of the Opposition, the doctrinal habits formed during the twenties remained in full force. Every act continued to require justification by theory; every reinterpretation of the scripture had to be added to the canon of obligatory belief.

Not the least remarkable feature of the unity mania in the Communist Party was its acceptance by the Opposition. Though perhaps not taking so seriously all the strictures about a monolithic and iron-disciplined party, the Opposition had long since been committed—explicitly since the Tenth Congress in 1921—to a conception of party unity which ruled out the existence of any organized special-opinion groups within the ranks of the party. "We categorically reject the theory and practice of 'freedom of factions and groupings,' " asserted the Opposition leaders in their temporary capitulation of October 1926, "realizing that such a theory and practice contradict the foundations of Leninism and decisions of the party. We consider it our obligation to put into effect the decision of the party refusing to permit factionalism."[164] Doctrinal purity was also accepted by the Opposition, though they might hold differing opinions on where the responsibility lay for the corruption of Bolshevik belief. Trotsky said in August 1926, "The real guarantee of the ideological purity of the party consists in the return to the Leninist political line and to the Leninist party regime."[165]

The Opposition were horrified by the idea of becoming a second party standing against the Communist organization. They never failed to cringe whenever the party leadership made the charge that their factional activity would inevitably lead to such a split. "We will carry out all decisions of the Communist Party and of its Central Committee," the Opposition leaders stated when they found themselves under pressure in the summer of 1927. With some rancor they conceded, "We are prepared to do everything possible to destroy all factional elements which have formed themselves as a consequence of the fact that, because of the intraparty regime, we were compelled to inform the party of our opinions that had been falsely reported in the press of the whole country."[166] Transfixed by the mirage of Leninist unity, the Opposition were never able to escape from the fatal irresolution and hopeless self-contradiction which this imposed on them.

The efforts of the Opposition to prove their fidelity to the united party were entirely unavailing, even aside from the violation of their own pledged submission by their periodic resumption of a critical stance. The oppositionists seem never to have realized that their existence as opposition was actually *required*. Castigation of the Opposition was the main device whereby the party leaders reassured themselves and kept their followers from error. An incarnation of evil to keep the party in perpetual anxiety; target for scorn; permissable object of hostility; scapegoat for difficulties; justification for the organizational control by which the leadership retained its position—such were the services which the existence of the Opposition provided. The Opposition was the anvil on which were hammered out the control machinery, the doctrine, and the system of ideological rationalization known as the party line, which have become lasting features of Communist rule.

A particular source of the hostility which was directed at the Opposition was the firmly established myth that the Opposition leaders, in contrast to the leaders of the party majority, were by and large a group of impractical, blowhard intellectuals. Stalin called the Opposition "a group of petty-bourgeois intellectuals, divorced from life, divorced from the revolution, divorced from the party, from the working class."[167] Trotsky, protesting the whole course of the leadership's policy, declared, "This deviation is being covered up by thoroughly reactionary speeches against the 'émigrés' and in favor of people rooted in the 'native soil.'"[168] Molotov alluded snidely to the prerevolutionary émigré status of the leading oppositionists: "Writing articles and making speeches is by no means sufficient to make one a consistent and enduring revolutionary. A genuine proletarian fighter must be well tempered in the fire of the real fight, in the fire of revolutionary work."[169] Here we see the old antagonism between the lowly undergrounder dodging the police and the émigré publicist arguing philosophy in a Swiss café.

No proletarian himself, Molotov manifests here the odd psychology of nonproletarians in Communist parties who feel guilty because they are not real workers and require some form of atonement for this.[170] Some such underlying state of mind must have been present to account for the bitter fanaticism with which individuals like Bukharin recounted the political and social sins of people whose background and outlook they once shared. They wished, it seems, to make up for their defective social origin by a studied display of the "proletarian" virtues of party discipline, solidarity, and closed-mindedness. Proletarian romanticism led many of the old Ultra-Leftists to make peace with the regime, even while the Trotskyists were still firmly protesting its abuses. Perhaps Bukharin falls into this category, together with Larin; the former Workers' Opposition leaders—Shliapnikov, Medvedev, and Kollontai—seem to also. Even the resolute Osinsky had abandoned the fight by this time.

Kollontai had still preserved her eloquent idealism, though she now turned it to the service of Stalin's organization. She described the near-unanimous votes against the Opposition in 1927 (in the selection of delegates to the Fifteenth Party Congress) as "the outcome of *a definite mental and spiritual growth among this rank and file,* a growth in the direction of consolidating collectivist thinking." It was the victory of the "collectivist system of work" over "individual initiative," with the enforcement of "the fundamental demand of the masses: *observance of* discipline." She heaped scorn on "the petty-bourgeois interpretation of democracy . . . dormant in the Opposition." Kollontai declared that collective work "produces an utterly new idea of the meaning of discipline . . . as merging one's own will with the will of the collective body."[171] The mythology of the collective will could leave room for only one individual.

The pattern of anxious leaders striving through any and all means to forestall criticism becomes vividly clear in 1926 and 1927. Fearful of committing blunders, almost overwhelmed by the practical difficulties confronting their government, the party leaders took every opportunity to justify their policies. The consequence was still greater need for organizational repression. "The less political practice conforms to the resolutions, i.e., to the social composition of the party and its traditions," Trotsky observed, "the less possible it is to carry out this policy in the normal party way, the more necessary are the appointive system and repression."[172] The party leaders finally prepared to dispose of their critics by force.

Repression within the party followed logically from the party's monopoly of political activity. Effective criticism could come only from other Communists, and only through Communist Party channels was an overturn in the country's political leadership at all likely. Therefore, the indicated steps for the party leaders to assure their continuity in office were to suppress criticism in the party and employ their organizational power to prevent any opposition movement from making headway. The Opposition actually made just such a charge, that office holding was the motive for the perversion of party democracy: "In the ruling faction there is a minority which puts factional discipline above the party. The purpose of all this factional mechanics is to keep the party from making a change, in the normal, lawful way, in the composition and policy of the party apparatus."[173]

All such machinations had to be justified and clothed in the forms of democratic procedure. In part, this was mere propaganda to mollify the rank and file. On the other hand, the extreme self-righteousness manifested by the party leaders suggests that they wanted to convince themselves of their political virtue. The universal fictions of democratic election and unanimous approval seem to have been psychologically necessary. Only on such a deeply irrational basis could the Communist leaders solemnly declare, as they often did, that the weakness or absence of opposition in most party organizations and meetings demonstrated the overwhelming unity of the party, and not merely the efficacy of the secretarial machinery. Bukharin, for example, offering the Opposition one last chance to submit, reminded them that their weakness made continued resistance hopeless, but he warned of the grave danger which threatened if the Opposition should openly become a second party and the mouthpiece for anti-Soviet elements.[174] On another occasion *Pravda* had denounced the Opposition for "a proclamation of disloyalty toward the party," and proceeded to rage about "the evil-smelling, nauseating lies regarding the 'Thermidor'" and about "an invisible, anti-Bolshevik, anti-Comintern bloc" with Trotsky as its "field marshal." But, *Pravda* reassured its readers, the Opposition were doomed: "The political opposition in the AUCP has burst like a soap bubble."[175]

Fear of the Opposition for their strength and contempt for their weakness combined to produce remarkable feats of name calling such as Stalin's sneer at "the Opposition, hobbling behind the party like a decrepit old man with rheumatism in his legs, pains in the side and pains in the head, the Opposition sowing pessimism and poisoning the atmosphere with its whining to the effect that nothing will come of our efforts to construct socialism in the USSR."[176] A local party paper found sadistic exultation in a line by Alexander Blok which it addressed to the Opposition: "Are we then to blame if your bones crack and break in our powerful claws?"[177]

The full blossoming of this schizoid state of mind about the internal alien had to wait for Vyshinsky's fulminations against the hapless defendants in the 1936–1938 trials. The echo of this bombast in the 1938 official party history is, to say the least, picturesque: "The fiendish crimes of the Bukharin-Trotsky gang" were held to be responsible for almost every difficulty, disagreement, or misfortune experienced by the Soviet regime since the revolution. But, the account goes on, "These White-guard pigmies, whose strength was no more than that of a gnat, apparently flattered themselves that they were the masters of the country. . . . These contemptible lackeys of the fascist forgot that the Soviet people had only to move a finger, and not a trace of them would be left."[178] It is hard to comprehend, without delving into the psychology of the irrational, how such insignificant foes could be charged with causing or threatening the damage attributed to them.

Without undertaking the baffling task of explaining the individual psychological traits of the various Communist leaders, it is nonetheless revealing to point out the typically authoritarian behavior pattern which prevailed in the Communist Party.[179] Bolshevism was in its essence the projection of an authoritarian mind, and Bolshevik political life exercised a powerful selective influence among the people involved in it. Those who had the psychological make-up requisite for adaptation to the movement were successful within it. Those who could not stomach the terms of party life eventually withdrew or were expelled.

The process of psychological selection was a decisive factor in prerevolutionary Bolshevism. It gave the definition of a Bolshevik—a "hard." Through the realignments of 1914–1917, the Bolshevik movement acquired much unsifted material. Here was a prime source of restiveness: the Left Opposition were the wrong kind of people. During the years of adjustment after the seizure of power, the screening process set in again. As the principles of Leninism were once more implemented through the elaboration of the party organization, the most suitable personalities—the authoritarians—were drawn to the fore. The year 1921 was the turning point. Disciplined and unrelenting, narrow and pettifogging, the *apparatchiki* placed their stamp on the brave new way of life.

Given the authoritarian make-up of the people who were successful in the positions of real power, together with the circumstances of insecurity following the loss of Lenin, the grave responsibility shouldered by those at the helm of state, the difficulty of deducing unquestionably correct policies from scriptural sources, and what must have seemed from the point of view of the leaders the carping criticism of irresponsible intellectuals, the party mentality formed in the twenties becomes more or less intelligible. It was a state of mind among leaders who were unsure of themselves but determined never to be found wrong: a psychology of weakness desperately masquerading as strength.

DESTRUCTION OF THE LEFT OPPOSITION

The implications of the doctrine of party unity were quick to be realized. Late in the summer of 1927 the party leadership finally announced plans for holding the next party congress, by then six months overdue. During the period of preliminary discussion before this congress, the Fifteenth, the Left Opposition made their last effort to win a hearing and force changes in the party's political course. The outcome was their total defeat at the hands of the omnipotent apparatus.

In September the Opposition leaders prepared a new platform, the last and much the longest of the three major political documents setting forth the position of the United Opposition.[180] With bountiful detail the platform reiterated earlier Opposition criticism. The party leadership was denounced for their errors in every sphere of political life—industrial policy, peasant policy, party organization and the problem of bureaucracy, foreign affairs, the Comintern, and military policy. The leadership were fully charged with the sins which they were simultaneously attributing to the Opposition: they were "opportunist," bending before petty-bourgeois influences, deviating from the Leninist line. There was no longer any suggestion of conciliation; the Opposition was making a clear bid for party members to support them in deposing the current leaders: "We are going to correct, in good time, the course of the party leadership."[181]

As the Opposition never ceased to complain, the tightening strictures of the party organization had made it increasingly difficult to get a case heard. Routine organizational affairs, local party meetings, and the press were entirely under the thumbs of the party secretaries. Party congresses, however, still required a certain amount of planning and effort to render them wholly manageable. The leadership were determined to avoid the kind of public discord as had marred the proceedings at the Fourteenth Congress in 1925. The next meeting was postponed and when a date was finally set, the customary period of precongress discussion (when any issue theoretically could be brought up for debate and decision) was cut from the usual three months to only one. As the Opposition observed, "It appears that the Central Committee *fears* a discussion like fire, that it has no hope at all of defending its political line in any sort of regular and honest intraparty discussion."[182] Trotsky and Zinoviev charged that "Stalin's group has decided to allow no discussion and to make up the Fifteenth Congress out of secretaries alone." At times the Opposition leaders were even deprived of the opportunity of stating their criticisms before the top party bodies: debate was simply prohibited.[183]

The party leadership had no intention of letting the Opposition platform go before the membership. They defined any criticism of themselves as illegal factionalism. This was precisely the form of Stalin's defense, after the Politburo decided on September 8 that the Opposition platform could not be printed.[184]

Why did the Central Committee not print the well-known "platform" of the Opposition . . . ? It is absurd to say that the party or the Central Committee were afraid of the truth. . . .

Above all [it was] because the Central Committee did not wish to legalize Trotsky's faction, and was not entitled to legalize it, as it is altogether not entitled to legalize factional groups. Lenin said, in the resolution of the Tenth Party Congress on unity, that the existence of "platforms" is one of the most important signs of a factional struggle going on. In spite of this, the Opposition worked out a "platform" and demanded its publication, which was in contradiction to the resolution of the Tenth Party Congress.[185]

The Opposition were not in a mood to let the suppression of their platform go unchallenged. They were well prepared to defy the Politburo's order: an underground printing plant under the direction of Trotsky's follower, Mrachkovsky, was immediately set in motion to reproduce the document for wide distribution. Four days after the Politburo's ban, agents of the GPU raided the printing shop and arrested its operators.[186] Mrachkovsky and his assistants in the printing enterprise were expelled from the party forthwith.[187] They were quickly followed by Preobrazhensky and Serebriakov, the Opposition leaders held responsible for organizing the printing activity. Expelled with them was the director of the state printing plant in Moscow, who had betrayed his secret sympathies by permitting the surreptitious reproduction of Opposition literature in his establishment.[188]

The party leaders were clearly determined to make as much political capital as they could out of the printing episode. The GPU report on the raid alleged that one of the Opposition printers was in contact, through a "Wrangel officer,"* with a counterrevolutionary organization that was planning to overthrow the Soviet government. This charge of Opposition ties with the counterrevolutionaries was immediately made known to the party. The Opposition quickly protested, and the leadership, lacking a case, did not attempt to press the charges; the "Wrangel officer" turned out to have been a GPU *agent provocateur*.[189] Nevertheless, the objective of further discrediting the Opposition had been accomplished. "The myth about the 'Wrangel officer' is being broadcast through the land, poisoning the minds of a million party members and tens of millions of nonparty men," reported the Opposition leaders. They charged Stalin with a deliberate fraud—"Without his consent, approval, and encouragement, no one would have ever dared to throw into the party ranks fraudulent accusations about the participation of Opposition Communists in a counterrevolutionary organization."[190]

In the meantime the vise was tightened still more. Trotsky was called before the presidium of the Comintern executive committee on September 27. He protested: "Bureaucratic discipline upon the basis of a wrong policy is not an instrument for unity, but an instrument making for the disorganization and undermining of the party."[191] This statement of Trotsky's was actually quoted by the ECCI presidium as evidence of his "political-renegade type of argumentation," which was taken to justify his expulsion from the Comintern executive.[192]

The next stage of the struggle paralleled almost exactly the events of a year before, when the Opposition had attempted a direct appeal for support through public meetings, only to be disciplined and humiliated. A series of

* The reference was to the last White resistance of 1920, led by Baron Wrangel.

demonstrations was organized. In Moscow the oppositionists, lacking a legal meeting place, boldly occupied a school building and held it while Trotsky and Kamenev addressed an audience estimated at two thousand, not counting the crowd outside.[193] In Leningrad Trotsky and Zinoviev appeared at a workers' parade and drew all the honors at the expense of the regular party official-dom.[194] But attempts to carry the fight to regular party meetings were rudely rebuffed. Kamenev and Rakovsky tried to address the Moscow organization and were forced to stop by what the official report described as "indignation" and "storm"—the organized uproar which Trotsky preferred to call "fascist methods." The vote reported was twenty-five hundred to one.[195]

Effective countermeasures were being taken by the leadership both in the form of direct organizational reprisals and in steps to steal the thunder of the Opposition. The occasion chosen for the latter maneuver was the tenth anniversary of the October Revolution, which was to be observed, as was the practice in accordance with the 1918 calendar reform, on November 7. The Soviet Central Executive Committee drew up an "anniversary manifesto," which among other things proclaimed the government's intention to introduce a seven-hour working day with no reduction in total pay, and ordered the complete exemption of poor peasants from taxes. The Opposition were caught off base; they had insistently argued that the leaders were neglecting the cause of the workers and poor peasants and were now trapped into voting against this obvious, if somewhat theoretical, advantage to their supposed clients.[196] Trotsky attacked this "Left anniversary zigzag" as "individual adventuristic gestures," which would inevitably be repudiated. Current policies were shaped, in Trotsky's mind, by "the forces that are pressing down on the proletarian vanguard—the bureaucrat, the labor faker, the admin-istrator, the industrial manager, the new private capitalist, the privileged intel-ligentsia of the town and country."[197]

The Central Committee met on October 21 to take definitive action against the Opposition. It was proposed to expel Trotsky and Zinoviev from the Central Committee. Trotsky, making his last speech as a Communist leader, countered with a slashing attack on the party leaders for betraying the masses, who would look to the Opposition for salvation. "We openly say to the party: the dictatorship of the proletariat is in danger. And we firmly believe that the party, its proletarian nucleus, will hear, will understand, will meet this danger. The party is already deeply stirred." The "anniversary zigzag" was an "indubitable and solemn recognition of the rightness of the Opposition's views upon all the fundamental problems of our life . . . a political disavowal of themselves on the part of the ruling faction, a con-fession of their bankruptcy."[198]

In a final effort to embarrass the general secretary, the Opposition managed at the same Central Committee session to force, for the first and last time, an open discussion of Lenin's "Testament" and the disparaging remarks about

Stalin which it contained. Asserted Trotsky, with perceptive vision, "The rudeness and disloyalty of which Lenin wrote are no longer mere personal characteristics. They have become the character of the ruling faction, both of its political policy and its organizational regime. . . . The fundamental character of our present leadership is its belief in the omnipotence of methods of violence—even in dealing with its own party."[199] Stalin rose to the occasion:

Now on the "Testament" of Lenin. Here the oppositionists have cried out—you have heard this—that the Central Committee of the party "has concealed" the "Testament" of Lenin. Several times this question has been discussed among us at the plenum of the Central Committee and the Central Control Commission—you know this. [Voice: "dozens of times."] It has been proved over and over again that nobody has concealed or is concealing anything, that Lenin's "Testament" was addressed to the Thirteenth Party Congress [cries of "quite true!"], that the congress resolved unanimously not to publish it, among other reasons because Lenin himself did not wish or demand its publication. . . .

It is said that in this "Testament" Comrade Lenin suggested to the congress that it consider, in view of Stalin's "rudeness," the question of replacing Stalin in the post of general secretary by another comrade. This is quite true.* Let us read that passage, although it has already been read repeatedly at the plenary session: "Stalin is too uncouth and this fault of his, which is tolerable within our intimate group and in view of the connections between us, becomes unbearable from one who holds the post of general secretary. I therefore suggest that the comrades should discuss the question of dismissing Comrade Stalin from this post and appointing for it another person who, in all respects is only distinguished from Stalin by one quality, i.e., that of being more tolerant, loyal, civil, and considerate toward the comrades, less moody, etc."† Yes, I am rude, comrades, in regard to those who are rudely and disloyally ruining and splitting the party. I have never concealed this and will not conceal it. . . . At the very first session of the plenum after the Thirteenth Congress, I asked the plenum of the Central Committee to relieve me of the duty of general secretary. . . . The congress itself considered this question. . . . All the delegates, including Trotsky, Kamenev, and Zinoviev, unanimously *obliged* Stalin to remain in his post.

Then Stalin managed to turn the "Testament" against his opponents:

It means that neither Trotsky . . . nor Kamenev and Zinoviev . . . can be trusted politically. It is a characteristic fact that not a single word, not a single allusion in the "Testament" touches on Stalin's mistakes. Only his rudeness is

---

* The foregoing is translated from the text of Stalin's speech as published in 1949 in his *Collective Works* (X, 173, 175). Up to this point it does not differ significantly from the English translation published by the Comintern in 1927 (*International Press Correspondence,* no. 64, November 17, 1927, pp. 1428–1429). But here the parallel breaks off, and it is evident that a portion of the speech has been expurgated from the later edition. The following is taken directly from the 1927 version. (The quotation from Lenin may be compared with the Eastman translation, p. 181 above.)

† At this point the 1949 text resumes.

mentioned. Lack of civility, however, is not a shortcoming in Stalin's political attitude or political positon and cannot be so.

The forensic agility of the general secretary had again averted a potential crisis, and once again an Opposition sally had been turned into a humiliation.

The expulsion of Trotsky and Zinoviev from the Central Committee proceeded as scheduled, as the two Opposition leaders were charged with "carrying the factional struggle against the party and its unity to a degree bordering on the formation of a new anti-Leninist party in conjunction with bourgeois intellectuals"[200] Action against the Opposition was given a prominent place on the agenda of the impending congress. From this the logical inference was drawn by the Left leaders concerning what they still termed Stalin's "factionalism": "Its final goal is the expulsion of the Opposition from the party. Maneuvering, not refraining from any means, Stalin relentlessly moves toward this goal."[201]

Two weeks later there occurred the last public demonstration of political opposition in the history of Soviet Russia. Acting now out of sheer desperation, the Opposition took the occasion of the revolutionary anniversary, November 7, to attempt a direct appeal to the populace. The demonstration was well organized: Trotsky headed it in Moscow, Zinoviev in Leningrad; the oppositionists put up posters, made balcony appearances, and rode in automobile processions through the streets, all in the name of "Leninism." The results were anticlimactic: a show of force by the government, and the oppositionists were ignominiously dispersed. The appearance of Zinoviev and Radek in Leningrad ended in their temporary arrest, and Trotsky's procession in Moscow was halted by the police with warning shots. Trotsky alleged "Black-hundred, anti-Semitic shouts," though he claimed that the crowd was mostly sympathetic. The Opposition placards were torn down, and a balcony appearance by Smilga and Preobrazhensky was broken up, again by a "fascist gang."[202]

In quick retaliation for the Opposition's boldness, the party leadership proceeded to inflict the most severe penalties on their critics. An instruction issued by the Central Committee ordered that "oppositionists who oppose the policy of the party in nonparty meetings are to be immediately expelled. . . . Illegal meetings called by the Opposition . . . are to be dissolved with all the forces of the party and the working class."[203] The Central Control Commission, backed up by the Central Committee, declared that the Opposition leaders "are transgressing the limits of Soviet legality and are openly becoming the mouthpiece for those forces which are hostile to the regime of the proletarian dictatorship." Trotsky and Zinoviev, summoned before the presidium of the Central Control Commission, refused to abandon their oppositional agitation and stalked out of the meeting. Thereupon the commission took the final step of expelling them from the party, on November

15. At the same time, all other prominent oppositionists were relieved of their positions on the party's governing bodies: Kamenev, Smilga, Rakovsky, and the Zinovievists Yevdokimov and Avdeyev were dropped from the Central Committee, and the six Opposition sympathizers who had remained on the Central Control Commission were finally removed.[204] Trotsky was evicted from his apartment in the Kremlin.[205] On the day following the expulsions, one of Trotsky's closest associates, Adolf Ioffe, despairing over his personal health and that of the country as well, committed suicide. His funeral was the occasion for one last assemblage of oppositionists—ten thousand, Trotsky claimed.[206]

Trotsky continued to manifest hope. He wrote on November 18 that a "semi-opposition," fearing to voice openly its sympathy for the Left, was nonetheless growing.[207] When thirty-one oppositionists submitted a declaration of unity to the Politburo, Trotsky endeavored to explain that this was not a capitulation but only an agreement, exacted by threat of force, to refrain from open demonstrations.[208] Stalin called it "hypocritical" and went on to say, "And now? It is not possible to go further, comrades, for all the boundaries of the permissible in our party have been overstepped. Two parties cannot continue to exist together, the old Leninist party which is a united party and the new Trotskyist party."[209] The intentions of the leadership were subject to no further doubt.

Preparations for the Fifteenth Party Congress, completed while the crackdown on the Opposition was in progress, were almost entirely dictated by the Secretariat. The Opposition managed to have recorded in their favor the votes of six thousand members—the last time that opposition in a party election was admitted—but the leadership claimed 99 per cent of the membership, and not a single oppositionist was permitted to be elected as a voting delegate.[210]

By the time the congress convened on December 2, the intense pressure applied by the Secretariat had proved to be too much for the weak seam in the Opposition's front. The alliance of Trotsky and Zinoviev and their respective followings, though it had stood firm since the spring of 1926, now finally broke down, as the despairing Zinovievists abandoned the struggle for the last time and threw themselves upon the mercy of the leadership. Kamenev, joined by one hundred and twenty other Zinovievists who still retained their party membership, submitted to the congress a declaration again renouncing all factional activity and any action which might tend toward the formation of a second party.[211]

Leninist orthodoxy had a fatal hold on the Zinoviev-Kamenev group. These people were only oppositionists by accident, not by principle, and their complete repudiation of opposition activity was easily won when the threat of expulsion from the party became imminent. Kamenev exclaimed at the Fifteenth Congress:

Before us stands the queston of choosing one of two roads. One of these roads is a second party. This road, under the conditions of the dictatorship of the proletariat, is ruinous for the revolution. This is the road of political and class degeneration. For us this road is forbidden to us, excluded by the whole system of our views, by all the teaching of Lenin on the dictatorship of the proletariat. . . . There remains, therefore, the second road. This road is . . . to submit completely and fully to the party. We chose this road, for we are profoundly convinced that a correct Leninist policy can triumph only in our party and through it, not outside the party and against it.[212]

The substance of the proceedings at the congress was less a debate than a spectacle of mob psychology, in which the delegates chorused contemptuous abuse of those left-wingers who dared entertain thoughts at variance with the infallible pronouncements of the leadership. Stalin, making his second appearance as the leading party figure by delivering the political report for the Central Committee, set the keynote of sarcastic denigration. Following a lengthy exposition of the international   situation and domestic economic progress, he took up the question of the Opposition.[213] Opposition charges of an absence of democracy in the party were unfounded, Stalin cooly asserted; the exclusion of Opposition delegates from the congress and the 99 per cent vote for the party leadership proved that the party membership had freely repudiated the Opposition. Political rights did not have to be accorded them, nor was it of import to Stalin that they promised to defend the government in the event of war: "They, a tiny group, representing scarcely half of one per cent of our party, graciously promise to assist us if the imperialists attack our country. We don't believe in your assistance, and we don't need it!" Demands for democratic rights on the part of such an insignificant group meant only that Trotsky and Zinoviev wanted to be a "privileged nobility" within the party.

Stalin enumerated again the familiar charges of Opposition heresy— denial of the proletarian character of the Soviet state, denial of the possibility of building socialism in one country, denial of the principle of Leninist party unity: in sum, Menshevism. The "Left" Opposition was really Right— "Objectively, the Opposition have become a tool of the bourgeois elements." Stalin combed party history again for instances of Trotsky's independent-mindedness to prove his anti-Leninist taint.

Anticipating the capitulation of the one hundred and twenty-one Zinovievists, Stalin rejected it in advance, as he recalled the violation of the Opposition's no-factionalism pledges of October 1926 and August 1927. Total and abject submission was the price demanded for suffering the remaining oppositionists to remain in the party:

The question is raised about terms. We have only one set of terms: the Opposition must disarm wholly and entirely, in ideological and organizational respects. [Voices: "Quite right!" Prolonged applause.]. . .

They must renounce their anti-Bolshevik views openly and honestly, before the whole world. [Voices: "Quite right!" Prolonged applause.]. . .

They must denounce the mistakes they have committed, mistakes which have grown into crimes against the party, openly and honestly, before the whole world. They must surrender their nuclei [cells] to us in order that the party may be able to dissolve them without leaving a trace. [Voices: "Quite right!" Prolonged applause.]

That is how the matter stands with the Opposition, comrades.

The ensuing discussion, largely a re-echoing of Stalin's propositions, was punctuated by violent heckling of the few voteless oppositionists who were allowed to speak. Rykov, who was shortly to come to grief himself, was among the fiercest in his castigation of the Opposition—they were worse than the Anarcho-Syndicalist deviators expelled in 1921; they were behaving as a separate party openly fighting the Soviet government; they must condemn themselves absolutely to qualify as good Bolsheviks.[214] Krupskaya, who had mended her ways after lending the Zinoviev Opposition the prestige of her support, expressed the belief that the Opposition had lost "the feeling for what animates the working class," and that the mass feeling represented by the party could no longer allow conciliation with unrepentent deviators.[215] The terms of the resolution on the Central Committee report were inevitable. The Opposition were an anti-Leninist second party of Menshevik persuasion; they slandered the Soviet Union; they had capitulated to the bourgeoisie. "Adherence to the Trotskyist Opposition . . . is incompatible with membership in the ranks of the Bolshevik Party."[216]

A special commission of congress delegates, headed by Ordzhonikidze, was set up to recommend definitive action on the question of the Opposition. The Opposition was for the last time accorded a hearing, the commission receiving two statements on December 10, one from the Zinovievists and one from the Trotskyist remnant led by Rakovsky and Radek. After the commission rejected the Zinovievists' December 3 contention that their factionalism had been necessary for the defense of their Leninist views, Kamenev and three other leading Zinovievists subscribed to a statement once more renouncing all factionalism and submitting to the congress's ban on the propagation of Opposition ideas.[217] The Rakovsky group still showed some spine: they agreed to cease factional activity but contended nonetheless that the expression of Opposition views was compatible with the rules of the party. Renunciation of their beliefs, they boldly asserted, would be the real violation of party tradition.[218]

Reporting to the congress, Ordzhonikidze's commission found the Opposition guilty as charged: their agreement to abandon factionalism was fraudulent; to persist in asserting the correctness of their platform was to maintain the stance of a second party. Nevertheless, even so steadfast an *apparatchik* as Ordzhonikidze could bring himself to pass sentence only with some reluctance; "We know perfectly well how difficult it is—but they forced it on us, I repeat, forced it on us—to expel a part of the former Bolsheviks who brought not a little benefit to our party and fought more than for just a year in our ranks."[219] The congress unanimously ratified the expulsion from the party of seventy-five Opposition leaders, including the Zinovievists Kamenev, Yevdokimov, and Lashevich, and the Trotskyists Rakovsky, Piatakov, Radek, Smilga, and Muralov. The earlier expulsion of Trotsky and Zinoviev was approved, and the independent Opposition group of Democratic Centralists led by Sapronov and Vladimir Smirnov (but abandoned by Osinsky) was also put beyond the pale.[220]

A final act of defiance was staged by the Trotskyist spokesmen. Rakovsky, Radek, Muralov, and Smilga submitted a statement on the expulsion resolution, in which they insisted on the Leninist correctness of their beliefs. They warned that a further rightward, prokulak drift in the policy of the government would result from the expulsion of the Opposition and the continued absence of democracy in the party. They foreswore factionalism but promised adherence to their program even in the event of their expulsion; they were sure that events would prove them the true and correct guardians of the interests of the working class.

The Zinovievists had no stomach for further resistance. They complied with the "ideological disarmament" demanded of them by totally repudiating the Opposition. The thesis of unity had resulted in the self-annihilation of resistance—"Whoever tries to build a special party against the Communist Party places himself inevitably in opposition to the Comintern and to the Soviet Union and is inevitably forced into the camp of the enemy."[221] There remained, for the time being, one more humiliation. The groveling submission of the Zinovievists was rejected, and the miscreants were dismissed with the instruction to wait six months and then try to qualify for readmission to the party.[222]

With the adjournment of the Fifteenth Congress the history of the Left Opposition as an active political force came to an end. Rank-and-file support for the Left was quickly dispersed as the result of recantations and expulsions.[223] Vain protest and futile intrigue were all that remained for the Left oppositionists, until exile, trial, and execution brought their tragic history to an end. The destruction of the Left Opposition put an end to the dual character of Russian Communism. The Leftist current of thought was liquidated, as unquestioned Leninism triumphed. The Western-oriented, intellectual, idealistic, bent in Russian radical Marxism gave way at last to the complete domination of the nativist, practical, and power-oriented movement to which Lenin gave form. The means of the revolution had finally become ends in themselves.

A final installment in the history of the Communist Opposition was still to come, however: a latent crisis erupted within the confines of the Leninist current of thought. With the Left eliminated and the Leninists unchallenged, the question of the ultimate nature of the regime arose to produce a serious, if brief, conflict among the party leaders. Leninism experienced a cleavage between the cautious pragmatists and the organizers of total power.

13

THE RIGHT OPPOSITION

For all its affirmation of the virtue and necessity of monolithic unity, the Bolshevik Party could not yet dispense with the function provided by an opposition. Stalin and Bukharin had hardly finished congratulating themselves on their triumphant victory over the Trotskyists when a new party split began. In a matter of months, Stalin's senior associates in the Politburo —Bukharin, Rykov, and Tomsky—found themselves the victims of precisely the same political tactics whose use against the Left they had so vigorously applauded such a short time before.

The Right Opposition led by these three men was quite different in character from the previous Trotskyist movement. The Left oppositionists had exhibited a certain continuity of ideological tradition over a considerable span of years, and their disagreements with the Leninist leadership were substantially grounded in deep-seated intellectual and social differences. By contrast, the Right Opposition was a phenomenon of the moment, emerging on the political scene with little forewarning. The Right Opposition had no background as a deviation, for the simple reason that before its appearance as an opposition it had been, both as a group of men and as a program, an indistinguishable part of the party leadership itself. In the form of its origin the Right Opposition thus closely resembled the Left Communists of 1918. Each group represented the previously prevailing line of the party from which the leading individual in the party suddenly swerved. In both instances the split thus produced was deep, and the manner in which the party crisis would be resolved was not immediately apparent.

The Grain Crisis and Stalin's Left Turn

For a time, the debates between the Rightist party leadership and the Left Opposition had obscured the basic agreement of almost all Communists on certain ultimate principles or objectives of socialist economics. As the Left Opposition waned, a few figures among the leadership began to refer with increasing emphasis to these first principles: state economic planning, reorganization of agriculture from individual farms to large-scale collective units, and the transformation of Russia into a modern industrial country. On such basic aims there was no disagreement, but a great deal of room remained for controversy regarding the means and particularly the timing for attaining the goals.

The outbreak of a new factional struggle after the defeat of the Left was foreseen by Trotsky, or at least he guessed correctly. In the fall of 1926, he asserted the existence of three groups within the ruling bloc—"proprietary" [propeasant], trade-unionist, and "pure apparatus."[1] Trotsky adhered to this perception of incipient cleavage throughout 1927, while adding the warning that a struggle among these groups would be the natural outcome of the suppression of the Left.[2] Finally he named names, with considerable accuracy: Stalin, Molotov, Kaganovich, Mikoyan, Kirov, and (erroneously) Uglanov, in the "Center" group; Tomsky as a trade-unionist; Rykov and A. P. Smirnov in the propeasant group, together with Kalinin, about whose Rightist inclinations there was much rumor though no evidence.[3]

With the passage of time, and as the economic condition of the country steadily improved from its low point during War Communism, the question of ultimate objectives began more and more to share the scene with problems of the moment. So it was in the latter part of 1927, when the party leadership, with no evidence of dissension, put itself on record in favor of comprehensive economic planning and a collectivized agriculture. This general approval was given in resolutions adopted by the Central Committee plenum of October 1927, confirmed by the Fifteenth Party Congress in December. The authors of the statements were Rykov for the economic plan and Molotov for agriculture. Both spoke largely in the cautious vein of the prevailing economic policy, though a somewhat more vigorous approach can be seen in Molotov's resolution. Rykov attacked the "super-industrialist" Opposition once again and stressed the need for caution and balance in the work of economic planning: not too much heavy industry, not too fast a tempo, adequate reserves, and so on. "It is essential to proceed from the optimal combination of both factors" was his recurring phrase.[4] His panacea was still the consolidation of industry to cut costs and placate the peasants with lower consumer-goods prices. Molotov spoke confidently of the progressive victory of socialist elements and the middle peasant over the kulaks, stressed cooperatives as the road to socialism, and specifically endorsed the established policy for collectivizing agriculture—gradual and voluntary.

The pronouncements of the Fifteenth Congress were sufficiently vague to allow a variety of interpretations, as would soon become apparent. Indications are that the Stalinists still had no definite idea of the policy changes which they were soon to make, nor of the immediate economic and political problems which would force this shift. As usual in Soviet politics, the departure from the NEP and the new cleavage in the party were precipitated when expedients had to be devised to meet a sudden crisis.

The problem was a familiar one—the peasantry and the food supply. Even before the sessions of the Fifteenth Party Congress had been completed with the formal expulsion of the whole Left Opposition, the party leadership began to express alarm about grain procurement. Two directives issued from the Central Committee to local party organizations, warning of a decline in the collections of grain from the peasants. These were followed in January 1928 by an order threatening disciplinary action against local party leaders if they failed to remedy the situation.[5] By February the entire party was agitated over the suddenly looming grain crisis.

The causes of the food-supply problem were of course not new. Russian agriculture during the period of the NEP was a weak foundation for an industrial economy; the need to remedy this condition had been made only too clear by those economists supporting the party leadership against the "super-industrialism" of the Left Opposition. Because of the subdivision of the land after the revolution, a much larger proportion of the country's food production was now in the hands of poor peasants who were much more inclined to eat their produce than to sell it, especially because of the chronic scissors problem.[6] As a result, the supply of marketed grain was cut in half. The city population, while not starving, was not in a secure position, and the possibility of its future growth was severely limited. The grain-export trade, on the other hand, had almost disappeared, though this was a time when the Soviet government required maximum resources in foreign exchange to procure machinery for its industrial construction projects.

The situation worsened in the winter of 1927–28, though it hardly warranted the sudden alarm with which the party leadership reacted. Because of low grain prices and in the hope of future increases, the peasants were increasingly withholding part of their grain production from the market. This, coupled with local crop failures, caused the rate of grain deliveries for the market to fall more than 25 per cent between the beginning of 1927 and January 1928.[7] The party's immediate response was to blame the kulaks, and since the prosperous peasants ordinarily marketed a much larger proportion of their output than did the others, there was no doubt some truth to the charge.

It was obvious even to foreign observers that the quick and vigorous action which the party took to counter the grain crisis was the work of Stalin.[8] No sooner were the serious dimensions of the crisis apparent than Stalin, accompanied by Molotov, set off personally for western Siberia, the only main grain surplus area not hit by drought.[9] True to character, he ordered the inauguration of "emergency measures." These included forced loans, increased tax assessments, certain purely economic measures such as stopping competition between government grain-purchasing agencies and expediting consumer goods for sale to the peasant. But most significant was the application of Article 107. This clause of the criminal code provided for the confiscation of the holdings of "speculators," and this term was applied to the kulaks who were found with stocks of grain. To facilitate the exposure of such individuals, the government rewarded the "village poor" with a quarter of the grain confiscated in each instance.[10] Trotsky commented that the *Pravda* editorial of February 15—which in substance merely reprinted Stalin's communication to the party of February 13—read almost like the Opposition platform.[11]

At the same time, Stalin was extending blame for the grain crisis to a broad group of local government and party officials, whose weakness allegedly allowed the problem to assume its current proportions. In his statement of February 13 Stalin reported, "In our organizations, party as well as others, there have recently grown up certain elements, alien to the party, which do not see the classes in the village, do not understand the basis of our class policy, and try to carry on work in such a way that no one in the village will be offended, to live in peace with the kulak and in general to preserve popularity among 'all strata' of the village."[12] This marked the appearance of a theme which soon became dominant in party discussions—the danger of those who would attempt to "conciliate" the kulaks, promote "peaceful evolution," and thereby reflect the influence of "kulak ideology."

Trotsky saw all his charges vindicated. How, he sarcastically inquired, could all these kulak elements have penetrated the party despite fits of "Bolshevization"? "In February 1928, we heard for the first time from [*Pravda*] what we knew long ago . . . that in the party of Lenin there has . . . taken shape a strong right wing which is pulling toward a neo-NEP, i.e., to capitalism by gradations."[13]

The commissar of agriculture, A. P. Smirnov, who had been closely associated with the previously lenient peasant policy of the party leadership, was removed on the reported grounds of a "peasant deviation."[14] According to Stalin's statement after the April meeting of the Central Committee, a purge of personnel in the grain-collecting agencies and in local party organizations in the grain areas was effectively carried out. Those eliminated were the "obviously corrupt elements, who do not recognize classes in the village and do not want to 'quarrel' with the kulak."[15] Subsequent concern about the "Right danger," however, suggests that this preliminary tightening of the ranks was comparatively mild.

Though there was general agreement among the party leadership on the gravity of the grain crisis and on the need for an effective remedy, serious behind-the-scenes differences concerning the proper course of action quickly arose. Harsh words were reportedly exchanged between Stalin and Rykov when Stalin returned from Siberia with plans for a sweeping purge in that region. Rykov cursed the general secretary and walked out of the Politburo meeting. Later, with the support of Tomsky and Kalinin, he was able to restrain Stalin's plans.[16] Apparently Rykov was the first to provide a rallying point for people opposed to Stalin's innovations in economic policy. In July 1928, Trotsky still termed the whole Rightist faction "Rykovist."[17] Stalin perhaps had Rykov in mind when in April he referred to opponents of his efforts to eliminate alleged friends of the kulaks: "I know that certain comrades do not willingly accept this principle. . . . He who believes that our alliance with the peasantry . . . means an alliance with the kulaks, has nothing in common with the spirit of Leninism."[18]

There was restive talk about the NEP's giving way to a revival of War Communism. Stalin sternly retorted, "Talk that we would abolish the NEP, introduce requisitioning, de-kulakization, etc., is counterrevolutionary gossip. . . . The NEP is the basis of our economic policy, and will remain such for a long historical period."[19] (Such statements show how little Stalin foresaw his own future policies.) Bukharin went to great lengths to deny the suggestion that the party's new policy toward the kulaks followed the platform of the Left Opposition.[20] Rykov conceded that the grain crisis and the kulak threat had taken the party by surprise, and, to judge by a comparison with earlier attacks on the Left Opposition's warnings, it actually did.[21]

In April the Central Committee expressed something of a compromising tone in criticizing "excesses" such as forced loans and confiscations without the formality of invoking Article 107. Trotsky reported privately that a majority at the plenum, under the prodding of provincial party officials, had administered a direct rebuff to Stalin.[22] On the other hand, the Central Committee affirmed the idea, suggested earlier by Stalin, that the party was engaged in an "offensive against the kulak," based upon the "decisions of the Fifteenth Congress" (a phrase that was to recur frequently). While the usual call for improved economic organization and planning was repeated, the committee statement sounded a new note in its appeal for "revolutionary discipline in the fulfillment of general economic plans" and for "the greatest straining of all forces and resources of the proletarian state."[23]

By May the tension in the Soviet political atmosphere had increased sharply. The affair of alleged counterrevolutionary "wrecking" activities by some mining engineers in the Donets Basin reached the trial stage (the so-called Shakhty trials), and for two months the press whipped up alarm over the external and internal bourgeois threat which the "plot" supposedly indicated. Reportedly Stalin was using the affair to embarrass Rykov as the governmental head.[24]

An extensive campaign of propaganda and agitation among the party members was undertaken at this point, ostensibly to promote "self-criticism" and to fight "bureaucratism." In the loftiest of tones, the Central Committee affirmed "the possibility of replacing any secretary, any bureau, any committee, etc."[25] As one might expect, this amounted in practice to criticism and removal of the "bureaucrats" who happened at the time to have incurred the displeasure of those in control of the party organization. Self-criticism became an effective device for prosecuting the struggle against nascent oppositionist tendencies. Stalin himself indicated the limits for the campaign, in a surprisingly frank statement: "Of course, the fact that there has developed among us a group of leaders who have been raised very high and have great authority is itself a great achievement for our party. It is obvious that without the existence of such an authoritative group of leaders the control of a great realm is unthinkable."[26] A measure of ten years' evolution is afforded by contrasting these remarks with the view toward public officials which Lenin put forth in "State and Revolution."

Late in April it appeared that the grain crisis had broken out all over again. *Pravda,* with the Stalinist Yaroslavsky now on its board,[27] sounded the alarm: the decline observed in the rate of grain collections was due to a tendency toward "demobilization." "In no way," warned an editorial, "may we slacken the *class pressure* on the well-to-do kulak strata."[28] Two weeks later *Pravda* put even more emphasis on the grain problem.[29] The successful grain collections of the winter months were attributed to the special efforts made at that time, and the lesson was drawn that "a system of energetic measures" was required to terminate the endemic grain-supply difficulty. The activist mentality was stressed: "The main thing depends on us ourselves, on our energy, our intelligent approach to the matter, on our qualities of discipline." Stalin later admitted the resumption of emergency measures to collect grain by force, and he adduced this as the reason "why certain of our party functionaries lacked the calmness and firmness to estimate the situation soberly and without exaggeration."[30] In reality, Stalin's heavy-handed response to the grain situation could only confirm the anxieties of those who had the specter of War Communism before their eyes.

Despite the growing misgivings of many party figures, Stalin proceeded toward the statement of a basically new agricultural policy, though he disclaimed innovation by speaking of "implementing the decisions of the Fifteenth Congress." In a talk to a gathering of Communist scholars late in May, Stalin made public his new approach: "The solution lies in the transition from individual peasant farming to collective, common farming." He did make a gesture in the direction of improving individual farming while it lasted, but the toughness of his new orientation was reaffirmed in his comment on industry: "Should we, perhaps, as a measure of greater 'caution,' retard the development of heavy industry and make light industry, which produces chiefly for the peasant market, the basis of our industry as a whole? Not under any circumstances! That would be suicidal; it would mean undermining our whole industry, including light industry. It would mean the abandonment of the slogan of the industrialization of our country, and the transformation of our country into an appendage of the capitalist system of economy."[31] Here Stalin announced what was to become the main theme of the economic discussions and controversies of the ensuing year. He had opted for the high-tempo industrialization which had just been condemned along with the Left Opposition, and he went even further with his refusal to recognize any limits either on the country's need for heavy industry or on its capacity for building it.[32]

Bukharin's first response to the new stress on collectivization was a panegyric on the "cultural revolution," which would put an end to "the contrast of city and country,"[33] but soon he removed his rose-colored glasses. By the first of June, Bukharin had privately attacked Stalin as the representative of a "Trotskyist danger,"[34] and he soon became the leading spokesman for a determined though still behind-the-scenes faction committed to the defeat of Stalin's line on agriculture.

Before the month of June was out, the storm clouds had gathered. The peasants had begun to riot in many areas, particularly in the grain-rich North Caucasus.[35] Among the industrial workers growing unrest was occasioned both by irregularities in the urban food supply and by the sympathetic personal ties which were still often maintained with the countryside.[36] Alarmed and also emboldened by this evidence of crisis, the critics of Stalin's forceful policy prepared to attack. The Moscow secretary, Uglanov, declared to his subsidiary organizations that Stalin's policy was wrong and that it was based on the wrong statistics.[37] In Leningrad there was disaffection among Kirov's subordinates, and Kirov found himself openly challenged by Bukharin's supporter, Slepkov.[38] Tomsky was reportedly preparing for a contest in the trade unions and had sought the advice of the repentant Trotskyist, Piatakov.[39] "Heated disputes" in the Politburo became known to the lower-level officialdom.[40] "Rykov's faction," wrote Trotsky, "is clearly taking shape not only in Moscow but also in the outlying regions."[41] The party press and the governmental bureaucracy appeared to be firmly on the side of Stalin's critics, though Stalin had scored a preliminary victory in the Institute of Red Professors under the cover of his self-criticism campaign.[42]

Meanwhile Stalin had initiated the tactic of attacking potential opposition supporters one at a time, while feigning conciliation with his rivals at the top to delay their open resistance. The commissar of finance, M. I. Frumkin, had written a letter protesting reliance on high-pressure methods in grain collecting. Stalin seized upon this as evidence of a prokulak tendency. Frumkin, he charged, was retiring in panic from the position of the Fifteenth Congress to that of the Fourteenth Congress and thus abandoning the offensive against the kulaks and the drive for collectivization.[43] Stalin made some barbed remarks concerning the deviant notion that the "alliance with the middle peasantry" could be upheld by any course other than the "struggle with the kulaks," though, lest the Trotskyist heresy be forgotten, he noted the danger of allowing the middle peasants to suffer from the anti-kulak measures.[44] How the fine line was to be drawn between ally and enemy was not explained. This was characteristic of Stalin's use of rigid, black-and-white formulas which, imposed on the complexities of reality, demanded the most minute and arbitrary distinctions.

By the time of the July meeting of the Central Committee, rumors of dissension in the highest councils of the party were rife.[45] Trotsky took note of "the existing breach between the apparatus and the right wing," although the make-up of the latter was not entirely clear to him.[46] Stalin apparently contemplated some kind of drastic action, though he may not yet have been sure of its precise direction.

Among Stalin's potential supporters and critics the lines had not definitely formed. Molotov spoke on June 30 with weighty caution, stressing the burden of backwardness in Russian agriculture and warning against excessive reliance on planning alone.[47] At the same meeting, Uglanov, who was about to take the Moscow organization into the Right Opposition, expressed precisely the opposite, optimistic, view of planning.[48] Earlier, Kaganovich had supposedly wavered.[49] Kalinin, Voroshilov, Andreyev, Ordzhonikidze, and the deputy GPU chief, Yagoda, among others, were rumored to be sympathetic toward Stalin's opponents. They were reportedly afraid to act or restrained by threats of blackmail by Stalin.[50] Voroshilov, for example, apparently feared the exposure of his sin of patriotic fervor which prompted him to volunteer for the tsarist army during World War I.[51]

The Central Committee assembled for its regular meeting in Moscow on July 4. Again the focus of its deliberations was the peasant problem, which was the subject of a climactic debate on July 9 and 10.[52] Reports were delivered by Kalinin, Molotov, and Mikoyan, dealing respectively with state farms, collective farms, and grain collections; they spoke in relatively moderate terms, with emphasis on maintaining the tie with the middle peasant. The principal resolution, proposed by Mikoyan, was a compromise document which stressed the need for raising the productivity of individual peasant farming, underscored the temporary nature of the extraordinary measures, and even admitted the necessity of raising the price of grain to correspond with the price of other agricultural products.[53] It was, in fact, essentially Bukharin's resolution, "stolen from my declaration," as he put it.[54]

Mikoyan's presentation was the signal for a series of right-wing comments, by Osinsky, Andreyev, A. I. Stetsky, and Sokolnikov, that the agricultural situation was still serious and that further concessions to the middle peasants (especially price increases) were imperative. Uglanov and Rykov followed with warnings about the general state of popular discontent and the danger of allowing the extraordinary measures to become an accepted system. Kaganovich entered the argument to protest that the extraordinary measures had been criticized too much, and that it was equally wrong to rely wholly on price policy. Some of his remarks were the harshest heard at the plenum: "The kulak's struggle with us will be cruel. . . . We must prepare for this. We must quicken the pace of the grain collection campaign." Rykov replied emotionally to Kaganovich, "It would be wrong to make a distinction between the extraordinary measures and 'excesses.' 'Excesses' sometimes include criminal or semicriminal offenses committed by individual persons in the process of collecting grain. This is altogether wrong. A crime is a crime. A whole series of 'excesses' was an organic part of the entire system of grain collections which we resorted to in January." Kaganovich, according to Rykov, was an apologist for violence as an end in itself: "The whole meaning of Kaganovich's speech reduces to the defense of extraordinary measures as such for any time and under any conditions." Kaganovich was "cut to pieces," in Sokolnikov's estimation.[55]

Stalin took part in the discussion with a major speech on July 9.[56] His point of departure was the Osinsky-Sokolnikov price-raising proposal, which he denounced as "putting the brakes on the industrialization of the country." By concentrating his fire against the most extreme representatives of the right-wing view (whom Rykov himself repudiated), Stalin endeavored to identify their heresy with all the opposition to his own view. The substance of Stalin's speech was to give the NEP a new meaning—it was not a retreat but an offensive, in which vigorous measures against the kulaks and the collectivization of the rest of the peasants had an appropriate place. Thus, in his usual fashion, Stalin was able to indulge himself in a new policy and still profess orthodox adherence to past authority. He anticipated objections to accelerated collectivization by classing them with opposition to the collectivist goal per se: "Those who fail to understand that, or who do not want to admit it, are not Marxists or Leninists, but peasant philosophers, looking backward instead of forward."[57]

Stalin took pains to distinguish his new policy from the Trotskyist program, with which many people had naturally associated it.[58] In fact he was moving rapidly toward the Left position and was soon to go far beyond it with the initiation of violent, rapid, and wholesale collectivization of the peasants. Trotsky took note of a Rightist hope that a fear of conceding the correctness of the Left would inhibit the Stalinists in changing their policy.[59] But Stalin again evidenced that doctrinal adroitness which belies the impression that he was clumsy and unlettered in matters of theory. His interest in theory was, to be sure, primarily a weapon to use against his enemies, but he wielded it with dexterity. As Bukharin confided to Kamenev, "Stalin . . . is an unprincipled intriguer who subordinates everything to the preservation of his power. He changes his theories according to whom he needs to get rid of at any given moment."[60]

Stalin's problem in the summer of 1928 was to borrow the Leftist policy of increased pressure on the peasants without appearing to adhere to the Trotskyist heresy. At the same time he was determined to maneuver those who held to the old official policy into a position where they appeared to be deviators. Bukharin complained, "He maneuvers in such a way as to make us stand as the schismatics."[61] Stalin's strategy for accomplishing these simultaneous feats of political sleight of hand was his usual redefinition of old party clichés, with the support of appropriately culled quotations from Lenin, to make accepted ideas mean something quite different. At the same time his firm adherence to the authoritative pronouncements of the party would be loudly proclaimed, and anyone who ventured to suggest divergence in the actual application of such pronouncements would immediately find himself charged with an un-Leninist attitude. So it was with those who complained that the actual trend of peasant policy was violating the spirit of the NEP. They were dismissed as a "kulak deviation."

On July 10, as recriminations between the factions at the Central Committee plenum grew increasingly bitter, Bukharin rose to make the major statement of his case. He was in deadly earnest, throughout frequent clownish heckling by the Stalinists, and sincerely alarmed over the security of the Soviet state, which he feared was threatened by a mass uprising under the leadership of the kulaks. "To undertake the slightest campaign in the country," he warned "means to mobilize against us to an ever greater degree the kulak element, the petty bourgeoisie . . . the middle bourgeoisie . . . etc. The reserves of these forces remain very great, and the slightest vacillation on the question in the ranks of our party will have a disproportionately great political significance."

The grain crisis, Bukharin explained, was a reflection of the country's basic economic weakness: reserves were seriously lacking, and it was proving impossible to advance simultaneously in agriculture, industry, and consumer satisfaction. "Give us your panacea," interjected Voroshilov, who was at pains to demonstrate by his repeated heckling of Bukharin that he sided firmly with the Stalinists.

"I don't want to give you a panacea, and please don't you make fun of me," replied Bukharin, stung by the remark but apparently unable to grasp the factional vindictiveness of his critics. He went on to criticize Stalin for suggesting that industrial development inevitably implied a threat to the worker-peasant alliance: this was a Trotskyist notion. It was wrong to attack reliance on price measures as capitalistic: prices were the decisive means whereby the government could regulate the individual peasants. Poor planning and incorrect pricing were responsible for the crisis that required such special measures. The extraordinary measures had tended to become a system of War Communism; their economic value was questionable and their political effect was indisputably bad. At all costs the allegiance of the middle peasants had to be kept, and this meant that their individual farms should be allowed to prosper more. The offensive against the kulaks could be continued, but only in the form of exploiting their productive capacity through taxation; the kulaks would be no threat as long as the middle peasants did not decide to follow them. Conciliation of the peasants was the key to the future—"We must in no case allow a threat to the smychka."

The compromise resolution on the grain collections was passed unanimously by the Central Committee after the close of debate on July 10. It gave many people the impression that the issues between the Stalinists and the

Rykov-Bukharin group had been completely settled.[62] The shifting balance was subtly revealed, however, where the resolution condemned the Rightists' principal complaint that the extraordinary measures were becoming an established policy: "Interpretations of these measures as organic consequences of the decisions of the Fifteenth Congress . . . testify only to the fact that at certain levels of the party an alien ideology has had influence."[63] The Rightist leaders discovered that their position was crumbling, as a number of the people on whom they thought they could count—including Voroshilov, Kalinin, and Kuibyshev—lined up on Stalin's side.[64] Stalin's attitude on July 11, the last day of the session, was correspondingly tougher. The general secretary was confidently unyielding about suggestions for further leniency toward the peasantry.[65]

Stalin's opponents now decided to act. It is not hard to imagine how their feelings took form—after enthusiastic collaboration with a strong and resourceful comrade, the growing discord, the verbal altercation when unleashed tempers turned uneasy friends into vengeful enemies, the nursing of grudges and the restrained growling in public encounters, and finally the horrifying realization that the old associate was a power-hungry intriguer who now held most of the cards and would stop at nothing in his determination to destroy them. While reports flew about that the Right was planning to depose Stalin,[66] Bukharin took the risky step of establishing contact with former members of the Left Opposition. Sokolnikov arranged a meeting between Bukharin and Kamenev.[67] For some reason Bukharin had come to fear a rapprochement between Stalin and the Zinoviev-Kamenev group, and he hastened to seek out the old oppositionists to be his own allies on the ground that they had a common cause to make.

On the morning of July 11, Sokolnikov and Bukharin slipped into Kamenev's Moscow apartment without ringing, and Bukharin, in a desperate mood, at once revealed his fears: "Stalin's line is ruinous for the whole revolution. It can make us collapse. . . . The differences between us and Stalin are many times more serious than all our former differences with you. Rykov, Tomsky, and I agree on formulating the situation thus: 'It would be much better if Zinoviev and Kamenev were in the Politburo instead of Stalin.' . . . I have not spoken with Stalin for several weeks. . . . Our arguing with him reached the point of saying, 'You lie!' He has made concessions now, so that [later] he can cut our throats." In the comments which he appended to the record of the talk, Kamenev observed, "Stalin knows only one method . . . to plant a knife in your back."

The strategy of the Right after the July Plenum was to make their defeat look like a victory and conceal the depth of the split in the leadership. This suited Stalin's purposes well, since he had neither the program nor the secure organizational position to guarantee him success in a public test of strength.

Pravda, still under Rightist control, put heavy stress on the theme of leniency toward the peasants. The editorial of July 14 gave an exaggerated impression of the Central Committee's critique of the extraordinary measures, while the "offensive against the kulaks" was almost completely overlooked.[68]

On July 13 Rykov spoke about the plenum to the Moscow party organization with such an aggressive air of factional victory that the printed text of his remarks had to be toned down. He let it be understood that the "left turn" of February had definitely been reversed and warned that if the extraordinary measures should be resumed, "This will be the end of the NEP. . . . Then there will certainly be an uprising in the army. I have Voroshilov's word on this." Trotsky was led to prophesy a right-wing victory and "the last stage of Thermidor." He thought time was running out for Stalin because he had overplayed his waiting game.[69]

Meanwhile, rumors of the split at the top had spread widely throughout the party, though there was much confusion about the specific issues and personalities involved and complaints that the membership was being kept in the dark.[70] The Moscow organization, where Stalin had begun to maneuver for the removal of Uglanov, was particularly agitated. Records have been preserved of typical questions asked by the rank and file at membership meetings in Moscow following the plenum.[71] "How serious was the dispute at the plenum between Stalin and Bukharin, and what came out of it?" inquired one man. "Which of the deviations—Rykov's or Stalin's—is worse?" another naively queried. Other typical questions were: Was the party returning to Trotsky's policy on the peasantry? Were there really two camps within the Politburo? What about the controversy in unpublished documents among the Politburo members? Why did Rykov say that he was speaking only for himself? What was the issue between Rykov and Stalin in the evaluation of individual peasant farming?

While steadfastly denying the reports of a split, the leaders of both factions took steps to prepare for an organizational struggle. Stalin, with a majority of the Politburo behind him, scored a strategic advance when he wrested control of *Pravda* and *Bolshevik* away from the Right.[72] (The Bukharinist editor Slepkov was exiled to the agitprop department in Yakutsk.[73]) Stalin allowed the rumor to spread that he intended to oust Uglanov, while Uglanov confided to a Moscow associate, "Stalin is sitting on the party's neck, and we've got to remove him."[74] By the end of July it was clear that reconciliation of the factions was impossible. Trivial policy differences had grown into a life-and-death struggle for power, the open resolution of which could not be long delayed. Into this supercharged atmosphere came the delegates to the Sixth World Congress of the Communist International—pawns to be moved by the rival Russian leaders in a new series of maneuvers.

While serious frictions over economic policy were accumulating within the Communist Party, no suggestion of a party split was publicly admitted. There was one arena, however, where Stalin could emphasize the danger of a split without the embarrassment of an untimely challenge to his still popular right-wing rivals. This opportunity was provided by the Communist International, whose intricate politics made it easy to develop the idea of a new factional deviation before applying such a charge against Stalin's right-wing critics in Russia. As in the case of the Trotskyists, the Comintern reflected an enlarged and sharpened likeness of the cleavages developing in the Russian leadership, and in the factional controversies in various foreign Communist parties there was extensive opportunity for both sides to test out their ideas before becoming committed to them with respect to Russia itself.

The Communist parties of Germany and the United States were torn by bitter dissension between Right and Center factions even before Trotsky's Leftist sympathizers were condemned and expelled. Other parties, particularly the French, British, and Czechoslovakian, had gone far in the direction of right-wing moderation under the "united front" policy.[75] By the beginning of 1928, the Soviet leaders had begun to turn against the Comintern Rightists now that their usefulness in combating the Trotskyists was coming to an end. This was the origin of the so-called "left turn" which took place during 1928 and which set the Comintern's aggressive tactical line for the next six years.

At the Fifteenth Party Congress Stalin had taken the stand, previously defended only by the Left Opposition, that the era of capitalist stabilization was drawing to a close—"We are living on the eve of a new revolutionary upswing."[76] The new orientation was expressed more definitely at the Ninth Plenum of the Comintern's executive committee, held in Moscow in February 1928. Developing the idea of the "third period" of revolutionary crisis (following the postwar chaos and the period of stabilization), Stalin felt his way toward a position from which he could later embarrass his political rivals.

By the time the February ECCI session closed, it was clear that the "united front" policy was at an end. A new revolutionary line was endorsed for the Chinese, British, and French Communists, and Social Democrats everywhere were denounced as the worst enemies of the Communist movement.[77] With respect to Communist deviation, however, the Trotskyists were still of paramount concern. Bukharin spoke at great length on the need for continued vigilance against them despite their defeat in the Russian party, and he constantly identified the Left deviation with the Social Democrats: "There is frequently talk about various Left and Right tendencies in the Comintern. . . . In my opinion, the real danger . . . is the Trotskyist danger."[78] This matter of estimating the relative threats on the Left and on the Right was later to become a sensitive test for Rightist deviation in the Soviet Union itself.

In July 1928, the delegates of the Communist parties gathered in Moscow for the Sixth World Congress of the Comintern (the first held in four years and the next to last ever to be assembled). By this time, the contending factions among the German and American Communists were openly expressing sympathies regarding the still concealed and obscure split in the Russian party. Bukharin was called down by some for overstating the capacity of capitalism to continue growing during the "third period," while his American and German sympathizers expressely defended him against such criticism.[79]

Efforts to embarrass Bukharin were afoot in the Russian party itself. Bukharin had submitted a draft of a program for the Comintern directly to the congress, and the Stalinists took advantage of this by demanding certain amendments, which had to be accepted in public. As Stalin later described them, these amendments all concerned points where a particular refinement or new twist of definition was desired.[80] Evidently the purpose was to show that Bukharin's thinking was out of date or in error, wherever such failings could plausibly be suggested. One amendment concerned the struggle with the Social Democrats: Bukharin allegedly forgot to put special stress on the fight against the *Left* Social Democrats. On fighting Right deviations in the Comintern parties, Bukharin forgot to include the necessary fight against the "conciliatory tendency" toward the Right. Bukharin assertedly forgot, as the prime defense against the Right deviation, "the necessity of maintaining iron discipline in the Communist parties"—though he had actually endorsed such a norm for years. Above all, Bukharin was said to have exaggerated the stabilization of capitalism in its "third period" of postwar growth.

By the time of the congress Bukharin himself agreed that right-wing factionalism was more serious than the Trotskyists, but his conception of the "Right danger" remained nebulous. He spoke of it not as a movement of specific people and factions, but only as a likelihood that ordinary Communists might commit mistakes of a rightward nature, such as cooperating too freely with Social Democrats or relying excessively on people like Chiang Kai-shek.[81] He did agree now that this threat of Rightist error was a real danger which had to be combated resolutely. At a Moscow party meeting following the adjournment of the Comintern congress, Bukharin stated, "The congress . . . imposed upon all members of the Communist International the obligation to struggle with the Right Opposition, and at the same time to overcome resolutely those tendencies within the Communist parties which underestimate this danger."[82] Behind the scenes, Bukharin expressed opinions which belied his official view of the Right danger. To the Swiss Comintern secretary, Humbert-Droz, then under attack as a Rightist deviator, Bukharin wrote to express sympathy with the idea that the

Communists' best interest lay in alliances with the Social Democrats against Fascism. He apologized for not being able to support this position in public because of the critical situation which he faced within the Communist Party in Russia.[83]

Bukharin took an open step in a dangerously conciliatory direction by appealing for "tact" in preserving Comintern unity and holding the allegiance of all who would respect the authority of the leadership: "We must in every way and with every means bring together the comrades who stand for . . . the decisions of the Communist International and who promise to carry on a relentless struggle against the Right danger. We wish here at the congress to create the conditions for a situation that will make any split within the future leading organs impossible."[84] To back up this call for circumspection in the enforcement of party discipline, Bukharin quoted from a letter Lenin had writen to him: "If you are going to expell all the not particularly obedient but clever people, and retain only the obedient fools, you will *definitely* ruin the party."[85] But Bukharin's equivocation never ceased, for when he used this quotation a second time, he qualified it with the comment, "This rule . . . must not, however, be allowed to degenerate into the needless tolerance of deviations. Deviations must be fought and overcome."[86]

The furor about the "Right danger" in the summer of 1928 did not publicly involve the Russian Communist Party, despite the numerous hints which had been dropped earlier respecting weakness in the face of the kulak threat. The only aspect of Russian party affairs which the Comintern discussed was the recent defeat of the Trotskyists. To put an end to the rumors about dissension in the Russian leadership, Stalin had the Politburo submit to the Comintern congress a declaration stating that they "most determinedly protest against the spreading of any kind of rumors about disagreements among the members of the Politburo of the Central Committee of the AUCP(b)."[87] Bukharin was naive enough to think that he increased his chances of victory by concealing his misgivings from the rank and file.

For the Stalin group the Comintern question served a useful purpose. Without risking a challenge inside Russia, they were able to create a sense of alarm and, particularly, to establish a new category, accepted by all the Russian leaders, of axiomatic political evil: "Right opportunism." Proceeding further, a second degree of error was established, hardly less damnable than the first—"the conciliatory attitude in regard to Right dangers," as Bukharin himself put it.[88] Both classifications were carefully confined to the non-Russian Communist parties for the time being so that there would be no question of disagreement in principle among the Russians. Once the character of these deviations had been established, however, it was a simple matter for the Stalinists to include within their terms, particularly in the "conciliatory" category, any Russian leaders whom they wished to discredit. In Russia this reasoning was actually taken further, to condemn people who would conciliate even the "conciliators." Stalin's political trap for the Rightists was well constructed, with Bukharin's unwitting assistance.

THE CRISIS IN THE MOSCOW ORGANIZATION

By the end of the summer of 1928 the differences between the Stalinists and the Bukharin-Rykov group were acute. Tension at the top began to have its effects on the lower levels, and the Right Opposition took form as a movement in the party organization. One brief engagement was fought, and its outcome was a victory for the Stalinists that was both easy and decisive.

The scene of the organizational struggle between Stalin and the Right was Moscow. The party machine in the Moscow province was the only major organizational force at the disposal of the Rightists and accordingly was of strategic significance. In contrast to the spontaneous and relatively democratic surge of Opposition sentiment among the Moscow Communists in 1923 and earlier, the 1928 Moscow Opposition was an apparatus affair, on the order of Zinoviev's Leningrad Opposition of 1925. Uglanov's Moscow Opposition was no more a democratic protest movement than was Stalin's central party machine. Uglanov was a typical organization man, installed in the key Moscow post in 1924 and rewarded for his loyalty to the general secretary by elevation to the Politburo as a candidate member in 1925.

The fact that a man such as Uglanov should have thrown his lot in with the Bukharin group indicates that the issues between Stalin and the Right had driven a deep wedge into the ranks of the party officialdom. While the motive of personal political advantage cannot be ruled out, Uglanov's stand during and after the July Plenum of the Central Commitee leaves no doubt that he was genuinely concerned over economic policy and that he took the Bukharinist alarm to heart. Like the other Rightist leaders, he linked the success of the Communist Party with the well-being of the country and recoiled before the social conflict which Stalin's aggressive line portended.

The misgivings which had initiated the cleavage between the Bukharinists and the Stalinists were intensified when indications of coming harvest difficulties prompted a noisy resumption of the grain-crisis talk. At this juncture, a regular plenary session of the Moscow party committee was held (from September 11 to September 15), at which opinions were aired that were clearly suggestive of a Bukharinist attitude in Uglanov's organization. Uglanov recalled the warnings expressed at the Fifteenth Congress on the grain problem, the "goods famine," and the problem of capital accumulation. He quoted the July Plenum of the Central Committee on the importance of raising the productivity of the individual peasants, the voluntary character which collectivization should have, and the observance of "revolutionary legality."[89] Such was the device of the Rightists for criticizing present policies without incurring the onus of a violation of discipline: they would simply stress an earlier party statement issued before the Stalinists began revising policy and reinterpreting the statements.

While both sides professed the strictest orthodoxy, a test for Rightist sympathies was provided by attitudes toward the various deviationist trends in the party. Uglanov's remarks on this score aroused the most violent objection later on, and such was the concern felt already that *Pravda* held up his September report for ten days before publishing it. Uglanov did have words of criticism for those in various organizations who opposed the offensive against the kulaks, but the bulk of his fire was aimed at the Trotskyists. He and his Moscow Committee dismissed talk of a Right-Center cleavage as a slander inspired by "splinters of Trotskyist groups" who were trying to embarrass the party.[90]

The Stalinists' reaction to the Rightist tendency in the Moscow Committee was quick, though still oblique. *Pravda* appeared on September 15 with an editorial advancing the slogan, "Struggle on two fronts." This was the first public suggestion that there was in Russia, as well as in the Comintern, a right-wing deviation equal to the Trotskyists in the seriousness of its threat. "The openly opportunist deviation," *Pravda* warned a few days later, "finds its expression . . . in the misunderstanding of the tasks set by the Fifteenth Congress and subsequent party decisions regarding the intensification of the struggle against the kulak and the development of the work of collectivization."[91]

Insisting on literal doctrinal correctness and claiming strict observance of official party decisions, the Stalinists were bent on proving that their every action was the necessary and correct implementation of "the decisions of the Fifteenth Congress." By 1929, the economic policy of the congress had become ancient history; yet the party leaders continued to insist that they were observing the 1927 resolutions and that their actions were thus sanctioned. Conversely, any attempt to argue that the Stalinists were transgressing the lines laid down by the congress would be denounced as a "misunderstanding," or even as an effort to undermine the congress decisions. To take action vigorously and to denounce critics for what the leadership itself was actually guilty of—and to make these denunciations stick through the power of the party's organization, propaganda apparatus, and press monopoly—was the Stalinist formula for political success.

A more direct critique of the Bukharinist trend of thought came in a speech on September 19 by Kuibyshev, who as chairman of the Supreme Economic Council had emerged as a leading spokesman for the economic policies which the Stalinists were developing. Kuibyshev warned of the

resistance and discontent which the program of vigorous industrial development was bound to generate:

> This same discontent penetrates through all sorts of channels even as far as cer-
> tain parts of our soviet apparatus, the result being doubts as to the possibility of
> executing such great tasks and as to the wisdom of aspiring to such difficult
> objectives as are involved in the industrialization of our entire economy. By pene-
> trating into our soviet apparatus, such sentiments also find entrance in a small
> measure into our party. The party will have recourse to all available measures for
> the purpose of nipping in the bud such sentiments as pessimism or lack of
> confidence.[92]

With what must have been a remarkable sense of journalistic balance,
Kuibyshev took *Pravda* to task for giving too much emphasis to the danger
of Trotskyism and for "ignoring the pessimistic tendencies which occur in
certain degenerated sections of our party organism." He charged that this
was "a sign of shortsightedness, a sign of undue tolerance in regard to the
said tendencies, and a failure to pursue the directives set up by the July
plenum on the subject of a fight upon two fronts." This was just the point
that *Pravda* itself had apparently made.

The central party leadership then proceeded to deal with the Opposition
in Moscow with the usual organizational measures. Under the convenient
pretext provided by the current campaigns for "self-criticism" and "intraparty democracy," and utilizing the scheduled elections for new bureaus or
directing committees for all party cells, the Stalinists by-passed the Moscow
leadership in order to apply pressure and seek supporters in the district
organizations nominally under the jurisdiction of the Moscow Committee.
"It is true" the Central Committee announced, "that some members of the
Moscow Committee and the leaders of some districts have recently shown a
certain inconsistency and vacillation in the struggle against the Right deviations from the Leninist line by tolerating a conciliatory attitude toward these
deviations which is inacceptable to the Bolshevik Party. This has aroused the
dissatisfaction of a certain section of the active membership of the Moscow
organization who wished to correct these mistakes."[93] Here were the tactics
employed so effectively against the Zinovievists in Leningrad in January
1926. They demonstrated the top leadership's ability to go outside the normal
lines of bureaucratic authority and make use of democratic forms in order
to buttress central control over the middle echelons.

Soon there were subtle indications of the effect of central pressure. Some
of the Moscow district organizations, passing resolutions about the Comintern congress, began to express the new central line against "petty-bourgeois
opportunism" in the Russian party itself. Other Moscow districts confined
themselves to vague exhortations for the "struggle on two fronts." As it was

later officially confirmed, the district secretaries had divided in their allegiance between Uglanov and the central leadership. The party organization at Moscow University, reflecting the intellectuals' predilection for any form of opposition, took a firm pro-Rightist stand.[94]

To appease the central leadership, Uglanov issued a declaration to the Moscow membership early in October, in which he heavily stressed the danger of the Right deviation as well as the Left.[95] But he did not put an end to the tolerance of Rightist opinions within his organization and lamely had to plead the "sickness" of himself and his two co-secretaries as the excuse.[96] Uglanov was evidently encouraged by the publication of Bukharin's thoughtful critique of the Stalinist economic program, his "Notes of an Economist," in *Pravda* on September 30. On October 3 he warned publicly that Soviet agriculture was now seriously lagging, to the detriment of both industry and consumers.[97] On the following day, one of Uglanov's district secretaries, Penkov, echoed these agriculture-first remarks and urged the study of Bukharin's article, but he met with an ominous response—direct contradiction by his own subordinates in the debate which ensued.[98]

On or about October 11, the central leadership initiated a violent press and organizational campaign against the still anonymous "Right deviation," and simultaneously took direct action against the Moscow Opposition. Uglanov suddenly found that he could no longer control transfers in his own organization.[99] While the bureau of the Moscow Committee was compelled to share responsibility for the move, it was on the acknowledged initiative of the Central Committee that the two most recalcitrant district leaders in Moscow, Penkov and Riutin, were removed, on the grounds that they had "recently allowed individual deviations from the correct Leninist line of the party."[100] Confirmation of the central victory came at the meeting of the Moscow Committee on October 18 and 19. Uglanov made the customary report but was given a portent of his coming fall as the committee members withheld the usual applause.[101] Sensing the forces against him, Uglanov remarked ironically that his removal would be justified if the membership really wanted it. He admitted weaknesses in his organization and vaguely conceded "lack of clarity in evaluating the economic situation," but he tried to stand his ground against the Stalinists' attacks: "We will consider it our duty . . . to defend ourselves by struggling against slander." Guardedly he recalled Lenin's warning about Stalin's character.[102]

Uglanov's defensive gestures were fruitless, for the great majority of the Moscow Committee had evidently gone over to the Stalinists. The proceedings of the session were largely taken up with criticism of Uglanov's errors, attacks on the Right deviation, and appeals for discipline and self-criticism. The oppositionists were accused of a "keep it in the family" attitude and of conniving against the Central Committee.[103] A number of Uglanov's supporters, including the ousted district secretaries Penkov and Riutin, made their confessions and boarded the band wagon.[104] "The party is *exclusively* correct," declared district secretary Safronov, "and I find in myself enough courage to admit my errors."[105] A hold-out, the dismissed agitprop chief, Liadov-Mandelshtam (the old Otzovist), pleaded that his friends had no honor because they avoided him as "a traitor to the party line."[106]

On October 19 Stalin appeared in person before the Moscow Committee to deliver a long warning against the Right deviation, though he still allowed it to remain anonymous. Affirming that a Right deviation did in fact exist among the Russian Communists as well as in the Comintern, he described it as "a tendency, an inclination of a part of the Communists, not yet formulated, it is true, and perhaps not yet consciously realized, but nevertheless a tendency, to depart from the general line of our party toward bourgeois ideology." This was not, Stalin argued, a new development, but it had been revealed more clearly by the "vacillations" which the government's recent economic problems had produced. Cleverly he twisted the Rightist efforts to defend the old party line and created an antiproletarian scapegoat: "In order to overcome the difficulties we must first defeat the Right danger . . . which is hindering the fight against our difficulties and is trying to shake the party's will to fight to overcome these difficulties."

Stalin followed this warning with an attack on people who spoke against the Right deviation but did not back up their words with action. "It is impossible to overcome the Right opportunist deviation," he asserted, "without conducting a systematic fight against the conciliationist tendency which takes the opportunists under its wing."[107] As he later put the case, like the confident cat giving the mouse a brief play before the next pounce, "I do not think there were any Rights among the leading Moscow comrades. . . . It should rather be said that this was a case of a conciliationist tendency." Stalin did concede that "there was an organizational fight . . . inasmuch as the elections in Moscow are taking place on the basis of self-criticism and the regional active members have the right to change their secretaries." The joke was obvious; "laughter" was the response recorded in the minutes.[108] Uglanov's resistance collapsed completely in the face of the general secretary's attack. The Moscow Committee confessed the "mistake" in its work and approved without reservation the removals which had been ordered by the Central Committee.[109] The disgrace of Uglanov was confirmed by his subordinates' criticizing him to his face for "insufficient" recognition of his "errors."[110]

By this time rank-and-file party members in Moscow were openly demanding to know whether it was really true that Bukharin, Rykov, and Tomsky were to be classified in the Right deviation.[111] Stalin went so far as to "admit," as he put it, that "elements of a conciliatory nature toward the Right danger" had appeared in the Central Committee as well as in the Moscow organization, though he denied that there were any such attitudes

in the Politburo: "It is time to get rid of the gossip spread by the enemies of
the party and by the oppositionists of all kinds to the effect that there is a
Right deviation, or a conciliatory attitude toward it, in the Politburo of our
Central Committee."[112] Until February 1929, Stalin refused to admit even
a suggestion that his opponents Bukharin, Rykov, and Tomsky were connected with the Right deviation. By then he found it appropriate for people
other than "enemies of the party" to announce that the three men had been
indulging in oppositional activities for months prior to the Moscow crisis.

Alarmed by the Moscow debacle, when he had allowed Uglanov to be
crushed without a single public word in his defense, and fearful that Rykov
was making undue concessions to Stalin on economic policy, Bukharin
decided to challenge Stalin directly. To obstruct and delay the Opposition,
Stalin is said to have employed the GPU at one point to frustrate Bukharin's
efforts to fly back to Moscow for a Politburo meeting. Then the Right leaders
undertook an "offensive," insisted on a meeting of the Politburo, and presented demands for an organizational shake-up. To gain time, Stalin agreed
to the establishment of a Politburo subcommittee to consider such changes,
composed of himself, Molotov, Ordzhonikidze (chairman of the Central
Control Commission), Bukharin, and Rykov. But the subcommittee was not
convened, despite the demands of the Opposition. Bukharin exploded in
protest and walked out of a session of the Politburo.[113]

This gesture was followed by a concerted effort on the part of the Right
to express their concern over Stalin's power and policies. Bukharin, Rykov,
and Tomsky handed in their resignations from their respective official positions as chairman of the Comintern and editor of *Pravda,* premier, and trade-
union chief.[114] Stalin, so the report goes, received the statement of resignation
with trembling hands and turned pale.[115] Well he might, for nothing, at this
juncture, could have been more embarrassing to Stalin's plans than an open
declaration of opposition by the Right leaders. Hastily, Stalin made adroit
verbal concessions and secured unanimous Politburo agreement on the economic resolution which the November Plenum of the Central Committee
was to pass.[116] Piatakov remarked, "Stalin makes concessions about everything, no matter what, just so that he can maintain unanimity." This was no
mean feat, for, according to a Trotskyist report, Stalin risked losing some of
his own headstrong followers when he made tactical concessions to the
Right.[117] The resolution itself bore all the marks of compromise, to the point
of a patent contradiction on the priority of agriculture as against heavy industry.[118] It was sufficient, however, to induce Bukharin, Rykov, and Tomsky to
withdraw their resignations. Stalin exacted another unanimous declaration
of Politburo unity and sanctimoniously proclaimed to the Central Committee,
with Rykov's endorsement, that there were absolutely no differences at the
top level of the party leadership.[119]

While differences at the top were being hushed up, a steady campaign against the still largely anonymous Right deviation was kept up in the party press and in the party organizations. In the latter part of November 1928, the Central Committee assembled for a plenary session that was to be devoted largely to exorcising the Rightist menace. To explain to the plenum the complexities of simultaneously fighting criticism from the Rightists and from the Trotskyists, Stalin simply identified the two groups: "Wherever there is a Right deviation there must be a 'Left' deviation. The 'Left' deviation is the shadow of the Right deviation. . . . Those who incline toward Trotskyism are in fact Rights turned inside out, they are Rights concealing themselves behind 'Left' phrases." Leninism was the real Left, as Stalin went on to explain, "without quotation marks." Pointedly referring to the fate of the Trotskyists, Stalin warned those who might incline toward the Rightists that the current "ideological" campaign against them would be supplemented by "organizational penalties" if they should attempt to form a faction.[120]

Taking its cue from Stalin, the Central Committee condemned not only the Rightists and the conciliatory tendency toward them, but also any inclination to conciliate the conciliators: "The overcoming of these deviations presupposes a systematic struggle against Philistine unprincipled tolerance regarding . . . conciliationism." But confidence in defeating the great danger of the deviations was once again found in the assurance that they had no strength against "the unanimous Bolshevik resistance on the part of the whole party."[121]

The objective of eliminating actual or potential oppositionists was conveniently served by stressing the party organization's spurious campaign for "intraparty democracy," to permit, as the Central Committee resolved, "the replacement of any secretary and any leading party organ . . . in accordance with the real will of the organization."[122] It is not strange, in the light of the previous evolution of the party, that the wishes which triumphed on the local level were always in accord with the desires of the very top. This "democracy" was supplemented by the device of the party purge, ostensibly a measure to weed out substandard members, but also effective against malcontents. Such a purge was initiated by this plenum; it continued steadily through the first half of 1929 and was highly effective in cleaning out rank-and file supporters of the Right Opposition.[123]

All the party leaders, including those who were subsequently "exposed" as Right deviationists, gave full endorsement to this attack on the Rightist and conciliationist tendencies. The Bukharinists, in their effort to avoid being labeled an opposition group, strove desperately to maintain the pose of unanimity in the party leadership and gave unqualified public support to the organizational campaign against their own supporters. Rykov, addressing the Leningrad party organization on the work of the November Plenum, repeated Stalin's description of the Right tendency as a vacillation expressing kulak pressure; he reaffirmed the unity of the Politburo and spoke of going beyond the methods of ideological campaigning: "This supposes in the future, if the Right deviation takes form in the ideological respect and leaves the path of unconditional obedience to party decisions and party discipline, the application to them of other measures of struggle." [124]

Immediately after the November session of the Central Committee, the Moscow Committee met to complete its housecleaning. Molotov was now in charge of the proceedings, and he commended the Moscow organization for its staunch resistance to right-wing vacillations. [125] "Requests for resignation," as the current euphemism went, were accepted from Uglanov, his co-secretary Kotov, and two more members of the bureau of the Moscow Committee. Molotov and four others were confirmed as new members of the bureau, and Molotov, K. Y. Bauman, and K. B. Ukhanov (Kamenev's successor in the Moscow Soviet) were selected for the new Moscow secretariat. Comparable changes were carried out down the line; the overturn was complete and secure. [126]

THE RIGHT OPPOSITION IN THE TRADE UNIONS

After the defeat of the Rightists in the Moscow organization there remained one center of Opposition organizational strength: the trade-union bureaucracy headed by Tomsky. Despite Tomsky's long-standing hold on this organization, however, the Opposition stood no greater chance there. Stalin was master of the party, and no force outside the party structure could long survive in defiance of his will.

Both the political position and the industrial functions of the trade unions had remained relatively stable under Tomsky's leadership since his position had been confirmed in 1922. The activities of the unions were adjusted to the conditions of the NEP, to the extent that the unions' position largely paralleled that of unions under capitalism. While the unions continued to exercise the political function of a "transmission belt" to ensure party influence over nonparty industrial workers, and while the overall interest of the state in maintaining production was of course respected, the primary work of the unions was to represent the interests of the workers and to provide miscellaneous social services for them. The ideal of wage equalization continued to exert influence; Tomsky spoke in 1926 in favor of reducing wage differentials in the name of "elementary class justice." [127]

On the other hand, the administration of the trade unions could be termed democratic only by a considerable stretch of the imagination. With the full sanction of the party organization behind it, Tomsky's leadership was unchallengeable until he himself fell from party grace. The impression Tomsky gives of himself, at least as manifested in his public pronouncements, is that of a long-winded party hack. His interest in trade-union autonomy was certainly linked closely with personal power considerations. Tomsky was consequently vulnerable to the anti-"bureaucracy" tactics which the Stalinists were about to employ against him.

The reason for Tomsky's involvement in the Right Opposition seems to lie less with him than with Stalin, who was evidently determined to discredit all party figures who did not owe their positions to the general secretary by forcing them into opposition. To this end the super-industrialization program proved to be as effective in provoking overt resistance from the professional trade-unionists as it was in driving into a fatal opposition those who were alarmed over economic theory or political principle. The policy of fast development with stress on the building of heavy industry clearly implied a drastic change in the relationship of the trade unions to the workers and to the state. The function of protecting the workers during a regime of "state capitalism," which had been considered the unions' primary role since the resolution of the trade-union controversy in 1921, was now to go by the boards; maximizing labor productivity would henceforth be the unions' chief responsibility.[128] Tomsky was determined to oppose such a basic change in Soviet society, and, while the new orientation had not yet definitely crystallized, he wrote repeatedly of the continuing need for the trade unions to protect the workers against the state no less than against private capitalists.[129] His apprehensions were indeed justified, for after three years of the new regime of planned economy and muzzled trade unions, the average real wages of Soviet workers had declined 40 per cent or more.[130]

There were no definite indications of pressure upon the trade-union leadership until the late fall of 1928, although Tomsky had openly sided with the Right in the Politburo in July. He incurred Stalin's ire for "capitulationism and lack of faith."[131] However, the July elections for delegates to the next trade-union congress proceeded under the firm and effective control of the Rightist union leaders. Lozovsky, one of the few Stalinists then in the Central Trade Union Council, proposed new discussions and elections, but the majority voted this down.[132] The actual convening of the Eighth Trade Union Congress was delayed until December. This worked to the advantage of the Stalinists, who were spared a test of strength in the unions until they had destroyed the organized forces of the Right Opposition within the party machinery. In the meantime, there occurred a series of minor frictions involving the unions and other organizations and pointing to the impending clash.

As early as June 1928, a Central Committee statement made pointed reference to violations of "democracy" in the trade unions and to the need to combat bureaucratism there. The Communist Party fractions in the union organizations were called upon to assume this task—thus threatening to short-circuit the regular organizational channels of the unions which were in the hands of the Rightists.[133] Disagreements arose periodically between the unions and the managerial organizations over the union complaints that genuine collective bargaining was not being conducted.[134] The economic planners, seeking to alleviate their own problems, began to blame all the troubles of the economy on low labor productivity, an insinuation which the unionists angrily resented.[135]

The sharpest dispute in which the trade unions were involved before December 1928 was an altercation with the Komsomol, the repercussions of which animated much of the open debate at the Eighth Trade Union Congress. The focus of discord was the question of jurisdiction over young workers and their indoctrination. The *Komsomolskaya pravda* and the trade-union organ *Trud* (Labor) indulged in heated polemics, in which the charge of bureaucratism in the trade unions figured prominently. At the trade-union congress, the controversy reached the bitter stage, as Andrei Zhdanov, in his first major political role, spoke out to back the Komsomol and hinted that the whole trade-union leadership, including Tomsky, ought to be removed.[136]

After the Stalinists crushed the Opposition in the Moscow organization, they turned abruptly to deal with the trade-unionists. A quiet shake-up of the editorial staff of *Trud* deprived the Tomsky forces of their capacity to reply.[137] Then, while the Central Committee was still in session to dispose of the Moscow deviators, *Pravda* opened the offensive against the trade-unionists. In an article entitled, "Let Us Strengthen Party Leadership in the Trade Union Movement," the official organ piously protested against the curtailment of "self-criticism" and "democracy" in the unions, and the lack of ties between the union organizations and the membership. It went on to suggest the implications of the Stalinists' industrialization drive by pointing out the need to emphasize to the workers the connection that must prevail between wage increases and productivity increases.[138] Three days later another spokesman called for public discussion in preparation for the coming trade-union congress; he complained of a "conspiracy of silence" regarding the important issues of self-criticism and bureaucracy in the unions.[139] Simultaneously the Central Committee gave pointed attention to the trade-union question. It had suddenly discovered that the trade unions were failing to mobilize the working class sufficiently well for the new tasks of industrial construction and that they were suffering seriously from bureaucratism and a lack of contact with the masses.[140]

During late November and early December, while preparations for the Eighth Trade Union Congress were in progress, the atmosphere of extreme tension was maintained in the party organization and in the press. Agitational campaigns for "self-criticism," for the fight against "bureaucracy," and for the proper conclusion of collective agreements were vigorously waged. "Solidarity," "activeness," "militancy," were *Pravda*'s watchwords, as the campaign reached its peak.[141] With the mention of no names whatsoever, the issue was made clear to all concerned. Sufficient organizational pressure was brought to bear to give the Stalinists a comfortable majority for the decisive tests in the Communist Party group at the trade-union congress.

Aside from the Komsomol issue, the plenary sessions of the congress were singularly free of explicit controversy, considering the state of affairs in the party by that time. The atmosphere was nonetheless tense, and much can be read between the lines in the remarks of the speakers supporting or criticizing the Tomsky leadership—those who thought that "too much attention" was being given to "shortcomings," as against those who objected to undue stress on alleged achievements. Tomsky had to yield some ground on the bureaucratic theme and conceded in his report that the unions had become divorced from the workers and had given inadequate attention to their personal needs. His answer to this shortcoming, however, was equally unacceptable to the Stalinists: he urged efforts to make industrial administrators live up to their obligations and pay fair wages.[142] One revealing instance showed what could happen to a Communist leader who let himself be swayed by principle. A Trotskyist holdover on the Central Trade Union Council tried to present a resolution and was howled down. Tomsky thereupon rose to admonish the delegates for denying the floor to a man whose official status traditionally entitled him to speak before the congress. The matter was then put to a vote and Tomsky lost, as the whole congress, excepting four delegates opposed and two abstaining, called for the deviator to be silenced.[143]

The decisive steps at the congress were taken not in the open sessions, but by the delegates who met as the Communist Party fraction behind closed doors on the last day of the congress. In the resolution pushed through the party meeting with a "unanimous" vote there was a tone distinctly different from the regular congress proceedings: it was the new harsh voice of Stalinism. High-tempo industrialization was endorsed, while "panicky assertions about the degradation of agriculture" were denounced. Maximum effort on the part of everyone was demanded, and the "purely worker" view of the unions was repudiated: "The tasks of overcoming the difficulties of the reconstruction period demand much more participation of the trade unions in all branches of socialist construction, and more mobilization than ever before of the working masses and the village toilers for the active solution of the next tasks of socialism."[144]

Corresponding to the new line were the changes in union personnel which the Communist fraction meeting ordered. Five Stalinist party leaders —Rudzutak, Ordzhonikidze, Kuibyshev, Kaganovich, and Zhdanov—were elected to the Central Trade Union Council.[145] Tomsky's supporters concentrated their efforts on resisting the election of Kaganovich because he was a member of the party Secretariat and evidently the most unpopular of Stalin's leading aides, but the attempt failed completely.[146] Tomsky complained that the inclusion of Kaganovich in the Central Trade Union Coun-

cil had created a "double center" in the organization. He vented his disgust
by repeating the threat which he had successfully used in November, to resign as chairman of the council. This time Tomsky simply refused to continue his work in the council, despite the rejection of his resignation.[147]
Vainly the Right leaders protested the intrusion of the party apparatus into
the trade-union organization as a "Trotskyist shake-up of the trade unions."
In return Tomsky, like Bukharin, was accused (not without some truth) of
having tried to make a "feudal principality" out of his trade-union domain.[148]

In April 1929, the Central Committee called for Tomsky's formal removal as trade-union head, and on June 2, 1929, Tomsky and his supporters
were eliminated from the membership of the Central Trade Union Council.[149] Tomsky was replaced as chairman by a reliable Stalinist, Nikolai
Mikhailovich Shvernik, who, except for his service as nominal head of state
(chairman of the Presidium of the Supreme Soviet) from 1946 to 1953,
headed the Soviet trade unions continuously until his retirement in March
1956.[150]

With the organizational triumph of the Stalinists, the productivity function of the trade unions became unquestioned doctrine. In April 1929, the
Central Committee commanded the unions to assume "a decisive role in the
work of building socialist industry, raising the productivity of labor and
labor discipline, in the organization of the productive initiative of the working class and of socialist emulation, and also of the class education of the
new strata of the proletariat."[151] Any lingering attachment to the earlier
policy came under attack in almost the same terms with which Lenin had
launched his Bolshevik philosophy. "Face to production," was the trade-
union slogan for the new era, with "a decisive struggle against elements of
trade unionism and opportunism in the trade-union movement."[152] The
NEP was clearly at an end.

THE ISSUE OF ECONOMIC PLANNING

While Stalin was destroying the foothold of the Right Opposition in the
party organization and in the trade unions, the policy cleavage between his
forces and the Right grew wider. From the specific issue of the kulaks and
the grain problem the controversy broadened to include the most general
problems of economic life and the country's future prospects. Ramifications
of the controversy reached to the core of Marxian doctrine and into the most
abstruse philosophical matters.

The political origins of the industrialization policy formulated by the
Stalinists late in 1928 are abundantly clear when the problem is viewed in
the context of the debates of 1925–1927. The issues were essentially the same,
with the Stalinists taking the position of Preobrazhensky and the Trotskyists
against the Rightists who adhered to the earlier official position. Stalin's new
affinity with the former Leftist program of intensive planned industrializa-

tion at the expense of the peasantry was only emphasized by the vigorous efforts which he made to refute the insinuation that he was merely copying the Trotskyist policy two years too late.[153] (As late as November 1928, the charge "super-industrialist" was still being hurled at the Trotskyists.[154]) The "capitulations" of exiled Trotskyists who decided that Stalin's program was close enough to their own show clearly enough how the new line actually appeared (see Chapter 14). In part, Stalin's espousal of the Leftist program was an acknowledgment of the country's economic impasse as the Left Opposition had analyzed it. His immediate interest in industrialization, however, was mainly political. It was a device to provoke the Rightists into making protests that could be called deviation.

While the Right-Left political battle raged in 1926 and 1927 over the speed of industrialization, a parallel cleavage developed among the professional economists. Two distinct conceptions of the nature of planning had emerged by 1927, represented respectively by the "geneticists" and the "teleologists." The geneticists stressed the work of predicting uncontrollable economic tendencies, and adapting plans accordingly, while the teleologists argued that the laws of economics could be transcended by the action of the socialist state. "Our task is not to study economics but to change it," wrote the leading professional exponent of the latter view, S. G. Strumilin, in a paraphrase of Marx. "We are bound by no laws. There are no fortresses which Bolsheviks cannot storm"—a slogan which Stalin was later to plagiarize. "The question of tempo is subject to decision by human beings."[155]

Contrary to the impression created by Stalinist denunciations, this attitude was not entirely rejected by the geneticists. They and the Bukharinist wing of the party were quite prepared to endorse extensively planned governmental economic effort as long as it remained within the limits of feasibility which circumstances imposed. Vladimir Bazarov, one of the leading economists in the State Planning Commission (Gosplan) until 1928, pointed out as early as 1924 that the planning of production in state-owned industry could and should proceed according to the teleological conception. Outside the nationalized sector of the economy, however, and specifically in agriculture, the prospects for economic development would have to be viewed genetically.[156] Owing to the dictates of proportionality, this meant a strict natural limit on the possible rate of industrial growth in Russia. "We are not determinists," affirmed the geneticists in the course of the debate, "but we believe that economic laws hold sway even in Soviet Russia. In working out the plan our first task is to take account of reality and its laws."[157]

The beginnings of the First Five Year Plan were laid down in the State Planning Commission between 1925 and 1928. Within the confines of the geneticist assumption about the agricultural limitations on Russia's economic development, substantial progress was made in the development of sets of "control figures." By 1928 these actually served to guide the country's annual economic activity. Longer projections were embodied in the so-called perspective plans of 1926 and 1927, though these had no practical import.[158] This development of the idea of long-range planning confirmed the readiness of the Stalin-Bukharin leadership to move toward a program of systematic state-directed economic development at the same time that they were attacking the Trotskyists as super-industrializers.

General party sanction for a five-year plan of development was given by the Fifteenth Party Congress, which endorsed the theses prepared by Rykov. Caution and the maintenance of balance were still prevailing themes, however. Rykov took special care to note how the economic plan would necessarily be limited by defects of organization and accounting and by the uncertainties of the harvest and of foreign-trade conditions.[159]

While Gosplan wrestled with the formulation of a plan that would take all such contingencies into account, a rival organization was moving into the planning field. This was the Supreme Economic Council (which actually functioned as the commissariat of industry), headed since 1926 by Kuibyshev, the former chairman of the Central Control Commission and a dedicated, if somewhat colorless, Stalinist.[160] Under Kuibyshev, the Supreme Economic Council proceeded to draw up its own drafts of a five-year plan, with considerably more emphasis on heavy industry. "Castles in air," scoffed the Gosplan economists.[161] In May 1928, the Supreme Economic Council presented its plan, which called for an industrial expansion on the order of 130 per cent in five years. Gosplan immediately protested that this proposal disregarded every sort of limit, natural, technical, and social. In turn, Gosplan presented its own plan in August 1928, with two variants: conservative and optimal. The latter envisaged an industrial growth of about 90 per cent for the five-year period.[162] But the cleavage in the party leadership was already a fact; considerations other than economic were to play a decisive role in the resolution of the complicated question of planning.

After the Central Committee plenum of July 1928, questions of economic policy were hopelessly intertwined with the contest between the Stalinists and the Bukharinists over control of the party. The Stalinists began to hint at a more drastic economic approach in the evident hope of forcing the Rightists to oppose the changes and make themselves easy targets. Such a maneuver was represented by the remarks of Kaganovich at the July Plenum on the limitations of price manipulation and the offensive against the kulaks. By August, having improved their organizational position, the Stalinists began to tighten their line, with emphasis on poor-peasant organizations and progress toward collectivization.[163] Molotov cautioned against any measure which might benefit the kulaks as "an essentially petty-bourgeois, or if you will, 'peasantophile' policy, which leads, in substance, to rejection of the leading role of the proletariat in the worker-peasant alliance."[164] These warnings against leniency were followed in mid-August by the discovery—somewhat contrived—of a new grain crisis. Thereafter, a state of constant alarm over the agricultural situation was maintained while the new Stalinist economic line was formulated and the Rightists in Moscow were purged. Genuine or artificial, the grain problem served the obvious purpose of magnifying the potential dangers which the party leadership ascribed to the views of the still vaguely defined right wing.

Aside from political pyrotechnics, the party's agricultural policy continued for a time to follow the earlier orthodoxy defended by the Rightists. A variety of official statements throughout the fall of 1928 stressed the importance of agriculture as the base for the program of intensive industrialization. The economic resolution of the November Plenum of the Central Committee, for instance, while taking care to reject the charge (made by Frumkin) that agriculture was actually retrogressing, conceded that the lag in agricultural development was the country's central economic problem.[165] On the other hand, new devices for raising the level of agriculture were receiving increased attention—in particular, the accelerated formation of collective and state farms. These, it was argued, would serve as centers for the propagation of modern techniques and socialist forms of organization, and would moreover provide nuclei for waging class warfare against the kulaks. Without any abrupt change of policy, ominous signs of the impending storm were building up.

A sharper turn was made with respect to industry. Gosplan, with the qualms of its economists, was largely ignored. Its August plan was by-passed on the grounds, Kuibyshev later explained, that it was "defective" and "did not fully calculate our resources." The Supreme Economic Council gave its planners directives to rework the plan.[166] At the same time, following up its high-tempo May plan, the Supreme Economic Council presented detailed control figures to govern the economy during the harvest-to-harvest accounting year 1928–1929. Kuibyshev, speaking as if he had formal party endorsement, called on all enterprises to cooperate in working out the final plan.[167] Criticism of the stepped-up tempo of industrialization was condemned in advance.

Kuibyshev's speech to the Leningrad party organization on September 19 was the firmest declaration yet heard of a determination to drive ahead and to eliminate any discontent engendered by the drive. "We must be fully aware," Kuibyshev asserted, "that it would be wrong from every point of view to speak of a reduction of the rate of industrialization. . . . We are told we are 'overindustrializing,' and 'biting off more than we can chew.'" This was a patent reference to the warnings from the Bukharin-Rykov group —but the objection was overruled: "Any careful student of our economy will, I am sure, agree with me that the most serious disproportion . . . is the one between the output of the means of production and the requirements of the country."[168] The vindication of Preobrazhensky could not have been more explicit. It would take uncanny dialectical subtlety to distinguish between the new Stalinist analysis and the warnings which the Left Opposition had been making for years.

Kuibyshev's statement does not appear to have evoked an immediate chorus of responses, and this suggests that it was still only a trial balloon. The fervor with which Kuibyshev spoke on repeated occasions in the fall of 1928 for the policy of intensive industrialization indicates that he was animated by a genuine "super-industrializing" enthusiasm, and he may well have advanced the program on his own initiative. It was his good fortune that his program appealed to Stalin as a means for making the Rightists look like deviators.

Kuibyshev's remarks in September clearly indicated that the Stalinists' desire for a faster tempo had encountered resistance. Most dramatically this opposition was expressed by Bukharin himself, in his "Notes of an Economist," published in *Pravda* on September 30. Bukharin complained that the plan drawn up by the Supreme Economic Council violated the directives of the Fifteenth Congress in several important respects—it neglected the need for reserves, failed to resolve the consumer-goods shortage, and proposed a dangerously excessive rate of investment. "The overstraining in capital expenditure," he warned, "will ultimately *retard the speed of development.*"[169]

Bukharin's article was immediately censured by the Stalinist majority in the Politburo for expressing "a whole series of disputed questions," and the party apparatus was evidently instructed to discourage members from reading it.[170] Shortly afterwards, at the climax of the organizational struggle in Moscow, an official answer to Bukharin's plea for observing the conditions of economic equilibrium was published. A radically new view of the nature of economics and of the relation between economic activity and political force was implied in this statement by the Central Committee: "In view of our technical backwardness it is impossible to develop industry at such a rate that it does not lag behind the capitalist countries, but reaches and overtakes them . . . without the greatest exertion of the means and forces of the country, without great perseverance, without iron discipline of the proletarian ranks."[171] Thus, according to the new economics, the function of the planning authority is not simply to allocate resources but to evoke effort, whether through exhortation or by force. The essence of the system was the application of military discipline to *create* economic resources where they otherwise would not exist. Here we have the heart of the Stalinist planned economy based upon the omnipotence of government. This approach to economic development should not be underrated; it is responsible for the undeniably immense achievements of the Soviet economic system since 1929, and it is today a serious contender for the destiny of the vast underdeveloped portions of the globe.

It was clearly seen by the Stalinists that the idea of forced-draft development would immediately evoke criticism, and they took care to mobilize all the carefully accumulated alarm over the Right deviation for use against potential dissidents:

The difficulties arising on this path—the straining of our material resources, the shortage of goods, etc.—create certain vacillations both in some strata of the working class and in some sections of our party. On this basis there sometimes arise inclinations toward a revision of the course of the party, toward a slowing down of the rate of development of industry in general and heavy industry in particular. In place of a Bolshevik overcoming of the difficulties there is in this manner a flight from them.[172]

In justification of the new line, the nationalist theme came increasingly to the fore. Speaking to the plenum of the Central Committee in November 1928, Stalin gave new emphasis to the goal of overtaking the capitalist countries and putting an end to "the age-long backwardness of our country."[173] Instead of being the product of capitalistic development, as Marx conceived it, Stalin's socialism was an alternative, a system for forcibly accelerating the development of those areas left behind in the progress of the industrial West.

Meanwhile, the planners in the Supreme Economic Council produced a new draft for the five-year plan, but this one too failed to measure up to the increasingly ambitious standards laid down by the Stalinist leadership.[174] The new plan, completed in October, was withheld, according to Kuibyshev, because "it would incorrectly orient the whole working mass, the party, the trade unions, and the managers, about the possibilities which we have concerning further development."[175] While the economists were once again trying to write a satisfactory draft for the five-year plan, the Central Committee at its November session gave its official approval to the August control figures of the Supreme Economic Council as the economic plan for the fiscal year 1928–1929.[176] Curiously, this was later taken as the beginning date of the First Five Year Plan, though at the time no complete plan had yet been approved. Not until May 1929 was a plan ready for endorsement by an official party gathering, when, with bland indifference to logic, it was simply back-dated to October 1928.

The leaders of the Right Opposition undoubtedly stood on principle as they tried to resist the policy innovations of the Stalinists in the fall of 1928. Bukharin, for all his political error and naiveté, was an honest and serious thinker in matters of theory. He and his philosophical followers were the last genuine practicing Marxists in Soviet Russia. But their devotion to a definite theoretical position only made the task of the Stalinists easier in contriving to have the Rightists marked off as a group with distinctly deviant ideas.

As for Rykov and Tomsky, opportunism and caution had reached the point where they became matters of principle. Both had been in the right wing of the party, almost without interruption, from the time they became members; temperamental predispositions were probably at the root of this in both cases. Their softness had a positive side, to be sure—Rykov's condemnation of the excesses against the peasants and Tomsky's interest in the welfare of the workers appear to have been sincere. Their circumspection, whatever its foundation, had so wedded them to the policies of the NEP that it transcended the course which political opportunism would dictate, that of joining the Stalin camp. Like Zinoviev and Kamenev in 1917, Rykov and Tomsky, if not Bukharin, put themselves in opposition to Stalin's new revolution primarily because they thought it would fail.

Bukharin's alarm over the new direction of economic policy stemmed from the same proposition which he had formulated when the controversy with the Zinovievists was brewing in 1925. Socialism in one country was the Russian reality, but its success hinged on the maintenance of peasant support for the proletarian dictatorship. In one of the foreboding articles published just before his downfall, Bukharin reiterated this assertion: "If this especially favorable combination of class forces is *removed,* then the whole basis for developing the *socialist* revolution in our country will collapse."[177] Bukharin derived further grounds for alarm from the anarchistic political philosophy upon which he had drawn from time to time. Political power and the bureaucratic organization of social life, according to his prerevolutionary views, were at best necessary evils. In his 1916 article, "The Theory of the Imperialist State," he warned of a general European trend toward "militaristic state capitalism," a totalitarian order in which economic life and every other kind of activity would be directly administered by an all-embracing governmental bureaucracy, "a new Leviathan, in comparison with which the fantasy of Thomas Hobbes seems like child's play." It was Bukharin's fervent expectation that the socialist revolution would put an end to this trend.[178]

Bukharin never abandoned this attitude toward the capitalist world. Near the end of his political career he expressed it in the idea of "organized capitalism," wherein governmental or monopolistic controls were overcoming the anarchy of individual enterprise. The ultimate elaboration of this concept of bureaucratized society, however, was to extend it, as a fearful possibility, to Soviet Russia as well. Bukharin, like Trotsky, was driven by the logic of his oppositionist situation to a theory of the bureaucratic degeneration of socialism. As early as March 1918, Bukharin and his Left Communist associates had expressed the fear that the revolution might, under certain conditions, lose its socialist character. Periodically Bukharin returned to this line of thought, particularly in 1922 in a speech before the Fourth Comintern Congress (which he made use of again in September 1928, thus presumably shielding himself by its time-tested orthodoxy). His argument centered on the question of how much of an organizational effort the proletariat could undertake in reconstructing society and directing economic activity:

If it takes too much upon itself, it is obliged to create a colossal *administrative apparatus*. To perform the economic functions of the small producers, small peasants, etc., it needs too many employees and administrators. The attempt to replace all these small people with state officials [*chinovniki*]—call them what you want, they are in fact state officials—begets such a colossal apparatus that the expenditure for its maintenance is incomparably more significant than the unproductive expenses which appear in consequence of the anarchistic conditions of small production; as a result, this whole form of administration, the whole economic apparatus of the proletarian state, does not facilitate, but only *hinders the development of the forces of production*. In reality it leads to the direct opposite of what it is supposed to do, and for this reason iron necessity compels the proletariat to destroy such an apparatus. . . . If the proletariat does not do it, other forces will overthrow its rule.[179]

When his dispute with Stalin was coming to a climax in mid-1928, Bukharin repeated the antibureaucratic theme. At the July Central Committee meeting he made it the concluding point of his speech, with a strong warning against the overcentralization that stifled initiative and induced provincialism.[180] In guarded terms he continued to express his concern through the medium of three articles published in *Pravda*. The first, and most substantial, was his "Notes of an Economist" of September 1928. Here, in addition to his defense of economic equilibrium, Bukharin returned to the antibureaucratic theme: "We are *much too* centralized. We must ask ourselves whether we cannot take a few steps in the direction of Lenin's Commune state." Thus, for Bukharin, as for Lenin in 1923, the anarchistic ideal of "State and Revolution" regained its attractiveness when he began to feel himself out of touch with the direction of affairs and thus was led to perceive an impending perversion of the revolutionary program.

The occasion of Bukharin's next warning was the fifth anniversary of Lenin's death, for which he published an article in *Pravda* under the title, "The Political Testament of Lenin."[181] Referring to Lenin's last articles and the admonitions they contained, Bukharin emphasized the necessity for further cultural development of the masses and the need to accomplish this social transformation without recourse to bureaucratic devices: "Lenin . . . advances the slogan, *all possible associations of workers, avoiding by all means their bureaucratization.*" The proletarian state, Bukharin asserted, should "constitute a certain stage in the transition to the state-commune, from which we are still, unfortunately, very, very far away. Thus, Vladimir Ilich asks: if the question of the state apparatus stands thus, how can we fix it, where should we turn, what sort of levers should we take hold of? And he gives back a significant formulation. He says: we should turn to the deep historical source of the dictatorship; and this deepest source is 'the progressive workers.' " That Bukharin was appealing to Lenin to support a call for a political overturn is easy to deduce; but no one knew better how to manipulate that "deepest source" of the dictatorship than the general secretary, for whom the votes of the "progressive workers" had always been the most reliably disciplined support.

Bukharin had to phrase his last article as an independent thinker in a roundabout fashion. It took the form of a book review on the work of a little-known German sociologist, Bente by name, whose comments on the contemporary evolution of the institutions of capitalism remarkably paralleled Bukharin's own emphasis on the drawbacks of excessive bureaucracy and centralization.[182] "The people for the official, and not the official for the people"—such was the evil against which Bukharin set himself. "Mass participation" was his socialist panacea, to be "the basic guarantee against a bureaucratic transformation of the cadre group." But the art of mass manipulation, highly developed by the Secretariat with Bukharin's connivance, effectively eliminated such a defense. The totalitarian state was well on its way to perfection.

The foundation of Bukharin's protest against the new economic line of the Stalinists, as it had been against the program of the Trotskyists, was his theory of equilibrium, stated most fully in his "Notes of an Economist." Equilibrium was not a static ideal; to Bukharin it meant a condition under which economic development would in the long run be fastest and easiest. Equilibrium was not automatic; he cited Marx to argue that economic crises under capitalism were due to the failure to maintain equilibrium. Economic planning by a socialist regime was to consist primarily in finding out what had to be done to maintain equilibrium: "The conditions for the correct coordination of the various spheres of production, or, in other words, the conditions of *dynamic economic equilibrium,* may be ascertained. This is the essential part of the task of working out . . . a consciously drawn-up plan, which is at the same time a prognosis and a directive." The economic planner, we might say, could work only like the physician with his patient—diagnose the ills, seek out remedies, and try to facilitate the natural process of healing. For Bukharin there existed certain hard facts (or what Marxists might call "objective circumstances")—the "conditions of equilibrium." Whether or not to admit the existence of such obstacles was the crux of the economic debate. Failure to recognize the limitations imposed by the country's material situation was, in Bukharin's eyes, the primary cause of economic dislocations. Economic planning meant the successful observation of the conditions of equilibrium, not their defiance: "Those who believe that the growth of planned economy brings with it the possibility . . . of working just as one desires to work, do not understand the ABC's of economic science."

Translated into specific terms for Russia, equilibrium meant above all the proper balance between industry and agriculture, and the conditions for undisrupted growth required in particular the development of agriculture as the basis for industrial expansion. "The greatest sustained speed," Bukharin argued, "is obtained by a combination in which industry develops on the basis afforded by a *rapidly growing* agriculture. . . . The Trotskyists do not grasp the fact that the development of industry is dependent on the development of agriculture." To this attack on the philosophy of exploiting the peasantry in order to finance industry, one of the Trotskyists, Smilga, replied from his Siberian exile: "Bukharin long ago forgot how to think and write like a Leninist. . . . The twentieth-century physiocrat Bukharin reasons not like a Marxist but like a genuine descendant of Slavophilic reaction."[183] Bukharin's deference toward the peasantry was not based, however, on sentiment, but on a central assumption about the nature of economic life—the same that governed the planning work of the genetic economists.

Paradoxical as it may seem, Bukharin, like Marx before him, was something of a liberal in his economic views. His analysis proceeded from the postulate of the classical economists that society is made up of a host of independent units, whose economic performance cannot effectively be governed by direct compulsion. Applied to the agricultural sector of the Russian economy, this model of atomistic capitalism was obviously appropriate. The Gosplan economists made this very point: economic laws such as supply and demand unquestionably held sway, and agricultural development could be accomplished only through such forms of indirect state intervention as price manipulations. The Stalinists also took cognizance of this state of affairs, though it only fortified their determination to put an end to such "anarchy" by collectivizing agriculture. But Bukharin went further in the direction of classical economics; he put the problem of the development of state-owned industry in the same light. The essence of the right-wing approach was that industry would have to develop in response to the monetary demand for its product; consumer-goods industry would respond in the first instance to the needs of a prosperous peasantry, while heavy industry would develop in answer to the need for expanding the facilities for the production of consumer goods.

Bukharin did not dispute the ideal of collectivization, but his espousal of the goal was conditioned by an insistence on gradualness and justified as a long-term system for increasing the productivity of agriculture. Reliance on compulsion rather than on a balance of economic accomplishment and reward were steadfastly rejected as economically disastrous: "One thing is clear: if any branch of production fails to receive back systematically the costs of production, plus a certain addition corresponding to a *part* of the surplus labor, to serve as a source of increased reproduction, then it stagnates or *declines*."[184]

Bukharin's economic thought, premised on a recognition of unpleasant realities and at the same time making human welfare a cardinal concern, stands in dramatic contrast to the philosophy being worked out by the party leadership. The Stalinists demanded not the recognition of natural limitations but direct assaults upon them, regardless of the cost. Molotov said of the Rightist attitude, before the Bukharinists were openly attacked, "The Right deviation leads to a leveling down to these 'tight spots,' instead of mobilizing the forces of the working class for the purpose of surmounting the obstacles in the path of industrialization."[185] The meaning of the new approach was deliberate political action to squeeze from society the resources needed by the state to realize its objectives. "Military-feudal exploitation," the Rightists termed the new system as it swung into action.[186] It accorded more with the economics of Ivan the Terrible than with those of Karl Marx.

The reflection of the party split in the work of economic planning reached the point of crisis in the winter of 1928–29. The right-wing Gosplan could not overcome its scruples and repeatedly failed to give the party leadership what was wanted, while the Supreme Economic Council went forging ahead with ever more optimistic visions. "Our planning," read a statement of the latter organization, "must include not only forecasting, not only the discovery of economic laws, but a creative, deliberate building of a socialist economy."[187] This was the teleological approach with a vengeance.

At the end of November 1928, too late for the Central Committee to act upon it, the planners in the Supreme Economic Council finally produced an optimal five-year plan which was acceptable to the leadership. The draft had been completed under such pressure for haste that Kuibyshev was unable to carry out his promise to go through the motions of "mass participation" in the preparation of the plan.[188] According to this new version, industrial investment would not only be undertaken at a high rate, but the percentage of the national income devoted to it would increase, year after year, through the five-year period.[189] The party leadership immediately turned, for a convenient forum, to the Eighth Trade Union Congress, and Kuibyshev appeared there to expound at great length the virtues of the new plan, which excluded all previous versions—"Only this variant can be placed under consideration."[190] Brought to heel by party pressure, the trade-unionists gave their endorsement to the plan.[191] Gosplan still remained critical. Bazarov warned, with courage that was remarkable at this late date, "Here there can be the worst results, here you can get such a clearly irrational distribution of resources as will discredit the whole idea of industrialization."[192]

By the early months of 1929, the party leadership was locked in bitter controversy with Bukharin, Rykov, and Tomsky. The Stalinists became unalterably committed to the highest conceivable speed of economic development, if only to assure that the Right would be branded as fainthearted deviators. At the same time they accused the Rightist critics of playing politics—compunctions about economic equilibrium were dismissed as "a mere convenient screen for political rather than methodological attacks."[193]

In the meantime, the uncooperative economists were disposed of. Quietly but thoroughly Gosplan was purged; everyone associated with the geneticist position was ousted. The planning efforts already accomplished were rejected for following the "wrong class approach," and the party leadership proclaimed the exclusive orthodoxy of the "purposive-teleological method."[194] A number of the former Gosplan economists, especially those who had originally been associated with the Mensheviks, were involved on charges of "sabotage" in the "Industrial Party" trial of 1930 and the Menshevik trial of 1931.[195] But the shake-up did not stop here. The Stalinist drive for heavy industrial development transcended even what the teleological economists thought feasible, and they in their turn were thrust aside into academic positions.[196]

In retrospect, the real planning controversy was not between the genetic and the teleological economists in Gosplan. The differences here were neither wide nor sharp. The real contest was between all the economists and Gosplan as a whole, backed by the Right Opposition leaders, on the one hand, against the politicians of the Supreme Economic Council and the party Secretariat. It was a choice between the science of economics and the art of dictatorship. This explains why the academic controversy over the methodology of economic planning was never resolved. It simply lapsed. When the genetic theory was condemned there was nothing left to take its place; the Soviet regime still has no overall theory of economic planning.[197] Soviet discussion of planning methods since the onset of the five-year plans has been confined to the elaboration of directives handed down by political authority.[198] At that level it became entirely a matter of wish and command. Party decisions and the effectiveness of their execution were frankly acknowledged to be more important than any of the mathematical subtleties of a scientific plan.[199]

In March 1929, the renovated Gosplan finally produced a full-dress plan with two complete variants. The times were changing fast, however; Kuibyshev now replied, "The optimal variant of the five-year plan is the plan for building socialism."[200] The Rightists protested and vainly proposed alternatives—Rykov suggested a "middle variant" and a subsidiary two-year program for agriculture. This brought down on him the charge that he opposed the five-year plan and defended the kulaks.[201]

The First Five Year Plan was finally approved as official party policy at the Sixteenth Party Conference in April 1929, and confirmed in May by the Council of People's Commissars and the Congress of Soviets. The new optimal variant was declared to have been in effect as of October of the previous year.[202] The role of chance was dismissed by governmental decree. Any concern for such bothersome economic considerations as statistical relationships or laws of equilibrium was swept aside as "class-alien." The new mentality was epitomized in the slogan, "There are no objective obstacles—obstacles must be overcome."[203] Speaking at the Seventeenth Party Congress in 1934, Stalin declared that "objective conditions" could no longer be admitted as factors limiting the will of the Soviet government.[204] Henceforth, there was no excuse for failure—treason could be the only explanation.

THE PHILOSOPHICAL CONTROVERSY

While Stalin's supporters were working out their new economic program, the doctrinal implications of the new approach were being debated by Soviet philosophers. At the opportune moment the party leadership found the interpretations it desired, gave them official sanction, and used them as one more weapon with which to beat the Bukharinists. The philosophical controversy was important, however, not merely as a step in the ideological campaign against the Right Opposition. It revealed a radically new official mentality, involving a substantially different interpretation of the tenets of Marxism. The conventional deterministic reading of the Marxian philosophy of history was replaced by a doctrine, not without a certain foundation in the writings of Marx himself, which put primary stress on the power of voluntaristic forces—individual will and governmental coercion—to effect fundamental social changes in defiance of material circumstances and the "laws" of history. The complex of ideas which guided the Soviet regime during the storm and stress of the collectivization and First Five Year Plan era was established in the course of this doctrinal evolution of 1928–1929; it has continued to give to both Soviet thought and Soviet political practice an aspect utterly different from that of the revolutionary era.

The background of the philosophical controversy was a nonpolitical though acrimonious debate which had been going on among Soviet philosophers since the middle twenties. The issue between the opposing sides, the "mechanists" and the "dialecticians," as they were styled, boiled down to the question of continuity or discontinuity in the organization of nature. The mechanists, who represented the initially prevailing outlook and who enjoyed the support of most natural scientists, stressed the continuity in developmental processes and the links between the various levels of phenomena (physical, biological, mental, and so on). The dialecticians, on the contrary, emphasized the qualitative jumps in development and the disparities between the different levels of phenomena; it was their contention that the higher organization of nature involved entirely new orders of lawfulness. In their scheme, mental phenomena, for example, could not be reduced to and explained solely in terms of the physical. Nor could the socialist economic system be adequately treated according to the "laws" of capitalist economics.

Between 1925 and 1928 the dialecticians, led by A. M. Deborin and A. S. Martynov (two former Mensheviks), attracted increasing attention, but in keeping with its pre-Stalinist reserve the party did not venture to take sides in the issue. As late as March 1928, a writer in *Pravda* could make the impartial complaint that neither faction was making its philosophy sufficiently comprehensible to the masses.[205] The situation was radically changed with the outbreak of dissension between the Stalinists and the Right Opposition. Casting about for issues to use against the Right, and for theories to uphold the new policies which they were contriving, the Stalinist leadership seized upon the doctrines of the dialectical philosophers as an ideal rationalization. There was, in fact, a close correspondence between the genetic-teleological controversy in economics and the mechanist-dialectician debate in philosophy. The idea of a dialectical "jump" to a new order of lawfulness was precisely the kind of argument needed to justify economic plans which flaunted the laws appealed to by the cautious economists. Moreover, in the dialectical view of the transition from one system to another, there was room for a decisive part to be played by leading personalities, and this suited Stalin's plans perfectly. Finally, the philosophical issue was one easily applicable to the needs of factional politics because Bukharin had explicitly associated himself with the mechanist position in his theoretical writings.

The cleavage between the two points of view, both in philosophy and in politics, can be traced to a fundamental ambivalence in Marxism.[206] This is the paradoxical combination of determinism, which declares the proletarian revolution and socialism to be inevitable, and voluntarism, which exhorts people to strive desperately for the victory. Up to the mid-1920s, the deterministic emphasis officially prevailed, but voluntarism was increasingly implied in the role played by the Bolshevik Party and its leaders. The dialecticians responded to this discrepancy between theory and practice by rejecting the mechanistic determination of events and stressing discontinuous jumps in historical development as elsewhere in nature. The new philosophy began to assert the independent historical role of human consciousness and the power of purpose (particularly Bolshevik purpose) over the deterministically analyzed conditions of society.

In April 1929, when the Right Opposition had been rendered harmless but was not yet subject to public disgrace, the party leadership took the offensive on the philosophical front. The official nod was given to the dialectical school of thought, and at a conference of "Marxist-Leninist Scientific Research Institutions" the mechanists were duly condemned for a "clear departure from the Marxist-Leninist philosophical position."[207] The dialectical view was enjoined on all loyal Communists, with particular stress on its application in rooting out bourgeois influences in science. The edifice of Stalinist thought control was rising rapidly.

The immediate advantage which the Stalinists derived from this incursion into philosophy was to set up the category of criminal deviation in this field. At the opportune moment, the Right Opposition leaders were herded into it, after the public denunciation of Bukharin in August 1929.

The focus of the charges against Bukharin which then filled the party's theoretical press was his theory of equilibrium, both as a general philosophical concept and as an approach to economic problems.[208] Everything which preceded the new Stalinist interpretation was dismissed as a "revision" of Marxism. The theory of equilibrium was held responsible for Bukharin's idea of "organized capitalism" and his overemphasis on the stability of the capitalist world. Allegedly it caused Bukharin to neglect the class struggle and to believe that the kulaks could be converted to socialism. Said Stalin, "it is not difficult to understand that this theory has nothing in common with Leninism. It is not difficult to understand that this theory objectively has the aim of defending the position of the individual peasant farm, of arming the kulak elements with a 'new' theoretical weapon in their struggle with the collective farms."[209] Not maintenance of equilibrium, but action to smash the existing equilibrium, was the Stalinist demand.

As philosophy was mobilized for political purposes, all trace of academic restraint and respect for accuracy disappeared. The dialecticians as a group appear to have been ambitious mediocrities angling for party support, and as soon as they received it they tore into the defenders of the right-wing and mechanist positions with wild invective and fanatic heresy hunting. Most independent accounts of the controversy give the exponents of the official line too much credit: there was little philosophical substance, and less logic, in their case. What the dialectical philosophers, like the Stalinist economists, implicitly stood for was blind defiance of rational analysis wherever it balked the party. Their victory was won by political pressure alone. But Soviet justice is impartial: within a year, the dialecticians were in turn condemned as anti-Marxist deviators, and their place was filled with hacks who had no purpose at all except to glorify the Leader.

The philosophical controversy represents the culmination of the process of doctrinal reinterpretation through the medium of party politics, and of the pursuit of political advantage with the help of doctrinal reinterpretation. With the final defeat of all opposition, Stalin had also overcome the limitations of Marxian theory. Henceforth he was free to rule as he pleased, while satisfying himself that every step was the logical implementation of Marxism-Leninism. Reinterpretation of ideology was henceforth to be obstructed neither by scruples about the truth nor by voices of criticism. With the fall of the Right, the last political and intellectual obstacles to Stalin's dictatorship were removed.

THE OPEN BREAK AND THE DISGRACE OF THE RIGHT

The history of the Right Opposition offers the singular spectacle of a political group's being defeated first and attacked afterwards. Stalin carefully avoided public top-level debate until he had disarmed his prospective foes, both ideologically and organizationally. Despite the intensity of the campaign against the Right deviation in the late fall of 1928, no individual names other than those involved in the Moscow organizational fight were brought into public controversy. While the issues and the factional lines were by this time quite clear to all those on the inside, Stalin and his supporters took great care to preserve the public illusion of stability and agreement among the top party leaders. In December 1928, Stalin came close to absolving all the Rightists of factional intent: "Indeed, the Rights in the AUCP(b) do not yet represent a faction, and it is indisputable that they loyally carry out the decisions of the Central Committee of the AUCP(b)."[210]

Failure to undertake a public struggle against Stalin was the major blunder of the Rightists. They began their opposition with much prestige, as Stalin's alarm over their threats to resign testified. Yet such was their own Leninist training that they carefully avoided a transfer of the controversy to the public arena. They were hemmed in by their orthodoxy and their respect for party unity. They could see public—or party—opinion only as a subject for manipulation, not as a court of appeal. While sparing the Rightist leaders for the time being, Stalin perfected his trap for them. Denying reports of their disaffection, he made it appear that his own policy modifications had the unanimous support of the Politburo as the continuation of an accepted line. When Bukharin and his supporters belatedly resisted, they were placed in the position of attacking accepted party policies to which they themselves had previously offered no public objection.

The official condemnation of the Bukharin group developed by stages, as the Right leaders were labeled with the tag of deviation before progressively wider audiences. Bukharin, Rykov, and Tomsky were first denounced by Stalin at a joint session of the Politburo and the presidium of the Central Control Commission early in February 1929. The attack was carried to the forum of the Central Committee in April, but the pose of united leadership was still observed at the Sixteenth Party Conference in May. The open secret of the Rightists' condemnation came before the Comintern executive committee in July, but it was not until late August, with the announcement of Bukharin's ouster as leader of the Comintern, that the disgrace of the three Rightist leaders was made a matter of public record. The strategy of the Stalinists was to keep all differences as quiet as possible, until the Rightists, in their disciplined silence fostered by hopes of a comeback within the organization, had lost all chance of threatening the leadership by an appeal to the public.

The occasion which prompted Stalin's first explicit attack on Bukharin, Rykov, and Tomsky in February 1929 was the Trotskyists' publication of the record of the theretofore secret discussions between Bukharin and Kamenev. Ordzhonikidze, who as chairman of the Central Control Commission was directly responsible for dealing with such individual breaches of the antifactional rule, summoned both Bukharin and Kamenev to account for their behavior; they are reported to have conceded the accuracy of the report of their talk.[211] When the Politburo and the presidium of the Central Control Commission met to consider the affair, Bukharin countered with a statement vigorously criticizing the policies of the party leadership.[212] He denied the charge of factionalism (the customary Opposition mistake) and attacked in turn the violation of democratic practices in the party organization, where, he contended, not one provincial secretary had been legitimately elected. Such was the natural evolution of defeated Leninists, not excepting those who with such zest had joined in badgering Trotsky, into the role of professed civil-libertarians. With respect to economic policy, Bukharin bitterly attacked the leadership for "military-feudal exploitation of the peasantry," through a tax policy that was equivalent to the exaction of "tribute," while the country's reserves of foreign exchange were being squandered. Bureaucratism was running wild, and the opposition was being "worked over."[213]

In reply, the Politburo set up a subcommittee to draft a condemnation of Bukharin's "political errors." A "compromise" was then proposed—the condemnatory resolution would be withheld if Bukharin would abjure his mistakes and withdraw his resignation from *Pravda* and the Comintern executive committee—that is, if he would condemn himself and spare the leadership the trouble.[214] Bukharin failed to comply, and the attack on him was put on the record as a resolution of the Politburo.[215] This document summarized Bukharin's misdeeds in tones of injured astonishment—Bukharin had slandered the party; Bukharin had deceitfully pretended to respect party unity while he organized a factional movement; Bukharin by conspiring with Kamenev had given aid and comfort to the enemy when the talks were made known. Past slips were now recalled—Bukharin's days as a Left Communist and the "Get rich" slogan (minimized by Stalin when Zinoviev had objected to it in 1925). Evidently the Right leaders had threatened to resign again, and this drew special reproof, indicating the anxiety Stalin felt about it. The gesture was "an appeal to discontented elements in the party . . . which cannot but create a serious threat to the unity of the party and the Comintern."[216]

Still defiant, Bukharin, Rykov, and Tomsky had meanwhile prepared a platform, which they presented to the Politburo on the same day, February 9, 1929.[217] This occasion marks the high point of the Right Opposition in the vigor of their criticisms. They accused the Stalinists again of "military-feudal exploitation" of the peasants, "a policy of propagating bureaucratism," and "a policy of dissolving the Comintern." In what the Stalinists referred to as a "liberal" interpretation of the NEP, the three Rightist leaders called for a reduction in the tempo of industrialization and the preservation of the free market. Once more they protested the absence of democracy within the party.

This clash had loud echoes. *Pravda* charged for the first time that the still unnamed Rightists represented a break from Leninism.[218] Molotov put the ideological condemnation of the Right Opposition in the most forceful manner yet: "Between our policy of an offensive against the kulak and the theory of the peaceful growth of the kulak into socialism there is a deep chasm. . . . In this question the party cannot tolerate any vacillation. . . . The theory of the peaceful growth of the kulak into socialism in practice means the abandonment of the offensive against the kulak; it leads to an emancipation of the capitalist elements and finally to the re-establishment of the power of the bourgeoisie."[219] Here again is the familiar Leninist dualism: everyone not bound to the movement by unquestioning doctrinal conformity is basically against it. The critic of the "proletarian" line can only be, "objectively" speaking, the mouthpiece of the bourgeois counterrevolution. He who would conciliate the conciliators must in turn be disgraced and silenced.

In April 1929, the attack on Bukharin, Rykov, and Tomsky, by name, was extended to the forum of the Central Committee. Struggling to evade the organization steamroller, the Rightists professed their basic adherence to the Stalinists' policy of high-tempo industrialization, though they continued the effort to introduce a note of caution by pleading for a two-year emphasis on agricultural development within the context of the five-year plan and warning against the "abolition of the NEP." Their tactic of avoiding straightforward opposition was so successful that in order to keep the sense of controversy alive the party leadership was forced to denounce the Rightists for "concealing their real attitude" and for "rhetorical declarations concerning the acceptability of the plan." Any surreptitious opposition thus camouflaged was to be dealt with stringently.[220]

Opposition complaints about repression in the party were now (with justice) compared with Trotskyism. The Right was denounced by the Central Committee for its repeated violation of discipline, just as the Left had been, and similarly was accused of representing "the least reliable elements in the nonproletarian sector of the party, those most subject to petty-bourgeois influence and the danger of degeneration, and the most backward. . . . segments of the workers." The party was called on to "expose" the Right deviation, which was most dangerous where it was concealed. Party democracy was affirmed, but with the usual qualification that rendered it meaningless: "The Leninist party rejects with all decisiveness the 'democracy' which legalizes deviations and factional groupings within the party. Intraparty democracy serves the goals of strengthening the Leninist unity and solidarity of the party. . . ."[221]

Stalin took the occasion of this meeting of the Central Committee to give the first systematic exposition of his "differences" with Bukharin. Bukharin was charged and convicted, in the course of Stalin's long report, with culpable error in every field—failure to attack "conciliationists" in the Comintern; "theoretical blindness" with respect to the kulak menace; neglecting the danger to the NEP posed by excessive free trade; failing to appreciate the collective farms as a "new form" of the worker-peasant smychka; advocating a "bourgeois-liberal policy and not a Marxian policy" in his allegedly absolute opposition to "emergency measures" against the kulaks; indulging in factionalism and obstructing the "collective leadership" of the Politburo. Bukharin's complaints of the lack of democracy were described with some justification as "the false words of a Communist gone liberal who is trying to weaken the party in its fight against the Right deviation. . . . Does Bukharin's group understand," Stalin exclaimed in conclusion, "that to refuse to fight the Right deviation is to *betray* the working class, to *betray* the revolution?" [222]

A certain note of restraint lingered on with respect to the party's peasant policy. Collectivization was still urged primarily as a source of technical aid and example for individual farming, which would continue to be "the main factor in the growth of agricultural production during the next few years." [223] In public Rykov was still a leading spokesman for this official compromise: "Only such a combination of our aid for the peasantry, the struggle for the extension of the socialized sector in agriculture, and the economic interest of the individual peasant who produces for the market, will make it possible for us to cement the alliance between the working class and the main mass of the peasantry, thereby enhancing the possibility of a rapid industrialization of the country, a rapid transformation of agriculture on the basis of collective wholesale production, and a successful offensive against the kulaks, the capitalist elements." [224]

Such statements, coupled with the fact that Rykov was the man who made the principal report on the five-year plan at the Sixteenth Party Conference, suggest that Rykov lacked firm conviction as a member of the Right Opposition. His name, to be sure, was the first to appear in reports of open friction between Stalin and the Right, but this affair of February 1928 may have been more of a personal flare-up at a time when Stalin's cultivation of policy differences had not proceeded far enough to cause the Right Opposition to take shape. There are indications that Rykov was rather less resolute than Bukharin throughout the course of the controversy. According to Stalin's account, Rykov broke the united front of Rightist resignations in February by withdrawing his own threat to resign before the Stalinist leaders took final action. [225] Possibly Rykov was persuaded in the spring of 1929 that he was not meant to be included among the Rightists scheduled for condemnation, and thus lent his name to the Stalinists for use as a demonstration of the continuity of their policy with past orthodoxy. By way of reward, Rykov was spared when the public pillorying of Bukharin commenced in August 1929, and his expulsion from high party and government office came considerably later than Bukharin's.

None of the speeches or resolutions of the April Plenum that pertained to the individual Rightist leaders were published at the time, even though the Central Committee appears to have taken the first material step in disciplining the Rightist leaders by recommending the removal of Bukharin from his chairmanship of the executive committee of the Comintern. This act was not officially put into effect until July, when it served as the signal for the first torrent of published abuse of Bukharin. During the Sixteenth Party Conference, which immediately followed the Central Committee session late in April, the pose of top-level unanimity was assiduously maintained, though there can be no doubt that reports of the cleavage between the Stalinists and the Bukharinists had spread far and wide by that time.[226] The Bukharinists cooperated fully in keeping their potential supporters in a state of uncertainty about the real extent and nature of the top-level split, and so contributed to the stillbirth of their own cause.

The Sixteenth Conference approved the Five Year Plan, endorsed the party purge, and condemned the still anonymous right-wing vacillations as an "openly opportunist surrender of the Leninist positions under the pressure of the class enemy."[227] Rykov backed the Five Year Plan like the staunchest Stalinist: "Every essential element of the Five Year Plan *must deeply penetrate the consciousness of every worker, every peasant,* in order that every one of them become conscious of the connection between his exertions and the results of his exertions." He forsook his personal reservations with an appropriate confession: "Many of us were mistaken in supposing that with the transition from the so-called restoration period to the reconstruction period the rate of development of our economy, and especially of industry, would suffer a decisive reduction."[228] Nevertheless, an ominous note was sounded by Kuibyshev, the man chiefly responsible for working out the industrial policy of the Stalinists. "There are a few party workers among us who have great doubts about the possibility of the high tempo of our development," he warned. "In this question . . . the Bolshevik Party must not make the slightest concession to the defeatist mood, to the lack of faith, to those trends which find their way into our ranks from . . . the petty-bourgeois element." Purging was thus in order to maintain the new orthodoxy, which Kuibyshev described in the Stalinist fashion as merely the fulfillment of old orthodoxy: "the five-year economic plan strictly follows the Bolshevik line, the line laid down by the Fifteenth Party Congress."[229]

Immediately after the Sixteenth Conference, Uglanov, who was unfortunate enough to have become involved in public controversy the previous fall, was removed from his top party positions as condidate member of the Politburo and member of the Secretariat. He was replaced by Bauman, who had already succeeded him as secretary of the Moscow party organization. Reporting to his constituents on the work of the conference, Bauman made the most violent public statement yet to appear against the Right. His personal attack on the Rightist leaders was but thinly veiled, as he denounced them for "the struggle in the Moscow organization, the attempt to form an unprincipled bloc with the former Trotskyists, the sabotage of party decisions, and the policy of resignations."[230] The public disgrace of the Right Opposition was not long in following.

Tomsky was the first of the right-wing trio to fall from a long-enjoyed position; he was officially ousted in June as chairman of the All-Union Central Council of Trade Unions. Bukharin's turn came next. On July 3, 1929, the executive committee of the Comintern obligingly executed the wishes of the Politburo by formally depriving Bukharin of his chairmanship and of his membership in the ECCI as well.[231] Public mention of the removal of Bukharin was for a time carefully avoided, but Right deviation in general continued to be the target for incessant abuse. The Rightist heresy of overestimating the sustaining power of world capitalism was denounced all the more violently as the last remnants of Right Opposition sympathizers were being extirpated from the ranks of the Comintern.[232] The economist Eugene Varga, for example, suffered a severe personal attack for observations about the stabilization of capitalism which smacked excessively of Rightist deviation.[233] (Surviving the purges of the thirties, Varga was once again attacked in 1947 for the same fault of failing to predict the imminent collapse of capitalism.)

The curious delay in the open denunciation of Bukharin was apparently brought to an end by evidence of a recrudescence of Rightist activity in certain party organizations.[234] Even so, a week elapsed between *Pravda*'s attack on the Rightists Sten and Shatskin and the first publication, on August 21, 1929, of the ECCI resolution which denounced and deposed Bukharin. Three days more passed before *Pravda* appeared with an editorial specifically attacking him—but this finally provided the signal for an obviously well-prepared hail of denunciations in the press and party meetings which kept up until Bukharin was completely broken as a political figure.

The anticlimactic performance was ended at the session of the Central Committee held in November 1929. The second-string Rightist leaders, headed by Uglanov, succumbed and endorsed a declaration repudiating the Bukharin movement.[235] Bukharin, Rykov, and Tomsky submitted a statement which acknowledged the correctness of the official party line but urged their own approach to achieve the same goal.[236] An outburst of rage was the reply: the Bukharin group was slandering the party, arrogating to itself the right of unfettered factionalism, and refusing to retract its opportunist errors. Their declaration of submission was rejected as a mere "factional maneuver" on a par with the Trotskyist tactic. Bukharin was forthwith expelled from the Politburo, just three years after Trotsky's fall was signaled in the same manner. The others were warned that "in case of the slightest attempt on their part to continue the struggle," the same punishment lay in store for them.[237] Thenceforth the status of the Rightist leaders was to be little better than that of convicts on parole. *Pravda* announced the party's demand—abject confession—for remission of the sin of failing to retract old accusations.[238]

Too late to save themselves, the Rightist leaders nonetheless finally performed the public recantation demanded of them. Here in full is the confession of error signed by the three of them, which appeared in *Pravda* on November 26, 1929:

In the course of the last year and a half there have been differences between us and the majority of the Central Committee of the CPSU on a series of political and tactical questions. We presented our views in a series of documents and statements at the plenums and other sessions of the Central Committee and the Central Control Commission of the CPSU.

We consider it our duty to declare that in this dispute the party and its Central Committee have proven right. Our views, presented in documents which are familiar, have proven erroneous. Recognizing these mistakes of ours, we for our part will apply all our efforts toward carrying on, together with the whole party, a decisive struggle against all deviations from the general line of the party and above all against the Right deviation and conciliation toward it, in order to overcome any difficulty and guarantee the complete and quickest victory of socialist construction.

The history of open political opposition in Soviet Russia had come to an end.

14

"ENEMIES OF THE PEOPLE"

With the fall of the Right in 1929 the Communist Opposition ceased to exist as a politically significant movement. Manifestations of opposition which have appeared in the Communist Party since 1929 have been personal, behind-the-scenes, and episodic, and they are hardly to be considered a part of the same historical phenomenon as the factional struggles before that date. All such later opposition was formless, without organization or platform. It took place within the context of Stalin's supreme leadership, which was never seriously challenged, and behind the veil of unanimity imposed by Stalin on all public party activity and pronouncements after he gained full power. No longer were great issues of doctrine or principle to be hammered out through factional controversy. The Opposition as a vital force reflecting the complex inner development of the Soviet regime had come to an end. With the elimination of all effective opposition by 1930, the Soviet regime had attained the form—in political structure, program, and ideology—which has characterized it ever since.

Partly for this reason and partly because the problems of data and interpretation become so much more difficult for the years after 1929, the present chapter is not designed to be a full history as the earlier ones have been. It is in the nature of an epilogue, to trace the fate of the old oppositionists who had gone down fighting. The story from this point on is inherently anti-climactic, though not without surprises.

At the time Stalin became an absolute dictator, it was still impossible to anticipate the common disposition which he would make of his broken opponents. The leaders of the Left Opposition had been banished to Siberian exile. The Right leaders still retained their party cards and some of their official positions. For a time, the courses of Left and Right ran separately. But, in the end, the same heading of "enemy of the people" covered anyone unfortunate enough to have been one of Stalin's peers or better in the formative years, as the "bloc of Rights and Trotskyists" was marched to meet the executioner.

THE LEFT IN EXILE

The leaders of the Left Opposition did not long remain at liberty following their exclusion from the ranks of the party and hence from the sole arena of legal political activity. In January 1928, Trotskyist charges of factional disloyalty against the repenting Zinovievists came to light, and this was taken as evidence that an organized political grouping was continuing among the oppositionists.[1] The response of the party leadership was to deliver Trotsky and some thirty other leading Leftists, including Radek, Preobrazhensky, Rakovsky, Smilga, Serebriakov, and Ivan Smirnov, and the Democratic Centralists Sapronov and Vladimir Smirnov, into the hands of the GPU for administrative exile to various remote points. Trotsky has described his departure from Moscow in dramatic detail. To foil the Opposition sympathizers who planned to demonstrate at the station from which he was scheduled to leave, the GPU transferred Trotsky at the last minute to another station, and he was whisked away from the capital without ceremony.[2]

Trotsky's designated place of residence was the city of Alma-Ata, deep in Central Asia and the capital of the Kazakh Republic. Apart from the remoteness of the location, the conditions of his exile were by no means onerous. He had a house, his family, even secretaries. He was able to conduct a voluminous correspondence, some open, some secret, with his sympathizers who had been banished to other parts of the country.[3]

In contrast with the original Trotskyists, the Zinoviev-Kamenev group tried to recant immediately at the Fifteenth Congress, even prior to their expulsion from the party. This was of little avail, for they were expelled from the party anyway. They continued thereafter to protest their orthodoxy and their rejection of the very idea of opposition: "Outside of the AUCP(b) there is only one fate facing our Leninist ideas—degeneration and decline."[4] At length, the submissiveness of the Zinovievists was rewarded, and they were readmitted to the party in June 1928. This was only a probationary rehabilition, as it were; no important positions were restored to the Zinovievists and, as it became all too clear later, there was no escape for them when victims were required for sacrifice.

Like the Zinoviev group, some of the Trotskyist leaders escaped exile. No doubt the party leadership had perceived signs that certain of them could be induced by pressure or argument into repudiating the Opposition, as had Zinoviev and Kamenev, on the grounds that it really constituted that political anathema, a second party. Just this sort of recantation was expressed between February and May 1928, by Piatakov, Krestinsky, and Antonov-Ovseyenko, as well as by various lesser figures among the Opposition.

Piatakov had wavered at the critical point in the fall of 1927. He told the Fifteenth Congress' Commission on the Opposition that he disapproved of the Opposition printing and demonstrations undertaken in defiance of party orders, though he was sure the Opposition platform was correct.[5] A man who appeared, even as Lenin described him in 1922, to be primarily interested in industrial administration, Piatakov was more concerned with the proper economic policy than with the condition of party democracy. Consequently he was readily won over when Stalin began to shift toward intensive industrialization. Applying for readmission to the party in February 1928, Piatakov stated that he could not discern a Thermidorean reaction and therefore felt compelled to devote his energies to the cause of the single party,[6] which in fact he did with some distinction. Readmitted to the party, he was restored to membership in the Central Committee and made deputy commissar of heavy industry, in which capacity he earned a reputation as "the real leader and chief executive in creating the new Soviet heavy industry."[7] Nonetheless he was in the prisoners' dock at the 1937 trial and was sentenced to death.

Krestinsky pleaded that he had never been an active member of the Trotskyist Opposition, which was true after 1921 when his support of Trotsky had caused his transfer from the party Secretariat to the important but conveniently distant post of ambassador to Germany. In 1928, after his profession of loyalty, Krestinsky was promoted to the post of deputy foreign commissar under Litvinov. His trial in 1938 was noteworthy for an outward instance of a miscarriage of Soviet justice. When summoned to testify in open court, Krestinsky stunned everyone present with a flat repudiation of the confession which he had made during the customary "preliminary examination." The court was hurriedly recessed and Krestinsky was returned to the police for further processing. The next day he obliged the prosecution with a repudiation of his repudiation. Then he was shot.[8]

Antonov-Ovseyenko completely repudiated the Opposition. He conceded that Stalin had been fundamentally right in his criticisms of the Opposition ever since 1923: the Opposition tended to become a second party and violated fundamental Bolshevik principles. Antonov-Ovseyenko went as far back as 1915 to claim that while associated with Trotsky—and not yet a Bolshevik Party member—he had really agreed with Lenin. Most interesting of all was his explicit absolution of the general secretary from the criticisms advanced by Lenin in the "Testament": "You . . . have shown that you have accepted Lenin's personal remarks about you"—Stalin had put the interests of the party first.[9] Whether it was a matter of the interests of the party or of Stalin's "rough" character, the sequel to Antonov's further years of service in the Comintern (culminating in the job of chief Soviet agent in Spain in 1936–1937), was his secret execution in 1938.[10]

In 1928 the "capitulators" among the Trotskyists were still a minority. Most of the Left Opposition maintained their stand as a matter of principle and continued as far as possible to propagate their views. Evidently the Left Opposition still commanded enough respect in the party to cause considerable anxiety to Stalin at the time when his struggle with the Bukharinists was sharpening.[11] Accordingly, in January 1929, Stalin took the grave step of ordering Trotsky expelled from the country—forcibly exiled abroad. A pretext was found, again, in one of Trotsky's particularly critical articles that had found its way to publication abroad. Trotsky's allegation that a Bonapartist coup was in the making and his call for the workers to strike against the regime were held to be clear evidence of his counterrevolutionary role.[12] Following negotiations to find a foreign government willing to admit Trotsky, arrangements were concluded for his reception by Turkey, and on February 11, 1929, Trotsky left for the last time the territory of the country whose revolution he had organized.[13]

In retrospect, the deportation of Trotsky is difficult to explain. Aside from the risks which Trotsky's freedom entailed, it would seem much more in character for the Stalinist regime to have held him in prison, with execution to follow in time. Trotsky abroad was in a position to become the center of a movement of Communist anti-Soviet criticism—the most embarrassing sort of opposition for the Stalinists. He quickly began to build an organization with the aid of foreign sympathizers, and soon was able to establish underground contacts with his forces inside the USSR. A periodical was founded by the group—*Biulleten Oppozitsii*—and successfully smuggled into the Soviet Union. More important, anti-Stalin Communists in the foreign parties and people whom the Comintern had already expelled were drawn into an organized movement. Eventually the Trotskyists reached the point of an absolute break with the regular Communist parties, finally freed from the dogma of the single united proletarian party. The upshot was the Fourth International, a curiously futile imitation of the Third, devoted to the embarrassment of the parent movement.

Did the deportation of Trotsky yield any advantage to the Soviet leadership offsetting the obvious external embarrassment which it caused? Perhaps the move seemed the only recourse for a regime too insecure to let Trotsky live in the country as a potential rallying point for his supporters or to invoke against Communist Party members the death penalty for political crime. The first such execution of an oppositionist sympathizer was soon to follow, however, with the liquidation of a secret-police official, Y. Bliumkin (who as a Left SR had shot the German ambassador in 1918), for the indiscretion of paying a visit to Trotsky in Turkey.[14] It is doubtful that more complex calculations were involved in the decision to deport Trotsky. Nevertheless, a certain utility did accrue to the regime by having its enemy alive outside the country. Trotsky was the scapegoat; he served as the focal point around which the web of alleged plotting was spun to ensnare the victims whom Stalin was preparing to dispose of after 1934. Treasonable dealings with Trotsky provided the main theme of all three of the big show trials of the oppositionists, in 1936, 1937, and 1938.

Trotsky's odyssey as a prophet cast out by his own country was to last eleven years. The wheel had turned full circle, and he was once again the lone political exile. From the Turkish island of Prinkipo Trotsky managed to arrange a move to France; from there he went on to Norway. In 1936 the Soviet government brought pressure to bear, and Trotsky was forced to seek still another asylum, this time in Mexico.

After the liquidation of all of his alleged accomplices, Trotsky was no longer of use to Stalin. Two attempts on Trotsky's life occurred; the first, in May 1940, by unknown assailants employing submachine-gun fire, failed. Meanwhile a Spanish Communist, Ramon Mercader, had won the confidence of the Trotsky household. On August 20, 1940, Mercader buried a pickax in Trotsky's brain.[15] The Soviet government has always denied responsibility, but to Stalin it could hardly have been a tragedy that the man whom he had harried so long had come to this grisly end.

Stalin's break with the Right and the promulgation of radically new economic policies had a telling effect on the resistance of the Trotskyists still in exile at remote points in the Soviet Union. Stalin's policies with respect both to the peasantry and to industry were clearly based on the ideas advanced by the Leftists between 1923 and 1927. Economically, Stalin's chief difference with the Trotskyists lay in the exaggeration and intensity with which he applied the program of intensive industrialization. To some of the exiles Stalin himself started to look like a Leftist, and they began to wonder why they should hold out against his leadership. Preobrazhensky declared in April 1929 that the Stalin group and the Left were now essentially in agreement: "One has to make the fundamental and overall conclusion that the policy of the party did not deviate to the right after the Fifteenth Congress, as the Opposition described it ... but on the contrary, in certain substantive points it has seriously moved ahead on the correct path." He referred to the change in the economic policies of the leadership as a "great moral victory of the views of the Opposition," and called on both the Opposition and the leadership to put aside the enmity between them.[16]

Preobrazhensky's reasoning illustrates the crippling effect which the limitations of Marxian categories had on the thinking of the Left oppositionists. Axiomatically the regime had to be either bourgeois or proletarian. They could conceive of no other alternative, since they ignored all other non-"bourgeois" possibilities. Theory obscured for these Leftists the vast difference between Stalin's policies and their own ideas—for example, between the gusto with which the Stalinists drove forward the program of forced collectivization and the qualms which Preobrazhensky had expressed about economic development based on governmental compulsion.

The combination of Marxian blinders and Stalin's super-industrialism was sufficient to produce in the middle of 1929 a wave of capitulations among the Trotskyists in exile. Radek hailed the "great class struggles" now going on, and proclaimed his eagerness to return and join in the fray.[17] A joint declaration from a group headed by Radek, Preobrazhensky, and Smilga backed the five-year plan and the struggle against the Right Opposition, condemned factionalism, and repudiated Trotsky's attempts to organize an opposition movement abroad. They viewed this as the establishment of a new party, which was doomed to degenerate. They appealed for readmission to the Communist Party and urged the rest of the Left to do likewise.[18] Readmission was soon granted those who recanted their factional past with sufficient fervor. Radek again rose to the highest councils of the party, not in an official position but as one of Stalin's principle spokesmen and propagandists. Reportedly he was a coauthor, with Bukharin, of the 1936 constitution.[19] His reward was special consideration when he stood trial for treason in 1937—a mere ten-year sentence. There has since been no definite word of him, though there were rumors during World War II that he was again writing for the party press. He is presumed to have died in prison either then or subsequently.

A small minority of the Trotskyist leaders continued to hurl defiance at Stalin's regime and chose to endure their exile rather than submit to the humiliation of recantation. Chief among these holdouts was Rakovsky, who devoted his efforts with considerable originality to a theoretical description of the evolving Soviet system. Rakovsky premised his new analysis on the observation that economic deficiencies in Russia had compelled the socialist ideal to give way to a progressive economic differentiation and social stratification, even within what was supposed to be the ruling class of proletarians. This idea was later developed at length and presented to the world by Trotsky; it formed the underlying thesis in his indictment of Stalin's "Bonapartism" in *The Revolution Betrayed*.[20] (More recently, the theory has been presented in a new version by the Yugoslav Milovan Djilas.[21])

That such a trend has long been in progress is obvious from the study of Soviet history; it is remarkable only in that it took so long for an awareness of this deep and enduring evolution to penetrate the Marxian consciousness of the Left Opposition. With the exception of the transitory fears of some Left Communists in 1918, there was among the Opposition leaders almost no grasp of the possibility of a third alternative to the prospects of the proletarian dictatorship or of a capitalist counterrevolution, until Rakovsky in exile worked out his justification for refusing to endorse the ruthless revolution practiced by Stalin.

The proletarian society, Rakovsky found, had been converted into an essentially bureaucratic social order, as the most active workers were drawn into the party and government machinery where they were able to enjoy economic preferment.[22] The Opposition was on the right track, he contended, when it began in 1923 to protest the contravention of democracy within the party: "The Opposition of 1923–1924 foresaw the great harm for the proletarian dictatorship which stemmed from the perversion of the party regime. Events have completely borne out its prognosis: the enemy crawled in through the bureaucratic window." Communist ideology was being reworked into a creed of bureaucratic authoritarianism: "The centrist leadership elevates into Communist dogma . . . the methods of commanding and compulsion, refining and reworking them with a virtuosity rarely achieved in the history of bureaucracy."[23] Rakovsky found the operations of this bureaucracy based on compulsion intrinsically repugnant. Vainly he pleaded with his former Opposition colleagues impressed by the material accomplishments of the Stalin regime that the economic and cultural foundations for real progress toward a socialist society were still lacking in Russia. Though such reasoning had long since been condemned as Menshevik heresy, it merits note, as does Rakovsky's less orthodoxly Marxian appeal to the importance of political principle. He lamented the capitulators' satisfaction over the state's economic progress alone: "[They] do not give thought to the fact that without the realization of the political part of the platform the whole socialist structure can tumble head over heels."[24]

THE RIGHT IN DISGRACE

While the Stalinists proceeded to implement their new economic policies, the issues raised by the Right Opposition had not ceased to exist. Collectivization and intensive industrialization led to precisely the economic and political problems which the Right had feared. Aggravation of the country's difficulties apparently engendered new waves of right-wing qualms, even among people hitherto unaffiliated with the Right Opposition. But such misgivings only made Stalin pursue his course more determinedly, as he strove to deny any shred of validity to the warnings of the Right Opposition. More alarm, more ruthless action, more anxiety about the Opposition leaders as a potential nucleus for the crystallization of new disaffection—such were, in brief, the political dynamics of the collectivization era.

The winter of 1929–30 was the first period of forced collectivization. Within the space of four months the Soviet government achieved the staggering feat of collectivizing over one half of the peasants in the entire country and much higher proportions in the grain-surplus-producing regions of southeastern European Russia. The consequences of this violent thrust soon became apparent; Stalin announced "dizzyness from success," and a retreat was ordered, undoing half of the winter's work.[25] The advance was then resumed somewhat more moderately; the half-way mark in collectivization was reached again in 1931, and by 1936 almost all of the peasantry had been brought within the new system.[26]

To justify himself in this time of crisis Stalin made dramatic use of the repentant Right leaders at the Sixteenth Party Congress, held in June 1930. The recantations followed the now standard form initiated by Zinoviev and Kamenev two and a half years before. Tomsky performed as a virtuoso, leaving no aspect of his oppositional career uncriticized. Referring in particular to the trade-union opposition, Tomsky confessed that it "brought on demoralization of the ranks of the trade-unionists, disorganization of the work of the trade unions, and compelled the Central Committee of the party to take the only correct measure . . . to remove the whole leadership of the trade-union movement."[27] The delegates were highly entertained and even showed something of an amiable indulgence toward Tomsky. Rykov, still the executive head of the government, tried to defend himself with the argument that he had not really been much of an oppositionist. This was a mistake—the congress received him with hostility.[28] Bukharin, against whom the most extreme attacks and the more severe penalties had been directed, chose to avoid— or was spared—the opportunity of unburdening himself; he was not present. The most demeaning ordeal was inflicted not on the top leaders of the Opposition but on their hapless organizational henchman, Uglanov. Uglanov confessed in no uncertain terms, to the accompaniment of repeated abuse from his audience, but his acknowledgement of error was presumably found inadequate, for he was compelled to submit a special supplementary declaration amplifying his recantation. He found himself guilty of "a departure from Leninism, reflecting petty-bourgeois elements," and "antiparty factional methods of struggle."[29] The verbal abuse of the Right was exemplified by Kirov: "Every single percentage point in the tempo of our industrialization, every single Kolkhoz—all this was achieved not only in the struggle with the kulak and other counterrevolutionary elements in our country; this was achieved in the struggle against comrades Bukharin, Rykov, Tomsky, and Uglanov."[30]

An absence of opposition was the last thing the leadership wanted at this juncture. Confession availed the Right not at all, but only led to new charges:

The congress directs the attention of the whole party to the fact that the opportunists of all suits, especially the Rights, are adopting a new maneuver, which is expressed in the formal admission of their errors and in formal agreement with the general line of the party but without confirmation of their admission by work and struggle for the general line, and which in fact signifies merely the transition from open to covert struggle against the party or the awaiting of a more favorable moment for renewing attacks on the party.

The party must declare the most merciless war on this kind of duplicity and deceit, and demand that all who admit their errors shall prove the sincerity of their admissions by active defense of the general line of the party. Nonfulfillment of this demand must bring on the most determined organizational measures.[31]

Rudzutak revealed whose sensitivities demanded the disgrace of the Right. He was quoting the declaration which the Rightist leaders presented to the Politburo in February 1929—"We are against one-man decisions of questions of party leadership. We are against control by a collective being replaced by control by a person, even though an authoritative one." This,

Rudzutak charged, was "direct slander of the party, direct slander of Comrade Stalin, against whom they try to advance accusations of attempting the single-handed direction of our party."[32] Rudzutak was purged by the slandered Comrade Stalin in 1938.

A further series of demotions for the Rightists was ordered at the Sixteenth Congress.[33] Uglanov and his Moscow men—Kotov, Kulikov, and Riutin—were dropped from the Central Committee. Tomsky's trade-unionists—Schmidt, Dogadov, and V. M. Mikhailov—were demoted to candidate status on the Central Committee. Tomsky was dropped from his seat in the Politburo, while three candidate members of loyal Stalinist standing—Kirov, Kosior, Kaganovich (one assassinated in 1934, one purged in 1938, one disgraced by a newcomer in 1957)—were elevated to full Politburo membership. Stalin's control of the top decision-making body was now secure, even allowing for vacillation among his own following.

By comparison with the Trotskyists, or by the retrospective application of later Stalinist standards, the Rightists were still being treated with remarkable leniency. Rykov remained a member of the Politburo. Bukharin and Tomsky retained their membership in the Central Committee. The former commissar of agriculture, A. P. Smirnov, and the trade-unionist Dogadov were kept in the Orgburo, though lowered to candidate status. This restraint recalls Lenin's concessions to the Workers' Opposition in 1921 or the jobs Stalin left to the Zinovievists in 1925—concessions to a broken opposition to inhibit their possibly embarrassing lamentations.

Bukharin, having abandoned all hope of opposing Stalin, went on to play an important role in the ideological sphere. He was made editor of *Izvestiya* and published extensively on theoretical and cultural topics. In all this work, however, he had abandoned his independence and his own original ideas: he was only the mouthpiece for the Stalinist line.

Toward the end of 1930 signs of stress began to appear again. In November the so-called Industrial Party trials were held, and a number of people identified as "bourgeois specialists" confessed profusely to the terms of their respective indictments for sabotage and "wrecking." The scapegoat device was rapidly gaining ground as a customary response to the government's economic difficulties. Then, early in December, it was suddenly announced that two party officials, S. I. Syrtsov and V. V. Lominadze, had been ousted from their positions and charged with organizing an "antiparty 'Left'-Right bloc."[34]

The Syrtsov-Lominadze affair is puzzling. Neither of the alleged leaders had been politically prominent, though Syrtsov had risen to high administrative status. A candidate to the Central Committee in 1924 and a full member in 1927, he was selected to relieve Rykov in the capacity of premier of the Russian Republic in May 1929, and at the Sixteenth Congress he was made a candidate member of the Politburo. The Trotskyists described him as a self-seeking "double-dealer," secretly sympathizing with the Right Opposition but posing as a loyal Stalinist.[35] Lominadze had figured largely in Comintern affairs—he was one of Stalin's emissaries to China in 1927 when the belated and fruitless revolutionary policy was attempted—and had just risen to Central Committee status at the Sixteenth Congress. What the real extent of the alleged conspiracy was, or what these apparently successful party figures hoped to gain, remain a mystery. In 1936, with liquidation impending, Lominadze reportedly committed suicide. Syrtsov disappeared at about the same time.[36] The "plot" served the party leadership well: further measures to restrain dissent were in order. Shortly after the Syrtsov-Lominadze affair broke, Rykov was finally ousted from the Politburo and from his office of chairman of the Council of People's Commissars. Ordzhonikidze was moved from the Central Control Commission to assume the Politburo seat, and the position of premier was taken over by Stalin's number-one henchman, the ever-reliable Molotov.[37]

Early in 1931, another spectacle was staged—the trial of the Menshevik "wreckers." Involved as defendants or witnesses were many of the Gosplan economists who had criticized the rate of industrialization. Also implicated was Riazanov, the last independent-minded party ideologist, who was now removed from the directorship of his Marx-Engels Institute.[38] Thereafter no academic scruples were to stand in the way of Stalin's determination to justify himself by whatever ideological manipulation seemed expedient. "Rotten liberalism" was his reproach for any attachment to truth that embarrassed his own interpretation of the Marxist-Leninist verities.[39]

With the disciplinary measures taken at the end of 1930 and early in 1931, political calm was maintained for a time. In the latter part of 1932, however, crisis erupted again, under the impact of the fearsome famine that was the result of collectivization. The pattern of events was markedly similar to the previous episode. A plot was discovered, wreckers were tried, and the regime endeavored to conceal the magnitude of the economic crisis in which it found itself. The alleged plot was the work of Riutin, the former Moscow supporter of Uglanov and the Right. Though dropped from the Central Committee in 1930, Riutin had apparently retained his position in the agitprop department. In October 1932, he was arrested. The decision of the Central Control Commission expelling Riutin's group from the party termed them "traitors to the party and the working class, trying to create by underground means, under the fraudulent cover of the banner of Marxism-Leninism, a bourgeois-kulak organization for the restoration of capitalism and especially the kulaks in the USSR."[40] Riutin's clandestine platform was a characteristically right-wing document in its appeal for a reduction in the tempo of industrialization and the outright abandonment of the collective farms. It went further to face the main issue by calling for the removal of Stalin.[41] The Trotskyists voiced a similar hope for a change. Ivan Smirnov, a capitulator, now reconsidered: "In view of the incapacity of the present leadership to get out of the economic and political deadlock, the conviction about the need to change the leadership of the party is growing."[42]

Stalin's response was nervously severe. Riutin himself was imprisoned, and it was reportedly only the objection of the Politburo that saved him from execution.[43] Riutin had committed the indiscretion of listing the names of those he thought were his sympathizers, and the government seized upon this opportunity to implicate a considerable number of oppositionists. Uglanov and certain other right-wing figures were arrested, interrogated, and forced to perform again the ritual of confession.[44] The hapless Zinoviev and Kamenev were also implicated in the Riutin affair, and for the second time expelled from the party.[45] Six months later their self-effacing compliance won them a second readmission, but their subsequent tenure in good standing was destined to be short-lived.

For Stalin this period was one of the most desperate of his career. Even his wife rebelled, though it meant her death. (Rumors differed on whether she perished by her own hand or her husband's.[46]) Stalin, for once, was reportedly close to losing his own nerve, and he took the risk of offering to resign in order to exact a vote of confidence from his Politburo.[47]

In January 1933, still another underground opposition cell was unearthed, this one organized by the former commissar of agriculture, A. P. Smirnov, and two other Rightists, Eismont and Tolmachev. They were accused of organizing "bourgeois degenerates" to attempt, like the Riutin group, the "restoration of capitalism and in particular of the kulaks." Smirnov was removed from the Central Committee and the other two were expelled from the party. The outcome of the episode was further ignominy for the former Right leaders: Rykov and Tomsky were attacked because they failed to fight the Smirnov deviation and because "by all their conduct they gave to all antiparty elements grounds for counting on the support of the former leaders of the Right Opposition."[48]

The Riutin and Smirnov plots, and a new "wrecking" trial, this time of the British Metro-Vickers engineers in January 1933, provided the cover for a change of course. Stalin made a strategic retreat and weathered the famine crisis. Substantial concessions to the peasants, particularly the parceling out of plots of an acre or two for free individual use, alleviated the worst features of the collective-farm system, and collective agriculture in Russia settled down into something like a stable existence. At the same time, with the inauguration of the Second Five Year Plan in industry, the needs of consumers were given more attention, though the characteristic emphasis on heavy industry continued.

To strengthen his position, Stalin resorted again to the technique of purging the party membership, already employed in 1921 and in 1929. The operation was launched in January 1933, with its announced objective "to guarantee iron proletarian discipline in the party and to cleanse the party's ranks of all unreliable and irresolute elements and hangers-on."[49] This time the weeding-out process was much more extensive. It continued for more than three years, on into 1936, when it issued into the volcanic era of mass imprisonment and liquidation. Between the beginning of 1933 and the end of 1936 the ranks of the party, including full and candidate members, were reduced from about three and a half million to less than two million.[50] Among the people expelled in 1933 were the last of the active Workers' Opposition leaders, Shliapnikov and Medvedev.[51] A particular objective of the purge was apparently to eliminate Communists overly inclined to support the interests of the national minorities. The most spectacular instance of this was Skrypnik, at the time a Central Committee member and Ukrainian commissar of education, who committed suicide to avoid disgrace.[52]

Was a political crisis over collectivization averted? Such was the pretense, at least, when the Seventeenth Party Congress convened in January 1934. Stalin proclaimed the attainment of unity firmer and more unquestioned than ever before.[53] The Rightist leaders lent authenticity to this claim with a repetition of their familiar self-denunciations, while the last Trotskyist holdout, Rakovsky, worn down by six years of exile, gave way and signed a paean to Stalin's infallibility.[54] Graciously, Stalin relinquished his right to reply to the debate: "Comrades, the debate at the congress has revealed complete unity of opinion among our party leaders. . . . There have been no objections to the report. Thus the extraordinary ideological-political and organizational solidarity in the ranks of our party has been demonstrated." Stalin dismissed the Opposition as "defeated and scattered."[55] Five years later, over one half of the participants in this gathering of the solid Leninist party were among the missing, victims of the insatiable purge.[56]

There were already signs of deepening trouble. Changes in the composition of the Central Committee in 1934 had interesting implications regarding the loyalty of the presumably steadfast Stalinists in the leadership. By contrast with 1930, when despite the sanctions in effect against the Right only six Central Committee members were dropped, in 1934 thirteen of the seventy-one members failed to be re-elected (not counting Skrypnik, a suicide). In the ranks of the candidate members the turnover reached the proportions of an upheaval: thirty of the sixty-three men receiving this honor in 1930 were ousted. There is no evidence of an organized and principled opposition movement of such proportions; apparently these were simply people whose Bolshevik resolution failed them in the years of crisis.

Rumor had it that new and fundamental divergences had arisen within the very core of the Stalinist ruling group. Reportedly the Politburo had split into two factions, hard and soft.[57] The liberal group is said to have included Voroshilov and Kalinin, who had already wavered in 1928, Rudzutak (who had just slipped to candidate member of the Politburo), and above all Kirov, the Leningrad party boss who was thought to be next in line to Stalin.

Molotov and Kaganovich figured most prominently in the group adhering firmly to the line of toughness. In 1934 the "liberals" appeared to have the upper hand; the populace got an economic breathing spell, and the harrying of the old oppositionists was eased. It may have seemed that the period of storm and stress was now a thing of the past.

In retrospect, Stalin seems to have been waiting for a calmer period so that he could deal more securely with the potential threat to his power which the old oppositionists still represented to him. His treatment of the oppositionists was hesitant and inconsistent; he may not yet have decided on his eventual course of action, or may have anticipated dangerous sympathy for the oppositionists if he took violent measures prematurely. Possibly the new external threat from Germany and Japan, or fear of criticism of his impending alliance with democratic forces abroad, contributed to his decision to liquidate the oppositionists.

Like his ambition to rule, Stalin's plans for his enemies probably grew in the process of dealing with them. Caution was certainly a factor. It was well after the collectivization crisis, and following the cultivation of the illusion that an era of good feeling was at hand, that Stalin seized upon a pretext for the total liquidation of every man who could arouse his suspicion. Whether Stalin's power was seriously challenged by the Right Opposition during the collectivization era is a question which may never be answered. The study of Soviet history after 1929 is balked by puzzles that the absence of documentation makes insoluble. Some observers see a constant threat from the Right which made Stalin acutely fearful for the security of his power, a challenge which failed only because of irresolute leadership. The evidence is scanty; one is forced to rely on inference from the little that is actually known about right-wing activities within the party organization during this period.

The weakness of the Right Opposition even at the time when their warnings were borne out so vividly is to be explained by the basic character of the right-wing tendency in the party. They were never a clearly defined group with an organization and a definite set of principles to which they could appeal against the leadership. All the potential Rightist feelings of cautious Leninism was never activated at the same moment; at various times, from 1928 until almost a decade later, individuals in the Stalinist leadership would suddenly begin to view the situation with alarm and turn to the growing group of personally squeamish but politically paralyzed oppositionists.

The weakness of the Right Opposition—its lack of definition and principle, as compared with the Left—was at the same time the basis for its endurance. There was always untapped Rightist potential ready to make itself felt in each new crisis. It is hard to distinguish sharply between the original

Right and the Stalinists who rebelled later at the rigorous application of their chief's policies. Therefore, any go-easy tendencies appearing at the policy-making level of the party—such as the "liberal" group of 1934, if it really existed—could justifiably be linked by the leadership with the Right deviation, even if direct influences were absent. This is why it has been possible for charges of Bukharinism or "Right opportunism" to recur since the purge period, while the Left Opposition was completely eradicated.

Echoes of the Right Opposition were heard during World War II in the Vlasov movement of Russian prisoners in Germany. A direct link with the Bukharinists was provided by the chief ideologist of the movement, M. A. Zykov. Zykov, the son of a Menshevik intellectual, had become an assistant editor of *Izvestiya* under Bukharin. Even in collaborating with the Germans he continued to profess with remarkable frankness the views of right-wing moderated Communism; his target was simply Stalin.[58]

When Communists came to power in Eastern Europe after World War II, and found themselves confronted with the burdens of governmental responsibility, the potential Right deviation broke out all over again. Wladyslaw Gomulka, secretary general of the Polish Communist Party until his temporary disgrace in 1948, was clearly following in Bukharin's footsteps with his hopes for a more gradual and less violent course toward socialism.[59] Accordingly, "a nationalist-Rightist deviation" was the charge when Gomulka and his associates were expelled from the movement.[60]

Bukharin's name was explicitly used in Stalinist charges against Yugoslavia when Tito defied Soviet domination in 1948.[61] The Communist Information Bureau charged the Yugoslav leaders with "the opportunist tenet that the class struggle does not become sharper during the period of transition from capitalism to socialism, as Marxism-Leninism teaches, but dies down, as was affirmed by opportunists of the Bukharin type, who propagated the theory of the peaceful growing-over of capitalism into socialism."[62] The Yugoslav Communist leaders returned the barrage of epithets measure for measure, and during the first three years after their break with Moscow they developed a systematic theoretical repudiation of Stalin's whole regime.[63] This counterattack savored in certain respects of both the Bukharinist and Trotskyist oppositions; Yugoslav ideologists resurrected the anarchistic ideas of "State and Revolution" and Marx's *Civil War in France* on the "commune state," and announced the discovery that the Soviet Union was a bureaucratic perversion of socialism. In the perspective of the Russian Opposition, the phrases were familiar: "bureaucratic dictatorship over the worker," "a new exploitation of the working masses," "the bureaucratic revision of Marxism."[64]

Inside Soviet Russia, the Right danger has not been permitted to die out (in contrast to the menace of Trotskyism, which is ancient history). Recurrent use has been made of the Bukharinist specter in the course of disciplining economists whose views failed to measure up to the standards of rigor demanded by the party leadership. In 1947 Eugene Varga was denounced for overestimating the staying power of capitalism in terms paralleling the condemnation of the Right Opposition.[65] In 1952, in his last published work, Stalin went out of his way to berate an academic economist, L. D. Yaroshenko, for ideas that assertedly matched Bukharin's on the limits of economic science.[66]

More important was the reference to the Right deviation just prior to the removal of Malenkov from the post of premier in February 1955. The crucial issue at this point was the relative emphasis on heavy industry and consumer-goods production, and the editor of *Pravda,* D. T. Shepilov, tore into the economists who had stressed the latter: "It would be difficult to imagine a more antiscientific, rotten, and nationally disruptive 'theory.' . . . Unmasking the theory of the Right capitulators, who were trying to force upon the party a program of 'cotton industrialization' to protect the preferential tempo of development in light industry [*sic*], Stalin pointed out: 'This has nothing in common with Marxism, with Leninism.' "[67] Echoes of the consumer-goods deviation were also heard at the Twentieth Party Congress in February 1956. In April the unfortunate economist Yaroshenko, who had taken the down-grading of Stalin to mean a new birth of intellectual freedom, was again attacked along with other "individual rotten elements" for "provocative antiparty statements."[68]

Vindication of right-wing Communism was won by the Poles in 1956 when Gomulka was restored and a measure of independence against Soviet dictation was asserted. In line with Bukharin's thinking, though with no specific reference to it, Gomulka undid the partially completed collectivization of agriculture, repudiated the worst excesses of the secret police and cultural controls, and temporarily allowed the industrial workers a certain degree of autonomy in their factory councils. The limits to Gomulka's system would seem to be those inherent in Bukharin's Communism: one-party dictatorship with ultimate organizational and doctrinal authority vested in the party leadership, however cautiously that leadership might proceed.*

Especially dramatic was the role played by right-wing Communism in Hungary after Stalin's death. Imre Nagy, premier in the Communist government from 1953 to 1955, made a notable effort to reduce the economic strain which had been imposed on the population by Stalinist industrialization and collectivization policies. In the crisis of October 1956, when it seemed that

---

* In Polish parlance, "Rightist" has been applied to the "Stalinist" wing, while the "Leftists" are the "revisionists" who would relax party controls. Gomulka stands in the "center," though policy-wise he most closely resembles the Right Opposition in Russia. The switch of labels may be attributed simply to the sequence of regimes in Poland: the Stalinists were the most "conservative" about dismantling their own system.

mass revolt might destroy Hungarian Communism altogether, right-wing Communism as represented by Nagy was recalled from disgrace and installed in power. Potentially Nagy was a Hungarian Gomulka, but the events of the revolution proceeded so fast that he found himself forced to forswear the one-party dictatorship and even the Soviet alliance, therefore falling victim to Soviet military intervention. Even the Soviet-satellite government of Kadar, however, has manifested a certain right-wing forbearance in order to minimize economic discontent.

Opposition of the Rightist type has been the characteristic form of political dissent within fully consolidated Communist regimes. The Right deviation does not, like the Left Opposition, depend on definite theories or traditions for its inspiration; it stems from psychological dispositions which are bound to appear again and again—fear, caution, the temptation to ameliorate the insecurity of dictatorial rule by giving the people a little satisfaction. Traces of "Right opportunism" will no doubt be found as long as the Communist system continues to include consumers.

THE RITUAL OF LIQUIDATION

On December 1, 1934, a young Communist student, Nikolaev by name, made his way ostensibly on party business into the Smolny Institute, the former school building made famous as the headquarters of the October Revolution and subsequently used as the seat of the Communist Party administration in the Leningrad region. At work within was Sergei N. Kirov, the first secretary of the party organization for Leningrad, member of the Politburo, the Orgburo, and the central Secretariat, Communist satrap in the northwest and heir apparent to the general secretary himself. Gaining admission to Kirov's office, Nikolaev produced a revolver and fired; Kirov was killed outright, the first official to fall a victim to political terrorism in Russia since revolutionary days.

Such was the reputation of Stalin's regime that no death, whether by violence or natural processes, could come to pass in the Soviet Union without engendering speculation about the hand of the leader in the demise of the individual in question. Various accounts have attributed Kirov's murder to Stalin's disfavor, expressed either through direct action or deliberate negligence. Party secretary Khrushchev himself fueled the flames of suspicion in 1956 with his reference to "many things which are inexplicable and mysterious . . . , reasons for the suspicion that the killer of Kirov was assisted by someone from among the people whose duty it was to protect the person of Kirov." [69] Whether or not Stalin planned the assassination because he feared a challenge from Kirov as the defender of the people's well-being against the worst excesses of the industrialization program, he moved quickly to make the murder serve as the pretext for a sweeping purge. Dozens of people who allegedly conspired in the assassination were shot out of hand, even before the actual assassin was sentenced to death. Broadening circles of people were arrested or deported from Leningrad to other parts of the country. The Leningrad secret police were rewarded for their part in the affair by the arrest of their principal officials. The "liberal" interlude was rudely terminated.[70]

As the work of interrogating those implicated in the assassination produced an accumulation of confessions, the tactic of linking the murder of Kirov to the Opposition became clear. Zinoviev and Kamenev again became the top-level scapegoats, the obvious connection this time being their former strength in the Leningrad party organization. Together with many of their former supporters, they were put on trial in January 1935, charged with encouraging the Opposition sentiment that inspired Kirov's assassin. They were inevitably convicted and sentenced to prison.

By the following year, Stalin's plans for utilizing the oppositionists had matured. He began the familiar and yet fantastic series of staged judicial processes that have gone down in history as the Moscow Trials. The subject is enormously complicated; whole books have been written about them, and there is ample room for more. The trials are important as evidence about the developing mentality of Stalin's regime. On the other hand, from the standpoint of interest in the oppositionists themselves, they are entirely anticlimactic. There was little substance to the charges of plotting against the regime; many of the defendants in the dock could only confess to hypothetical crimes —actions that their thoughts *might* have led to.

In August 1936, Zinoviev and Kamenev were disinterred from prison and brought to trial a second time, together with fourteen others, including their former Leningrad henchmen, Yevdokimov and Bakaev, and the Trotskyist Ivan Smirnov. The charge this time was based on alleged new evidence that the culprits had directly planned, in cooperation with Trotsky, the assassination not only of Kirov but of Stalin and the whole Soviet government. All the accused confessed elaborately to the charges; all were shot.[71] It was not long before the next group of traitors was paraded before the public. In January 1937, seventeen individuals, mostly former Trotskyists, were brought to the bar of justice on truly fantastic counts—plotting with German and Japanese intelligence agencies to overthrow the government, partition the country, and restore capitalism. Piatakov, Radek, Sokolnikov, and the one-time party secretary, Serebriakov, headed the list of victims. Most were shot; Radek and Sokolnikov inexplicably drew prison terms.[72] Both are presumed to have perished in prison.

In June, 1937, the top army command, including the long-time chief of staff, Tukhachevsky, was tried and liquidated.[73] A special trial in Tiflis disposed of most of the Georgians from both sides of the 1922 controversy.[74] Another death of questionable cause occurred in 1937, when Ordzhonikidze, at the time commissar of heavy industry, fell victim to what was announced as a heart attack. There were rumors as to his purge or suicide, possibly as the consequence of his opposing the liquidation of his deputy Piatakov,[75] though he still remained a hero in party history. At length, in 1956, it was asserted that Ordzhonikidze was the victim of a plot by Beria (then deputy commissar of internal affairs) which Stalin condoned, and that he had been forced to shoot himself.[76]

The turn of the Right Opposition followed soon after the first two trials. Most of the Rightist leaders were arrested in 1937 and brought to trial in March 1938. Bukharin and Rykov headed the list of defendants—Tomsky had committed suicide in 1936 when arrest was imminent. Also in the dock were the surviving Trotskyists Rakovsky and Krestinsky, and an assortment of former people's commissars (including the commissar of internal affairs, Yagoda, responsible for the preparation of the 1936 trial), officials of the non-Russian Soviet republics, and physicians accused of medical murder at Yagoda's instigation. The latter charge, respecting the deaths of GPU chief Menzhinsky in 1934, industrial chief Kuibyshev in 1935, and writer Maxim Gorky in 1936, added a particularly bizarre aspect to the otherwise repetitious indictment for espionage, treason, and plotting to restore capitalism in alliance with the Germans and Japanese. All of the accused were sentenced to death, except for Rakovsky and a few of the minor defendants, who went to prison and have not been heard of since.[77]

Less spectacular than the trials but of more real importance was the liquidation of the disaffected Stalinists—the incredible purge of Stalin's own party machinery. Everyone who had incurred Stalin's displeasure or suspicion—which extended to most of the party apparatus—was done away with in the utmost secrecy. There were no trials, no reports of execution, no explanation of circumstances, no blame, no charges of wrecking—simply no mention. (At one time Stalin may have planned a show trial based on charges of "bourgeois nationalism" against the fallen Ukrainian party leaders, Kosior, Postyshev, and Petrovsky.[78] Rudzutak was brought to trial *in camera,* but he repudiated his confession and was shot without public notice.[79]) The names of those who disappeared in the early months of 1938 were literally expunged from the historical record; from then until February 1956 there was not the slightest published suggestion that any of the people liquidated in this secret purge ever so much as existed. They had become "unpersons."

The reasons for the purge of the Stalinists may never be known. Were Stalin's men really plotting against him? Were they disturbed by the marked conservatism of Stalin's new social and cultural policies? Did they offend Stalin's ego by exceeding in height the Napoleonic stature of the general secretary? (All the prominent survivors were notably short men.) Did the *Yezhovshchina*—the Yezhov regime, so called after the commissar of internal affairs who directed the purge in 1937 and 1938 before he fell into the vortex himself—with its ramifying accusations, denunciations, arrests, and confessions, simply get out of control and sweep all the way up to the top? Was it sheer paranoic madness? Stalin's revenge may have been triggered by a general uneasiness about executing the oppositionists. Under the leadership of the Ukrainian secretary, P. P. Postyshev, the Central Committee actually rebelled against Stalin early in 1937, in protest against his plans to execute the Right Opposition leaders. Stalin reportedly let the matter rest, bided his time, and then struck mercilessly.[80]

Not even the highest levels were immune. Five out of the six candidate members of the Politburo were purged—only Zhdanov escaping—and two members of the Politburo itself, Kosior and Chubar, were liquidated. Of the seventy-one members of the Central Committee, fifty-five failed to reappear in the list voted by the Eighteenth Party Congress in 1939. A few of these had died publicly, if under mysterious circumstances; a few (old oppositionists) were publicly tried and executed; most simply disappeared during the winter of 1937–38, presumably dispatched by NKVD executioners. Among the candidates to the Central Committee, the purge was even more severe: sixty of the sixty-eight dropped out of sight, almost all without the slightest public mention. Of the fourteen new candidate members introduced by Stalin into the Central Committee in 1923, all but one (Kaganovich) saw their careers now come to an end. Not one in the 1924 crop of twenty-two candidates survived. Andrei Zhdanov was the lone survivor of the 1925 group. The whole Stalinist phalanx which acquired its "monolithic unity" during the struggle with the Opposition was literally annihilated, with the exception only of the Politburo and a mere handful of lucky subordinates.*[81] At the Eighteenth Party Congress in 1939, there were only thirty-four delegates of the 1570 in attendance whose party membership dated from before 1917.[82] Outside of the people who were members or candidates in the Politburo, there remained at liberty only seven individuals in the whole party who had held any significant position in the 1920s or before: Litvinov, Yaroslavsky, Lozovsky, Manuilsky, Alexandra Kollontai, K. I. Nikolaeva, and the one-time Duma deputy, A. E. Badaev. (To these might be added five obscure figures who were on the Central Control Commission in the twenties; but there are no others.) All of these people are known or presumed to have died since 1939.

The vast majority of former oppositionists were disposed of in the same manner as the fallen Stalinists—without trial and without confession. Among the Opposition figures who simply disappeared were the Trotskyists Preobrazhensky, Antonov-Ovseyenko, Beloborodov, Smilga, and Sosnovsky; the Zinovievists Safarov, Zalutsky, and Avdeyev; all of the Democratic Cen-

---

* Among the lesser vanished *apparatchiki* who had figured in the struggle with the Opposition were the Moscow secretary Bauman; Gusev of the Central Control Commission; Stalin's organization director, Antipov; Bubnov, who had defected from Trotsky to Stalin in 1923; Solts, the tough chairman of the Central Control Commission in 1921; Unshlikht of the GPU; Ukhanov of Moscow; the Ukranian Leninists, Yakovlev and Kviring; and the old undergrounders, Krzhizhanovsky, Goloshchekin, and Muranov.

tralists; the Workers' Oppositionists Shliapnikov and Medvedev; the Bukharin Rightists Uglanov, Kotov, V. M. Mikhailov, Liadov, Shmidt, A. P. Smirnov, and Dogadov; the early Rightists Riazanov, Miliutin, Teodorovich; the early Leftists Lomov and Krylenko.

The only important oppositionist to escape the purge was Alexandra Kollontai. Only one other of any note is known to have survived—K. I. Nikolaeva, one of the Central Committee members who joined the Zinoviev Opposition in 1925 but who managed to remain as a candidate or full member as late as 1939. It is interesting that these two were both women, and that they were the only two women of any prominence in the party in the 1920s who were still living when the Great Purge began. It is quite improbable that such a singular exception in the purge was the result of chance; Stalin's conservative streak apparently extended to the standards of chivalry, and he spared the women.

Many writers have pondered the reasons for the confessions of the Bolsheviks who were brought to trial. Suggested explanations range from hypnotic drugs to the guilt-complex of the Slavic soul, but reality was undoubtedly more prosaic—threats of reprisal against families or friends, promises of clemency in exchange for cooperation. Where such measures did not suffice, execution without trial was the answer. If one recalls the obvious lack of backbone manifested repeatedly by such individuals as Zinoviev and Kamenev, there is no mystery in comprehending their bowing again to the master's dictates and going a little further this time in self-incrimination.

One important exception, at least, is Bukharin. Bukharin would not make the false confession which was demanded of him. Time after time he disputed with the prosecutor, Vyshinsky, over the accuracy of factual points. He refused, for example, to admit that he had planed to kill Lenin when, during the heat of the Brest-Litovsk controversy in 1918, he had entered into negotiations with the Left SRs. On the other hand, he readily conceded the inferences drawn by the prosecution concerning the treasonable implications of his opposition record, or concerning the acts of desperation which might by some conceivable logic flow from certain of his ideas. While curiously determined to maintain his personal integrity in some respects, Bukharin perceived that he could not escape the necessity of making an overall repudiation of opposition, and of giving Stalin the measure of justification that the general secretary was grasping at. Probing his own mind to find reasons for thus complying, Bukharin undertook what can only be described as a sheer act of faith in the revolutionary labels of the Soviet regime. He told the court:

When you ask yourself: "If you must die, what are you dying for?"—an absolute black vacuity suddenly rises before you with startling vividness. There was nothing to die for, if one wanted to die unrepentant. And, on the contrary, everything positive that glistens in the Soviet Union acquires new dimensions in a man's mind. This in the end disarmed me completely and led me to bend my knees before the party and the country. And when you ask yourself: "Very well, suppose you do not die; suppose by some miracle you remain alive—again what for? Isolated from everybody, an enemy of the people, in an inhuman position, completely isolated from everything that constitutes the essence of life.". . . The result is the complete internal moral victory of the USSR over its kneeling opponents.[83]

Only if Bukharin could repent and convince himself that Stalin was the best representative of the socialist ideal, rather than its betrayer, could the Soviet Union be to him something both to live and to die for. In this desperate way he strove for the conviction that his life-long toils had not been wholly in vain.

THE DEAD DON'T DIE

When Joseph Stalin died in March 1953, there were many in the outside world who believed that this would mean a serious and perhaps crippling shock for the state which he had built. With consummate irony the ensuing years have shown that it was not the Soviet state but Stalin's own memory which was most vulnerable.

The reaction to Stalin's demise was surprising by contrast with the effect which Lenin's death had in 1924. In 1953 there was little lamenting and no anxiety; after the first few days, there was no special concern about tightening up the unity of the party in order to replace the firm hand of the departed leader. The sense of relief was obvious as the successor leadership hastily moved to tone down the memory of the late dictator and to correct some of the most obnoxious features of his rule. The revulsion of Stalin's former lieutenants against him was clear long before they decided, in February 1956, to denounce openly his conduct of the state in his later years.

The deflation of the Stalin legend began an indecently short time after the dictator's death. The frequency of Stalin's name in the Soviet press fell drastically, and the familiar tone of adulation disappeared altogether. On April 16, 1953, *Pravda* editorialized at length on the virtues of "the collective principle and the collegial principle." In terms which pointedly suggested Stalin without naming him, *Pravda* attacked people who failed to listen to the advice of their subordinates and who "conduct themselves as if they alone knew everything, as if only they can say anything sensible and intelligible and it remains to the lot of others only to support their opinion." Oddly enough, support for this position was found in the words of Stalin himself—a statement of 1931 praising the Central Committee (the same Central Committee which was later decimated in the purges). In June the theoretical journal *Kommunist* took up the same theme and elaborated on the "anti-Marxist" idea that heroes can accomplish historic wonders apart from the force of the masses: "Our party . . . resolutely struggles against the cult of personality, which means the idealistic inflation of the role of personality, imputes to it a supernatural mind, superstitiously bowing before it, and ignores the role of the masses, classes, and the party."[84]

The policy, if such it was, of quietly forgetting Stalin while collective Leninist leadership was extolled came abruptly to an end with the Twentieth Party Congress (the first since Stalin's death and the first to be held nearly on schedule since 1924). On February 24, 1956, party secretary Khrushchev addressed a secret session of the congress and presented a sensational case against Stalin.[85]

Khrushchev depicted Stalin as a bungler and an egomaniac, corrupted by power and consumed by the suspicion that his subordinates were plotting against him. Hardly since the era of Ivan the Terrible had the history of the world, let alone that of Russia itself, known such a psychopathic despotism. "Stalin showed in a whole series of cases his intolerance, his brutality, and his abuse of power."[86] His bloody injustice was matched, according to Khrushchev, by blundering incompetence, irresponsibility, and sheer pig-headedness, both in war and in peace, in foreign policy and domestic. Declared the secretary, formerly Stalin's own party agent for the Ukraine: "We have to consider seriously and analyze correctly this matter in order that we may preclude any possibility of a repetition in any form whatever of what took place during the life of Stalin, who absolutely did not tolerate collegiality in leadership and in work, and who practiced brutal violence, not only toward everything which opposed him, but also toward that which seemed to his capricious and despotic character, contrary to his concepts."[87] Khrushchev repudiated the cult of personality altogether, and even promised the renaming of cities and factories to undo the un-Marxist glorification of individuals.[88]

The strong hints of psychopathology which the historical record offers were at last borne out in Khrushchev's revelation, though Stalin's paranoia is not the whole story; few people have given their countrymen more incentive to plot assassination. Once, reported Khrushchev, when he was alone with Bulganin, the latter confided to him, "It has happened sometimes that a man goes to Stalin on his invitation as a friend. And when he sits with Stalin, he does not know where he will be sent next, home or to jail."[89] For his own part, Khrushchev commented:

Stalin was a very distrustful man, sickly suspicious; we knew this from our work with him. He could look at a man and say: "Why are your eyes so shifty today," or "Why are you turning so much today and avoiding looking me directly in the eyes?" The sickly suspicion created in him a general distrust even toward eminent party workers whom he had known for years. Everywhere and in everything he saw "enemies," "two-facers," and "spies."[90]

Stalin was clinically insane, if Khrushchev's characterization can be considered accurate: "You see to what Stalin's mania for greatness led. He had completely lost consciousness of reality. . . ."[91]

The picture of Stalin's mind as his record in the 1920s revealed it—his mania for self-justification and his determination not to admit the slightest criticism—was dramatically underscored by Khrushchev. He recalled the discussion after World War II of a Soviet defeat caused by Stalin's stubborness:

Anastas Ivanovich Mikoyan mentioned that Khrushchev must have been right when he telephoned concerning the Kharkov operation and that it was unfortunate that his suggestion had not been accepted. You should have seen Stalin's fury! How could it be admitted that he, Stalin, had not been right! He is, after all, a "genius," and a genius cannot help but be right! Everyone can err, but Stalin considered that he never erred, that he was always right. He never acknowledged to anyone that he made any mistake, large or small.[92]

From this Khrushchev deduced the whole catastrophe of the purges:

Stalin acted not through persuasian, explanation, and patient cooperation with people, but by imposing his concepts and demanding absolute submission to his opinion. Whoever opposed this concept or tried to prove his viewpoint and the correctness of his position, was doomed to removal from the leading collective and to subsequent moral and physical annihilation. This was especially true during the period following the Seventeenth Party Congress, when many prominent party leaders and rank-and-file party workers, honest and dedicated to the cause of Communism, fell victim to Stalin's despotism.[93]

Even the mere objection to Stalin's unfounded suspicions could place a person on the list of victims, as Khrushchev noted in reference to Postyshev's vain opposition in 1937.[94]

The impact of Khrushchev's attack was highly unsettling within the Soviet Union as well as among Communists abroad. Tiflis rioted—and this was the ultimate irony, that the most serious civil disturbance in Soviet Russia since collectivization days should come as a demonstration in *support* of the late dictator. The ferment in the party soon reached proportions where *Pravda* had to draw the line: "Under the guise of condemning the cult of the individual, some rotten elements try to cast doubt on the correctness of the party's policy. . . . The party has never tolerated and will not tolerate petty-bourgeois license, much less antiparty utterances, in its midst."[95]

At the same time that the principle of party discipline was reaffirmed, however, the case of the new leadership against Stalin was being publicized in further detail. Stalin was openly saddled with personal responsibility for mismanaging the Soviet defense effort in the first months after the German invasion in 1941, and grave damage in fields ranging from military science to literature and the arts was attributed to the cult of personality. *Pravda* queried rhetorically, "Why has our party opened a resolute struggle against the cult of the individual and its consequences?" The response recalls the attacks of 1953, though this time the individual concerned was named quite explicitly: "Because the cult of the individual signifies an inordinate glorification of individuals, ascribing supernatural features and qualities to them, making them almost miracle workers and worshipping them. Such incorrect conceptions of man, and specifically of J. V. Stalin, which are alien to the spirit of Marxism-Leninism, developed and were cultivated among us for many years."[96]

Echoes of the new anti-Stalin line came from other Communist regimes in a tone still clearer and manifestly emotional. Radio Warsaw, to take one example, called the Stalin era "a period of great hypocrisy." Then it came directly to the point—the 1938 purge of the Stalinist apparatus: "How monstrously and pathologically suspicious must have been the thoughts of the man who could suppose that numerous members of the Central Committee, most of them Old Bolsheviks, were enemies or imperialist agents. And yet it was Stalin himself who approved the lists of members of the Central Committee about to be arrested. The list of false accusations is long."[97] Thus the line developed—he did great work, until his power-madness turned him against his own supporters.

Hand in hand with the repudiation of Stalin's excesses, his victims—or some of them—were posthumously depurged. The first such steps were taken soon after Stalin's death. Without mention of their past vicissitudes, two living purge victims were unearthed and given the Order of Lenin as birthday presents. One was M. K. Muranov, once a Bolshevik deputy in the tsarist Duma and a member of the Central Control Commission from 1922 to 1934, after which time he dropped out of sight.[98] The other was G. Y. Petrovsky, who until his fall in 1938 was the chairman of the presidium of the Ukrainian Supreme Soviet and a candidate member of the Politburo in Moscow.[99]

These early moves were taken with no explicit reference to the purges of the thirties, but at the Twentieth Congress the purge of the Stalinists in 1937 and 1938 was specifically recalled and denounced. Its victims, who had been expunged from the official history without a trace, were restored to honorable positions in the party's memory. There were two groups of people thus favored: the military men, headed by Marshal Tukhachevsky, who were tried and liquidated in 1937, and the Stalinist party chiefs who disappeared in 1938.

The rehabilitation of the military group was first revealed in Khrushchev's secret speech, and confirmed by the journal *Voprosy istorii* in April 1956. Those exculpated included, together with the generals, two former heads of the military political department—Antonov-Ovseyenko and Bubnov (both one-time Left oppositionists).[100] Included in a later list of men readmitted to history was N. V. Krylenko, the left-wing military chief immediately after the revolution and then commissar of justice.[101] Depurging of the party group was hinted at even before Khrushchev's secret speech. In an open session of the Twentieth Congress Mikoyan made passing references to Antonov-Ovseyenko and to S. V. Kosior (the former Ukrainian party chief) as people whom party historians had unjustly attacked.[102] Rudzutak had quietly reappeared in a *Voprosy istorii* article on the trade-union controversy of 1921 (approved for the press on February 11, 1956, before the congress).[103]

In his secret talk Khrushchev dwelt at great length on the purge of the Stalinists in 1937–1938; this was, in his mind, the greatest crime Stalin had committed. He mentioned all the ranking figures who had disappeared and cited at length the vain pleas for justice which some of them had composed. Those rehabilitated included the former Politburo members Chubar, Rudzutak, and Kosior; the former candidate members Postyshev and Eikhe (in addition to Petrovsky, who was the only purge victim among the top leadership who escaped with his life); and a number of lesser party figures.[104] Stalin's purge of the Stalinists seems to have been repudiated in its entirety.

Khrushchev gave figures for the incidence of the purge among the members of the 1934 Central Committee and among those who had been delegates to the Seventeenth Party Congress of that year. The statistics come as no surprise, but the toll was now official: "It was determined that of the 139 members and candidates of the Party's Central Committee who were elected at the Seventeenth Congress, 98 persons, i.e., 70 per cent, were arrested and shot (mostly in 1937–38). [Indignation in the hall] . . . The same fate met . . . the majority of the delegates to the Seventeenth Party Congress. Of 1966 delegates with either voting or advisory rights, 1108 persons were arrested on charges of antirevolutionary crimes. . . . How then can we believe that such people could prove to be 'two-faced' and had joined the camps of the enemies of Socialism . . . ? This was the result of the abuse of power by Stalin, who began to use mass terror against the party cadres."[105]

To further substantiate his case against Stalin, Khrushchev turned to unimpeachable authority, and the story of Lenin's rupture with Stalin at long last became a part of the officially acknowledged history of the party. The text of Lenin's "Testament" was distributed to the congress delegates, and Khrushchev quoted the document at length as evidence that Lenin "detected in Stalin in time those negative characteristics which resulted later in grave consequences." Khrushchev then went on to read two letters, the texts of which were previously unknown—one from Krupskaya to Kamenev and one from Lenin to Stalin—which corroborated the long-standing allegation that Lenin was on the verge of a complete rupture with Stalin when he suffered his final stroke.[106]

Toward the end of his talk Khrushchev faced up to the obvious question: "Some comrades may ask us, 'Where were the members of the Political Bureau of the Central Committee? Why did they not assert themselves against the cult of the individual in time? And why is this being done only now?'" They were taken in, he had to admit, but the heat of controversy and Stalin's leading role during the struggle with the Opposition were important factors: "At that time Stalin gained great popularity, sympathy, and support."[107] Khrushchev preferred to ignore the fact that Stalin's evil propensities were, by force of circumstances, made painfully obvious to the oppositionists at that early date.

Despite the acknowledgment of Lenin's "Testament" and the documents associated with it, the official position since the Twentieth Congress has been an almost unqualified defense of Stalin's record in the elimination of the Opposition and in the violent reconstruction of the nation's economy. "The party," Khrushchev asserted, "had to fight those who attempted to lead the country away from the correct Leninist path; it had to fight Trotskyites, Zinovievites and Rightists, and the bourgeois nationalists. This fight was indispensable."[108] The year 1934, roughly, is the point at which Stalin's "negative characteristics" suddenly begin to emerge. It was "particularly in the later period of his life," according to the Central Committee's pronouncement of June 1956, when Stalin was "guilty of many lawless acts."[109] The rehabilitation of victims has been confined entirely to persons who stood in Stalin's good graces before the Great Purge.

Nevertheless, while Stalin's campaign against the "anti-Leninist" Opposition is still upheld, this no longer holds for the manner in which he finally disposed of them. "Worth noting," said Khrushchev in his secret speech, "is the fact that even during the progress of the furious ideological fight against the Trotskyites, the Zinovievites, the Bukharinites, and others—extreme repressive measures were not used against them. The fight was on ideological grounds. But some years later when socialism in our country was fundamentally constructed, when the exploiting classes were generally liquidated, when the Soviet social structure had radically changed, when the social basis for political movements and groups hostile to the party had violently contracted, when the ideological opponents of the party were long since defeated politically, then the repression directed against them began." This was thought to be particularly evil because it paved the way for similar treatment of "many honest Communists . . . who actively fought against the Trotskyites and the Rightists for the Leninist party line."[110]

In contrasting the political methods of Lenin and Stalin, Khrushchev made a remarkable admission. He cited the opposition to the October Revolution by Zinoviev and Kamenev as an example of how Lenin won deviators back and secured valuable collaboration from them: "After the Great Socialist October Revolution, as is known, Zinoviev and Kamenev were given leading positions in which they carried out most responsible party tasks. . . . Lenin did not pose the question of their arrest and certainly not their shooting." Even the Trotskyists came within the terms of Khrushchev's posthumous amnesty: "At present, after a sufficiently long historical period, we can speak about the fight with the Trotskyites with complete calm and can analyze this matter with sufficient objectivity. . . . These . . . individuals took an active part in the workers' movement before the revolution, during the Socialist October Revolution itself, and also in the consolidation of the victory of this greatest of revolutions. Many of them broke with Trotskyism and returned to Leninist positions. Was it necessary to annihilate such people? We are deeply convinced that had Lenin lived, such an extreme method would not have been used against many of them."[111]

Khrushchev bitterly denounced the method of establishing "guilt" through confessions extracted by torture. While the specific subject of his remarks was the treatment of the purged Stalinists, an article published shortly afterwards on the same theme linked the repudiated method of confession with its most noted practitioner, Andrei Vyshinsky, chief prosecutor at the trials of the oppositionists.[112] After the Twentieth Congress the analogous purge trials held in Hungary and Bulgaria in 1949 were publicly repudiated. Following this obvious precedent, and in the light of Khrushchev's new stand on the Opposition, it would be logical for the Soviet government to announce the falsity of the three great show trials of 1936, 1937 and 1938. In later references to the old Opposition, the tone of vituperation was conspicuously diminished. Trotsky was actually referred to in one historical connection as "Comrade Trotsky."*[113] Osinsky and Rykov were mentioned without censure when *Pravda* published a letter attacking bureaucratic cover-ups which Lenin addressed to them in 1922.[114]

Probably more significant than these isolated gestures was the call emanating from the Twentieth Congress for completely revising and reinvigorating the study of party history. Mikoyan delivered a sweeping indictment of the inadequacy of work on party history and did not spare even Stalin's *Short Course*. His attack was followed up by a detailed critique from the politically most prominent Soviet historian, A. M. Pankratova. She revealed in startling terms the effect of the Stalinist strait jacket: "It cannot but alarm us now that almost no serious scientific work is being done on the history of the party, that the journal dealing with party history questions, which existed before the war, is not published, and that there is no scientific center for studying the history of the party." Citing a variety of deficiencies, which ranged from the suppression of unpleasant facts to the uncritical defense of tsarist foreign policy, Pankratova observed, perhaps with conscious irony, "The work of Lenin's comrades-in-arms, the Old Bolsheviks, is very feebly reflected in our literature on party history."[115]

In line with these injunctions, the Marx-Engels-Lenin-Stalin Institute was reorganized in the spring of 1956 as the Institute of Marxism-Leninism, with responsibility for the study of general party history as well as the works of

---

* I noted remarkably dispassionate mentions of Trotsky in lectures on party history and the Soviet Army which I heard in Leningrad and Moscow in the fall of 1956, but the lecturers reverted to the familiar denunciations when I questioned them specifically on him.

the prophets. Some long-banned material, including the works of rehabilitated purge victims, certain strictly anti-Communist tracts, and the second and third editions of Lenin's collected works (with their abundance of historically objective footnotes), could again be used freely by Soviet scholars, though the writings of the Opposition leaders remained proscribed.[116] Republication of the minutes of the party congresses has commenced. In 1957 a new journal of party history, *Voprosy istorii KPSS* (Questions of the History of the CPSU), was launched, though to date it has not distinguished itself in critical-mindedness.

Logically, the Soviet repudiation of Stalin, particularly with the references that have been made to the time of Lenin's "Testament," would imply the rehabilitation of the memory of all those oppositionists who stood against Stalin from that time on and who warned against the perversion of power which actually took place. Such a reversal on the Opposition, however, would be extremely disruptive—far more so than the admission of injustice in the cases of the Stalinists and the military. The present Soviet leaders have inherited their basic mode of thought from Stalin and the years of his climb to power. This is the psychology of unity, unanimity, and self-justification, the evolution of which figured so prominently in the era of factional struggle within the Russian Communist Party. In all of Khrushchev's expostulation on the virtues of Leninist collective leadership, there was not the remotest reference to the taking of votes and the public expression of disagreement among the leadership, which constantly recurred while Lenin was still governing. Stalin's fixation on unity has been preserved by his followers, even though it was the root of the cult of personality which the followers, now dominant themselves, profess to repudiate. They cannot dispense with authorities and leaders, nor with demigods and devils. The new attitude both toward Lenin and toward the old Opposition remains a Stalin-like one. A cult of Lenin has replaced that of Stalin, with barely diminished proportions, though ancestor worship, to be sure, is by its nature less offensive than the deification of a ruling prince.

We have witnessed, moreover, the institution of the cult of personality in reverse—Stalin as an individual became a scapegoat for countless failings of the Soviet state, and particularly for the near-defeat of the Red Army in 1941. It is hardly necessary to mention Beria, whose place in the new demonology rivals Trotsky's a generation back. Meanwhile, individual leadership was finally restored when Khrushchev ousted Malenkov, Molotov, and Kaganovich from the party and governmental command in June 1957. Khrushchev's power was only underscored when he assumed the premiership himself in March 1958. Stalin has been desanctified, but Stalinism, purged of some of its more insane abuses, lives on.

15

WHY THE OPPOSITION FAILED

There is a certain romance in the history of lost causes. Heroes who go down to defeat can be glorified at will and contrasted to those whose character is revealed in the glare of victory and its responsibilities. Success is often determined by the winner's qualities of evil, and this was notably true in the history of the Russian Revolution. The revolutionaries who fought for an ideal were overwhelmed by those who contented themselves with the defense or enlargement of a system of power. The task which remains here, however, is not to praise or to lament, but to extract the understanding that events may yield. The Opposition failed: what does this imply about the political and social circumstances in which their cause came to grief?

Political Weaknesses of the Opposition

The failure of the Communist Opposition movements in Russia is easy to account for, though the immediate explanation has deeper implications. The Opposition's record was an unmitigated series of defeats at the hands of an apparently omnipotent party organization. At each critical juncture the Opposition displayed such vacillation, disunity, tactical obtuseness, and organizational ineptness that one can only wonder how the forces of Communist dissent managed to survive as long as they did.

The history of the Opposition affords a number of obvious political morals. First of all it points up the vital role which leadership can sometimes play in history, and the grievous consequences which the lack of resolute leadership can have for a movement. There is another lesson in the various tactical blunders which were committed by the Opposition leaders. Disunity within the Opposition, as different currents of criticism mistook each other for the real enemy, made it still easier for the organization men to assert their power. Finally, the oppositionists were crippled by doctrine: acceptance of the principles of the Leninist party deprived them of any ultimate appeal to basic beliefs.

If politics is an art at all, it is the art of leadership. The Communist Opposition movements were conspicuously lacking in this essential. The talent, it seems, was scarce; the vision was myopic; and the will, which was crucial, failed at every decisive turn. It is difficult to avoid the feeling that the Bolshevik leaders, whether in command or in opposition, were on the whole an undistinguished lot. There was, to be sure, much intelligence among them and a measure of integrity, very unevenly distributed. Force of will was much less common, and where it was found it was unlikely to be accompanied by strength of character. There were few top Bolsheviks who could be effective not only as followers but as leaders also. Lenin and the kind of party he built up did not provide a congenial atmosphere for men of stature.

There was in the Opposition one outstanding exception to this rule: he, of course, was Trotsky, whose place in history is secure as one of the three figures of heroic proportions which the Russian Revolution produced. Trotsky was a born leader, and he probably comes closer to the Western image of a statesman than any of his colleagues. Yet Trotsky had fatal limitations. In times of crisis he could rise to heights of inspired greatness and command the impassioned loyalty of his movement in unyielding struggle against the foe. This was Trotsky as the voice of the St. Petersburg Soviet in 1905, the leader of the Bolshevik insurrection in 1917, the organizer of victory in the Civil War. Trotsky was an outstanding leader, but no politician. When the question was a contest for power and influence within the movement, Trotsky was ineffective. Throughout the years between 1905 and 1917 he stood alone, refusing to follow another, unable to draw followers to himself. His attitude toward Lenin from 1917 on was ambivalent. He was a follower only with reservations and almost a power unto himself as the acknowledged second-in-command of the movement. He made an effort to comply with the Bolshevik habit of revering Lenin—more so than did some Bolsheviks, perhaps to compensate for his earlier opposition. But still he had a mind of his own and continued to clash with Lenin. He could be neither the docile follower nor the uninhibited opponent. Trotsky in opposition, while Lenin still lived, was always the vacillator, the proponent of half-measures, the man who could only annoy the one faction while failing to give the other the resolution which it needed. Thus did he act in the Brest-Litovsk controversy, in the trade-union controversy of 1920–1921, in the New Course controversy of 1923.

From the very beginning, the record of the Opposition was one of high-minded irresolution and ineffectiveness. The Left Communists could easily have deposed Lenin in 1918 in order to form a government with the Left SRs, but their nerve failed. The Workers' Opposition and the Democratic Centralists were unable to achieve any results from the political capital which they had accumulated in 1920. The most fateful lost opportunity was Trotsky's in 1923. With more foresight, a little of his former boldness, willingness to use the army, and moderate good fortune, Trotsky very probably could have made himself the successor to Lenin. He preferred to connive behind the scenes, where his disadvantage was greatest, while his potential followers were left floundering. When his supporters were forced out into the open in the December debates, Trotsky fled from the field of battle.

Between 1925 and 1927 the record of Opposition leadership was considerably better, but then it was too late: the power of the secretarial machine had grown too strong. In organizational durability and political determination the Opposition made its best showing during these years. Much of this is to the credit of the Leninist offshoot—the Zinoviev group—which found itself driven into the arms of the Left. Trotsky too showed himself more of a fighter in 1926 and 1927 than he had since Civil War days. No one can deny him tribute for the courage which he displayed in adversity, then and in exile, right up to the time of his murder.

But even the United Opposition made serious mistakes. Their tactics of thrust and retreat repeatedly mystified their followers. The controversy was always shrouded in semisecrecy, as the Opposition tried to confine the debate to the top levels of the party. The bold course of open and repeated appeal to the public could have been no more harmful. The blunder of secrecy was a major factor in the undoing of the Right Opposition. No one outside the inner circles could be sure what the furor was all about, let alone who stood for what, until the Right had been stripped of all means of defense. The Right Opposition was the most deficient of all in the will and courage of their leadership—but this, after all, was the quality which drew them to the Leninist Right in the first place.

Weaknesses or mistakes of leadership cannot be held solely responsible for the defeat of the Opposition, for the men in command of the party organization were no more distinguished as imaginative statesmen. Disunity within the Opposition ranks made the victory of the organization an easy matter. Against Lenin the Opposition was hopelessly divided by the cleavage between the moderate Left and the Ultra-Left. This permitted the decisive Leninist advance of 1921 and the eradication of the Ultra-Left as a significant political force. Later the issues changed, as emergent Stalinism began to alienate not only the Left but the cautious Leninists as well. Only after it was too late did men in both currents of Bolshevism—anyone who still had any concern for the human values which the revolution was supposed to promote—awake to appreciate their common concerns and see them go down to ignominious defeat. The Leninist-Leftist cleavage was decisive during Stalin's rise in dividing the potential resistance: first when it kept Trotsky and Zinoviev at swords' points; later when it made antagonists of the united Left and the Right. Traditional disputes made the Opposition concentrate their fire on the wrong targets, their potential friends, while the latter in the meantime outdid themselves in closing the last loopholes of political freedom in the party.

The disunity and the irresolution of the Opposition are traceable to a deeper defect: the Opposition lacked the necessary vision or self-consciousness about what it was and where it wanted to go. The movement needed a clear doctrine which would give it a realistic sense of the problems it faced and the goals it could achieve. The democracy of the oppositionists was felt rather than thought, and they had no assurance of their rightness. Intellectually they had only the illusions of Marxism and the organizational strictures of Leninism to turn to, and could never disenchant themselves from the myth of the proletarian dictatorship.

A good measure of poetic justice is to be found in the fate of the Opposition. There was scarcely a Bolshevik who could not temper his ideals of democratic procedure as long as his party was in power and he himself was in the good graces of the leadership. Rare indeed were the party members who made a principle of tolerance for non-Communists: Dmitri Riazanov, on the far right of the party, and Gabriel Miasnikov, on the far left, were almost alone in holding such standards. Democracy for all Communists was more stoutly defended, largely by the Ultra-Left, and even a success in these terms, such as might have occurred in 1920, could have made the course of Soviet history far different. Certain of the Ultra-Left leaders, particularly Valerian Osinsky and Timofei Sapronov of the Democratic Centralists, deserve much more recognition by history for sustaining as long as they did the courage of their antiauthoritarian convictions. It is the moderate Left, and above all Trotsky, whose compromises with principle made their fate unlamentable. When they shared power, until they found themselves victimized, they felt little compunction about the rigors of the collective dictatorship. They tolerated the curtailment of free expression until the machinery of curtailment could no longer be kept in check. As for the Leninists who went over to the Opposition—the Zinoviev group and the Right—they compromised no democratic principles, for in no real sense did they have any.

THE PREMISES OF LENINISM

As obvious lesson can be drawn from the Opposition's neglect of democratic principles. Rosa Luxemburg wrote in 1918, to rebuke the Bolsheviks: "Freedom only for the supporters of the government, only for the members of one party . . . is no freedom at all. Freedom is always and exclusively freedom for the one who thinks differently. . . . Its effectiveness vanishes when 'freedom' becomes a special privilege."[1] Yet it is not enough to berate the Opposition; the reason for their failing must be sought out.

It might be said that almost everyone in the Communist Party lived under a spell, transfixed by the political witchcraft of the party's founder. The term Leninism and the codification of its principles did not come into vogue until after Lenin's death, but its elements were by then well established in party belief and practice. The principles were the same ones that Lenin had elaborated in the early 1900s and confirmed in all their force in 1921. Unity was the watchword, with all that it implied concerning centralization, authority, discipline, and orthodoxy. There was no room for a second voice. Trotsky wrote in 1924, when he was trying to prove his orthodoxy: "The party must, at the price of whatever violence and harsh measures are expedient, guarantee the unity of its revolutionary method, its political line, its traditions—the unity of Leninism. In this case it would even be incorrect to refrain from 'repression.' "[2]

Lenin's conception of party discipline did not go so far beyond European parliamentary practice as to be fatal in itself. The critical step was the political monopoly of the Communist Party established during the Civil War. Disciplinary action by the party could then mean political annihilation. The party monopoly per se did not inevitably imply the eradication of democracy within the party; for a time there were signs of the development of a multi-faction system within the party which could have established considerable political latitude. Such a possibility was abruptly ruled out, however, by the organizational decisions of 1921. Thenceforth the combination of Leninist discipline within the party and the threat of oblivion outside it made the existence of opposition a fruitless anomaly.

The Opposition from 1923 on were hopelessly crippled by their accept-ance of these party standards. They were paralyzed by the fear that they might be forced to become a second party, which, according to the pseudo-Marxist reasoning then current, could only be a reflection of antiproletarian and hence counterrevolutionary forces. The psychology of proletarian relativ-ism was unchallenged: everything the Communist Party leadership did was "proletarian" by definition; and the only steps which were "proletarian" were those authorized by the Communist Party leadership. No one seems to have inquired why the proletariat could not, like the bourgeoisie, be represented by two or more parties. Years of exile finally brought Trotsky to admit the original political sin of one-party rule: "It is necessary to prepare the arena for two parties . . . maybe three or four. It is necessary to smash away the dictatorship of Stalin. . . . If this new political upheaval is successful, the masses, with these experiences, will never permit the dictatorship of one party, of one bureaucracy."[3]

Within the ever-narrowing confines of the disciplined party the currents of Communist Opposition swirled and died without effect. At each critical turning point the pattern was the same: disagreement over principle and expediency; controversy; settlement of the controversy by organizational pressure in favor of the people who controlled the organization and favored expediency; and curtailment of the freedom to oppose in the future. Some-thing of this sequence can be seen even in prerevolutionary Bolshevism, at the time of the 1909 split. With the Brest-Litovsk controversy of 1918 it had clearly become established and was then repeated in 1921, 1923, 1925, 1926-1927, 1928-1929. With each victory of the organization over the dissenters, the path for later opposition became more difficult; each successive victory of the principles of Leninism was easier and more certain.

The power of the party machine was the other side of the coin. The machinery was built to implement the principles of Leninism, and the two reciprocally reinforced one another. Stalin's victory, in the last analysis, was not a personal one, but the triumph of a symbol, of the individual who embodied both the precepts of Leninism and the techniques of their enforcement.

For the rank-and-filer, the movement and its constituted authorities were everything. Identification with the movement was important even for the Opposition: they could only insist that they were its genuine defenders, the purest Leninists. Despite their treatment at the hands of the organization, the Opposition could never break with the Leninist premise of the sole and united proletarian party. They were unable to deny that the party embodied the cause, and they could not admit that the cause to which they had dedicated their lives had gone wrong. This is why Bukharin had to confess as he did. The subordination of the self to the movement, while it may have its roots in the psychology of the irrational, nevertheless has to be acknowledged as a demonstration of principle. Karl Radek said, when the new discipline was being debated in 1921, "I feel that it may be turned against us; but in spite of this, I stand for the resolution. . . . Let the Central Committee at the moment of danger take the sternest measures against the best comrades, if it finds this necessary."[4] Such self-sacrifice is not always the noblest course. Here it undermined other principles, democratic expectations, and revolutionary hopes, and in the end all was lost. The party principle pointed directly to the destruction of the Opposition and the perfection of the totalitarian state. But Leninism was not solely responsible for this; there were other and greater forces at work.

THE TIDE OF SOCIAL EVOLUTION

Russia after the revolution was in a unique state of flux and acutely sensitive to a complex set of historical forces which were molding the future character of the society in the shape of a monolithic authoritarianism. The Leninist party was one of these factors, but combined with it were the effects of revolution and civil war, the autocratic background of Russian politics, the needs and costs of economic development, and the general drift of industrialized societies toward more elaborate and centralized systems of organization and communication. The combination of these forces exerted an overwhelming pressure on Russia to adopt a form of social organization which, broadly speaking, can be described as bureaucratic or totalitarian. The Communist Opposition took their stand against the march of history, fitfully and inconsistently, though often valiantly. In retrospect there was little hope for their success. Stalin was victorious because he embodied the totalitarian trend and did everything in his power to accelerate it and capitalize on it.

Total revolution is a rare phenomenon in history, with its own distinctive laws. The kind of revolution which Russia experienced, with the fanatic devotion and violent hatreds unleashed during its course, leads almost inevitably to dictatorship—in this case a rule more despotic than that which was overthrown. The Russian revolutionaries were inexorably caught up in the cataclysm which they had helped to bring on.

Probably the most decisive single event impelling the Communists to dictatorial rule was the outbreak of the Civil War, which itself was an integral phase of the revolutionary process. The emotions of life-or-death struggle and the militarization of the Communist organization between 1918 and 1920 confirmed and reinvigorated Lenin's conspiratorial model of the party, and bequeathed the institution of one-party rule, where opposition was synonymous with treason. Paradoxically, it was the end of open conflict and the relaxation of the revolution in 1921 that put a premium on the dictatorial aspect of Bolshevism. From this time on it was no longer revolutionary emotion but their monopoly of political organization which sustained the Communists in power, and they felt compelled to adhere to the system of command which the Civil War had called forth.

The Bolsheviks were well aware of their position at a historic turning point, and they always acted with the model of the French Revolution vividly in their minds. They naturally envisaged themselves as the Jacobins, and, while they hoped to avoid the fate of the latter, they were disquieted by the idea of a possible "Thermidorean" reaction and a "Bonapartist" dictatorship. The rival factions were fond of hurling charges about such tendencies back and forth. While the Communists did maintain political continuity in Russia, and thus distinguished their revolution from the kaleidoscopic sequence of events in France, basic changes nonetheless took place. From the vantage point of two or three decades, one can discern remarkable analogies between the Russian Revolution and the French, with a "Thermidorean" reaction in 1921 and a "Bonapartist" dictatorship after 1929.

More important than tagging the phases of the Communist regime with the labels of French revolutionary governments is the comprehension of the basic process of social psychology which seems to characterize all the major revolutions. Revolutionary emotion and utopian fervor reach a peak, as in Russia in 1918, after which they must inevitably subside. In this perspective the history of the Communist Opposition is the history of the ebbing revolutionary wave. As the idealistic excesses of revolution lose their impetus, they yield to excesses of unlimited power: the dictatorship to which revolutionary emotion gives rise continues independently of its origin and seeks to expand and perpetuate itself. If it is a law of revolution that the means of violent change tend to become ends in themselves, the Soviet record conforms closely.

It is remarkable that, although the revolution involved such a consciously violent break with the past, the tradition and habit bequeathed by the Russian past were by no means swept away. Indeed, they seem to have emerged again, step by step, with renewed vigor. No tsar since Peter attempted such a grandiose national transformation by governmental command, until Stalin made his appearance on the historical scene. One must turn back to the days of Ivan the Terrible for an analogue of the devious duplicity and paranoiac vengeance with which the Communist dictator consolidated and maintained his rule. Violent revolutionary upheaval, though a political impasse may make it inescapable, cannot be counted on as a force for progress; more likely it means turning the clock back.

Direct political continuity between tsarism and Communism is not hard to demonstrate. The historical legacy, the habits of despotic government by the rulers and of fatalistic, if sullen, submission by the ruled, could not be quickly overcome. The Communist, finding himself a bureaucrat, proceeded to act according to the notions of bureaucratic behavior which he had gained from his experience with the old officialdom, either as his overlords before the revolution or as his colleagues afterwards. If the Communists did in fact "smash" the tsarist governmental machinery, as they claimed, they were compelled to build a new one immediately and, as they candidly admitted, had to use the old materials or copy them. The upsets of revolution and the problem of reconstructing the administrative machinery actually exaggerated the despotic tradition of the Russian bureaucracy.

It should occasion no surprise that Communist Russia sooner or later returned to so many of the traits of the tsarist past. No nation could be expected to digest immediately the new fruits of political freedom. To the victim of despotism, all authority is suspect; anarchism was the universal response of the Bolsheviks' revolutionary forebears in Russia. Democracy requires the acceptance of authority, not its repudiation, and a widely diffused sense of cooperation and self-discipline, which a nation can only acquire gradually. Utter defiance can be hammered into a political order only by an authority powerful enough to crush all those who defy it. In revolutionary Russia, it is hard to conceive of any regime that could have fulfilled the minimum requirements of governing without resorting to force and becoming a dictatorship.

Together with the crippling political legacy of tsarism, Soviet Russia inherited a set of economic problems which could well bring any high-minded government to grief. The country was in the throes of the industrial revolution when the political upheaval struck, and most of the people had not accomplished the transition from their own peasant culture to the modern European mode of life. Russia was the first of the nations outside the orbit of Western European civilization to feel the Western impact and to attempt to reconstitute itself on Western lines. The revolution was not the product of the situation that Marx had anticipated; it was not the result of industrial maturity, but the outcome of the stressful beginnings of rapid industrialization in imitation of Europe. This explains the crucial anomaly of a movement espousing socialism and coming to power in a locale where the preconditions of the ideal were absent.

Russia's relative backwardness was realized only too well by the Communists. Trotsky's theory of permanent revolution was the most sophisticated explanation of the situation and its dangers, and logically became the target when Stalin commenced arguing that backwardness had nothing to do with the prospects for socialism. The inescapable task of the revolutionary regime in Russia—of any regime which would successfully hold power in Russia and realize the nation's potential—was the modernization and industrialization of the country. This, however, demanded policies and methods which made socialism as originally conceived seem even more remote. The Left Opposition clearly diagnosed the problems of industrialization, but the remedy, posed in the "Preobrazhensky dilemma," was one from which they shrank. The Right Opposition were even more apprehensive when such an industrialization program became imminent. It was Stalin, committed to the ruthless amassing of power in and through the party organization, who equipped himself with the instruments and the determination to apply the totalitarian solution.

Industrialization, when and insofar as it was achieved, did not bring any abatement of the pressure toward bureaucratic social organization. The Communists were never more wrong than when they supposed that the growth of the industrial way of life would make the functions of control and administration simpler, and that an equalitarian democracy, devoid of official hierarchies, would naturally ensue. Rapid construction of large-scale industry and its continued operation both required elaborate arrangements of discipline, managerial authority, and administrative centralization (whether corporate or governmental). Meanwhile, the revolution had caused a loosening of all habits and institutions and a readiness to use violent measures to introduce change and also to deal with immediate problems. In consequence, the flux of revolution made Russian society unusually responsive to certain of the organizational implications of industrialization.

The Soviet regime lost little time in restoring managerial authority in the factories and, with the collectivization of agriculture, extended it to the farms as well. Over the agonized protests of the Opposition, the collegial principle of administration was rapidly liquidated in favor of strict individual authority vested in a hierarchy of officials—party, administrative, and industrial. Ultimately, except for state ownership and the substitution of the plan for profit making, Soviet industry revived all the internal forms and social distinctions that characterize capitalism. It was actually a more perfect bureaucracy, freed from the anomalies of competition and independent trade unions.

Russia, though a relative newcomer among the industrial nations, has gone beyond all the others in the adaptation of its social order to the centralizing and disciplinary logic of modern industry. That it could do so is the result, again, of the flux of revolution, together with the unconscionable pragmatism of the Leninist Bolsheviks. Soviet institutions were molded to the demands of industrial growth and efficiency much more freely than their counterparts in the established industrial societies of the West. Society at large became one great factory, with its discipline and its ranks of skill. The dominant class, if any could be so styled, was not the proletariat but the new "intelligentsia" of administrators and technicians—those who won reward and prestige by virtue of education and officeholding. The idea of the "managerial revolution" is not far wrong.[5] The forms of civil bureaucracy and military command have coincided in the totalitarian industrial order.

The pressure of historical circumstances, exerted equally by backwardness and by its successful liquidation, makes it appear that the goal of socialism to which the Russian revolutionaries had initially dedicated themselves was an unattainable vision. On the other hand, the Soviet regime as it actually developed was not the only possible response to the problems of industrialization. The outcome of events in Russia was the result of a complex (and in their particular combination unique) set of social forces, accidents, and personalities. The Communist perversion of socialist ideals was caused by this specific historical situation, not by any logic inherent in the idea.

If socialism is defined concretely and undogmatically as a social order where both equality and the democratic control of economic institutions are maximized as far as is practicable, it is easy to see how events in Russia frustrated such an objective. The experience of total revolution and its retrogressive political implications would alone delay a development toward socialism as here defined. Economic and cultural backwardness poses impassable barriers until it is overcome, while a successful effort to accomplish this is likewise incompatible with the proximate realization of the ideal. Industrialism itself poses serious obstacles to the progress of democracy and equality, as the Soviet experience has demonstrated so graphically.

There is one further factor distinctive to Russia until the Soviets began to export it—the political methods of Leninism, embodied in the theory and practice of the Communist parties. Leninism became, in effect, a movement and philosophy competing with and antagonistic to socialism. This was the significance of the long contest between the means of revolution, represented by Lenin and the Stalinists, and the revolutionary goals which the Opposition tried to defend.

Stalin succeeded for the same reason that the Opposition failed: he put himself on the side of all the pressures which were working in the bureaucratic and totalitarian direction, and made himself their personification. He linked Lenin's conception of the party with this trend by proclaiming the party to be the natural and for all practical purposes permanent form of rule for the postrevolutionary society. Meanwhile, he could maintain continuity with the revolutionary past and the socialist ideal only by the most farfetched doctrinal reinterpretations. To sustain them he felt compelled to annihilate every person and every thought that threatened to challenge the official image of the regime. Stalin's historical role was to effect a particular resolution of the forces acting on postrevolutionary Russian society. The power of Stalin and his party, and the bureaucratic trend in the country at large, mutually reinforced each other. With the die of his sinister will, Stalin stamped Russia into the totalitarian mold.

MARX, TROTSKY, STALIN

Retrospectively it is clear that the Russian Revolution was not the revolution which Marx expected, but one which made false claims to the Marxian legitimacy. How it came about that the protagonists of socialism shifted their sights while imagining that they were still on the same target has been described here at length. On this score there was an unbridgeable gulf between the party leadership and the Left Opposition at every stage; the historical import of the Opposition was to record in their protests the evolution of the Soviet regime away from Marxism.

The irony of events was that a movement professing certain aims came to power in the wrong place and ultimately had to recast its goals in conformance with the actual problems which confronted it. Lenin and Stalin between them arrived at a completely new meaning of socialism: not an ideal system based on established industry and stressing the even distribution of economic value and political power throughout the population, but a system for accomplishing industrialization and overcoming backwardness, with stress on bureaucratic authority and economic hierarchy. In this contraposition of old and new aims lay the most fundamental difference between the factions, with the Opposition committed to the old Marxist vision and the Stalinists blazing a new path of deliberate history making.

The doctrinal import of the factional cleavage—the Western perspective of postindustrial utopianism versus the Russian perspective of a dictatorial assault on backwardness—was paralleled by the contrasting intellectual backgrounds of the two currents. The oppositionists were typically Westernized émigrés, both Bolshevik and Menshevik, who had assimilated basic Western assumptions of socialism as a democratically constituted system based on prior industrial development. The Stalinists were Russia-oriented undergrounders, who took for granted the real political and economic implications of the Russian Revolution. Reality was on the side of the latter.

This cleavage between Europe-oriented and Russia-oriented revolutionaries had a series of analogues in the prerevolutionary history of Russian thought, extending back to the mid-nineteenth-century controversies between the "Westerners" and the "Slavophiles" over whether Russia's national development should or would take a European or a native course. Among the revolutionaries of the late nineteenth century the same sort of issue divided the Marxists and the Populists, who predicated their socialism respectively on the furtherance or the avoidance of the Western example of industrialization. Finally, among the Marxists another such split occurred, between the Mensheviks, who would copy European democracy and wait for socialism to follow the Europeanization which capitalism implied, and the Bolsheviks, who would use the workers but rely mainly on the Russian type of conspiratorial organization to accelerate and guarantee the revolution. All these divisions between the pro-Westerners and the anti-Westerners were characteristic for a country feeling the impact of a more advanced culture—in this case, the example of industrialized Western Europe. The challenge could be met by submitting and joining the dominant culture, or by nativistic defiance. Small wonder that when the latter course prevailed under Stalin, the Europeanists of the Left Opposition became devils incarnate.

As the foregoing discussion has suggested, the divergence between the Communist Left and the Leninists was in many respects a repetition of the original Menshevik-Bolshevik division. At least in relative terms the Left Opposition corresponded to the Mensheviks: more Western-oriented, more conscious of the industrial prerequisites for the socialist ideal, more democratic than the Lenin-Stalin current. This likeness was far from being an accidental parallel: the core of the Left Opposition leadership was Menshevik in its political beginnings, and the basic premises of the old split continued to rule down to the very end of the Communist factional controversies.

It was therefore with good reason that the Stalinist apparatus echoed and re-echoed the charge that the Left Opposition was a Menshevik deviation from Leninism. Molotov was correct in saying, "Trotskyism . . . was and is a remnant of the Social Democracy within our own ranks."[6] The oppositionists never ceased to protest that such charges were unfounded, that the Leninist orthodoxy of their views was not only above question but superior to the position of the party leadership. However, they had no real chance to rebut the charge of Menshevism because it was, in the deeper sense of the term, true.

The Menshevik character of the Opposition pervades their whole history. Menshevism, broadly speaking—and the Stalinists were speaking broadly when they used the term—is Marxist socialism which rebels at the political methods and organizational strictures of Leninism. It was this which distinguished the Mensheviks, including Trotsky and so many other future Left oppositionists, when the Russian Social Democrats first split in 1903. It was the same scruple, though usually not untarnished, which agitated the Communist Left throughout the decade following the revolution. While the Leninists were dominated by considerations of expediency alone, the Leftists could not abandon principles. In spite of themselves, the Left could never really stomach the discipline of Leninism. In 1924 Rudzutak (then a staunch Stalinist) observed crudely but with some justification: "I would say that the creation of a symbol of faith out of democratism is a real Menshevik belch, and this constitutes for the most part the position of our Opposition."[7] The tragedy of the Left Opposition was that they could not fully admit their own un-Leninist nature, which would have been their strongest defense.

Insofar as the Opposition were Menshevik, they were also better Marxists. Here the charges of deviation made against the Opposition were deserved more by the accusers. The oppositionists were attached to theory for its own sake and not just as a device for political manipulation. In particular they were able to employ Marxian reasoning about the historical process and the limitations which social and economic conditions might impose on political endeavors. Whereas for Lenin and for Stalin the party could accomplish nearly anything, given the requisite discipline and means of force, the Opposition were usually aware that Russia's historical circumstances made the attainment of the objectives of socialism a remote goal at best. This was precisely the Menshevik line of reasoning. Stalin's regime, as both Mensheviks and Trotskyists pointed out, was doing the work of capitalism, albeit in a different manner, and the nature of the regime was experiencing a corresponding metamorphosis. Here again the label of "Menshevik" officially pinned on the Opposition was entirely justified.

On the other hand, the differences between Menshevism and the Communist Left are by no means to be neglected. Trotsky was no fatalist; his program for the Opposition, after all, centered on planned industrial development to lay the foundations for socialism, although he did not pretend that the situational limitations on the revolution isolated in Russia could easily be overcome. Neither was Trotsky overly constrained by democratic scruple when it might be inconvenient (that is, when he was in power). The Leftists —particularly the moderate Left—could combine ruthless expediency with their principles. This, in the last analysis, proved to be their undoing. The Communist Left sealed their doom when they made the fatal error of committing themselves to Leninism. It was no defense for them to accept Leninist party standards and dispute the charge of Menshevik deviation; at every stage the Opposition's merit lay precisely in what the party leadership attacked them for.

STALIN'S RUSSIA

The era of the Opposition was the phase of Communism in evolution. As Lenin and those who followed him attacked the problems of political and economic success, the rigors of Russian circumstances came into play. The mentality of Leninism made adaptation to these circumstances a virtue, while it simultaneously pretended that the circumstances were being overcome. Leninism begat Stalinism in two decisive respects: it prepared a group of people ready to use force and authority to overcome any obstacles, and it trained them to accept any practical short-cut in the interest of the immediate success and security of the movement. Leninism thus made Russian Marxists ready to alter the basic nature of their movement and to execute a revolution far different from the one they had originally contemplated. Communism became, in essence, a movement to conquer backwardness, by force, violence, deceit, and control—in short, through the application of totalitarian politics. Communism is militaristic industrialism fortified with an irrelevant dogma.

In the struggle of the Leninists with the Opposition it is easy to observe both the developing political characteristics of the regime and the outlines of the problems which impelled the country toward totalitarianism. Cultural and economic backwardness, as well as the problems of managing the elements of modernity in the society, pressed for the solution of bureaucratic industrialism. The one-party dictatorship and the repression of factional activity, the political principles of Leninism, were relentlessly unfolding toward the time when but one voice was left, that of the omniscient dictator. Doctrine became dogma; intellectual life was doomed to total regimentation as the logical outcome of the frenzied reinterpretation of theory and history to justify the dictatorship in every step it took.

Personalities played a decisive role. The Bolshevik Party, to begin with, was Lenin's image writ large. In the transformations which Bolshevism underwent, the hand of Stalin, devious, vengeful, and self-deifying, was guiding the course of destiny. Here there can be no dispute that Trotsky's victory would have meant a vast difference: party dictatorship, undoubtedly, but without the clever perfection of one-man domination and hardly with such insane thought control or paranoiac ruthlessness. Furthermore, Trotsky's success would have been a victory against the party apparatus rather than through it, and would have reflected circumstances much less compelling toward dictatorship than was actually the case.

The rise of the party apparatus and the factional struggles between its representatives and the oppositionists were the specific conditions for the growth of Stalinism. Stalinism was not simply the manifestation of the party organization, but a product of the conflict between the instruments of the Communist movement and its standards of achievement—between political action and the revolutionary conscience. The conscience of the revolution, embodied in the Communist Opposition groups, failed to make itself effective. The Communist movement succumbed to the pressures and temptations of power; it defied its conscience and then proceeded to attack it. There was obviously deep uneasiness about this among the *apparatchiki,* similar to the guilt felt by anyone involved in action contrary to principles which have been ingrained in him. Rationalization was not enough to set at ease the minds of Stalin and his followers—they had to condemn every person and extirpate every thought which threatened to recall the proddings of their ideological heritage.

The history of the Soviet experiment is the record of the betrayal and perversion of great ideals. This fate was rigorously logical because of two original deficiencies—one material, one moral. On the one hand, the historical conditions were wrong. Both ancient Russia and industrial Russia combined to make the goals of socialism chimerical. On the moral side, the revolution was corroded from within by the methods adopted in pursuit of the goal. The effect of evil means was bad enough; but it was the destiny of Communism for the means to displace the ends and become ends in themselves.

Such is the nature of Communism as the historical study of the Opposition reveals it. It moved, in unplanned evolution, far from its initial aims and its original meaning. The people who stood up for these were trapped in the failings of the original scheme, and were crushed. Now all terms have lost their sense, as a new specter stalks the globe in the guise of another of a century ago. Its devotees and its enemies are equally deceived.

APPENDIXES
BIBLIOGRAPHY
NOTES
INDEX

APPENDIX I

Chronology of Important Events in the History of the Communist Party of the Soviet Union*

1898
March 1–3: First Congress of the RSDWP, Minsk.

1902
Lenin's "What is to be Done?" published in Stuttgart.

1903
July 30–August 23 (N.S.): Second Congress of the RSDWP, Brussels and London.

1904
August: Bolshevik "Conference of the Twenty-two," Geneva.

1905
January 9: "Bloody Sunday."
April 25–May 10 (N.S.): Third Party Congress, London.
September 7–9: Conference of the Social Democratic Organizations in Russia, Riga.
October: General strike.
October 13: Formation of the First St. Petersburg Soviet (suppressed December 3).
October 17: "October Manifesto."
December 12–17: First Conference of the RSDWP, Tammerfors.
December 6–17: General strike and insurrection, Moscow.

1906
March: Election of the First Duma (convened April 27; dissolved July 8).
April 23–May 8 (N.S.): Fourth Party Congress, Stockholm.
November 3–7: Second Party Conference, Tammerfors.

1907
January: Election of the Second Duma (convened February 20; dissolved June 3).
May 13–June 1: Fifth Party Congress, London.
July 21–23: Third Party Conference, Kotka (Finland).
November 5–12: Fourth Party Conference, Helsingfors.

1909
January 3–9 (N.S.): Fifth Party Conference, Paris.
June 21–30 (N.S.): Consultation of the Augmented Editorial Board of *Proletari*, Paris. Split in Bolshevik faction with expulsion of Otzovists-Ultimatists.

* Dates Old Style until February 1, 1918, unless indicated as New Style (N.S.).

1910

January 15–February 5 (N.S.): Plenum of the Central Committee of the RSDWP, Paris. Last Bolshevik-Menshevik unity effort.

1912

January 18–30 (N.S.): Sixth Party Conference, Prague.

1914

August 1 (N.S.): German declaration of war on Russia. Socialist splits.

1915

February 27–March 4 (N.S.): Conference of the Émigré Sections of the RSDWP, Berne.
September 18–21 (N.S.): Conference of Anti-War Socialists, Zimmerwald (Switzerland).

1917

February 27: February Revolution—Overthrow of Tsar Nicholas II. Formation of Provisional Government (March 2)—Prince Lvov Prime Minister.
March 12: Stalin and Kamenev return to Petrograd from Siberia.
March 28: Conference of Bolshevik delegates to the First Congress of Soviets.
April 3: Return of Lenin to Petrograd. "April Theses."
April 24–29: Seventh (April) Party Conference.
July 3–5: "July Days."
July 8: Kerensky becomes Prime Minister in Provisional Government.
July 26–August 3: Sixth Party Congress. Trotsky et al. admitted to Bolshevik Party.
September 12–14: Lenin calls for insurrection.
October 10: Bolshevik Central Committee decides on insurrection.
October 25: October Revolution—Overthrow of the Provisional Government by the Bolsheviks. Soviet government proclaimed; Lenin becomes Chairman of the Council of People's Commissars.
November 4: Resignation of Bolshevik leaders favoring free press and coalition.
December 2: Armistice with Germany. Brest-Litovsk negotiations begin.

1918

January 5–6: Convocation and dispersal of Constituent Assembly.
January 7: Lenin calls for peace—Brest-Litovsk controversy begins.
February 1 (O.S.) [February 14 (N.S.)]: Gregorian calendar put into effect.
February 23: Central Committee accepts German peace terms.
March 3: Treaty of Brest-Litovsk signed.
March 6–8: Seventh Party Congress.
March 10–14: Capital moved from Petrograd to Moscow.
March 13: Trotsky appointed Commissar of War.
May 25: Czecho-Slovak revolt. Beginning of large-scale civil war.
June 28: Decree of general nationalization. Beginning of War Communism.
July 6: Left SR revolt.
August: High point of Whites' Volga offensive.

1919

March 2–7: First Comintern Congress. Zinoviev elected Chairman of the Comintern.
March 18–23: Eighth Party Congress. Politburo, Orgburo, and Secretariat established.
April: High point of Kolchak's offensive in Urals.
October: High point of Denikin's offensive in South Russia. Yudenich's drive on Petrograd.
December 2–4: Eighth Party Conference.

1920

January: Collapse of Whites in Siberia.
March 29–April 5: Ninth Party Congress.
May–September: War with Poland.
July 21–August 6: Second Comintern Congress.
September 22–25: Ninth Party Conference. Control Commissions established.
November: Conquest of Crimea from Wrangel. End of Civil War.
November–March 1921: Trade-union controversy.

1921

March 2–17: Kronstadt Rebellion.
March 8–16: Tenth Party Congress. Beginning of NEP. "Resolution on Unity" condemns factional groupings within the Communist Party.
May 26–28: Tenth Party Conference.
June 22–July 12: Third Comintern Congress.
Summer–Fall: Party "purge."
December 19–22: Eleventh Party Conference.

1922

February: "Declaration of the Twenty-two" to the Comintern.
March 27–April 2: Eleventh Party Congress.
April 3: Stalin appointed General Secretary of the Communist Party.
May 26: Lenin's first stroke (returns to work, October).
August 4–7: Twelfth Party Conference.
September–April 1923: Controversy over Georgia and the nationality question.
November 4–December 5: Fourth Comintern Congress.
December 16: Lenin's second stroke.
December 25: Lenin's "Testament" (postscript January 4, 1926).
December 30: USSR established.

1923

January–March: Lenin's last articles. Controversy over party reform.
March 6: Lenin's break with Stalin.
March 9: Lenin's third stroke.
April 17–25: Twelfth Party Congress.
Summer: Scissors crisis and strike wave.
August (?): Kislovodsk conference on reorganizing the Secretariat.
October 8: Trotsky's letter attacking the party leadership.

October 15: "Declaration of the Forty-six."

October 21–23: German Communist revolution misfires.

November 7: Beginning of discussion on "Workers' Democracy."

December 5: Resolution of the Politburo on Workers' Democracy.

December 8: Trotsky's New Course letter.

December 14: Campaign against the Opposition begins.

1924

January 16–18: Thirteenth Party Conference. Opposition condemned.

January 21: Death of Lenin. Rykov becomes Chairman of the Council of People's Commissars.

February: "Lenin Enrollment."

April: Stalin's lectures, "Foundations of Leninism."

May 23–31: Thirteenth Party Congress.

June 17–July 8: Fifth Comintern Congress.

October: Trotsky's "Lessons of October" published. Anti-Trotsky campaign (to December).

December: Stalin proposes theory of "Socialism in one country."

1925

January 15: Trotsky forced to resign as Commissar of War.

April 27–29: Fourteenth Party Conference. High point of NEP.

December 18–31: Fourteenth Party Congress. Defeat of Zinoviev Opposition.

1926

February 12: Zinovievists removed from leadership of the Leningrad party organization.

April 6–9: Central Committee Plenum. United Opposition formed by Trotsky-Zinoviev coalition.

May 12: Collapse of general strike in Great Britain.

July 14–23: Central Committee Plenum. Lashevich Affair and "Declaration of the Thirteen." Removal of Zinoviev from Politburo.

October 16: Opposition capitulation.

October 23–26: Central Committee Plenum. Trotsky and Kamenev removed from Politburo. Zinoviev replaced by Bukharin as Chairman of the Comintern.

October 26–November 3: Fifteenth Party Conference. "Socialism in one country" debated.

1927

February 7–12: Central Committee Plenum. Need for economic planning stressed.

April 12: Anti-Communist coup by Chiang Kai-shek, Shanghai.

May: Rupture of relations with Great Britain. War scare (through summer).

May 25: "Declaration of the Eighty-four."

July 29–August 9: Central Committee Plenum. Issue of defeatism and threats to expell Opposition.

October 21–23: Central Committee Plenum. Trotsky and Zinoviev removed from Central Committee. Discussion of Lenin's "Testament."

November 7: Last Opposition demonstration.

November 15: Trotsky and Zinoviev expelled from Communist Party by Central Control Commission.

December 2–19: Fifteenth Party Congress. Left Oppositionists expelled from Communist Party.

1928

January: Left Opposition leaders exiled from Moscow (January 16—Trotsky sent to Alma-Ata).

January: Crisis over grain collections begins.

April 6–11: Central Committeee Plenum. Discussion of the grain problem.

May 18–July 5: Shakhty trial.

June: Zinovievists readmitted to the party.

July 4–12: Central Committee Plenum. Dispute between Stalin and the Right comes to a head.

July 11: Secret talk of Bukharin and Kamenev.

July 17–September 1: Sixth Comintern Congress.

September–October: Defeat of the Right Opposition in the Moscow party organization.

September 19: Kuibyshev calls for intensive industrialization.

September 30: Bukharin's "Notes of an Economist" published in *Pravda*.

October 1: Beginning of First Five Year Plan (set retroactively, April 1929).

October 18–19: Plenum of the Moscow party committee. Capitulation of Uglanov and the Right.

November 16–24: Central Committee Plenum. Stalin condemns the Right deviation and proclaims industrialization drive.

December 10–24: Eighth Trade Union Congress. Defeat of Right Opposition in the trade-union leadership.

1929

February 9–10: Politburo condemns Bukharin, Rykov, and Tomsky.

February 11: Trotsky deported from the USSR to Turkey.

April: Conference of Marxist-Leninist Scientific Research Institutions. Mechanist philosophy condemned.

April 16–23: Central Committee Plenum. Right deviation condemned.

April 23–29: Sixteenth Party Conference. First Five Year Plan declared to be in effect (retroactive to October 1, 1928).

June 2: Tomsky replaced by Shvernik as trade-union chairman.

July: Capitulation of Radek, Preobrazhensky, Smilga, et al.

July 3: Bukharin replaced by Molotov as Comintern chairman.

August 21: Public attack on Bukharin and the Right Opposition begins.

November 10–17: Central Committee Plenum. Capitulation of the Right Opposition. Bukharin removed from Politburo.

December 27: Stalin calls for accelerated collectivization of the peasantry and liquidation of the kulaks.

1930

June 26–July 13: Sixteenth Party Congress. Tomsky removed from Politburo.

December: Syrtsov-Lominadze affair.

December 17-21: Central Committee Plenum. Rykov removed from Politburo. Rykov replaced by Molotov as Chairman of the Council of People's Commissars (December 20).

1932

January 30–February 4: Seventeenth Party Conference.
October: Riutin affair. Zinoviev and Kamenev expelled from party for second time.

1933

January 1: Second Five Year Plan begins. (First Five Year Plan declared complete after four years and three months.)
January 7–12: Central Committee Plenum. Affair of A. P. Smirnov et al. Party purge begins (continuing until trials and liquidations of 1936–1938).

1934

January 26–February 10: Seventeenth Party Congress.
December 1: Assassination of Kirov.

1935

January 15–16: First trial of Zinoviev, Kamenev, et al.

1936

August 19–24: First of the Moscow Trials: Zinoviev, Kamenev, et al. convicted and executed.
August 23: Tomsky commits suicide.

1937

January 23–30: Second Moscow Trial: Radek, Piatakov, Sokolnikov, et al. convicted.
June: Secret trial and execution of Tukhachevsky and other military leaders.

1937–1938

Yezhovshchina—mass arrests and executions. Secret purge of Stalinist party leaders.

1938

March 2–13: Third Moscow Trial: Bukharin, Rykov, et al. convicted and executed.

1939

March 2-13: Eighteenth Party Congress.

1940

August 20: Trotsky assassinated, Coyoacan, Mexico.

1941

February 15–20: Eighteenth Party Conference.
May 6: Stalin becomes Chairman of the Council of People's Commissars.
June 22: German invasion of USSR.

1952
October 5–14: Nineteenth Party Congress.

1953
March 5: Death of Stalin. Malenkov becomes Chairman of the Council of Ministers.
June 27: Arrest and removal of Beria from party and government posts (tried and executed December 1953).

1955
February 8: Malenkov replaced by Bulganin as Chairman of the Council of Ministers.

1956
February 14–25: Twentieth Party Congress. Secret denunciation of Stalin by Khrushchev. "Rehabilitation" of Stalinist purge victims.

1957
June 29: Removal of Malenkov, Molotov, Kaganovich from party and government posts.

1958
March 27: Khrushchev becomes Chairman of the Council of Ministers.

APPENDIX II

Composition of the Chief Party Organs

January 1912—Sixth Conference

Central Committee

Goloshchekin, F. I.
Lenin, V. I.
Malinovsky, R.
Ordzhonikidze, G. K.
Schwartzman, D.
Zinoviev, G. Y.
(J. V. Dzhugashvili-Stalin
coopted afterwards)

Central Committee Candidates

Bubnov, A. S.
Kalinin, M. I.
Smirnov, A. P.
Spandarian, S.
Stasova, Y. D.

April 1917—Seventh Conference

Central Committee

Fedorov, G. F.
Kamenev, L. B.
Lenin, V. I.
Miliutin, V. P.
Nogin, V. P.
Smilga, I. T.
Stalin, J. V.
Sverdlov, Y. M.
Zinoviev, G. Y.

Central Committee Candidates

Bubnov, A. S.
Glebov-Avilov, N. P.
Pravdin, A.
Teodorovich, I. A.
(record of one lost)

August 1917—Sixth Congress

Central Committee

Berzin, Y. A.
Bubnov, A. S.
Bukharin, N. I.
Dzerzhinsky, F. E.
Kamenev, L. B.
Kollontai, A. M.
Krestinsky, N. N.
Lenin, V. I.
Miliutin, V. P.
Muranov, M. K.
Nogin, V. P.
Rykov, A. I.
Sergeyev, F. A.
Shaumian, S. G.
Smilga, I. T.
Sokolnikov, G. Y.
Stalin, J. V.
Sverdlov, Y. M.
Trotsky, L. D.
Uritsky, M. S.
Zinoviev, G. Y.

Central Committee Candidates

Dzhaparidze, P. A.
Ioffe, A. A.
Kiselev, A. S.
Lomov, G. I.
Preobrazhensky, Y. A.
Skrypnik, N. A.
Stasova, Y. D.
Yakovleva, V. N.
(record of two lost)

Sources: For the Central Committee: The Great Soviet Encyclopedia, 1st ed., LX (Moscow, 1934), 555–556. For the Politburo, Orgburo, and Secretariat, 1926–1933, *ibid.*, pp. 558–559; prior and subsequent years, as reported in *Pravda*.

March 1918—Seventh Congress

Central Committee

Bukharin, N. I.	Sokolnikov, G. Y.	
Dzerzhinsky, F. E.	Stalin, J. V.	
Krestinsky, N. N.	Stasova, Y. D.	
Lashevich, M. M.	Sverdlov, Y. M.	
Lenin, V. I.	Trotsky, L. D.	
Sergeyev, F. A.	Vladimirsky, M. F.	
Shmidt, V. V.	Zinoviev, G. Y.	
Smilga, I. T.		

Central Committee Candidates

Berzin, Y. A.
Ioffe, A. A.
Lomov, G. I.
Petrovsky, G. I.
Shliapnikov, A. G.
Stuchka, P.
Uritsky, M. S.

March 1919—Eighth Congress

Central Committee

Beloborodov, A. G.	Serebriakov, L. P.
Bukharin, N. I.	Smilga, I. P.
Dzerzhinsky, F. E.	Stalin, J. V.
Kalinin, M. I.	Stasova, Y. D.
Kamenev, L. B.	Stuchka, P.
Krestinsky, N. N.	Tomsky, M. P.
Lenin, V. I.	Trotsky, L. D.
Muranov, M. K.	Yevdokimov, G. Y.
Radek, K. B.	Zinoviev, G. Y.
Rakovsky, K. G.	

Central Committee Candidates

Bubnov, A. S.
Danishevsky, K.
Mitskevich-Kapsukas, A.
Sergeyev, F. A.
Shmidt, V. V.
Smirnov, I. N.
Vladimirsky, M. F.
Yaroslavsky, Y. M.

Politburo	*Politburo Candidates*	*Secretariat*
Kamenev	Bukharin	Krestinsky
Krestinsky	Kalinin	
Lenin	Zinoviev	*Orgburo*
Stalin		(varying composition)
Trotsky		

April 1920—Ninth Congress

Central Committee

Andreyev, A. A.	Rudzutak, Y. E.
Bukharin, N. I.	Rykov, A. I.
Dzerzhinsky, F. E.	Serebriakov, L. P.
Kalinin, M. I.	Sergeyev, F. A.
Kamenev, L. B.	Smirnov, I. N.
Krestinsky, N. N.	Stalin, J. V.
Lenin, V. I.	Tomsky, M. P.
Preobrazhensky, Y. A.	Trotsky, L. D.
Radek, K. B.	Yevdokimov, G. Y.
Rakovsky, K. G.	Zinoviev, G. Y.

Central Committee Candidates

Beloborodov, A. G.
Gusev, S. I.
Miliutin, V. P.
Molotov, V. M.
Muranov, M. K.
Nogin, V. P.
Petrovsky, G. I.
Piatnitsky, I. A.
Smilga, I. T.
Stuchka, P.
Yaroslavsky, Y. M.
Zalutsky, P. A.

424 APPENDIX II

April 1920—Ninth Congress—*Continued*

Politburo	Orgburo	Secretariat
(unchanged)	Serebriakov	Krestinsky
	Stalin	Preobrazhensky
	Krestinsky	Serebriakov
	Preobrazhensky	
	Rykov	

March 1921—Tenth Congress

Central Committee

Central Committee Candidates

Bukharin, N. I.	Rakovsky, K. G.	Chubar, V. Y.
Dzerzhinsky, F. E.	Rudzutak, Y. E.	Gusev, S. I.
Frunze, M. V.	Rykov, A. I.	Kirov, S. M.
Kalinin, M. I.	Sergeyev, F. A.	Kiselev, A. S.
Kamenev, L. B.	Shliapnikov, A. G.	Kuibyshev, V. V.
Komarov, N. P.	Stalin, J. V.	Miliutin, V. P.
Kutuzov, A.	Tomsky, M. P.	Osinsky, V. V.
Lenin, V. I.	Trotsky, L. D.	Piatakov, G. L.
Mikhailov, V. M.	Tuntul, I.	Safarov, G. I.
Molotov, V. M.	Voroshilov, K. Y.	Shmidt, V. V.
Ordzhonikidze, G. K.	Yaroslavsky, Y. M.	Smirnov, I. N.
Petrovsky, G. I.	Zinoviev, G. Y.	Sulimov, D. Y.
Radek, K. B.		Uglanov, N. A.
		Zalutsky, P. A.
		Zelensky, I. A.

Politburo	Politburo Candidates	Secretariat
Kamenev	Bukharin	Molotov
Lenin	Kalinin	("responsible secretary")
Stalin	Molotov	Mikhailov
Trotsky		Yaroslavsky
Zinoviev		

Orgburo		Orgburo Candidates
Komarov	Stalin	Dzerzhinsky
Mikhailov	Tomsky	Kalinin
Molotov	Yaroslavsky	Rudzutak
Rykov		

April 1922—Eleventh Congress

Central Committee

Central Committee Candidates

Andreyev, A. A.	Kamenev, L. B.	Badaev, A. Y.
Bukharin, N. I.	Korotkov, A.	Bubnov, A. S.
Chubar, V. Y.	Kuibyshev, V. V.	Gusev, S. I.
Dzerzhinsky, F. E.	Lenin, V. I.	Kirov, S. M.
Frunze, M. V.	Molotov, V. M.	Kiselev, A. S.
Kalinin, M. I.	Ordzhonikidze, G. K.	Komarov, N. P.
Petrovsky, G. I.	Stalin, J. V.	Krivov, T.
Radek, K. B.	Tomsky, M. P.	Lebedev, N.

Central Committee—Continued		*Central Committee Candidates—Continued*
Rakovsky, K. G.	Trotsky, L. D.	Lepse, I. I.
Rudzutak, Y. E.	Voroshilov, K. Y.	Lobov, S. S.
Rykov, A. I.	Yaroslavsky, Y. M.	Manuilsky, D. Z.
Sapronov, T. V.	Zelensky, I. A.	Mikhailov, V. M.
Smirnov, A. P.	Zinoviev, G. Y.	Mikoyan, A. I.
Sokolnikov, G. Y.		Piatakov, G. L.
		Rakhimbaev, A.
		Safarov, G. I.
		Shmidt, V. V.
		Smilga, I. T.
		Sulimov, D. Y.

Poltiburo	*Politburo Candidates*	*Secretariat*
Kamenev	Bukharin	Stalin (General Secretary)
Lenin	Kalinin	Kuibyshev
Rykov	Molotov	Molotov
Stalin		
Tomsky		
Trotsky		
Zinoviev		

	Orgburo		*Orgburo Candidates*
Andreyev	Rykov		Kalinin
Dzerzhinsky	Stalin		Rudzutak
Kuibyshev	Tomsky		Zelensky
Molotov			

April 1923—Twelfth Congress

Central Committee		*Central Committee Candidates*
Andreyev, A. A.	Petrovsky, G. I.	Badaev, A. Y.
Bukharin, N. I.	Piatakov, G. L.	Bubnov, A. S.
Chubar, V. Y.	Radek, K. B.	Chudov, M. S.
Dzerzhinsky, F. E.	Rakovsky, K. G.	Kaganovich, L. M.
Frunze, M. V.	Rudzutak, Y. E.	Kolotilov, N. N.
Kalinin, M. I.	Rykov, A. I.	Kosior, S. V.
Kamenev, L. B.	Sokolnikov, G. Y.	Lebed, D. Z.
Kharitonov, M.	Stalin, J. V.	Lepse, I. I.
Kirov, S. M.	Sulimov, D. Y.	Miasnikov, A. F.
Komarov, N. P.	Smirnov, A. P.	Morozov, D.
Korotkov, A.	Tomsky, M. P.	Moskvin, I. M.
Kubiak, N. A.	Trotsky, L. D.	Narimanov, N.
Kviring, E. I.	Tsuriupa, A. D.	Orakhelashvili, M. D.
Lashevich, M. M.	Uglanov, N. A.	Rumiantsev, I. P.
Lenin, V. I.	Ukhanov, K. V.	Ryskulov, G.
Manuilsky, D. Z.	Voroshilov, K. Y.	Skrypnik, N. A.
Mikhailov, V. M.	Yevdokimov, G. Y.	Uryvaev, M. Y.
Mikoyan, A. I.	Zalutsky, P. A.	
Molotov, V. M.	Zelensky, I. A.	
Ordzhonikidze, G. K.	Zinoviev, G. Y.	

April 1923—Twelfth Congress—*Continued*

Politburo	Politburo Candidates	Secretariat
Kamenev	Bukharin	Stalin (General Secretary)
Lenin	Kalinin	Molotov
Rykov	Molotov	Rudzutak
Stalin	Rudzutak	Zelensky
Tomsky		
Trotsky		
Zinoviev		

	Orgburo	Orgburo Candidates
Andreyev	Rykov	Kalinin
Dzerzhinsky	Stalin	Zelensky
Molotov	Tomsky	
Rudzutak		

May 1924—Thirteenth Congress

Central Committee

Andreyev, A. A.	Krzhizhanovsky, G. M.	Rumiantsev, I. P.
Antipov, N. K.	Kubiak, N. A.	Shvarts, I. I.
Bubnov, A. S.	Kuklin, M.	Sokolnikov, G. Y.
Bukharin, N. I.	Lashevich, M. M.	Smirnov, A. P.
Chubar, V. Y.	Lepse, I. I.	Stalin, J. V.
Dogadov, A. I.	Manuilsky, D. Z.	Sulimov, D. Y.
Dzerzhinsky, F. E.	Medvedev, A. V.	Tomsky, M. P.
Frunze, M. V.	Mikhailov, V. M.	Trotsky, L. D.
Kaganovich, L. M.	Mikoyan, A. I.	Tsuriupa, A. D.
Kalinin, M. I.	Molotov, V. M.	Uglanov, N. A.
Kamenev, L. B.	Nikolaeva, K. I.	Ukhanov, K. V.
Kharitonov, M.	Ordzhonikidze, G. K.	Voroshilov, K. Y.
Kirov, S. M.	Petrovsky, G. I.	Yevdokimov, G. Y.
Kolotilov, N. N.	Piatakov, G. L.	Zalutsky, P. A.
Komarov, N. P.	Rakovsky, K. G.	Zelensky, I. A.
Kosior, S. V.	Rudzutak, Y. E.	Zinoviev, G. Y.
Krasin, L. B.	Rukhimovich, M. L.	

Central Committee Candidates

Artiukhina, A. B.	Krinitsky, A. I.	Shmidt, V. V.
Badaev, A. Y.	Lobov, S. S.	Skrypnik, N. A.
Chaplin, N. P.	Markov, A. T.	Smilga, I. T.
Chudov, M. S.	Miasnikov, A. F.	Strievsky, K. K.
Gei, K. V.	Morozov, D.	Syrtsov, S. I.
Glebov-Avilov, N. P.	Moskvin, I. M.	Tolokontsev, A. F.
Goloshchekin, F. I.	Narimanov, N.	Tseitlin
Ivanov, N.	Orakhelashvili, M. D.	Uryvaev, M. Y.
Ivanov, V. L.	Rakhimbaev, A.	Vareikis, I. M.
Kabakov, I. D.	Rumiantsev, K. A.	Vladimirov, M. K.
Kirkizh, K. I.	Ryndin, K. V.	Zorin
Korostelev, G.	Safarov, G. I.	

Politburo	Politburo Candidates	Secretariat
Bukharin	Dzerzhinsky	Stalin (General Secretary)
Kamenev	Frunze	Andreyev
Rykov	Kalinin	Kaganovich
Stalin	Molotov	Zelensky
Tomsky	Rudzutak	
Trotsky	Sokolnikov	
Zinoviev		

	Orgburo	Orgburo Candidates
Andreyev	Nikolaeva	Antipov
Bubnov	Smirnov	Chaplin
Dogadov	Stalin	Frunze
Kaganovich	Uglanov	Lepse
Kalinin	Voroshilov	
Molotov	Zelensky	

December 1925—Fourteenth Congress

Central Committee

Andreyev, A. A.	Kotov, V. A.	Rykov, A. I.
Antipov, N. K.	Krasin, L. B.	Shmidt, V. V.
Artiukhina, A. B.	Krzhizhanovsky, G. M.	Shvarts, I. I.
Badaev, A. Y.	Kubiak, N. A.	Shvernik, N. M.
Bauman, K. Y.	Kulikov, Y. F.	Smilga, I. T.
Bubnov, A. S.	Kviring, E. I.	Smirnov, A. P.
Bukharin, N. I.	Lepse, I. I.	Sokolnikov, G. Y.
Chicherin, G. V.	Lobov, S. S.	Stalin, J. V.
Chubar, V. Y.	Manuilsky, D. Z.	Stepanov-Skvortsov, I. I.
Chudov, M. S.	Medvedev, A. V.	Sulimov, D. Y.
Dogadov, A. I.	Mikoyan, A. I.	Tolokontsev, A. F.
Dzerzhinsky, F. E.	Mikhailov, V. M.	Tomsky, M. P.
Kabakov, I. D.	Molotov, V. M.	Trotsky, L. D.
Kaganovich, L. M.	Ordzhonikidze, G. K.	Tsiurupa, A. D.
Kalinin, M. I.	Petrovsky, G. I.	Uglanov, N. A.
Kamenev, L. B.	Piatakov, G. L.	Ukhanov, K. V.
Kirkizh, K. I.	Radchenko, A. F.	Voroshilov, K. Y.
Kirov, S. M.	Rakovsky, K. G.	Yevdokimov, G. Y.
Kolotilov, N. N.	Rudzutak, Y. E.	Zelensky, I. A.
Komarov, N. P.	Rumiantsev, I. P.	Zinoviev, G. Y.
Kosior, S. V.	Rukhimovich, M. L.	Zhukov, I. P.

Central Committee Candidates

Avdeyev, A. D.	Kaminsky, G. N.	Lukhashin, S. L.
Chaplin, N. P.	Kiselev, A. S.	Markov, A. T.
Eikhe, R. I.	Klimenko, I. Y.	Matveyev, D. I.
Gamarnik, Y. B.	Kondratev, T.	Melnichansky, G. P.
Gei, K. V.	Kosior, I. V.	Moskvin, I. M.
Goloshchekin, F. I.	Krinitsky, A. I.	Musabekov, G. K.
Ikramov, A.	Lashevich, M. M.	Nikolaeva, K. I.
Ivanov, V. L.	Liubimov, I. Y.	Nosov, I. P.
Kadatsky, I. F.	Lominadze, V. V.	Orakhelashvili, M. D.
Kalygina, A. S.	Lomov, G. I.	Osinsky, V. V.

December 1925—Fourteenth Congress—*Continued*

Central Committee Candidates—Continued

Postyshev, P. P.
Rumiantsev, K. A.
Ryndin, K. V.
Semenov, B. A.
Serebrovsky, A. P.

Skrypnik, N. A.
Strievsky, K. K.
Syrtsov, S. I.
Ugarov, F. Y.
Unshlikht, I. S.

Uryvaev, M. Y.
Vareikis, I. M.
Zhdanov, A. A.

Politburo

Bukharin
Kalinin
Molotov
Rykov
Stalin

Tomsky
Trotsky
Voroshilov
Zinoviev

Politburo Candidates

Dzerzhinsky
Kamenev
Petrovsky
Rudzutak
Uglanov

Secretariat

Stalin (General Secretary)
Kosior (S.)
Molotov

Uglanov
Yevdokimov

Secretariat Candidates

Artiukhina
Bubnov

Orgburo

Andreyev
Artiukhina
Bubnov
Dogadov
Kosior (S.)
Kviring

Molotov
Smirnov
Stalin
Uglanov
Yevdokimov

Orgburo Candidates

Chaplin
Lepse
Mikhailov
Shmidt
Ukhanov

December 1927—Fifteenth Congress

Central Committee

Akulov, I. A.
Andreyev, A. A.
Antipov, N. K.
Artiukhina, A. B.
Badaev, A. Y.
Bauman, K. Y.
Bubnov, A. S.
Bukharin, N. I.
Chicherin, G. V.
Chubar, V. Y.
Chudov, M. S.
Dogadov, A. I.
Gamarnik, Y. B.
Goloshchekin, F. I.
Kabakov, I. D.
Kaganovich, L. M.
Kalinin, M. I.
Kirkizh, K. I.
Kirov, S. M.
Knorin, V. G.
Kolotilov, N. N.
Komarov, N. P.
Kosior, I. V.
Kosior, S. V.

Kotov, V. A.
Krupskaya, N. K.
Krzhizhanovsky, G. M.
Kubiak, N. A.
Kuibyshev, V. V.
Kulikov, Y. F.
Kviring, E. I.
Lepse, I. I.
Liubimov, I. Y.
Lobov, S. S.
Lomov, G. I.
Manuilsky, D. Z.
Medvedev, A. V.
Menzhinsky, V. P.
Mikoyan, A. I.
Mikhailov, V. M.
Molotov, V. M.
Moskvin, I. M.
Orakhelashvili, M. D.
Petrovsky, G. I.
Piatnitsky, I. A.
Postyshev, P. P.
Rudzutak, Y. E.
Rukhimovich, M. L.

Rumiantsev, I. P.
Rykov, A. I.
Shmidt, V. V.
Shvarts, I. I.
Shvernik, N. M.
Skrypnik, N. A.
Smirnov, A. P.
Sokolnikov, G. Y.
Stalin, J. V.
Stepanov-Skvortsov, I. I.
Stetsky, A. I.
Strievsky, K. K.
Sulimov, D. Y.
Syrtsov, S. I.
Tolokontsev, A. F.
Tomsky, M. P.
Tsiurupa, A. D.
Ugarov, F. Y.
Uglanov, N. A.
Ukhanov, K. V.
Voroshilov, K. Y.
Zelensky, I. A.
Zhukov, I. P.

Central Committee Candidates

Alekseyev, P. A.
Antselovich, N. M.
Baranov, P. I.
Briukhanov, N. P.
Chaplin, N. P.
Chuvyrin, P. Y.
Chutskaev, S. Y.
Eikhe, R. I.
Eliava, S. Z.
Gei, K. V.
Griadinsky, F. P.
Ikramov, A.
Ivanov, V. L.
Kadatsky, I. F.
Kalygina, A. S.
Kaminsky, G. N.
Khataevich, M. M.

Kiselev, A. S.
Klimenko, I. Y.
Kolgushin, F. T.
Kondratev, T.
Krinitsky, A. I.
Leonov, F. G.
Lokatskov, F. I.
Lominadze, V. V.
Lozovsky, S. A.
Markov, A. T.
Melnichansky, G. P.
Mezhlauk, V.
Mirzoyan, L. I.
Mikhailov-Ivanov, M. S.
Musabekov, G. K.
Nikolaeva, K. I.
Nosov, I. P.

Oshvintsev, M. K.
Osinsky, V. V.
Polonsky, V. I.
Riutin, M. N.
Rumiantsev, K. A.
Ryndin, K. V.
Semenov, B. A.
Serebrovsky, A. P.
Sobolev, S. M.
Stroganov, V. A.
Sukhomlin, K. V.
Tsikhon, A. M.
Unshlikht, I. S.
Uryvaev, M. Y.
Vareikis, I. M.
Zhdanov, A. A.

Politburo

Bukharin
Kalinin
Kuibyshev
Molotov
Rudzutak

Rykov
Stalin
Tomsky
Voroshilov

Politburo Candidates

Andreyev
Chubar
Kaganovich
Kirov
Kosior (S.)
Mikoyan
Petrovsky
Uglanov

Secretariat

Stalin (General Secretary)
Kosior (S.)
Kubiak

Molotov
Uglanov

Secretariat Candidates

Artiukhina
Bubnov
Moskvin

Orgburo

Andreyev
Artiukhina
Dogadov
Bubnov
Kosior (S.)
Kubiak
Molotov

Moskvin
Rukhimovich
Smirnov
Stalin
Sulimov
Uglanov

Orgburo Candidates

Chaplin
Lepse
Lobov
Mikhailov
Kotov
Shmidt
Ukhanov

July 1930—Sixteenth Congress

Central Committee

Alekseyev, P. A.
Andreyev, A. A.
Antipov, N. K.
Badaev, A. Y.
Bauman, K. Y.
Bubnov, A. S.
Bukharin, N. I.

Chubar, V. Y.
Chudov, M. S.
Chuvyrin, P. Y.
Eikhe, R. I.
Gamarnik, Y. B.
Goloshchekin, F. I.
Kabakov, I. D.

Kadatsky, I. F.
Kaganovich, L. M.
Kalinin, M. I.
Khataevich, M. M.
Kirov, S. M.
Knorin, V. G.
Kolotilov, N. N.

July 1930—Sixteenth Congress—*Continued*

Central Committee—*Continued*

Komarov, N. P.
Kosior, I. V.
Kosior, S. V.
Krupskaya, N. K.
Krzhizhanovsky, G. M.
Kubiak, N. A.
Kuibyshev, V. V.
Kviring, E. I.
Lebed, D. Z.
Leonov, F. G.
Liubimov, I. Y.
Lobov, S. S.
Lominadze, V. V.
Lomov, G. I.
Manuilsky, D. Z.
Menzhinsky, V. P.
Mikoyan, A. I.

Molotov, V. M.
Moskvin, I. M.
Nosov, I. P.
Orakhelashvili, M. D.
Petrovsky, G. I.
Piatakov, G. L.
Piatnitsky, I. A.
Postyshev, P. P.
Rudzutak, Y. E.
Rukhimovich, M. L.
Rumiantsev, I. P.
Rykov, A. I.
Ryndin, K. V.
Sheboldaev, B. P.
Shvarts, I. I.
Shvernik, N. M.
Skrypnik, N. A.

Smirnov, A. P.
Stalin, J. V.
Stetsky, A. I.
Strievsky, K. K.
Sulimov, D. Y.
Syrtsov, S. I.
Tolokontsev, A. F.
Tomsky, M. P.
Tsikhon, A. M.
Ukhanov, K. V.
Vareikis, I. M.
Voroshilov, K. Y.
Zelensky, I. A.
Zhdanov, A. A.
Zhukov, I. P.

Central Committee Candidates

Afanasev, S. I.
Amosov, A. M.
Antselovich, N. M.
Baranov, P. I.
Bergavinov, S. A.
Briukhanov, N. P.
Bulat, I. L.
Bulatov, D. N.
Bulin, A. S.
Chaplin, N. P.
Chutskaev, S. Y.
Eliava, S. Z.
Gei, K. V.
Goloded, N. M.
Griadinsky, F. P.
Ikramov, A.
Isaev, U. D.
Ivanov, V. L.
Kakhiani, M. I.
Kalygina, A. S.
Kalmanovich, M. I.

Kaminsky, G. N.
Kartvelishvili, L.
Khlopliankin, M. I.
Kiselev, A. S.
Klimenko, I. Y.
Kosarev, A. V.
Kozlov, I. I.
Krinitsky, A. I.
Kuritsyn, V. I.
Lozovsky, S. A.
Mezhlauk, V.
Mirzoyan, L. I.
Mikhailov-Ivanov, M. S.
Musabekov, G. K.
Nikolaeva, K. I.
Oshvintsev, M. K.
Osinsky, V. V.
Pakhanov, N. I.
Perepechko, I. N.
Polonsky, V. I.
Popov, N. N.

Pozern, B. P.
Ptukha, V. V.
Rumiantsev, K. A.
Savelev, M. A.
Sedelnikov, N. I.
Semenov, B. A.
Serebrovsky, A. P.
Smordin, P. I.
Stroganov, V. A.
Sukhomlin, K. V.
Terekhov, R. Y.
Tsarkov, F. F.
Uborevich, I. P.
Unshlikht, I. S.
Uryvaev, M. Y.
Veinberg, G. D.
Volkov, P. Y.
Voronova, P. Y.
Yagoda, G. G.
Yakir, I. Y.
Yurkin, T. A.

Politburo

Kaganovich
Kalinin
Kirov
Kosior (S.)
Kuibyshev

Molotov
Rykov
Rudzutak
Stalin
Voroshilov

Politburo Candidates

Andreyev
Chubar
Mikoyan
Petrovsky
Syrtsov

Secretariat	*Secretariat Candidates*

Bauman	Postyshev	Moskvin
Kaganovich	Stalin (General Secretary)	Shvernik
Molotov		

Orgburo	*Orgburo Candidates*

Akulov	Molotov	Dogadov
Bauman	Moskvin	Kosarev
Bubnov	Postyshev	Smirnov
Gamarnik	Stalin	Tsikhon
Kaganovich	Shvernik	
Lobov		

February 1934—Seventeenth Congress

Central Committee

Alekseyev, P. A.	Knorin, V. G.	Postyshev, P. P.
*Andreyev, A. A.	Kosarev, A. V.	Razumov
Antipov, N. K.	Kosior, I. V.	Rudzutak, Y. E.
*Badaev, A. Y.	Kosior, S. V.	Rukhimovich, M. L.
Balitsky, V. A.	Krinitsky, A. I.	Rumiantsev, I. P.
Bauman, K. Y.	Krzhizhanovsky, G. M.	Ryndin, K. V.
*Beria, L. P.	Krupskaya, N. K.	Sheboldaev, B. P.
Bubnov, A. S.	Kuibyshev, V. V.	*Shvernik, N. M.
Chernov, M. A.	Lavrentev, L. I.	*Stalin, J. V.
Chubar, V. Y.	Lebed, D. Z.	Stetsky, A. I.
Chudov, M. S.	Litvinov, M. M.	Sulimov, D. Y.
Chuvyrin, P. Y.	Liubimov, I. Y.	Ukhanov, K. V.
Eikhe, R. I.	Lobov, S. S.	Vareikis, I. M.
Gamarnik, Y. B.	*Manuilsky, D. Z.	*Voroshilov, K. Y.
Ivanov, V. L.	Mezhlauk, V.	Yagoda, G. G.
Ikramov, A.	*Mikoyan, A. I.	Yakir, I. Y.
Kabakov, I. D.	Mirzoyan, L. I.	Yakovlev, Y. A.
Kadatsky, I. F.	*Molotov, V. M.	Yenukidze, A. S.
*Kaganovich, L. M.	*Nikolaeva, K. I.	Yevdokimov, G. Y.
*Kaganovich, M. M.	Nosov, I. P.	Yezhov, N. I.
*Kalinin, M. I.	Ordzhonikidze, G. K.	Zelensky, I. A.
Khataevich, M. M.	Petrovsky, G. I.	*Zhdanov, A. A.
*Khrushchev, N. S.	Piatakov, G. L.	Zhukov, I. P.
Kirov, S. M.	Piatnitsky, I. A.	

* Indicates re-election at the Eighteenth Party Congress, 1939. All others dead or purged.

Central Committee Candidates

*Bagirov, M. A.	Demchenko, N. N.	Kalmanovich, M. I.
Blagonravov, G. I.	Deribas, T. D.	Kalygina, A. S.
Bliukher, V. K.	Eliava, S. Z.	Kaminsky, G. N.
Broido, G. I.	Filatov, N. A.	Komarov, N. P.
*Budenny, S. M.	Gikalo, N. F.	Kubiak, N. A.
Bukharin, N. I.	Goloded, N. M.	Kulkov, M. M.
*Bulganin, N. A.	Griadinsky, F. P.	Kuritsyn, V. I.
Bulin, A. S.	Grinko, G. F.	Lepa, A. K.
Bykin, Y. B.	Isaev, U. D.	Liubchenko, P. P.

February 1934—Seventeenth Congress—*Continued*

Central Committee Candidates—Continued

*Lozovsky, S. A.	Ptukha, V. V.	Tomsky, M. P.
†Makarov, I. G.	Rozengolts, A. P.	Tovstukha, I. P.
*Mekhlis, L. Z.	Rykov, A. I.	Tukhachevsky, M. N.
Mikhailov, M. E.	Sarkisov, S. A.	Uborevich, I. P.
Mikhailov, V. M.	Sedelnikov, N. I.	Ugarov, A. I.
Musabekov, G. K.	Semenov, B. A.	Unshlikht, I. S.
Osinsky, V. V.	Serebrovsky, A. P.	†Veinberg, G. D.
Pakhanov, N. I.	Shvarts, I. I.	Vereg, Y. I.
Pavlunovsky, I. P.	Shteingardt, A. M.	Yegorov, A. I.
Polonsky, V. I.	Shubrikov, V. P.	Yeremin, I. G.
*Popov, N. N.	Smordin, P. I.	Yurkin, T. A.
*Poskrebyshev, A. N.	Sokolnikov, G. Y.	Zatonsky, V. P.
Pozern, B. P.	Strievsky, K. K.	Zaveniagin, A. P.
Pramnek, E. K.	Struppe, P. I.	

* Indicates elected member († indicates re-elected candidate) at the Eighteenth Party Congress, 1939. All others dead or purged. (Zaveniagin restored as candidate to Central Committee at Nineteenth Party Congress, 1952; died, 1956.)

Politburo		*Politburo Candidates*
Andreyev	Kuibyshev	Chubar
Kaganovich (L.)	Molotov	Mikoyan
Kalinin	Ordzhonikidze	Petrovsky
Kirov	Stalin	Postyshev
Kosior (S.)	Voroshilov	Rudzutak

Secretariat

Stalin (General Secretary)	Kirov
Kaganovich (L.)	Zhdanov

Orgburo		*Orgburo Candidates*
Gamarnik	Shvernik	Kaganovich (M.)
Kaganovich (L.)	Stalin	Krinitsky
Kirov	Stetsky	
Kosarev	Yezhov	
Kuibyshev	Zhdanov	

March 1939—Eighteenth Congress

Politburo		*Politburo Candidates*
Andreyev	Khrushchev	Beria
Kaganovich (L.)	Stalin	Shvernik
Kalinin	Voroshilov	
Mikoyan	Zhdanov	
Molotov		

October 1952—Nineteenth Congress

Presidium of the Central Committee		*Candidates to the Presidium*
Andrianov, V. M.	Bulganin, N. A.	Brezhnev, L. I.
Aristov, A. B.	Chesnokov, D. I.	Ignatov, N. G.
Beria, L. P.	Ignatev, S. D.	Kabanov, I. G.

Presidium of the Central Committee—Continued

Kaganovich, L. M.

Khrushchev, N. S.

Korotchenko, A. Y.

Kuznetsov, V. V.

Kuusinen, O. V.

Malenkov, G. M.

Malyshev, V. A.

Melnikov, L. G.

Mikoyan, A. I.

Mikhailov, N. A.

Molotov, V. M.

Pervukhin, M. G.

Ponomarenko, P. K.

Saburov, M. Z.

Shkiriatov, M. F.

Shvernik, N. M.

Stalin, J. V.

Suslov, M. A.

Voroshilov, K. Y.

Kosygin, A. N.

Patolichev, N. S.

Pegov, N. M.

Puzanov, A. M.

Tevosian, I. F.

Vyshinsky, A. Y.

Yudin, P. F.

Zverev, A. G.

March 1953—Reorganization

Presidium

Candidates to the Presidium

Beria, L. P.

Bulganin, N. A.

Kaganovich, L. M.

Khrushchev, N. S.

Malenkov, G. M.

Mikoyan, A. I.

Molotov, V. M.

Pervukhin, M. G.

Saburov, M. Z.

Voroshilov, K. Y.

Bagirov, M. A.

Melnikov, L. G.

Ponomarenko, P. K.

Shvernik, N. M.

February 1956—Twentieth Congress

Presidium

Candidates to the Presidium

Bulganin, N. A.

Kaganovich, L. M.

Khrushchev, N. S.

Kirichenko, A. I.

Malenkov, G. M.

Mikoyan, A. I.

Molotov, V. M.

Pervukhin, M. G.

Saburov, M. Z.

Suslov, M. A.

Voroshilov, K. Y.

Brezhnev, L. I.

Furtseva, Y. A.

Mukhitdinov, N. A.

Shepilov, D. T.

Shvernik, N. M.

Zhukov, G. K.

June 1957—Plenum of the Central Committee

Presidium

Candidates to the Presidium

Aristov, A. B.

Beliaev, N. I.

Brezhnev, L. I.

Bulganin, N. A. (out, September 1958)

Furtseva, Y. A.

Ignatov, N. G.

Khrushchev, N. S.

Kirichenko, A. I.

Kozlov, F. R.

Kuusinen, O. V.

Mikoyan, A. I.

Shvernik, N. M.

Suslov, M. A.

Voroshilov, K. Y.

Zhukov, G. K. (out, October 1957)

Kalnberzin, Y. E.

Kirilenko, A. P.

Korotchenko, A. Y.

Kosygin, A. N.

Mazurov, K. T.

Mukhitdinov, N. A. (full member, December 1957)

Mzhavanadze, V. P.

Pervukhin, M. G.

Pospelov, P. N.

(New candidates, June 1958:

N. V. Podgorny

D. S. Poliansky)

APPENDIX III

The Graphic Analysis of "Left" and "Right"

Graphically represented, the two political scales of program (left-right) and method (hard-soft) create a rectangular field. A party or movement with any given program and methods is described by the appropriate location in the field. See Figure 1.

An interesting picture of the development of revolutionary Russia can be drawn with the use of this field analysis. See Figure 2. The sweep from extreme "right" to extreme "left" describes a vast arc. At first the movement was largely in the dimension of political organization—this was the democratic revolution which began in 1905 and was completed in February 1917. Then the movement began to swing around into the dimension of economic and social policy, and proceeded rapidly in the direction of mass-oriented programs. This was the revolutionary wave of 1917 which culminated in the Bolsheviks' seizure of power. From this point the course of the revolution swung around once again into the dimension of political methods, in the direction of hardness, as the Bolshevik dictatorship was forged during the Civil War. Finally, as the Soviet regime became more intensely dictatorial, it also began to draw away from radicalism in the policy dimension, and, as it did so, various Communist Opposition groups split off in vain efforts to halt this retreat.

The field analysis can be further employed to map out a visual approximation of the factional history of the Russian Communist Party. See Figure 3.

FIGURE 1. The Two-dimensional Political Classification

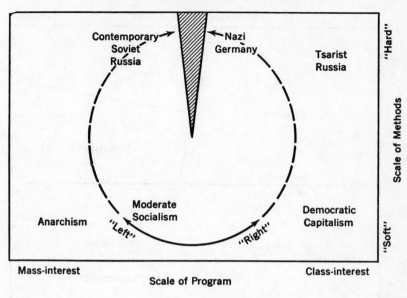

FIGURE 2. The Evolution of Soviet Politics

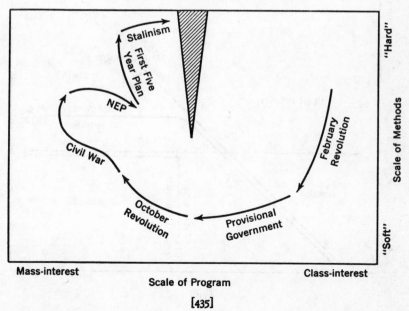

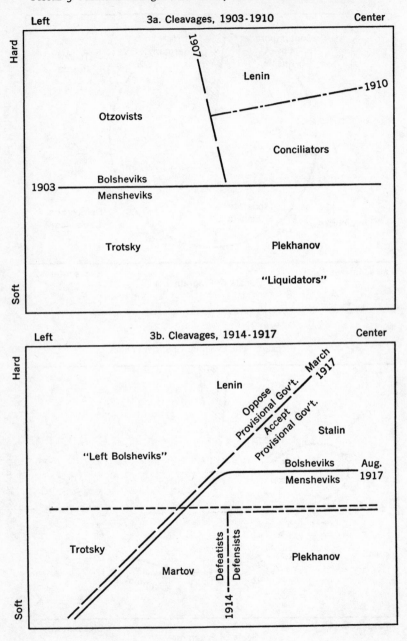

FIGURE 3. Factional Cleavages in the History of the Russian Communist Party

3a. Cleavages, 1903-1910

Left — Hard — Center

1907

Lenin

1910

Otzovists

Conciliators

1903 — Bolsheviks / Mensheviks

Trotsky

Plekhanov

"Liquidators"

Soft

3b. Cleavages, 1914-1917

Left — Hard — Center

Lenin

Oppose Provisional Gov't.

Accept Provisional Gov't.

March 1917

"Left Bolsheviks"

Stalin

Bolsheviks / Mensheviks — Aug. 1917

Trotsky

Martov

Defeatists / Defensists

1914

Plekhanov

Soft

[436]

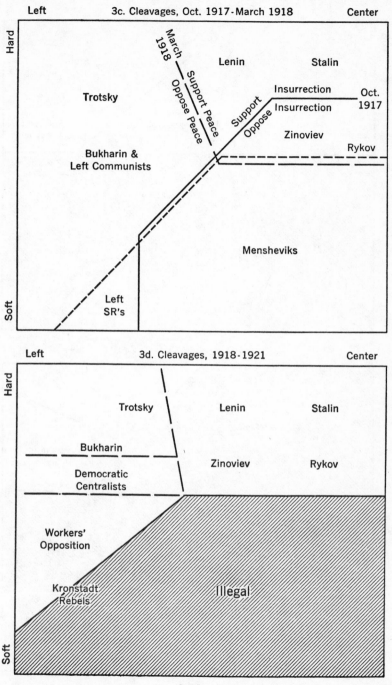

3c. Cleavages, Oct. 1917-March 1918

Left · Center

Hard · Soft

March 1918
Support Peace
Oppose Peace

Support
Oppose

Trotsky

Lenin

Stalin

Insurrection
Insurrection

Oct. 1917

Zinoviev

Rykov

Bukharin & Left Communists

Mensheviks

Left SR's

3d. Cleavages, 1918-1921

Left · Center

Hard · Soft

Trotsky

Lenin

Stalin

Bukharin

Zinoviev

Rykov

Democratic Centralists

Workers' Opposition

Kronstadt Rebels

Illegal

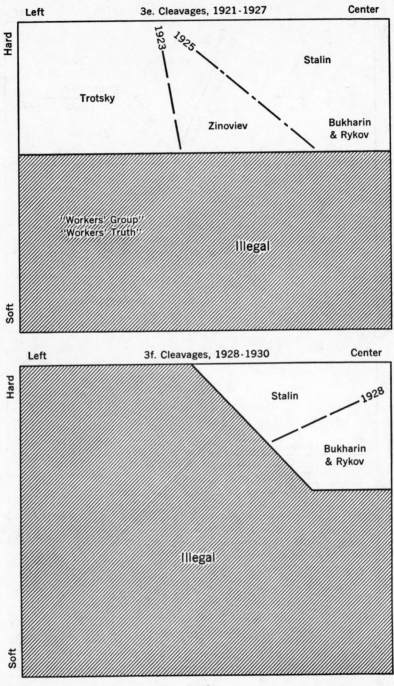

3e. Cleavages, 1921-1927

Left / Center
Hard / Soft

1923 1925

Trotsky

Stalin

Zinoviev

Bukharin & Rykov

"Workers' Group"
"Workers' Truth"

Illegal

3f. Cleavages, 1928-1930

Left / Center
Hard / Soft

Stalin

1928

Bukharin & Rykov

Illegal

BIBLIOGRAPHY

The accessibility of Soviet political history to scholarly study is related to the events themselves, which mark off two sharply different periods in the availability of source material (just as in the character of Communist rule). Until 1929 Soviet politics had not yet become absolutely totalitarian, nor had the Communist treatment of the historical record. Thus this study of the era during which opposition, controversy, and development marked the Soviet political scene coincides with the period of Soviet political history which has reasonably full and varied documentation and which can therefore be readily investigated with the normal methods of the historian.

After Stalin achieved complete personal power, his mania for absolute justification of his actions extended to the record of the past. Not only were the policies and decisions of the government from this time on cloaked in secrecy and official unanimity; but history itself began to be rewritten. Barring drastic political changes, no history in depth can be written of Soviet politics since 1930, for the sources have been and still are controlled by an authority which regards the record of the past as an instrument for present political advantage.

Official or semiofficial Communist Party history falls neatly into three periods. Up to 1927—the demise of the Left Opposition—a variety of views could appear in print; history was the work of an author rather than an official mouthpiece. The bias of Communist against non-Communist was intense, but the record of the Communist movement itself was kept relatively straight. After the expulsion of the Trotskyists polemics held the field; all history had to condemn the now voiceless Opposition, though facts remained more or less facts. The most damaging change came with the onset of the purges in 1936—from history which was highly prejudiced to history which was completely rewritten. Up to this time the oppositionists had been described as misguided un-Leninist deviators, which was a matter of arguable opinion; subsequently the oppositionists became imperialist agents plotting counterrevolution, which was an absurdity. Previously a man's record in office would be acknowledged, whatever his final defects; subsequently every notable achievement of an anti-Stalinist would be ignored altogether, while the Stalinist victims of the secret purge of 1938 literally became "unpersons," whose historical existence was totally ignored from that time until after Stalin died. Up to 1936 documents were published in great volume, even though nothing but approved conclusions from them would be allowed. After 1936 most such publications dealing with the Opposition period stopped altogether, and other publications full of embarrassing source material—including the extant editions of Lenin's collected works—were apparently withdrawn from circulation. Deliberate textual falsifications of earlier documents, on the other hand, are rare: this author has encountered them only in later versions of Stalin's own works, which had to be subjected to judicious expurgation. Finally, the relaxation on the historical front that accompanied the criticism of Stalin in 1956 must be noted. It might be fair to say that the Soviet regime has returned approximately to the 1927–1936 type of history, still governed by a party-dictated bias but refreshed with a revival of some respect for the actual record.

The overwhelming bulk of documentation for the history of Soviet politics is to be found in official publications, with the limitations that this implies (depending on the period). Granted critical judgment, considerable use can be made of the various monographs and official texts on party history, with the value, of course, decreasing with later dates of publication. Many worthwhile articles appeared in the party historical journal *Proletarskaya revoliutsiya* (The Proletarian Revolution) in the 1920s. A number of valuable collections of documents were issued during that period, and even if the purpose of publishing Opposition views was to attack them, it is nonetheless possible for the historian to use the material.

The most important published source for the study of the internal politics of the Russian Communist Party is the debates of the party congresses. For the period from 1917 to 1925 these give a vivid and detailed picture of the stands taken and arguments advanced by the various factions. In addition they throw much light on the development of the party as an institution and on the general course of events. The intensity of some of the criticisms of the party leadership by various oppositionists, and the freedom with which they were made, are quite startling. Originally the congresses were reported in full in *Pravda* and published in book form soon afterwards under the title of *Stenograficheski otchet* (Stenographic Report). In the early 1930s the Marx-Engels-Lenin Institute undertook the editing and republication of the verbatim records of all of the early congresses. The new edition covered all the congresses through the Eleventh (1922), with the exception of the Seventh, under the general title *Protokoly sezdov i konferentsi Vsesoyuznoi Kommunisticheskoi Partii (b)* (Protocols of the Congresses and Conferences of the All-Union Communist Party [Bolshevik]), and appeared between 1933 and 1936. The Protocols are rendered especially useful by the editorial work incorporated in them—voluminous and highly informative footnotes, resolutions and relevant documents, and, in the "index of names," hundreds of thumbnail sketches of party personalities. The texts do not appear to have been tampered with; the most damaging sort of Opposition criticism is included.

Equally indispensable as a source is the party organ *Pravda*. The myriads of relevant articles, reports, and records of party gatherings contained in its pages are invaluable in filling out the details of party history through 1928. A large proportion of the party documents available in more convenient form were originally published in *Pravda*. Unfortunately, where availability is not the limiting factor in the use of the early years of *Pravda*, legibility often is.

There is one source of unpublished documentary material which is crucially important for certain portions of the history of the Opposition. This is the Trotsky Archive at the Houghton Library, Harvard University.* The archive contains a large quantity of correspondence and political literature, either in the original or in copies, written by Trotsky or received by him. It is richest for the years just before Trotsky's exile, and for the present study has its greatest relevance for the 1926–1927 period. It includes copies of a number of key Opposition statements not available elsewhere in any form.

Occasional use in this work has also been made of the Humbert-Droz Archive, copies of which are held by the Russian Research Center, Harvard University.

The scholarly study of Soviet political history has made great progress in recent years, though there is much still to be desired in the way of detailed treatment of many aspects and policies of the Communist regime. The inevitable problem of bias or partisanship still exists, even among the specialists, but despite this an imposing body of objective work has been building up. Until after World War II, detailed outside studies of Soviet politics were largely confined to people who had been involved with the Communist movement either as participants or as opponents. Since that time, investigation of various aspects of Soviet history and society by Western scholars has expanded at a

* For the full contents of the archive, see George Fischer, *A Guide to the Trotsky Archive* (in preparation). I was privileged to assist in this analysis of the archive under a grant from the Social Science Research Council.

commendable rate, and this writer owes a major debt of gratitude to a number of authors whose work has done much to prepare the ground for the present study.

The listings which follow are not intended to be an exhaustive catalogue of works in the field of Soviet history, but merely a guide to the sources employed in the present work. Minor articles and works which have simply been mentioned in passing are indicated in the notes but are not included here.

A. Official Communist Party Documents or Collections

1. Congresses and conferences of the Communist Party

Vtoroi sezd RSDRP (The Second Congress of the RSDWP [1903]). Moscow: Marx-Engels-Lenin Institute (IMEL), 1932.

Chetverty (Obedinitelny) sezd RSDRP (The Fourth [Unification] Congress of the RSDWP [1906]). Moscow: IMEL, 1934.

Piaty sezd RSDRP: Protokoly (The Fifth Congress of the RSDWP [1907]. Moscow: IMEL, 1935.

Sedmaya ("Aprelskaya") Vserossiskaya i Petrogradskaya obshchegorodskaya konferentsii RSDRP(b) (The Seventh ["April"] All-Russian and Petrograd City-Wide Conferences of the RSDWP[b]; 1917). Moscow: IMEL, 1934.

Shestoi sezd RSDRP(b): Protokoly (The Sixth Congress of the RSDWP[b]: Protocols [1917]). Moscow: IMEL, 1934.

Sedmoi sezd RKP: Stenograficheski otchet (The Seventh Congress of the RCP: Stenographic Report [1918]). Moscow: 1923.

Vosmoi sezd RKP(b): Protokoly (The Eighth Congress of the RCP[b]: Protocols [1919]). Moscow: IMEL, 1933.

Deviaty sezd RKP(b): Protokoly (The Ninth Congress of the RCP[b]: Protocols [1920]). Moscow: IMEL, 1934.

Desiaty sezd RKP(b): Protokoly (The Tenth Congress of the RCP[b]: Protocols [1921]). Moscow: IMEL, 1933.

Odinnadtsaty sezd RKP(b): Protokoly (The Eleventh Congress of the RCP[b]: Protocols [1922]). Moscow: IMEL, 1936.

Dvenadtsaty sezd RKP(b): Stenograficheski otchet (The Twelfth Congress of the RCP[b]: Stenographic Report). Moscow: 1923.

Trinadtsaty sezd RKP(b): Stenograficheski otchet (The Thirteenth Congress of the RCP[b]: Stenographic Report). Moscow: 1924.

Chetyrnadtsaty sezd VKP(b): Stenograficheski otchet (The Fourteenth Congress of the AUCP[b]: Stenographic Report [1925]). Moscow: 1926.

Piatnadtsaty sezd VKP(b): Stenograficheski otchet (The Fifteenth Congress of the AUCP[b]: Stenographic Report [1927]). Moscow: 1928.

Shestnadtsaty sezd VKP(b): Stenograficheski otchet (The Sixteenth Congress of the AUCP[b]: Stenographic Report). Moscow: 1930.

Semnadtsaty sezd VKP(b): Stenograficheski otchet (The Seventeenth Congress of the AUCP[b]: Stenographic Report). Moscow: 1934.

Vosemnadtsaty sezd VKP(b): Stenograficheski otchet (The Eighteenth Congress of the AUCP[b]: Stenographic Report). Moscow: 1939.

2. Proceedings of other official organs

People's Commissariat of Justice of the USSR, Report of Court Proceedings: *The Case of the Trotskyite-Zinovievite Terrorist Center; The Case of the Anti-Soviet Trotskyite Center; The Case of the Anti-Soviet Bloc of Rights and Trotskyites.* Moscow: 1936, 1937, 1938.

Proletari, "Iz neopublikovannykh protokolov rasshirennoi redaktsii 'Proletariya': Borba Lenina s bogostroitelstvom" (From the Unpublished Protocols of the Expanded Editorial Board of *Proletari:* Lenin's Struggle with God-Building [June, 1909]), *Literaturnoe nasledstvo* (Literary Heritage; Moscow), no. 1, 1931.

Protokoll des III Kongresses der Kommunistischen Internationale. Hamburg: Hoym, 1921.

Protokoll des Vierten Kongresses der Kommunistischen Internationale [1922]. Hamburg: Hoym, 1923.

Protokoll des 6. Weltkongresses der Kommunistischen Internationale. 3 vols. Hamburg: Hoym, 1928.

Protokoly Tsentralnogo Komiteta RSDRP(b), Avgust 1917 g.–Fevral 1918 g. (Minutes of the Central Committee of the Russian Social Democratic Workers Party [Bolshevik], August 1917–February 1918). Moscow and Leningrad: State Press, 1929.

Trudy pervogo vserossiskogo sezda sovetov narodnogo khoziaistva (Proceedings of the First All-Russian Congress of Economic Councils). Moscow: Supreme Economic Council, 1918.

Vtoroi vserossiski sezd professionalnykh soyuzov: Stenograficheski otchet (The Second All-Russian Congress of Trade Unions: Stenographic Report). 2 vols. Moscow: Central Trade Union Press, 1919.

Sedmoi vsesoyuzny sezd profsoyuzov: Stenograficheski otchet (Seventh All-Union Congress of Trade Unions: Stenographic Report). Moscow: Central Trade-Union Press, 1927.

Vosmoi vsesoyuzny sezd profsoyuzov: Stenograficheski otchet (Eighth All-Union Congress of Trade Unions: Stenographic Report). Moscow: Central Trade-Union Press, 1929.

3. Collected Writings

Lenin, Vladimir Ilich, *Sochineniya* (Works), 3rd ed. 30 vols. Moscow: Marx-Engels-Lenin Institute, 1928–1937. This may be taken as the standard edition, on the whole more complete and far better annotated than the fourth edition of 1941–1952.

Leninski sbornik (The Lenin Collection), 33 vols. Moscow: Lenin Institute, 1924–1940. Notes, manuscripts, and fragments by Lenin.

The Selected Correspondence of Marx and Engels, tr. Dona Torr. New York: International, 1942.

Stalin, Joseph, *Sochineniya* (Works). Moscow: Marx-Engels-Lenin Institute, 1946–195–. Not textually reliable. Contemporary versions of Stalin's writings have been used where possible.

———— *Voprosy leninizma* (Problems of Leninism). Moscow: State Social-Economic Press, 1931, and Political Press of the CC of the AUCP(b), 1941. This is the basic volume of Stalin's selected works (primarily speeches), issued in a number of editions with slightly varying content and entitled either "Leninism" or "Problems of Leninism" (not to be confused with Stalin's essay, "Problems of Leninism," of January 1926).

Trotsky, Leon, *Kak vooruzhalas revoliutsiya* (How the Revolution Armed Itself). 3 vols. Moscow: Higher Military Editorial Council, 1923–1925. Collection of Trotsky's writings of the Civil War period.

———— *Sochineniya* (Works). 21 vols. (incomplete). Moscow: State Press, 1924–1927.

4. Special Collections

Kommunisticheskaya Partiya Sovetskogo Soyuza v rezoliutsiyakh i resheniyakh sezdov, konferentsi i plenumov TsK (The Communist Party of the Soviet Union in Resolutions and Decisions of its Congresses, Conferences, and Plenums of the Central Committee), 7th ed. 3 vols. Moscow: State Press for Political Literature, 1954.

Meller, V. L., and A. M. Pankratova, *Rabochee dvizhenie v 1917 godu* (The Workers' Movement in 1917). Moscow and Leningrad, State Press, 1926.

Novaya oppozitsiya—Sbornik materialov o diskussii 1925 g. (The New Opposition— Collection of Materials on the Controversy of 1925). Leningrad: Workers' Press "Surf," 1926.

Revoliutsiya i RKP (The Revolution and the RCP). Moscow: Institute of Party History, 192-.

Sorin, V., *Partiya i Oppozitsiya* (The Party and the Opposition), I: "Fraktsiya levykh kommunistov" (The Faction of Left Communists). Moscow: Moskovsky Rabochi, 1925.

TsKK-RKI v osnovnykh postanovleniyakh partii (The Central Control Commission— Workers' and Peasants' Inspection in the Basic Decisions of the Party). Moscow: State Press, 1927.

Voprosy partinogo stroitelstva (Questions of Building the Party). Moscow: Iskra Revoliutsii, 1923.

Vsesoyuznaya Kommunisticheskaya Partiya (bolshevikov) v rezoliutsiyakh i resheniyakh sezdov, konferentsi i plenumov TsK (The All-Union Communist Party of Bolsheviks in Resolutions and Decisions of its Congresses, Conferences, and Plenums of the Central Committee). 2 vols. Moscow: Party Press, 1931. Contains appended material omitted in later editions.

Za leninizm: Sbornik statei (For Leninism: A Collection of Articles). Moscow and Leningrad: State Press, 1925.

B. UNOFFICIAL COLLECTIONS OF DOCUMENTS AND WRITINGS

The Anti-Stalin Campaign and International Communism, edited by the Russian Institute, Columbia University. New York: Columbia University Press, 1956.

Avant Thermidor: Revolution et contrerevolution dans la Russie des Soviets—Platforme de l'Opposition de Gauche dans le parti Bolchevique. Lyon: 1928.

The Preliminary Commission of Inquiry, John Dewey, Chairman, *The Case of Leon Trotsky: Report of Hearings on the Charges Made Against Him in the Moscow Trials.* New York: Harper, 1937.

The Soviet-Yugoslav Dispute. London: Royal Institute of International Affairs, 1948.

Trotsky, Leon, *The New Course,* tr. and ed. Max Shachtman. New York: The New International, 1943.

—— *Problems of the Chinese Revolution,* tr. Max Shachtman. New York: Pioneer, 1932.

—— *The Real Situation in Russia,* tr. Max Eastman. New York: Harcourt, Brace, 1928.

—— *The Stalin School of Falsification,* introduction and notes by Max Shachtman; tr. John G. Wright. New York: Pioneer, 1937.

—— *The Third International After Lenin,* tr. John G. Wright. New York: Pioneer, 1936.

United States Department of State, Press Release of June 30, 1956. Contains documents believed to have been distributed to the delegates at the Twentieth Congress of the CPSU.

C. OFFICIAL COMMUNIST PERIODICALS

Bolshevik (theoretical organ of the Central Committee of the Communist Party). Moscow: 1924-1952. Continued as *Kommunist,* 1952- .

International Press Correspondence (organ of the Executive Committee of the Communist International; published also in French and German editions). London: 1922–1938.

Iskra (The Spark; organ of the Russian Social Democratic Workers' Party). London and Geneva: 1900–1905.

Izvestiya TsK (Central Committee News; organizational journal of the Central Committee of the Communist Party). Moscow: 1920–1929.

Krasnaya nov: Literaturno-khudozhestvenny i nauchno-publitsisticheski zhurnal (Red Virgin Soil: A Literary-Artistic and Scientific-Publicist Journal). Moscow: 1921–1942.

Planovoe khoziaistvo (Planned Economy; organ of the Supreme Economic Council). Moscow: 1923– .

Pod znamenem marksizma (Under the Banner of Marxism; philosophical organ of the Central Committee of the Communist Party). Moscow: 1922–1944.

Pravda (Truth; daily organ of the Central Committee of the Communist Party). Petrograd: 1917–1918; Moscow: 1918– .

Proletarskaya revoliutsiya (The Proletarian Revolution; organ of the Bureau of Party History under The Central Committee of the Communist Party, to 1929; after 1929 of the Marx-Engels-Lenin Institute). Moscow: 1921–1932.

Voprosy istorii (Questions of History). Moscow: Institute of History of the All-Union Academy of Sciences, 1945– .

Voprosy istorii KPSS (Questions of the History of the CPSU). Moscow: Institute of Marxism-Leninism, 1957– .

Voprosy sovetskogo khoziaistva i upravleniya (Questions of the Soviet Economy and Administration; organ of the Central Control Commission of the Communist Party and of the Workers' and Peasants' Inspection). Moscow: 1924 only.

D. OPPOSITION AND MENSHEVIK PERIODICALS

Biulleten oppozitsii (The Bulletin of the Opposition; Trotskyist organ). Paris: 1929–1939.

Kommunist (The Communist; organ of the Moscow Regional Bureau of the Communist Party). Moscow: April–May 1918.

Nashe slovo (Our Word; Left Menshevik organ). Paris, 1915–1916.

The New International (organ of the Socialist Workers' Party [Trotskyist]). New York: 1934–1940.

Sotsialisticheski vestnik (The Socialist Herald; organ of the Menshevik Party). Berlin, Paris, New York: 1921– .

E. CONTEMPORARY PROGRAMMATIC AND POLEMICAL WORKS

Bukharin, N. I., *Oekonomik des Transformationsperiode*. Hamburg: Verlag der Kommunistischen Internationale, 1922.

——— "Teoriya imperialisticheskogo gosudarstva" (The Theory of the Imperialist State; 1916), in *Revoliutsiya prava* (The Revolution of Law). Moscow: Communist Academy—Collection I, 1925.

The Errors of Trotskyism. London: Centropress, 1925.

Grinko, G. F., *The Five-Year Plan of the Soviet Union*. New York: International, 1930.

Kollontai, Alexandra, *The Workers' Opposition*. Chicago: Kerr, 1921.

Letter of an Old Bolshevik. New York: Rand School, 1937.

Luxemburg, Rosa, *The Russian Revolution* (1918), tr. Bertram D. Wolfe. New York: Workers' Age, 1940.

Lunacharsky, A. V., *Veliki perevorot* (The Great Overturn). Petrograd: Grzebin, 1919.

Pasić, Najdan, "Izvrtanje marksistickog učenja o državi u teoriji i praksi savremenog revizionizma" (The Perversion of the Marxist Doctrine of the State in the Theory and Practice of Contemporary Revisionism), *Komunist* (The Communist: Belgrade), January 1951.

Pravda o Kronshtadte (The Truth about Kronstadt). Prague: Volia Rossii, 1921.

Preobrazhensky, Y. A., *Ekonomicheskie krizisy pri NEPe* (Economic Crises under the NEP). Moscow: Socialist Academy, 1924.

—— *Novaya ekonomiya* (The New Economy). Moscow: Communist Academy, 1926.

Stalin, *Ekonomicheskie problemy sotsializma v SSSR* (Economic Problems of Socialism in the USSR). Moscow: State Press, 1952.

Shliapnikov, A. S., *Die russischen Gewerkschaften*. Leipzig: Kleine Bibliothek der russischen Korrespondenz, 1920.

Stepanov-Skvortsov, I. I., *Ot rabochego kontrolia k rabochemu upravleniyu* (From Workers' Control to Workers' Administration). Moscow: 1918.

Trotsky, Leon, *Dictatorship vs. Democracy (Terrorism and Communism): A Reply to Karl Kautsky*. New York: Workers' Party of America, 1922.

—— *Nashi politicheskie zadachi* (Our Political Tasks). Geneva: Russian Social Democratic Workers' Party, 1904.

—— *Our Revolution: Essays on the Working Class and International Revolution.* New York: Holt, 1918 (an abridged translation by M. J. Olgin of *Nasha revoliutsiya* [Our Revolution], Geneva, 1906).

—— *The Permanent Revolution,* tr. Max Shachtman. New York: Pioneer, 1931.

—— *Zadachi XII sezda RKP* (The Tasks of the Twelfth Congress of the Russian Communist Party). Moscow: Ninth of January Press, 1923.

Zinoviev, G. Y., *Leninizm* (Leninism). Leningrad: State Press, 1925.

F. Official Communist Histories

Avdeyev, N., *Revoliutsiya 1917 goda: Khronika sobyti* (The Revolution of 1917: Chronicle of Events). 5 vols. Moscow: State Press, 1923–1926.

Badaev, A. Y., *The Bolsheviks in the Tsarist Duma*. London: Lawrence, [1932].

Beria, L. P., *On the History of the Bolshevik Organizations in Transcaucasia*. London: Lawrence and Wishart, 1935.

Bolshaya sovetskaya entsiklopediya (The Great Soviet Encyclopedia), 1st ed. Moscow: "Soviet Encyclopedia" State Scientific Institute 1926–1947. Contains various articles pertaining to the history of the Communist Party. 2nd ed., 1949–1958.

Bubnov, A. S., ed., *VKP(b)* (The All-Union Communist Party of Bolsheviks). Moscow and Leningrad: State Social-Economic Press, 1931.

Burdzhalov, E. N., "O taktike bolshevikov v marte-aprele 1917 goda" (On the Tactics of the Bolsheviks in March and April, 1917), *Voprosy istorii* (Questions of History; Moscow), no. 4, 1956.

Drabkina, F., "Priezd tov. Lenina i martovskoe soveshchanie predstavitelei bolshevistskikh organizatsiyakh" (The Arrival of Comrade Lenin and the March Conference of Representatives of the Bolshevik Organizations), *Proletarskaya revoliutsiya*, no. 4, 1927. Further abbr. *Prol. revol.*

Entsiklopedicheski slovar (Encyclopedic Dictionary). Moscow and Petrograd: Granat. Appendixes to vols. 41–43 (1925–1928) contain biographies of Communist leaders.

Fotieva, L., *Poslednye gody zhizni i deyatelnosti V. I. Lenina* (The Last years of V. I. Lenin's Life and Activity). Moscow, 1947.

Gladkov, I., "K istorii pervoi piatiletnego narodnokhoziaistvennogo plana" (On the History of the First Five Year Economic Plan), *Planovoe khoziaistvo*, no. 4, 1935.

History of the Communist Party of the Soviet Union (Bolsheviks): Short Course. New York: International, 1939.

Kanev, S. N., "Partinye massy v borbe za edinstvo RKP(b) v periode profsoyuznoi diskussii (1920–1921)" (The Party Masses in the Struggle for the Unity of the RCP[B] in the Period of the Trade Union Controversy, 1920–1921), *Voprosy istorii*, no. 2, 1956.

Kritsman, L., *Geroicheski period russkoi revoliutsii* (The Heroic Period of the Russian Revolution). Moscow and Leningrad: State Press, 1926.

Liadov, M. N., *Dvadtsat-piat let RKP(b)* (Twenty-five Years of the Russian Communist Party of Bolsheviks). Nizhni-Novgorod: Krasnaya Nov Press and Nizhni-Novgorod Party Committee, 1923.

Ostroukhova, K., "Gruppa 'Vpered'" (The "Vperiod" Group), *Prol. revol.*, no. 1, 1925.

—— "Otzovisty i Ultimatisty" (The Otzovists and the Ultimatists), *Prol. revol.*, no. 6, 1924.

Popov, N. N., *Narys istorii Kommunistichnoi Partii (bolshevikiv) Ukrainy* (Sketch of the History of the Communist Party of Bolsheviks of the Ukraine). Kharkov: 1929.

—— *Outline History of the Communist Party of the Soviet Union*. 2 vols. New York: International, 1934.

Pukhov, A. S., *Kronshtadtski miatezh v 1921 g.* (The Kronstadt Revolt of 1921). Leningrad: Young Guard, 1931.

Ravich-Cherkassky, M., *Istoriya Kommunisticheskoi Partii (bolshevikov) Ukrainy* (History of the Communist Party of Bolsheviks of the Ukraine). Kharkov: State Press of the Ukraine, 1923.

—— ed., *Pervy sezd Kommunisticheskoi Partii (bolshevikov) Ukrainy* (The First Congress of the Communist Party of Bolsheviks of the Ukraine). Kharkov: 1923.

Ruban, N. V., "Borba partii protiv trotskistsko-zinovevskoi oppozitsii" (The Party's Struggle against the Trotskyist-Zinovievist Opposition), *Voprosy istorii KPSS*, no. 5, 1958.

Shelavin, K., *Rabochaya oppozitsiya* (The Workers' Opposition). Moscow: Young Guard, 1930.

Shliapnikov, A. G., *Semnadtsaty god* (The Year 1917). Moscow: State Press, 1925.

Sidorov, A., "Ekonomicheskaya programma oktiabria" (The Economic Program of October), *Prol. revol.*, no. 6, 1929.

Sorin, V., *Rabochaya Gruppa: "Miasnikovshchina"* (The Workers' Group: The "Miasnikov Movement"). Moscow: State Press, 1924.

Syromiatnikov, M., "Bernskaya konferentsiya 1915 g." (The Berne Conference of 1915), *Prol. revol.*, no. 5, 1925.

Voitinsky, N., "Boikotizm, otzovizm, ultimatizm" (Boycottism, Otzovism, Ultimatism), *Prol. revol.*, no. 8–9, 1929.

—— "O gruppe 'Vpered' (1909–1917)" (On the "Vperiod" Group, 1909–1917), *Prol. revol.*, no. 12, 1929.

Yaroslavsky, Yemelian, "A Brief History of the Russian Communist Party." Mimeographed ed., 2 vols. [Moscow: ca. 1926–27].

—— ed., *Istoriya VKP(b)* (History of the All-Union Communist Party of Bolsheviks). 4 vols. Moscow and Leningrad: State Press, 1926–1930.

Yurenev, I., "Mezhraionka, 1911–1917" (The Interdistrict Committee, 1911–1917), *Prol. revol.*, nos. 1–2, 1924.

Zinoviev, G. Y., *Istoriya Rossiskoi Kommunisticheskoi Partii (bolshevikov)* (History of the Russian Communist Party of Bolsheviks). Leningrad: State Press, 1924.

G. Other Histories and Memoirs by Participants

Agabekov, G. S., *Ogpu—The Russian Secret Terror*. New York: Brentano, 1931.

Bajanow, B., *Stalin, Der rote Diktator*. Berlin: Aretz, 1931.

Balabanova, Angelica, *My Life as a Rebel*. London and New York: Harper, 1938.

Barmine, Alexander, *One who Survived*. New York: Putnam, 1945.

Beck, F., and W. Godin, [pseud.] *Russian Purge and the Extraction of Confession*. New York: Viking Press, 1951.

Berkman, Alexander, *The Bolshevik Myth*. London: Hutchinson, 1925.

Borkenau, Franz, *The Communist International*, London: Faber and Faber, 1938.

Ciliga, Anton, *The Russian Enigma*. London: Routledge, 1940.

Dan, F. I., *Proiskhozhdenie bolshevizma* (The Origin of Bolshevism). New York: New Democracy Press, 1946.

Dmitrievsky, S. V., *Sovetskie portrety* (Soviet Portraits). Berlin: Strela, 1932.

—— *Stalin*. Berlin: Strela, 1931.

Eastman, Max, *Since Lenin Died*. London: Labour Publishing Co., 1925.

Fischer, Ruth, *Stalin and German Communism*. Cambridge: Harvard University Press, 1948.

Ouralov, Alexandre, (A. Avtorkhanov), *Staline au pouvoir*. Paris: Les Iles d'Or, 1951.

Serge, Victor, *Portrait de Staline*. Paris: Grasset, 1940.

Sukhanov (Himmer), N. N., *The Russian Revolution, 1917: A Personal Record*, tr., ed., and abridged by Joel Carmichael. London: Oxford University Press, 1955.

Trotsky, Leon, *History of the Russian Revolution*, tr. Max Eastman. 3 vols. New York: Simon & Schuster, 1932.

—— *The Lessons of October*, introduction and notes by Maurice Spender; tr. John G. Wright. New York: Pioneer, 1937.

—— *My Life: An Attempt at an Autobiography*, New York: Scribners, 1931.

—— *Stalin: An Appraisal of the Man and his Influence*, ed. and tr. Charles Malamuth. New York and London: Harper, 1946.

—— *The Suppressed Testament of Lenin*. New York: Pioneer, 1935.

Voline (V. M. Eikhenbaum), *Nineteen-Seventeen: The Russian Revolution Betrayed*. London: Freedom Press, 1954.

Volsky, N., *Memoirs*. Unpublished manuscript, 1956, made available to the author through the courtesy of the Research Program on the History of the CPSU, Columbia University.

H. Independent and Scholarly Studies

Aleksandrov (A. S. Michelson), *Kto upravliaet Rossiei?* (Who Rules Russia?). Berlin: Parabola, 1933.

Baykov, Alexander, *The Development of the Soviet Economic System*. New York: Macmillan, 1947.

Brandt, Conrade, *Stalin's Failure in China, 1924–1927*. Cambridge: Harvard University Press, 1958.

Bunyan, James, and H. H. Fisher, *The Bolshevik Revolution, 1917–1918*. Stanford: Stanford University Press, 1934.

Carr, Edward Hallett, *A History of Soviet Russia*, including *The Bolshevik Revolution, 1917–1923* (3 vols., New York, Macmillan, 1950–1953), and *The Interregnum, 1923–1924* (New York, Macmillan, 1954).

Chamberlin, William Henry, *The Russian Revolution, 1917–1921*. New York: Macmillan, 1935.

Daniels, R. V., "The State and Revolution: A Case Study in the Genesis and Transformation of Communist Ideology," *The American Slavic and East European Review*, February 1953, pp. 22–43.

Deutscher, Isaac, *The Prophet Armed—Trotsky: 1879–1921*. London: Oxford University Press, 1954.

—— *Stalin: A Political Biography*. New York and London: Oxford University Press, 1949.

Dobb, Maurice, *Soviet Economic Development Since 1917*. New York: International, 1948.

Duranty, Walter, *Duranty Reports Russia*. New York: Viking, 1934.

——— *I Write as I Please*. New York: Simon & Schuster, 1935.

Engels, Friedrich, *The Peasant War in Germany*. New York: International, 1926.

Erlich, Alexander, "Preobrazhensky and the Economics of Soviet Industrialization," *Quarterly Journal of Economics*, February 1950, pp. 57–88.

——— "The Soviet Industrialization Controversy." Unpublished dissertation, The New School for Social Research, 1953.

Fainsod, Merle, *How Russia is Ruled*. Cambridge: Harvard University Press, 1953.

——— *International Socialism and the World War*. Cambridge: Harvard University Press, 1935.

——— *Smolensk under Soviet Rule*. Cambridge: Harvard University Press, 1958.

Fischer, George, *Soviet Opposition to Stalin: A Case Study in World War II*. Cambridge: Harvard University Press, 1952.

Jakobson, Michael, *Die russischen Gewerkschaften, ihre Entwicklung, ihre Zielsetzung, und ihre Stellung zum Staat*. Berlin: 1932.

Jasny, Naum, "A Soviet Planner—V. G. Groman," *The Russian Review*, January 1954, pp. 53–58.

Kennan, George, *Soviet-American Relations, 1917–1920*. Vol. 1: *Russia Leaves the War*. (Princeton, Princeton University Press, 1956).

Koch, Waldemar, *Die Bolshevistischen Gewerkschaften*. Jena: Sozialwissenschaftliche Bausteine, 1932.

Korey, William, "Zinoviev's Critique of Stalin's Theory of Socialism in One Country, December, 1925–December, 1926," *The American Slavic and East European Review*, December 1950, pp. 255–267.

Kostiuk, Hryhory, *The Fall of Postyshev*. New York: Research Program on the USSR, 1954.

Labour Conditions In Russia. London: The Russian Economist, 1921.

Levin, Alfred, *The Second Duma*. New Haven: Yale University Press, 1940.

Majstrenko, Iwan, *Borotbism: A Chapter in the History of Ukrainian Communism*. New York: Research Program on the USSR, 1954.

Maynard, John, *Russia in Flux*. New York: Macmillan, 1948.

Meyer, Alfred G., *Leninism*. Cambridge: Harvard University Press, 1957.

——— "Soviet Politics and the War Scare of 1927." Unpublished manuscript, 1958.

Pipes, Richard, *The Formation of the Soviet Union: Communism and Nationalism, 1917–1923*. Cambridge: Harvard University Press, 1954.

Prokopowicz, S. N., *Russlands Volkswirtschaft unter den Sowjets*. Zurich and New York: Europa, 1944.

Schapiro, Leonard, *The Origin of the Communist Autocracy: Political Opposition in the Soviet State—First Phase, 1917–1922*. London: The London School of Economics and Political Science, 1955.

Schwarz, Solomon, *Labor in Soviet Russia*. New York: Praeger, 1952.

Schwartz, Benjamin, *Chinese Communism and the Rise of Mao*. Cambridge: Harvard University Press, 1951.

Shub, David, *Lenin: A Biography*. New York: Doubleday, 1948.

Souvarine, Boris, *Stalin: A Critical Survey of Bolshevism*, tr. C. L. R. James. London: Secker and Warburg [1939].

Wolfe, Bertram, *Three Who Made a Revolution*. New York: Dial, 1948.

Yugow, Aaron, *Piatiletka* (The Five Year Plan). Berlin: 1931.

——— *Russia's Economic Front for Peace and War*. New York: Harper, 1942.

NOTES

INTRODUCTION

1. Engels to Vera Zasulich, April 23, 1885, in *The Selected Correspondence of Marx and Engels* (New York, 1942), pp. 437-438.
2. Stalin, in *Piatnadtsaty sezd VKP(b): Stenograficheski otchet* (Fifteenth Congress of the All-Union Communist Party [Bolshevik]: Stenographic Report [1927]; Moscow, 1928), p. 371.
3. This method of political classification was originally formulated jointly by the author and Professor Alfred G. Meyer.
4. Isaiah Berlin, "The Silence in Russian Culture," *Foreign Affairs*, October 1957, p. 7.

CHAPTER 1. THE FORMATION OF THE BOLSHEVIK PARTY

1. Organizational rules of the RSDWP adopted at the Second Party Congress, and draft of the organizational rules of the RSDWP introduced at the congress by Lenin, *Kommunisticheskaya Partiya Sovetskogo Soyuza v rezoliutsiyakh i resheniyakh sezdov, konferentsi i plenumov TsK* (The Communist Party of the Soviet Union in Resolutions and Decisions of the Congresses, Conferences, and Plenums of the Central Committee; 7th ed., Moscow, 1954), I, 45, 43. All subsequent citations of CPSU in Resolutions refer to this edition, unless otherwise specified.
2. *Vtoroi ocherednoi sezd RSDRP* (The Second Regular Congress of the RSDWP, Protocols; Geneva, 1903), pp. 169-170.
3. *Protokoly II sezda RSDRP* (Protocols of the Second Congress of the RSDWP; Moscow, Party Press, 1932), pp. 263-285.
4. *Ibid.*, p. 376.
5. See F. I. Dan, *Proiskhozhdenie bolshevizma* (The Origin of Bolshevism; New York, 1946), pp. 278-279.
6. V. I. Lenin, "Chto delat?" (What is to be Done?), *Sochineniya* (Works; 3rd ed., Moscow, 1932-1935), IV, 465, 477. All subsequent references to Lenin's Works are to this edition unless otherwise specified.
7. *Ibid.*, pp. 384, 456.
8. Lenin, "Shag vpered, dva shaga nazad" (One Step Forward, Two Steps Back), Works, VI, 311.
9. See Alfred G. Meyer, *Leninism* (Cambridge, 1957), ch. 5.
10. Lenin, "Svoboda kritiki i edinstvo deistviya" (Freedom of Criticism and Unity of Action), Works, IX, 275.
11. Lenin, "What is to be Done?" Works, IV, 391-392.
12. "Tovarishch Lenin o nashikh organizatsionnykh zadachakh" (Comrade Lenin on Our Organizational Tasks), by "Praktik," *Iskra* (The Spark), Supplement to no. 64, April 18, 1904.
13. See E. H. Carr, *The Bolshevik Revolution, 1917-1923* (New York, 1951-1953), I, 32-33.
14. Starover, "Nashi zlokliucheniya" (Our Misfortunes), *Iskra*, no. 78, November 20, 1904.

15. Rosa Luxemburg, "Organizatsionnye voprosy rossiskoi sotsial-demokratii" (Organizational Questions of Russian Social Democracy), *Iskra,* July 10, 1904.

16. Trotsky, *Nashi politicheskie zadachi* (Our Political Tasks; Geneva, 1904), pp. 54, 105.

17. Participants listed in Yemelian Yaroslavsky, ed., *Istoriya VKP(b)* (History of the All-Union Communist Party [Bolshevik]; Moscow and Leningrad, 1926–1930), I, 376, and in Bertram Wolfe, *Three Who Made a Revolution* (New York, 1948), p. 263.

18. A. A. Bogdanov, *Nashi nedorazumeniya* (Our Misunderstandings), excerpts in *Revoliutsiya i RKP* (The Revolution and the Russian Communist Party; Moscow, 192?), II, 520–521.

19. David Shub, *Lenin: A Biography* (New York, 1948), pp. 65–66; biography of Bogdanov in *Entsiklopedicheski slovar* (The Encyclopedic Dictionary; Moscow and Petrograd, 1925–1928), XLI-1, appendix, 30–31. Hereafter abbreviated *Ency. Dict.*

20. Yaroslavsky, I, 377.

21. M. N. Liadov, "Treti sezd" (The Third Congress), *Proletarskaya revoliutsiya* (The Proletarian Revolution), no. 3, 1922, p. 62. Hereafter abbreviated *Prol. revol.*

22. N. N. Popov, *Outline History of the Communist Party of the Soviet Union* (New York, 1934), I, 135–136.

23. Lenin to the Secretary of the Central Committee, January 29, 1905, *Leninski sbornik* (The Lenin Collection; 33 vols., Moscow, 1924–1940), V, 149.

24. Resolution of the Third Party Congress, "Ob otkolovsheisia chasti partii" (On the Schismatic Part of the Party), CPSU in Resolutions, I, 81.

25. Lenin, "Dve taktiki sotsial-demokratii v demokraticheskoi revoliutsii" (Two Tactics of Social Democracy in the Democratic Revolution), Works, VIII, 120.

26. Wolfe, pp. 306–308.

27. Autobiography of Melnichansky, *Ency. Dict.,* XLI-2, appendix, 31.

28. Popov, I. 139–140; Resolution of the Third Party Congress, "O podgotovke uslovi sliyaniya s menshevikami" (On the Preparation of Conditions for a Merger with the Mensheviks), CPSU in Resolutions, I, 90.

29. "Otkrytoe pismo k organizatsionnoi kommissii" (Open Letter to the Organizational Commission, written by Bogdanov and signed by the Central Committee), reprinted in Lenin, Works, VIII, 449–451.

30. CPSU in Resolutions, I, 91, 96–99.

31. Popov, I, 194–195.

32. *Ibid.,* pp. 202, 211.

33. Wolfe, p. 376; CPSU in Resolutions, I, 145–149.

34. Trotsky, *Stalin: An Appraisal of the Man and his Influence,* ed and trans. Charles Malamuth (New York and London, 1946), p. 99; Wolfe, p. 377.

35. A. V. Lunacharsky, *Vospominaniya o Lenine* (Recollections of Lenin; Moscow, 1933), p. 21, as quoted in Shub, p. 86.

36. CPSU in Resolutions, I, 108–109, 129–131.

37. *Chetverty (obedinitelny) sezd RSDRP* (The Fourth [Unification] Congress of the RSDWP, Protocols; 3rd ed., Moscow, 1934), p. 420; Wolfe, p. 376.

38. J. V. Stalin, speech at a meeting of the Moscow Committee of the RCP(b) in connection with the fiftieth birthday of Lenin, *Sochineniya* (Works; Moscow, 1946–1951), IV, 316–317.

39. See Wolfe, p. 349.

40. Resolution of the First Party Conference, "O gosudarstvennoi dume" (On the State Duma), CPSU in Resolutions, I, 101.

41. Fourth Party Congress, p. 385.

42. CPSU in Resolutions, I, 114–116; Dan, pp. 410–411.

43. CPSU in Resolutions, I, 118–119; Dan, pp. 414–415; Fourth Party Congress, pp. 341, 373–374.

44. Alfred Levin, *The Second Duma* (New Haven, 1940), p. 70.

45. See Trotsky, *Stalin*, p. 89.

46. *Ibid.*, p. 92.

47. N. Voitinsky, "Boikotizm, otzovizm, ultimatizm" (Boycottism, Otzovism, Ultimatism), *Prol. revol.*, no. 8–9, 1929, p. 35.

48. CPSU in Resolutions, I, 173, 178; K. Ostroukhova, "Sotsial-demokratiya i vybory v III gosudarstvennuyu dumu" (The Social Democracy and the Elections to the Third State Duma), *Prol. revol.*, no. 2, 1924, pp. 91–92, 198–199.

49. Voitinsky in *Prol. revol.*, no. 8–9, 1929, p. 44.

50. A. S. Bubnov, ed., *VKP(b)* (The All-Union Communist Party [Bolshevik]; Moscow and Leningrad, 1931), p. 533.

51. Resolution of the Fourth Party Conference, "O taktike sotsial-demokraticheskoi fraktsii v gosudarstvennoi dume" (On the Tactics of the Social Democratic Fraction in the State Duma), CPSU in Resolutions, I, 182–184.

52. Bubnov, p. 533; M. N. Liadov, *Dvadtsat-piat let RKP(b)* (Twenty-five Years of the Russian Communist Party [Bolshevik]; Nizhni-Novgorod, 1923), pp. 56–57.

53. Voitinsky in *Prol. revol.*, no. 8–9, 1929, p. 58.

54. K. Ostroukhova, "Otzovisty i ultimatisty" (The Otzovists and the Ultimatists), *Prol. revol.*, no. 6, 1924, pp. 27–30.

55. *Ibid.*, pp. 30–32; biography of Zinoviev in *Ency. Dict.*, XLI–1, appendix, 143.

56. Liadov, "Twenty-five Years of the RCP," p. 57; Ostroukhova in *Prol. revol.*, no. 6, 1924, p. 20.

57. See G. Y. Zinoviev, *Istoriya Rossiskoi Kommunisticheskoi Partii (bolshevikov)* (History of the Russian Communist Party [Bolshevik]; Leningrad, 1924), pp. 154–155; Voitinsky in *Prol. revol.*, no. 8–9, 1929, p. 63.

58. Lenin to Gorky, February 25, 1908, Works, XXVIII, 527–531.

59. N. Voitinsky, "O gruppe 'Vpered' (1909–1917)" (On the "Vperiod" Group, 1909–1917), *Prol. revol.*, no. 12, 1929, p. 73; Liadov, "Twenty-five Years of the RCP," pp. 58–59.

60. Lenin to Gorky, February 25, 1908, Works, XXVIII, 529. For the Menshevik attack see A. M. Deborin, "Filosofiya Makha i russkoi revoliutsiya" (The Philosophy of Mach and the Russian Revolution), *Golos sotsial-demokrata* (The Voice of the Social Democrat; Geneva), no. 4–5, April 1908.

61. Bubnov, p. 542.

62. "Izveshchenie o soveshchanii rasshirennoi redaktsii 'Proletariya' " (Notice on the Consultation of the Expanded Editorial Board of "Proletari"), CPSU in Resolutions, I, 213. (Bogdanov and Shantser are here referred to only by their pseudonyms of Maksimov and Marat, respectively.)

63. *Ibid.*, p. 217.

64. "Iz neopublikovannykh protokolov rasshirennoi redaktsii 'Proletariya': Borba Lenina s bogostroitelstvom" (From the Unpublished Protocols of the Expanded Editorial Board of "Proletari": Lenin's Struggle with God-Building), *Literaturnoe nasledstvo* (Literary Heritage), no. 1, 1931, pp. 17–38; CPSU in Resolutions, I, 222.

65. Resolutions of the consultation of the expanded editorial board of *Proletari* (June 1909), "Ob otzovizme i ultimatizme" (On Otzovism and Ultimatism) and "Zadachi bolshevikov v partii" (The Tasks of the Bolsheviks in the Party), CPSU in Resolutions, I, 220, 227.

66. Voitinsky in *Prol. revol.*, no. 8–9, 1929, pp. 59–60.

67. Resolution of the board of *Proletari*, "On Otzovism and Ultimatism," CPSU in *Resolutions*, I, 221.

68. Notice on the consultation of the board of *Proletari, ibid.*, pp. 214-215.

69. Resolutions of the board of *Proletari, ibid.*, pp. 215-216, 221-222, 228-229.

70. Resolutions of the board of *Proletari*, in Lenin, *Works*, XIV, 98-99, 109-110.

71. Voitinsky in *Prol. revol.*, no. 12, 1929, pp. 88-89.

72. S. I. Gusev, letter to the Bolshevik Center on Otzovism and Ultimatism (1909), *Prol. revol.*, no. 6, 1924, pp. 197-199.

73. K. Ostroukhova, "Gruppa 'Vpered'" (The "Vperiod" Group), *Prol. revol.*, no. 1, 1925, p. 214; Popov, I, 243n.

74. Voitinsky in *Prol. revol.*, no. 12, 1929, pp. 93-103.

75. Liadov, "Twenty-five Years of the RCP," p. 59.

76. See Voitinsky in *Prol. revol.*, no. 12, 1929, p. 84.

77. Gusev, letter to the Bolshevik Center, *Prol. revol.*, no. 6, 1924, p. 197.

78. Bogdanov, letter, "K vsem tovarishcham" (To All Comrades; 1910), quoted by Ostroukhova in *Prol. revol.*, no. 1, 1925, p. 200. The Octobrists were a conservative party content with the government's concessions of October 1905.

79. Voitinsky in *Prol. revol.*, no. 12, 1929, p. 103.

80. M. N. Liadov, "Po povodu partinogo krizisa" (In Regard to the Party Crisis; 1911), as quoted in Voitinsky, *ibid.*, p. 104.

81. Bogdanov, *Vera i nauka* (Faith and Science; 1910), quoted in Wolfe, p. 508.

82. Bogdanov, "Sotsializm v nastoyashchem" (Socialism in Actuality), *Vpered* Collection no. 2, February, 1911, p. 63.

83. D. Kin, "Vpered" (Vperiod), *Bolshaya sovetskaya entsiklopediya* (The Great Soviet Encyclopedia), XIII, 388.

84. Voitinsky in *Prol. revol.*, no. 12, 1929, p. 109.

85. Quoted by Ostroukhova in *Prol. revol.*, no. 1, 1925, p. 213.

86. Information from George Denicke.

87. Kin in The Great Soviet Encyclopedia, XIII, 389; Wolfe, p. 469; Zinoviev, "History of the RCP," p. 146; Shub, p. 403.

88. Zinoviev, "History of the RCP," p. 162; Bubnov, p. 549.

89. Zinoviev, *ibid.*; Shub, p. 151.

90. Listed in Bubnov, p. 549, and Popov, I, 248.

91. Popov, pp. 248-249.

92. Lenin to Gorky, April 11, 1910, *Works*, XIV, 269-270; Bubnov, p. 555.

93. Popov, pp. 267-269; Wolfe, pp. 528-529.

94. Wolfe, *ibid.*

95. Listed in Popov, I, 274. Spandarian died in Siberia in 1916.

96. Collection, "Na temi dnia" (On Themes of the Day; 1912), as quoted in Ostroukhova, *Prol. revol.*, no. 1, 1925, p. 212.

97. Ostroukhova, *ibid.*, pp. 212-213.

98. Wolfe, pp. 540-562 *passim;* Trotsky, *Stalin*, p. 141.

99. Trotsky, *ibid.*, pp. 147-149, 159-160.

100. See A. Badaev, *The Bolsheviks in the Tsarist Duma* (London [1932]), chs. 12-14. Malinovsky left the Duma and the Bolshevik Party in 1914, to avoid exposure. Lenin, despite the suspicions of a number of his associates, refused to doubt the revolutionary loyalty of the man who had virtually become the second-in-command of the Bolshevik movement, until the opening of the police archives in 1917 put an end to all doubts. Malinovsky was tried and shot in 1918 (see Shub, pp. 126, 194-195, 333-335; Wolfe, pp. 549-557).

101. Khoniavko, "V podpole i v emigratsii, 1911-1917 gg." (In the Underground and in the Emigration, 1911-1917), *Prol. revol.*, no. 4, 1923, pp. 168-169.

102. Trotsky, *Stalin*, p. 169. Bubnov (p. 600) attributes this to Kamenev alone.

103. A. V. Lunacharsky, *Veliki perevorot* (The Great Overturn; Petrograd, 1919), p. 52.

104. Isaac Deutscher, *The Prophet Armed—Trotsky: 1879–1921* (London, 1954), pp. 221–222.

105. Autobiography of Antonov-Ovseyenko in *Ency. Dict.*, XLI-1, appendix, 8–9.

106. Biography of Riazanov, *ibid.*, XLI-2, appendix, 231–232.

107. Listed in Deutscher, pp. 222–223.

108. *Nashe slovo* (Our Word; Paris), January 19, 1916, as quoted in Deutscher, p. 233.

109. Deutscher, pp. 225n2, 226–235 *passim*.

110. See I. Yurenev, "Mezhraionka, 1911–1917" (The Interdistrict Committee, 1911–1917), *Prol. revol.*, nos. 1 and 2, 1924.

111. *Ibid.*, no. 2, p. 125.

112. Quoted in Ostroukhova, *Prol. revol.*, no. 1, 1925, p. 218.

113. Popov, I, 336; see Deutscher, ch. 8.

114. Merle Fainsod, *International Socialism and the World War* (Cambridge, 1935), p. 53; Voitinsky in *Prol. revol.*, no. 12, 1929, pp. 118–119.

115. Lenin to Shliapnikov, September or October 1916, Works, XIX, 274–275.

116. Autobiography of Bukharin, *Ency. Dict.*, XLI-1, appendix, 55–56.

117. Biography of Krylenko in *Ency. Dict.*, XLI-1, appendix, 242.

118. M. Syromiatnikov, "Bernskaya konferentsiya 1915 g." (The Berne Conference of 1915), *Prol. revol.*, no. 5, 1925, pp. 154–171 *passim*.

119. Trotsky in *Nashe slovo*, as quoted in Y. Yaroslavsky, "Brief History of the Russian Communist Party" (mimeographed English edition, Moscow, *ca.* 1926–27), II, 34.

120. Syromiatnikov in *Prol. revol.*, no. 5, 1925, pp. 154–162; Trotsky, " 'Vpered,' " *Nashe slovo*, November 28, 1915; Voitinsky in *Prol. revol.*, no. 12, 1929, pp. 114–116.

121. Lenin, "O lozunge soedinennykh shtatov Evropy" (On the Slogan of the United States of Europe; August 23, 1915), Works, XVIII, 232–233. This passage later became the basis of Stalin's doctrine of "socialism in one country." It should be noted, however, that Lenin at this time had no idea of Russia as the one socialist state; he deemed only the industrial powers of Western Europe ripe for socialism.

122. Richard Pipes, *The Formation of the Soviet Union: Communism and Nationalism, 1917–1923* (Cambridge, 1954), pp. 47–48.

123. *Ibid.*, p. 48; autobiography of Dzerzhinsky in *Ency. Dict.*, XLI-1, appendix, 123.

124. Trotsky in *Nashe slovo*, February 4, 1916.

125. *Ibid.*, April 12, 1916, as quoted in Deutscher, p. 238.

126. Pipes, p. 47.

CHAPTER 2. THE BOLSHEVIK FACTIONS IN THE REVOLUTION OF 1917

1. Deutscher, *The Prophet Armed*, pp. 101–105, 148.

2. Trotsky, "Itogi i perspektivy—dvizhushchie sily revoliutsii" (Results and Prospects—The Driving Forces of the Revolution), in *Nasha revoliutsiya* (Our Revolution; Geneva, 1906), translated in abridged form under the title, "Prospects for a Labor Dictatorship," in Trotsky, *Our Revolution: Essays on the Working Class and International Revolution* (New York, 1918).

3. Lenin, "Two Tactics of Social Democracy," Works, VIII, 32, 104–105.

4. Lenin, "O dvoevlastii" (On Dual Power), Works, XX, 94.

5. See Carr, *The Bolshevik Revolution*, II, 13.

6. See *Piaty sezd RSDRP: Protokoly* (Fifth Congress of the RSDWP: Protocols; Moscow, 1935), pp. 109–110.

7. Biography of Pokrovsky, *Ency. Dict.*, XLI-2, appendix, 119. Cf. Trotsky, *The Permanent Revolution* (New York, 1931), p. 24.

8. *Ibid.*

9. The fact that Lenin did not explicitly acknowledge his conversion to Trotsky's point of view gave Trotsky's later opponents the opportunity to argue that he and Lenin were always in opposition over "permanent revolution." However, the scholastic efforts which had to be made to force a distinction between Trotsky's ideas and the theory attributed to Lenin, of "the growth of the bourgeois-democratic revolution into the socialist revolution," simply underscore the essential agreement which was reached between the two men during 1917. See Meyer, *Leninism,* pp. 143-144. See also, for example, Y. Rezvushkin, "Lenin o teorii pererastaniya burzhuazno-demokraticheskoi revoliutsii v sotsialisticheskuyu" (Lenin on the Theory of the Growth of the Bourgeois-Democratic Revolution into the Socialist), *Prol. revol.,* nos. 10 and 11-12, 1928.

10. Lenin, "A Few Theses," Works, XVIII, 312.

11. Lenin, "Proshchalnoe pismo k shveitsarskim rabochim" (Farewell Letter to the Swiss Workers), Works, XX, 68.

12. Lenin, "Nabrosok tezisov 17-ogo marta, 1917" (Draft of Theses of March 17, 1917 [New Style]), Works, XX, 10.

13. Trotsky in *Novy mir* (The New World; New York), March 16, 19, 20, 1917 [New Style]), as quoted in Trotsky, *History of the Russian Revolution,* (tr. Max Eastman, New York, 1932), I, appendix 2, 471-474.

14. N. I. Bukharin, "From the Collapse of Tsarism to the Fall of the Bourgeoisie," as quoted in Trotsky, *The Stalin School of Falsification* (New York, 1937), p. 78.

15. A. G. Shliapnikov, *Semnadtsaty god* (The Year 1917; Moscow, 1925), II, 176-177, 187.

16. *Ibid.*, I, 186, 208; II, 144.

17. Quoted, *ibid.*, I, appendix 24, 261-262.

18. *Ibid.*, I, 97; Trotsky, *History of the Russian Revolution*, I, 285.

19. Shliapnikov, II, 173.

20. *Ibid.*, II, 183; N. N. Sukhanov, *The Russian Revolution, 1917: A Personal Record* (tr., ed., and abridged by Joel Carmichael, London, 1955), pp. 226-227.

21. Stalin, "O voine" (On the War), *Pravda,* March 16, 1917, in Works, III, 8.

22. The Bolsheviks' March conference is known chiefly through the minutes published by Trotsky: "The March, 1917, Party Conference," in *The Stalin School,* pp. 231-303. See Trotsky, *Stalin,* p. 194.

23. See Leonard Schapiro, *The Origin of the Communist Autocracy: Political Opposition in the Soviet State—First Phase, 1917-1922* (London, 1955), pp. 27-28.

24. Skrypnik, in "The March, 1917, Party Conference," *The Stalin School,* pp. 253, 272.

25. Shliapnikov, III, 204-205.

26. Quoted, *ibid.*, p. 208.

27. Stalin, in "The March, 1917, Party Conference," *The Stalin School,* pp. 238-239. In 1924 Stalin admitted that his policy before Lenin returned had been wrong: "This was a profoundly erroneous position, for it produced pacifist illusions, poured water into the mill of defensism and hindered the revolutionary education of the masses" ("Trotskizm ili leninizm?" [Trotskyism or Leninism; speech to the Communist Party Fraction of the All-Union Central Council of Trade Unions, November 19, 1924], in *Za leninizm—Sbornik statei* [For Leninism: A Collection of Articles; Moscow, 1925], p. 132). Later accounts published during Stalin's lifetime overlooked this error altogether, but following the desanctification of Stalin at the Twentieth Party Congress in 1956, his old right-wing deviation was once again recalled. See E. N. Burdzhalov, "O

taktike bolshevikov v marte-aprele 1917 goda" (On the Tactics of the Bolsheviks in March and April, 1917), *Voprosy istorii* (Problems of History), no. 4, 1956.

28. Trotsky, *Stalin,* pp. 192–193.

29. Sukhanov, p. 257.

30. Recounted in F. F. Raskolnikov, "Priezd tov. Lenina v Rossiyu" (Comrade Lenin's Arrival in Russia), *Prol. revol.,* no. 1, 1923, p. 221.

31. Recounted in Sukhanov, p. 273.

32. *Ibid.,* p. 280.

33. Lenin, speech at a meeting of the Bolshevik members of the All-Russian Conference of Soviets, April 4, 1917, Works, XX, 78–83.

34. F. Drabkina, "Priezd tov. Lenina i martovskoe soveshchanie predstavitelei bolshevistskikh organizatsiyakh" (The Arrival of Comrade Lenin and the March Conference of Representatives of the Bolshevik Organizations), *Prol. revol.,* no. 4, 1927, p. 157.

35. Kamenev, "Nashi raznoglasiya" (Our Differences), *Pravda,* April 8, 1917.

36. Carr, I, 81.

37. Quoted in Trotsky, *Stalin,* p. 198.

38. Minutes of the Petrograd City Party Conference of April 1917, in *Sedmaya* ("Aprelskaya") *vserossiskaya i petrogradskaya obshchegorodskaya konferentsi RSDRP(b), Aprel 1917 g.: Protokoly* (The Seventh ["April"] All-Russian and Petrograd City-Wide Conferences of the RSDWP[b], April, 1917, Protocols; Moscow, 1934), pp. 29, 53, 242–243, 258.

39. N. Avdeyev, *Revoliutsiya 1917 goda: Khronika sobyti* (The Revolution of 1917: Chronicle of Events; Moscow, 1923), II, 60–61.

40. Seventh Party Conference, p. 51.

41. *Ibid.,* pp. 66–70.

42. *Ibid.,* pp. 87–91.

43. CPSU in Resolutions, 335–338.

44. *Ibid.,* pp. 338–339.

45. Rykov, Seventh Party Conference, p. 93.

46. Resolution of the Seventh Party Conference, "O tekushchem momente" (On the Current Moment), CPSU in Resolutions, I, 352.

47. Seventh Party Conference, p. 190.

48. See Sukhanov, pp. 457–458; Deutscher, *The Prophet Armed,* pp. 273–278. Recently published materials from the German archives strongly suggest that the Bolsheviks accepted German funds, but there was certainly no such German control over them as the 1917 charges alleged; Lenin bowed to no one. See Z. A. B. Zeman, ed., *Germany and the Revolution in Russia, 1915–1918* (London and New York, 1958), and F. L. Carsten, "Was Lenin a German Agent?" *Problems of Communism,* January–February, 1959, pp. 44–48.

49. "The March, 1917, Party Conference," *The Stalin School,* pp. 256–268, 274–275.

50. Schapiro, pp. 28–29.

51. "The March, 1917, Party Conference," *The Stalin School,* p. 263.

52. Lenin at the meeting of Bolshevik members of the Soviet Conference, April 4, 1917, Works, XX, 83.

53. Avdeyev, II, 10–11.

54. Resolution of the Seventh Party Conference, "Ob obedinenii internatsionalistov protiv melkoburzhuaznogo oboroncheskogo bloka" (On the Unification of the Internationalists against the Petty-Bourgeois Defensist Bloc), CPSU in Resolutions, I, 347.

55. "Lenin na konferentsii Mezhraiontsev" (Lenin at the Conference of the Mezhraiontsy), The Lenin Collection, IV, 300–303.

56. Deutscher, *The Prophet Armed*, pp. 257–258n2.

57. Lenin's notes on Trotsky's speech in "Lenin at the Conference of the Mezhrai-ontsy," The Lenin Collection, IV, 303.

58. See Angelica Balabanova, *My Life as a Rebel* (London, 1938), pp. 155–156.

59. Deutscher, *The Prophet Armed*, p. 258, citing A. V. Lunacharsky, *Revoliutsionnya siluety* (Revolutionary Silhouettes; Moscow, 1923), p. 69; Yurenev in *Shestoi sezd RSDRP(b): Protokoly* (The Sixth Congress of the RSDWP[b]: Protocols; Moscow, 1934), pp. 47–48.

60. See, for example, the remarks of Kalinin at the Petrograd City Conference in April 1917, in Seventh Party Conference, p. 42.

61. *Protokoly Tsentralnogo Komiteta RSDRP(b), Avgust 1917 g.–Feveral 1918 g.* (Protocols of the Central Committee of the RSDWP[b], August 1917–February 1918; Moscow and Leningrad, 1929), pp. 5, 56.

62. Listing in The Great Soviet Encyclopedia, LX, 555.

63. Shliapnikov, II, 187; III, 209.

64. Lenin, Works, XX, 648n125.

65. Autobiographies of Bukharin, Piatakov and Osinsky, *Ency. Dict.*, XLI, appendixes, pt. 1, pp. 54–55; pt. 2, pp. 92–93, 133.

66. On the background of Lenin's doctrine of the "commune state," see R. V. Daniels, "The State and Revolution: A Case Study in the Genesis and Transformation of Communist Ideology," *The American Slavic and East European Review*, February 1953, pp. 25–33.

67. Resolution of the Seventh Party Conference, "O peresmotre partinoi programmy" (On the Revision of the Party Program), CPSU in Resolutions, I, 352.

68. Lenin, "Gosudarstvo i revoliutsiya" (State and Revolution), Works, XXI, 396–400; Cf. Marx, *The Civil War in France* (Chicago, n.d.), p. 42ff.

69. Lenin, "State and Revolution," Works, XXI, 403.

70. Lenin, "Odin iz korennykh voprosov revoliutsii" (One of the Fundamental Questions of the Revolution), Works, XXI, 145.

71. Lenin, "On Dual Power," Works, XX, 95.

72. Lenin, "State and Revolution," Works, XXI, 386. Cf. Daniels in *The American Slavic and East European Review*, p. 23.

73. Lenin, "Pisma o taktike" (Letters on Tactics), Works, XX, 106.

74. Lenin, "On Dual Power," Works, XX, 96.

75. Resolution of the Sixth Party Congress, "Tekushchi moment i voina" (The Current Moment and the War), CPSU in Resolutions, I, 373–374.

76. Trotsky, "Programma mira" (A Program of Peace; May 25, 1917); *Sochineniya* (Works; Moscow, 1925–1927), III–1, 73.

77. Lenin, "Proekt rezoliutsii o voine" (Draft Resolution on the War; introduced to the Petrograd City Conference of the Bolshevik Party, April 1917), Works, XX, 189.

78. Bukharin, Sixth Party Congress, p. 101.

79. *Ibid.*, pp. 109, 192–193.

80. Preobrazhensky and Stalin, *ibid.*, pp. 192, 233–234.

81. CPSU in Resolutions, I, 394.

82. Lenin to the Bolshevik members of the Regional Congress of the Soviets of the Northern Region, October 8, 1917, Works, XXI, 322.

83. Lenin, "K lozungam" (On Slogans), Works, XXI, 33.

84. *Ibid.*, p. 38; see Meyer, pp. 173–175.

85. Trotsky, *Stalin*, pp. 215–216.

86. Resolution of the Sixth Party Congress, "O politicheskom polozhenii" (On the Political Situation), CPSU in Resolutions, I, 376.

87. Molotov, Sixth Party Congress, pp. 132–133.

88. Sokolnikov, *ibid.,* p. 121.

89. William Henry Chamberlin, *The Russian Revolution, 1917-1921* (New York, 1935), I, 277.

90. Lenin, "O kompromissakh" (On Compromises), Works, XXI, 133-134.

91. *Ibid.,* p. 136.

92. Lenin, "Proekt rezoliutsii o sovremennom politicheskom momente" (Draft Resolution on the Present Political Situation), Works, XXI, 137-141.

93. Lenin, "One of the Fundamental Questions of the Revolution" (published September 14, 1917), Works, XXI, 142-148.

94. Chamberlin, I, 277-278.

95. Lenin, "Bolsheviki dolzhny vziat vlast" (The Bolsheviks Must Take Power) and "Marksizm i vosstanie" (Marxism and Insurrection), Works, XXI, 193-199.

96. Lenin, "The Bolsheviks Must Take Power," Works, XXI, 193-194.

97. Trotsky, *Stalin,* p. 222.

98. Protocols of the Central Committee, pp. 64-65; Bukharin, speech at an evening of reminiscences, 1921, *Prol. revol.,* no. 10, 1922, p. 319.

99. Protocols of the CC, pp. 70-71; Trotsky, *Stalin,* p. 227. The vote in the fraction is also given as 72 to 50 (see Chamberlin, I, 283).

100. Lenin, "Iz dnevnika publitsista" (From the Diary of a Publicist), entries for September 22 and 23, 1917, Works, XXI, 218-219.

101. Lenin, "Krizis nazrel" (The Crisis is Imminent), Works, XXI, 240.

102. *Ibid.,* p. 241.

103. Protocols of the CC, p. 87.

104. Sukhanov, pp. 537-538.

105. Protocols of the CC, pp. 90-91.

106. Trotsky, declaration of the Bolsheviks at the session of the Democratic Conference, October 7, 1917. Works, III-1, 323. See Sukhanov, pp. 539-540.

107. Lenin to the Central Committee, Moscow Committee, Petrograd Committee, and the Bolshevik members of the Petrograd and Moscow Soviets, October 3-7, 1917, Works, XXI, 293.

108. Chamberlin, I, 299-300.

109. Protocols of the CC, p. 99. The meeting was held secretly in the apartment of the left-wing Menshevik Sukhanov, whose Bolshevik wife had persuaded him to spend the night near his office (see Sukhanov, p. 556). Eleven of the twenty-one Central Committee members were in Petrograd to participate in the vote: in favor were nine— Lenin, Trotsky, Stalin, Sverdlov, Uritsky, Dzerzhinsky, Kollontai, Bubnov, and Sokolnikov—together with the candidate member Lomov (Protocols of the CC, p. 101). A vote of the full committee, including the absent right-wingers Rykov, Nogin, and Miliutin, would in all probability have shown much stronger opposition to the insurrection (see Schapiro, p. 59).

110. Declaration of Zinoviev and Kamenev, "K nastoyashchemu momentu" (On the Present Situation), Protocols of the CC, pp. 102-108.

111. Kamenev, *ibid.,* p. 118.

112. *Ibid.,* pp. 124-125.

113. *Ibid.,* p. 124.

114. Lenin to Comrades, October 16-17, 1917, Works, XXI, 336, 346.

115. Text in Protocols of the CC, p. 137.

116. Quoted in Lenin to Comrades, postscript, Works, XXI, 348.

117. "Yu. Kamenev o 'vystuplenii'" (Y. Kamenev on the "Move"), reprinted in Protocols of the CC, pp. 136-137.

118. Lenin to the members of the Bolshevik Party, October 18, 1917, Works, XXI, 350-351.

119. Lenin to the Central Committee, October 19, 1917, Works, XXI, 355.

120. Protocols of the CC, pp. 127–129.

121. Lenin, "Sovety postoronnego" (Advice of a Bystander), Works, XXI, 320.

122. Lenin, report at the Central Committee session of October 16, 1917, Protocols of the CC, p. 111.

123. Sukhanov, p. 636.

124. Protocols of the CC, pp. 144–146.

125. I. N. Liubimov, *Revoliutsiya 1917 goda: Khronika sobyti* (The Revolution of 1917: Chronicle of Events; Moscow and Leningrad, 1930), VI, 22, as quoted in Schapiro, p. 71.

126. Carr, I, 147.

127. Protocols of the CC, pp. 148–155.

128. Minutes of the session of the Petrograd Committee of the Bolshevik Party, November 1, 1917, in Trotsky, *The Stalin School,* pp. 107, 110–112.

129. V. Maksakov, "Moskovskoe Oblastnoe Biuro pered oktiabrskimi dniami" (The Moscow Oblast Bureau before the October Days), *Prol. revol.,* no. 10, 1922, p. 476.

130. Deutscher, *The Prophet Armed,* p. 333.

131. Resolution of the Central Committee, November 2, 1917, "Po voprosu ob oppozitsii vnutri TsK" (On the Question of the Opposition Inside the CC), CPSU in Resolutions, I, 401–402.

132. Protocols of the CC, pp. 162–164.

133. Lenin, Works, XXI, 580n14; see Trotsky, *Stalin,* p. 240.

134. Reported from *Novaya zhizn* (New Life), November 5, 1917, in S. Oldenbourg, ed., *Le Coup d'état bolcheviste* (Paris, 1929), p. 406.

135. Text in Protocols of the CC, p. 167.

136. Text, *ibid.,* p. 169.

137. Lozovsky in *Rabochaya gazeta* (The Workers' Gazette), November 5, 1917, as quoted in Trotsky, *The Lessons of October* (New York, 1937), p. 76.

138. The Central Committee of the Russian Social Democratic Workers' Party (Bolshevik), to all party members and to all the toiling classes of Russia, November 4–6, 1917, in Lenin, Works, XXII, 59–61.

139. Zinoviev, "Pismo tovarishcham" (Letter to the Comrades), Protocols of the CC, p. 177.

140. Uritsky, report to the Petrograd Party Committee, December 12, 1917, as quoted in Trotsky, *The Lessons of October,* p. 78.

141. Protocols of the CC, pp. 181, 184–185.

142. James Bunyan and H. H. Fisher, *The Bolshevik Revolution, 1917–1918* (Stanford, 1934), p. 384.

143. Resolution of the First All-Russian Congress of Trade Unions, *ibid.,* pp. 639–641.

144. Schapiro, pp. 226n35, 231.

145. The Great Soviet Encyclopedia, 2nd ed., LI, 180.

CHAPTER 3. THE BREST-LITOVSK CONTROVERSY AND THE LEFT COMMUNISTS

1. Trotsky, in *Vtoroi vserossiski sezd sovetov R. i S.D.* (The Second All-Russian Congress of Soviets of Workers' and Soldiers' Deputies; Moscow, 1928), pp. 86–87.

2. See Carr, *The Bolshevik Revolution,* III, 14–33.

3. "Dekret o mire" (Decree on Peace), *Pravda,* October 27 and 28, 1917.

4. Yaroslavsky, "Brief History of the Russian Communist Party," II, ch. 6, p. 20.

5. Trotsky, "K trudiashchimsia, ugnetennym i obeskrovlennym narodam Evropy" (To the Toiling, Oppressed, and Bled Peoples of Europe), December 6, 1917, Works, III-2, 206.

6. V. Sorin, *Partiya i oppozitsiya* (The Party and the Opposition), I, "Fraktsiya levykh kommunistov" (The Faction of Left Communists; Moscow, 1925), p. 15.

7. Lenin, "Tezisy po voprosu o nemedlennom zakliuchenii separatnogo i anneksionistskogo mira" (Theses on the Question of Immediately Concluding a Separate and Annexationist Peace), Works, XXII, 198.

8. Protocols of the Central Committee, p. 200.

9. *Ibid.*, pp. 204–206.

10. Stalin, statement at a session of the Central Committee concerning the question of peace with the Germans, Works, IV, 27.

11. Protocols of the CC, p. 203.

12. *Ibid.*, p. 207.

13. See Schapiro, *The Origin of the Communist Autocracy*, p. 132.

14. Quoted in Sorin, p. 17.

15. Lenin, in *Sedmoi sezd RKP—Stenograficheski otchet* (The Seventh Congress of the RCP—Stenographic Report; Moscow 1923), p. 29.

16. Schapiro, p. 105.

17. Protocols of the CC, pp. 226–229, and Lenin, Works, XXII, 605n114, 607–609n119, 122–124. On the basis of the votes taken between February 17 and February 23, the Central Committee members who were present can be classified politically as follows, from Right to Left: Lenin and his hard core (Stalin, Sverdlov, Smilga, Zinoviev); inclining toward the Leninists—Sokolnikov; intermediate (moderate Left)—Trotsky; Left, inclining toward the intermediate—Krestinsky and Dzerzhinsky; Left, inclining toward the extreme—Uritsky and Ioffe; extreme Left—Bukharin, Lomov, and Bubnov. The Rightists Kamenev, Rykov, Nogin, and Miliutin had not yet resumed the Central Committee seats which they resigned in November 1917 over the press and coalition issues.

18. Protocols of the CC, p. 238.

19. Proclamation of the Council of People's Commissars, To the Toiling Population of All Russia, *Pravda,* February 21, 1918 (morning ed.).

20. Lenin, "Sotsialisticheskoe otechestvo v opasnosti" (The Socialist Fatherland is in Danger), *Pravda,* February 22, 1918 (morning ed.).

21. Trotsky, *My Life* (New York, 1931), p. 387.

22. Protocols of the CC, p. 248.

23. *Ibid.*, pp. 249–251.

24. *Ibid.*, p. 252.

25. Petrograd *Kommunist,* no. 2, as quoted in Sorin, pp. 19–20.

26. Protocols of the CC, p. 253.

27. Quoted in Lenin, Works, XXII, pp. 296n, 296–297.

28. Quoted in Sorin, p. 20.

29. Lenin, Works, XXII, 609n124.

30. Schapiro, pp. 107–108.

31. Quoted in Trotsky, *My Life,* p. 389.

32. See Kennan, *Russia Leaves the War* (Princeton, 1956), pp. 370–371, 491.

33. *Pravda,* March 6, 1918.

34. Lenin, Works, XXII, 611n132.

35. Lenin, "Serezny urok i sereznaya otvetstvennost" (A Serious Lesson and a Serious Responsibility), Works, XXII, 306–310.

36. Seventh Party Congress, pp. 76–77.

37. Lenin, "Strannoe i chudovishchnoe" (Strange and Monstrous), Works, XXII, 303.

38. Lenin, Seventh Party Congress, p. 23.

39. Lenin, "Strange and Monstrous," Works, XXII, 300.

40. Zinoviev, Seventh Party Congress, p. 56.

41. Lenin, "A Serious Lesson and a Serious Responsibility," Works, XXII, 307.

42. Lenin, Seventh Party Congress, p. 22.
43. Lenin, "Strange and Monstrous," Works, XXII, 301.
44. Bubnov, Seventh Party Congress, pp. 60–63.
45. Bukharin, *ibid.,* p. 33.
46. Trotsky, *ibid.,* pp. 84–85.
47. Bukharin, *ibid.,* p. 125.
48. Uritsky, *ibid.,* p. 55.
49. Trotsky, *ibid.,* p. 85.
50. Bukharin, *ibid.,* pp. 40–48, 82.
51. Trotsky, *ibid.,* p. 80.
52. *Ibid.,* p. 139.
53. *Ibid.,* pp. 140–157.
54. Recounted in Voline (V. M. Eikhenbaum), *Nineteen-Seventeen: The Russian Revolution Betrayed* (London, 1954), p. 98.
55. Trotsky, Seventh Party Congress, pp. 83, 86.
56. *Ibid.,* pp. 189–194.
57. Resolution of the Seventh Party Congress, "Po povodu otkaza 'levykh kommunistov' voiti v TsK" (In Regard to the Refusal of the "Left Communists" to Enter the Central Committee), CPSU in Resolutions, I, 406.
58. Radek, "Posle piati mesiatsev" (After Five Months), *Kommunist,* no. 1, April 1918, pp. 3–4.
59. Lenin, "State and Revolution," Works, XXI, 446.
60. Lenin, answer to a question from the Left SRs at a session of the Central Executive Committee, November 4, 1917, Works, XXII, 45.
61. Lenin, "Uderzhat li bolsheviki gosudarstvennuyu vlast?" (Will the Bolsheviks Retain State Power?), Works, XXI, 261.
62. Lenin, "The Threatening Catastrophe and How to Fight It," Works, XXI, 157.
63. Quoted in V. L. Meller and A. M. Pankratova, *Rabochee dvizhenie v 1917 godu* (The Workers' Movement in 1917; Moscow and Leningrad, 1926), pp. 74–75.
64. Quoted in S. O. Zagorsky, *State Control of Industry in Russia during the War* (New Haven, 1928), pp. 174–175.
65. See Maurice Dobb, *Soviet Economic Development since 1917* (New York, 1948), p. 90; A. Sidorov, "Ekonomicheskaya programma oktiabria" (The Economic Program of October), *Prol. revol.,* no. 6, 1929, p. 46.
66. Lenin, "Proekt polozheniya o rabochem kontrole" (Draft Regulations on Workers' Control), Works, XXII, 25–26.
67. N. Filippov, "Ob organizatsii proizvodstva" (On the Organization of Production), *Vestnik metallista* (The Metalworker's Herald), January 1918, pp. 40, 43.
68. Quoted in A. S. Shliapnikov, *Die Russischen Gewerkschaften* (Leipzig, 1920), pp. 20–21.
69. Carr, II, 105–106.
70. See Osinsky in *Trudy pervogo vserossiskogo sezda sovetov narodnogo khoziaistva* (Proceedings of the First All-Russian Congress of Economic Councils; Moscow, 1918), pp. 61–64.
71. Lenin, "Ocherednye zadachi sovetskoi vlasti" (Immediate Tasks of the Soviet Regime), Works, XXII, 444–446.
72. Sidorov, "The Economic Program of October," *Prol. revol.,* no. 6, 1929, pp. 45–46.
73. Carr, II, 75, 86.
74. Lenin, First Congress of Economic Councils, p. 3.
75. Carr, II, 85–87.
76. *Ibid.,* 109–115; Lenin, Works, XXII, 622n186.
77. Carr, II, 394–396.

78. Preobrazhensky in *Kommunist,* no. 4, May 1918.
79. Lenin, "The Immediate Tasks of the Soviet Regime," Works, XXII, 446-447, 461-462, and *passim.*
80. "Tezisy o tekushchem momente" (Theses on the Current Situation), *Kommunist,* no. 1, April 1918, p. 7. See Lenin, Works, XXII, 620n117.
81. Osinsky, "O stroitelstve sotsializma" (On the Building of Socialism), *Kommunist,* no. 2, April 1918, p. 5.
82. Lenin, "O levom rebiachestve i melkoburzhuaznosti" (On Left Childishness and the Petty-Bourgeois Quality), Works, XXII, 524.
83. Lenin, First Congress of Economic Councils, p. 5.
84. Radek, *ibid.,* pp. 14-19.
85. Osinsky, *ibid.,* pp. 64-65.
86. Lomov, *ibid.,* p. 75.
87. Osinsky, *ibid.,* p. 65.
88. "Polozhenie ob upravlenii natsionalizirovannymi predpriyatiyami" (Regulations for the Administration of Nationalized Enterprises), *ibid.,* pp. 477-478.
89. "Theses on the Current Situation," *Kommunist,* no. 1, April 1918, p. 8.
90. Quoted in Sorin, pp. 21-22.
91. *Ibid.,* pp. 22-23.
92. *Krasnaya gazeta* (The Red Gazette), March 14, 1918, as quoted in Lenin, Works, XXII, pp. 176n620.
93. See *Kommunist,* no. 4, May 1918, pp. 13-14.
94. Sorin, pp. 23-24.
95. "Theses on the Current Situation," *Kommunist,* no. 1, April 1918, p. 9.
96. Y. Yaroslavsky, "Nam s nimi ne po doroge" (The Road with Them is not for Us), *Pravda,* July 3, 1918.
97. Piatakov, Stukov, Radek, V. Yakovleva, V. Smirnov, Pokrovsky, Preobrazhensky, Sheverdin, and Maksimovsky to the editorial board of *Pravda,* December 20, 1923, in *Pravda,* January 3, 1924.
98. See People's Commissariat of Justice of the USSR, *Report of Court Proceedings: The Case of the Anti-Soviet Bloc of Rights and Trotskyites* (Moscow, 1938), pp. 30, 440-445, 773-774.
99. *Ibid.,* pp. 445-446.
100. Yaroslavsky, "The Road with Them is not for Us," *Pravda,* July 3, 1918.
101. Lenin, Works, XXII, 160n131.

CHAPTER 4. WAR COMMUNISM AND THE CENTRALIZATION CONTROVERSIES

1. See Dobb, *Soviet Economic Development since 1917,* pp. 89-90.
2. I. I. Stepanov-Skvortsov, *Ot rabochego kontrolia k rabochemu upravleniyu* (From Workers' Control to Workers' Administration; Moscow, 1918), p. 24.
3. Bubnov, "VKP(b)" (The All-Union CP[b]), The Great Soviet Encyclopedia, 1st ed., XI, 453.
4. Lenin in *Protokoly sezdov i konferentsi Vsesoyuznoi Kommunisticheskoi Partii* (b): *Vosmoi sezd RKP(b)* (Protocols of the Congresses and Conferences of the All-Union Communist Party [b]: Eighth Congress of the RCP[b]; Moscow, 1933), p. 250.
5. L. Kritsman, *Geroicheski period russkoi revoliutsii* (The Heroic Period of the Russian Revolution; Moscow and Leningrad, 1926), pp. 71, 77.
6. Bukharin, *Oekonomik des Transformationsperiode* (Hamburg, 1922), pp. 55-60.
7. Kritsman, p. 129.
8. Trotsky, *Stalin,* p. 202.
9. Resolution of the Seventh Party Conference, "Po natsionalnomu voprosu" (On the Nationality Question), CPSU in Resolutions, I, 345-346.

10. Eighth Party Congress, pp. 47–53.

11. Bukharin, Eighth Party Congress, pp. 48–49.

12. See Carr, *The Bolshevik Revolution*, I, 261, 265–266.

13. Piatakov, Eighth Party Congress, pp. 79–83.

14. Lenin, *ibid.*, pp. 54–57, 107–108.

15. *Ibid.*, pp. 70–71, 91–94.

16. M. Ravich-Cherkassky, *Istoriya Kommunisticheskoi Partii (bolshevikov) Ukrainy* (History of the Communist Party [Bolshevik] of the Ukraine; [Kharkov], 1923), pp. 51–55.

17. See E. I. Kviring, "Nashi raznoglasiya" (Our Differences), in *Pervy sezd Kommunisticheskoi Partii (bolshevikov) Ukrainy* (The First Congress of the Communist Party [Bolshevik] of the Ukraine), M. Ravich-Cherkassky, ed. (Kharkov, 1923), pp. 6, 11.

18. See V. P. Zatonsky, "K piatiletiyu KP(b)U" (On the Fifth Anniversary of the CP[b]U), *ibid.*, p. 15.

19. Kviring, *ibid.*, pp. 8–9.

20. Ravich-Cherkassky, "History of the CP(b)U," pp. 58–64, 84–86, 90–96.

21. See N. N. Popov, *Narys istorii Kommunistichnoi Partii (bolshevikiv) Ukrainy* (Sketch of the History of the CP[b]U; 2nd ed., Kharkov, 1929, pp. 186–187.

22. Ravich-Cherkassky, "History of the CP(b)U," pp. 55–56.

23. *Ibid.*, pp. 117–118.

24. Carr, II, 159–160n4; Popov, "History of the CP(b)U," p. 190.

25. See Iwan Majstrenko, *Borotbism: A Chapter in the History of Ukrainian Communism* (New York, 1954), pp. 120–121.

26. Ravich-Cherkassky, "History of the CP(b)U," p. 55.

27. Zatonsky, in "The First Congress of the CP(b)U," p. 15.

28. See Ravich-Cherkassky, "History of the CP(b)U," pp. 123–125; Popov, "History of the CP(b)U," pp. 183–184.

29. Ravich-Cherkassky, "History of the CP(b)U," pp. 107–118.

30. Resolution of the Eighth Party Congress, "Po organizatsionnomu voprosu" (On the Organizational Question), CPSU in Resolutions, I, 443.

31. Eighth Party Congress, pp. 79–83, 91–94.

32. Resolution of the Central Committee of the RCP, "O sovetskoi vlasti na Ukraine" (On Soviet Power in the Ukraine), *Izvestiya TsK* (News of the Central Committee), December 2, 1919.

33. Central Committee circular dated December 12, 1919, *ibid.*, January 14, 1920.

34. Yakovlev, in *Protokoly: Deviaty sezd RKP(b)* (Ninth Congress of the RCP[b]; Moscow, 1934), p. 62.

35. Popov, "History of the CP(b)U," p. 220; Ravich-Cherkassky, "History of the CP(b)U," pp. 156, 158–160.

36. *Ibid.*, p. 160–162.

37. *Ibid.*, pp. 149–150, 155–156.

38. Bubnov, Ninth Party Congress, pp. 63–65.

39. Ravich-Cherkassky, "History of the CP(b)U," p. 152.

40. Lenin, Ninth Party Congress, p. 94.

41. Central Committee Order, "Vsem organizatsiyam KP(b)U" (To All Organizations of the CP[b]U), April 7, 1920, text in Ravich-Cherkassky, "History of the CP(b)U," appendix 12, pp. 235–238.

42. Popov, "History of the CP(b)U," pp. 234–245.

43. Trotsky, report to the Moscow city conference of the RCP, March 27, 1918, "Trud, distsiplina, poriadok" (Work, Discipline, Order), Works, XVII–1, 155ff.

44. Autobiography of Krylenko, *Ency. Dict.*, XLI–1, appendix, 246.

45. Trotsky, "Work, Discipline, Order," Works, XVII–1, 171–172.

46. See Schapiro, *The Origin of the Communist Autocracy*, pp. 241–243.

47. Trotsky, "Work, Discipline, Order," pp. 162, 170–171.

48. Quoted in Sorin, "The Faction of Left Communists," p. 137.

49. A. F. Ilin-Zhenevsky, *Bolsheviki u vlasti* (The Bolsheviks in Power; Leningrad, 1929), pp. 87–98, cited in Deutscher, *The Prophet Armed*, p. 412.

50. V. Smirnov, Eighth Party Congress, p. 156. Cf. Sokolnikov, Eighth Party Congress, pp. 147–149.

51. Smirnov, *ibid.*, pp. 158–159.

52. Resolution of the Eighth Party Congress, "Po voennomu voprosu" (On the Military Question), CPSU in Resolutions, I, 432–433.

53. Trotsky, *My Life,* p. 437.

54. See Deutscher, p. 431, where the record is reconstructed on the basis of documents in the Trotsky Archive.

55. Trotsky, *Stalin,* p. 302.

56. Lenin, Works, XXIV, 750.

57. Excerpt from the Protocols of the Central Committee, March 25, 1919, Trotsky Archive T147; Trotsky to the Central Committee, March 1919, T2954.

58. CPSU in Resolutions I, 433–436.

59. Trotsky, *Stalin,* pp. 297–298.

60. Trotsky to the Central Committee, December 1918, T2953. See also Deutscher, pp. 425–426.

61. *Ibid.,* pp. 433–436.

62. Schapiro, pp. 247–252.

63. Tomsky, theses, "Zadachi professionalnykh soyuzov" (The Tasks of the Trade Unions), Ninth Party Congress, p. 535.

64. Kritsman, p. 83.

65. Lenin, speech to the Second All-Russian Congress of Economic Councils, Works, XXIII, 447.

66. Preobrazhensky, Ninth Party Congress, p. 72.

67. Lenin, speech to the Third All-Russian Congress of Economic Councils (January 1920), Works, XXV, 17.

68. Carr, II, 190; Schapiro, p. 230.

69. Lenin, theses presented on behalf of the Central Committee, "Professionalnye soyuzy i ikh zadachi" (The Trade Unions and their Tasks), Ninth Party Congress, appendix 12, p. 532.

70. Lenin, Ninth Party Congress, pp. 26, 28.

71. Trotsky, *Dictatorship vs. Democracy* (New York, 1922), p. 115.

72. *Ibid.,* p. 161.

73. Ninth Party Congress, p. 571n75.

74. Maksimovsky, *ibid.,* p. 54.

75. Trotsky, *Dictatorship vs. Democracy,* p. 16.

76. V. V. Osinsky, T. V. Sapronov, and V. N. Maksimovsky, "Tezisy o kollegialnosti i edinolichii" (Theses on the Collegial Principle and Individual Authority), Ninth Party Congress, appendix 14, p. 538.

77. Resolution of the Ninth Party Congress, "Ob ocherednykh zadachakh khoziaistvennogo stroitelstva" (On the Next Tasks of Economic Construction), CPSU in Resolutions, I, 482–484.

78. To cite one example, the proportion of enterprises in the city of Petrograd under collegial administration declined from 52 per cent in December 1919, to 17 per cent a year later. See *Labour Conditions in Russia* (London, 1921), p. 50.

79. Sapronov, Ninth Party Congress, p. 56.

80. Trotsky, *ibid.*, p. 116.

81. Resolution of the Ninth Party Congress, "Tasks of Economic Construction," CPSU in Resolutions, I, 485.

82. Osinsky, Eighth Party Congress, pp. 196–198.

83. Lenin, *ibid.*, p. 28.

84. Skrypnik, *ibid.*, p. 176.

85. Osinsky, *ibid.*, pp. 30, 168.

86. *Isvestiya TsK,* December 2, 1919.

87. "Organizatsionny otchet tsentralnogo komiteta" (Organizational Report of the Central Committee), *ibid.*

88. Resolution of the Eighth Party Congress, "On the Organizational Question," CPSU in Resolutions, I, 443.

89. Biography of Krestinsky, *Ency. Dict.*, XLI-2, appendix, 233.

90. Krestinsky, organizational report to the Ninth Party Conference, *Pravda,* September 24, 1920.

91. Lenin, "Detskaya bolezn 'levizny' v kommunizme" (The Infantile Disease of "Leftism" in Communism), Works, XXV, 179–180.

92. *Ibid.*, p. 190.

93. Resolution of the Eighth Party Congress, "On the Organizational Question," CPSU in Resolutions, I, 444.

94. Krestinsky, Ninth Party Congress, pp. 47–48.

95. Yurenev, *ibid.*, pp. 51–52.

96. Kamenev, *ibid.*, p. 77.

97. Osinsky, *ibid.*, pp. 132–133; cf. Kamenev, *ibid.*, pp. 76–77.

98. Sapronov, *ibid.*, pp. 57–58.

99. Zinoviev, Eighth Party Congress, p. 220.

100. *Izvestiya TsK,* March 7, 1921, p. 5. Text, *ibid.*, September 4, 1920.

101. Report of the Central Committee for the period from the Ninth to the Tenth Party Congress, *Izvestiya TsK,* March 7, 1921, p. 5.

102. *Pravda,* September 25, 1920.

103. *Ibid.*, September 26, 1920.

104. *Ibid.*, September 30, 1920.

105. Report of the Central Committee of the RCP(b) for the period from the Ninth Congress to September 15, 1920, *Izvestiya TsK,* September 18, 1920, p. 7.

106. Resolution of the Ninth Party Conference, "Ob ocherednykh zadachakh partinogo stroitelstva," (On the Next Tasks of Building the Party), CPSU in Resolutions, I, 511–512.

107. *Ibid.*, p. 507.

108. Zinoviev at the Fifteenth Party Conference (October 1926), *Pravda,* November 9, 1926.

Chapter 5. The Trade-Union Controversy

1. "Programma Rossiskoi Kommunisticheskoi Partii (bolshevikov)" (Program of the Russian Communist Party [Bolshevik]), CPSU in Resolutions, I, 422.

2. Bukharin, *Oekonomik des Transformationsperiode*, pp. 81–82.

3. *Vtoroi vserossiski sezd professionalnykh soyuzov: Stenograficheski otchet* (The Second All-Russian Congress of Trade Unions: Stenographic Report; Moscow, 1919), I, 97.

4. *Ibid.*, I, 99.

5. See Carr, *The Bolshevik Revolution*, II, 202–209.

6. See Kritsman, "The Heroic Period of the Russian Revolution," pp. 78–93.

7. See Waldermar Koch, *Die Bolshevistischen Gewerkschaften* (Jena, 1932), pp. 81–82.

8. Riazanov, Eighth Party Congress, p. 72.

9. Trotsky, *Dictatorship vs. Democracy*, pp. 151–155.

10. Trotsky, Ninth Party Congress, p. 100.

11. Trotsky, *Dictatorship vs. Democracy*, p. 143.

12. Trotsky, "Tezisy TsK–RKP po trudu" (Theses of the CC of the RCP on Labor), *Pravda*, January 22, 1920.

13. Trotsky, *Dictatorship vs. Democracy*, p. 14.

14. Trotsky, Ninth Party Congress, p. 112.

15. Resolution of the Ninth Party Congress, "Ob ocherednykh zadachakh khoziaistvennogo stroitelstva" (On the Immediate Tasks of Building the Economy), CPSU in Resolutions, I, 478–479.

16. Rykov, Ninth Party Congress, p. 139.

17. Carr, II, 190, 370–371.

18. Trotsky, *Dictatorship vs. Democracy*, p. 14.

19. Trotsky to a friend, "Po nauke ili koe-kak?" (Scientifically or Any Old Way?), January 10, 1919, in Trotsky, *Kak vooruzhalas revoliutsiya* (How the Revolution Armed Itself; Moscow, 1923–25), I, 170.

20. Vladimir Smirnov, "Trudovaya povinnost i militarizatsiya" (Labor Duty and Militarization), *Pravda*, March 27, 1920.

21. Deutscher, *The Prophet Armed*, p. 492.

22. *Ibid.*, p. 493; Lenin, letter of March 2, 1920, "K organizatsiyam RKP(b) po voprosu o poriadke dnia partinogo sezda" (To the Organizations of the RCP[b] on the Question of the Agenda of the Party Congress), Ninth Party Congress, appendix 2, p. 473.

23. Molotov, *ibid.*, pp. 252–253.

24. Resolution of the Ninth Party Congress, "Po voprosu o professionalnykh soyuzakh i ikh organizatsii" (On the Question of the Trade Unions and their Organization), CPSU in Resolutions, I, 493.

25. See Carr, II, 220; Schapiro, *The Origin of the Communist Autocracy*, p. 256.

26. See Tenth Party Congress, pp. 867–868n128.

27. See Schapiro, pp. 257–258.

28. Tomsky, "Zadachi profsoyuzov" (Tasks of the Trade Unions), Ninth Party Congress, appendix 13, p. 534.

29. Bukharin, *ibid.*, pp. 234, 237–238.

30. *Ibid.*, p. 564n32.

31. Osinsky, *ibid.*, pp. 123–124.

32. Lutovinov, *ibid.*, pp. 254–255.

33. Lenin, "To the Organizations of the RCP(b) on the Question of the Agenda of the Party Congress," March 2, 1920, *ibid.*, appendix 2, p. 474.

34. Polidorov, *ibid.*, p. 81.

35. Krestinsky, *ibid.*, pp. 88–89, and in *Pravda*, March 12, 1920.

36. Ninth Party Congress, p. 564n32.

37. Theses of the Moscow Provincial Committee of the RCP, *ibid.*, appendix 15, p. 542.

38. Krestinsky, *ibid.*, p. 44, and p. 564n32; Lutovinov, *ibid.*, p. 60.

39. Resolution of the Ninth Party Congress, "On the Question of the Trade Unions," CPSU in Resolutions, I, 492.

40. Lenin, Ninth Party Congress, p. 96.

41. K. Shelavin, *Rabochaya oppozitsiya* (The Workers' Opposition; Moscow, 1930) p. 26.

42. Tomsky, in *Desiaty sezd RKP(b): Protokoly* (The Tenth Congress of the RCP[b]: Protocols; Moscow, 1933), pp. 371–372.

43. See statistics on political strikes in Meller and Pankratova, "The Labor Movement in the Year 1917," pp. 16, 20; and M. G. Fleer, *Rabochee dvizhenie v gody voiny* (The Labor Movement in the War Years; Moscow, 1925), pp. 4–7.

44. Workers' Opposition Theses on the Trade Unions, January 18, 1921, *Vsesoyuznaya Kommunisticheskaya Partiya (bolshevikov) v rezoliutsiyakh sezdov, konferentsi i plenumov TsK* (The All-Union Communist Party [Bolshevik] in Resolutions and Decisions of the Congresses, Conferences, and Plenums of the Central Committee; Moscow, 1931), I, appendix, 813.

45. Alexandra Kollontai, *The Workers' Opposition* (Chicago, 1921), p. 5.

46. *Ibid.*, p. 9.

47. Lenin, "What is to be Done?" Works, IV, 391.

48. Rosa Luxemburg, *The Russian Revolution* (New York, 1940; tr. and introduction by Bertram D. Wolfe; written in 1918), p. 52.

49. Kollontai, pp. 10–11.

50. Medvedev, Tenth Party Congress, p. 140.

51. Resolution on party organization proposed by the Workers' Opposition, Tenth Party Congress, p. 663.

52. Kollontai, p. 45.

53. Trotsky, "Profsoyuzy i ikh dalneishaya rol" (The Trade Unions and Their Further Role), Tenth Party Congress, appendix 10, p. 786.

54. Biography of Rudzutak in *Ency. Dict.*, XLI–2, appendix, 213, 222.

55. *Pravda*, November 6, 1920, reporting speech by Rudzutak to the Fifth Trade Union Conference.

56. Tenth Party Congress, p. 872n153; Lenin, speech to the Second All-Russian Congress of Miners, January 23, 1921, Works, XXVI, 100.

57. Tenth Party Congress, p. 825n1.

58. Resolution of the RCP fraction at the Fifth Trade Union Conference, "O zadachakh profdvizheniya" (On the Tasks of the Trade Union Movement), *Pravda*, November 13, 1920.

59. Tenth Party Congress, p. 825n1.

60. *Ibid.*

61. Trotsky, *O zadachakh profsoyuzov* (On the Tasks of the Trade Unions; Moscow, 1921—speech of December 30, 1920), pp. 15–21, cited in Schapiro, p. 276.

62. Tenth Party Congress, p. 825n1.

63. *Ibid.*, pp. 825–826n1; Schapiro, p. 280.

64. Trotsky, speech at the enlarged plenum of the Tsektran, December 2, 1920, Works, XV, 422–423.

65. Tenth Party Congress, p. 826n1; text in *Pravda*, December 14, 1920.

66. Tenth Party Congress, p. 826n1.

67. Lenin, "O professionalnykh soyuzakh, o tekushchem momente, i ob oshibkakh tov. Trotskogo" (On the Trade Unions, the Current Situation, and the Mistakes of Comrade Trotsky), Works, XXVI, 63–81.

68. *Ibid.*, p. 67.

69. AUCP(b) in Resolutions (1931), I, 790–800.

70. Shliapnikov, "Organizatsiya narodnogo khoziaistva i zadachi soyuzov" (The Organization of the Economy and the Tasks of the Unions—Speech of December 30, 1920), Tenth Party Congress, appendix 11, pp. 789–793.

71. AUCP(b) in Resolutions (1931), I, 810–815.

72. Bukharin, *Oekonomik des Transformationsperiode*, p. 86.

73. Platform of the Bukharin group, "O zadachakh i strukture profsoyuzov" (On the

Tasks and Structure of the Trade Unions; January 16, 1921), Tenth Party Congress, appendix 16, p. 802.

74. AUCP(b) in Resolutions (1931), I, 809.

75. Lenin, "Krisis partii" (The Crisis of the Party), *Pravda*, January 21, 1921.

76. It may be noted that this characterization of the three positions differs from the usual one, in which the Leninist group occupies the mean between the two extremes. See, for example, John Maynard, *Russia in Flux* (New York, 1948), pp. 228–229; Isaac Deutscher, *Stalin: A Political Biography* (New York and London, 1949), pp. 222–223; Carr, II, 223–244.

77. Friedrich Engels, *The Peasant War in Germany* (New York, 1926), pp. 135–136.

78. For example, see Bukharin, *Oekonomik des Transformationsperiode*, pp. 76–81.

CHAPTER 6. THE CRISIS OF 1921

1. Sapronov, "O raspredelenii partinykh sil" (On the Distribution of Party Forces), *Pravda*, November 12, 1920.

2. Bukharin, "K vyboram na moskovskuyu konferentsiyu" (On the Elections to the Moscow Conference), *ibid.*, November 16, 1920.

3. *Ibid.*, editorial, "Tekushchi moment i zadachi partii" (The Current Moment and the Tasks of the Party), November 19, 1920.

4. Tenth Party Congress, p. 829n2.

5. *Ibid.*, p. 851n60.

6. Theses of the Democratic Centralists, "Ocherednye zadachi partii" (The Next Tasks of the Party), *Pravda*, January 22, 1921.

7. Perepechko, Tenth Party Congress, p. 93.

8. Yaroslavsky, *ibid.*, reporting statement by Y. K. Milonov. The reference is to the hierarchs of the tsarist bureaucracy.

9. "Ocherednye zadachi partinogo stroitelstva: Proekt postanovleni X sezda RKP, predlagaemy gruppoi aktivnykh rabotnikov raionov g. Moskvy" (The Next Tasks of Party Construction: Draft of Decisions for the Tenth Congress of the RCP, Proposed by a Group of Active Workers from the Districts of the City of Moscow), *Pravda*, February 12, 1921.

10. Kollontai, Tenth Party Congress, p. 103.

11. *Pravda*, January 19, 1921.

12. Declaration to the party from the Petrograd organization of the RCP, *ibid.*, January 13, 1921.

13. Trotsky, "Otvet petrogradskim tovarishcham" (Answer to the Petrograd Comrades), Tenth Party Congress, appendix 7, pp. 779–781.

14. *Ibid.*, pp. 826–827n1.

15. Resolution of the Moscow Party Committee, January 13, 1921, *ibid.*, appendix 6, p. 779.

16. See Schapiro, *The Origin of the Communist Autocracy*, pp. 269–271.

17. Excerpt from the minutes of the Central Committee, in *Izvestiya TsK*, January 27, 1921, p. 16.

18. Solts, Tenth Party Congress, pp. 61, 67.

19. Quoted in *TsK-RKI v osnovnykh postanovlenniyakh partii* (The Central Control Commission–Workers' and Peasants' Inspection in the Basic Decisions of the Party; Moscow, 1927), pp. 12–13.

20. Tenth Party Congress, p. 827n1.

21. Statement of the Moscow Party Committee, "Nashi raznoglasiya" (Our Differences), *Pravda*, January 19, 1921.

22. Preobrazhensky, "Kak ne nado diskussirovat" (How the Controversy Should Not Be Conducted), *Pravda*, January 22, 1921.

23. *Pravda,* January 27, 1921.

24. Quoted in A. S. Pukhov, *Kronshtadtski miatezh v 1921 g.* (The Kronstadt Revolt of 1921; Leningrad, 1931), p. 52.

25. *Ibid.,* p. 53.

26. *Pravda,* January 27, 1921.

27. *Ibid.,* January 26, 1921.

28. *Ibid.,* February 23, 1921.

29. Report of the Central Committee for the period from the Ninth to the Tenth Congress, *Izvestiya TsK,* March 7, 1921, p. 6.

30. "Novy belogvardeiski zagovor" (A New White Guard Plot), *Pravda,* March 3, 1921. For a more extensive discussion of the circumstances and motives of the revolt, see R. V. Daniels, "The Kronstadt Revolt of 1921," *American Slavic and East European Review,* December 1951, pp. 241–254.

31. Alexander Berkman, *The Bolshevik Myth* (London, 1925), pp. 300–301, diary entry for March 5, 1921.

32. *Pravda,* March 6, 1921.

33. Tenth Party Congress, p. 861n97.

34. *Izvestiya vremennogo revoliutsionnogo komiteta* (News of the Temporary Revolutionary Committee), entire file reprinted as an appendix to *Pravda o Kronshtadte* (The Truth about Kronstadt; Prague, 1921).

35. "Etapy revoliutsii' (Stages of the Revolution), *ibid.,* March 12, 1921.

36. *Ibid.,* March 10, 13, 1921.

37. *Ibid.,* March 9, 1921.

38. *Ibid.,* March 5, 7, 13, 12, 1921.

39. Resolution of 240 defecting prisoners, *ibid.,* March 16, 1921.

40. See Chamberlin, *The Russian Revolution,* II, 443.

41. Lenin, Tenth Party Congress, pp. 29, 119.

42. Resolution of the Tenth Party Congress, "O sindikalistskom i anarkhistskom uklone v nashei partii" (On the Syndicalist and Anarchist Deviation in Our Party), CPSU in Resolutions, I, 530.

43. Lenin, Tenth Party Congress, pp. 382–383.

44. See, for instance, Smilga, *ibid.,* p. 258.

45. Reported in Trotsky, letter to friends in the USSR, 1930 (T3279).

46. Resolution of the Tenth Party Congress, "On the Syndicalist Deviation," CPSU in Resolutions, I, 531.

47. Resolution of the Tenth Party Congress, "O edinstve partii" (On the Unity of the Party), *ibid.,* I, 527–530.

48. Radek, Tenth Party Congress, p. 540.

49. Resolution of the Tenth Party Congress, "Po voprosam partinogo stroitelstva" (On Questions of Building the Party), CPSU in Resolutions, I, 517–520.

50. *Ibid.,* pp. 522–526.

51. Lenin, Tenth Party Congress, pp. 121–122.

52. Lenin, *Ibid.,* pp. 382–383.

53. Resolution of the Tenth Party Congress, "On the Unity of the Party," CPSU in Resolutions, I, 529; Lenin, Tenth Party Congress, p. 544.

54. Lenin, *ibid.,* p. 546.

55. The Great Soviet Encyclopedia, 1st ed., LX, 555.

56. Lenin, Tenth Party Congress, p. 563.

57. Preobrazhensky, "How the Controversy Should Not Be Conducted," *Pravda,* January 22, 1921.

58. *Izvestiya TsK,* July 20, 1921, p. 7; The Great Soviet Encyclopedia, 1st ed., LX,

555; *Protokoly: Odinnadtsaty sezd RKP(b)* (Eleventh Congress of the RCP[b]: Protocols; Moscow, 1936), index of names.

59. Biography of Molotov, *Ency. Dict.*, XLI-2, appendix, 65.
60. *Izvestiya TsK*, July 20, 1921, p. 7.
61. Aleksandrov (A. S. Michelson), *Kto upravliaet Rossiei?* (Who Rules Russia?; Berlin, 1933), pp. 380–381.
62. *Pravda*, December 5, 1943.

CHAPTER 7. LENINISM RESTORED

1. Lenin, Eleventh Party Congress, p. 16.
2. Dobb, *Soviet Economic Development since 1917*, p. 143.
3. Lenin, Tenth Party Congress, pp. 406, 407, 411.
4. Merle Fainsod, *How Russia is Ruled* (Cambridge, 1953), p. 244.
5. Lenin, Works, XXVII, 536–537n119.
6. Y. Larin, "O predelakh prisposobliaemosti nashei ekonomicheskoi politiki" (On the Limits of Adaptability of Our Economic Policy), *Krasnaya Nov* (Red Virgin Soil), November-December 1921, pp. 150–151.
7. Preobrazhensky, "Perspektivy novoi ekonomicheskoi politiki" (Prospects of the New Economic Policy), *ibid.*, September-October 1921, p. 202.
8. See *ibid.*, pp. 209–211.
9. Tenth Party Congress, p. 828n1.
10. Resolution of the Tenth Party Congress, "O roli i zadachakh profsoyuzov" (On the Role and Tasks of the Trade Unions), CPSU in Resolutions, I, 536–542ff.
11. See Schapiro, *The Origin of the Communist Autocracy*, p. 323.
12. Tenth Party Congress, index of names, p. 925.
13. Report of the Central Committee of the RCP for the period May 1–June 1, 1921, *Izvestiya TsK*, August 6, 1921, pp. 3–4.
14. *Ibid.*, pp. 2–3. The congress is discussed in detail in Schapiro, pp. 324–325, and Carr, *The Bolshevik Revolution*, II, 324–325.
15. Reported by Riazanov, Eleventh Party Congress, pp. 277–278. Cf. resolution of the Tenth Party Congress, "On the Role of the Trade Unions," CPSU in Resolutions, I, 540, and report of the Central Committee of the RCP for the period May 1–June 1, 1921, *Izvestiya TsK*, August 6, 1921, pp. 1–2.
16. Biography of Rudzutak, *Ency. Dict.*, XLI-2, appendix, 222.
17. Carr, II, 325–326.
18. *Ibid.*, pp. 326–327. The resolution was repassed by the Eleventh Party Congress: "Rol i zadachi profsoyuzov v usloviyakh novoi ekonomicheskoi politiki" (The Role and Tasks of the Trade Unions under the Conditions of the New Economic Policy), CPSU in Resolutions, I, 603–612.
19. See Carr, II, 321–322, 327–329.
20. Resolution of the Eleventh Party Congress, "The Trade Unions under the Conditions of the NEP," CPSU in Resolutions, I, 607, 610–612.
21. Autobiography of Andreyev, *Ency. Dict.*, XLI-1, appendix, 6.
22. *Izvestiya TsK*, March 1922, p. 11.
23. *Ibid.*
24. Lenin to Miasnikov, [July] 1921, Works, XXVI, 472–475.
25. *Izvestiya TsK*, March 1922, pp. 71–72.
26. See V. Sorin, *Rabochaya gruppa: "Miasnikovshchina"* (The Workers' Group: The "Miasnikov Movement"; Moscow, 1924), in which the manifesto is quoted extensively.
27. Quoted, *ibid.*, pp. 61–62.

28. Ruth Fischer, *Stalin and German Communism* (Cambridge, 1948), p. 247n.

29. See "Vozzvanie gruppy 'Rabochei Pravdy'" (Appeal of the "Workers' Truth" Group), *Sotsialisticheski vestnik* (The Socialist Herald; Berlin), January 31, 1923, p. 14.

30. N. Karev, "O gruppe 'rabochaya pravda'" (On the "Workers' Truth" Group), *Bolshevik*, July 15, 1924, pp. 31ff.

31. "Appeal of the 'Workers' Truth' Group," *Sotsialisticheski vestnik*, January 31, 1923, pp. 12–14.

32. Shliapnikov, "Nashi raznoglasiya" (Our Differences), *Pravda*, January 18, 1924.

33. Schapiro, p. 326.

34. Shelavin, "The Workers' Opposition," pp. 28–29.

35. Resolution of the Eleventh Party Congress, "O nekotorykh chlenakh byvshei 'rabochei oppozitsii'" (On Certain Members of the Former "Workers' Opposition"), CPSU in Resolutions, I, 650–651.

36. Kollontai, Eleventh Party Congress, p. 208; see also Schapiro, pp. 330–332.

37. *Protokoll des III Kongresses der Kommunistischen Internationale* (Hamburg, 1921), pp. 778–781; Fischer, pp. 181–182.

38. Text of the Declaration of the Twenty-two in *Izvestiya TsK*, March 1922, pp. 69–70. See also Report of the Commission to Investigate the Workers' Opposition, Eleventh Party Congress, p. 696.

39. Central Committee circular on the Declaration of the Twenty-two, *Izvestiya TsK*, March 1922, p. 70.

40. Resolution of the enlarged plenum of the executive committee of the Communist International, February 28, 1922, on the Declaration of the Twenty-two, *ibid.*, p. 70.

41. Report of the Commission to Investigate the Workers' Opposition, Eleventh Party Congress, pp. 694–698.

42. Resolution of the Eleventh Party Congress, "On Certain Members of the Former Workers' Opposition," CPSU in Resolutions, I, 650–653.

43. Lenin, Eleventh Party Congress, p. 26.

44. Resolution passed by a conference of party secretaries and confirmed by the Eleventh Party Congress, "Prakticheskie predlozheniya po organizatsionnym voprosam partstroitelstva" (Practical Proposals on the Organizational Questions of Party Construction), CPSU in Resolutions, I, 633.

45. Osinsky, Eleventh Party Congress, p. 94.

46. Kollontai, *ibid.*, pp. 211–212.

47. Riazanov, *ibid.*, p. 188.

48. Solts, *ibid.*, pp. 175–178.

49. *Ibid.*, pp. 218–219.

50. *Ibid.*, p. 220.

51. Resolution of the Eleventh Party Congress, "Ob ukreplenii i novykh zadachakh partii" (On the Strengthening and New Tasks of the Party), CPSU in Resolutions, I, 621.

52. Declaration of the Forty-six, October 15, 1923, Trotsky Archive T802a.

53. S. Gusev, "Zadachi Tsentralnoi Kontrolnoi Kommissii otnositelno sovetskoi i partinoi linii" (Tasks of the Central Control Commission regarding the Soviet and Party Line), *Voprosy sovetskogo khoziaistva i upravleniya* (Questions of Soviet Economy and Administration), January 1924, pp. 5–6.

54. For a detailed discussion of the Secretariat, its agencies, and the development of its control over the local party organizations, see R. V. Daniels, "The Secretariat and the Local Organizations in the Russian Communist Party, 1921–1923," *American Slavic and East European Review*, February 1957, pp. 32–49.

55. Stalin in *Dvenadtsaty sezd RKP(b): Stenograficheski otchet* (Twelfth Congress of the RCP[b]: Stenographic Report; Moscow, 1923, p. 187.

56. V. Kosior, *ibid.*, p. 93.

57. Trotsky to the Central Committee and the Central Control Commission, October 8, 1923, extracts in Shachtman, "The Struggle for the New Course," in Trotsky, *The New Course* (New York, 1943), p. 154 (first published in *Sotsialisticheski vestnik*, May 28, 1924, p. 10).

58. Tenth Party Congress, pp. 848–849n48, and index of names, p. 925.

59. Molotov, Eleventh Party Congress, pp. 57–58.

60. Stalin, "Lenin kak organizator i rukovoditel Rossiskoi Kommunicheskoi Partii" (Lenin as the Organizer and Leader of the Russian Communist Party), Works, IV, 309.

61. Trotsky, *Stalin*, pp. 373, 357.

62. Information from George Denicke, who was at the time on the staff of the Marx-Engels Institute; the report came to him from another member of the Institute who was present at the meeting of the heads of delegations.

63. Preobrazhensky, Eleventh Party Congress, p. 89.

64. Biography of Kuibyshev, *Ency. Dict.*, XLI–1, appendix, 246–248.

65. S. V. Dmitrievsky, *Stalin* (Berlin, 1931), p. 296.

Chapter 8. The Interregnum

1. Lenin's illness is discussed in chronological detail, apparently accurate as far as it goes, in L. Fotieva, *Poslednye gody zhizni i deyatelnosti V. I. Lenina* (The Last Years of V. I. Lenin's Life and Activity; Moscow, 1947).

2. Quoted in N. S. Khrushchev, report to a closed session of the Twentieth Party Congress, February 25, 1956, "On the Cult of Personality and its Consequences," presumed text released by the United States Department of State (in *The Anti-Stalin Campaign and International Communism*, New York, 1956, p. 13).

3. The existence of the troika was openly discussed in the debates at the Twelfth Party Congress; see, for example, p. 122 (Osinsky) and p. 183 (Stalin).

4. *Pravda*, June 4, 1922.

5. See, for example, Balabanova, *My Life as a Rebel*, pp. 220–222.

6. Biography of Zinoviev, *Ency. Dict.*, XLI–1, appendix, 143.

7. Boris Souvarine, *Stalin: A Critical Survey of Bolshevism* (London, [1939]), pp. 249, 505.

8. Autobiography of Kamenev, *Ency. Dict.*, XLI–1, appendix, 161–165.

9. Khrushchev at the Twentieth Party Congress, *The Anti-Stalin Campaign*, p. 76.

10. Biographies of Rykov, *Ency. Dict.*, XLI–2, appendix, 223ff, and of Tomsky, *ibid.*, XLI–3, appendix, 146.

11. See Deutscher, *Stalin*, p. 273.

12. Trotsky, *My Life*, p. 488.

13. Autobiography of Antonov-Ovseyenko, *Ency. Dict.*, XLI–1, appendix, 10.

14. Zinoviev, report to the executive committee of the Communist International, January 6, 1924, *International Press Correspondence*, no. 20, March 14, 1924, pp. 175, 178.

15. L. P. Beria, *On the History of the Bolshevik Organizations in Transcaucasia* (London, 1935), p. 177; *Sotsialisticheski vestnik*, January 17, 1923, p. 19.

16. Lenin to Kamenev (copies to the members of the Politburo), September 27, 1922, Trotsky Archive T754 (excerpts in Trotsky to the Bureau of Party History, October 21, 1927, in *The Stalin School of Falsification*, pp. 65–66, and summary in *Kommunist*, no. 9, June 1956, p. 26n1).

17. Stalin to Lenin, September 27, 1922, T755 (excerpts in *The Stalin School*, pp. 66–67).

18. Volsky, *Memoirs*, pp. 62, 65.

19. Lenin, "Doklad v Politbiuro o borbe s veliko-derzhavnym shovinizmom" (Report

to the Politburo on the Struggle with Great-Power Chauvinism; October 6, 1922), Works (4th ed.), XXXIII, 335.

20. Beria, p. 179. See also *Sotsialisticheski vestnik*, January 17, 1923, p. 19.

21. See E. H. Carr, *The Interregnum, 1923–1924 (History of Soviet Russia,* IV; New York, 1954), p. 262n.

22. Quoted in *Sotsialisticheski vestnik,* January 17, 1923, p. 19. See also Beria, p. 179.

23. Trotsky, *Stalin,* p. 357.

24. Beria, p. 178. Cf. Trotsky, *Stalin,* p. 360.

25. Makharadze, Twelfth Party Congress, pp. 156–158.

26. Pipes, *The Formation of the Soviet Union,* pp. 153, 272.

27. Mdivani, Twelfth Party Congress, p. 150.

28. Quoted in full in Khrushchev, secret speech to the Twentieth Party Congress, *The Anti-Stalin Campaign,* p. 8.

29. A partial translation of Lenin's "Testament" was first published by Max Eastman in *Since Lenin Died* (New York, 1925), after he acquired the text through his contacts with the Trotsky Opposition. It appeared in full in the *New York Times* of November 18, 1926. Diehard foreign Stalinists occasionally tried to deny the authenticity of the "Testament" altogether, though Stalin himself discussed the document and actually quoted from it at length before the Central Committee of the party in October 1927. The "Testament" was quoted extensively by Khrushchev in his secret attack on Stalin at the Twentieth Party Congress, and then at long last was published by the Soviet authorities in the theoretical journal *Kommunist,* no. 9, June 1956.

30. The letter was included among the documents distributed at the Twentieth Party Congress, and was finally published together with the "Testament" in *Kommunist,* no. 9, June 1956.

31. Quoted in full in Khrushchev, secret speech to the Twentieth Party Congress, *The Anti-Stalin Campaign,* pp. 8–9.

32. Lenin to Trotsky, March 5, 1923 (dictated and telephoned), reproduced in Trotsky to the Bureau of Party History, October 21, 1927, in *The Stalin School,* p. 69. Reportedly distributed at the Twentieth Party Congress (see U. S. Department of State, press release of June 30, 1956, p. 23).

33. Trotsky, *My Life,* p. 483.

34. Trotsky to the Bureau of Party History, October 21, 1927, in *The Stalin School,* p. 71.

35. Recounted in Trotsky, *Stalin,* p. 362.

36. Lenin to Mdivani et al., March 6, 1923, reproduced in Trotsky to the Bureau of Party History, October 21, 1927, in *The Stalin School,* p. 69.

37. Recounted in Trotsky to the Bureau of Party History, October 21, 1927, *ibid.,* p. 71.

38. Trotsky, *My Life,* pp. 485–486.

39. Stalin, Twelfth Party Congress, p. 185.

40. Mdivani and Makharadze, *ibid.,* pp. 151–152, 157.

41. Trotsky, "Natsionalny vopros i vospitanie partinoi molodezhi" (The Nationality Question and the Education of the Party Youth), *Pravda,* March 20, 1923.

42. Trotsky to the Secretariat, March 28, 1923, protesting the delegations from the record, Trotsky Archive T792.

43. L. Fotieva to Kamenev (copy to Trotsky), April 16, 1923, in U. S. Department of State release of June 30, 1956, p. 24. (Copy of original text in Trotsky Archive T793.)

44. Kamenev to the Secretariat, April 16, 1923, *ibid.,* p. 25.

45. Trotsky to Stalin and all members to the Central Committee, April 16, 1923, *ibid.,* p. 16. (Copy of original text in Trotsky Archive T794, not specifically addressed to Stalin.)

46. Fotieva to Stalin, April 16, 1923, *ibid.*, p. 25.

47. Stalin to the members of the Central Committee, April 16, 1923, *ibid.*, p. 26.

48. Trotsky to the members of the Central Committee, April 17, 1923, "Comrade Stalin's Declaration of April 16 [1923]," quoted in full in Trotsky, *Stalin*, pp. 362–363.

49. Trotsky to Stalin, April 18, 1923, quoted in full, *ibid.*, p. 363.

50. Stalin, Twelfth Party Congress, pp. 183–185, 441–448.

51. Mdivani, *ibid.*, pp. 454–455.

52. Makharadze, *ibid.*, p. 156.

53. Rakovsky, *ibid.*, pp. 528–534.

54. Bukharin, *ibid.*, p. 563.

55. See Yenukidze and Zinoviev, *ibid.*, pp. 540–542, 552.

56. See Carr, I, 399–401.

57. Deutscher, *Stalin*, p. 245.

58. Carr, IV, 289.

59. *Ibid.*, pp. 286–287; Pipes, pp. 260–262.

60. Trotsky, *Stalin*, p. 417 (quoting Kamenev's account); Stalin, "O pravykh i 'levykh' v natsresbublikakh i oblastiakh" (On The Right and 'Lefts' in The National Republics and Regions; speech at the Fourth Consultation of the CC of the AUCP[b] with Responsible Workers of the National Republics and Regions), June 10, 1923, Works, V, 305.

61. Resolution of the Conference of the Central Committee with Responsible Workers of the National Republics and Regions, June 9–12, 1923, "Delo Sultan-Galieva" (The Sultangaliev Affair), CPSU in Resolutions, I, 760.

62. Lenin, Tenth Party Congress, p. 41.

63. Trotsky, report to the Seventh Conference of the Communist Party of the Ukraine, April 5, 1923, published as *Zadachi XII sezda RKP* (The Tasks of the Twelfth Congress of the RCP; Moscow, 1923), p. 24.

64. Lenin, "Piat let russkoi revoliutsii i perspektivy mirovoi revoliutsii" (Five Years of the Russian Revolution and the Prospects of the World Revolution), Works, XXVII, 353.

65. Lenin, "Luchshe menshe da luchshe" (Better Less but Better), Works, XXVII, 407.

66. Trotsky, statement to the Central Control Commission, [September] 1927, quoted in Trotsky to the Bureau of Party History, October 21, 1927, in *The Stalin School*, pp. 73–74. Trotsky reported an abbreviated version to the Politburo on January 15, 1923 (T773).

67. Texts published in *Kommunist*, no. 9, June 1956, pp. 16–26.

68. Lenin, "O kooperatsii" (On Cooperatives), Works, XXVII, 397.

69. *Ibid.*

70. Lenin, continuation of notes, December 26, 1922, in *Kommunist*, no. 9, June 1956, p. 19.

71. Lenin, "Letter to the Congress," December 23, 1922, and continuation of notes, December 26, 1922, *ibid.*, pp. 16–19. The expansion idea is also mentioned in the "Testament."

72. Lenin, "Kak nam reorganizovat Rabkrin" (How We Should Reorganize the Workers' and Peasants' Inspection), Works, XXVII, 402–405.

73. Trotsky to the Central Committee and the Central Control Commission, October 23, 1923, excerpts in Trotsky to the Bureau of Party History, October 21, 1927, in *The Stalin School*, pp. 72–73.

74. Trotsky's enemies tried to hit back with the insinuation that he was working against Lenin's wishes. Trotsky spoke before the Central Committee on February 22, 1923, to defend himself against the charges that he opposed Lenin's reform plan and

advocated instead a "double center arrangement" of the party's governing institutions. His declaration provides contemporary substantiation of the article-suppressing episode: "A simple factual statement of the history of comrade Lenin's letter and my relation to this letter . . . leaves nothing of this malicious house of cards. The fact is just the reverse. At the time when the majority of the members of the Politburo considered it impossible even to print Comrade Lenin's letter, I, on the contrary, not only insisted on—and with the cooperation of Comrade Kamenev and in the absence of Comrade Zinoviev successfully insisted on—the printing of the letter, but defended its basic idea, or to be more exact, the idea in it which seemed to me basic." Trotsky, declaration, "K proektu reorganizatsii raboty tsentralnykh uchrezhdeni partii" (On the Project of Reorganizing the Work of the Central Institutions of the Party), in minutes of the Central Committee, February 22, 1923, excerpts furnished to Trotsky, T2963.

75. "Predpolozheniya sekretariata o raspredelenii funktsi mezhdu plenumom TsK, Politbiuro, Orgbiuro, i Sekretariatom TsK" (Proposals of the Secretariat on the Distribution of Functions among the Plenum of the CC, the Politburo, the Orgburo, and the Secretariat of the CC), January 29, 1923, T776.

76. Stalin, Twelfth Party Congress, p. 60.

77. Trotsky, "On the Project of Reorganizing the Work of the Central Institutions of the Party," T2963.

78. Trotsky, "Mysli o partii" (Thoughts on the Party), published as an appendix in Trotsky, "Tasks of the Twelfth Congress of the RCP," pp. 54–55.

79. Lenin, "Better Less but Better," Works, XXVII, 410.

80. Stalin, Twelfth Party Congress, p. 181.

81. Declaration of the Forty-six, October 15, 1923, T802a.

82. Izvestiya TsK, March 1923, pp. 7–8.

83. Trotsky, "Tasks of the Twelfth Congress of the RCP," pp. 26–30.

84. Trotsky, Stalin, p. 366.

85. Vladimir Kosior, Twelfth Party Congress, pp. 94–95.

86. Preobrazhensky, ibid., p. 133.

87. Biography of Krasin, Ency. Dict., XLI–1, appendix, 231.

88. Krasin, Twelfth Party Congress, pp. 114–115.

89. Bukharin, ibid., p. 171.

90. Belenki, ibid., p. 107.

91. Riutin, ibid., pp. 165–166.

92. Stalin, ibid., pp. 49ff.

93. Kamenev, ibid., p. 3.

94. Zinoviev, ibid., pp. 46–47.

95. Stalin, ibid., p. 61.

96. Zinoviev, ibid., p. 207.

97. Ibid., p. 183.

98. Stukov, ibid., pp. 128–129.

99. Osinsky, ibid., p. 122.

100. See lists, ibid., p. 608.

101. Ibid., pp. 608–609.

102. Declaration of the Forty-six, October 15, 1923, T802a.

103. The "scissors crisis" derived its name from the graphic representation, first demonstrated by Trotsky at the Twelfth Party Congress in 1923, of the trends in the relative prices of agricultural and industrial products. In 1921, the famine had driven agricultural prices much higher than the prewar relative norm ("parity," in the American formulation of the problem), but after the spring of 1922 they fell steadily in relation to industrial prices, while the latter rose correspondingly. Graphically, the situation

resembled the diverging blades of an open pair of scissors, extending to the fall of 1923, when the widest disparity was reached.

104. See Dobb, *Soviet Economic Development since 1917*, pp. 158–160; Resolution of the Central Committee, December 24, 1923, "Ob ocherednykh zadachakh ekonomicheskoi politiki" (On the Immediate Tasks of Economic Policy), *Pravda*, December 25, 1923.

105. See Carr, IV, 21, 86–87.

106. See letters from Lenin to Trotsky, December 1922, in Trotsky to the Bureau of Party History, October 21, 1927, in *The Stalin School*, pp. 59–63; esp. Lenin to Trotsky, December 13, 1922, cited in Trotsky to the Politburo, October 24, 1923 (first published in *Sotsialisticheski vestnik*, May 28, 1924, p. 11; copy in Trotsky Archive T766).

107. Dobb, p. 153.

108. Trotsky to the Bureau of Party History, citing Lenin at the Eleventh Party Congress, *The Stalin School*, pp. 55–56.

109. Trotsky, Twelfth Party Congress, pp. 296–297.

110. Dobb, p. 174.

111. Trotsky to the Bureau of Party History, *The Stalin School*, pp. 53–54.

112. Dobb, pp. 160–161, 171.

113. Quoted by Zinoviev, Twelfth Party Congress, pp. 42, 204.

114. Krasin, *ibid.*, p. 113.

115. Safarov, *ibid.*, p. 138.

116. Yevdokimov, *ibid.*, pp. 147–148.

117. Safarov, *ibid.*, p. 139.

118. Preobrazhensky, *ibid.*, pp. 131–133.

119. Resolution of the Twelfth Party Congress, "O promyshlennosti" (On Industry), CPSU in Resolutions, I, 701–705.

120. See Carr, II, ch. 20, "The Beginnings of Planning."

121. Zinoviev, Twelfth Party Congress, p. 195.

122. Kamenev, *ibid.*, pp. 388ff.

123. See, for example, P. A. Bogdanov, *ibid.*, p. 330.

124. See Trotsky, "Po povodu postanovleniya o rabote Zamov" (In Regard to the Decision on the Work of the Deputies), April 18, 1922, T746, and Trotsky to the Politburo, April 19, 1922, T747.

125. Lenin to Frumkin and Stomoniakov, December 12, 1922 (copy to Trotsky; Trotsky Archive T765); Lenin, continuation of notes, December 27, 1922 ("Concerning the Assignment of Legislative Functions to Gosplan"), in *Kommunist*, no. 9, 1956, pp. 19–20.

126. Trotsky, "Tezisy o promyshlennosti" (Theses on Industry), March 6, 1923, T2964.

127. Trotsky, Twelfth Party Congress, pp. 321–322.

128. "Svodka k predlozheniyu tov. Zinoveva" (Summary of Comrade Zinoviev's Proposal) [June 1923], T797.

129. Excerpt from the minutes of the Central Committee, February 20, 1923, T780.

130. Tenth Congress of Soviets (December 1922), pp. 101–102, 110–111, cited in Carr, II, 317.

131. Trotsky to the Politburo, Sokolnikov, Tsiurupa, and Piatakov, February 13, 1923, T778; Trotsky, Twelfth Party Congress, p. 304.

132. See, for instance, Preobrazhensky, *Ekonomicheskie krizisy pri NEP'e* (Economic Crises under the NEP; Moscow, 1924).

133. See Alexander Erlich, "Preobrazhensky and the Economics of Soviet Industrialization," *Quarterly Journal of Economics*, February 1950, pp. 68–70.

134. Trotsky, Twelfth Party Congress, p. 321; Krasin, *ibid.*, pp. 352–353.

135. Resolution of the Twelfth Party Congress, "On Industry," CPSU in Resolutions, I, 687–688.

136. Quoted by Kamenev, Twelfth Party Congress, p. 145.

137. Osinsky, *ibid.*, p. 122; Sorin, *ibid.*, pp., 136–137; Zinoviev, *ibid.*, p. 203.

138. *Das Manifest der Arbeitergruppe der Russischen Kommunistischen Partei* (Berlin, 1924), quoted in Carr, IV, 82.

139. "Obrashchenie gruppa 'rabochei pravdy' k XII sezdu RKP" (Appeal of the Workers' Truth Group" to the Twelfth Congress of the RCP), *Sotsialisticheski vestnik*, October 18, 1923, pp. 13–14.

140. Lutovinov, Twelfth Party Congress, p. 105.

141. Zinoviev, *ibid.*, p. 200.

142. See "Na sezde RKP—pismo ot Moskvy" (At the Congress of the RCP—A Letter from Moscow), dated August 10, 1923, *Sotsialisticheski vestnik*, September 1, 1923, p. 14.

143. Trotsky, Twelfth Party Congress, p. 365.

144. *Ibid.* See also Volsky, *Memoirs*, p. 90.

145. Alexander Barmine, *One Who Survived* (New York, 1945), p. 212. Anton Ciliga, *The Russian Enigma* (London, 1940), pp. 85–86, also reports the belief that Trotsky could have won in 1923.

146. See, for example, Petrovsky in *Izvestiya*, April 7, 1923.

147. Eastman, p. 17.

148. Trotsky, *My Life*, p. 481.

149. B. Bajanow, *Stalin, Der Rote Diktator* (Berlin, 1931), p. 61.

150. Zinoviev, report to the executive committee of the Communist International, January 6, 1924, *International Press Correspondence*, no. 20, March 14, 1924, pp. 175–176.

151. "At the Congress of the RCP," *Sotsialisticheski vestnik*, September 1, 1923, p. 14. Cf. Politburo to Trotsky, October 1923, quoted in the present work, pp. 217–218.

152. Volsky, *Memoirs*, pp. 97–98.

153. The Kislovodsk affair is known principally through the remarks concerning it made at the Fourteenth Party Congress in 1925, by Zinoviev, Stalin, and Voroshilov. See *Chetyrnadtsaty sezd VKP(b): Stenograficheski otchet* (Fourteenth Congress of the AUCP[b]: Stenographic Report; Moscow, 1926), pp. 398–399, 455–456, 484, 950, 953.

154. *Izvestiya TsK*, October-November 1923, p. 21.

CHAPTER 9. THE NEW COURSE CONTROVERSY

1. *Izvestiya TsK*, August-September 1923, p. 7, and October-November, 1923, p. 9; Dobb, *Soviet Economic Development since 1917*, pp. 168–170.

2. *Izvestiya TsK*, August-September 1923, pp. 11–12.

3. See Carr, *The Interregnum* (History of Soviet Russia, IV), pp. 93–94.

4. Central Committee circular, May 9, 1923, *Izvestiya TsK*, July 1923, p. 81.

5. Sorin, "The Workers' Group," p. 116.

6. See "GPU o 'rabochei gruppe' RKP(b)" (The GPU on the "Workers' Group" of the RCP[b]), *Sotsialisticheski vestnik*, July 6, 1924, pp. 9–10.

7. Report from Moscow, "Vnutri-partinye dela" (Intraparty Affairs), *ibid.*, November 3, 1923, p. 14.

8. Decision of the Central Control Commission on the Workers' Truth organization, *Pravda*, December 30, 1923.

9. *Isvestiya TsK*, October-November 1923, p. 10.

10. Reported in the resolution of the combined plenum of the Central Committee and the Central Control Commission with representatives of ten party organizations, October 25, 1923, "O vnutripartinom polozhenii" (On the Intraparty Situation), CPSU in Resolutions, I, 767.

11. Carr, IV, 107–112.

12. *Ibid.*, pp. 104, 113–114.

13. Recounted by Kamenev in a speech to the Moscow party organization, December 11, 1923, in *Pravda,* December 13, 1923.

14. Trotsky to the Central Committee and the Central Control Commission, October 8, 1923, *Sotsialisticheski vestnik,* May 28, 1924, p. 10.

15. *Ibid.*

16. Bajanow, *Stalin,* pp. 52–53; Cf. Stalin, concluding remarks on the Report on Building the Party, Thirteenth Party Conference, January 18, 1924, in Works, VI, 38–39.

17. Trotsky to the CC and the CCC, October 8, 1923, *Sotsialisticheski vestnik,* May 28, 1924, p. 10.

18. See Trotsky to the Bureau of Party History, October 21, 1927, *The Stalin School of Falsification,* pp. 33–34.

19. Zinoviev, in minutes of the Comintern Program Commission, June 28, 1922, pp. 7–8 (Humbert-Droz Archive, copies at Russian Research Center, Harvard University).

20. Radek, in *Protokoll des Vierten Kongresses der Kommunistischen Internationale* (Hamburg, 1923), pp. 317–318.

21. See Ruth Fischer, *Stalin and German Communism,* chs. 9, 13.

22. Radek, "A propos du programme de l'Internationale Communiste—Remarques preliminaires," July 7, 1922, pp. 8–9 (Humbert-Droz Archive).

23. See Ruth Fischer, chs, 10, 12, and pp. 279–281.

24. *Ibid.*, pp. 305–306.

25. Carr, IV, 186–187.

26. Stalin to Zinoviev, August 1923 (text in Ruth Fischer, p. 306). This letter was never published in the Soviet Union, but Stalin confirmed its authenticity in a debate with Zinoviev before the Central Committee in August 1927 (Stalin, Works, X, 61–62).

27. See Carr, IV, 202–203; Ruth Fischer, p. 316.

28. *Ibid.*, pp. 312–316.

29. *Ibid.*, pp. 373–375; Carr, IV, 234–235.

30. Resolution of the Thirteenth Party Conference, "O mezhdunarodnom polozhenii" (On the International Situation), CPSU in Resolutions, I, 802–803.

31. Radek, speech to the presidium of the executive committee of the Communist International, in *Die Lehren der Deutschen Ereignisse* (Hamburg, 1924), p. 23, cited in Carr, IV, 237.

32. Trotsky to Albert Treint, September 13, 1931, in *The New International,* February 1938, pp. 56–58.

33. Trotsky to the CC and the CCC, October 8, 1923, in Trotsky, *The New Course,* pp. 153–156.

34. Politburo to Trotsky, October 1923, in Eastman, *Since Lenin Died,* pp. 143–145.

35. Trotsky to the CC and the CCC, October 23, 1923, excerpts in *Sotsialisticheski vestnik,* May 28, 1924, pp. 11–12.

36. Copy in the Trotsky Archive, T802a (statements of signatories, T802b). For published translation of the full text see Carr, IV, 367–373. Most of the signatories qualified their assent in various respects, but all agreed that the situation was critical.

37. Eastman, *Since Lenin Died,* p. 37.

38. CPSU in Resolutions, I, 767.

39. See Trotsky, *My Life,* pp. 508–509.

40. Preobrazhensky at the Thirteenth Party Conference, *Pravda,* January 20, 1924.

41. Resolution of the CC and the CCC, October 25, 1923, "On the Intraparty Situation," CPSU in Resolutions, I, 767–768.

42. Zinoviev, "Novye zadachi partii" (New Tasks of the Party), *Pravda,* November 7, 1923.

43. Ne-Zamraionets [pseud.], "Apparat oboroniaetsia" (The Apparatus Defends Itself), *Pravda,* November 21, 1923.

44. Preobrazhensky, "O nashem vnutripartinom polozhenii" (On Our Intraparty Situation), *Pravda,* November 28, 1923.

45. Zinoviev, speech at the Fourteenth Petrograd Provincial Party Conference, December 1, 1923, in *Voprosy partinogo stroitelstva* (Questions of Building the Party; Moscow, 1923), pp. 21–22.

46. Stalin, "O zadachakh partii" (On the Tasks of the Party), *Pravda,* December 2, 1923.

47. Zinoviev, speech of December 1, 1923, in "Questions of Building the Party," p. 20.

48. Trotsky, *My Life,* p. 499; Stalin, Report on Building the Party, Thirteenth Party Conference, Works, VI, 33.

49. Stalin, *ibid.,* and concluding remarks on the political report to the Thirteenth Party Congress, Works, VI, 224; Eastman, p. 38.

50. Text in *Pravda,* December 7, 1923: resolution of the Central Committee and the Central Control Commission, "O partstroitelstve" (On Building the Party).

51. Stalin at the Thirteenth Party Congress, Works, VI, 224.

52. S. I. Gusev at a session of the Central Control Commission in 1926, quoted by Trotsky in a declaration to the Politburo, August 13, 1926 (T2998).

53. Preobrazhensky at the Thirteenth Party Conference, *Pravda,* January 20, 1926.

54. Text in Trotsky, *The New Course,* pp. 89–98.

55. *Pravda,* December 12, 1923.

56. Sapronov, speech to the Moscow party organization, December 11, 1923, *Pravda,* December 14, 1923.

57. Preobrazhensky, speech to the Moscow party organization, December 11, 1923, *Pravda,* December 16, 1923.

58. Radek, speech to the Moscow party organization, *Pravda,* December 15, 1923.

59. Trotsky, *Stalin,* p. 387.

60. *Trinadtsaty sezd RKP(b): Stenograficheski otchet* (Thirteenth Congress of the RCP[b]—Stenographic Report; Moscow, 1924), pp. 111–112.

61. Quoted by Trotsky, *ibid.,* p. 155.

62. Kuibyshev, "Pervy god raboty" (The First Year of Work), *Voprosy sovetskogo khoziaistva i upravleniya,* April-May 1924, p. 4.

63. Carr, IV, 319, 322–323.

64. Eastman, p. 81.

65. Zelensky, Twelfth Party Congress, p. 111.

66. Zinoviev, Fourteenth Party Congress, pp. 459–460.

67. Shliapnikov, "Nashi raznoglasiya" (Our Differences), *Pravda,* January 19, 1924.

68. See Eastman, p. 84.

69. G. S. Agabekov, *Ogpu—The Russian Secret Terror* (New York, 1931), pp. 38–39.

70. Sapronov at the Thirteenth Party Conference, *Pravda,* January 22, 1924.

71. See Eastman, p. 82.

72. Stalin, concluding remarks on the Report on Building the Party, Thirteenth Party Conference, Works, VI, 42–43.

73. Quoted in Yaroslavsky, "A Brief History of the Russian Communist Party," II–2, 183.

74. See biography of Bubnov, *Ency. Dict.,* XLI–1, appendix, 49.

75. See, for instance, Declaration of the Forty-six (T802a) and resolution proposed by Preobrazhensky at the Eleventh Moscow Provincial Party Conference, *Pravda,* January 12, 1924.

76. Resolution of the Thirteenth Party Conference, "Ob itogakb diskussii i o

melkoburzhuaznom uklone v partii" (On the Results of the Controversy and on the Petty-Bourgeois Deviation in the Party), CPSU in Resolutions, I, 781.

77. Bukharin, "Doloi fraktsionnost" (Down with Factionalism), Pravda, January 1, 1924.

78. Ibid., installments of December 28 and 29, 1923.

79. See Ruth Fischer, p. 360.

80. Stalin, concluding remarks to the Thirteenth Party Conference, Works, VI, 28–29, 33–34.

81. Bukharin, "Down with Factionalism," Pravda, December 28, 1923.

82. Ibid., installment of January 1, 1924.

83. Piatakov, Stukov, Radek, et al., to the editorial board of Pravda, December 20, 1923, in Pravda, January 3, 1924.

84. See Trotsky, "O smychke goroda i derevni" (On the Bond between the City and the Village), Pravda, December 6, 1923.

85. Resolution of the Central Committee, December 24, 1923, "Ob ocherednykh zadachakh ekonomicheskoi politiki" (On the Immediate Tasks of Economic Policy), Pravda, December 25, 1923.

86. Resolution proposed by Osinsky to the Moscow party organization, "Ob ocherednykh zadachakh ekonomicheskoi politiki" (On the Immediate Tasks of Economic Policy), Pravda, January 1, 1924.

87. See Carr, IV, 27, 126.

88. CPSU in Resolutions, I, 771; Souvarine, Stalin, p. 348.

89. Stalin, report and concluding remarks to the Thirteenth Party Conference, Works, VI, 7, 16, 21, 33–34.

90. Ibid., pp. 25, 44.

91. Volsky, Memoirs, pp. 129–131 and passim.

92. Stalin, report to the Thirteenth Party Conference, Works, VI, 24. Contrary to Stalin's statement, the existence of the clause was not entirely secret; it had been publicly referred to in connection with the Shliapnikov affair of mid-1921.

93. Resolution of the Thirteenth Party Conference, "On the Results of the Controversy," CPSU in Resolutions, I, 782.

CHAPTER 10. THE PARTY AFTER LENIN

1. Quoted in Walter Duranty, I Write as I Please (New York, 1935), pp. 225–226.

2. Trotsky, My Life, pp. 508–509.

3. Stalin, "Po povodu smerti Lenina" (In Regard to the Death of Lenin), Works, VI, 46–51.

4. Factional dissension reportedly arose even over the disposition of Lenin's remains. Lenin was not yet dead when Stalin, backed by Kalinin and Rykov, urged plans for a "Russian" type of entombment of the embalmed body. Trotsky denounced this as an intention to create new holy "relics" and called for cremation, which Bukharin and Kamenev endorsed. After Lenin died, Stalin engineered a demand that the body be preserved, and carried the move over the protests of the same group of critics. The present mausoleum was the result. See Volsky, Memoirs, pp. 147–152.

5. Zinoviev, Thirteenth Party Congress, p. 115.

6. See Stalin, ibid., pp. 240–248 passim.

7. Zinoviev, speech to the executive committee of the Communist International, March 25, 1925, International Press Correspondence, no. 34, April 17, 1925, p. 452.

8. Trotsky, My Life, p. 514.

9. Stalin, "Ob osnovakh leninizma" (On the Foundations of Leninism), Pravda, April 26, 1924.

10. *Ibid.,* installment of May 18, 1924.

11. See Zinoviev, Thirteenth Party Congress, p. 112.

12. Preobrazhensky, *ibid.,* p. 196.

13. "XIII sezd partii" (The Thirteenth Congress of the Party), *Pravda,* April 3, 1924; Thirteenth Party Congress, pp. 12–13.

14. Preobrazhensky, *ibid.,* pp. 202–203.

15. Editorial, "Nashi zadachi" (Our Tasks), *Bolshevik,* no..1, April 1924, p. 3.

16. Biographies of Skliansky and Frunze, *Ency. Dict.,* XLI–3, appendix, 45, 193.

17. Reported by Zinoviev, declaration on the stenogram of the combined plenum of the Central Committee and the Central Control Commission, July 19, 1926, Trotsky Archive T886.

18. Stalin, Thirteenth Party Congress, p. 133.

19. Note by Krupskaya accompanying documents transmitted to Kamenev, May 18, 1924, in U. S. Department of State release, June 30, 1956, p. 3.

20. See Bajanow, *Stalin,* pp. 30–32; Trotsky, "On Lenin's Testament," in *The Suppressed Testament of Lenin* (New York, 1935), p. 22; Stalin, speech to the combined plenum of the Central Committee and the Central Control Commission, October 1927, Works, X, 244.

21. Bajanow, p. 33.

22. Stalin, speech to the plenum, October 1927, Works, X, 175–176.

23. Zinoviev, Thirteenth Party Congress, p. 115.

24. Resolution of the Thirteenth Party Congress on the report of the Central Committee, CPSU in Resolutions, II, 10.

25. Trotsky, Thirteenth Party Congress, p. 164.

26. Editorial, "Bolshevistski sezd bez Lenina" (A Bolshevik Congress without Lenin), *Bolshevik,* no. 3–4, May 20, 1924, p. 14.

27. Stalin, "Ob itogakh XIII sezda RKP(b)" (On the Results of the Thirteenth Congress of the RCP[b]), Works, VI, 253.

28. Trotsky, Thirteenth Party Congress, pp. 166–167.

29. Stalin, *ibid.,* p. 235, and Krupskaya, *ibid.,* p. 244.

30. Krupskaya, *ibid.,* pp. 236–237.

31. Zinoviev, *ibid.,* pp. 267, 269.

32. See resolution of the Thirteenth Party Congress, "Ob ocherednykh zadachakh partinogo stroitelstva" (On the Immediate Tasks of Building the Party), CPSU in Resolutions, II, 14–28.

33. Resolution of the Thirteenth Party Congress, "O rabote kontrolnykh komissi" (On the Work of the Control Commissions), CPSU in Resolutions, II, 28–34.

34. *Pravda,* June 3, 1924.

35. The Great Soviet Encyclopedia, XXX, 516–517.

36. *Pravda,* June 3, 1924.

37. Eastman, *Since Lenin Died,* p. 120.

38. See Preobrazhensky, Thirteenth Party Congress, pp. 202–203.

39. Kuibyshev, *ibid.,* pp. 280–282.

40. The essay was written by Trotsky as an introduction to the collection of his writings of the revolutionary year then being issued under the title, *1917* (Works, III–1); it was published separately in book form as *The Lessons of October* (New York, 1937).

41. *Ibid.,* pp. 37, 52.

42. Aleksandrov, "Who Rules Russia?" pp. 127–129.

43. Trotsky, "Tsel etogo obiasneniya: Nashi raznoglasiya" (The Object of This Explanation: Our Differences), unpubl. article, November 1924 (T2969).

44. Trotsky to the Central Committee, January 15, 1925, in *The Errors of Trotsky-ism* (London, 1925), p. 372.

45. Zinoviev, "Bolshevizm ili trotskizm" (Bolshevism or Trotskyism), in *Za lenin-izm: Sbornik statei* (For Leninism: A Collection of Articles; Moscow, 1925), p. 132.

46. Stalin, "Trotskizm ili leninizm" (Trotskyism or Leninism; speech to the Com-munist faction of the All-Union Central Council of Trade Unions, November 19, 1924), *ibid.*, p. 93.

47. See Trotsky, *The New Course*, p. 59.

48. Kamenev, "God bez Ilicha" (A Year without Ilich), *Pravda*, January 14, 1925.

49. Trotsky to M. Olminsky, December 6, 1921, "For Leninism," pp. 487–488.

50. Rykov, "Novaya diskussiya" (A New Controversy), *ibid.*, p. 8.

51. Bukharin, "Teoriya permanentnoi revoliutsii" (The Theory of Permanent Revo-lution; speech to the propagandists of the Moscow party organization, December 13, 1924), *ibid.*, p. 372.

52. Zinoviev, "Bolshevism or Trotskyism," *ibid.*, pp. 126–129.

53. Kamenev, "Partiya i trotskizm" (The Party and Trotskyism; speech to the Moscow party organization, November 18, 1924), *ibid.*, pp. 84–85.

54. Stalin, "Trotskyism or Leninism," *ibid.*, p. 108.

55. Krupskaya, "K voprosu ob urokakh oktiabria" (On the Question of the Lessons of October), *ibid.*, p. 153.

56. Eastman, p. 106.

57. Trotsky, "Our Differences," T2969, pp. 1, 3, 8–9.

58. Bukharin, "The Theory of Permanent Revolution," in "For Leninism," p. 367.

59. Stalin, "Trotskyism or Leninism," *ibid.*, p. 108.

60. Zinoviev, "Bolshevism or Trotskyism," *ibid.*, p. 151.

61. Quoted in Eastman, p. 128.

62. Barmine, *One Who Survived*, pp. 213–214.

63. Resolution of the Central Committee, "O vystuplenii Trotskogo" (On Trotsky's Move), January 17, 1925; CPSU in Resolutions," II, 107, 113.

64. Trotsky, *My Life*, p. 518.

65. Stalin, "Trotskyism or Leninism," in "For Leninism," pp. 87–92. Cf. *History of the Communist Party of the Soviet Union (Bolsheviks): Short Course* (New York, 1939), p. 206; Trotsky, letter to the Bureau of Party History, October 21, 1927, in *The Stalin School of Falsification*, pp. 12–15.

66. Stalin, "Trotskyism or Leninism," in "For Leninism," p. 95.

67. "Osveshchenie voprosa o trotskizme v RLKSM" (Clarification of the Question of Trotskyism in the Komsomol), *Izvestiya TsK*, January 5, 1925, p. 4.

68. Text of the findings of the Supreme Court of the USSR in the case of L. P. Beria et al., *Pravda*, December 24, 1953.

69. Kamenev, "The Party and Trotskyism," in "For Leninism," p. 70.

70. Stalin, "On the Foundations of Leninism," *Pravda*, May 9, 1924.

71. Bukharin, "The Theory of the Permanent Revolution," in "For Leninism," pp. 349–356.

72. Bukharin, "A New Revelation as to Soviet Economics, or How the Workers' and Peasants' Bloc can be Destroyed," *International Press Correspondence*, no. 6, January 20, 1925, p. 40.

73. Bukharin, "The Theory of the Permanent Revolution," in "For Leninism," p. 367.

74. *Ibid.*, pp. 355–356.

75. Stalin, "Oktiabrskaya revoliutsiya i taktika russkikh kommunistov," (The Octo-ber Revolution and the Tactics of the Russian Communists), in Stalin, *Voprosy leninizma* (Problems of Leninism; Moscow and Leningrad, 1931), pp. 107–114.

CHAPTER 11. THE ZINOVIEV OPPOSITION

1. Stalin, "On the Results of the Thirteenth Congress of the RCP(b)" (June 17, 1924), Works, VI, 255–259. Cf. CPSU in Resolutions, II, 12.

2. Autobiographies of Zelensky and Uglanov, Ency. Dict., I, 142–143, and III, 175–176; Uglanov, Fourteenth Party Congress, p. 193. Bajanow (Stalin, pp. 37–38) reports a confidential meeting between Stalin and Uglanov just before the latter's appointment. On the 1921 dispute, see the declaration by Semenov, in Fourteenth Party Congress, pp. 510–512.

3. See Ruth Fischer, Stalin and German Communism, p. 403.

4. Stalin, Fourteenth Party Congress, p. 502.

5. Stalin, ibid.

6. Stalin, ibid., p. 503.

7. Fourteenth Party Congress, speeches of Bukharin (pp. 140–141), Komarov (pp. 217–219), Zalutsky (pp. 230–232), and Stalin (p. 505).

8. Stalin, ibid., pp. 44–45; Popov, Outline History of the CPSU, II, 247.

9. Stalin, Fourteenth Party Congress, p. 505; Popov, II, 248–249.

10. Resolution of the Fourteenth Moscow Provincial Party Conference on the report of the Central Committee, in Novaya oppozitsiya—Sbornik materialov o diskussii 1925 g. (The New Opposition—Collection of Materials on the Controversy of 1925; Leningrad, 1926), pp. 36–40.

11. Declaration of the Twenty-second Leningrad Provincial Party Conference, ibid., pp. 40–44.

12. The Moscow Party Committee to the Leningrad party organization, November 1925, ibid., pp. 44–51.

13. Safarov, "Kak bylo delo" (How the Matter Was), Leningradskaya pravda, December 27, 1925, ibid., p. 11; Popov, II, 248.

14. Trotsky to Bukharin, January 9, 1926, Trotsky Archive T2976.

15. Erich Wollenberg, letter to the editor, Ost-Probleme, July 21, 1951, p. 896. Wollenberg, a German ex-Communist, had worked with the Red Army.

16. See Souvarine, Stalin, p. 398; Trotsky, Stalin, p. 418; E. H. Carr, "Pilniak and the Death of Frunze," Soviet Studies, October 1958, pp. 162–164.

17. Souvarine, p. 398; cf. Wollenberg in Ost-Probleme, pp. 896–897.

18. Stalin, Fourteenth Party Congress, p. 507.

19. Zinoviev, ibid., pp. 706–708.

20. Stalin, ibid., p. 54.

21. Bukharin, speech to the executive committee of the Communist International, April 1925, IPC, April 20, 1925, p. 161.

22. Kamenev and Stalin, reports to the Moscow Provincial Party Conference, January 1925, Pravda, January 29 and 30, 1925.

23. Zinoviev, "Proletariat i krestianstvo: Chto oznachaet lozung 'Litsom k derevne'?" (Proletariat and Peasantry: What Does the Slogan, "Face to the Village," Mean?), Pravda, January 13, 1925.

24. Stalin, Fourteenth Party Congress, p. 504.

25. Bukharin at the Fourteenth Party Conference, Pravda, May 3, 1925.

26. Stalin, Fourteenth Party Congress, p. 44.

27. See resolutions of the Fourteenth Party Conference, "O partinom stroitelstve" (On Building the Party) and "O kooperatsii" (On Cooperation), CPSU in Resolutions, II, 140–142, 145–158.

28. Resolution of the plenum of the Central Committee, April 30, 1925, "Ocherednye zadachi ekonomicheskoi politiki partii v sviazi s khoziaistvennymi nuzhdami derevni"

(The Immediate Tasks of the Party's Economic Policy in Connection with the Economic Needs of the Village), CPSU in Resolutions, II, 116–126.

29. Zinoviev, *Leninizm* (Leningrad, 1925), pp. 221–224. Cf. Zinoviev, Twelfth Party Congress, p. 33.

30. Zinoviev, *Leninizm*, p. 226.

31. Zinoviev, "Filosofiya epokha" (The Philosophy of the Epoch), *Pravda*, September 19–20, 1925.

32. Stalin to Molotov, September 12, 1925, quoted by Stalin, Fourteenth Party Congress, p. 500. Stalin had seen Zinoviev's article prior to its publication.

33. *Pravda*, August 11, 1925; Yevdokimov, Fourteenth Party Congress, p. 214.

34. Moscow Party Committee to the Leningrad party organization, November 1925, "The New Opposition," p. 47.

35. Stalin, Fourteenth Party Congress, p. 43; Souvarine, pp. 399–402.

36. Stalin, Fourteenth Party Congress, pp. 44–45, 489; Zinoviev, *ibid.*, pp. 113–114.

37. Safarov in *Leningradskaya pravda*, December 27, 1925, in "The New Opposition," p. 9.

38. Tomsky, Fourteenth Party Congress, p. 276.

39. AUCP(b) in Resolutions (1936), II, 32.

40. Resolution of the plenum of the Central Committee, October 1925, "O rabote partii sredi derevenskoi bednoty" (On Party Work Among the Village Poor), CPSU in Resolutions, II, 180–184.

41. Moscow Party Committee to the Leningrad party organization, November 1925, "The New Opposition," p. 45.

42. Zinoviev, Fourteenth Party Congress, pp. 101–110.

43. Kamenev, *ibid.*, pp. 252–253.

44. See Tomsky, *ibid.*, p. 279.

45. Zalutsky, *ibid.*, p. 230.

46. Resolution of the Fourteenth Moscow Provincial Party Conference, on the report of the Central Committee, "The New Opposition," p. 37.

47. Stalin, Fourteenth Party Congress, p. 32.

48. Stalin, *ibid.*, p. 489.

49. Stalin, *ibid.*, pp. 487–488. The reference is to the Dawes Plan for German reparations payments, which according to Stalin envisaged Russia as a market for German industrial products. See Alexander Erlich, "The Soviet Industrialization Controversy" (unpubl. dissertation, The New School for Social Research, 1953), pp. 32–35.

50. See *History of the CPSU* (1939), pp. 276–277, 280ff.

51. Resolution of the Fourteenth Party Congress on the report of the Central Committee, CPSU in Resolutions, II, 196–197; Kamenev, Fourteenth Party Congress, p. 521. Trotsky's criticism is contained in corrections to the draft of a resolution by Rykov, April 12, 1926, T2983.

52. Resolution of the Fourteenth Party Congress on the report of the Central Committee, CPSU in Resolutions, II, 198.

53. Zinoviev, "Über die Lage der Dinge in der KPD," March 26, 1924 (Humbert-Droz Archive).

54. Ruth Fischer, pp. 392, 394.

55. *Ibid.*, chs. 16, 17 *passim*.

56. *Ibid.*, pp. 420–425.

57. Zinoviev, "International Prospects and Bolshevization," speech to the plenum of the ECCI, March 25, 1925, *International Press Correspondence*, no. 34, April 17, 1925, pp. 448, 453–455.

58. Zinoviev, "The Epoch of Wars and Revolutions," *IPC*, no. 55, July 9, 1925, and

"An Estimate of the International Situation," report to the Metalworkers' Congress, November 25, 1925, *ibid.*, no. 87, December 17, 1925; Kamenev, "The International Situation and the Soviet Union," report on the activity of the Central Committee to a Moscow *raion* conference, November 22, 1925, *ibid.*, no. 86, December 10, 1925. See William Korey, "Zinoviev's Critique of Stalin's Theory of Socialism in One Country, December, 1925–December, 1926," *American Slavic and East European Review*, December 1950, pp. 255–267.

59. Zinoviev, Fourteenth Party Congress, p. 681.

60. "Tezisy o zadachakh Kominterna i RKP(b) v sviazi s rasshirennym plenumom IKKI" (Theses on the Tasks of the Comintern and the RCP[b] in Connection with the Enlarged Plenum of the ECCI), adopted by the Fourteenth Party Conference; CPSU in Resolutions, II, 163–172. This statement of the theory by the conference was by no means as clear-cut as it has been represented in later official histories. Many qualifications were introduced—the role of foreign proletarians in support of Russian socialism, the continuing threat of a bourgeois restoration in the absence of international revolution, and the dangers inherent in passivity toward the building of socialism in Russia and in lack of concern for Russian dependence on the world revolution. Zinoviev and Kamenev reportedly raised some doubts about this resolution when the Politburo discussed it, but the substance of their objections is not clear, and they did not as yet see fit to make a public issue of the question (Tomsky, Fourteenth Party Congress, p. 277).

61. Stalin, report on the work of the Fourteenth Party Conference to the Moscow party organization, May 9, 1925, *Pravda*, May 13, 1925.

62. Ruth Fischer, pp. 442–444.

63. Franz Borkenau, *The Communist International* (London, 1938), p. 267.

64. Ruth Fischer, pp. 444–450.

65. *Ibid.*, p. 568.

66. Zinoviev, *Leninizm*, p. 302.

67. *Ibid.*, pp. 302–307; Korey in *The American Slavic and East European Review*, p. 256.

68. Stalin, "Voprosy i otvety" (Questions and Answers), June 9, 1925, "Problems of Leninism" (1931), p. 242.

69. Zinoviev, Fourteenth Party Congress, p. 98.

70. Stalin, *ibid.*, p. 55.

71. Bukharin, *ibid.*, p. 135.

72. Stalin, "K voprosam leninizma" (On Problems of Leninism; January 1926), "Problems of Leninism" (1931), pp. 306–310.

73. CPSU in Resolutions, II, 197.

74. Zinoviev, *Leninizm*, p. 377.

75. Lashevich, Fourteenth Party Congress, pp. 183–184.

76. Uglanov, *ibid.*, p. 193.

77. Resolution of the Fourteenth Moscow Provincial Party Conference on the report of the Central Committee, "The New Opposition," p. 39.

78. Stalin, Fourteenth Party Congress, p. 53.

79. Resolution of the Fourteenth Moscow Provincial Party Conference on the report of the Central Committee, "The New Opposition," p. 39.

80. Safarov in *Leningradskaya pravda*, December 27, 1925, "The New Opposition," p. 12.

81. Kamenev, Fourteenth Party Congress, pp. 274–275.

82. Sokolnikov, *ibid.*, pp. 334–335.

83. Zinoviev, *ibid.*, p. 99; Badaev, *ibid.*, p. 317.

84. For instance, see Tomsky, *ibid.*, p. 289.

85. Rudzutak, *ibid.*, p. 344.

86. Stalin, *ibid.*, pp. 504–508; cf. Stalin, *Political Report to the Fourteenth Congress of the CPSU(b)* (Moscow, 1950), pp. 162, 165.

87. Stalin, Fourteenth Party Congress, p. 504, 508.

88. Stalin, "On Problems of Leninism," in "Problems of Leninism," pp. 301–302.

89. Fourteenth Party Congress, p. 524.

90. Declaration to all members of the Leningrad organization of the RCP(b), *ibid.*, pp. 710–711.

91. Zinoviev, *ibid.*, pp. 711–712.

92. *History of the CPSU* (1939), p. 278. For details of the purge, see "Ochetnaya kampaniya v Leningrade o rabotakh XIV partinogo sezda (Beseda s sekretarem TsK VKP(b) tov. Molotovym" (The Report Campaign in Leningrad on the Work of the Fourteenth Party Congress—Talk with the Secretary of the CC of the AUCP(b), Comrade Molotov), "The New Opposition," pp. 271–274. See also Popov, II, 273, and N. V. Ruban, "Borba partii protiv trotskistsko-zinovevskoi oppozitsii" (The Party's Struggle against the Trotskyist-Zinovievist Opposition), *Voprosy istorii KPSS* (Problems of the History of the CPSU), no. 5, 1958, pp. 125–128.

93. Aleksandrov, "Who Rules Russia?" p. 160; *Pravda,* February 13 and 16, 1926; *IPC,* no. 13, February 18, 1926.

94. *Pravda,* January 17, 1926; Aleksandrov, p. 161.

95. *Pravda,* January 3, 1926.

96. *Ibid.,* January 1, 1926.

97. See Antonov-Ovseyenko to Trotsky (protesting Trotsky's decision not to act against Zinoviev and Kamenev), cited by Rykov in *Pravda,* November 26, 1927.

98. Trotsky, note of December 22, 1925, T2975.

99. Trotsky, *My Life,* p. 520.

CHAPTER 12. THE UNITED OPPOSITION

1. Zinoviev, Fourteenth Party Congress, p. 467.

2. Bukharin, *ibid.,* p. 857.

3. Ruth Fischer, *Stalin and German Communism,* p. 548.

4. Trotsky in *Biulleten oppozitsii* (The Bulletin of the Opposition; Paris, March 1937, pp. 11–12.

5. In Eastman, *Since Lenin Died,* pp. 28–32.

6. Trotsky, "Po povodu knigi Istmena 'Posle smerti Lenina' " (In Regard to Eastman's Book, "Since Lenin Died"), *Bolshevik,* September 1, 1925, p. 68.

7. Krupskaya to the editor of the *London Sunday Worker,* July 7, 1925, *ibid.,* p. 73.

8. Trotsky to Muralov, September 11, 1928, *The New International,* November 1934, pp. 125–126.

9. Trotsky, speech to the Central Committee, "Dva slova ob armii" (A Couple of Words on the Army), July 1926, Trotsky Archive T2990.

10. Trotsky to Bukharin, March 4, 1926, T868.

11. Trotsky to Serebriakov, April 2, 1926, T873.

12. G. Tsypin, *Blok bezprintsipnosti—rukovoditeli oppozitsionnogo bloka drug o druge* (The Bloc of Unprincipledness—The Leaders of the Opposition Bloc on Each Other; Kharkov, 1927).

13. Stalin, report to the Fifteenth Party Conference, "Ob oppozitsii i o vnutripartinom polozhenii" (On the Opposition and the Intraparty Situation), *Pravda,* November 5, 1926.

14. Trotsky at the Seventh ECCI Plenum, as quoted in Y. Rezvushkin, "O poslednikh otkroveniyakh Trotskogo" (On Trotsky's Latest Revelations), *Proletarskaya revoliutsiya,* no. 10, 1928, p. 4.

15. Quoted by Trotsky in note to comrades, November 21, 1927, *Biulleten oppozitsii,* no. 9, February-March 1930, p. 32.

16. Trotsky, *My Life,* p. 521.

17. Trotsky, corrections to the draft of a resolution by Rykov on the economic situation, April 12, 1926, T2983; Stalin, report on the Opposition to the Fifteenth Party Conference, *Pravda,* November 5, 1926.

18. Trotsky, *My Life,* pp. 521–522.

19. *Pravda,* April 13, 1926.

20. Trotsky, declaration to the Politburo, June 6, 1926, T2986.

21. Declaration of the Thirteen, July 1926, T880a.

22. Bukharin, speech to the Moscow party organization, June 8, 1926, "Questions of the International Revolutionary Struggle," *IPC,* no. 52, July 15, 1926, p. 852.

23. Resolution of the combined plenum of the Central Committee and the Central Control Commission, July 23, 1926, "Po delu Lashevicha i dr. i o edinstve partii" (On the Affair of Lashevich et al. and on the Unity of the Party), CPSU in Resolutions, II, 281–282. See also Ruban, "The Party's Struggle against the Trotskyist-Zinovievist Opposition," *Voprosy istorii KPSS,* no. 5, 1958, p. 129, citing "materials of the October [1926] Plenum" from the Central Party Archive of the Institute of Marxism-Leninism.

24. Resolution, "On the Affair of Lashevich," CPSU in Resolutions, II, 282.

25. Text in Trotsky Archive, T880a.

26. See Trotsky, speech at the plenum of the Central Committee, July 1926, T2989.

27. Souvarine, *Stalin,* p. 425.

28. Resolution, "On the Affair of Lashevich," CPSU in Resolutions, II, 282.

29. Bukharin, report to the Leningrad party organization on the results of the Central Committee plenum, July 28, 1926, *Pravda,* August 3, 1926.

30. Resolution, "On the Affair of Lashevich," CPSU in Resolutions, II, 284.

31. Aleksandrov, "Who Rules Russia?" p. 164.

32. *Pravda,* July 25, 1926.

33. Rykov, report to the Moscow party organization on the results of the Central Committee plenum, July 26, 1926, *Pravda,* August 1, 1926.

34. Resolution, "On the Affair of Lashevich," CPSU in Resolutions, II, 286.

35. Text of the letter in Trotsky Archive T804. Summary and critique in "Pravaya opasnost v nashei partii" (The Right Danger in Our Party), *Pravda,* July 10, 1926.

36. *Pravda,* editorial, "Za leninskoe edinstvo, za proletarskuyu distsiplinu" (For Leninist Unity, for Proletarian Discipline), July 30, 1926.

37. Trotsky, draft of theses for the Fifteenth Party Conference, September 19, 1926, T3006.

38. Popov, *Outline History of the CPSU,* II, 293.

39. Resolution of the Bureau of the Moscow Committee, "Po voprosu o fraktsionnom vystuplenii oppozitsii" (On the Question of the Opposition's Factional Move), October 2, 1926, in *Pravda,* October 3, 1926.

40. *Pravda,* editorial, "Nashi trudnosti i oppozitsiya" (Our Difficulties and the Opposition), October 2, 1926.

41. Stalin, report on the Opposition to the Fifteenth Party Conference, *ibid.,* November 5, 1926.

42. Decision of the Politburo, "O narushenii edinstva" (On the Violation of Unity), *Pravda,* October 9, 1926.

43. Declaration of Zinoviev, Kamenev, Trotsky, Piatakov, Sokolnikov, and Yevdokimov, October 16, 1926, in *Pravda,* October 17, 1926.

44. Despite allegations to the contrary (for instance, Popov, II, 295–296), the Opposition seem to have been sincere in the hope that by respecting party discipline they

could survive and best exert their influence. See Trotsky, note of October 16, 1926, T896, and Kamenev at the Fifteenth Party Conference, *Pravda,* November 5, 1926.

45. See, for instance, Anton Ciliga, *The Russian Enigma* (London, 1940), p. 5.

46. Stalin, theses for the Fifteenth Party Conference, "Ob oppozitsionnom bloke v VKP(b)" (On the Opposition Bloc in the AUCP[b]), *Pravda,* October 26, 1926.

47. Bukharin at the Fifteenth Party Conference, *Pravda,* November 10, 1926.

48. Decision of the combined plenum of the Central Committee and the Central Control Commission, October 23, 1926, "O vnutripartinom polozhenii v sviazi s fraktsionnoi rabotoi i narusheniem partinnoi distsipliny so storony riada chlenov TsK" (On the Intraparty Situation in Connection with the Factional Work and Violation of Party Discipline on the Part of a Series of Members of the Central Committee), CPSU in Resolutions, II, 291.

49. *Pravda,* October 24 and November 5, 1926.

50. Declaration by Shliapnikov and Medvedev to the Politburo and the Presidium of the Central Control Commission, October 29, 1926, in *Pravda,* October 31, 1926. See Stalin, report on the Opposition to the Fifteenth Party Conference, *ibid.,* November 5, 1926.

51. Stalin, concluding remarks on the report on the Opposition, Fifteenth Party Conference, *ibid.,* November 12, 1926.

52. Krupskaya, letter to *Pravda,* May 20, 1927.

53. Rykov, speech concluding the Fifteenth Party Conference, *Pravda,* November 5, 1926.

54. Quoted in Souvarine, p. 439.

55. Ciliga, pp. 7–8.

56. *Pravda,* editorial, "Novaya vylazka oppozitsii" (A New Attack by the Opposition), December 9, 1926; Zinoviev, declaration on the Seventh ECCI Plenum, T906.

57. Stalin, report to the Seventh Plenum of the ECCI, "Vnutripartinye voprosy VKP(b)" (Intraparty Questions of the AUCP[b]), *Pravda,* December 9, 1926.

58. Stalin, concluding remarks to the Seventh Plenum of the ECCI, *Pravda,* December 19, 1926.

59. See Benjamin Schwartz, *Chinese Communism and the Rise of Mao* (Cambridge, 1951), pp. 44, 50, 58–59.

60. Zinoviev, declaration on the stenogram of the combined plenum of the Central Committee and the Central Control Commission, July 19, 1926, T886; Trotsky, theses of September 19, 1926, T3006; Trotsky, "Kitaiskaya kompartiya i Gomindan" (The Chinese Communist Party and the Kuomintang), September 27, 1926, T3008a.

61. Zinoviev, "Theses on the Chinese Revolution," April 14, 1927, in Trotsky, *Problems of the Chinese Revolution* (New York, 1932), p. 381.

62. Trotsky, "The Chinese Revolution and the Theses of Comrade Stalin," May 7, 1927, *ibid.,* p. 25.

63. Rykov, report to the Moscow party organization on the plenum of the Central Committee, August 11, 1927, *Pravda,* August 16, 1927.

64. See Conrad Brandt, *Stalin's Failure in China* (Cambridge, 1958), pp. 115–119.

65. *Pravda,* editorial, "Spekuliatsiya na trudnostiakh" (Speculation on Difficulties), May 14, 1927.

66. Text in Trotsky Archive, T941.

67. Trotsky, Zinoviev, Smilga, and Yevdokimov to the Politburo, May 25, 1927 (transmitting the Declaration of the Eighty-four), T955.

68. Resolution of the combined plenum of the Central Committee and the Central Control Commission, August 9, 1927, "O mezhdunarodnom polozhenii" (On the International Situation), CPSU in Resolutions, II, 367–372. See Schwartz, pp. 86–93; Brandt, pp. 141–151, 162.

69. Schwartz, ch. 7; Brandt, pp. 162–163.

70. Trotsky, declaration of June 28, 1927, T3075; Trotsky and Zinoviev to the Politburo, the presidium of the Central Control Commission, and the executive committee of the Communist International, September 12, 1927, T1015b.

71. Alfred G. Meyer, in "Soviet Politics and the War Scare of 1927" (unpubl. manuscript, 1958), demonstrates the spuriousness of the crisis.

72. Trotsky to the Central Committee, June 27, 1927, T3074.

73. Quoted in Souvarine, 451.

74. Trotsky, speech before the Central Control Commission, June 1927, in *The Stalin School of Falsification,* pp. 132–133.

75. Trotsky, declaration of June 28, 1927, T3075.

76. Resolution of the combined plenum of the Central Committee and the Central Control Commission, August 9, 1927, "O narushenii partinoi distsipliny Zinovevym i Trotskim" (On the Violation of Party Discipline by Zinoviev and Trotsky), CPSU in Resolutions, II, 389–390.

77. *Sotsialisticheski vestnik,* July 2, 1927, p. 12.

78. *Ibid.,* August 1, 1927, p. 14.

79. Trotsky to Ordzhonikidze, July 11, 1927, quoted by Stalin in speech to the plenum of the Central Committee and the Central Control Commission, August 1, 1927 (Works, X, 52). See also Trotsky, "Clemenceau," August 2, 1927, T3081; Trotsky, speech to the plenum, August 6, 1927, T3085; Meyer, "The War Scare of 1927," p. 132.

80. Trotsky, Kamenev, Zinoviev, et al., "Zayavlenie po povodu rechi T. Molotova o povstanchestve oppozitsii" (Declaration regarding the Speech of Comrade Molotov on the Insurrectionism of the Opposition), August 4, 1927, T993b.

81. Deutscher, *Stalin,* p. 310. The reference is to the British foreign secretary, Austen Chamberlain.

82. Resolution, "On the Violation of Party Discipline," CPSU in Resolutions, II, 391–392.

83. Declaration of the Opposition to the plenum of the Central Committee and the Central Control Commission, August 11, 1927, in *IPC,* no. 48, August 18, 1927, pp. 1078–1079.

84. Resolution, "On the Violation of Party Discipline," CPSU in Resolutions, II, 392–393.

85. Rykov, report to the Moscow party organization on the results of the plenum of the Central Committee, August 11, 1927, in *Pravda,* August 16, 1927.

86. Stalin, report on the Opposition to the Fifteenth Party Conference, *Pravda,* November 6, 1926.

87. Trotsky to Ordzhonikidze, June 28, 1927, T965; Trotsky to Krupskaya, May 17, 1927, T951.

88. Basic sources for the ensuing discussion of economic issues include the following:

For the Left Opposition view: Trotsky, corrections to the draft of a resolution by Rykov on the economic situation, April 12, 1926, T2983; Declaration of the Thirteen, July 1926, T880a; Trotsky, theses for the Fifteenth Party Conference, September 19, 1926, T3006; speeches of Kamenev and Trotsky at the Fifteenth Party Conference, *Pravda,* November 5 and 6, 1926; speech of Kamenev at the Seventh Plenum of the ECCI, *ibid.,* December 15, 1926; the "Platform of the Thirteen," September 1927, published as "The Real Situation in Russia and the Tasks of the Communist Party," in Trotsky, *The Real Situation in Russia* (New York, 1928); the countertheses of the Opposition on the Five Year Plan and on work in the villages, *IPC,* no. 70, December 12, 1927.

For the view of the leadership: resolution of the plenum of the Central Committee, April 1926, "O khoziaistvennom polozhenii i khoziaistvennoi politike" (On the Economic Situation and Economic Policy), CPSU in Resolutions, II, 258–267; Rykov, report to the Moscow party organization on the results of the Central Committee plenum, July 26, 1926, *Pravda*, August 1, 1926; Bukharin, report to the Leningrad party organization on the results of the Central Committee plenum, July 28, 1926, *ibid.*, August 3, 1926; Rykov, report on the economic situation to the Fifteenth Party Conference, *ibid.*, October 30–31, 1926; Rykov and Krzhizhanovsky, draft of theses for the Fifteenth Party Congress, "Direktivy po sostavleniyu piatiletnego plana narodnogo khoziaistva" (Directives on Drawing up the Five Year Economic Plan), CPSU in Resolutions, II, 395–413 (authorship indicated only in earlier editions—see *IPC* no. 67, November 26, 1927, p. 1512); Molotov, theses for the Fifteenth Party Congress, "O rabote v derevne" (On Work in the Village), CPSU in Resolutions, II, 414–430.

89. Dobb, *Soviet Economic Development since 1917*, p. 189; Baykov, *The Development of the Soviet Economic System* (New York, 1947), pp. 148–149.

90. Preobrazhensky, Thirteenth Party Congress, p. 197.

91. A basic work on the industrialization controversy is Erlich, "The Soviet Industrialization Controversy." See also Erlich, "Preobrazhensky and the Economics of Soviet Industrialization," *Quarterly Journal of Economics*, February 1950, pp. 57–88.

92. Preobrazhensky's most important exposition of his position was the book *Novaya ekonomiya* (The New Economy; Moscow, 1926). See Erlich in *Quarterly Journal of Economics*, pp. 58ff.

93. Preobrazhensky, "The New Economy," pp. 98–99.

94. Erlich in *Quarterly Journal of Economics*, pp. 73–74.

95. *Pravda*, editorial, "Pochemu uklon oppozitsii est uklon sotsial-demokraticheski" (Why the Opposition Deviation is a Social Democratic Deviation), November 3, 1926.

96. *Biulleten oppozitsii*, no. 29–30, September 1932, p. 34.

97. See Erlich, "The Soviet Industrialization Controversy," ch. 6.

98. Erlich in *Quarterly Journal of Economics*, pp. 80–81.

99. Preobrazhensky, "Khoziaistvennoe ravnovesie v sisteme SSSR" (Economic Equilibrium in the System of the USSR), *Vestnik Kommunisticheskoi Akademii* (Herald of the Communist Academy), no. 22 (1927), p. 70, quoted *ibid.*, p. 80.

100. Stalin, Fourteenth Party Congress, pp. 27–28.

101. Resolution of the Central Committee, April 1926, "On the Economic Situation," CPSU in Resolutions, II, 258–267.

102. Trotsky, speech to the plenum, [July] 1926, T2989.

103. Trotsky, "Tekushchi moment" (The Current Moment), February 19, 1927, T3028; resolution of the Central Committee, February 1927, "O kapitalnom stroitelstve promyshlennosti v 1926/27 godu" (On Capital Construction in Industry in the Year 1926/27), CPSU in Resolutions, II, 343–344.

104. "Countertheses of the Opposition on Work in the Village," *IPC*, no. 70, December 12, 1927.

105. "Directives for Drawing up a Five Year Economic Plan," CPSU in Resolutions, II, 395–413 (esp. pp. 396, 412). See Erlich in *Quarterly Journal of Economics*, p. 81.

106. "Theses on Work in the Village," CPSU in Resolutions, II, 414–430.

107. Erlich in *Quarterly Journal of Economics*, p. 83, and "The Soviet Industrialization Controversy," pp. 138, 244–245.

108. Stalin in *Piatnadtsaty sezd RKP(b): Stenograficheski otchet* (Fifteenth Congress of the RCP[b]: Stenographic Report; Moscow, 1928), pp. 49–59.

109. Trotsky, declaration of June 28, 1927, T3075.

110. Trotsky, "The Russian Opposition: Questions and Answers," *The New International*, May 1938, p. 155 (written in 1927).

111. Trotsky, theses for the Fifteenth Party Conference, September 19, 1926, T3006.

112. Kamenev, speech to the Seventh ECCI Plenum, December 11, 1926, in *Pravda*, December 15, 1926.

113. *Ibid.*

114. S. Ossovsky, "Partiya k XIV sezdu" (The Party up to the Fourteenth Congress), *Bolshevik,* July 30, 1926, pp. 59–80.

115. Trotsky, statement to the members of the Politburo and declaration against expelling Ossovsky, both of August 13, 1926, T2997 and T2998; Ruth Fischer, pp. 566–567n.

116. Bukharin, report to the Leningrad party organization, *Pravda,* August 3, 1926.

117. Trotsky, Kamenev, Zinoviev, et al., "Declaration regarding the Speech of Comrade Molotov on the Insurrectionism of the Opposition," August 4, 1927, T993b.

118. Stalin, report on the Opposition to the Fifteenth Party Conference, *Pravda,* November 6, 1926.

119. Zinoviev at the Fifteenth Party Conference, *ibid.,* November 9, 1926; Stalin, concluding remarks to the Fifteenth Party Congress, *ibid.,* November 12, 1926. On Stalin's misinterpretation of Engels' internationalism, see Daniels, "The State and Revolution," *American Slavic and East European Review,* February 1953, pp. 30, 40.

120. Kamenev at the Fifteenth Party Conference, *Pravda,* November 5, 1926, citing Lenin, "Neskolko tezisakh" (A Few Theses), October 13, 1915 (Works, XVIII, 312).

121. Trotsky at the Fifteenth Party Conference, *Pravda,* November 6, 1926.

122. Stalin at the Fifteenth Party Conference, *ibid.,* November 12, 1926.

123. Trotsky, speech to the plenum, August 6, 1927, T3085.

124. Stalin at the Fifteenth Party Conference, *Pravda,* November 12, 1926.

125. Trotsky at the Fifteenth Party Conference, *ibid.,* November 6, 1926, citing Lenin, "Otvet na zapros krestianina" (Answer to a Peasant's Inquiry; *ibid.,* February 15, 1919); Stalin at the Fifteenth Party Conference, *ibid.,* November 12, 1926.

126. Trotsky, "The 'Clemenceau Thesis' and the Party Regime," September 24, 1927, in *The New International,* July 1934, p. 25.

127. The Declaration of the Thirteen described the "factional septemvirate" (composed of the Politburo minus Trotsky, with Kuibyshev, as chairman of the Central Control Commission, included), which in 1923 and 1924 decided party policy secretly, in advance of regular Politburo meetings. There may have been some substance to the charge, for two of the seven—Zinoviev and Kamenev—were now supporting the Opposition complaint. See Zinoviev, declaration on the stenogram of the combined plenum of the Central Committee and the Central Control Commission, July 19, 1926, T886.

128. Trotsky, declaration to the Politburo, June 6, 1926, T2986.

129. Declaration of the Eighty-four, T941.

130. Trotsky, declaration to the Politburo, June 6, 1926, T2986.

131. Trotsky, Kamenev, Zinoviev, et al., "Declaration regarding the Speech of Comrade Molotov on the Insurrectionism of the Opposition," August 4, 1927, T993b.

132. Trotsky, speech to the presidium of the ECCI, September 27–28, 1927, T3094.

133. Trotsky, theses for the Fifteenth Party Conference, September 19, 1926, T3006, pp. 23–24.

134. Stalin at the Fifteenth Party Conference, *Pravda,* November 12, 1926.

135. Rykov, report to the Moscow party organization on the plenum of the Central Committee, July 26, 1926, in *Pravda,* August 1, 1926.

136. Stalin, theses on the Opposition bloc, *Pravda,* October 26, 1926; resolution of the plenum of the Central Committee, August 9, 1927, "On the Violation of Party Discipline," CPSU in Resolutions, II, 389.

137. See Bukharin, report on the plenum of the Central Committee to the Leningrad party organization, August 11, 1927, in *Pravda,* August 18, 1927.

138. Barmine, *One Who Survived,* pp. 216–217.

139. F. I. Dan, "Novy fazis mezhduusobitsy" (A New Phase of the Dissension), *Sotsialisticheski vestnik,* September 18, 1926, p. 6.

140. Stalin, report on the Opposition to the Fifteenth Party Conference, *Pravda*, November 5, 1926.

141. See Trotsky, declaration of June 28, 1927, T3075.

142. Declaration of the Thirteen, July 1926, T880a.

143. See Ruth Fischer, p. 584.

144. Smilga, Rakovsky, et al., draft of a resolution on the affair of Lashevich et al., July 1926, T883.

145. See Trotsky, *Stalin*, p. 391.

146. Platform of the Fifteen, presented to the Politburo, June 27, 1927; published as *Avant Thermidor: Revolution et contrerevolution dans la Russie des Soviets—Platforme de l'Opposition de Gauche dans le parti Bolchevique* (Lyon, 1928), p. 57.

147. Trotsky to the Central Committee, June 27, 1927, T3074.

148. Declaration of Trotsky, Zinoviev, Peterson, and Muralov to the Politburo, etc., September 6, 1927, T1010.

149. *Ibid.*; Trotsky, speech of October 23, 1927, in *The Real Situation in Russia*, pp. 14-15; Trotsky (et al.?) to the Politburo and the presidium of the Central Control Commission, November 9, 1927, T1048; Barmine, pp. 224-225.

150. Merle Fainsod, *Smolensk under Soviet Rule* (Cambridge, 1958), p. 48.

151. Note, "Kak oni boroyutsia s oppozitsiei" (How They Fight the Opposition), 1927, T1001.

152. Minutes of a meeting of the candidate group of the AUCP, Sokhond-Chitinsky District, September 1927, T1006. *Nepach* was a particularly derogatory term denoting the *nouveau-riche* profiteer of the NEP period.

153. Trotsky, *Stalin*, pp. 399-400.

154. Bukharin, report to the Leningrad party organization, *Pravda*, August 3, 1926.

155. Stalin, Fifteenth Party Congress, p. 379.

156. Rykov, report to the Moscow party organization, July 26, 1926, *Pravda*, August 1, 1926.

157. Resolution of the Moscow Provincial Party Committee, October 19, 1926 "O vnutripartiinom polozhenii" (On the Intraparty Situation), *ibid.*, October 20, 1926.

158. Bukharin, report to the Leningrad party organization, August 11, 1927, in *Pravda*, August 18, 1927.

159. Stalin, report on the Opposition, Fifteenth Party Conference, *ibid.*, November 6, 1926 (italics added).

160. *Pravda*, editorial, "Za leninskoe edinstvo, za proletarskuyu distsiplinu!" (For Leninist Unity, for Proletarian Discipline), July 30, 1926.

161. Stalin, report on the Opposition, Fifteenth Party Conference, *ibid.*, November 6, 1926.

162. Stalin, concluding remarks at the Seventh Plenum of the ECCI, *ibid.*, December 19, 1926.

163. Trotsky, second speech to the Central Control Commission, June 1927, in *The Stalin School*, p. 155.

164. Declaration of Zinoviev, Kamenev, Trotsky, Piatakov, and Sokolnikov, October 16, 1926, *Pravda*, October 17, 1926.

165. Trotsky, declaration against expelling Ossovsky, August 13, 1926, T2997.

166. Declaration of the Opposition to the plenum of the Central Committee and the Central Control Commission, August 4, 1927, in *IPC*, no. 48, August 18, 1927, p. 1078.

167. Stalin, Fifteenth Party Congress, p. 74.

168. Trotsky, "The Russian Opposition: Questions and Answers," *The New International*, May 1938, p. 156.

169. Molotov, speech at the opening of the fourth session of the Central Committee School for District Party Workers, October 2, 1926, in *Pravda*, October 5, 1926.

170. See Donald C. MacRae, "The Bolshevik Ideology," *Cambridge Review*, December 1951, p. 171.

171. Kollontai, "Oppozitsiya i partinye nizy" (The Opposition and the Rank and File of the Party), *Pravda*, November 1, 1927.

172. Trotsky, draft of theses for the Fifteenth Conference, September 19, 1926, T3006.

173. Declaration of the Thirteen, July 1926, T880a.

174. Bukharin, report to the Leningrad party organization, August 11, 1927, *Pravda*, August 18, 1927.

175. *Pravda*, editorial, "Za t. Zinovevym—t. Trotski" (After Comrade Zinoviev, Comrade Trotsky), December 10, 1926.

176. Stalin, concluding remarks to the Seventh Plenum of the ECCI, *ibid.*, December 19, 1926.

177. From the Saratov party organ, quoted by Zinoviev at the Fifteenth Party Conference, *ibid.*, November 9, 1926.

178. *History of the CPSU* (1939), pp. 346–347.

179. On the concept of the authoritarian personality, see particularly, Erich Fromm, *Escape from Freedom* (New York, 1941), and T. W. Adorno et al., *The Authoritarian Personality* (New York, 1950). These works make no direct reference to Soviet developments, but their applicability to Communism affords a persuasive confirmation of the theory, as well as a revealing insight into the official Soviet mind. The attraction which the military-like hierarchy and discipline of the party organization had for the type of member who became a good functionary is aptly described by Fromm's "symbiotic complex" of simultaneous impulses toward dominance and submission. The Adorno model of the authoritarian's rigid mode of thought is borne out markedly by the either-or, black-and-white frame of mind of the Communist leaders, by their extreme literalism and rigidity of conceptualization, and most dramatically by their attitude of simultaneous fear and contempt directed toward the internal but alien out-group. The Opposition apparently provided the party leaders with the same sort of psychological release as the scapegoat group does for the typical authoritarian. Public castigation of the Opposition had much the same role in the construction of Stalin's dictatorship as anti-Semitism played in the establishment of the Nazi dictatorship in Germany. In each case, the menace of the out-group was employed to cultivate the atmosphere of irrational fear, loyalty, and submission, and to secure the abnegation of individual will—prerequisites to real dictatorial power over the mass mind. One important difference should be noted: whereas the movement of political authoritarianism in Germany involved the population at large, in Russia it appears to have applied chiefly to the membership of the Communist Party.

180. "The Real Situation in Russia and the Tasks of the Communist Party," in Trotsky, *The Real Situation in Russia*, pp. 1–195.

181. *Ibid.*, p. 190.

182. Declaration of Trotsky, Zinoviev, Peterson, and Muralov to the Politburo, etc., September 6, 1927, T1010.

183. Trotsky and Zinoviev to the Politburo, etc., September 12, 1927, T1015b.

184. Report on the plenum of the Central Committee, *IPC*, no. 60, October 27, 1927, p. 1328.

185. Stalin, "Trotskistskaya oppozitsiya, prezhde i teper" (The Trotskyist Opposition, Then and Now), October 1927, *Works*, X, 177–179.

186. Trotsky, Zinoviev, Yevdokimov, Smilga, and Bakaev to the Politburo, October 1, 1927, published as "The Opposition and the Wrangel Officer," *The New International*, November 1934, p. 120.

187. Decisions of the Moscow Control Commission and the Central Control Commission, September 28, 1927, in *Pravda*, September 29, 1927.

188. Decisions of the presidium of the Central Control Commission, *Pravda,* October 13, 1927.

189. "The Opposition and the Wrangel Officer," *The New International,* November 1934, p. 120.

190. Trotsky, Zinoviev, Yevdokimov, Bakaev, Peterson, and Smilga to all party members, October 4, 1927, *ibid.,* p. 124.

191. Trotsky, speech to the presidium of the ECCI, September 27–28, 1927, Trotsky Archive T3094.

192. Report of the presidium of the ECCI and the International Control Commission on the expulsion of Trotsky and Vuyovich from the ECCI, September 27, 1927, *Pravda,* October 1, 1927.

193. Trotsky, *My Life,* p. 532.

194. Report in the French Communist Opposition paper, *Contre le courant,* quoted in *The Real Situation in Russia,* p. 16, translator's note.

195. *IPC,* no. 61, November 3, 1927, p. 1361; Trotsky, speech to the Central Committee, October 23, 1927, in *The Real Situation in Russia,* p. 15.

196. Popov, II, 318; Solomon Schwarz, *Labor in Soviet Russia* (New York, 1952), pp. 259–260.

197. Trotsky, speech to the Central Committee, October 23, 1927, *The Real Situation in Russia,* p. 10.

198. *Ibid.,* pp. 12, 15–16.

199. *Ibid.,* p. 7.

200. Decision of the plenum of the Central Committee and the Central Control Commission, October 23, 1927, "Ob iskliuchenii Zinoveva i Trotskogo iz TsK VKP(b) (On the Expulsion of Zinoviev and Trotsky from the CC of the AUCP[b]), CPSU in Resolutions, II, 431.

201. Unsigned collective declaration written by Trotsky, late October 1927, T1030.

202. Trotsky, *My Life,* pp. 533–534; Trotsky, "Posle slovesnogo zigzaga vlevo—gluboki zdvig vpravo" (After the Verbal Zigzag, to the Left, a Profound Shift to the Right), November 8, 1927, T3103a; Trotsky to the Politburo and the presidium of the Central Control Commission, November 9, 1927, T1048.

203. Central Committee to all organizations of the AUCP(b), November 10, 1927, in *Pravda,* November 11, 1927.

204. Decision of the Central Committee and the Central Control Commission, "Ob antipartinykh vystupleniyakh liderov oppozitsii" (On the Antiparty Moves of the Leaders of the Opposition), *Pravda,* November 15, 1927.

205. Trotsky to the secretary of the Central Executive Committee, November 15, 1927, T1053.

206. Trotsky, *My Life,* p. 537.

207. Trotsky, note of November 18, 1927, T3107.

208. Trotsky, " 'Zayavlenie' oppozitsii i polozhenie v partii" (The "Declaration" of the Opposition and the Situation in the Party), November 17–20, 1927, T3105.

209. Stalin, speech to the Sixteenth Moscow Provincial Party Conference, November 23, 1927, Works, X, 267.

210. See Popov, II, 323.

211. Declaration of the Hundred and Twenty-one, December 3, 1927, Fifteenth Party Congress, pp. 1333–1335.

212. Kamenev, *ibid.,* pp. 251–252.

213. Stalin, *ibid.,* pp. 68–82.

214. Rykov, *ibid.,* pp. 255–266.

215. Krupskaya, *ibid.,* p. 177.

216. Resolution of the Fifteenth Party Congress on the report of the Central Committee, CPSU in Resolutions, II, 441.

217. Declaration of Kamenev, Bakaev, Avdeyev, and Yevdokimov to the Commission on the Opposition, December 10, 1927, Fifteenth Party Congress, p. 1337.

218. Declaration of Muralov, Rakovsky, and Radek to the Commission on the Opposition, December 10, 1927, *ibid.*, p. 1338.

219. Ordzhonikidze, report of the Commission on the Opposition, *ibid.*, pp. 1244–1245.

220. Resolution of the Fifteenth Party Congress, "Ob oppozitsii" (On the Opposition), CPSU in Resolutions, II, 490.

221. Declaration of the Twenty-three, December 18, 1927, Fifteenth Party Congress, pp. 1266–1267.

222. Decision of the Fifteenth Congress on the declaration of Zinoviev, Kamenev, et al., *ibid.*, pp. 1267–1268.

223. See Popov, II, 327n2.

Chapter 13. The Right Opposition

1. Trotsky, theses for the Fifteenth Party Conference, September 19, 1926, Trotsky Archive T3006.

2. Trotsky, "The Russian Opposition: Questions and Answers" (1927), *The New International*, May 1938, p. 156.

3. Platform of the Thirteen, September 1927, in Trotsky, *The Real Situation in Russia*, pp. 122–123.

4. Rykov and Krzhizhanovsky, "Directives on Drawing up a Five Year Economic Plan," CPSU in Resolutions, II, 453–454, 469. On their authorship, see above, Chapter 12, note 88.

5. Stalin, "Pervye itogi zagotovitelnoi kampanii i dalneishie zadachi partii" (The Initial Results of the Collection Campaign and the Further Tasks of the Party; February 13, 1928), Works, XI, 11.

6. According to figures presented by Stalin in 1928 ("Na khlebnom fronte" [On the Grain Front], *Pravda,* June 2, 1928), the percentage of the national production of grain which found its way to market and hence became available for the urban food supply or for export declined from 26 per cent in 1913 to 13.3 per cent in 1926–27. Total grain production was almost as high at the latter date, but 85 per cent of it was contributed by poor and middle peasants as against only 50 per cent in 1912. In 1939, after collectivization was complete, grain marketed or delivered to the state totaled 41.5 per cent of the crop (*Izvestiya,* March 29, 1941).

7. Stalin, "The Initial Results of the Collection Campaign," Works, XI, 10.

8. See Walter Duranty, *Duranty Reports Russia* (New York, 1934), pp. 155–156.

9. Stalin, Works, XI, Biographical Chronicle, pp. 369–370.

10. Stalin, "The Initial Results of the Collection Campaign," Works, XI, 14; Resolution of the Plenum of the Central Committee and the Central Control Commission, April 11, 1928, "O khlebozagotovkakh tekushchego goda i ob organizatsii khlebozagotovitelnoi kampanii na 1928/29 g." (On the Grain Collections of the Current Year and the Organization of the Grain Collection Campaign for 1928–29), CPSU in Resolutions, II, 494.

11. Trotsky, "What Now?" July 12, 1928, in *The Third International After Lenin* (New York, 1936), pp. 274–275.

12. Stalin, "The Initial Results of the Collection Campaign," Works, IX, 13.

13. Trotsky, "What Now?" *The Third International After Lenin,* pp. 285–286. See also Ciliga, *The Russian Enigma,* p. 28.

14. *Sotsialisticheski vestnik,* March 6, 1928, p. 1.

15. Stalin, report to the Moscow party organization on the work of the April com-

bined plenum of the Central Committee and the Central Control Commission (April 13, 1928), *Pravda*, April 18, 1928.

16. *Sotsialisticheski vestnik*, July 23, 1928, p. 15; see also Smilga, "Platforma pravogo kryla VKP(b)" (The Platform of the Right Wing of the AUCP[b]), October 23, 1928, in Trotsky Archive T2825.

17. Trotsky, "Iyulski plenum i pravaya opasnost" (The July Plenum and the Right Danger), July 22, 1928, T 3126.

18. Stalin, report to the Moscow organization (April 13, 1928), *Pravda*, April 18, 1928.

19. Stalin, "The Initial Results of the Collection Campaign," Works, XI, 15.

20. Bukharin, "Uroki khlebozagotovok, shakhtinskogo dela, i zadachi parti" (Lessons of the Grain Collections, the Shakhty Affair, and the Tasks of the Party; speech to the Leningrad party organization, April 13, 1928), *Pravda*, April 19, 1928.

21. Rykov, speech to the Moscow Soviet, *ibid.*, March 11, 1928; Trotsky "What Now?" *The Third International After Lenin*, pp. 271–272, 282.

22. Trotsky to "Dear Friend," June, 1928, T1588.

23. Resolution of the Central Committee, "On the Grain Collections," CPSU in Resolutions, II, 496, 500.

24. *Sotsialisticheski vestnik*, August 3, 1928, p. 14.

25. Appeal of the Central Committee of the CPSU to all party members and all workers, *Pravda*, June 3, 1928.

26. Stalin, report to the Moscow organization (April 13, 1928), *ibid.*, April 18, 1928.

27. Trotsky to "Dear Friend," June 1928 (T1588).

28. *Pravda*, editorial, "Na khlebozagotovkakh" (On the Grain Collections), April 26, 1928.

29. *Ibid.*, editorial, "Na zagotovkakh" (On the Collections), May 13, 1928.

30. Stalin, Report on the July Plenum of the Central Committee, to the Leningrad party organization, July 13, 1928, *Pravda*, July 15, 1927.

31. Stalin, "On the Grain Front," *Pravda*, June 2, 1928.

32. It has been the burden of subsequent Communist historiography to obscure the suddenness of Stalin's turn in economic affairs in 1928 and to play down both his close association with the Bukharin-Rykov school of thought before that date and his debt to the Left Opposition for the ideas which he applied thereafter. It is not true that the program of intensive industrialization was clearly in the minds of the Stalin group but withheld from application on the grounds that the time was not yet quite ripe. (as suggested, for example, in Dobb, *Soviet Economic Development since 1917*, pp. 206–207). Together with the other party leaders, Stalin repeatedly denounced the Opposition program and never made any reference to its possible future validity. There is no evidence that before the end of 1927 Stalin ever really questioned the industrial gradualism of the Rightists. The timing idea does not even make good economics. It was in great measure due to the insufficiency of gradual capital construction previously that the economic situation became so critical in 1928 as to impel the program of high-speed industrialization at any cost.

33. Bukharin, "Na dnia" (On Themes of the Day), *Pravda*, May 27, 1928.

34. Trotsky to "Dear Friend," June 1928 (T1588).

35. Bukharin and Andreyev at the plenum of the Central Committee, July 1928 (partial copy of minutes in Trotsky Archive T1901 and T1834).

36. Uglanov and Rykov, *ibid.* (T1835); report by the GPU, cited in a statement of the All-Union Central Council of Trade Unions, signed by Tomsky, on the report of the Supreme Economic Council on the work of industry for the half-year (summer 1928), T1829.

37. Letter to "Dear Comrade," September 1928 (T2442).

38. *Ibid.;* Trotsky to "Dear Friend," June 1928 (T1588).

39. Letter to "Dear Comrade," September 1928 (T2442).

40. Riutin in Protocols of the Sixth Plenum of the Moscow Committee and the Moscow Control Commission of the Communist Party, October 18–19, 1928, p. 114 (excerpts in Trotsky Archive T2814).

41. Trotsky to "Dear Friend," June 1928 (T1588).

42. Letter to "Dear Comrade," September 1928 (T2442).

43. Stalin to the Politburo (answer to Frumkin), Works, XI, 120–121.

44. Stalin, "Lenin i vopros o soyuze s seredniakom" (Lenin and the Question of the Alliance with the Middle Peasant; June 12, 1928), Pravda, July 3, 1928.

45. See Sotsialisticheski vestnik, July 23, 1928, p. 13, and August 3, 1928, p. 14.

46. Trotsky, "What Now?" The Third International After Lenin, p. 289.

47. Molotov, "Partinaya liniya i khoziaistvennaya praktika" (The Party Line and Economic Practice; speech to the plenum of the Moscow Party Committee, June 30, 1928), Pravda, July 4, 1928.

48. Uglanov, "Voprosy khoziaistvennogo stroitelstva" (Questions of Economic Construction; speech to the Moscow Party Committee, June 30, 1928), ibid., July 5, 1928.

49. Trotsky to "Dear Friend," June 1928 (T1588).

50. Kamenev, notes on talk with Bukharin, July 11, 1928, T1897 (see note 67, below); Trotsky, Stalin, pp. 388–390.

51. Erich Wollenberg, letter to the editor, Ost-Probleme, July 21, 1951, p. 895.

52. The proceedings of the July 1928 plenum have been reconstructed here on the basis of the incomplete but nearly verbatim copy of the minutes in the Trotsky Archive (T1832–1836, 1900–1901) and the account of the meeting in the letter, "Dear Comrade" (T2442), which was written by someone who was either present or who had intimate access to the full record. Stalin's speeches at the plenum have been published in his Works, XI. Comparison with the notes on his speech of July 9 in T1900 indicates that the published text was reworded and perhaps amplified but otherwise is accurate, except for the elimination of most of his specific references to individuals in the Opposition.

53. Resolution of the plenum of the Central Committee, "Politika khlebozagotovok v sviazi s obshchim khoziaistvennym polozheniem" (The Grain Collection Policy in Connection with the General Economic Situation), July 10, 1928, CPSU in Resolutions, II, 511–517.

54. Kamenev, notes on talk with Bukharin, July 11, 1928 (T1897).

55. Ibid. (preliminary talk with Sokolnikov).

56. Stalin, "Ob industrializatsii i khlebnoi probleme" (On Industrialization and the Grain Problem; July 9, 1928), Works XI, 166, and T1900.

57. Stalin, Report to the Leningrad party organization on the results of the July Plenum of the Central Committee, Pravda, July 15, 1928.

58. See "Informatsionnaya spravka ob itogakh obsuzhdeniva resheni iyulskogo plenuma TsK na sobraniyakh raionnogo partaktiva g. Moskvy" (Informational Guide on the Results of the Discussion of the Decisions of the July Plenum of the Central Committee at the Meetings of the District Party Organization of the City of Moscow), Organization and Assignment Division of the Moscow Committee of the AUCP(b), July 21, 1928 ("secret"; copy in Trotsky Archive T2021), p. 6. See also notes on Stalin's speech to the plenum, July 9 (T1900).

59. Trotsky, "What Now?" The Third International After Lenin, pp. 289–290.

60. Kamenev, notes on talk with Bukharin, July 11, 1928 (T1897).

61. Ibid.

62. See Trotsky, "Krizis pravo-tsentristskogo bloka i perspektivy" (The Crisis of the Right-Centrist Bloc and the Prospects; fall 1928), T3143.

63. Resolution of the CC, July 10, 1928, "The Grain Collection Policy," CPSU in Resolutions, II, 515.

64. Kamenev, notes on preliminary talk with Sokolnikov, July 11, 1928 (T1897); letter to "Dear Comrade," September 1928 (T2442).

65. Stalin, "O smychke rabochikh i krestian i o sovkhozakh" (On the Union of the Workers and Peasants and on the State Farms), Works, XI, 188–196.

66. Ciliga, pp. 34–35; Sotsialisticheski vestnik, July 23, 1928, p. 13, and August 3, 1928, p. 14.

67. The talk was recorded in notes made by Kamenev immediately afterwards (copy in Trotsky Archive T1897). The record was first published by the Trotskyists in Paris in January 1929; it is summarized and quoted at some length in Souvarine, Stalin, pp. 482–485, and discussed in the Politburo resolution of February 9, 1929 (CPSU in Resolutions, II, 556–557, 564).

68. Pravda, editorial, "Khlebozagatovki i sniatie ekstraordinarnykh mer" (The Grain Collections and the Recision of the Extraordinary Measures), July 14, 1928.

69. Rykov, report to the Moscow party organization, July 13, 1928, as described in Trotsky, "The July Plenum and the Right Danger," July 22, 1928 (T3126), and in letter to "Dear Comrade," September 1928 (T2442); excerpts from unofficial text, T2003.

70. Zvezdov in protocols of the Moscow Committee plenum, October 1928, pp. 30–31 (T2786).

71. "Informational Guide," July 21, 1928 (T2021), and "Informatsionnaya spravka o khode obsuzhdeniya itogov plenuma TsK VKP(b) na yacheikakh gor. Moskvy" (Informational Guide on the Course of the Discussion of the Results of the Plenum of the CC of the AUCP[b] in the Cells of the City of Moscow), July 25, 1928, T2167.

72. Letter to "Dear Comrade," September 1928 (T2442).

73. Trotsky to "Dear Friend," June 1928 (T1588).

74. Polonsky in protocols of the Moscow Committee plenum, October 1928, p. 77 (T2801); Zapolsky, ibid., p. 96 (T2811); letter to "Dear Comrade," September 1928 (T2442).

75. See Bukharin in Protokoll des 6. Weltkongresses der Kommunistischen Internationale (Hamburg, 1928), I, 548–549.

76. Stalin, Fifteenth Party Congress, p. 45 and passim.

77. See Borkenau, The Communist International, pp. 333–334; Pravda, editorial, "K plenumy IKKI" (To the Plenum of the ECCI), February 7, 1928.

78. Bukharin, "The Opposition in the CPSU and in the Comintern," report to the Ninth Plenum of the ECCI, February 9, 1928, in IPC, no. 10, February 25, 1928, p. 218.

79. Sixth Comintern Congress, I, 159, 345.

80. Stalin, "O pravom uklone v VKP(b)" (On the Right Deviation in the AUCP[b]; excerpts from a speech to the plenum of the Central Committee, April 1929), "Problems of Leninism" (1931), pp. 541–544.

81. Bukharin, Sixth Comintern Congress, I, 66, 547.

82. Bukharin, report to the Moscow party organization on the results of the Sixth Congress of the Communist International, September 6, 1928, Pravda, September 12, 1928.

83. Bukharin to J. Humbert-Droz, September 1928 (Humbert-Droz Archive).

84. Bukharin, Sixth Comintern Congress, I, 550.

85. Ibid., pp. 552–553.

86. Bukharin, report to the Moscow party organization on the Sixth Comintern Congress, Pravda, September 12, 1928.

87. Quoted in the Politburo resolution of February 9, 1929, CPSU in Resolutions, II, 558–559.

88. Bukharin, Sixth Comintern Congress, p. 550.

89. Uglanov, "O blizhaishikh zadachakh moskovskoi organizatsii" (On the Immediate Tasks of the Moscow Organization), report to the plenum of the Moscow Committee and the Moscow Control Commission, September 11, 1928, *Pravda*, September 21, 1928.

90. Resolution of the Moscow Committee and the Moscow Control Commission, "Ocherednye zadachi moskovskoi organizatsii" (Regular Tasks of the Moscow Organization), *ibid.*, September 13, 1928.

91. *Pravda*, editorial, "Komintern o borbe s pravymi uklonami" (The Comintern on the Struggle Against the Right Deviations), September 18, 1928.

92. Kuibyshev, "O khoziaistvennom polozhenii SSSR" (On the Economic Situation of the USSR), report to the Leningrad party organization, September 19, 1928, *ibid*, September 25, 1928.

93. Central Committee to the Moscow party organization, October 18, 1928, *ibid.*, October 19, 1928.

94. Protocols of the Moscow Committee plenum, October 1928, p. 25 (T2783).

95. Notice to the Moscow party organization, "Gotovtes k perevyboram biuro yacheek" (Prepare for the Re-election of the Cell Bureaus), *Pravda*, October 3, 1928.

96. Uglanov, report to the Krasnaya-Presnia district organization, *ibid.*, October 24, 1928.

97. Report on a meeting of cell secretaries of the Moscow province, *ibid.*, October 4, 1928.

98. Report on a meeting of the Rogozhsko-Simonovski district organization, *ibid.*, October 5, 1928; Penkov in protocols of the Moscow Committee plenum, October 1928, p. 44 (T2792).

99. Uglanov, *ibid.*, p. 119 (T2815).

100. Decisions of the Moscow Committee and the Moscow Control Commission, *Pravda*, October 20, 1928; Stalin, "O pravoi opasnosti v VKP(b)" (On the Right Danger in the AUCP[b], speech to the Moscow Committee plenum, October 19, 1928), in "Problems of Leninism" (1931), p. 493.

101. Tsifrynovich in protocols of the Moscow Committee plenum, October 1928, p. 22 (T2782).

102. Uglanov, *ibid.*, pp. 9–19 (T2780).

103. Polonsky, *ibid.*, p. 80 (T2801); Akopian, *ibid.*, p. 86 (T2804).

104. Penkov, *ibid.*, p. 44 (T2792); Riutin, *ibid.*, p. 117 (T2814).

105. Safronov, *ibid.*, p. 64 (T2797).

106. Mandelshtam, *ibid.*, p. 68 (T2798).

107. Stalin, "On the Right Danger," in "Problems of Leninism" (1931), pp. 485, 491–492.

108. Stalin, "Ob industrializatsii strany i o pravom uklone v VKP(b)" (On the Industrialization of the Country and on the Right Deviation in the AUCP[b], speech to the Central Committee plenum, November 19, 1928, in "Problems of Leninism" (1931), p. 528.

109. Decisions of the plenary session of the Moscow Committee and the Moscow Control Commission, *Pravda*, October 20, 1928.

110. *Pravda*, October 24, 1928.

111. Report of the Moscow Party Committee, "O nastroeniyakh v partorganizatsiyakh (v sviazi s plenunom MK i MKK)" (On the Tendencies in the Party Organizations—in Connection with the Plenum of the Moscow Committee and the Moscow Control Commission; October 1928), copy in Trotsky Archive T2852.

112. Stalin, "On the Right Danger," in "Problems of Leninism" (1931), p. 492.

113. "Vnutri pravo-tsentristskogo bloka" (Inside the Right-Centrist Bloc), *Biulleten oppozitsii* (The Bulletin of the Opposition; Paris), July 1929, pp. 15–16 (written by

Trotsky—see T3179). This account is based on talks reportedly held by Bukharin and Kamenev in December 1928 and January 1929, at the residence of Piatakov.

114. Resolution of the Politburo, February 9, 1929, CPSU in Resolutions, II, 558, 564.

115. "Inside the Right-Centrist Bloc," *Biulleten oppozitsii*, p. 16.

116. Resolution of the Politburo, February 9, 1929, CPSU in Resolutions, II, 566.

117. Unsigned letter to "Friends," mid-November 1928, T2850.

118. Resolution of the CC, November 24, 1928, "O kontrolnykh tsifrakh narodnogo khoziaistva na 1928/29 god" (On the Control Figures of the National Economy for the year 1928/29), CPSU in Resolutions, II, 530–531ff.

119. Resolution of the Politburo, February 9, 1929, *ibid.*, pp. 559, 566.

120. Stalin, "On the Industrialization of the Country," in "Problems of Leninism" (1931), pp. 521–522, 527–528.

121. Resolution of the CC, "On the Control Figures," CPSU in Resolutions, II, 538–539.

122. Resolution of the CC, November 24, 1928, "O verbovke rabochikh i regulirovanii rosta partii" (On the Recruiting of Workers and the Regulation of the Growth of the Party), *ibid.*, p. 544.

123. See Popov, *Outline History of the CPSU*, II, 376; Fainsod, *Smolensk under Soviet Rule*, pp. 211–219.

124. Rykov, report to the Leningrad party organization on the Central Committee plenum of November 1928 (November 30, 1928), *Pravda*, December 4, 1928.

125. Molotov, speech to the Moscow Party Committee, *ibid.*, November 28, 1928.

126. Decisions of the Moscow Party Committee, *ibid.*

127. Tomsky, in *Sedmoi vsesoyuzny sezd profsoyuzov: Stenograficheski otchet* (Seventh All-Union Congress of Trade Unions: Stenographic Report; Moscow, 1927), p. 51.

128. See Michael Jakobson, *Die russischen Gewerkschaften, ihre Entwicklung, ihre Zielsetzung, und ihre Stellung zum Staat* (Berlin, 1932), pp. 138–139.

129. See Tomsky, *Novye zadachi russkikh profsoyuzov* (The New Tasks of the Russian Trade Unions; Moscow, 1928), pp. 12–13, cited in Jakobson, p. 140.

130. Solomon Schwarz, *Labor in Soviet Russia*, p. 139.

131. Letter to "Dear Comrade," September 1928 (T2442), quoting statement by Mikoyan at the plenum of the Central Committee, July 1928.

132. Letter to "Friends," November 1928 (T2850).

133. Appeal of the Central Committee, "To All Party Members, to All Workers," *Pravda*, June 3, 1928.

134. See Maynard, *Russia in Flux*, pp. 357–358.

135. Yaglom, Tomsky, and Ginzburg, in *Vosmoi vsesoyuzny sezd profsoyuzov: Stenograficheski otchet* (Eighth All-Union Congress of Trade Unions: Stenographic Report; Moscow, 1929), pp. 180, 201, 411.

136. *Ibid.*, pp. 110–113, 116, 130, 177–178, 189–195.

137. Letter to "Friends," November 1928 (T2850).

138. "Ukrepim partrukovodstvo profdvizheniem" (Let Us Strengthen Party Leadership in the Trade Union Movement), *Pravda*, November 21, 1928.

139. I. Niurnberg, *ibid.*, November 24, 1928.

140. Resolution of the CC, "On the Recruiting of Workers," CPSU in Resolutions, II, 542.

141. See, for example, *Pravda*, editorial, "Profsoyuzy i massa" (The Trade Unions and the Masses), December 7, 1928.

142. Eighth Trade Union Congress, pp. 24–54 *passim*.

143. *Ibid.*, pp. 206–207.

144. Resolution of the Communist Party fraction at the Eighth Trade Union Con-

gress, December 24, 1928, on the November Plenum of the Central Committee, *ibid.*, pp. 504–505.

145. *Ibid.*, p. 573.

146. Popov, II, 377.

147. Politburo resolution of February 9, 1929, CPSU in Resolutions, II, 558, 564.

148. Resolution of the combined plenum of the Central Committee and the Central Control Commission, April 23, 1929, "Po vnutripartinym delam" (On Intraparty Affairs), *ibid.*, p. 554, and Politburo resolution of February 9, 1929, *ibid.*, p. 562.

149. *Ibid.*, p. 556; Aleksandrov, p. 377.

150. *Pravda,* March 17, 1956.

151. Resolution of the combined plenum of the Central Committee and the Central Control Commission, April 23, 1929, "On Intraparty Affairs," CPSU in Resolutions, II, 553.

152. Resolution of the Sixteenth Party Congress, "O zadachakh profsoyuzov v rekonstruktivny period" (On the Tasks of the Trade Unions in the Reconstruction Period), CPSU in Resolutions, III, 64–65. The English loan term *tred-yunionizm* has a specifically derogatory sense in Russian Communist jargon.

153. See Stalin, "On the Right Deviation in the AUCP(b)" (April 1929), "Problems of Leninism" (1931), p. 570.

154. Resolution of the CC, November 24, 1928, "On the Control Figures," CPSU in Resolutions, II, 539.

155. S. G. Strumilin, "Industrializatsiya SSSR i epigony narodnichestva" (The Industrialization of the USSR and the Epigones of Populism), *Planovoe khoziaistvo* (Planned Economy), no. 7, 1927, p. 11.

156. V. Bazarov, *K metodologii perspektivnogo planirovaniya* (On the Methodology of Long-term Planning; Moscow, 1924), p. 8, quoted in S. N. Prokopowicz, *Russlands Volkswirtschaft unter den Sowjets* (Zurich and New York, 1944), p. 254.

157. *Piatiletka* (The Five Year Plan; Moscow, Communist Academy, 1929), p. 26, quoted in Aaron Yugow, *Russia's Economic Front for Peace and War* (New York, 1942), p. 5.

158. See Dobb, pp. 230–234, 320–334.

159. "Directives on the Five Year Plan," CPSU in Resolutions, II, 452.

160. See S. V. Dmitrievsky, *Sovetskie portrety* (Soviet Portraits; Berlin, 1927), pp. 188–189.

161. Dobb, pp. 232–233.

162. I. Gladkov, "K istorii pervoi piatiletnego narodnokhoziaistvennogo plana" (On the History of the First Five Year Economic Plan), *Planovoe khoziaistvo,* no. 4, 1935, pp. 126–130.

163. *Pravda,* editorial, "Vazhny uchastok nashei raboty" (An Important Part of Our Work), August 3, 1928.

164. Molotov, "K tekushchemu momentu" (On the Current Moment), *ibid.*, August 5, 1928.

165. Resolution of the CC, "On the Control Figures," CPSU in Resolutions, II, 528–530.

166. Kuibyshev, Eighth Trade Union Congress, pp. 446–447.

167. Gladkov in *Planovoe khoziaistvo,* no. 4, 1935, p. 131.

168. Kuibyshev, "On the Economic Situation of the USSR," *Pravda,* September 25, 1928.

169. Bukharin, "Zametki ekonomista (k nachalu novogo khoziaistvennogo goda)" (Notes of an Economist—at the Beginning of a New Economic Year), *Pravda,* September 30, 1928.

170. Glezarov in protocols of the Moscow Committee plenum, October 1928, p. 102 (T2812).

171. The Central Committee to the Moscow party organization, October 18, 1928, *Pravda,* October 19, 1928.

172. *Ibid.*

173. Stalin, "On the Industrialization of the Country," in "Problems of Leninism" (1931), p. 499.

174. Ginzburg, Eighth Trade Union Congress, p. 410.

175. Kuibyshev, *ibid.,* pp. 446–447.

176. Resolution of the CC, November 24, 1928, "On the Control Figures," CPSU in Resolutions, II, 525–540.

177. Bukharin, "Politicheskoe zaveshchenie Lenina" (The Political Testament of Lenin), *Pravda,* January 24, 1929.

178. Bukharin, "Teoriya imperialisticheskogo gosudarstva" (The Theory of the Imperialist State), *Revoliutsiya prava* (The Revolution of Law; Moscow, Communist Academy), Collection I, 1925, pp. 21, 30.

179. Requoted by Bukharin in his report to the Moscow party organization on the Sixth Congress of the Comintern, *Pravda,* September 12, 1928.

180. Bukharin at the plenum of the Central Committee, July 1928 (T1901).

181. Bukharin, "The Political Testament of Lenin," *Pravda,* January 24, 1929.

182. Bukharin, "Teoriya organizovannoi bezkhoziaistvennosti" (The Theory of Organized Mismanagement), *ibid.,* June 30, 1929.

183. Smilga, "The Platform of the Right Wing of the AUCP(b)," October 23, 1928 (T2825).

184. Bukharin, "Notes of an Economist," *Pravda,* September 30, 1928.

185. Molotov, "Ob uspekhakh i trudnostiakh sotsialisticheskogo stroitelstva" (On the Achievements and Difficulties of Socialist Construction), report to the Seventeenth Moscow Provincial Party Conference, February 23, 1929, *ibid.,* February 27, 1929.

186. Bukharin-Rykov-Tomsky declarations of February 9, 1929, cited by Stalin, "Pravy uklon v VKP(b)" (The Right Deviation in the AUCP[b]), speech to the Central Committee plenum, April 1929, Works, XII, 3–4. This is the first and only unabridged version of the speech.

187. Supreme Economic Council, "Diskussiya metodologii plana" (Discussion of the Methodology of the Plan), November 1928, quoted in Yugow, *Russia's Economic Front,* p. 6.

188. Kuibyshev, Eighth Trade Union Congress, p. 446.

189. Ginzburg, *ibid.,* p. 410.

190. Kuibyshev, *ibid.,* p. 446.

191. See Gladkov in *Planovoe khoziaistvo,* no. 4, 1935, p. 132.

192. Quoted, *ibid.,* p. 136.

193. G. F. Grinko, *The Five-Year Plan of the Soviet Union* (New York, 1930), p. 281.

194. Aaron Yugow, *Piatiletka* (The Five Year Plan; Berlin, 1931), p. 10; Yugow, *Russia's Economic Front,* pp. 3, 6.

195. *Ibid.,* p. 6; Naum Jasny, "A Soviet Planner—V. G. Groman," *The Russian Review,* January 1954), pp. 53–58.

196. *Ibid.,* p. 54.

197. For a sympathizer's admission of this point, see Dobb, pp. 332, 334.

198. See Harry Schwartz, *Russia's Soviet Economy* (New York, 1950), ch. 5.

199. See Strumilin, *Problems of Planning in the USSR* (Moscow, 1932), pp. 16–21, cited in Yugow, *Russia's Economic Front,* pp. 6–7.

200. Quoted by Gladkov in *Planovoe khoziaistvo*, no. 4, 1935, pp. 134–135.

201. *Ibid.*, p. 135; Stalin, "On the Right Deviation in the AUCP(b)," in "Problems of Leninism" (1931), pp. 582–583.

202. Yugow, "The Five Year Plan," p. 11; resolution of the Sixteenth Party Conference, "O piatiletnem plane razvitiya narodnogo khoziaistva" (On the Five Year Plan of Economic Development), CPSU in Resolutions, II, 569–573.

203. Yugow, "The Five Year Plan," pp. 12–13.

204. Stalin, in *Semnadtsaty sezd VKP(b): Stenograficheski otchet* (Seventeenth Congress of the AUCP[b]: Stenographic Report; Moscow, 1934), p. 33.

205. G. Dimitriev, "Dialekticheski materializm—v massy" (Dialectical Materialism —To the Masses), *Pravda*, March 9, 1928.

206. See Raymond A. Bauer, *The New Man in Soviet Psychology* (Cambridge, 1952), ch. 2.

207. Resolution of the Second All-Union Conference of Marxist-Leninist Scientific Research Institutions, "O sovremennykh problemakh filosofii marksizma-leninizma" (On the Contemporary Problems of the Philosophy of Marxism-Leninism), *Pod znamenem marksizma* (Under the Banner of Marxism), May 1929, p. 7.

208. See, for instance, Gessen and Podvolotsky, "Filosoficheskie korni pravogo opportunizma" (The Philosophical Roots of Right Opportunism), *ibid.*, September 1929, pp. 1–29, and A. S. Martynov, "Teoriya podvizhnogo ravnovesiya obshchestva i vzaimo-otnosheniya mezhdu obshchestvom i vneshnei sredoi" (The Theory of the Dynamic Equilibrium of Society and the Interrelation between Society and the External Milieu), *ibid.*, February-March 1930, pp. 59–76.

209. Stalin, "K voprosam agrarnoi politiki v SSSR" (On Problems of Agrarian Policy in the USSR; December 1929), "Problems of Leninism" (1931), p. 615.

210. Stalin, "O pravoi opasnosti v germanskoi kompartii" (On the Right Danger in the German Communist Party), speech to the presidium of the ECCI, December 19, 1928, Works, X, 307.

211. Stalin, "Gruppa Bukharina i pravy uklon v nashei partii" (The Bukharin Group and the Right Deviation in Our Party; statement to a session of the Politburo and the presidium of the Central Control Commission, February 9 or 10, 1929), Works, XI, 319; "Inside the Right-Centrist Bloc," *Biulleten oppozitsii*, July 1929, p. 17.

212. The statement is known only as described, *ibid.*, and in critiques of it, especially Stalin, "The Right Deviation," Works, XII, 3, 7, 90–91.

213. Resolution of the Politburo, February 9, 1929, CPSU in Resolutions, II, 558–561.

214. Stalin, "The Right Deviation," Works, XII, 6–7.

215. Resolution of the Politburo, February 9, 1929, CPSU in Resolution, II, 556–567.

216. *Ibid.*, p. 565.

217. The platform is known only as described in criticisms of it—Stalin, "The Right Deviation," Works, XII, 3–4, and resolution of the CC, April 23, 1929, "On Intraparty Affairs," CPSU in Resolutions, II, 551–554.

218. "Borba s pravym uklonom i ideologicheskoe vospitanie mass" (The Struggle with the Right Deviation and the Ideological Education of the Masses), *Pravda*, February 10, 1929.

219. Molotov, "The Achievements and Difficulties of Socialist Construction," *ibid.*, February 27, 1929.

220. *Pravda*, editorial, "V borbe za sotsialisticheskuyu rekonstruktsiyu" (In the Struggle for Socialist Reconstruction), April 24, 1929. See also Popov, II, 380.

221. Resolution of the CC, April 23, 1929, "On Intraparty Affairs," CPSU in Resolutions, II, 554.

222. Stalin, "On the Right Deviation in the AUCP(b)," in "Problems of Leninism" (1931), pp. 541–581 *passim*, 592.

223. Politburo theses on the report of Kalinin to the Sixteenth Party Conference, "The Development of Agriculture and the Tax Alleviations for the Middle Peasant," *IPC,* no. 19, April 19, 1929, p. 401.

224. Rykov, report to the Ninth Moscow Provincial Congress of Soviets, *Pravda,* April 13, 1929.

225. Stalin, "The Bukharin Group," Works, XI, 323.

226. The conference actually passed a brief resolution which named Bukharin in the course of approving the April Central Committee resolution against the Rightists, but this was not published with the rest of the conference material. See CPSU in Resolutions, II, 614–615, 619.

227. Resolution of the Sixteenth Party Conference, "On the Five Year Plan," *ibid.,* p. 575.

228. Rykov, report to the Sixteenth Party Conference on the Five Year Plan, *Pravda,* April 26, 1929.

229. Kuibyshev, *ibid.,* April 27, 1929.

230. K. Y. Bauman, report to the Moscow party organization on the results of the Central Committee plenum of April 1, 1929, and of the Sixteenth All-Union Party Conference, *ibid.,* May 14, 1929.

231. Resolution of the Tenth Plenum of the ECCI on Bukharin, July 3, 1929, *ibid.,* August 21, 1929.

232. See *ibid.,* July 21, 1929, editorial, "Itogi plenuma IKKI" (The Results of the Plenum of the ECCI), and theses of the Tenth ECCI Plenum, "O mezhdunarodnom polozhenii i ocherednykh zadachakh kommunisticheskogo internatsionala," (On the International Situation and the Next Tasks of the Communist International).

233. O. Kuusinen, "Mezhdunarodnoe polozhenie i zadachi Kominterna" (The International Situation and the Tasks of the Comintern, report to the Tenth ECCI Plenum), *ibid.,* July 28, 1929.

234. See S. V. Kosior, report to the Kharkov party organization, "On the Internal Situation of the CPSU," *IPC,* no. 64, November 15, 1929, pp. 1376–1377.

235. Text in *Pravda,* November 18, 1929.

236. Popov, II, 398.

237. Resolution of the plenum of the Central Committee, November 17, 1929, "O gruppe Bukharina" (On the Bukharin Group), CPSU in Resolutions, II, 662–663.

238. *Pravda,* editorial, "Itogi i perspektivy" (Results and Prospects), November 18, 1929.

CHAPTER 14. "ENEMIES OF THE PEOPLE"

1. See Souvarine, *Stalin,* pp. 471–472.

2. Trotsky, *My Life,* pp. 540–541.

3. *Ibid.,* p. 548.

4. Statement by Zinoviev and Kamenev, *Pravda,* January 27, 1928.

5. Ordzhonikidze, report of the Commission on the Opposition, Fifteenth Party Congress, p. 1243.

6. Piatakov's application for readmission to the party, *Pravda,* February 29, 1928.

7. F. Beck and W. Godin [pseud.], *Russian Purge and the Extraction of Confession* (New York, 1951), p. 112.

8. People's Commissariat of Justice of the USSR, *Report of Court Proceedings: The Case of the Anti-Soviet Bloc of Rights and Trotskyites,* pp. 36, 157–158.

9. Antonov-Ovseyenko to Stalin, April 4, 1928, *Pravda,* April 8, 1928.

10. Date confirmed in The Great Soviet Encyclopedia, 2nd ed., LI (1958), 20.

11. See *Sotsialisticheski vestnik,* January 9, 1929, pp. 14–15.

12. *Pravda,* editorial, January 24, 1929, attacking Trotsky's "Letter of Instruction" of October 21, 1928.

13. Trotsky, *My Life,* p. 569.

14. See *The Case of Leon Trotsky: Report of Hearings on the Charges Made Against Him in the Moscow Trials,* by the Preliminary Commission of Inquiry, John Dewey, chairman (New York, 1937), pp. 105–106.

15. See Victor Serge, *Vie et mort de Trotsky* (Paris, 1951), part 7; Isaac Don Levine, *The Mind of an Assassin* (New York, 1959).

16. Preobrazhensky, "Ko vsem tovarishcham po oppozitsii" (To All Comrades in Opposition), April 1929 (Trotsky Archive).

17. Radek to Smilga, May 19, 1929, quoted in Yaroslavsky, "Etot son konchen" (This Dream is Over), *Pravda,* May 30, 1929.

18. "Zayavlenie v TsKK byvshikh rukovoditelei trotskistskoi oppozitsii tt. Y. Preobrazhenskogo, K. Radeka, i I. Smilgi o razryve s oppozitsiei" (Declaration to the CCC by the Former Leaders of the Trotskyist Opposition, Y. Preobrazhensky, K. Radek, and I. Smilga, on their Break with the Opposition), *ibid.,* July 14, 1929.

19. See Deutscher, *Stalin,* pp. 359, 370.

20. Trotsky, *The Revolution Betrayed,* tr. Max Eastman (New York, 1937).

21. See Milovan Djilas, *The New Class* (New York, 1957).

22. Rakovsky, "O prichinakh pererozhdeniya partii i gosudarstvennogo apparata" (On the Causes of the Degeneration of the Party and the State Apparatus), August 2–6, 1928, published in *Biulleten oppozitsii,* no. 6, October 1929, pp. 14–20.

23. Excerpts from theses by Rakovsky, V. Kosior, and M. Okudzhava of August 1929, *ibid.,* no. 7, November-December 1929, p. 9.

24. *Ibid.,* p. 5.

25. Stalin, "Golovokruzhenie ot uspekhov" (Dizzy with Success), "Problems of Leninism" (1941), pp. 299–304.

26. See Baykov, *The Development of the Soviet Economic System,* p. 327.

27. Tomsky, Sixteenth Party Congress, p. 144.

28. Rykov, *ibid.,* pp. 130–132.

29. Uglanov, *ibid.,* pp. 744–745.

30. Kirov, *ibid.,* p. 158.

31. Resolution of the Sixteenth Party Congress on the Central Committee report, CPSU in Resolutions, III, 21.

32. Rudzutak, Sixteenth Party Congress, pp. 201–202.

33. The Great Soviet Encyclopedia, 1st ed., LX, 559.

34. *Pravda,* December 2, 1930, p. 6; *Biulleten oppozitsii,* November-December 1930, pp. 24–26.

35. *Ibid.,* p. 23.

36. Souvarine, p. 625.

37. The Great Soviet Encyclopedia, 2nd ed., XXVIII, 153; XXXI, 173.

38. See Trotsky, "Delo t. Riazanova" (The Affair of Comrade Riazanov), *Biulleten oppozitsii,* no. 21–22, May-June 1931, pp. 19–23.

39. Stalin, "O nekotorykh voprosakh istorii bolshevizma" (On Certain Questions of the History of Bolshevism), "Problems of Leninism" (1941), p. 359.

40. *Pravda,* October 11, 1932.

41. *Biulleten oppozitsii,* November 1932, p. 23 (Letter from Moscow).

42. Quoted in Deutscher, *Stalin,* p. 349.

43. Ciliga, *The Russian Enigma,* p. 279.

44. *Biulleten oppozitsii,* November 1932, p. 23.

45. Decision of the Central Control Commission, October 9, 1932, *Pravda,* October 11, 1932.

46. On the report that Stalin shot his wife, see *New York Times,* April 1, 1956. I heard the currency of this rumor confirmed in Moscow in the fall of 1956.

47. Barmine, *One Who Survived,* p. 264; Victor Serge, *Portrait de Staline* (Paris, 1940), pp. 94–95.

48. Resolution of the combined plenum of the Central Committee and the Central Control Commission, "Ob antipartinoi gruppirovke Eismonta, Tolmacheva, A. P. Smirnova i dr." (On the Antiparty Grouping of Eismont, Tolmachev, A. P. Smirnov, et al.), January 12, 1933, CPSU in Resolutions, III, 199.

49. Resolution of the combined plenum of the Central Committee and Central Control Commission, "O chistke partii" (On the Party Purge), January 12, 1923, *ibid.,* III, 198.

50. See Fainsod, *How Russia is Ruled,* pp. 223–224.

51. Popov, *Outline History of the CPSU,* II, 450, 456.

52. *Ibid.,* p. 456; Stalin, Seventeenth Party Congress, p. 31.

53. Stalin, *ibid.,* p. 28.

54. See Deutscher, *Stalin,* p. 351.

55. Stalin, Seventeenth Party Congress, pp. 259, 28.

56. See Khrushchev, secret speech at the Twentieth Party Congress, *The Anti-Stalin Campaign,* p. 23.

57. See *Letter of an Old Bolshevik* (New York, 1937), pp. 12–14; Deutscher, *Stalin,* pp. 353–354.

58. George Fischer, *Soviet Opposition to Stalin: A Case Study in World War II* (Cambridge, 1952), pp. 39–40, 148.

59. See Adam Ulam, *Titoism and the Cominform* (Cambridge, 1952), p. 158.

60. Resolution of the Central Committee of the Polish Workers' Party, November 14, 1949, reported in *New York Times,* November 15, 1949.

61. The Central Committee of the Communist Party of the Soviet Union to the Central Committee of the Communist Party of Yugoslavia, March 27 and May 4, 1948, in *The Soviet-Yugoslav Dispute* (London, Royal Institute of International Affairs, 1948), pp. 16, 43.

62. Cominform communiqué of June 28, 1948, *ibid.,* pp. 62–63.

63. See H. F. Armstrong, *Tito and Goliath* (New York, 1951), pp. 82–114, *passim.*

64. Najdan Pasić, "Izvrtanje marksistickog učenja o državi u teoriji i praksi savremenog revizionizma" (The Perversion of the Marxist Doctrine of the State in the Theory and Practice of Contemporary Revisionism), *Komunist* (Belgrade), January 1951, pp. 96, 103, 115.

65. See E. D. Domar, "The Varga Controversy," *American Economic Review,* March 1950, pp. 148–149.

66. Stalin, *Ekonomicheskie problemy sotsializma v SSSR* (Economic Problems of Socialism in the USSR; Moscow, 1952), pp. 166–168.

67. D. T. Shepilov, "Generalnaya liniya partii i vulgarizatory marksizma" (The General Line of the Party and Vulgarizers of Marxism), *Pravda,* January 24, 1955.

68. "Kommunisticheskaya partiya pobezhdala i pobezhdaet vernostiu leninizmu" (The Communist Party has Triumphed and is Triumphing through Loyalty to Leninism), *ibid.,* April 5, 1956.

69. Khrushchev at the Twentieth Party Congress, *The Anti-Stalin Campaign,* pp. 25–26.

70. See Trotsky in *Biulleten oppozitsii,* no. 41, January 1935, pp. 1ff, 11.

71. See People's Commissariat of Justice of the USSR, *Report of Court Proceedings: The Case of the Trotskyite-Zinovievite Terrorist Center* (Moscow, 1936).

72. See People's Commissariat of Justice of the USSR, *Report of Court Proceedings: The Case of the Anti-Soviet Trotskyite Center* (Moscow, 1937).

73. See Trotsky, "Obezglavlenie krasnoi armii" (Beheading the Red Army), *Biulleten oppozitsii*, no. 56–57, July-August 1937, pp. 1–7.

74. See N. Markin, "Delo Mdivani-Okudzhava" (The Mdivani-Okudzhava Affair), *ibid.*, pp. 7–9.

75. Deutscher, *Stalin*, pp. 378–379; *New York Times*, March 18, 1956.

76. Khrushchev at the Twentieth Party Congress, *The Anti-Stalin Campaign*, p. 69.

77. See People's Commissariat of Justice of the USSR, *Report of Court Proceedings: The Case of the Anti-Soviet Bloc of Rights and Trotskyites*.

78. Beck and Godin, p. 212.

79. Khrushchev at the Twentieth Party Congress, *The Anti-Stalin Campaign*, pp. 34–35.

80. Hryhory Kostiuk, *The Fall of Postyshev* (New York, Research Project on the USSR, 1954), pp. 20–24. For a slightly different version, see Alexandre Ouralov, *Staline au pouvoir* (Paris, 1951), pp. 36–40. Cf. Khrushchev at the Twentieth Party Congress, *The Anti-Stalin Campaign*, p. 29.

81. Cf. Central Committee lists, Seventeenth Party Congress, pp. 680–681, and *Vosemnadtsaty sezd VKP(b): Stenograficheski otchet* (Eighteenth Congress of the AUCP[b]: Stenographic Report; Moscow, 1939), p. 688.

82. *Ibid.*, list of delegates, pp. 693–724.

83. Bukharin in *The Case of the Anti-Soviet Bloc of Rights and Trotskyites*, pp. 777–778.

84. *Kommunist*, editorial, "Kommunisticheskaya Partiya Sovetskogo Soyuza—napravliayushchaya i rukovodiashchaya sila sovetskogo obshchestva" (The Communist Party of the Soviet Union—The Directing and Leading Force of Soviet Society), no. 8, May 1953, p. 15.

85. The substance of Khrushchev's speech was quickly transmitted to the party membership through the agitational channels of the party organization. A substantially complete and evidently quite authentic text, made available to one of the East European Communist governments, was obtained by the United States Department of State and released for publication in June 1956 (text in *The Anti-Stalin Campaign*.)

86. *The Anti-Stalin Campaign*, p. 18.

87. *Ibid.*, p. 10.

88. *Ibid.*, pp. 86–87.

89. *Ibid.*, p. 82.

90. *Ibid.*, p. 40.

91. *Ibid.*, p. 63.

92. *Ibid.*, pp. 52–53.

93. *Ibid.*, p. 10.

94. *Ibid.*, p. 82.

95. "The Communist Party has Triumphed and is Triumphing through Loyalty to Leninism," *Pravda*, April 5, 1956.

96. "Pochemu kult lichnosti chuzd dukhu markizma-leninizma?" (Why is the Cult of Personality Alien to the Spirit of Marxism-Leninism?), *ibid.*, March 28, 1956.

97. Reported in *New York Times*, April 8, 1956.

98. The Great Soviet Encyclopedia, 2nd ed., XXVIII, 565.

99. See *Pravda*, May 7, 1953. Petrovsky's award in honor of his seventy-fifth birthday, interestingly, was a year late—it had to wait for Stalin's demise. Petrovsky died in January 1958.

100. Reported in *New York Times*, April 14, 1956. The available text of Khrushchev's secret speech does not include the reference to the military.

101. The Great Soviet Encyclopedia, 2nd ed., LI, 167.

102. Mikoyan at the Twentieth Party Congress, *Pravda,* February 18, 1956.

103. S. N. Kanev, "Partinye massy v borbe za edinstvo RKP(b) v periode profsoyu-znoi diskussii (1920–1921)" (The Party Masses in the Struggle for the Unity of the RCP[b] in the Period of the Trade Union Controversy, 1920–1921), *Voprosy istorii* (Questions of History), no. 2, 1956, p. 20.

104. Among the few people who were still alive when restored to favor was the first state planning chief, Krzhizhanovsky, who enjoyed a brief period of honorable retirement before his death in 1959 (see *Pravda,* April 1, 1959).

105. Khrushchev at the Twentieth Party Congress, *The Anti-Stalin Campaign,* pp. 22–24.

106. *Ibid.,* pp. 6–9.

107. *Ibid.,* p. 81.

108. *Ibid.*

109. Decision of the Central Committee, June 30, 1956, "O preodolenii kulta lich-nosti i ego posledstvi" (On Overcoming the Cult of Personality and its Consequences), *Pravda,* July 2, 1956.

110. Khrushchev at the Twentieth Party Congress, *The Anti-Stalin Campaign,* pp. 11–12.

111. *Ibid.,* pp. 16–17.

112. "XX sezd i zadachi sovetskoi pravovoi nauki" (The Twentieth Congress and the Tasks of Soviet Legal Science), *Sovetskoe gosudarstvo i pravo* (Soviet State and Law), no. 2, 1956, pp. 3–14.

113. Kanev in *Voprosy istorii,* no. 2, 1956, p. 20.

114. *Pravda,* April 22, 1956.

115. Mikoyan and Pankratova at the Twentieth Party Congress, *ibid.,* February 22, 1956.

116. Observed by the author in Moscow in the fall of 1956. Works by oppositionists were not listed in the catalog of the Lenin Library, but were evidently kept in a "special preserve," from which any item could be withdrawn when its author was rehabilitated.

CHAPTER 15. WHY THE OPPOSITION FAILED

1. Luxemburg, *The Russian Revolution,* p. 45.

2. Trotsky, "Tsel etogo obiasneniya: Nashi raznoglasiya" (The Object of This Explanation: Our Differences; 1924), Trotsky Archive T2969, p. 2.

3. *The Case of Leon Trotsky: Report of Hearings on the Charges Made Against Him in the Moscow Trials,* pp. 440–441.

4. Radek, Tenth Party Congress, p. 540.

5. See James Burnham, *The Managerial Revolution* (New York, 1941).

6. Molotov at the Fifteenth Party Conference, *Pravda,* November 17, 1926.

7. Rudzutak, Thirteenth Party Congress, p. 209.

INDEX

Aleksinsky, G. A., 19–21, 25, 27, 29, 46
Anarchism, 23, 146–147
Anarcho-syndicalism, 94, 146–147
Andreyev, A. A.: in trade-union controversy, 130–131; dropped from Central Committee, 151; rise to party leadership, 158, 242, 279; trade-union head, 158–159; and Zinoviev Opposition, 269; and Right Opposition, 329
Anglo-Russian Trade-Union Unity Committee, 276
"Anonymous platform," 204–205
Antipov, N. K., 388
Anti-Semitism, 25, 275, 304, 316, 492n179
Antonov-Ovseyenko, V. A.: editor of *Nashe slovo*, 29; in Mezhrainontsy, 31; joins Bolsheviks, 49; and army political administration, 175, 229; and opposition of 1923, 218, 229; ambassador to Czechoslovakia, 303; repudiates opposition, 371–372; on Stalin, 372; purged, 372, 388; rehabilitated, 393–394
"Apparatus." *See* Communist Party
"April Conference," 44, 47
"April Days," 44
Armenia: and formation of USSR, 177
Army. *See* Military controversy; Red Army; *Spetsy*
"Article 107," 324, 326
"August Bloc," 27
Authoritarianism, 24, 311, 403, 492n179
Avdeyev, A. D., 317, 388
Avilov, N. P., 40
Azerbaijan: and formation of USSR, 177

Badaev, A. Y., 388
Bakaev, L. P., 386
"Baku Letter," 279
Bakuninism, 12, 24
Bauman, K. Y., 344, 367–368, 388
Bazarov, 13, 40, 62, 349, 358
Bazhanov, B., 206
Belenki, 195
Beloborodov, A. G., 388
Belorussia: and formation of USSR, 177
Beria, L. P., 178, 248, 387, 397
Berkman, Alexander, 143
Berne conference, 32

Berzin, Y. A., 49
Biulleten Oppozitsii (Trotskyist organ), 373
Blanquism, 53
Blok, Alexander, 310
Bliumkin, Y., 373
Bogdanov, A. A. (Malinovsky): leads left deviation, 5, 19–21; in Bolshevik leadership, 14, 17; expelled from Bolshevik faction, 22; returns to Mensheviks, 25; and "Workers' Truth," 159, 161, 210; death of, 25
   On party, 14; on Social Democratic unity, 16; on revolutionary militancy, 23–24; on Lenin, 24; on "proletarian culture," 25, 161
Bologna School, 23
Bolshevik (theoretical journal), 239
Bolshevik Party: formed, 10–13; realignment of, 28, 33–34, 45–51; "rearming" of, 43–44, 244–245; outlawed by Provisional Government, 45–46. *See also* Communist Party
"Bonapartism," 12, 175, 375, 404
Brandler, Heinrich, 213, 215–216
Brest-Litovsk: negotiations at 71; treaty of, 77–78, 88; controversy over, 35, 70–80, 88
Bubnov, A. S.: supports boycott of Duma, 19; in Central Committee, 27, 48; and October Revolution, 61, 247, 457n109; opposes coalition government, 66; opposes peace, 75, 79, 459n17; leads opposition in Ukraine, 98, 102; and Democratic Centralists, 116; and trade-union controversy, 130–131, 133; signs Declaration of the Forty-six, 218; heads army political administration, 229; purged, 388; rehabilitated, 393
Bukharin, N. I.: early deviation, 32, 50; and World War I, 32; on "April Theses," 44; in Central Committee, 49, 80; influence on Lenin, 52; and Constituent Assembly, 68; opposes peace, 72–76, 79–80; leads Left Communists, 76–77, 79–80, 85, 89; in Supreme Economic Council, 84; and anti-Lenin plot, 89–90; in 1938 trial, 89, 387; candidate to Politburo, 112; and trade-union controversy, 127, 131–134; and 1921 controversy, 138, 140; quits Left, 151; and issue of Georgia, 177, 186; opposes Lenin's reform plan, 190; opposes foreign-trade monopoly, 199; and Kislovodsk conference, 207–208; and German revolution, 214; fights

opposition of 1923, 225, 231–232; Politburo
member, 242; in attack on Trotskyism, 245–
246, 250; and Zinoviev Opposition, 258–261,
265–266, 269–270; and struggle with United
Opposition, 273, 278, 280, 283–285, 309–
310; head of Comintern, 281; in Right Opposition, 322, 326–336, 340–342, 348, 352–
358, 363–369; "Notes of an Economist,"
340, 352; theory of equilibrium, 352, 356–
357; and philosophical controversy, 361;
condemnation of, 363–368, 503n226; removed as Comintern head, 368; expelled
from Politburo, 368; capitulates, 368–369;
and Stalin Constitution, 375; absent from
Sixteenth Party Congress, 377; serves Stalin
as ideologist, 378; confession, 389–390, 403
    On world revolution, 32, 96, 250; on na-
tionality issue, 33, 186; on "permanent
revolution," 38–39, 250, 265–266; on revolutionary war, 53–54; on War Communism,
95; on trade unions, 119–120, 123, 125,
133–134, 157; on party centralism, 138,
195; on Trotsky, 175, 231–232, 257; on
Comintern, 213, 334–336; on repression of
opposition, 227; on role of leaders, 231; use
of party history, 231–232; on peasantry, 250,
257–258, 262, 326, 328, 331, 354, 357, 364;
on "socialism in one country," 265–266,
354; on China, 283, 285; on "workers'
state," 297; on proletarian orthodoxy, 305,
309; on planning, 331, 356–357; on Stalin,
332; on Marxism, 353; on bureaucracy, 354–
356, 364; humanism of, 358; and East European deviations, 383
    Lenin on, 96, 134; Stalin on, 269, 335–
336, 362, 365–366; Smilga on, 357
Bulganin, N. A., 391
Bund, 10, 19
Bureau of the Central Committee, 40–41, 43
Bureau of the Central Region, 20
Bureau of the Committees of the Majority, 14
Bureaucracy: debated, 115–117, 187–193, 223;
growth in party, 165–166; and failure of
opposition, 405–407; and industrialization,
406–407, 411
    Lenin on, 82, 188–193; Democratic Cen-
tralists on, 92; Workers' Opposition on, 92,
139, 162; Sapronov on, 116, 138; Preobrazhensky on, 116, 221; Kronstadters on, 145;
Trotsky on, 168, 188, 217, 224, 240, 301;
and Ultra-Left, 187; United Opposition on,
277, 296; Bukharin on, 354–356, 364; Rakovsky on, 375–376; Yugoslavs on, 383

Capitalism: control of, 82; and War Communism, 92; and NEP, 155; "stabilization"
of, 213, 263, 296, 368; function of, com-

pared with Stalinism, 410. See also "State
capitalism"
"Capitulations." See Trotskyists
Capri School, 21, 23
Central Committee of Communist Party: en-
largement of, 111–112, 190–192, 196–197,
241–242; "Military Center" of, 61
Central Control Commission: function debated,
164–165; and discipline, 167; Lenin on,
190; issue of reorganization of, 196–197,
242; under Stalin's control, 198; and re-
pression of Opposition, 227, 303. See also
Control Commissions
Centralism: debated, 94–95, 113–114, 147,
195–196
Cheka: and Kronstadt revolt, 145. See also
GPU
Chamberlain, Austen, 287
Chiang Kai-shek, 283, 335
Chicherin, G. V., 30
China, Communist Party of, 283–285, 334
Chubar, V. Y., 187, 281, 388, 394
Ciliga, A., 282
"Circle spirit," 11, 14
Civil War, 92–93, 100–101, 104, 115; and
Communist Party, 113; and dictatorship,
402, 404
"Clemenceau thesis," 286–287
Coalition government: debated, 63–67
"Collective leadership," 173, 377, 390–391
Collectivization, 323, 327–328, 330, 357, 376
Collegial principle, 108–109, 390, 406, 463n78
Comintern. See Communist International
Committees of the village poor, 94, 99
"Commune State," 52, 355, 383
Communism: nature of, 3–4, 145, 411–412;
duality in, 4–5
Communist International: planned, 32; and
Workers' Opposition, 162–163; Zinoviev
chairman, 174; tactics debated, 212–213;
Lenin on, 213; and Zinoviev Opposition,
262–264; United Opposition on, 277–278,
284; Bukharin chairman, 281; and Right
Opposition, 334–336; and fall of Bukharin,
363, 368. See also World revolution
Communist Information Bureau, 383
Communist Party: change of name, 3; dualism in, 4–5, 9, 16; factions in, 6–7; evolution from democracy to bureaucracy, 111,
113; "apparatus," 166–170, 193–194, 222–
224, 267–268, 301, 311, 411; history, political use of, 231–232, 247–248, 439; membership, debated, 267. See also Bureaucracy;
Central Committee; Central Control Commission; Democracy; Discipline; Party; Political Bureau; Organizational Bureau; Secretariat; Unity

Kulaks, issue over, 100, 258, 260–262, 288, 293–294, 306–307, 323–326, 329–331, 338, 365, 379. *See also* Peasantry

Kulikov, Y. F., 378

Kuomintang, 283, 285

Kutuzov, I. I., 150

Kuznetsov, N., 163, 210

Kviring, E. I., 99–100, 388

"Labor Group" (*Trudoviki*), 18

Larin, M. A.: joins Bolsheviks, 31, 49; and press and coalition issues, 66; and Constituent Assembly, 38; in Supreme Economic Council, 84; supports industrial administrators, 200; against United Opposition, 282

   On NEP, 155; on proletarian orthodoxy, 309

Lashevich, M. M.: in military controversy, 105, 107; dropped from Central Committee, 112; and Kislovodsk conference, 207; in war commissariat, 212, 256; and opposition of 1923, 229; demoted to Central Committee candidate, 271; punished for conspiratorial meeting, 277–279; expelled from party, 320

Latvia, Communist Party of, 100

Lebedev-Poliansky, P. I., 31

"Left," meaning of, 4–7, 302, 343

"Left Bolsheviks," 32

Left Communists: and Brest-Litovsk issue, 70–80, 88; and economic councils, 83–84; defeated, 87–91, 399; in anti-Lenin plot, 89–90, 232; rejoin Lenin, 91, 93–94

   On revolutionary war, 39–40, 71, 73–74; on industrial administration, 81, 85–87; on *spetsy*, 105

Left Socialist Revolutionaries: Zinoviev and Kamenev on, 60; in October Revolution, 63; and coalition government, 64, 67–68; oppose curb on press, 66; oppose peace, 88; in anti-Lenin plot, 89–90, 232; attempt insurrection, 90, 93; in Ukraine, 99; oppose *spetsy*, 105

Lenin, V. I. (Ulianov): and formation of Bolshevik Party, 9–17; opposes Social Democratic unity, 14, 17, 28, 30–31, 47; opposes boycott of Duma, 18–20; controversy with Otzovists, 5, 20–23; controversy with Vperiodists, 23–24; opposes World War I, 32; in revolution of 1917, 35–39, 42–46, 55–63; in Central Committee, 45, 48; Chairman of Council of People's Commissars, 63; opposes coalition government, 64–67; and Brest-Litovsk issue, 71–80; defeats Left Communists, 87–89; in Politburo, 112; and trade unions, 123–127, 130–134, 147, 157; and Workers' Opposition, 146–147, 150;

and NEP, 154–155, 164; and Miasnikov, 160; at Eleventh Party Congress, 164; illness, 172–173, 176, 183, 193, 198; conciliates opposition, 150, 173; breaks with Stalin, 177, 179–182, 193, 394; and issue of Georgia, 177–182, 186–187; attempts party and government reform, 188–193, 198, 473–474n74; supports foreign-trade monopoly, 199; emphasizes Gosplan, 202–203; death, 236, 241, 479n4

   Doctrine of the party, 11–12, 147; on discipline, 11, 84–85, 108, 113; on need for ideological purity, 12; on force vs. parliamentarianism, 15; on Bogdanov, 21; on "uneven development," 32–33; on nationality question, 33, 97, 177–181, 184–187; on soviets, 35, 52, 56; on Provisional Government, 38–39, 43–44; and "permanent revolution," 38–39, 43, 454n9; on Trotsky, 48, 179–180; on relations with other parties, 52–53, 56–57, 64; on revolutionary war, 53; on Blanquism, 53; on Germany, 54, 58, 72, 78; on Zinoviev, 61–62, 174; on Kamenev, 61–62, 188–189; on Lunacharsky, 65; on party unity, 65, 150, 164; on world revolution, 42, 78–79; on communist society, 81; on industrial administration, 82, 84–86, 108–109; on bureaucracy, 82, 188–193; on workers' control, 82–85; on peasantry, 94, 155; on Bukharin, 96, 134; on the Ukraine, 103; on decision-making, 111; on justification of opposition, 118; on deviation among workers, 147; on freedom of press, 160; on Stalin, 169–170, 179–181; on Rykov, 188–189; and Marxism, 193; on Comintern, 213; and meaning of socialism, 408; and Roman Malinovsky, 452n100

   Pragmatism of, 33; prestige of, 172–173; cult of, 237, 246, 397

   Mensheviks on, 12–13; Kollontai on, 129; Workers' Opposition on, 139; Stalin on, 169, 236–237; Kamenev on, 196; Bukharin on, 355–356

   Writings: "What Is To Be Done?" 11, 165, 169, 237; *Materialism and Empiriocriticism*, 21; "April Theses," 35, 43–44; "State and Revolution," 51–53, 81–82, 147, 383; "One Step Forward, Two Steps Back," 169; "Testament," 179–180, 238–239, 274, 301, 314–316, 372, 394–395, 472n29

"Lenin Enrollment," 238

Leningrad party organization: and Zinoviev Opposition, 255, 267, 270–271; rebuffs United Opposition, 280. *See also* Petrograd

Leninists: defined, 4–7; and prerevolutionary left deviation, 20–25; and Prague Conference, 27; and unity of internationalists, 29,

27؟; in United Opposition, 280–285, 287, 312–317; dropped as Comintern chairman, 281; expelled from Central Committee and party, 316–317; readmitted to party, 371; re-expelled from party, 380; and assassination of Kirov, 386; tried and executed, 386

Hostility to Trotsky, 48, 80, 106, 125, 176, 225–226, 245–255, 400; on revolution in West, 73; on trade unions, 156; on party unity, 196, 205, 237, 239–241, 280; on peasantry, 202, 258–260; on world revolution, 213–214, 263; and Germany, 214, 262–264; on democracy, 221, 267; on Leninism, 237; on Stalin, 239, 285, 298; on

"permanent revolution," 245; on petty-bourgeois danger, 259; on Russian backwardness, 261; on "state capitalism," 261; on NEP, 261; on "socialism in one country," 264–265, 484n60; internationalism of, 272; on repression of Opposition, 275, 312; on China, 283–284; on Engels, 298; and anti-Semitism, 304; and revisionism, 306; on "septemvirate," 490n127

Character, 69, 173–176, 400–401; Lenin on, 61–62, 174; Sverdlov on, 174; Trotsky on, 243, 272; Stalin on, 253, 315, 318; Khrushchev on, 395

Zykov, M. A., 383

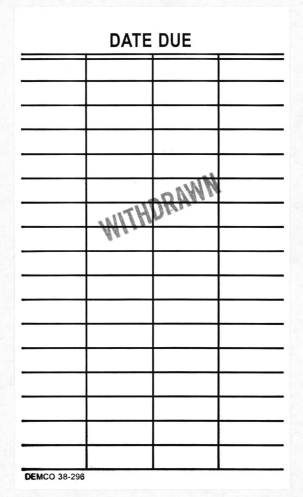

DATE DUE

DEMCO 38-296